Cinepoetry

VERBAL ARTS :: STUDIES IN POETICS

SERIES EDITORS :: Lazar Fleishman & Haun Saussy

Cinepoetry

IMAGINARY CINEMAS IN FRENCH POETRY

Christophe Wall-Romana

FORDHAM UNIVERSITY PRESS *New York* 2013

mLI the modern language initiative

THIS BOOK IS MADE POSSIBLE BY A COLLABORATIVE GRANT FROM THE ANDREW W. MELLON FOUNDATION.

Fordham University Press also publishes its books in a variety of electronic formats. Some content that appears in print may not be available in electronic books.

Library of Congress Cataloging-in-Publication Data

Wall-Romana, Christophe.
Cinepoetry : imaginary cinemas in French poetry / Christophe Wall-Romana. — 1st ed.
p. cm. — (Verbal arts: studies in poetics)
Includes bibliographical references and index.
ISBN 978-0-8232-4548-2 (cloth : alk. paper)
1. French poetry—20th century—History and criticism. 2. Motion pictures and literature—France. 3. Motion pictures in literature. 4. French poetry—19th century—History and criticism. I. Title.
PQ443.W35 2013
841'.91209357—dc23

2012033167

Printed in the United States of America

15 14 13 5 4 3 2 1

First paperback printing 2015

CONTENTS

ILLUSTRATIONS

PLATES
(following page 256)

FIGURES

ACKNOWLEDGMENTS

The topic of this book was first developed in Suzanne Guerlac's poetry and vision seminar in 2001 at the University of California at Berkeley, which led to my work with Ann Smock, also in the Department of French at Berkeley. My thanks go to both of them for their confidence in this project, as well as to the faculty, lecturers, staff, and graduate students in the Department of French at Berkeley for their personal kindness, active support of my work, and critical stimulation: Bertrand Augst, Karl Britto, Michael Cowan, Carol Dolcini, Ulysse Dutoit, Gail Ganino, Tim Hampton, David Hult, Michael Lucey, Lowry Martin, Darlene Pursley, Vesna Rodic, Debarati Sanyal, and Hélène Sicard-Cowan. I would like to thank others as well who had a hand in enlarging my intellectual horizons at Berkeley: Anne-Lise François, Lyn Hejinian, Robert Kaufman, Irina Leimbacher, Julio Ramos, Shaden Tageldin, and Omise'eke Natasha Tinsley. Special thanks go to Mark Feldman, coadventurer on the job market.

The too many years this project has taken have nonetheless allowed for the silver lining accrual of insights from sharp readers and listeners. My thanks to Tom Augst, Reda Bensmaia, Omar Berrada, Tom Conley, Claude Debon, George Didi-Huberman, Tom Gunning, Lynn Higgins, Sarah Keller, Muisi Krosi, Sydney Lévy, Laura U. Marks, Carrie Noland, Marjorie Perloff, Bill Smock, Maria Tortajada, Jennifer Wild, and Steven Winspur. My colleagues in the Department of French and Italian at the University of Minnesota have offered an incredibly generous and fostering environment to myself and other junior faculty, and I would like to honor them for being an abnormally friendly and functional academic collective. For the extra work they have carried out on my behalf, I thank especially Dan Brewer, Juliette Cherbuliez, and Eileen Sivert. Many colleagues at Minnesota have helped *de près ou de loin* with this book, in particular, members of a book proposal reading group—Siobhan Craig, Shaden Tageldin, and Omise'eke Natasha Tinsley—who did marvels to point out gently some of its and my worse blind-spots (many, many thanks!), as well as Maria Damon, Rembert Hueser, and Verena Mund.

I would like to thank the Centre National du Cinéma at Bois d'Arcy for granting access to their archive, the services and staff of La Cinémathèque française, especially Laure Marchaut and Monique Faulhaber, and the cheerful team at La Bibliothèque du film (BiFi): Waldo Knobler, Régis Robert, and Cécile Touret. My thanks also to the following institutions for their assistance: La Bibliothèque Nationale de France, la Bibliothèque littéraire Jacques Doucet, la Bibliothèque historique de la Ville de Paris, L'Institut Mémoire de l'édition contemporaine, the British Film Institute, le Musée Gaumont, Gaumont Pathé Archives, the Beinecke Rare Books and Manuscript Library, and le comité Jean Cocteau; the following publishers: Éditions Gallimard, Éditions P.O.L., Éditions du Seuil, Éditions Paris Expérimental, Éditions de l'Attente, Éditions Héros-Limite; and to the following individuals: Arlette Albert-Birot, Pierre Bergé, Jean-François Clair, Frédérique Devaux, Jacques Fraenkel, Catherine Goldstein, Jacques Goormaghtigh, Christiane Guymer, Michael Kasper, Marie-Ange L'Herbier, Suzanne Nagy, René Rougerie, and Marie-Thérèse Stanislas.

An early version of Chapter 1, "Mallarmé's Cinepoetics: The Poem Uncoiled by the *Cinématographe*, 1893–1898," appeared in *PMLA* 120, no. 1 (January 2005) 128–47. A draft of Chapter 2 appeared in French under the title, "Dispositif et cinépoésie, autour du *Raymond Roussel* de Michel Foucault," in *Dispositifs de vision et d'audition: épistémologie et bilan*, ed. François Albéra and Maria Tortajada (Lausanne: L'Âge d'homme, 2011), and portions of Chapter 11 were published in "Triangular Translation: Racism, Film, Poetry," *Valley Voices* 7, no. 1 (spring 2007): 49–52.

For her reading and editing of countless versions of chapters of this book, her suggestions and flair both in terms of substance and exposition, and her boundless gifts of time, reassurance, and love during writing bouts, Margaret Wall-Romana deserves a triumph. This book simply would not exist without her.

ABBREVIATIONS

ECU	extreme close-up (a small detail, part of something, an eye)
CU	close-up (a face filling the screen or a small object/area)
MCU	medium close-up (chest and face or a larger object/area)
MS	medium shot (a person from the waist up or equivalent)
FS	full shot (a person from the feet or knee up or equivalent)
LS	long shot (several persons in a large indoor or outdoor space, or equivalent)
VLS	very long shot (a crowd or a very large space or expanse)
ELS	extreme long shot (persons too small to identify, aerial establishing shot)
HA	high angle (camera pointed downward)
LA	low angle (camera pointed upward)

INTRODUCTION

Cinema as Imaginary Medium in French Poetry

Cinema with ink and paper ought to do the job faster than cinema on film.
—JEAN EPSTEIN[1]

(is it a "book," a "film"? the interval between the two?)
—MAURICE BLANCHOT[2]

CINEPOETRY

It is a well-known fact that French poets such as Antonin Artaud and Jean Cocteau worked in cinema, and several critics have examined at some length the thematic presence of film in modernist poetry, albeit mostly in the Anglo-American domain. Literary criticism has only begun probing the more complex ways in which relatively new technologies like cinema may have altered poetry's forms, practices, and theories. After all, cinema has profoundly inflected the whole cultural landscape of modernity, so why should poetry have been spared?

It is to this simple question apparently difficult to come to ask—how has cinema transformed poetry?—that this book tries bringing answers in the case of poetry written in French. Although some are more definitive than others, these answers open or reopen wide-ranging debates about the nature of poetry, cinema, spectatorship, imagination, writing, perception, mediality, and remediation, to cite only a few rubrics. Ultimately, this book has three main goals: to demonstrate that French poetry at large has been thoroughly and continuously impressed with and imprinted by cinema; to understand through specific examples what it means for poetry to be considered "filmic" and for poets to engage in filmic writing; and finally to draw the main historical and theoretical consequences of such cross-medial practices. It should be added at the outset that only the want of space and personal expertise account for limiting the scope of this study to the so-called French domain—even though we will see that it, too, comes out redefined.

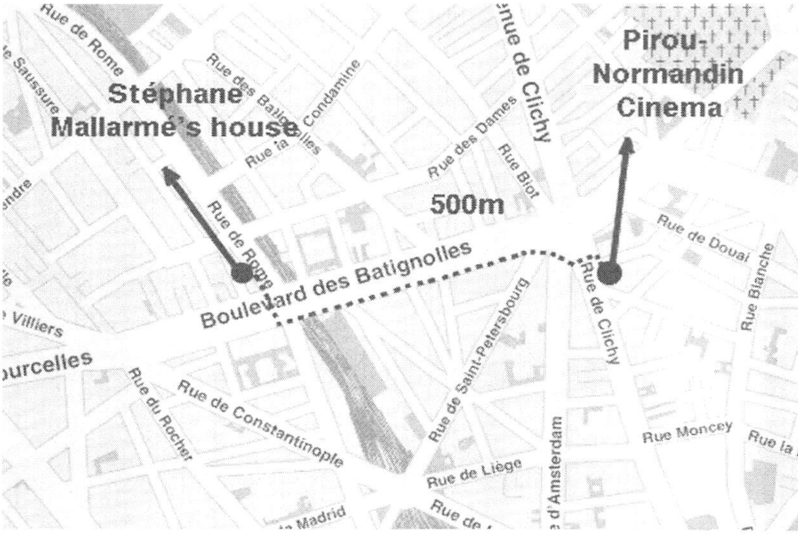

Figure 1. Stéphane Mallarmé's flat and the nearest movie theater (Le Pirou-Normandin) in Paris, 1896.

The intuition that cinema's emergence touched on some of the fundamental conditions of poetry writing was made plain as early as 1897 by none other than the paradigmatic figure of so-called pure poetry, Stéphane Mallarmé. Eighteen months after the commercial debut of cinema in Paris, the poet wrote a short, clearly theoretical note anticipating the changes the "cinématographe" would bring to the relationship between "images and text." This book began after, pondering on Mallarmé's note, I found other traces of cinema in his late works, soon discovering that the poet lived a few blocks from a movie theater that opened in 1896, Le Pirou-Normandin (Figure 1). As I started researching what I took to be a new critical object—surprised to find how little criticism existed on the topic of cinema "in" poetry—I stumbled upon a book published in 1921 that had tackled similar questions: *La Poésie d'aujourd'hui, un nouvel état d'intelligence* (Today's poetry: A new mindset). It had last been checked out of the library in 1974 (this was 2001), and neither it nor its author, Jean Epstein, figured in bibliographies of poetic theory.

Epstein's remarkable book correlates the experience of urban modernity—constituted by mass labor, mechanization, and pulp culture as collective management of psychosexual fatigue—with a new typology in poetry. At the very heart of this experience of modernity, Epstein located cinema. The postwar poetry of the late 1910s, he argued, took its cue from the pulp fiction of "subliterature" and serial movies that had adapted their forms and conditions of production to modernity. In other words, Epstein showed that modernist poets, piggy-backing on cinema, were writing smack across "the great divide" between high art and mass culture. To bolster his claim, he outlined specific features derived from cinema's perceptual immediacy, mapping them out on the modernist aesthetics of Louis Aragon, Blaise Cendrars, and Marcel Proust among others. What is most confounding about his original and far-ranging thesis is that only very recently have studies of modernism come to similar conclusions regarding interplays between modernity, literature, and mass culture including cinema—mainly under the inspiration of Walter Benjamin's pioneering 1930s work. Had that book, like Benjamin's theses, been too far ahead of its time to be appreciated by his contemporaries? Did Epstein's fame as an experimental filmmaker somehow disqualify him as a theoretician of poetry in the eyes of literary critics? Moreover, could Benjamin, who lived in Paris at the same time as Epstein, have known him, or of him?

The present book was begun after it became clear that between Mallarmé's inkling and Epstein's theory, and between that theory and today, a host of poets, writers, and thinkers had also conjectured that the future of poetry was somehow linked to cinema. Reflections on this linkage and experiments conducted to explore, deepen, or formalize it run through the entire corpus of twentieth-century poetry and poetics written in French. This is what I call *cinepoetry*.

At its most general, cinepoetry is a writing practice whose basic process is homological: it consists of envisioning a specific component or aspect of poetry as if it were a specific component of cinema, or vice versa, but always in writing. The screen becomes the page, a close-up turns into a metaphor, or conversely, the irregular spacing of words on the page is meant to evoke the movement of images on screen. Poets took cinema and film culture to be reservoirs of new textual genres and practices, but they also meditated on the apparatus and the industry as potential fields of poetic expansion and actualization. When such possibilities were foreclosed they fell back to envisioning cinema as an imaginary medium for utopian experiments in abeyance of social transformation. The readings offered herein, supported by archival research, make it possible to affirm that in the last phase of his work Mallarmé was unequivocally experimenting with ways of merging poetic writing and film and thus that he pioneered cinepoetry. This conclusion has important ramifications for literary history. Not only does it trouble current historiography concerning the constitution of historical avant-gardes as a reaction to late symbolism, but also it questions the narrative that high poetic modernism kept mass and technological cultures to the margins, in Surrealism in particular. In a more general way, cinepoetry permeates the work of poets and writers across practically all periods, aesthetic programs, and established schools, and directly contributed to a surprising number of key poetic concepts and practices of the last century.

What is both fascinating and challenging about cinepoetry is its paradoxical character. It is neither a form nor a movement and no poetic project ever rallied around it. Yet it has insistently reemerged in cyclical anamnesis either within successive avant-gardes or under the pen of isolated poets, almost without interruption from the 1890s to the contemporary poetics of the digital era. Its development took place within multiple dynamic tensions between high lyricism and low pulp, literary centers and peripheries, between text and image, avant-garde and arrière-garde, utopia and commercialism, embodied experiencing and writing, virtual imagination and actual films. As the association of Mallarmé and Epstein demonstrates, cinepoetry reveals transversal links and noncanonical practitioners, shadowing established poetic history with a transhistorical network of poets who never realized that they had cinema in common. This study explores the main features of this *inexplicit community* (to alter the translation of Blanchot's *communauté inavouable*) that strove nonetheless to reshape poetry on the common basis of a creative spectatorship taking the imaginary resonances of cinema as fodder for a new kind of writing. Much of the material this book covers has either not been studied at all or has dropped out of our critical canon, often having been willfully pushed aside by avant-garde gatekeepers. Cinepoetry is thus a *minor* component of poetics (to extend the sense of Deleuze and Guattari's "minor literature") that poses major questions about the role of cinema's *aisthesis*—the creative, embodied, and imaginary experience of cinema—in writing and poetic theory.

This study might appear intemperate on several counts. First, it might be associated with the traditionally literature-centered genre of adaptation studies, whose fortunes have rather ebbed, in spite of critics like Robert Stam who have endeavored to expand their range.[3]

Adaptations studies, however, focus overwhelmingly on the novel through the notion of an invariant *fabula* transferable across media.[4] Cinepoetry, though open to narrative, focuses more on imaginary immersion than fabula and appears little concerned with invariance. Second, a long-standing philosophical prejudice has consistently devalued *mediated experience*, especially when the mediation is embodied and technological, and especially when it comes to poetry's status of keystone among the arts. And third, because today's literary theory is not quite sure what to do with *imagining* (which I distinguish from the romantic imagination below) as a productive and critical force informing, alongside socially determined discourse, aesthetic activity such as writing. *Cinepoetry*'s premise is that poets' cinematically mediated practice, bypassing notions of cinema as an illusion or a factory of die-cast cultural products, gave rise to a new and distinctly virtual ecology of the text.[5] For more than a hundred years, anticipating many recent developments in digital poetry, it has been altering fundamental aspects of what we understand poetry to be.

CROSS-MEDIUM WRITING

Cinepoetry comprises only page-based artifacts, either textual or textual and visual, that are considered "poetic" and display features explicitly or implicitly cinematographic or filmic. Literary works that purport to relate to cinema but that have no demonstrably cinematic aspects are not analyzed.[6] This purely heuristic limitation also gently pushes to the background artworks and digital forms such as e-poetry, though clearly cinepoetry has tangible links with each of them. Films per se are also excluded from the definition, yet plainly cinepoetry, as a "*cinéma en encre et papier*" is a kind of cinema—especially when in dialogue with specific movies—and just as plainly not cinema, since it is print and it does not move.

The works examined here skirt the belle-lettrist tradition and the canons of figurality, rhetoric, genre, and intertextuality that remain today at the core of literature. Written mostly by poets, cinepoetic texts often forego the norms of verse, form, and genre usually considered synonymous with poetry. Hence we find poetic prose, poetic essays—"critical poems" as Mallarmé called them—and poetic novels, as well as visual poems and prose poems. What initially incited their transmutation away from more canonic practices has to do with the new forms of texts ancillary to film culture that began flourishing during the silent era: treatments, scenarios, decoupages, lyrical film reviews, utopian cinema theory, film industry exposés, star biographies, novelizations, screening programs, screening booklets, intertitles, rolling screen credits, and so on (Figure 2). When they came to write around, about, or for cinema, writers naturally had this new para-filmic spectrum of texts in mind. The year 1917–18 figures as a watershed, in that the first explicit cinepoems were published, sometimes jointly in a cinema journal—Louis Delluc's *Le Film*—and in literary journals—Pierre Reverdy's *Nord-Sud* and Pierre Albert-Birot's *S.I.C.*[7] Critics like Alain Virmaux and David Trotter who have looked at these works have tended to see them as exceptions, punctual moments of extreme hybridity between literature and cinema that do not, by and by, impinge on their respective and distinct histories and/or medium specificity.[8] But cinepoetry proves, if anything at all, that a very substantial number of writers in the twentieth century renounced the myth of literature's primacy, autonomy, and separation by opening it up to another medium—what's more, one that was pubescent and of still dubious repute. And while recent film studies have been weary of literary models and antecedents, the film work of Epstein, Cocteau, and Isou, for instance, can hardly be severed from their written oeuvre—although, again, their films are not the focus of this study.

The eclectic corpus of cinepoetry examined here reflects in important ways the similarly eclectic background of its authors. While several are canonical native French writers, others flicker at the edge of the canon, and many can be seen as peripherally "French." This is the case of Ivan Goll, born in German-occupied Alsace, or Italian-Polish-French Guillaume Apollinaire, anxious to be naturalized during World War I, or Max Jeanne, born in Guadeloupe and living in Canada. As for Marcel Mariën and Henri Michaux, both from Belgium, the former resisted the gravitational attraction of Paris to remain in Brussels, while the latter became a French citizen. Yet other cinepoets are Francophones coming from semi- or non-Francophone countries, such as Isidore Isou and Benjamin Fondane from Romania, and Nelly Kaplan from Argentina. Many cinepoets from the 1920s were homosexual or queer (Jean Cocteau, Jean Epstein, Irène Hillel-Erlanger), and a good number were Jewish (Goll, Isou, Epstein, Hillel-Erlanger, Kaplan, Gabriel Pomerand, Christian Rodanski, Maurice Lemaître), equally challenging circumstances in interwar France. Cinepoets' challenge to medium specificity and literary norms thus often went

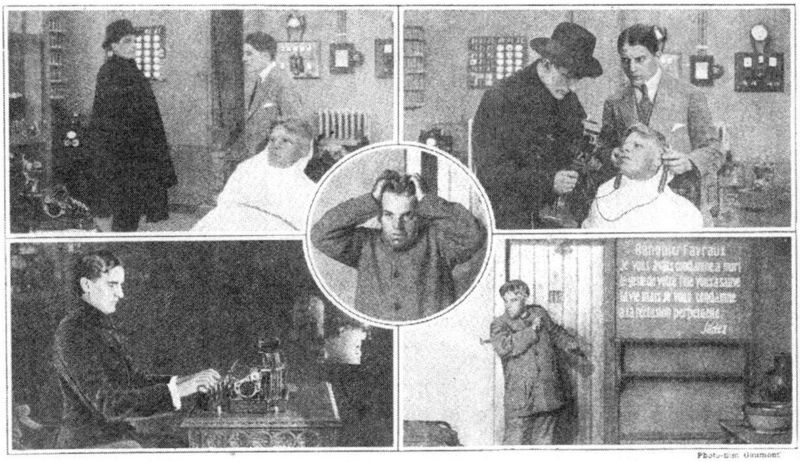

Photo-film Gaumont

Lorsqu'il revint à la vie, Favraux apprit avec épouvante qu'il était au pouvoir du mystérieux Judex. Le justicier le contraignit d'abord à demander pardon à sa fillle, puis le condamna à la réclusion perpétuelle.

made of many appliances and instruments utilized by the master himself.

Hence the Pasteur Film is, in the widest and most rigorous acceptation of the word, a historical and scientific film of reconstitution. Not only has it a dramatic and moral interest, but also that of authenticity, which makes it a subject worthy of meditation by everyone.

TWO EDUCATIONAL FILMS

The detailed visualization of the scientific work of Pasteur would have been too great and lessened the lessons of abnegation and civic virtue thrown into relief in the scientist's life. Therefore the *Édition Française Cinématographique* has had two educational films composed in addition tho the great film for the general public. One includes the whole extent of Pastorian science and is particularly suitable for advanced students. The other summarizes that science, making it intelligible to young minds, and is specially intended for children.

- 27 -

Figure 2. (Left) Page from the 1923 booklet accompanying the release of Jean Epstein's docudrama *Pasteur*; (Above) new hybrid of photo and text in the cine-novel version of Louis Feuillade's 1916 *Judex* (note the "imaginary" text set within the lower-right image, as both explanatory intertitle and handwritten note).

hand in hand with questioning norms of citizenship, cultural capital, social emplacement, and sexual identity.

Such diversity in the range of texts, their cross-medium modalities, and the status and perspectives of their authors call for a fluid methodological approach. Workaday models of poetry criticism find themselves out of their element when addressing texts envisioned through medium stereoscopy. While close reading remains central, literary criticism resting on the skillful analysis of high figural and rhetorical craft doubled with generic and intertextual references simply does not go far enough. At the same time, cinepoems display a textual, material, and corporeal singularity that does not lend itself to cultural studies analysis relying on discursive formation and power relations in the social sphere. Such a challenge represents an exciting opportunity to expand poetry theory and criticism toward underused afferent disciplines. For instance, the perspectives of pragmatics, discourse analysis, and cognitive poetics can be very useful to resituate linguistic artifacts within the field of social acts through embodied experience. Perception and sensation studies, including recent works in phenomenology, can offer new models that reassess the articulation of meaning with embodiment and technology—one of the main blind spots of close reading. And, of course, film and media studies contribute an invaluable understanding of how audiovisual spaces organize experience into meaning in ways that contrast with and supplement the ways texts do.

While this book is the first sustained attempt since Epstein's to rethink French poetics through cinema, it claims neither to have coined the compound "cinepoetry,"[9] nor to be the first contemporary critical effort to note and address cinema's permeation of poetry. The work of Alain and Odette Virmaux, who tirelessly researched and republished source texts starting in the 1970s, and that of Richard Abel, from the purview of film studies in the 1980s, has been vital for my research.[10] Since I began this project, several studies analyzing Anglo-American modernist poetry and literature in relation to cinema have appeared, and *Cinepoetry* partakes of this recent effort to acknowledge and examine cinema's epistemological impact on literature, especially given the increased cultural preeminence of moving images and concomitant visual and digital turns in the humanities.[11] New media criticism has indeed helped formalize a number of new concepts such as virtual experiencing, bodily immersion, multisensory perception, and text embedding in visual media. Yet many of these constructs were in one way or another originally deployed and limned out within cinepoetic writings. As for film studies, this book modestly intends to return the gift by helping to dispel the enduring notion that literature, or poetry, or the text, or language retain a de facto primacy preserving their purity and disciplinary priority. Poets have long embraced poetic practice as open to impurity, alterity, complexity, technology, experience, and the contingence of affect—in fact, the distension of the text by such forces has been one of the central interests for poets of modernity.

EXAMPLES AND LIMITATIONS

Let us look at an example of how cinepoetics strains the generic bounds and formalist hermeneutics of poetry. In 1914 Colette decided to write her first film review after watching the footage recovered intact from the Scott expedition; over a year had passed since all its members had died of starvation. Film reviews were not yet a normalized genre, and the bulk of Colette's review reads like a poetic experiment:

> How many seated travelers, chained wanderers, like me leaned forward yesterday toward the biting and dark salt water. . . . To know how snow soars thirty degrees below zero, to touch the down of a penguin chick that has just burst through its shell. . . . The wet and half-frozen velvet clothing a mother seal's olive-shaped body, with her calf nursing—this is ours now, it is within ourselves. . . .
>
> It took Scott, with his long adventurous and wise face, receding on the white desert, slowly, his hand holding the bridle of his horse, and sending—to whom? to *us*?—a supreme, an invaluable gesture of "good-bye." . . . It took his perishing, with all of them whose creviced cheeks are still smiling on the screen, while even in death, by preserving the films, the photos, the manuscripts, they thought only of *us*—us, their glory.[12]

The eulogistic style of this passage commands a series of classical meters surreptitiously embedded in the French prose. We find octosyllables ("Et que de voyageurs assis"; "vers l'eau salée, mordante et sombre"), and a distich: "Savoir comment vole la neige [/] par quarante degrés de froid." There are alexandrines such as "il a fallu que Scott, à la longue figure," with the distich: "il a fallu qu'il périsse avec tous ceux-là [/] dont les joues crevassées rient encor[e] sur l'écran." Through a series of hard /k/ and /r/ sounds this last alexandrine transduces the crunching of snow, as the men "recede" from the camera toward death. Colette keenly links this movement to the "leaning forward" of spectators otherwise immobilized, so that the crucial transmission of ethereal "glory" that film achieves takes place through a virtual transmission of embodied motion. On film, men and animals move, smile, are born in the sensorially perceivable present of the screening, so much so that their life physically enters our absorbed trance, "*en nous*." Cinema is not an aura-destroying apparatus faking the abridging of distances. The way it makes present the distant and the Other may awaken an audience to the ethics of the manifold[13] and to its own agency. In Colette's description, birthing, nursing, and sensing balance out the posthumous nature of the movie—and perhaps of cinema itself. She focuses on the senses of taste ("salty," "biting," "olive") and touch ("to touch the down," "the wet and half-frozen velvet") to create an imaginary sensory experience of hypermediacy corresponding to the images she saw. Her words also subtly redraw the hierarchy of media: "films, photos, manuscripts," in that order, as if to signal that animated photography opens up a new embodied apparatus and a new social medium to the resources of writing. And this is precisely what her review does, interweaving classical poetic devices, in particular the anaphora—"ours," "in ourselves," "to *us*?" "of us," "us"—within a new matrix of meaning in which film-mediated embodiment and sociality expand textual art.

A recent example, at the other end of film culture's permeation of writing, is the 2008 book by poet Nathalie Quintane: *Grand Ensemble, concernant une ancienne colonie*, a title translatable as both *Very long shot* (plan de grand ensemble) and *Housing project*, with the subtitle *Concerning a former colony*. Addressing the colonization and liberation of Algeria, the book presents itself as a poetic documentary of the year 2003, which was designated The Year of Algeria by presidents Chirac and Bouteflika. Cinema is omnipresent in the book, yet also curiously absent. Mixing prose and verse sections with titles such as "Faux barrage" (Fake check-point), "Dispositif" (Apparatus, but also Police deployment) and "Grand Récit" (Grand narrative), the book blends clipped poetic syntax, a short novel, and personal recollections of the narrator's father who fought in Algeria, with mentions of torture, rape, and mutilation during the Algerian war of independence. Behind its disorienting eclecticism, the book focuses on a critique of the state-sponsored cultural events the narrator attended, in particular screenings. It opens with a mention of Jean-Luc Godard's *Le Petit soldat* (1960), a film banned in France until the Évian agreements of 1962 because, though set in Geneva, it pits FLN and procolonist armed groups and includes a torture scene. The ambiguous status of Godard's film as a work of fiction that conceals a political documentary informs the paradoxical place of cinema in *Grand Ensemble*. In particular, the book carefully avoids describing what the untitled documentaries about the war and its aftermath show, the better to frame the state-sponsored cultural events of remembrance as a species of nonevent, erasure, and indeed counteranamnesis. The only film sequence described is from a movie starring Jackie Chan, whose playful invincibility morphs disturbingly into bits of inner monologue by French soldiers during a killing and raping spree in Algeria. When Quintane purports to show us a scene from one of the documentaries it is only to thwart our desire to see for ourselves:

> FALSE CHECK-POINT 5: DOCUMENTARY
>
> Repetition is, in contemporary poetry sometimes,
> a choral technique.
> It can be used in case of emergency.
>
> A former male nurse of Blida's psychiatric hospital talks about
> the hospital in the fifties:
> So then words follow in Arabic words follow in Arabic words
> follow in Arabic words follow in Arabic once it started words
> follow in Arabic . . . words follow in A[14]

The documentary-screened-in-writing foils our learning anything about this nurse on several counts: the Arabic is not provided, possibly because it is presumed that French readers couldn't read it if it were, and if the film alluded to was subtitled, no transcription is offered by Quintane. By puncturing the French with the palimpsestic label "Arabic," she deflates the conceit that we are participating in colonial history's anamnesis. We are not watching a film, we still don't understand the language of the other, and we are not remembering history: we have merely fallen prey to a "false check-point" in "contemporary poetry."

The tricky place of cinema in such a book seems to me threefold. First, it serves as a virtual metamedium loosely holding together various kinds of voices, forms, and discourses. Both the "meta" and the "loose" aspects are crucial, and although it is in a different key, we recognize in this a high modernist stance (Proust's architectonic is equally meta and loose). Second, by renouncing the ekphrastic fullness of described footage, this "acinema" deflates French readers' voyeuristic desire for narrative comfort and national redemption, and it rejects the poetic aestheticization of both politics and intermedia. This might be its postmodern way of undercutting "grand narratives." Lastly, and most importantly, *Grand ensemble* enacts through this acinema a sense of potential witnessing, a limning of the horizon of justice. In other words, *Grand ensemble* suggests that the task of historical justice might be taken up by poetry today as a form of acinema—the cinematic imaginary being equated with a potential collective witnessing that mitigates holes in the historical record. By forsaking grandstanding denunciations (à la Victor Hugo) while keeping open the ethical dimension of a virtual documentary on history, cinepoetry in *Grand ensemble* reveals its ethical potential. In all, "cinema," as a polyvalent object allows Quintane to circulate freely between experimental, modernist, postmodern, documentary, and ethical purviews, as a way to push the boundaries of poetry. (Another acinematic book of Quintane, *Mortinsteinck, le livre du film* [1999], is examined in the Conclusion.)

These examples show the inner limits of cinepoetry and make plain the reliance on the work of interpretation and corroboration. Blaise Cendrars's 1913 *La Prose du transsibérien et de la petite Jehanne de France* can serve as an outer liminal example (Plate 1). Published as a two-meter-long accordion strip with simultaneist verse in colored inks on the right column, and illustrated with bright geometrical gouache patterns by artist Sonia Terk-Delaunay on the left column, it is a multimedia, multiauthor work. While the text bears only tangential marks of cinema, its paratext (unfolding page), subtext (Cendrars's 1912 profession of faith toward cinema), and intermedial aspect (resemblance to a strip of dyed film stock from the period) make it flicker at the edge of the cinepoetic.[15] Prose can also be a liminal province of cinepoetry, as in pioneer film theoretician and poet Riciotto Canudo's 1923 novelization of Abel Gance's 1922 film *La Roue*, itself an adaptation of a 1912 novel by Pierre Hamp.[16] Illustrated with shooting stills, the book appears antithetical to poetry since it is (doubly) derivative, as well as narrative, pulp, and a medium hybrid. Yet just like Gance's film, Canudo's book is of far lesser interest as a narrative than as a modernist montage of mythopoetic pieces. Canudo's preface states that this book is not "an adaptation or narrative of the film," but instead its "psychological synthesis," and he cites Walt Whitman, Émile Verhaeren, and Aeschylus to link together "the literary ideal of the representation of the collective," the "broad poetry of the machine," and Gance's "lyricism."[17] Inaugurating a book-to-film-to-book pulp genre, Canudo's work does not allude to poetry for respectability, but as the default terrain for new experiments in writing.

My general approach in this study is not that texts with cinepoetic elements all resemble each other nor that they constitute a fully definable corpus amounting to the systematic addition of cinema to poetry.

On the contrary, I argue that the functional diversity of cinematic elements in these texts invites us to consider them in the singularity through which each expands poetics and poetry.

QUESTIONING ORIGINS: POETRY AND EARLY CINEMA

Historically speaking, in both France and the United States, the interrelation of poetry and cinema reached the public sphere in 1908, with several developments that serve as a starting point for overt cinepoetics.[18] As audiences demanded better and longer movies, the Film d'Art company was launched to offer single-reel literary films—chiefly, historical reconstructions and adaptations of novels. That same year a month-long international conference in Berlin tackled the question of intellectual ownership of scenarios, after Parisian writers and rights-owners sued production and distribution companies for infringement.[19] Cinema had suddenly made its appearance in the literary sphere.

At the premiere of the Film d'Art's new brand of cinema, attended by the *tout Paris* establishment, the main feature was a screening of *L'Assassinat du duc de Guise*, accompanied by music especially written for the film by Camille Saint-Saëns. It was earlier in the program that one of the first public encounters of poetry and cinema was staged. While a distinguished actor of the Comédie française read a longish rhymed ode by academician Edmond Rostand, "The sacred wood" ("Le Bois sacré"), a dance movie miming the ode was projected on the screen, with famed Cléo de Mérode playing one of the protagonists. A farcical pantomime, the poem revolves around the encounter by Greek gods and goddesses of a broken-down automobile—which they fix—while its two occupants are asleep. Journalists noted that the poem dramatized the clash between the moribund aesthetics of symbolism and modernity's technological materialism.[20] The poem in fact mirrored the very encounter of poetry with cinema. We might think for instance of Heidegger's contrasting the two main forms of "making": *poiesis* as making something appear (representation), and *tekhnê* as extracting something from the world (production). I read the gods fixing the car in the poem as a wink by Rostand: poetry might very well be needed to help fix cinema. Turgid as it is, the ode innovates in one surprising area: luxury product placement. It manages to mention the champagne Mumm, the perfumer Guerlain, the couturier Jacques Doucet (future benefactor of Surrealism), and the jeweler Kirby, Beard & Co.[21] Mallarmé had had a similar idea in his notes for "Le Livre."

The evening's program included the projection of photographic slides with commentary, so that all the beaux-arts of time—music, dance, theater, poetry—and all the new technologies of space—advertising, automobile, cinema, and photography—were united in a decidedly gentrified *Gesamtkunstwerk*. This event took place a full year before Marinetti's *Futurism Manifesto* launched the so-called historical avant-gardes, with their signature interart and multimedia practices, and their fascination with new technologies. Should we consider that the Film d'Art evening announced (or preempted) the innovations of the avant-garde? Or are we falling for the chronological illusion of a "first"? After all, multiart performances were already the hallmark of the early cinema of attractions that combined film, dance, and theater on stage after 1896. As for advertisement, some had been screened in Paris —including outdoors—from 1898 onward, while poems had been played on phonographs with movie projections as early as 1903. My point here is that the Film d'Art evening as *Gesamtkunstwerk* exemplifies a motif that runs throughout this study, namely, that claims of innovation, often from the avant-garde, entail the forgetting or erasure of already established practices.

In 1908 as well, poet Jules Romains published *Life Unanimous (La Vie unanime)* to great acclaim. Critics recognized in its everyday speech indifferent to tropes and exact rhymes, the first "modernist offensive" toward "a total modernism."[22] The book-length poem overcame the bogged down opposition between symbolism's high ideals and naturalism's pastoral nostalgia by paying attention to modernity: "With the latest developments of civilization," Romains had remarked already in 1905, "our way of being has been thoroughly transformed without poetry taking any notice whatsoever."[23] His work proceeded to remedy this, by positing that with urban modernity came a new collective consciousness he called *l'unanime* (the unanimous), not as a consensus or a crowd synergy but an intersubjective force or soul (animus). Related to Bergsonian vitalism and Gabriel Tarde's study of group mimesis, it differs from these by being a multilevel phenomenon at once psychosomatic, technological, political, and aesthetic, characterized by transference or tele-empathy with others, but also with the built world.[24]

Romains was trained as a medical doctor and figures this intersubjective sentience in the poem as a "communal flesh" at once fluid and viral. He describes for instance his own "flesh ooz[ing]" when he senses the fever of a child who is sick in an apartment several stories above his.[25] The unanimous is viral and telepathic, transiting through nonhuman structures: "the soul that seeps from groups to halls [*salles*]."[26] Romains is thinking about not only halls for political meetings (unanimism was originally labeled "communism") but also entertainment halls. Indeed, in 1907–8 huge movie halls were built in Paris as the movie industry consolidated to compete with fairground cinemas.[27] Romains's concept of the telepathic link between urban masses and spaces was very likely informed by the movie palace boom, even though *Life Unanimous* does not refer to cinema per se.[28]

Romains makes the role of cinema clear in "The Crowd at the Cinematograph" (1911), a text written shortly after the completion of *Life Unanimous*, suggesting that the animating principle of "l'unanime" has much to do with "vues animées" (animated views) as movies were still called. He describes spectators losing their sense of self into the group, before the group loses itself into the film: "Its eyes no longer see itself; it is no longer aware of its own flesh. In it there is but a flight of images, a gliding and rustling of daydreams" (*une fuite d'images, un glissement et un froufrou de songes*).[29] The collective dimension of the unanimous is double: the group "imagines" itself as a collective, and imagines other "groups like itself."[30] Romains singles out temporal and causal effects as central to the experience: "Time [on screen] . . . is not ordinary time . . . actions have no logical consequences, causes lay odd effects like golden eggs."[31]

The mention of "golden eggs" is far from casual. In 1905, the year of inception of *Life Unanimous*, an adaptation of a la Fontaine fable, "La Poule aux oeufs d'or" ("The hen with the golden eggs") became, according to Richard Abel, "the most popular of Pathé's féeries or follies . . . a four-part toned and stencil-colored film."[32] Romains was struck by a specific shot of the hatching of golden eggs in that film. It is more directly alluded to in his cinepoetic work, *Donogoo-Tonka* (1919), the first scenario text published by the NRF and subtitled "a cinematographic fable." He writes, "Suddenly under the tap of his finger, the brochure lets out a gold coin, then another . . . [each] grows, becomes rounder, fuller, taking the shape of a hen."[33] In Romains's 1919 recollection of the movie *La Poule aux oeufs d'or*, two-dimensional print produces gold coins that become both animal and animated. Print, in other words, generates a "vue animée." It does so on three distinct levels: Romains's scenario as meant to generate a movie; in the diegesis, the protagonist generates a film-within-the-scenario; and finally, our mind's eye as readers has no problem invoking our mind's eye as movie viewer to experience virtually this animation of a text.

I take Romains's twin references in 1911 and 1919 to the sensorimotor impress of this trick shot of coin-to-hen "morphing" dating back to a 1905 movie, as indicative of a broad change in poetics. Imagination had now found a new supplement in cinema, not in its content or in its social unanimism, but in its very texture: the miracle of filmic images plastically self-mutating. Poetry and imagination were both faced with a new regime of *automorphosis*.[34] This is what I call the *cinematic imaginary*.

In 1905, explaining his poem in progress, Romains had written, "Such a poetry . . . would not limit itself . . . to describing . . . the outside of modern things, and the *colored surface* of existence. . . . I believe that emotional links between a person and his city, that the total mind, the broad movements of consciousness, the vast enthusiasms of human groups, are capable of creating a penetrating lyricism."[35] The new imaginary of the poetry of modernity, I will argue, broke with the "colored surface" of poetic images to engage with the "broad movements" of embodied collective lyricism, through the revelation of the *automorphic* character of cinema's moving images. Symbolist theoretician and poet Remy de Gourmont in 1907, and Ricciotto Canudo in 1908, both single out cinema as such an automorphic new medium, disclosing a new sense of materiality and of the collective, and they cite writers that have in common a strong focus on bodily experiencing: Shakespeare, Poe, Emerson, and Nietzsche.[36] Canudo, whose 1908 text on cinema as art is held as the earliest example of "film theory," was directly influenced by Jules Romains's unanimism when he saw in cinema a better collective-oriented synthesis of the arts than that he had sought in music.[37] Cinematic automorphosis, with its embodied and collective resonances, began transforming the imaginary of poetry over the years 1907 to 1911.

The modernist historiography of poets' early fascination with cinema has skipped Rostand, Romains, Canudo, and de Gourmont almost entirely, and likely others as well.[38] The poet considered to have pioneered interest in cinema among the literary avant-garde is Apollinaire—a close friend of Canudo. There is no question that, in featuring cinema in a literary text in 1902, in cofounding in 1913, with Picasso, Max Jacob, and Maurice Raynal, the Société des amis de Fantômas, named after the commercially successful serial of Louis Feuillade, and in selling a coauthored scenario in 1917, he was indeed the most openly and actively cinephilic of French poets.[39] The discovery of the films of Chaplin and Griffith in 1916, and a national desire to bring France back to its prewar leadership status in world cinema, led more French poets to reflect on cinema toward the end of the war. Apollinaire seized upon this interest in a November 1917 talk-manifesto, "The New Spirit and the Poets." The future surrealist nucleus attended the talk, together with cubist avant-garde writers and artists and other figures of the Paris intelligentsia. Apollinaire called for a new lyrical inspiration in national poetry, based on surprise and innovation, and relying explicitly on cinema and the phonograph: "It would have been strange, in an era when the popular art par excellence, cinema, is a book of images, if poets had not tried their hand at composing images for the more meditative and refined spirits who cannot be content with the vulgar imaginations of film manufacturers."[40] The substance of his injunction was for poets to engage in and improve commercial cinema screenwriting. This "temptation of cinema" among postwar poets, as Alain Virmaux has dubbed their efforts, did result in several collaborations with avant-garde films: Apollinaire himself was doing his share with a scenario coauthored with André Billy in April 1917.[41] However, over the years 1918–29, poets responded mostly with a plethora of experimental cinepoetic writings, many of which were never really meant to become actual film projects.[42] Their singularities, as well as their inadequacies from the viewpoint of the film industry, led Virmaux to speak of a series of illusions and delusions, which another critic characterizes as "a mad love . . . unconsummated."[43]

If neither poetry criticism nor cinema studies have approached these cinepoetic texts for what they are—an original cross-medium writing practice demanding a new interpretive framework[44]—it is largely because of their disciplinary boundaries. To overcome them we may invoke Jacques Rancière's critique of "the distribution of the sensible."[45] For Rancière this expression denotes three concurrent processes that converged in the mid-nineteenth century: class stratification and modern democracy, increased discourses about the differentiation of the senses, and the rise of an "aesthetic regime of the arts," ultimately redefining the arts not according to their sensory modalities but to their joint removal from the sphere of useful products and practices. By breaching on the one hand the constitutive opposition of sensory distribution—that between vision/image and language/text—and on the other hand the great divide between mass culture and high art, cinepoetry represents a practice of "dissensus" contesting and subverting the "policing" of the distribution of the sensible.[46]

The very textual nature of the scenario was no doubt a major impetus for cinepoetry. As Pasolini remarked, the scenario functions all at once as a *virtual text*, in being formally and literarily subservient to the film that will proceed from it, and as a *virtual film*, since the scenario text describes a film that does not yet exist.[47] Such a double virtuality undermines the logos of literature and poetry, the primacy of language, and the authority of the text, without favoring the sheer sensorial power of actual images, as is usually the case. My sense is that poets saw this double virtualization on both the language and image sides, supported by the intuition of automorphosis as itself nonrepresentable in either language or fixed image, as a new kind or mode of imagining. This is reflected in the range of formulations poets used to label their cinepoetic experiments. In 1916, Cocteau wrote of "a supernatural film"; Philippe Soupault in 1918 spoke of "cinematographic poems"; Jules Romains subtitled *Donogoo-Tonka* a "cinematographic fable [*conte*]"; Yvan Goll in 1920 coined the term *Kinodichtung* (cinepoem); Benjamin Fondane in 1928 emphasized the virtual aspect with "unshootable scenarios" (*scénarios infilmables*); Maurice Lemaître echoes this in 1952 with his expression "imaginary film." While subsequently each of these poets had at least one scenario made into a movie, the texts they produced under invented labels purposefully avoid the scenario form in order to develop a new, cross-medium writing practice. Rather than "a poetry of cinema," as Cocteau would later call his films, this new practice aimed at making cinema in poetry. Not because of money, fandom, fad, or avant-garde experimentalism (though all were motivating factors), but because cinepoetry was a privileged channel to explore the shift in the literary imagination that cinema had triggered in modernity.

THE CINEMATIC IMAGINARY: "UN MAGASIN D'IMAGES ET DE SIGNES"

[Le cinéma] c'est de l'imaginaire pour les gens sans imagination (cinema is an imaginary for people without imagination).

—LOUIS VUILLERMOZ, ca. 1915[48]

Baudelaire's exultation, "Images, my one, my great passion!" can serve as a prologue to the new imaginary of cinema. As Rémi Brague has shown in *L'Image vagabonde* (*The wayward image*), Baudelaire sought a new integration of the romantic imagination with vision and the material image via specific sensorimotor experiences. He was perhaps the first French poet to theorize a concept of the imagination in line with earlier romantics such as Coleridge and members of the Atheneum group in Iena.[49] In proposing that "the whole visible universe is nothing but a store of images and signs [*magasin d'images et de signes*] to which the imagination will give a relative place and value," Baudelaire sounds like Schlegel or Coleridge—but for the decidedly consumerist and materialist simile anchored in Haussmannian modern life.[50] His poetics also rests on a more bodily dialectic than theirs, one of sensory multiplication and condensation, as well as visual decomposition and recomposition. This emphasis on fragmentation as an existential dynamics contrasts with the holistic fantasy of the romantic fragment. Other components of the Baudelairean imagination strain the romantic model, famously the notion of sensorial correspondences or synesthesia, as well as the theoretical reliance on hallucinogens and intoxicants for exploring the reach of the image. But nothing more than his meditation on material images in their relationship to poetry—doubled with a refusal to erase their materiality through the transpositional formula *ut pictura poesis*—marks Baudelaire's imaginary as belonging to this side of technological modernity. His passion for images *as such* dislodges the imagination (the freest faculty of the mind, pace Kant) from what Philippe Lacoue-Labarthe and Jean-Luc Nancy have called the "literary absolute," that is, the post-Kantian myth of literature's autonomy.[51] I suggest that Baudelaire, by entangling the imagination all at once with material images from art and mass culture, the body's hallucinogenic faculty, and the discontinuities of sensory experiences, largely contributed to reveal a precinematic imaginary.[52]

Because Brague's keen argument nonetheless disregards technology (photography and optical toys are not even mentioned), it is all the more striking how precinematic is the model of vision and imagination he reconstructs for Baudelaire. It focuses on *mobility* between observer and image, via a rhetoric of gleaning or *capturing* images such as faces, and looking *into* rather than *at* both faces and images.[53] The representational stasis of the image is thus transformed into a dynamic layering, as when Baudelaire writes that "a harmoniously made painting consists of a series of overlapping pictures, each new layer providing more reality to the dream."[54] For Brague, this crucial layering corresponds to what Baudelaire calls "the conjecture," a term Brague reads as translating the Greek word "symbol," meaning "throwing things together."[55] What Baudelaire favors most about the imagination is not its demiurgic or holistic or transcendental character, but its dynamic capacity to make the image move and dehisce so that, Brague explains, "the spectator enter[s] into the object's mobility, taking part in its aura."[56] This corresponds to sensorimotor experiences involving kinesthesia, hyperesthesia, and a haptic transduction of vision into physical touch that can be found in many of Baudelaire's descriptions of hallucination, such as in *Artificial Paradises*: "The harmony, the swaying of lines, the eurhythmy of motions, seem to the dreamer like necessities, like *duties*" (*L'harmonie, le balancement des lignes, l'eurythmie dans les mouvements, apparaissent au rêveur comme des* devoirs).[57] It is in this specific sensory register of dynamic phasing, of motion burgeoning from out of the image that I find early poetic traces of automorphosis. Baudelaire's wayward image drifts indeed remarkably close to chronophotography and cinema in *Fusées* (ca. 1862):

> Je crois que . . . le charme infini et mystérieux qui gît dans la contemplation d'un navire, et surtout d'un navire en mouvement, tient, dans le premier cas, à la régularité et à la symétrie qui sont un des besoins primordiaux de l'esprit humain, au même degré que la complication et l'harmonie, — et, dans le second cas, à la multiplication successive et à la génération de toutes les courbes et figures imaginaires opérées dans l'espace par les éléments réels de l'objet.
>
> L'idée poétique qui se dégage de cette opération du mouvement dans les lignes est l'hypothèse d'un être vaste, immense, compliqué, mais eurythmique, d'un animal plein de génie, souffrant et soupirant tous les soupirs et toutes les ambitions humaines.
>
> [I think that the infinite and mysterious charm that lies in the contemplation of a ship, and even more a moving ship, proceeds in the

> first case from regularity and symmetry that are one of the primordial needs of the human spirit, to the same degree than complication and harmony, —and, in the second case, from the successive multiplication and the production of all the imaginary curves and figures described in space by the real components of the object.
>
> The poetic idea emanating from this enactment of motion through lines is the hypothesis of a vast, immense, complicated, yet eurhythmic being—an animal full of genius suffering and exuding all the sorrows of human ambitions.][58]

With its precise contrast between the static ship (the first case) and the ship in movement (the second case), followed by a prescient description of an *automorphic image space* before cinema, then a mini poetic manifesto linking automorphosis to sentience, affect, and auto-affection, this passage heralds the new spectrum of the imaginary at play in cinepoetry.

This raises of course the difficult questions of origins, causality, and archaeology of the cinema apparatus: How can Baudelaire be said to herald cinepoetry before the invention of cinema? Does this not invalidate the main thesis of this study that takes the cinema apparatus as a direct cause? Underneath such questions is the old debate between Bazin's teleological belief that "the cinematographic idea" precedes the apparatus, and the atelic and factual approach of historians who can only attest to its progressive assembly once chronophotography emerged.[59] The measured answer of the present study is that over the years 1860–90 French writers in the wake of Baudelaire come to intuit an apparatus very much like what the cinema will be, not on the basis of an idea, as Bazin supposes, but of a twin interest in optical technology and poly-sensorial experience.

Philippe Ortel's magisterial study on photography and French literature in the nineteenth century establishes the fact that by the 1850s photography's constituent technologies—the camera obscura, mechanical mimesis, the inverting lens, chemical development, and so on—permeated the theory and poetics of various literary genres and practices, in particular poetry.[60] When Lamartine writes in the second preface, dated July 1849, to his 1821 *Poetic Meditations*, "I was born impressionable and sensitive [*impressionnable et sensible*]. . . . Exterior things, barely glimpsed at, left a vivid and profound imprint [*vive et profonde empreinte*] in me," we need not read between the lines to find that photo-sensitivity and photo-mimesis inform not just the tropes but the very construal of his own poetic genius.[61] The second half of the nineteenth century is replete with such photo-poetics,[62] and yet this contamination of the poetic by the material image and technological processes of its production has, until Ortel, simply not found its place in current theories of poetry. In Hugo Friedrich's diagnosis of modern poetry as showing symptoms of "disorientation, disintegration of the familiar, loss of order, incoherence, fragmentism, reversibility, additive style, depoeticized poetry, bolts of annihilation, strident imagery, brutal abruptness, dislocation, astigmatism, alienation,"[63] the forceful register of mechanical, optical, and electrical dysfunctions is a better clue that a shift may be at play in modern poetry than his controversial conclusions. Indeed, we find similar breakdowns of subjectivity already correlated with mechanical, optical, and electrical technologies in a text that had a key influence on the development of romanticism and fantastic literature in France—E. T. Hoffman's "The Sandman" (1816). In it, the hero Nathanael falls prey to a deadly series of phantasms, misperceptions, conspiracies, and trickeries precisely due to the blurring of boundaries between the psychic and the technological.

Literary criticism has resisted correlating—not to mention establishing direct causality between—modernity's mediated and technologized experience, and mutations in the postromantic imagination of poetry. Yet there is no a priori reason to believe that technologies such as photography and cinema damage or supplant the imagination in any way, rather than displacing, reterritorializing, reactivating, or expanding it. The facts and analyses from Ortel's or the present study rather suggest the opposite: that technology has been a powerful catalyst for the poetic imagination. So powerful that this has directly led to a crucial terminological shift, from *l'imagination* (the imagination) to *l'imaginaire* (the imaginary). It appears indeed that the spread of the substantive *l'imaginaire* closely parallels the progressive development of precinema and cinema. Let us make a detour through this separate theoretical episode since it illustrates the historical invisibility of cinema and technology as a correlation to epistemic changes.

Theories of the imagination are usually thought to culminate with romanticism.[64] Wolfgang Iser, for instance, sees the history of concepts of the imagination as going from a model external to consciousness (the passions for Descartes), before becoming internal as its highest faculty (Kant), then encompassing the very act of consciousness (Sartre), and finally evaporating into the social conditioning of consciousness (Castoriadis).[65] But all these models are ultimately romantic in that the imagination is thought of only as a kind of immaterial realm outside consciousness. This is true whether imagination is active as *imaginatio*, the manipulation of imaginary contents (*ars combinatoria*) by "genius," whether imagination is passive as *phantasia*, the uncontrolled exposure of the spirit to corporeal imaginings, and in both Enlightenment theories of the biological impress of visual shock among female subjects, and more recent theories of the unconscious.[66] John Sallis has skillfully deconstructed this model from the purview of phenomenology by showing that the "force of imagination" has little to do with abstraction or transcendence since it inheres to every step of our constituting experience as such.[67] If we bracket the romantic premise, three main features in the characterization of imagining surface. First, it is a process of image making rather than a container of images (Husserl and Sartre); second, it frees mental representations to open them to new affordances involving metamorphosis or movement;[68] and third, much more problematically, it is couched as the opposite of, if not the remedy against, material images (Kearney and Sallis).[69]

The imaginary, I claim, arose as a new term when it became clear that this third feature was untenable, that is, when cinema emerged as a dispenser of automorphic images that began informing the very process of our visual imaginings. Yet even before cinema, another apparatus had shaken the foundation of transcendent-immaterial imagination: Phantasmagoria.[70] This striking apparatus invented in 1795 by the Belgian Robertson, who coined its name, led viewers through dark halls with magic lanterns projecting images on veils and mirrors, often with smoke and musical accompaniment. The magic lanterns with glass slides were on wheels, and a belt connected the wheels to the lens to create zooming effects. It was a huge commercial success. What happened next is crucial for our purpose. Starting from the 1820s and until the emergence of cinema, the term "la phantasmagorie" was used as a common name, stripped of its complicated technological apparatus, as a limit metaphor for nonconceptualizable experiences. It figures in just about every text of the fantastic genre, and many poems and theoretical works of the romantics and symbolists. Generally, it is used only once, to mark an absolute linguistic limit beyond which the sensorial, the subjective, the cognitive, the imagined, but also the given *literary genre* of the text lose clear boundaries.[71] A precinematic technology of mass entertainment was thus condensed into a limit term and trope that inverted the abstract/immaterial nature of imagining.

The two new disciplines that revolutionized the understanding of the imagination in the fin-de-siècle—Husserl's phenomenology and Freud's psychoanalysis—were contemporaneous with the emergence of cinema.[72] Freud's *Traumdeutung* reinserted the uncontrolled *phantasia* within the psyche as both dreaming and phantasm, albeit through the split of the unconscious,[73] while Husserl erased the difference between imagination and ideation by subsuming them under "intentionality," the basic force pulling the mind toward its objects.[74] In perception, Husserl argues, there is always more than the sum of the given percepts at play, and he defines this excess as "free variation," the capacity to modify, project, interrelate, and ideate percepts. Husserlian analyses focus on vision, movement, virtuality, and seriality—the very conceptual array of precinema and early cinema. Husserl's student Eugen Fink explains perception itself in terms of *Abschattungen*—"adumbrations"—that is, the partial and changing percepts of an object that can never be perceived as a whole. Adumbrations imply the capacity to imagine that "hyletic flows"—the movements of our sensorial impresses—coalesce in distinct objects. This closely links kinesthesia, the faculty to perceive movement as such, and imagination.[75] Phenomenology's focus on mobile percepts was also contemporary with physiological movement studies conducted by Étienne-Jules Marey. His work during the 1880s on graphing movement via chronophotography directly led to the synthesis of photographed motion: cinema.

It is at this Husserlian and Mareysian crux that "the imaginary" as a *substantive* enters the picture.[76] Rarely attested in the first part of the nineteenth century (it seems to have been first used by Maine de Biran, a key source for Bergson, in 1820), the term gained currency among late nineteenth-century writers, especially in concert with technological images.[77] It is present in a critical passage of Villiers de l'Isle Adam's *L'Ève future* (1886), the most oft-cited literary precursor of cinema.[78] In 1909, poet Victor Segalen wrote *Imaginaires*, a collection of poetic tales about "The Mysterious," a neofantastic notion that crosses sensorial and mechanical registers and refers pointedly to Villiers's book.[79] In a tale about a beheaded statue, Segalen writes, "The Face is getting nearer, in the perfect stillness of the flat light [*lumière plate*]; it gets nearer, nearer, it grows to the extreme of what the human eye can see, and slowly it becomes virtual [*virtuelle*], flipped over on my face, forehead against forehead and mouth against mouth. . . . I must close my eyes, then, since its eyes have penetrated mine."[80] Historians of early cinema will recognize the haptic protrusion characteristic of early reception of the moving image, amplified in films such as *The Big Swallow* (1901) in which a man in LS advances toward the camera in a zoom effect, until his open mouth "swallows" the camera, or Méliès's *The Man with a Rubber Head* (1902), where a head seems to grow like a balloon then bursts, through means of a tracking shot in composite. Segalen's poetics of *l'imaginaire*, based on scalar optics, is clearly beholden to a new technologically mediated form of imagination.[81] In 1936, Georges Hugnet published a book of poems titled *La Hampe de l'imaginaire*, after having written the scenario of the first film to be deemed surrealist, *La Perle* (France, 1929, dir. H. D'Ursel).

It is Sartre's 1940 study, *The Imaginary: A Phenomenological Psychology of Imagination*, that first marked a philosophical difference between the imagination and the imaginary, considered its "noematic correlate," its conceptual structure in Husserlian language. Sartre follows Husserl in denying that the imagination is a container of either percepts or images, agreeing that it is rather a process, indeed intentionality itself. He insists that in conditioning the purest act of consciousness imagining is equal to freedom: "For a consciousness to be capable of imagining . . . it needs to be free."[82] Sartre accomplishes several things at once: he pushes aside the romantic imagination of poetry, relegates the imaginary to the structural sphere of cognitive functions, and bestows an intentional and existential primacy to imagining as the essence of free consciousness.

Yet greater scrutiny reveals his central argument to rest on an anti-cinematic stance—under the influence of Bergson. His thesis is that consciousness as an imagining flow may be either real (via percepts or percept-related concepts within duration) or unreal (as an imagining flow of representations removed from duration), but that it is free only when real. Hence Bergsonian duration alone vouchsafes freedom. The imagining flow of the dream presents him with an antinomy, since it must be deemed real even though the dreamer is not free. He resolves it by insisting that a dream is not similar to how "the projection of a film shot faster gives us the impression of 'slow-motion,'"[83] since in that case there would a secondary duration. Instead, he writes, the dream "is constituted by a few truncated scenes which, *I imagine*, form a coherent whole,"[84] adding that the illusion of continuity proceeds entirely from "belief." Hence the dream is a falsified montage, an un-free imagining held together by a further positing of (false) consciousness, rather than corresponding to a second duration compressed or distended, which could still qualify as possibly free. Rather symptomatically cinema is called upon on *both* sides of an opposition meant to define consciousness as the imaginary of real duration. In another passage, Sartre must gauge "whether kinesthetic sensations play an essential role in the constitution of the image,"[85] because if the body codetermines imagining flows, consciousness would not be the transparent "nothingness" that alone makes it free. His mental experiment consists of tracing "a figure 8" with his index finger while "his eyes are closed," to find out whether he perceives it as a sensorimotor experience or only an imaginary thing. "What comes to my consciousness," he observes, "is the trajectory of movement *as a form in process* . . . as do the letters in movie advertising taking shape by themselves on the screen" (*comme le font ces lettres des réclames cinématographiques qui se forment elles-mêmes sur l'écran*).[86] On this basis he concludes in quasi-Kantian terms that "it is naturally the unity of consciousness that makes the unity of the image."[87] Earlier, Sartre made a similar point when consciousness was couched as the agency animating photographic images: "We are conscious, in a way, that we *animate* the photo, to lend it its life, in order to make it into an image."[88]

Sartre's photographic and filmic illustrations, we see, are far from peripheral. Ultimately, his entire argument comes to revolve around the question of the cinema effect. As perception scholars have shown, retinal persistence, although a real phenomenon, was wrongly thought to be the optical explanation for cinematic perception, especially among French film theoreticians all the way to George Sadoul and André Bazin.[89] As early as 1912, Max Wertheimer had decisively demonstrated that it was rather due to the "phi-effect," the synthesis of stroboscopic positions of an object that our brain (not our eye) reads as fluid motion. In denying that the imaginary can produce a true imagining flow, Sartre alludes to Roget's stroboscopic illusion of seeing a wheel move opposite to its true motion: "It has happened to me that, annoyed to see a luminous wheel [*roue lumineuse*] turning clockwise, I wanted to make it turn in reverse without succeeding."[90] This wheel on film—for what else is a "luminous wheel"?—robs Sartre of his free consciousness, his knowing that it ain't so.[91] He resorts to bad faith as an explanation: it must be I who, somehow, render myself incapable of seeing the wheel's true movement. The same goes for retinal persistence: "The movements of this violet spot, that stays in my eyes after I looked at a light bulb" must be willed since they result from "the willed movements of my ocular globes."[92] So we must ask why Sartre is so eager to rid consciousness of stroboscopic perception and retinal persistence, if not for the reason that cinema resembles—I even would say, exemplifies—what the imaginary as pure consciousness does for Sartre? In order to protect his fundamental assertion that consciousness is a flow that takes up then cancels out (*anéantissement*)[93] imaginary contents, thereby remaining empty and free, Sartre paradoxically alludes directly to Wertheimer's phi-effect. He writes, "Already the works of Koehler, Wertheimer and Koffka allow us to explain, by *the persistence of formal structures through our positional variations,* certain anomalous constants in perception."[94] Hence Sartre in the end dismisses retinal persistence (which he takes to be the cinema effect) by invoking the phi-effect (which he does not know to be the cinema effect), in order to preserve the free imagining flow of consciousness.

Sartre's position that there are no images in consciousness, only intended objects, and that consciousness alone links imaginary contents together (including to produce the illusion of movement), sides with Bergson's condemnation of cinema as a false synthesis of consciousness. But he defines consciousness through the very processes that cinema best instantiates: the agency of the visual sense of motion (retinal persistence and the phi-effect), the editing of imaginary visual contents (dreams), even the trickster of stroboscopic illusions. In the end, the best definition of consciousness as free imaginary, which cannot be theorized without cinema, might be expressed as: *a purely immaterial camera.* Critics have recently pointed out that Sartre's early work on the cinema from 1925 to 1931, where he tried to reconcile French impressionist film theory (dominated by Epstein's thought) with Bergson, was a prototype for his later articulation of the "for-itself" of consciousness. In his 1925 "Apologie pour le cinéma," for instance, he writes, "film is itself a consciousness, because it is an indivisible flux."[95] Unbeknownst to Sartre, it would seem that his early sense of cinema as Bergsonian duration had carried into his conception of consciousness as the imaginary.

It then appears that the emergence of the imaginary as a theoretical construct is haunted by its being unwittingly but deeply embedded in the cinema apparatus. The thought of Gaston Bachelard, whose work on poetics has shaped the Geneva School of criticism and continues to influence much poetic theory to this day, shares the same predicament. In 1943, he published his key work, *Air and Dreams: An Essay on the Imagination of Movement.* It focuses on imagining flows as the thrust of the poetic image: "The fundamental term corresponding to imagination is not *image*, but *imaginary* [*l'imaginaire*]. The value of an image can be measured by the reach of its *imaginary* aura

[*aura imaginaire*]. Thanks to the *imaginary*, imagination is essentially *open, expansive*."[96] As in Baudelaire, the imaginary aura is synonymous with movement, albeit in a vitalistic vein: "We must systematically add to the study of a particular image the study of its mobility, its fecundity, its life."[97] This vitalist stance, albeit distinct from that of his old enemy Bergson, explains why Bachelard must reject cinema from his imaginary. He posits that "as soon as images offer themselves in series, they designate a primary form of matter, a fundamental element."[98] In other words, images in series are not related to cinematic perception. Offering no justification for this assertion, he does acknowledge that cinema is the target, since he adds that "this 'drive' [*duction*] caused by an intimacy with the real," must be held distinct from "visual mobilism [which] remains purely cinematic."[99] It is clear, nonetheless, that technology haunts Bachelard's conception of poetic movement. When he writes, "Try hard as you might, only flight in dreams allows you, as a whole self, to become a moving object, aware of its own unity, experiencing complete and unified mobility from the inside out,"[100] it is meant to deny that haptic-kinesthetic technologies such as cinema offer such a unified sense of auto-mobility. Yet a footnote on the same page concedes that experiential fusion with machines are possible (he gives as example Saint-Exupéry and his airplane, and Marinetti and his automobile), and that they come close to "a synthesis of the moved and the moving" that is the hallmark of the poetic image. But Bachelard then resorts to a finer distinction, asserting that "the passenger cannot benefit from" the dynamic imagination because only the pilot is "at one with [*faire corps avec*] his machine."[101] Bachelard maintains cinema outside of the poetic imaginary not by rejecting technology altogether—like Bergson—but rather by suggesting that the mind and cinema can never fuse and be at one, like the poet's mind and the poetic image, or the body and the airplane, because anything coming from cinema makes us spectators, that is, passengers rather than pilots. In spite of their differences, Sartre and Bachelard deny cinema any epistemological credit, yet they prove equally unable to theorize the imaginary without bringing back cinema as its sticky supplement.[102]

It is only after the rise of *Filmologie* studies after the Liberation that the cinematic imaginary finally received its dues.[103] Edgar Morin announced as much in the title of his path-breaking book: *The Cinema, or The Imaginary Man*. A transdisciplinary investigation of the phenomenology and sociology of cinema, the book finally tackled the obvious: "The psyche of the cinema not only elaborates our perception of the real, it also secretes the imaginary [*l'imaginaire*]. . . . The cinema makes us understand not only theater, poetry, and music, but also the internal theater of the mind: dreams, imaginings, representations: *this little cinema we have in our heads*."[104] Morin theorizes the reach of cinema into the imaginary by recognizing it as what Walter Ong later called a "technology of cognition" with regard to writing.[105] In many ways, Morin draws his inspiration directly from the cinema theory of the silent era, and chief among the filmmakers and theoreticians he mentions is Jean Epstein.[106]

Morin's keen analysis of the cinematic imaginary—and with it, the whole genealogy of the imaginary itself—was displaced by structuralism and poststructuralism's turn to language. This demotion was famously effected by Jacques Derrida's deconstruction of Jean-Pierre Richard's phenomenological criticism of Mallarmé's "imaginaire."[107] At stake for Derrida was the philosophical underpinning of the so-called thematic criticism linked to the Geneva School, which modeled the imaginary, pace Bachelard, as a regulative-stylistic domain rooted in the deepest sensorial and biographical strata of the writer. For Derrida—and rightly so—such a model was rife with dubious presuppositions that predetermined the text from the outside, robbing it of ontological relevance, and depriving the act of reading of its potential as an event. The imaginary, he objected, smuggled back romantic and vitalist notions of genius, sensibility and soul under the mask of phenomenology, and the term was unredeemable. Notwithstanding, Dee Reynolds has cogently shown that, while the objections of Derrida to Richard's romantic postulates hit the mark, his wholesale rejection of the imaginary overshoots it. For in dismissing the nontextual authorial imaginary, Derrida deprives his philosophy of any imaginary space, notably for the reader, even though the "imagining activity can be stimulated by the sensory characteristics of language itself," she notes.[108] In other words, the famed materiality of the signifier that Derrida defends, tacitly implies a technical agency, a space, and an event that could be called imaginary. Derrida's "Double séance" illustrates such a mode of imaginary experiencing on the part of the reader—Derrida himself. In fact, his reading of Mallarmé's is fully in line with Mallarmé's own poetics in which, Reynolds observes, "the imaginary dimension arises out of the medium."[109] Derrida had legitimate polemical reasons for rejecting, in the name of the text, the imaginary as the last remnant of the authorial doctrine of the "work," but this cannot be construed as a dismissal of imagining altogether. Chapter 1 will suggest that Derrida was in fact aware that what distinguished Mallarmé's writings, that is, the novelty of Mallarmé's conception that a text could be animated by its "spacing," was directly connected to cinema.

The imaginary, as distinct from the imagination, is haunted by cinema from its modern emergence in Villiers's *L'Ève future* in 1886 to its partial dismissal through Derrida's notion of spacing, or *espacement*, itself taken over from Mallarmé. Having shown the cinematic tenor of the notion of the imaginary, we now turn to the other pole of cinepoetry, that of the material field of graphic signifiers.

THE CINE-GRAPHIC FIELD

While the cinematic (and precinematic) imaginary pulled poetry toward a new performative, technological, and corporeal outside, it also had an opposite centripetal effect: it brought a new focus to the scene and materiality of writing, and to the spatial and visual dimensions of the page. As if through a reflex or refractive action, it made writing more aware of itself as a medium. In her 1995 study of literature as a visual practice, Anne-Marie Christin puzzles over the fact that only with Mallarmé's *Un Coup de dés* did the modern Western literary tradition remember the visual aspect of writing, which other eras (the Middle Ages) and other cultures (Japan and China) had considered obvious. She asks, "Why has a revolution consisting only, in the end, of using the alphabet as a true form of writing, not as the recording of speech, occurred so late?"[110] In other words, what caused a sudden break with the enduring rationalist view of the transparency of writing, and of language itself? We might find a broad answer in Rancière's conception of the aesthetic regime of the arts previously mentioned. This new regime synonymous with modernity broke, he claims, with a previous "regime of mimesis" in place until the nineteenth century, according to which each art depended on its own medium-specific form of codified imitation. The new regime instead held that all art products share "an autonomous form of life,"[111] distinct from other products and practices. One consequence is that such epistemic connection between the arts greatly facilitated transfers and contaminations, that is, interart innovation such as cinepoetry, "because the identification of art no longer occurs via a division within ways of doing and making, but it is based on distinguishing a sensible mode of being specific to art products."[112]

This is also a useful way of explaining how a new visuality for writing arose in the late 1800s since it posits an epistemic difference with the *ut pictura poesis* tradition centered on early modern oppositions/transpositions between text and image, without falling into the *Gesamtkunstwerk* vanguard with its teleology of interart fusion. Moreover, Rancière considers that the aesthetic regime of the art proceeds largely from literature, indeed, from the new status of the word as decidedly but problematically material. He asserts that "[modern] literature has been constructed as a tension between two opposing rationalities: a logic of disincorporation and dissolution, whose result is that words no longer have any guarantee, and a hermeneutic logic that aims at establishing a new body for writing."[113] On the one hand, then, literature "lives only by the separation of words in relation to any body that might incarnate their power," while on the other hand, "the written word is like a silent painting that retains on its body the movements that animate the logos."[114] Literary language's pull toward utter abstraction—"la parole muette" (mute speech)—comes with a counterthrust toward utter concretion—"la chair des mots" (the flesh of words). Rancière is well aware that this double movement takes place around the turn of the century when cinema presents itself as a new intermedium between words and things. Yet he is intent in suppressing any agency to technology. In his subsequent book on film, he even takes Jean Epstein as his primary target, strenuously dismissing altogether the cinema apparatus and cinema as art because "it is both the art of the afterward, that emerges from the romantic de-figuration of stories, and the art that returns the art of de-figuration to classical imitation."[115] Against cinema's rear-guard nostalgia, Rancière deploys what he calls "the sentence-image," which he defines thus: "By [sentence-image] I understand something different from the combination of a verbal and a visual form. The power of the sentence-image can be expressed in sentences from a novel, but also in forms of theatrical representation or cinematic montage or the relationship between the said and unsaid in a photograph."[116] It is not the place here to gauge Rancière's omnibus proposal. My point here is only that Rancière clearly wrestles with Christin's question about the sudden birth of modern visual poetry in 1897 by seeing it as a result of wide epistemic changes about writing and visibility from the mid-nineteenth century onward—changes that directly touch upon cinema as both medium and art.

Since the "sentence-image" amends the redefinition of cinema by Deleuze via the "movement-image" and the "time-image," we might turn to this thinker as more willing to look into technics for proximal causes of poetry's mutations. For Deleuze, indeed, the force of technics precipitates changes that reach immediately into poetry: "The action of this force follows two paths: the path of actual history and the development of technology, and the path of poetry and the poetic creation of fantastic imaginary machines. This conception demands . . . new forms of thought which integrate the old poetic unconscious and today's powerful machines."[117] Deleuze is addressing Alfred Jarry's mirroring in poetry some of the changes new technologies brought to the public sphere, and in so doing he opens the way for positing cinepoetry (including in Jarry) as part and parcel of the advent of technics rather than its secondary elaboration.

Rancière and Deleuze—both aware of the philosophy of cinema of Jean Epstein, let us remember—agree on one implicit point: that rearticulations of texts and images, of a visual graphic imaginary, necessarily involves cinema. Walter Benjamin shares this sense as well. In a section of *One-Way Street*, he characterizes a new technologically mediated sensible form of writing as "image-script," "picture-writing," and ultimately, under the sway of cinema, "moving script." Miriam Brattu Hansen glosses this last expression:

> More than simply a "moving script," *Wandelschrift* implies two senses in which writing has become at once more moving and more mobile: a new mutability and plasticity of script (*Wandel* in the sense of change), which heralds a resurgence of writing's imagistic, sensuous, mimetic qualities; and the connotation of the verb *wandeln* (to walk, amble, wander), which suggests writing's migration into three-dimensional, public space and which makes reading a more tactile, distracted experience.[118]

Benjamin explicitly links this cinematic "wandering script" to Mallarmé's visual poem, *Un Coup de dés*, as well as to the multiplication of billboards, placards, lettering, and pulp print within the increasingly mobile public sphere.[119]

Marjorie Perloff, Johanna Drucker, and Willard Bohn, among others, have theorized the direct relationship between this proliferation of public writings and signs, experimental typography, and the aesthetics of avant-garde poems.[120] What makes cinepoetics especially

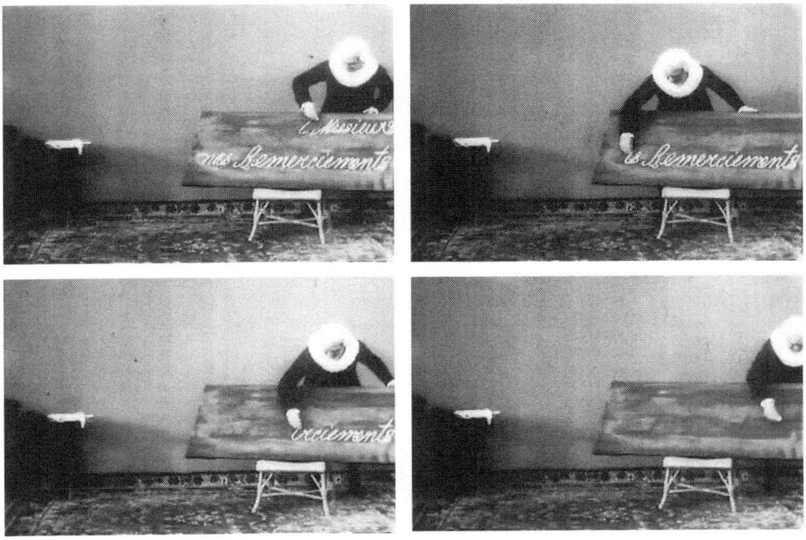

Figure 3. Stills from *Écriture à l'envers* (Reverse writing), Lumière Bros., catalogue no. 42, 1896.

relevant with regard to this linkage is that poets took early notice of how changed letters, writing, and print felt and looked when experienced through cinema's automorphosis. I propose that film was an integral and central agent in how the new mobility of letters after the turn of the century came to the attention of poets and artists. This conjunction might be called the cine-graphic field, and Mallarmé's experiment with visual poetry took place explicitly in it.

Early cinema documented in newsreels the superabundance of signage and commercial lettering in the built world and offered a new frame within which such lettering appeared fragmented, reflected, distorted, less inert, and thus renewed. But early showmanship also took writing and letters as direct subject matter, as "talents" to be manipulated in novel ways. A paradigmatic example is the 1896 short titled "Backward writing" ("Écriture à l'envers") that was shown as ersatz closing credits in many Lumière programs (Figure 3). It features a showman standing behind a low blackboard, writing on two lines: "Le Cinématographe vous remercie" (The Cinématographe thanks you). He does so by starting from the final –e– and writing in cursive backward to the capital L. Fittingly, "à l'envers" means at once "backward," "upside down," and "reversed," since the showman is writing

Figure 4. Stills from Émile Cohl, *Le Binettoscope*, 1908. © Musée Gaumont.

left to right, bottom to top, and traces the letters upside down. This fairground feat, however, becomes truly remarkable when the film is *itself* shown backward. For then, the written words on the board magically disappear while seemingly traced by the chalk in the normal fashion (left to right, top to bottom). Viewers are thus given to see an entirely new kind of ghost writing, writing undoing itself—*unwriting*. Poets like Mallarmé already attuned to the graphic visual field cannot have failed to be struck by how such a film performed what had remained for them abstract possibilities or limit aesthetic ideals. In his *Life Unanimous* (1908), Jules Romains seems intent on describing scenes of reading and writing as involving kinetic vision and visual projections in a way that makes writing come alive, animated, part of the cine-graphic field. Moreover, tableaux from specific movies are recognizable in filigree under some of these descriptions.[121]

In 1910, animation film pioneer Émile Cohl drew and shot *Le Binettoscope* (Mug-o-scope) (Figure 4), a short showing a page with the letters of the alphabet, each of which is progressively transformed into a still human face, before all the faces come to life in the last frames. Both the letters and the faces are drawn graffito style, which suggests that the animation of writing involved the street and ephemera: when Chaplin's hand signs his name on the credit of his *Shoulder Arms* (1918), he does so with chalk for a similar reason. But there is also a more highbrow version of the cine-graphic field in early cinema. In 1910, Léonce Perret's *Le Festin de Balthazar* (Belshazzar's feast) adapted a famous episode from the Book of Daniel in which Belshazzar is warned by supernatural handwriting that he is about to be met with divine punishment. As Richard Abel describes, "A magnified hand writes, 'Mane Thecel Phares,' against a black background wall—a spectacle that is then doubled when an angel (replacing the

Figure 5. Henri-Achille Zo, illustration for Raymond Roussel, *Nouvelles impressions d'Afrique*, 1932. Courtesy of Bibliothèque Nationale de France.

words) steps down to confront the king."[122] This diegetically cinegraphic scene seems to have profoundly marked the writers who saw it. Symbolist poet Saint-Pol-Roux, in his cinepoetic treatise from the 1920s, as well as in unpublished notes, even makes of this episode a cinema before cinema: "The first screening took place at Nebuchadnezzar's [Belshazzar's father's palace]. One night, there could be read on the palace wall that served as a screen for luminous letters prior to the Lumière Brothers: Mane Thecel Phares. The film projector was none other than the prophet Daniel."[123] Raymond Roussel ends his *Nouvelles Impressions d'Afrique* with an illustration showing the same three words surrounded with a comic-book-like jagged halo (Figure 5). As for Marcel Proust, in a crucial passage of *Sodom and Gomorrha* written in 1916, he stages his narrator's realization that Charlus is homosexual as an optical revelation of these words inscribing themselves on his pupils: "Mane Thecel Phares." What links all these intertextual, or rather interfilmic citations, appears to be the new status of the word acquiring a renewed power from its automorphic agency. Filmmakers like Louis Feuillade would have been impressed by such graphic automorphism—especially since Perret was his assistant. The first revelation of the identity of Fantômas in Feuillade's eponymous 1913 series is in fact staged as automorphic writing: his name appears in sympathetic ink on a card before disappearing again (Figure 6). A later example figures in an episode of *Judex* (1916) in which a kidnapped banker "sees" four lines writing themselves on a wall, as if an intertitle had suddenly entered the diegesis (see Figure 2, above).[124]

Such graphic automorphism no doubt stimulated critical interest among poets for Feuillade's crime serials, in particular *Les Vampires* in 1916. For the central enigma of the series—the identity of the mysterious, black-clad female criminal played by the famed Musidora—is resolved in a scene of self-animating letters. The protagonist, a

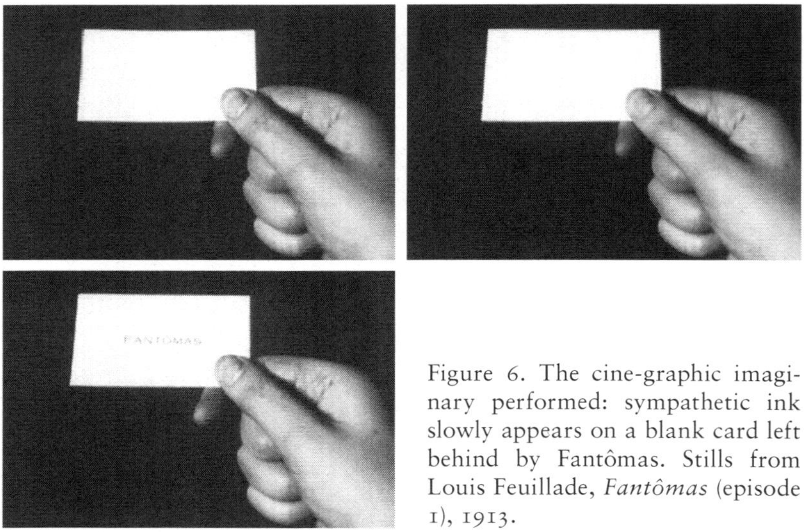

Figure 6. The cine-graphic imaginary performed: sympathetic ink slowly appears on a blank card left behind by Fantômas. Stills from Louis Feuillade, *Fantômas* (episode 1), 1913.

journalist investigating the "vampire" bandits, beholds a poster of cabaret singer Irma Vep, whom he suspects to be the she-vampire. The shot that reveals that they are indeed the same person is an MCU stop-action animation of the words "Irma Vep" rearranging themselves into the anagram "Vampire" (Figure 7). The scene sets up a striking correspondence between the journalist's thought process and the dancing letters, as well as between writing and the legibility of the filmic image. As Musidora's character can be read as lesbian,[125] it is very possible that in Proust, the cine-graphic field combines the queer hermeneutics of "Mane Thecel Phares" with this very shot from *Les Vampires*, since he develops also a trope around a self-traced anagram.[126]

Performances of automorphic lettering—in which letters become their own agents—may have also inspired the other source of renewal of the visual poem apart from Mallarmé, Apollinaire's *Calligrammes* published in 1918, but written from 1912 to 1917. Traditional calligrams, in which words visually mimic a thing, were mostly limited to objects and portraits. The first calligram Apollinaire drew brings together four disparate elements to form a landscape—it is titled "Paysage." Its original title from 1913 was "*Petit paysage animé*" (Small animated landscape), as Willard Bohn has discovered (Figure 8).[127] A "Paysage animé" traditionally denotes a landscape painting

Figure 7. Automorphic anagram, Louis Feuillade, *Les Vampires* (episode 4), 1916.

that includes people, like a Fernand Léger's 1924 painting of that title. However, starting in 1913, according to animation historian Donald Crafton, the term "dessin animé" (animated cartoon) became current, so that Apollinaire's Calligramme may very well be an attempt at remediating the cartoon.[128] In a 1913 letter to André Billy (with whom he coauthored his film scenario in 1917), Apollinaire writes, "As for the *Calligrammes*, they are an idealization of free verse poetry and a typographical enhancement at a time when typography is ending its brilliant career, and at the dawn of new means of reproduction such as cinema and the phonograph."[129] When the sketched "Petit paysage animé" became the final typeset "Paysage," it lost its dynamic and sequential-looking aspect. The single human figure in the poem is composed of the words: "Amants couchés ensemble vous vous séparerez mes membres" (Lovers lying together you will split up my limbs). This human figure thus conceals three different bodies: the speaker's and those of the two lovers (one of whom might also be him). The past participle "couchés ensemble" conceals the

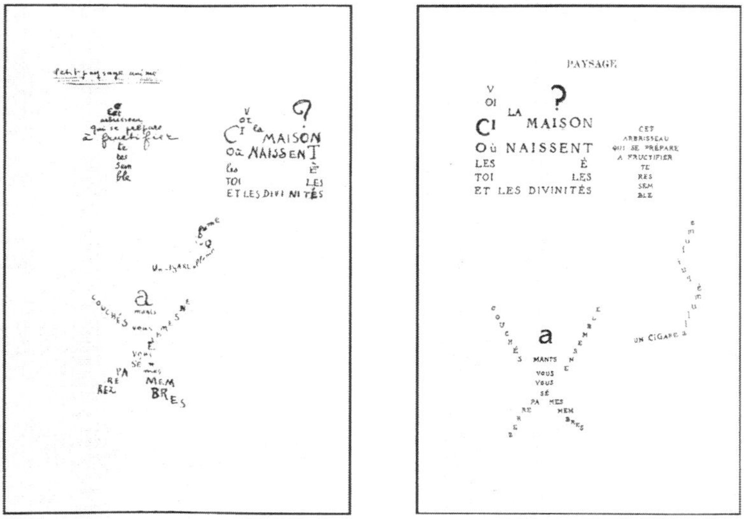

Figure 8. Guillaume Apollinaire's first calligram: "Petit paysage animé" (1913), and its final typeset version, "Paysage" (1918). Courtesy of Willard Bohn.

infinitive "coucher ensemble" (to sleep together), and "you will split up my limbs" hides "you will split up" (*vous vous séparerez*). Hence the wording, the meaning, and the visual figure are layered, spliced, or fragmented—as is the odd time frame, all at once present, future, and retrospective. Even if Apollinaire did not have the cartoon or cinema directly in mind—very unlikely given his acute cinephilia—his first calligramme belongs to the new cine-graphic field inflected by the automorphic imaginary. It is likely that the *Calligrammes* in turn rekindled cine-graphic inventiveness on screen. The letters of the title of Abel Gance's film *J'Accuse* (1919), for instance, are composed of persons (actual veterans, including Blaise Cendrars, Gance's shooting assistant) who move into place in VLS, thereby continuing the back-and-forth of self-animated anthropomorphized letters from cinema (Cohl) to literature (Apollinaire) to cinema (Gance), and back to poetry with Cendrars (Figure 9).

Most cinepoetic works rest on a homology between broad graphic or print components, and broad aspects of film or movie culture. An especially influential homology was /visual poem⇔intertitle card/.

Figure 9. "Dead" soldiers forming the letters of the title of Abel Gance's 1919 *J'Accuse.*

The intertitle or title-card was introduced in the early 1900s during the development of narrative cinema and ended in France with the arrival of the talkies in 1929–30.[130] Its principal use was for continuity support by giving titles or very short plot summaries of scenes to come or marking omitted diegetic events. As the feature film emerged in the early teens, it became increasingly used for notations of dramatic dialogue. Printed program notes and a live commentator often completed this important verbal/textual apparatus of the silent era, which has proved challenging to fully reconstruct. Although poets were of two minds about the use of intertitles in cinema, what is significant is that they registered the novelty of this didascalic form of writing. While in 1919, Pierre Albert-Birot advocates for "the suppression of any text projection," in cinema, Epstein argued that intertitles were needed both narratively and rhythmically, musing in 1924 that "advertising for a film by saying it has no intertitles, is it not like advocating for Mallarmé's poems because they have no punctuation?"[131] Parenthetically, Epstein's remark reveals all at once an intimate knowledge of Mallarmé's poetics, a new form of homology /poems+punctuation⇔film+intertitle/, and a tacit awareness of cinepoetry.

It is poet Pierre Reverdy who likely first grasped the homology /poem⇔intertitle/ by composing blocks of texts modeled on the distinctly squarish aspect of intertitle card texts, which was overdetermined by the squarish aspect ratio of the filmic image (Figure 10). His

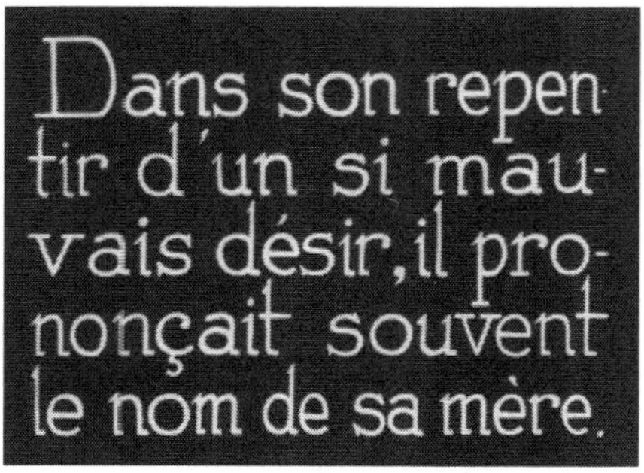

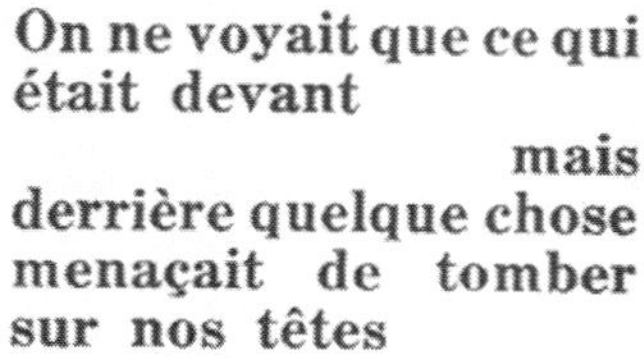
**On ne voyait que ce qui
était devant
mais
derrière quelque chose
menaçait de tomber
sur nos têtes**

Figure 10. (Left) Intertitle from Jean Epstein, *L'Auberge rouge* (1923). © Musée Gaumont. Compare to a page from Reverdy, *Le Voleur de Talan* (1917).

1916 poem titled "Carrés" (Squares), pioneered what has been called the "square-poem," a hallmark of his new poetics which, together with the "crenelated" (indented) poem, retains the squarish symmetrical feel of intertitles.[132] In the late war and early afterwar, poets and filmmakers seemed fully aware that reading a text on the screen, as well as texts embedded in filmic images, opened new avenues for reimagining the text. Take for instance the title shot of Chaplin's 1918 *Shoulder Arms* (Figure 11). It shows a CU of his hand signing his name in chalk on the title card, underneath his picture (a silhouette of himself in character as a soldier). The shot ends with his index finger first pointing to the silhouette, then mimicking a gun and shooting at his signature—a pun on "Chaplin shoots Chaplin." Chalk reappears in a troubling scene of the film: a dream-sequence where his character shoots at off-screen enemy soldiers, making a chalk mark on a small blackboard after each kill. Taken together, these two scenes link the kinetic act of writing to the automorphic image space of cinema with darker connections of ephemerality and death. For French poets, especially those obsessed with Chaplin, such a simple yet complex cine-graphic enactment of meaning—conflating authorship, fiction, identity, verbal/visual punning, automorphosis, killing, dying, joking—could not but trigger attempts at possible equivalences in poetry.

Around World War I, words also begin to figure *within* filmic images themselves. Griffith's 1916 *Intolerance*, one of the most influential American masterpieces for postwar French cinema culture, used lines of Walt Whitman as a leitmotiv, superimposing them directly on shots of a rocking cradle. Germaine Dulac's 1917 *La Belle*

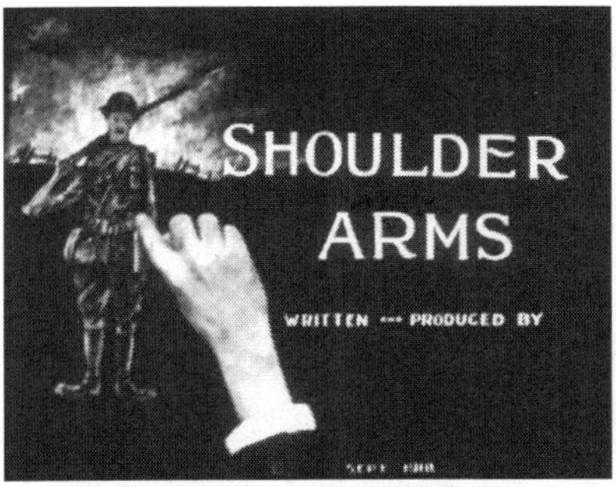

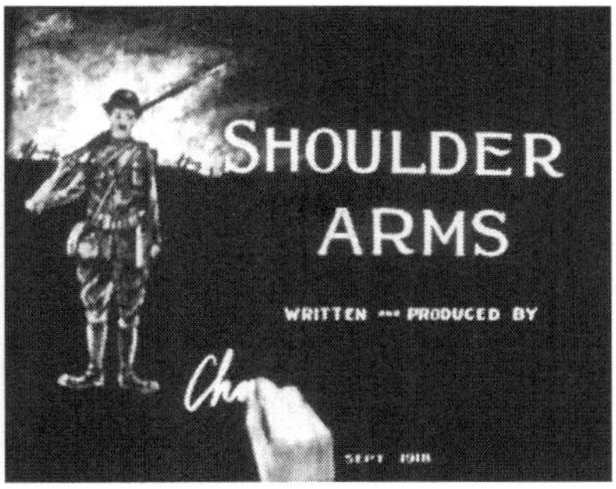

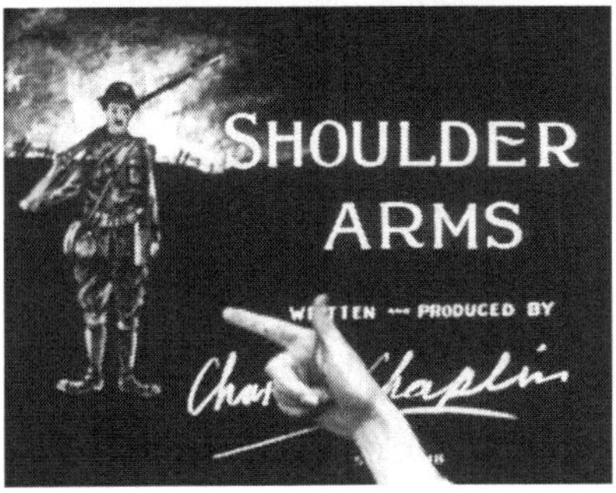

Figure 11. Opening credits of Chaplin's *Shoulder Arms* (1918): the index of Chaplin points to the Tramp-soldier, signs Chaplin's name underneath, then shoots at the still image. © Roy Ames Ltd.

dame sans merci echoed Griffith's intermedium breakthrough by rendering a song through the still shot of a singer's face on which the lyrics appears one line at a time from top to bottom. Amazingly, here the *text* moves while the image is still. The last line reaches just over her mouth as if to suture the words to it. The first French narrative avant-garde reveled in making words move on screen: the opening credit shot of Marcel L'Herbier's 1920 *L'Homme du large* and the closing shot of Germaine Dulac's 1927 *L'Âme d'artiste* both render extradiegetic words mobile, as a kind of *text-over* that may have inspired rolling credits (Figure 12). Marcel L'Herbier's *L'Homme du large* also emphasized the embedding of text within the filmic image. He integrated both text-over and dialogue into the margins of the image by using irises and mattes in various combinations (Plate 2). For such uses of text, we might speak of *intra*titles in a form later expanded by the likes of Jean-Luc Godard and Peter Greenaway.

Let us add that during the crucial years when cinepoetry as such developed (1916–19), all the pioneers of the new poetic avant-garde—Apollinaire, Cendrars, Reverdy, Jacob, Aragon, Goll, Soupault, Epstein, and Breton—were under the sway of the movies and, as

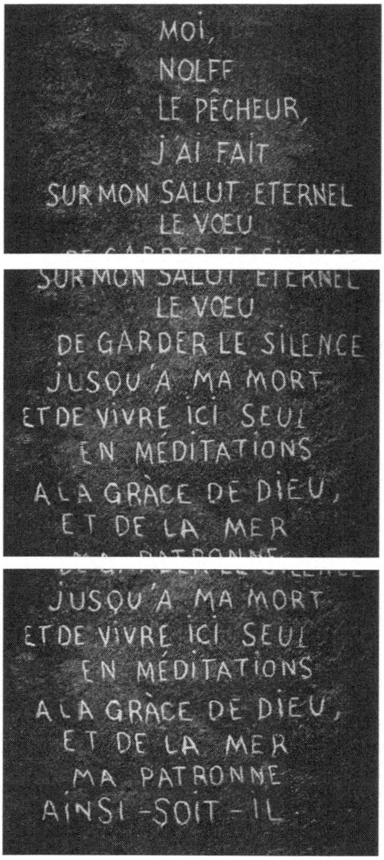

Figure 12a. Cine-graphemes on the margin of the film: Opening rolling credits of Marcel L'Herbier's 1920 *L'Homme du large*. © Musée Gaumont.

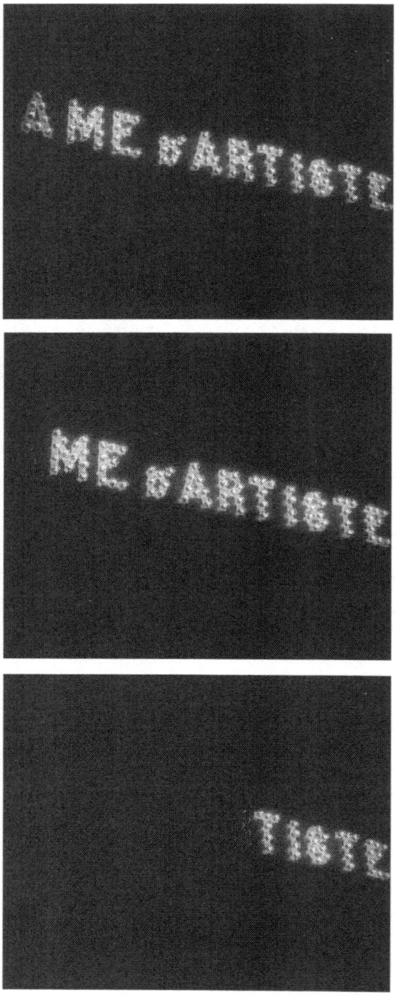

Figure 12b. Cinegraphemes within the film: closing shots of Dulac's 1925 *L'Âme d'artiste*. © Musée Gaumont.

Étienne-Alain Hubert has shown, of Mallarmé's *Un Coup de dés*.[133] The unpunctuated poems with floating lines that many of them wrote were influenced all at once by contemporary cinema and by Mallarmé's poem—itself, unbeknownst to them, already a cinepoem. This illustrates the difficulty, after the 1920s, of separating channels of influence in a poetic landscape which, as a whole, had become, albeit always quite tacitly, deeply cinepoetic.

METHODOLOGY AND OUTLINE

As much as cinepoems are experimental, this book experiments with how to do poetry criticism using film history and concepts, perception studies, and other noncanonical critical frameworks and tools. First, of course, is cinema studies, to which this book hopes to contribute modestly, if only by attempting not to mischaracterize film history and techniques. To this end, I have used the following terminology. I refer to "cinema" as the general technology for projecting automorphic image spaces, whether they be photographic or drawn. "Precinema" refers to the research in various fields and the cultural productions, including in mass performances, from about 1870 to 1895, that ultimately, and perhaps contingently led to cinema. The term "Films" refers to all the strips of images projected in cinema; whereas, the term "The movies" denotes the industry integrated vertically and horizontally, selling and controlling films and ancillary products. Cinema, films, and movies as generating discursive and imaginary effects that shape perception, cognition, subjectivity, and identity I call "the apparatus." Finally, the term "screenings" refers to the performing of films, historically in various venues (traveling shows and so on) and within heteroclite entertainment programs (live music, live acts, commentary, and so on). These intersecting aspects change throughout history and are neither independent of nor reducible to each other. Cinema historians insist that before tending toward normalization in the Hollywood studio production model, cinema's praxis, especially in its early and silent period, was pluralistic and contingent regarding what it showed, where, how, and to whom, and how it envisaged itself. Poets tended to regard the cinema likewise, as a techno-cultural project in progress, open to experimentation, and laden with a potential often as disproportionate as that which some attribute today to digital technology. This study also uses the standard way of describing film shots through their scale (ECU=extreme close up, and so forth), camera movements, and brief mise-en-scène. *Cinepoetry* puts in question the hierarchy (cultivated in "adaptation studies") that places literature above cinema, granting literary scholars a dispensation from addressing cinema as a discipline. Conversely, it invites cinema studies, in considering Jean Epstein as a critic of literature and a writer on the cinema, to take better stock of the poetics of writing on and around film.

The relationship of modernity, modernism, and cinema that is central to this study has led to a fractious debate around Walter Benjamin's influential "shock" model of perceptual change due to cinema. Let us address this question briefly. David Bordwell has called this model "the modernity thesis," claiming that scholars such as Tom Gunning argue that the aesthetics of shock in the early "cinema of attractions" correlates to changes in the human perceptual apparatus.[134] Bordwell asserts that modernity is a vacuous moniker and that perception systems result from evolutionary duration, meaning that cinema could cause no hard-wired changes. For Bordwell, conjectures about modernity distract from the true job of film studies: the analysis and typology of film forms. Gunning has given a measured rebuttal to the often caricatural critiques of Bordwell and his followers.[135] He points out that theory need not and does not exclude careful analysis and asserts that avant-garde film aesthetics, dismissed as unrepresentative by Bordwell, nonetheless altered the overall perceptual and cultural horizon in ways requiring no hard-wired changes. I consider that cultural and cognitive etiologies in the humanities need not exclude, but on the contrary can complement, each other. This said, I am indebted to Gunning's stance that "the avant-garde valued cinema for what it was *not*" while also "articulating aspects of what cinema was, isolating new—and for this generation defining—differences it displayed from other arts."[136] By deploying their texts between film and poetry, between the movies they saw and the utopian apparatus they dreamed of, weaving together the actual and the potential, cinepoets demonstrate the real effects imaginary resonances of cinema can have. Bordwell's statement that our sensory systems are unchanging "perceptual-cognitive-affective universals"[137] is just as hypothetical as the modernity thesis, since we can hardly peel away our contingent layers to access bare perceptual systems, nor can we measure whether they have changed. In the late 1920s Jean Epstein noted that silent films from the early 1920s were already felt to be too slow by general audiences, an indication that within the span of a few years the cadence of visual deciphering had changed.[138] This habituation represents a tangible shift in spectatorial practices for which "soft-wired" seems indeed too soft. In a sustained thought experiment, Walter Ong proposed that we can only conjecture what living, thinking, speaking, even maintaining social ties may have been like before the advent of writing and the deep cognitive hold of literacy. He calls writing a "cognitive technology."[139] For exactly the same reasons, so is cinema. Ong challenges the idea of an unchanging human nature as a myth, arguing instead that a technology like writing becomes internalized through such a complete experiential and cognitive adaptation that we simply can no longer step back from it. Metaphors such as "hard-wired" versus "soft-wired" and entrenched oppositions between cultural studies and cognitive approaches seem to me played out.[140] A reasoned middle position is possible whereby deep technologies such as writing and cinema, but also the contingent forms and power of their cultural deployment, reveal new and equally "real" cognitive-affective potentials. The modality common to both cultural and cognitive etiologies is that of psycho-sensorial *plasticity*. There again, cinema's automorphosis, intuited along similar lines by ideas such as Jean Epstein's "photogénie," Elie Faure's "cineplasticity," and Sergei Eisenstein's "plasmatics" could be enlisted to conceptually open the way.[141]

Plasticity represents a critical nexus where perception, metamorphosis, technology, and habitus interact.[142] Merleau-Ponty's embodied perception as haptic interface—the "intertwining" between perceiver and world—typifies the new primacy of mediating plasticity in phenomenology's overcoming of both Cartesian and Hegelian dualisms.[143] In a 1944 talk on cinema, Merleau-Ponty suggested that if film was able to synthesize the rhythms of poetry and the analytical power of philosophy it was because of its uniquely plastic capacity for rendering social and embodied situations.[144] One of the premises of cinepoetry is that poets took the cinema to be a perceptual prosthesis offering virtual tests of the plasticity of embodied experience. Hence this book uses theories of sensorial experience derived from Merleau-Ponty, relating especially to the motor apprehension of depth, through which I link cinematic space with new strategies of description in language. David Morris, analyzing depth—which, following Edward Casey and Merleau-Ponty, he calls "our first dimension"—argues that we must refrain from attempting to understand 3-D by translating from 2-D.[145] Rather than remaining within the "logic of solids," Morris continues, we should conceive perception as a dynamic engagement with a field, since "vision is inherently interactive and prospective," residing *in* the field of perception.[146] Space does not appear in discrete images but in voluminous flows amounting to a "topology of envelopment." Morris associates this evocative term on the one hand with the "peristaltic flows" of our experience of walking through a landscape as 3-D forms reveal themselves through "the continuous unfolding" of their mobile envelopes (not just through immaterial "perspectives"), and on the other hand with morphogenesis—the dynamic and autopoetic reorganization of an organism's inner and outer forms as it grows.[147] Lest this appear remote, let us remember that 1920s filmmakers of the photogénie movement, especially Germaine Dulac, pointed to accelerated films of the growth and visual plasticity of a wheat germ or a crystal as the very essence of cinema.[148]

Morris's Merleau-Pontyan topology of envelopment partakes of a recent ecological approach to perception that breaks radically with late Cartesian notions of perception as representations in the brain.[149] Alva Noë has theorized what he calls "enactive vision," proposing that vision takes place literally in the world. He writes, "Perception isn't something that unfolds in the brain *however characterized*, whether in information-processing terms, or those of neurophysiology." To the contrary, he continues, "*Vision is a mode of exploration of the environment drawing on implicit understanding of sensorimotor regularities.*"[150] Vision, in other words, is interdependently linked to other sensory modalities in the way it projects onto and tests the environment. Vision, we might say, is paradoxically antiocularcentric,[151] and writings derived from a fuller experience of cinema proceed from a similar intuition of reembodied vision. Coining a word, the poet Supervielle wrote in 1925 that, with cinema, "all our senses become ocularized [*s'ocularisent*]," by which he explicitly means a two-way relation that also integrates nonocular sensations within vision.[152] Cinepoetry breaks with the *ut pictura* poetics in a way that parallels the way enactive vision breaks with visual models based on internalism and mimesis. Cinepoetic works thus involve the reader's active filling-in of meaning through a virtual multisensory experience of cinematic image spaces. Noë insists that "the content of perceptual experience is *virtual*," with the proviso that "*virtual* presence is a kind of presence, not a kind of nonpresence or illusory presence."[153] Since the division between perception and imagination is largely based on the polar opposition of presence versus absence, the theory of enactive vision reopens channels between perception and imagination.[154] The scenario form, most notably, draws its poetic potential precisely from being a medium *in stereo*, writing doubled by the virtual presence of a film.

Edgar Morin pointed out in 1956 that "it is not pure chance if the language of psychology and that of cinema often coincide in terms of projection, representation, field, and images."[155] It is even truer today in pragmatic and cognitive linguistics where notions of situational "frame" and "script," of "actors" following "scenarios," and of "schemas" suggesting "possible worlds" have become normalized seemingly unawares how much such a conceptual apparatus owes to cinema. While this study only loosely refers to pragmatics—the analysis of "the functional relatedness of language with the other facets of human life"[156]—it shares with it an attention to the situational implications of language in spatial, temporal, embodied, social, and user-oriented contexts. Taking care not to generalize unduly either the romantic imagination or the cinematic imaginary, we will look for ruptures between these two creative modes of envisioning by carefully probing the role of the cinema apparatus in both constructing cinepoetry's possible worlds and shaping cinepoetry's textual economy.

The selected texts examined in *Cinepoetry* represent a unique corpus of more than a century of medium crossing, remediation, and postmedium practice—as such migrations and alterations have been described, often more theoretically than through the study of such a corpus.[157] My discussions of specific texts will engage with some of these theories to gauge their usefulness and their shortcomings. Hence this book contributes to cross-medium studies by proposing to make explicit the homologies cinepoetic writings developed between poetry and cinema. Whenever possible, these homologies will be indicated by a double arrow sign in between slashes. They range from the more general /poetry⇔cinema/, /poetic text⇔scenario/, to more specific: /act of writing words on paper⇔projected moving images on screen/, /textual trope⇔shot edit/, or /poetic stanza⇔film shot(s)/. Texts and passages that either break a homology or prove unable to sustain it are equally of interest, and it should be noted that often cross-medium transfers are a great deal more oblique than any single homology would suggest.

Since cinepoetry embraces the oldest of the new media as its imaginary, it has affinities with the longer historical view on media

Figure 13. George du Maurier's drawing of a "Telephonoscope," *Punch's Almanach*, 1878.

archaeology taken by the likes of Siegfried Zielinski,[158] as well as with the interest for "imaginary media," about which the editor of a recent collection on that topic notes, "For a long time cinema has obviously been a dominant medium to define the popular media imagination."[159] Imaginary cinema has in fact preceded in both written and visual form technical work on the apparatus. In 1878, Georges du Maurier published in *Punch's Almanack* a striking drawing of a "telephonoscope": it is a home teleconferencing apparatus with a large screen through which British parents speak to and see their daughter located in Africa (Figure 13).[160] Already in 1872, the poet Charles Cros—who invented a color photography process and conceived of the phonograph a year before Edison—published a short tale titled, "An Interastral Drama," that foresees cinema.[161] In this futuristic tale, astronomers from the Earth and Venus communicate through strong telescopes allowing them to see each other directly. The son of an astronomer from Earth and the daughter of an astronomer from Venus fall in love and seek more promiscuity:

> They believed they could vanquish the distance separating them by exchanging the most complete traces of their bodies. They sent each other serial photographs sufficient [*photographies en séries suffisantes*] for the reproduction of relief and movement. Glaux [the son] . . . would shut himself in a room to reproduce on smoke or dust clouds the moving image [*l'image mouvante*] of his beloved—an impalpable image made only of light.[162]

In late 1873, Cros presented a "Project of communication with the inhabitants of Venus," before the Académie des sciences. The astronomer Jules Janssen most certainly attended this conference, since he was elected to the Académie that very year,[163] and he was then developing his famous photographic revolver to shoot "serial photographs" (*photographies par séries*) of the 1874 transit of Venus.[164] This revolving camera, in turns, directly inspired Muybridge's *analytical* experiments in 1878, which developed into chronophotography, then inspiring Marey's own experiments. Subsequently, Edison's viewing of Marey's work in Paris led to his working toward chronophotographic *synthesis*, resulting in the Kinetograph of 1888. Quite remarkably, then, Cros had extrapolated both the *serial analysis* and the *serial synthesis* of movement by photographs, as well as envisioning its projection on an automorphic medium—smoke or dust. Cinema may well be the paradigmatic imaginary media of the twentieth century: yet even before its technological threshold of execution, nineteenth-century French poets—Cros and Villiers—first imagined it.[165] The contested category of "precinema" does not devolve from favoring superstructure or teleology over base or contingency, but of giving their due to historically documented expressions of imaginary cinema, rather than considering only actual technical apparatuses.

Regarding the organization of the book, it seemed that neither a purely chronological approach (because of cinepoets' lack of mutual awareness of each other) nor a purely thematic approach (since many texts are nonetheless informed by common historical conditions and aesthetic debates) was fully appropriate. I have adopted a compromise with a general chronological slant that includes several transhistorical exceptions.

The launching point in Part I, "The Early Poetic Sensorium of the Apparatus," is provided by Stéphane Mallarmé's little noticed comment about the Lumière's Cinématographe in 1897, which reveals his surprising familiarity with many major players in early French cinema. Disrupting commonplaces about symbolism, technology, and the rise of the prewar avant-gardes, Chapter 1 bridges the sensorium of the early cinema of attractions and the aesthetics of Mallarmé, by focusing on kinesthesia and textuality. Chapter 2 analyzes an epic poem of Raymond Roussel, "La Vue," which describes a miniature photograph in more than two-thousand verses, demonstrating how a new kind of ekphrasis, located at the brink between photography and cinema, informs mutations in poetic form, composition, and language, while later shaping an important moment in the thought of Foucault. In Chapter 3, Jean Cocteau's fascination with cinematic immersion from 1913 onward completes a sketch of the early cinepoetic sensorium in writing, with analyses of the embodied poetics of the cone of projection, the dimensional imaginary (Cocteau's drawn cartoons), and the immersive materiality of writing.

Part II, "Telepresence of the Marvelous: Cinepoetic Theories of the 1920s," centers on Jean Epstein and the contest between cinepoetics and Surrealism. Chapter 4 explores the written work of filmmaker Jean Epstein, who both theorized and practiced cinepoetry in 1920–22. His cinepoetic experiment, *Bonjour cinéma*, melds poetic and essayistic writing to explore on its own terms spectatorial experience, which formed the core of his later corporeal theory of cinema, *photogénie*. This chapter contains the first close examination of Epstein's *The Poetry of Today*, a book that offers an incisive and extensive theory of the poetic image in the age of cinema. Chapter 5 argues that Breton eschewed cinepoetry as prosthetic and tainted by commercialism while at the same time sublimating cinepoetics into surrealism. Breton's key allies in the 1924 *First Manifesto of Surrealism* were all pioneer cinepoets (Reverdy, Aragon, Soupault, Saint-Pol-Roux), and his theory of the "marvelous image" closely echoes Epstein's new model of film-mediated language. This chapter addresses theories of the avant-garde that take Surrealism as their paradigm and draws theoretical consequences from Breton's occlusion of cinepoetry. Since the whole French avant-garde was under the sway of Chaplin, Chapter 6 examines several cinepoems to elucidate the intersection of writing, body, ontology, and Chaplin's films and persona, in poetic terms.

Part III, "Cinepoetry and Postwar Trauma Cultures," puts in parallel the aftermaths of both world wars. Chapter 7, "The Poem-Scenario in the Interwar (1917–1928)," analyzes poem-scenarios written in the wake of World War I that explored cinema as a temporal and sensorial apparatus for diffracting trauma. Cendrars's 1918 *The End of the World Filmed by the Angel of Notre Dame*, Apollinaire and André Billy's 1917 *La Bréhatine*, Ricciotto Canudo's 1924 *The Other Wing*, and Artaud's 1926 *Dix-huit secondes* (Eighteen seconds) are all centered on traumatic aftermath, moments of blindness, and the imaginary reversibility generated by cinema. Two unfilmable film-scenarios, Romain Rolland's 1920 *La Révolte des machines* (The revolt of machines) and Irène Hiller-Erlanger's *Voyages en kaléïdoscope*

(*Trips Through the Kaleidoscope*), are examined also since their cine-poetics of war trauma does not exclude a new techno-utopianism. Chapter 8, "Reembodied Writing: Lettrism and Kinesthetic Scripts (1946–1959)" shows how cinema aided in the material reconceptualization of poetic writing after World War II and the Shoah. Jean Cayrol, Isidore Isou, Maurice Lemaître, Gabriel Pomerand, Christian Rodanski, Jean-Pierre Duprey, and Henri Michaux all redeployed cinepoetics in the 1950s in line with what Cayrol describes as a post-Shoah "Lazarean" aesthetics.

Part IV, "Cinema's Print Culture in Poetry," addresses the "subliterature" Epstein took to be at the source of cinepoetics. Chapter 9, "Postlyricism and the Movie Program: From Jarry to Alferi," presents the film program as a new mode of organization of poetic pieces and a new economy of meaning requiring a participatory poetics, a "filling-in" on the reader's part. A similar strategy is found in Jarry's 1897 *Exploits and Opinion of Dr. Faustroll* and in the 1997's *Kub Or* of Pierre Alferi. Other examples come from a Max Jacob poem and Irène Hille-Erlanger's 1919 *Voyages en kaléïdoscope*. Chapter 10, "Cine-Verse: Decoupage Poetics and Filmic Implicature," reads closely two intermedia books, the 1925 *Drames sur celluloïd* (Celluloid dramas) by Pierre Chenal (who later coined the term "Poetic Realism"), which is a film program with compact scenarios in verse, and the 1928 *Un Suicide* by novelist and film critic André Beucler, a shot-by-shot decoupage in verse with intertitle boxes.

Part V, "Skin, Screen, Page: Cinepoetry's Historical Imaginary," endeavors to read three major cinepoetic texts of the 1960s and 1970s addressing the posthistorical and postcolonial condition. In Chapter 11, we look at *Tel Quel* writer Maurice Roche's challenging "novel" *Compact,* which displays polyvocal paragraphs in colored inks, with themes of blindness and post-Shoah trauma, in post-Hiroshima Japan. Rarely analyzed, it reprises crucial aspects of the aesthetics of cinepoetry. Chapter 12 examines *Western*, a self-titled "cine-poem" by Guadeloupean author Max Jeanne, which denounces France's enslavement of the Caribbean by staging history as a sarcastic western. Its cinepoetics, I argue, provide an eschatological space of justice that follows in the footsteps of Guyanese poet Léon-Gontran Damas and Haitian poet Frankétienne. Finally, Chapter 13 reads through *Le Collier de ptyx* (The ptyx necklace), a cine-novel by poet and filmmaker Nelly Kaplan—Abel Gance's close friend and legal heir—that functions as a fitting synthesis of cinepoetic history since it involves a specialist of Mallarmé and a virtual film-within-a-film associated with André Breton, while addressing South American dictatorships from the 1970s.

The Conclusion, "The Film to Come in Contemporary Poetry," provides an overview of recent work by contemporary poets who are experimenting with radically new poetic forms, either by invoking the notion of *dispositif* (apparatus) and pointing toward digital culture and performance, or resorting to what I call the "photo-cinematic difference," by mixing photographs and poetry while trying to overcome the logic of collage. The open question is whether this work, partly inspired by electronic media, represents another chapter in the cyclical forgetting and rediscovery of cinepoetry, or whether it signals a break, and perhaps the emergence of a *post*cinematic imaginary.

Finally, two major preoccupations have informed the making of this book: first, a wish to show that poets and poetic works have much to tell us about the culture of moving images that is too often seen as antithetical to poetry, if not signaling its historical disappearance altogether; and second, a desire, in the face of a troubling canonical retrenchment within the humanities and literary studies, to keep looking for new voices (including old ones) and revive forgotten texts by established voices, so as to keep open the very question of what literature has been and might be in the eyes of the broadest section of its past and future practitioners.

PART ONE

The Early Poetic Sensorium of the Apparatus

CHAPTER ONE

Mallarmé Unfolds the *Cinématographe*

" . . . a series of <imaginary mental written> images <linked b[y]> connected by a thread . . . "

—STÉPHANE MALLARMÉ, draft preface for *Un Coup de dés*, April 1897[1]

In 1898, Stéphane Mallarmé became the first poet to comment in writing on the new *Cinématographe.*[2] Concurrently, he wrote the first poem mediated by cinema—*Un Coup de dés*—and began to plan a live performance combining poetry, cinema, and other media, an unfinished project that came to be known as *Le Livre*, possibly with the Paris World Fair of 1900 in mind.[3] We will examine what led him to consider cinema as at once a new imaginary medium for the text, a virtual expansion of the poem as a form, and the ideal technical supplement for poetry's public enactment.

Mallarmé's oeuvre has long been held as typifying modern literature's inner and outer limits. It signaled both the waning of the romantic sensibility and the dawning of "the great divide" of modernity, that between art as social participation (whether via popular literature or political vanguard) and art as withdrawal (whether as art for art's sake or reactive vanguard).[4] Critics like Blanchot, Barthes, Derrida, and Kristeva have sought to rescue Mallarmé from the "wrong" side of modernity by foregrounding the radical historicity of his conception of subjectivity, made famous by his injunction to "relinquish the initiative to words," and make language the primary agency within the poetic subject. For modernist studies, *Un Coup de dés*, the first modern visual poem, and Mallarmé's thoughts on music and dance, all point to notions of the total work of art, the dialectics of form and whole versus randomness and fragmentation, the materiality of signifiers, the writing of finitude, and a general philosophical alteration of the logos (Figure 14). Yet the myth of Mallarmé as pure

SOIT
que

l'Abîme

blanchi
étale
furieux
sous une inclinaison
plane désespérément

d'aile

la sienne
par
avance retombée d'un mal à dresser le vol
et couvrant les jaillissements
coupant au ras les bonds

très à l'intérieur résume

l'ombre enfouie dans la profondeur par cette voile alternative

jusqu'adapter
à l'envergure

sa béante profondeur en tant que la coque

d'un bâtiment

penché de l'un ou l'autre bord

Figure 14. A page from Stéphane Mallarmé's *Un Coup de dés*, 1897.

poet, fueled by disciples such as Paul Valéry and Wallace Stevens, has led to a sustained lack of critical attention to the breadth of his interests: sociality, commodity and specular culture, corporeality, and the everyday.[5] Rectifying this situation, recent commentators have studied Mallarmé's fascination with concerts, modern dance and theater, newspapers and the women's press, postal poetry, photography, and pulp novels.[6] For instance, in the Doucet archive in Paris I have found a small undated comic strip by Mallarmé, showing the arrival at the Melun train station of his muse/mistress Méry Laurent (nicknamed "The Peacock"). This is a significant clue that the poet was attentive to cartoon art, such as that of Émile Cohl, who later pioneered film animation in 1908, and that he was actively interested in the poetics of serial images (Figure 15). Cinema clearly belongs to this constellation of mass and visual culture interests. What sets it apart, however, is that as a new medium and apparatus reframing interrelations between language, image, time, and space, it had the potential to affect fundamental aspects of textual and literary representation. I will endeavor to show that Mallarmé's late projects—with *Un Coup de dés* and *Le Livre*—from roughly 1890 to his death in 1898, must be understood as a radical alteration of the medium of writing through its permeation by cinema and cinematic thought.[7]

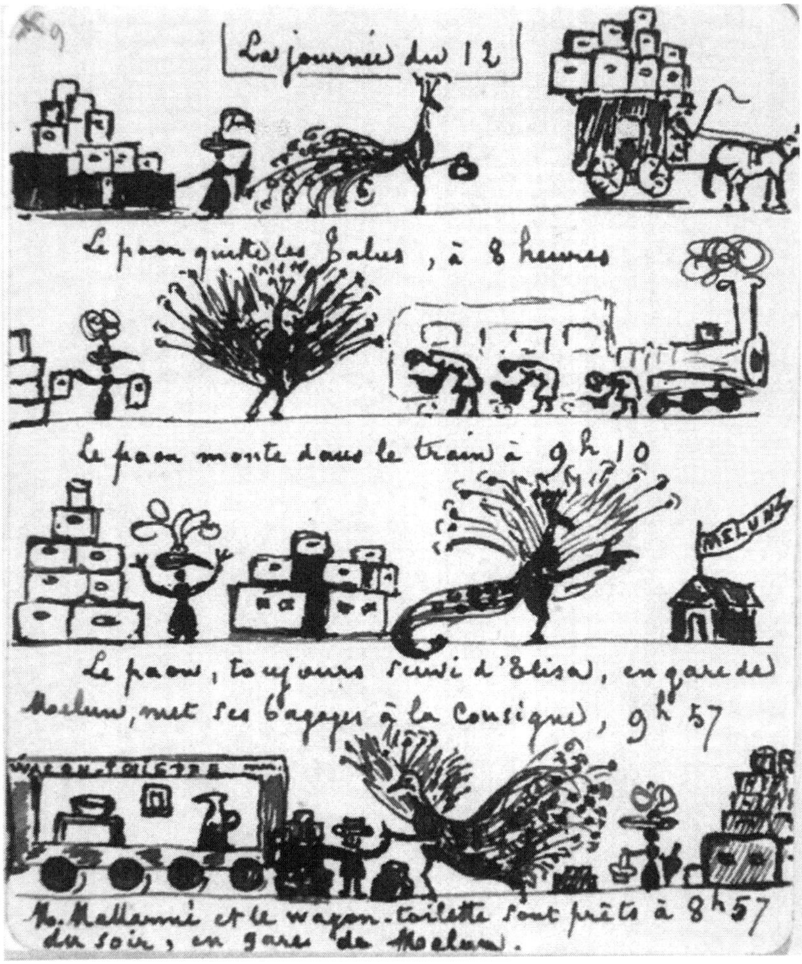

Figure 15. Comic strip by Stéphane Mallarmé, "La journée du 12," ca. 1890. It shows the arrival of Méry Laurent, nicknamed "Le Paon—the Peacock," at the train station of Melun. © Bibliothèque littéraire Jacques Doucet / Madame Marie-Thérèse Stanislas.

CINEMA IN MALLARMÉ

In the neat version of its origin tale, cinema sprang to life full-blown on December 28, 1895, in Paris, when the Lumière brothers opened their Cinématographe to the paying public. The record points instead to a great deal of exchange and rivalry among competitors throughout the late 1880s and 1890s.[8] Nonetheless, very quickly the Cinématographe spread through the public sphere, first for its magical photo-mimetic automorphism projected on screen, and second because its apparatus was remarkably compact and portable, as well as reversibly usable as camera and projector. The two journalists present at the inaugural December 28, 1895, show insisted on a third feature as well, exulting the fact that "it is life itself, it is motion recorded live [*sur le vif*]," "death will cease to be absolute . . . life will have left an indelible trace [*trace indélébile*]," "life is reproduced."[9] Their excitement sprang from the perceived dissolution of the barrier between life and death.

Only two weeks later, it would seem in a world apart, Mallarmé declared his candidacy for the honorary position of "Prince of Poets" left vacant by the death of his friend Paul Verlaine a week earlier. Traditionally bestowed by acclamation, the position was put up for election instead, in a spirit of democracy and because poets from different groups were vying for the position and publicity. Mallarmé, as presumptive heir, was asked to write and publish a short electoral platform:

> Poètes,
> D'un geste, se conçoit, à l'heure—où prestige matériel évanoui, hélas!—en lumière pure se résout le fantôme humain. . . .
>
> [Poets, It can be conceived through a gesture, now that—the material prestige having vanished, alas!—the human ghost resolves itself in pure light.][10]

The translation is approximate because of Mallarmé's willfully elliptical style. This "pure light," I argue, is not only a metaphor for the departed Prince of Poets' soul, but a multiple formulation pointing to the genesis of cinema. For while clearly addressing the posthumous glory of Verlaine, Mallarmé's image not only echoes the shock of cinema, still reverberating in the press, and the new posthuman era it opens,[11] but it also refers back to a crucial literary work of precinema.[12]

In 1886, Mallarmé's friend Villiers de l'Isle-Adam had published his poetic novel *L'Ève future*, the focus of which is a female automaton belonging to a new race of "electrical ghosts" (*fantômes électriques*).[13] With this work Villiers presciently extrapolated the cinema that was to come out of chronophotography, correctly positing that Edison would be its inventor:

> . . . on the large white canvas . . . was refracted the life-size apparition of a very pretty and quite young red-haired woman. The vision, transparent flesh, miraculously photochrome, was dancing. . . . The movements had the quality of flow of Life itself, thanks to the process of serial photography which, on a six-yard-long ribbon, can capture ten minutes of the motions of a being on microscopic glass-slides, later reflected back through a powerful lamposcope. . . . Suddenly a flat and heavy voice, silly and harsh resounded. . . . The gestures, gazes, lip movements . . . were reproduced.[14]

For Villiers, the "electrical ghost" and the filmic image are synonymous. In a written eulogy after the death of Villiers in 1889, Mallarmé speaks of him as a "luminous ghost" (*fantôme lumineux*)[15] and shows great familiarity with *L'Ève future,* quoting a long passage from the novel that mentions "the automaton [*automate*] . . . fabricated by Edison."[16] It seems to me that the luminous ghosts in Mallarmé have Villiers's cyborg, and thus cinema, as intertext.[17]

What directly links Villiers's 1886 *L'Ève future* and Mallarmé's 1896 tangential reference to cinema is a front-page article from May 8, 1893, in *Le Figaro* titled "*Une visite chez Edison*," the first eyewitness account of a picture show in a leading French newspaper.[18] The author, Octave Uzanne, recounts how "voiceless, incapable of the slightest possible expression, in sheer disbelief," he viewed a short movie of a Tyrolian man dancing, through the peephole of a Kinetograph box. Uzanne adds that "these shots . . . reproduce, with all the expression of life and the acceleration of movement, the human gesture [*le geste humain*] methodically recorded." For several reasons, we can be certain Mallarmé read this article. He was a regular subscriber of, and contributor to *Le Figaro*, and Uzanne was a close friend and correspondent; he and Mallarmé belonged to a tight circle called the "dinners of the occult," with Octave Mirbeau and Édouard Manet.[19] More to the point, Uzanne and Mallarmé had exchanged letters regarding the welfare of Villiers's widow. Uzanne could hardly have visited Edison's laboratory without thinking of Villiers's book—which takes place almost entirely in Edison's laboratory—and probably did so *because* Villiers's fiction was about to become reality. In the longer version of the interview published the same year in his book *Vingt jours dans le Nouveau Monde* (Twenty days in the New World), Uzanne indicates that he asked Edison point-blank "whether he had read *L'Ève future* or whether someone had told him of the novel"—the scientist muttering dismissively that he never read novels.[20] For these reasons it is very likely that Uzanne discussed his experience at Edison's Menlo Park laboratory with Mallarmé—including Edison's prognostic that production was "eighteen months to two years away."[21] It may have been at that point that the poet began to consider how the impending implementation of some kind of cinema apparatus would affect literature.

Let us now turn to a number of interactions and connections that Mallarmé had with figures key to the emergence of cinema in France. In November 1894, Arthur Meyer, owner of the Musée Grévin and the newspaper *Le Gaulois,* asked performer Émile Reynaud to start using "instantaneous photographs" in his projected *Pantomimes lumineuses.*[22] Mallarmé knew Meyer (having met him in December 1895 at the latest), and would have been fascinated by Reynaud's animated projections, in particular the *Pauvre Pierrot*—a key figure for Mallarmé.[23] In August 1894, a poem by Henri de Régnier, a close friend and disciple of Mallarmé, had been staged by Lugné-Poe at the Théâtre de l'Oeuvre, with "ghosts" (*fantocini*) moving "behind a veil of gauze" and "mimicking the words pronounced by actors."[24] Was this a performance akin to the shadow puppetry made popular at the Montmartre's *Chat noir* cabaret—or was it the earliest attempt at cinepoetic staging?[25] It is quite likely as well that Mallarmé knew firsthand of the development of the camera/projector. In May 1896, he writes a letter to his friend, the photographer Paul Nadar (son of pioneer photographer Félix Nadar, also a close friend), chiding him for working too hard and thanking him for going sailing together.[26] On June 24, Paul Nadar would apply for a patent for a reversible cinematographic camera, whose prototype he had been feverishly constructing, and about which he is more than likely to have talked on the boat with Mallarmé.[27]

On April 23, 1896, three months after winning his election, Mallarmé and cinema cross paths in the newspaper. The back page of that day's *Le Figaro* read, "Great success yesterday, at the Théâtre Mondain, for Stéphane Mallarmé and Charles Morice. In his series: *French poets*, Charles Morice gave a lecture on the new 'Prince of Poets.'" Four paragraphs later the author of the column, Jules Huret, writes that "the Cinématographe-Lumière," recorded "between two and six o'clock . . . over twelve hundred admissions."[28] Huret was a friend and correspondent of Mallarmé and had penned an influential literary survey in 1891 that helped define symbolism, in no small part through Mallarmé's transcribed interview.[29] Throughout 1896, Huret gave regular news of the Lumière cinema in *Le Figaro*, noting its expanding venues and multiple competitors such as the Kinetograph of Méliès and the Isolatographe of the Isola brothers.[30] Finally, Jules Clarétie, another friend of Mallarmé and the director of the Théâtre Français, published a long article on the Cinématographe in the newspaper *Le Temps* on February 13, 1896, in which he mused, "And this marvelous cinématographe, that sends us the specters of the living [*spectres des vivants*], will it give us, by allowing that we keep their ghost [*fantôme*], the gestures, and the sound of the voice, the sweetness and caresses of our dear departed?"[31]

This context of Mallarmé's overwhelmingly certain—though, to our frustration, not plainly attested—familiarity with the venues, actors, apparatus, and early criticism of cinema gives a powerful valence to his statement on cinema, which I will unpack as a manifesto for cinepoetry. It was written in June 1897, at a critical time for Mallarmé's experimental turn and for the history of cinema. *Un Coup de dés* had been published in April 1897, in the new trilingual journal *Cosmopolis*, and in late April and early May several notices about Mallarmé's poem came out in the press, including one in *Le Journal* on May 4, 1897.[32] On that fateful day for early cinema, the film projector in a tent of the Bazar de la Charité ignited into a fireball, killing 128 spectators in a few minutes, mostly women of high society.[33] Over the following days, Mallarmé wrote two sets of letters, one addressed to friends (Raffaëlli, Heredia, Régnier) whose wives or daughters were injured in the fire, the other set addressed to journalists and friends (Mégnin, Gide) who were reacting to and publicizing *Un Coup de dés,* then being printed by Didot.[34] On June 10, he wrote two more letters to his disciples Régnier and Montesquiou who had fought a duel over false allegations that the latter had escaped the fire by wielding his cane.[35]

On the heels of this most charged intertwining of cinema, his private life, and his experimental poetics, on June 31, 1897, Mallarmé wrote his single statement on cinema. In response to a survey by André Ibels asking several writers whether they favored illustrating books with photography, Mallarmé answered:

> Je suis pour—aucune illustration, tout ce qu'évoque un livre devant se passer dans l'esprit du lecteur; mais, si vous employez la photographie, que n'allez-vous droit au cinématographe, dont le déroulement remplacera, images et texte, maint volume, avantageusement.
>
> [I am in favor of—no illustration, since all that a book evokes must take place in the reader's mind; but, if you use photography, why not

> go straight to the cinematograph, whose unreeling (unfolding) will replace, images and text, many a volume, advantageously.][36]

Alone among the twenty-four writers surveyed (including Zola, Rachilde, Rodenbach, Uzanne) Mallarmé mentions cinema—whose popularity had precipitously dipped after the fire. André Ibels finds this sufficiently noteworthy in the 1898 introduction to the published survey that he draws a pointed comparison between the "cinematograph" and "The Book" (*Le Livre*).[37] The capital L he uses certainly suggests that the reference is to Mallarmé's (often capitalized) Book as an instrument and ideal, as in Mallarmé's title, *Le Livre, instrument spirituel* (The book, spiritual instrument).[38] Can it be concluded that Mallarmé opened up to Ibels about his cinepoetic ideas? Again, we have no archival confirmation.

The force of Mallarmé's compact statement hinges on three notions: *déroulement* as a new relation between image and text; the reader/viewer as creative agent; and the word *volume*. Both *déroulement* and *volume* have rich dual meanings: materially, the former denotes the "unreeling" of the filmstrip, while in textual terms it refers to the "unfolding" of a plot in drama. Volume conveys also a dual meaning, that of book—etymologically, a scroll of parchment (Lat. *volumen*) and thus one continuous strip—and of the haptic space of perspective which, before cinema, could not be replicated as an immersive mobile representation. Because Mallarmé's overall poetics placed such an emphasis on the choice of single words, this confluence of polysemic terms invites us to read his note as an incipient manifesto of the cinematicization of the text.

But these three notions might not be enough in themselves did they not figure in the explicit poetics of *Un Coup de dés*. Mallarmé's preface to the poem informs the reader that "a sort of general leitmotiv that unfolds [*leitmotiv qui se déroule*] constitutes the poem's unity: accessory motifs are grouped around it." This unfolding competes with Wagner's influential dramatic concept of "leitmotiv," since it points to the "movement," "succession," and "mobility" of reading with its cinematic connotations.[39] The preface also points to the reader's active role, mentioning the book as "volume" and insisting on spatiality through words such as "spacing" (*espacement*) and "simultaneous vision of the page." Hence the encounter of space, time, and creative readership/spectatorship shapes the common poetics of Mallarmé's visual poem and his note on the cinema. Two recently published drafts of the preface to *Un Coup de dés* demonstrate even more plainly that Mallarmé contrived it out of the very same textual matrix as the note: the parallelism in the syntactical arc and in the lexicon are plain.[40] We may therefore affirm that *déroulement* in the manner of the cinematograph constitutes the new literary "advantage" Mallarmé was experimenting with in *Un Coup de dés.*

UNFOLDING KINESTHESIA THROUGH WRITING

Terms like "unfolding," "uncoiling," "unreeling," and so forth connote the centrality of rotation in modernity's mechanized energetics (motors, train wheels, propellers, the bicycle, the gas engine, Tesla's dynamo, and electro-industrial applications such as public lighting, the telephone, radio, and so on). This constitutes a rotational "hybrid network" as Latour called interactions of new ideas and new material practices.[41] Such a rotational network emblematizes modernity's interpenetrations of forces, geometries, bodies, machinery, and the social.[42] The rise of rhythm as an operational norm echoes the cyclical aspect of forces, the cadence of engines, the regularity of geometric forms, and by the same token highlights the biorhythmic vitalism of the body.[43] Rhythm became central to Mallarmé's poetics as a way of overcoming the restricted economy of lyrical romanticism that modulates sensations and emotions into fixed-form verses stabilizing poetic subjectivity. Rhythm thus corresponds to the search for a general economy of "Verse" (to use Mallarmé's own capitalized term expanding the traditional fixed-form line) reflected in symbolism's dissemination toward prose poetry, free verse, even poeticized novelistic writing such as that of André Gide.

The rotational complex and the general economy of bodily rhythm coalesce into *kinesthetic uncoiling*, a sensorial spectrum ranging from experiencing actual motions to sensations derived from movement as well as their imaginary resonances and aesthetic refractions. Kinesthetic uncoiling explains why we find in Mallarmé such an intriguing convergence between propelled machinery, dancing, and poetics. In "L'Action restreinte" (1895), for instance, Mallarmé muses on the younger generation's "wish to evade the body" (*souci d'extravaguer du corps*), by way of the bicycle rather than reading. This seems an odd juxtaposition of activities, but when Mallarmé pushes this juxtaposition further, we see these antithetical activities blend into each other, hybridized within "the monotony of reeling [*enrouler*], between one's calves, on the roadway, according to the instrument in favor, the fiction of a mesmerizing continuous rail [*la fiction d'un éblouissant rail continu*]."[44] Reading and biking are both like riding a train: they are rhythmical, bodily, automatic, and entrancing. Yet these kinesthetic activities are also and foremost visual—*éblouissant* means all at once "beautiful," "mesmerizing," and "blinding." Hence the series easily extends to cinema as a new "fiction of a blindingly continuous rail."

What drew Mallarmé to cinema may well be the sudden possibility of an actualization of the kinesthetics of reading. The blindness and insight of cinematic *déroulement* inspired in Mallarmé a new sense of rhythm and (dis)continuity that he endeavored to graph as an intermittent pattern of blanks and text in *Un Coup de dés*. Before turning to the poem, let us provide a broader account of the permeation of kinesthesia across senses and disciplines, for it amounted to an epistemological shift. While language as voice and poetry from Plato to Husserl (as Derrida demonstrated) was held to be the very essence of the human, for Mallarmé language was foremost writing, and as such, subject to mediation by modernity's forces and forms, and the apparatuses then changing the conditions of the *graphic trace*. Other thinkers of the 1890s were grappling with kinesthetic *déroulement* under these new conditions of inscription: Henri Bergson with the analysis of duration, Jules-Étienne Marey with chronophoto*graphy*, and Loïe Fuller with choreo*graphy*. All three have in common an epistemological closeness to early cinema. Let us briefly examine how each can help us understand Mallarmé's cinematic experimentation.

Deleuze and his commentators have made plain the link between Bergson's theory of duration and the thought that arises from cinema. Bergson's central notion is that duration and intuition have their own lived phenomenology, irreducible to quantification. When trying to define them further Bergson's language falls on kinesthetic unwinding: "[psychological states] unfold [*se déroulent*] in time, they constitute duration," he writes in 1889.[45] Rather than discrete or narrative entities, they form a continuous chain of potential energy, "a wire coiled up [*fil enroulé*] like a spring."[46] Bergson reuses this kinesthetic program—more than an image—when later defining intuition as "like the tension of a spring-coil," in the penultimate sentence of *La pensée et le mouvant*.[47] Kinesthetic coiling and uncoiling even informs his redefinition of both life and the human in *Creative Evolution*: "Life appears on the whole as an immense wave propagated from a center and which, upon the quasi totality of its circumference, stops and converts itself into static oscillations: at only one point was the obstacle breached to let the impulsion freely pass through. It is this freedom the human form registers."[48] The human vortex or spiral wave alone moves out of the evolutionary center, freeing itself from its gravitational pull. Such freedom rests on a modern and modernist primacy of the active present, as a complete temporal synthesis over the past. This is what *Matter and Memory* describes painstakingly: "The very orientation of our psychological life [is a] veritable unfolding [*déroulement*] of states amidst which our interest focuses on what actually unfolds [*se déroule*], and not on what is entirely unfolded [*ce qui est . . . déroulé*]."[49] The subtle contrast between the present reflexive ("se dérouler") of process and agency—the human—and the transitive past ("est déroulé") of artifacts and memories shows the crucial nuance Bergson invested in the contrastive senses of the word *déroulement* as redefining the human.

With Marey we find the mirror opposite: the mechanical process is valued over agency. Marey's 1891 innovation over Muybridge's multiple cameras and Janssen's photographic revolver was the use of a continuous filmstrip recording separately with *quantifiable time intervals* the "series of photographic images representing the successive phases of a phenomenon"—his definition of chronophotography.[50] To achieve this, Marey's mechanical talent lays in making compatible two opposite motions of the filmstrip in his camera. On the one hand, he needed to insure "the regularity of the rolling and unrolling" (*l'enroulement et le déroulement*),[51] of the off-reel and on-reel. On the other hand, it was imperative that "the film unrolls with an intermittent motion" (*la pellicule se déroule d'un mouvement saccadé*),[52] so that it stops when taking the shot, moving only in-between frames. This allowed not only the stroboscopic recording of motion, but crucially its synthesis as cinematic projection. The two-stroke rhythm of the coiling and uncoiling of the filmstrip for both recording and projecting is the sine qua non condition to Edison's 1894 Kinetograph and the Lumières's 1895 Cinématographe.[53]

But Marey was motivated by a broader project that historian Dagognet calls, "the passion for tracing," that is, rendering motion visible and *legible*—quantifiable.[54] From graphing blood and pulmonary pressure to finding the precise pattern of horse or human steps, or wing-beats in birds or flies, Marey developed apparatuses tracing organic motion, according to a method he theorized as *The Graphic Method in Experimental Sciences* (1878). Trained as a doctor, Marey saw corporeal motion as inherently discontinuous, a series of jerks, falls, and breaks of different cadences within "the animal machine,"[55] in direct contrast, according to Dagognet, to Vitalists such as Bergson who insist on *élan vital* as unanalyzable life-in-movement. Dagognet interprets Marey as producing a representation of the neuro-motor unconscious, "made of rhythms, of inchoate pulsions and fluxes which traverse the corporeal machine . . . in short, the automatic writing of nature itself."[56] By contrast, for Bergson any representation of life as a discontinuous mechanical process is a simulation and a falsification, especially cinema's chronophotography: "It is because the cinematographic strip unfolds [*se déroule*], causing, in succession, the different photographies of the scene to prolong one another, that each actor in the scene reconquers its mobility. . . . The process thus consists, in short, in extracting from all the movements that are specific to all the figures, an impersonal motion, abstract and simple. . . . This is the artifice of the cinematograph. And so too is it that of our cognition."[57] Bergson is unable to think of cinema as other than a mechanical instance of Zeno's paradox (spatializing movement), the false notion of duration invented by our cognition.[58]

What is intriguing in Marey's and Bergson's use of *déroulement* is their common failure to stay on either side of the human versus mechanical divide. Bergson discounts cinema's inhuman unreeling only to appeal to the uncoiling of intuition, while Marey, rejecting *élan vital*, finds the technical inspiration for rolling and unrolling the filmstrip in an ellipsoid cam whose two-stroke motion in fact mimics the human gait, which since Aristotle's "featherless biped" quip, had been used to define the human.[59] Mallarmé's *déroulement* similarly brackets the division between the "human" and the "phantoms" of technological prostheses by questioning the very nature of the modern body.

It was during the 1892–93 season of the Folies-Bergères Theater that Mallarmé saw Loïe Fuller's celebrated "Serpentine dance" for the first time. Her body hidden under oversized robes and veils, and using prosthetic arm-extenders, Loïe Fuller performed the dance she had invented, whose aesthetic pleasure devolves from the dissolution of the human body into pure kinetic patterns of light and color.[60] Dance and pantomime fascinated Mallarmé partly because they represented arts of time (according to Lessing) complementing poetry, while he saw the operatic music of Wagner as well as contemporary theater as overly rooted in narrative. Devoid of narration, melodrama, supporting cast, or decor, but using complex arrangements of mirrors, electrical lighting, and even a radium-tipped dress, Fuller's dance exemplified in his eyes not just choregraphic artistry, but the spectacle of the human in modernity: "an industrial accomplishment," fusing "nuances of velocity," and "prismatic . . . passions," to form an "oxyhydric phantasmagoria" (*fantasmagorie oxyhydrique*)—a particularly apt use of the limit-figure of fantasmagorie as denoting the precinema apparatus.[61]

Already in the 1887 "Crayonné au théâtre," Mallarmé had reflected on the paradoxical corporeality of dancing. The (female) dancer, he wrote, retains her "feminine appearance," while also disappearing into a kind of "impersonality" when embodying the "mimed subject-matter" of her dance. Through this living paradox, "she unfolds [*déroule*] our conviction in a cypher of pirouettes prolonged toward another motif [*motif*]."[62] The ballet's "allegory" relies on the efficacy of kinesthetic transference from the dancer's body to the spectator's affective and aesthetic response. In the 1893 "Les Fonds dans le ballet," concerning Fuller, Mallarmé similarly celebrates "the solution she unfurls [*la solution qu'elle déploie*] through the sole emotion [*émotion*] of her dress," generating fugitive (e-)motions, or kinesthetic images: "visions dissipated as soon as known" (*vision éparses sitôt que sues*).[63] Again, the aesthetic "solution" implies *dissolution*, unwinding, and visual movement. Hence for Mallarmé kinesthetic uncoiling represents the actual medium of dance—that through which dancers and spectators communicate. On this basis he envisions a "poem free of any scribal apparatus," except for "corporeal writing,"[64] a notion he revisits in 1895 in his theoretical text "Le Mystère dans les lettres," where his ideal of the book form as displaying "transitory coilings [*enroulements transitoires*] . . . in argumentation of light,"[65] alludes to a kinetic performance of the text, possibly virtual—in contrast to the actual performance he had explicitly in mind for *Le Livre*. In any case, kinesthetic unwinding informs Mallarmé's sense of the fluid interchangeability of moving bodies and writing.

Some of his accounts of theatrical performances remain cryptic if we fail to notice that he invokes chronophotography as the technical model for this interchangeability:

> Seul principe! et ainsi que resplendit le lustre, c'est-à-dire lui-même, l'exhibition prompte, sous toutes les facettes, de quoi que ce soit et notre vue adamantine, une oeuvre dramatique montre la succession des extériorités de l'acte sans qu'aucun moment garde de réalité et qu'il se passe, en fin de compte, rien.

> [Unique principle! and in the manner in which a chandelier shines, that is to say itself, the quick display, under all its facets, of anything whatsoever and our diamondlike vision, a dramatic work shows the succession of an act's exteriorities without any single moment remaining real and (without) there occuring, in the end, anything at all.][66]

This 1887 formulation of dance as glass optics ("luster" [*lustre*], "facets," "diamondlike vision"), optical motion ("shines," "quick display," "succession of an act's exteriorities"), and performance ("display," "dramatic work," "act," "occuring,") anticipates the preface of *Un Coup de dés*, which develops this chronophotographic model into a more explicitly cinematic theory of poetic composition.

We can now return to the key sentence in the preface of *Un Coup de dés*, which we have shown to be generically related to his 1897 note on cinema, in order to flesh out Mallarmé's cinepoetics (I underline the main clause for clarity):

> Le papier intervient chaque fois qu'une image, d'elle-même, cesse ou rentre, acceptant la succession d'autres et, puisqu'il ne s'agit pas, ainsi que toujours, de traits sonores réguliers ou vers—plutôt, de subdivisons prismatiques de l'idée, l'instant de paraître et que dure leur concours, dans quelque mise-en-scène spirtuelle exacte, c'est à des places variables, près ou loin du fil conducteur latent, en raison de la vraisemblance, que s'impose le texte.

> [Paper intervenes each time an image, of its own accord, ceases or withdraws, accepting the succession of others and, since it is not a matter, as always, of regular sound features or verse—rather, of prismatic subdivisions of the Idea, in the instant of appearing and so long as their contribution lasts, in some exact spiritual staging, it is at variable places, near or far the latent conducting wire, by reason of verisimilitude, that the text imposes itself.][67]

The "succession" combined with "prismatic subdivisions of the Idea" corresponds closely to Marey's "successive phases of a phenomenon," and to the musical-balletic "succession of an act's exteriorities." Moreover, the play of "image" and "text" directed by "some exact spiritual staging" at "variable places" recalls rather pointedly Mallarmé's statement on cinema. In it, we'll recall, the book's virtuality ("everything . . . must take place in the reader's mind") is as if sublated by the play of "images and text" of cinema.

But this passage also has in common with Octave Uzanne's description of Edison's Kinetograph a number of very specific words (I cite Uzanne's text first): "Sound/sound features," "successive/succession," "movement/movement," "acceleration/accelerate," "copied/reproduce," and "noted/will note" (Figure 16). Another text of Étienne-Jules Marey describing the odometer that he invented, a machine that transforms walking into a trace on paper using a wheel also comes very close to Mallarmé's lexicon in his preface: "Let us suppose a clock driving, in a uniform movement, a strip of paper; a quill fastened above this strip lowers and raises itself alternatingly at certain intervals and for variable durations; contacts between this quill and the paper that moves will leave a trace in the form of lines, more or less spaced out and more or less long, that will express succession and duration."[68] Here is a second set of specific words in common with Mallarmé's preface (Marey is cited first): "spacing/spaced out," "paper/paper," "succession/succession," "lines/lines," "regular/uniform," "lasts/duration," "variable/variable," movement/movement," and "rises or falls/lowers and raises." This set is even closer than Uzanne's text because of the role of the strip of paper that moves in Marey, echoed by Mallarmé's "the paper intervenes," and "the mobility of writing." Whether Mallarmé actually read Marey's monograph as a work of reference in precinema—perhaps lent to him by Paul Nadar or Octave Uzanne?—matters less here than the striking epistemological convergence of the poet and the researcher describing virtually indistinguishable motion-transcribing apparatuses.

To make sense of Mallarmé's cinematic thought, we may argue that all the Greek etymons of chronophotography and cinematography—time (chronos), light (photos), movement (kino), and writing (graphy)—combine into a new idea of the literary work as a material book, as volume, read in space and time as a kind of performance by the reader.[69] In other words, the imaginary realm of poetry emanating from the two-dimensional page was theoretically expanded by Mallarmé to a four-dimensional performance involving three-dimensional space plus time, in which the page would be projected through a mechanical light-source. This is, I will argue, what Mallarmé's last project known as *Le Livre* was ostensibly aiming to achieve: the cinematic projection of a poem for an audience.

CINEPOETICS OF *LE LIVRE*

The idea of the mechanical projection of words—rather than images—goes back again to Villiers. One of his 1882 *Contes cruels*, which Mallarmé much admired, is titled *L'Affichage céleste* (Celestial billboard).[70] In this futuristic satire about advertising in the night sky,

Fig. 3. — Marcheur poussant devant lui l'odographe.

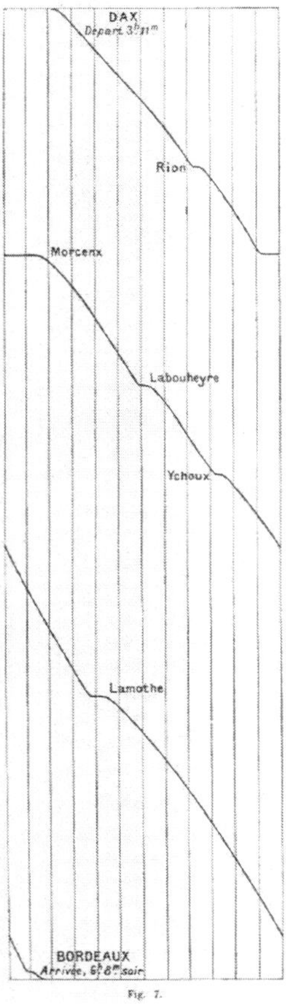

Fig. 7.

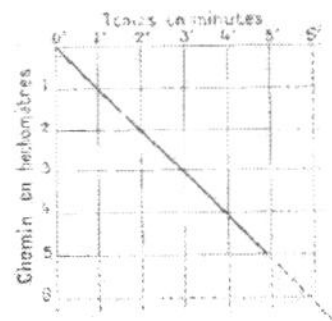

Fig. 1.

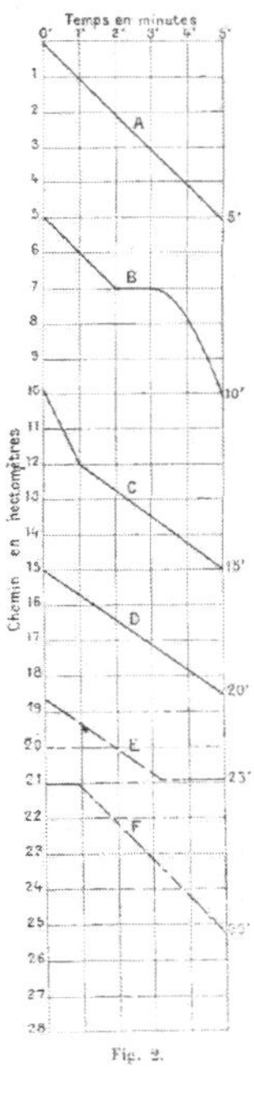

Fig. 2.

Figure 16. The odometer invented by Jule-Étienne Marey to measure and transcribe distance into a graph on paper (ca. 1890). Compare the variably descending lines with the descending text in Mallarmé's *Un Coup de dés* in Figure 14.

a powerful electrical apparatus called a *lamposcope* is used to implement "a luminous project of using the vast expanses of the night, so as to raise, to coin a phrase, the sky to the height of our era [*d'élever, en un mot, le ciel à la hauteur de l'époque*]."[71] It is worth noting that outdoor projections of writings through magic lantern were common in the last part of the nineteenth century, and that outdoor screenings began in France in 1898: a screen was placed at the Palais des Glaces ice rink for night projections, while both the Lumière Brothers and Méliès projected advertisements on the walls of Paris.[72]

Un Coup de dés's preface proposes "the simultaneous vision of the page," to the reader, so her gaze can open to "the spacing of reading" (*l'espacement de la lecture*), by scanning "the mobility of writing."[73] The project for *Le Livre* addresses the same kinesthetic poetics of quasi simultaneity through quick succession: "In one glance through the succession of sentences . . . everything must appear" (*Il faut que d'un coup d'oeil par la succession des phrases . . . tout apparaisse*).[74] These somewhat paradoxical formulations suggest that Mallarmé was pursuing an automorphic effect for the reader/spectator through the visual disposition of the text or pages. In fact, Mallarmé conceives of the very act of composing poetry, of *poetic thought itself*, as a projective and automorphic process. He writes in 1895:

> Les mots, d'eux-mêmes, s'exaltent à mainte facette reconnue la plus rare ou valant pour l'esprit, centre de suspens vibratoire; qui les perçoit indépendamment de la suite ordinaire, projetés, en parois de grotte, tant que dure leur mobilité ou principe, étant ce qui ne se dit pas du discours: prompts tous, avant exctinction, à une réciprocité de feux distante ou présentée de biais comme contingence.
>
> [Words exalt themselves through the rarest facets valued by the mind, center of vibrating suspension; which perceives them singly outside of the ordinary series, projected, on the cave wall, so long as lasts their mobility or principle, this being what is not said in speech; all of them quick, before fading, to reciprocate their light at a distance or sideways like a contingent aspect.][75]

In substance, this is another way of restating the relative autonomy of words flickering in the poet's mind, making semantic and rhythmic connections between themselves that the poet then transcribes by reshuffling syntax if needs be. At the more figural and material levels, Mallarmé's passage mixes at least three distinct fields of reference: that of the mind as a hanging crystal chandelier, a jumble of light beams interacting with each other; that of Plato's Allegory of the Cave, unmistakably referenced (later film theoreticians from Saint-Pol-Roux to Jean-Louis Baudry allude to the Cave as the philosophically problematic origin of cinema); and, finally, that of words as ephemeral images projected upward ("to exalt" means literally "to leave upward") on a wall in the dark. Chronophotography provided Mallarmé with an apparatus actualizing his theory of the word's multiple, latent, or potential meanings: cinema offers him an apparatus materializing his very conception of poetic language, and what is more, as both a continuation and an overcoming of Plato's archetypes. This is what transpires from the following note for *Le Livre*: "Undoing idea into book / its operating mechanism here / . . . / the Idea in it is visible there it is clear / glow within titles transparence" (*Défaire idée en livre / son mécanisme opérateur là / . . . l'Idée y est visible là c'est net / lueur en titres transparence*).[76] The capital to "Idea" indicates that the performance aims to make the book, the page, language, the word, its graphy, and the idea coalesce, thereby rescinding Plato's separate realms, again through an apparatus—"mechanism," "glow," "transparence" akin to the cinema.

Let us make a tighter case that Mallarmé ostensibly crafted the performance of *Le Livre* after the imaginary cinema apparatus disseminated in the French press from 1891 to 1895. The chronology fits well, since the project was devised in 1893—the year Uzanne reported on Edison's Kinetograph—and limned out in 1895. Commentators have noted the physical machinery of the notes, the focus on freeing reading and language into chains of signifiers more than fixed signifieds, and the secular dimension of the public performance placing poetry at the core of a new democratic communion.[77] All these aspects are synthesized and sublated by the cinema. There are also six specific arguments to support the fact that Mallarmé modeled *Le Livre* on cinema. First, he refers to the performance as a "double séance,"[78] directed by an "operator" (*opérateur*).[79] The words "*séance*" and "*opérateur*" were the very terms used respectively for a cinematographic projection and for the projectionist or camera operator from 1895 onward.[80] Mallarmé's séance is dual because each page was meant to be read twice, the second time a reversal of the first. Not only is the camera projector itself reversible, but one of the favorite tricks of projectionists of the cinema of attractions consisted precisely of cranking films backward, so that time and motion were perceived as bidirectional and entwined to their opposite. Second, the *séance* relies explicitly on electrically projected images. Mallarmé writes that the operator "saw clearly, the electr. glow was his spirit [*la lueur électr. fut son esprit*]."[81] The preface of *Un Coup de dés* also mentions a "latent conducting wire" (*fil conducteur latent*).[82] The signature substance of modernity—electricity—which Wagner and Fuller had used in their groundbreaking performances, becomes the new medium that suspends Platonism by creating a middle realm—imaginary and artificial, yet whose materiality and actuality are thereby exacerbated.[83] In "Ballets," Mallarmé calls for "some impersonal or flashing absolute gaze [*fulgurant regard absolu*], such as the flash enveloping . . . the Édens dancer, infusing an electrical starkness [*crudité électrique*] to the whitish hues of extracarnal powder, so as to make her, indeed, the prestigious being receding beyond any possible life [*l'être prestigieux reculé au-delà de toute vie possible*]."[84] We should hear in "the prestigious being" the magical connotations of prestidigitation (as in the film *The Prestige*) bestowing on the performer an "extracarnal" status because of the "flashing" of electricity. Third, Mallarmé makes the same claims as Edison, the Lumière brothers and early film critics such as Uzanne: his performance will bring life back to the frozen *punctum* of photography:

pureté lumière électr —
— le volume, malgré l'im-
pression fixe, devient par ce jeu,
mobi-
le—de mort il devient vie

purity electr. light
the volume, despite the fixed im-
pression, becomes by this play,
mobi-
le—from death it becomes life[85]

The ambiguity of "volume," as both book and lived kinesthetic space, is here directly related to the filmic abrogation of death. Fourth, we are dealing unequivocally with projections on a screen:

l'arabesque électrique
s'allume derrière—et les deux
voile
—sorte de déchirure sacrée du
voile, orchestre—ou déchire—
et deux êtres à la fois oiseau
et parfum—semblables aux
deux d'en
haut . . .

the electrical arabesque
lights up behind—and the two
veils
a kind of sacred tearing of the
veil, orchestra—or tears—
and the two beings at once bird
and perfume—akin to the
two
from above . . . [86]

The context of this passage is neither exactly a stage play nor a screen projection—but rather, a theatrical stage with veils used as screens, elsewhere described as "a dioramic curtain deepened [*un rideau dioramique s'aprofondit* (sic)] . . . [via a] stronger and stronger shadow."[87] Mallarmé is thinking of the use of an image-projection device together with a dance or pantomime performance. In 1896, cinematographic projections combined with still shots were used on stage for the first time in *La Biche au bois*.[88] Fifth, aside from reverse motion, the favorite trick of operators of the cinema of attractions was to heighten the film effect by starting the projection on a still "coming to life," then slowing down or accelerating the projection. The preface to *Un Coup de dés* appeals to the same visual mobility "to accelerate at times and to slow down the movement"[89] of reading, and we have seen this same double tension at play in *Le Livre* between simultaneity (rest) and succession (motion). Sixth, and finally, Mallarmé conceived of the performance of *Le Livre* as public, commercial, repetitive, highly profitable, and even containing advertising—which is mentioned three times.[90] Mallarmé's entrepreneurial drive is surprising but unambiguous: "pure financial operation through the book otherwise nothing."[91] Indeed, the profit structure he expected from the séances resembles very closely the exponential revenues of cinema in its first year.[92] For all these reasons, we must conclude that cinema is just as integral to the project of *Le Livre* as it was to *Un Coup de dés* on the basis of separate evidence.

It is not hard to conclude that Mallarmé may have envisaged projecting each page of *Un Coup de dés*—or another visual poem with a similar typesetting—on a stage, perhaps even on the veils born by a Loïe Fuller-like dancer that would literally embody the poem. Perhaps, Mallarmé planned on showing a film of the poem being written and then erased. We have seen that he fantasized "words . . . projected . . . before extinction"—which would be a fitting description for the Lumière's short film *Écriture à l'envers* (see my Introduction). In fact, one wonders if another meditation of Mallarmé on viewing spectacles, written in 1897, is not a direct description of that film. He celebrates: "the magic, perhaps unknown in literature, of turning off [*éteindre*] strictly one by one every sight [*toute vue*] that might sparkle [*éclaterait*] with purity; much like crossing-out [*raturer*] certain words."[93] The word "*vue*" was the contemporary term for a film, and perhaps this is Mallarmé's tacit appreciation of *Écriture à l'envers*, the "vue" that ended every show of the Lumière in 1897, and that he may have seen in an actual theater, perhaps the Pirou-Normandin, the nearest cinema only eight blocks from his home on rue de Rome.

Whatever the case may be, not a single technical, aesthetic, or conceptual component was lacking for Mallarmé to have made tangible plans to integrate cinema into the reading of poetry in a public performance. Perhaps the project was meant for the 1900 World Fair, which was very much on the mind of many pioneers of early cinema, and to which, as Prince of Poets, he may legitimately have contributed. A number of cinema-based spectacles were staged there, from a ten-screen circular panoramic projection of a balloon ride, to a giant water-cooled screen with the audience seated on either side. Such a venue would have been the ideal occasion for the political performance Rancière has theorized for Mallarmé: a rebirth of social participation where the poem means or represents nothing other than its own production, only a secular celebration of democracy acted by its own masses, through the intermediary of poetry.[94] Mallarmé died two years before the World Fair opened.

In *Un Coup de dés* and the notes for *Le Livre*, Mallarmé began experimenting with the very cinematic hybridization of the poetic text that is implicit in his manifesto-statement on cinema. This cinepoetics at once theory and practice solved and synthesized a number of his concerns: the complementarity for poetry of other arts of time like music and dance; the materiality and modality of the book made of flat pages unfolding in space and time; the centrality of kinesthetic rhythm in both modernity and postmetric verse or poetic prose; and finally, an urge to redeem poetry within the mass culture and politics of the Third Republic. We may note from this constellation of interests one of the central paradoxes that will accompany the development of cinepoetry throughout the twentieth century: the decentering of questions of vision, description, ekphrasis, and more generally, of aesthetics driven by optical mimesis. While symbolism has been rightly analyzed as a break with Parnassian aesthetics' focus on the visual, and with the romantic cult of the beautiful image—both the picturesque and the simile—it has been too often mischaracterized as breaking with reality effects and perception altogether, in a show of indifference toward the social sphere and the real world. The cinepoetic aesthetics Mallarmé sketched out engages with the social and with experiential aspects of reality: reading a book, playing music, attending a kinesthetic spectacle, communing with others in performing the political rites of the secular socius. Mallarmé's cinepoetics paradoxically suggests that one of the overlooked aspects of symbolism might be its deemphasizing of verbal depictions of the visual, the better to foreground the haptic work of words, the experiential realism of kinesthesia, and the immersive effects of turn-of-the-century performance culture.

Two close friends and disciples of Mallarmé, André Gide and Paul Valéry, also registered the shift brought about to late symbolism by the kinesthetic unfolding linked to the imaginary of moving images. It was no longer the suggestive allegory and its surfeit of poetic images that interested them, but the flow of images itself as phenomenal, imaginary, and dynamic. Other poets such as Maurice Maeterlinck theorized a similar shift within Belgian symbolism, rejecting the centrality of "symbolic productions" based on "deliberate symbols" in favor of "affecting" productions based on "unconscious" symbols.[95] In other words, aesthetic ideas were overtaken by embodied experience.

My sense is that the term "phenomenon" marks this change from poetic idealism to pragmatic embodiment in late symbolism, as when de Gourmont writes in the 1896 introduction to his *Book of Masks*, that "we know only phenomena. . . . I don't see what is, what is is what I see."[96] In his "Traité du Narcisse: théorie du symbole" ("Treatise of Narcissus: Theory of the symbol"), published in 1892, Gide had enlarged the symbol in the same direction, as synonymous to "the phenomenon, what is," while Valéry in his 1894 "Introduction to the Method of Leonardo" focuses on "a concrete mental relation between phenomena, or rather, to be more rigorous, between the images of phenomena."[97] Such *experiential realism*—the word "concrete" here is more important than "mental"—finds a middle road between the deliberate symbols of earlier symbolism and the call to naturalist transparency. By focusing on phenomenological intentionality as a flow of images, experiential realism is bound to refract the cinema apparatus. Hence Gide describes Narcissus in his traditional posture with his "hands on the frame [*cadre*]. . . . As he gazes down, suddenly in the water a flimsy image appears . . . a set of rapidly fleeting images [*une fuite de rapides images*] only waiting for him to come to be . . . visions that undulate in the running water," until he can't tell "whether his soul guides the flux or the flux guides it."[98] The reference to the frame suggests more than a mirror—a screen upon which a series of automorphic images projects themselves, melding the subjective and the objective in their temporal flux. This phenomenal temporality of the psyche's encounter with itself in the world is also at the core of Valéry's reenactment of Leonardo:

> He surmises the sheets of air generated by a flying bird, the curves upon which glides a rock thrown, the surfaces defining our gestures, and the extraordinary rips, the fluid arabesques, the formless chambers, created through an all-pervading network, by the squeaking scratches of trembling insects, the lurching of trees, wheels, the human smile, the tide. Sometimes the trace of what he imagines can be seen on the sand, on the waters; sometimes his own retina can compare, in real time, an object to the form of its own movement.[99]

This kinetic poetics of automorphic volumes and flows ultimately leads to the inscription of retinal persistence, through which moving images would be (wrongly) explained. Such "kinetic mania,"[100] Valéry notes in 1930, is inherently chronophotographic: "[Leonardo's] precise imagination represents what photography has made perceptible today."[101] Valéry, conflicted about the kinetic power of cinema as a 1944 text makes clear, may conceal under the reference to (chrono)photography what was actually more properly a reference to cinema.[102]

While partaking of late symbolism's turn toward the phenomenal flow of consciousness informed by the cinematic imaginary, Valéry and Gide did not share in Mallarmé's cinepoetic experimentalism, even though the latter became involved in cinema through his partner and lover Marc Allégret.[103] But other late symbolist poets, without being aware of Mallarmé's cinepoetics, blazed their own path parallel to it, notably Alfred Jarry and Raymond Roussel, but also Abel Gance. Born in 1889, Gance considered himself a symbolist poet in his late teens, particularly influenced by the work of Mallarmé.[104] In 1907 he began acting for the stage, and soon for the camera as well, playing Molière in a Léonce Perret film in 1909. When he turned to scriptwriting in 1910, he became the first French poet to write for cinema: he must have intuitively taken to writing mediated by the cinematic imaginary because his biographer indicates that he would write film scenarios first then turn them into plays—against the grain of the literature-to-cinema model of adaptation.[105] He became a director in 1912 and through his two best films, *J'accuse* (1919) and *La Roue* (1923), he was the central figure in the first French film avant-garde, in particular for Jean Epstein. Looking back on his evolution from symbolist poetry to cinema in 1914, he concluded drily, "The era of the cinématographe? Probably."[106] The quip conceals the deep affinities between symbolism and the cinema apparatus that informed Gance's work over the next fifteen years, prompting Germaine Dulac and Jean

Epstein to adapt to the screen the twin founders of French symbolism, respectively Charles Baudelaire and Edgar Poe.

Because of the history of their publication, Mallarmé's writings have had a delayed effect. Between the first publication of *Un Coup de dés* in 1897 (a small run in the short-lived journal *Cosmopolis*) and 1914, when it was finally republished in full (Albert Thibaudet had reproduced one page of the poem in his 1912 book on Mallarmé) the poem was not in public circulation. The copious drafts and notes around the unfinished project of *Le Livre* were published only in 1957, and we had to wait until 1998 to discover that drafts of the preface of *Un Coup de dés* were written together with the note on cinema. With each new layer of Mallarmé's work that resurfaced, a new cinepoetic impulse resulted. Apollinaire's visual poetry sprung up after Thibaudet's reprints of *Un Coup de dés*. Starting in the late 1940s Marcel Broodthaers's cinepoems and later film work drew their inspiration from Mallarmé, in part through the publication of the drafts of the dramatic and theoretical poem "Igitur"[107]; and Jacques Derrida's momentous reinvention of Mallarmé's "spacing" (*espacement*) in his 1967 "La Double séance," owes much to the publication of the notes on *Le Livre* in 1957 and expressly cites his note on cinema. What is remarkable is how many times Mallarmé has been subsequently invoked by either cinepoetic writers or thinkers of the cinema without any of them having a direct idea of the cinepoetic nature of his late work.[108]

CHAPTER TWO

The Pen-Camera

Raymond Roussel's Freeze-Frame Panorama

While the writings of Mallarmé are rarely read from the purview of scientific and technological developments, those of Raymond Roussel (1877–1933) have in many ways initiated such readings. Imbued with Jules Verne's science fiction and the vulgarization of scientific culture in journals such as *La Nature*, his writings connect nineteenth-century scientism and avant-garde aesthetics, in close parallel to the work of Marcel Duchamp in art.[1] Roussel's mechanical imaginary has left its imprint on the novels of Raymond Queneau and Alain Robbe-Grillet, the films of René Clair, Jean-Luc Godard, Terry Gillian, and the Brothers Quay, and the criticism of Michel Carrouges, Jean-Louis Baudry, and Michel Foucault, to cite only a few. For all this, the relationship of his work to cinema has never been properly elucidated, and his early poems in particular remain *lettre morte*, since when they are read at all they are considered failed prototypes of his later "method" writing. This is not so much a misreading as a missed reading. In particular, the poem titled "La Vue" (1902), of epic size at 2,100 lines (the length of *Hamlet* and *Macbeth* combined!), may be read as bringing the cinematographic imaginary to bear on writing by altering the very economy of the poetic text.

Among the first studies of the myth of machinism in modern literature was Michel Carrouges's 1954 *Les Machines célibataires*, examining works by the likes of Villiers, Jarry, Kafka, and Roussel.[2] The "bachelor machines" at their core represented, for Carrouges, a "modern myth" at the intersection of Surrealism, George Bataille's notion of expenditure, and Carl Jung's archetypes. His thesis that mechanistic literature amounts to "triumphal shouts of hope" from the modern imagination against "the simultaneous sway of machinism and the world of terror,"[3] exemplifies a humanistic tradition that insists on making the machine into something either abstract or foreign to human embodied subjectivity. My focus on the cinematic imaginary aims to counter this obfuscation of the robustness of technology by emphasizing its epistemic integration within our psycho-affective makeup.[4]

Roussel went to the movies—that is certain.[5] His biographer mentions as evidence a letter written by Roussel to René Clair in 1924 apologizing for having missed a projection of the latter's *Entr'acte*. Clair apparently had intended to make a film with Roussel once he finished *Entr'acte*, having read *Locus Solus* (1914) and *Impressions d'Afrique* (1910).[6] In both works transparently cinematographic passages appear, especially in the second:

> . . . the patient saw flashing by [*défiler*] on a white background, with the help of electrical projections, all kinds of colored images . . .
>
> . . .
>
> . . . an electrical light . . . was brightly projecting on the wall a large square of light produced by the combined effect of a lens and a reflector . . . Darriand . . . now slowly turned a silent hand-crank. . . . Soon, produced by some colored film [*pellicule*] placed in front of the lamp, an image took shape on the white screen. . . . Darriand turned the hand-crank again, thus activating, through a system of rolls [*rouleaux*] and diaphanous strips, a series of films [*vues*] ready to flash by [*défiler*] in front of the lit lens.[7]

Following this description of a film apparatus are nine titled "*tableaux*"[8]—a synonym for short dramatic films—forming a clear and complete movie program. (See Chapter 6 for the movie program as new genre.)[9]

Cinema is never ostensibly referred in "La Vue," written in 1902 and published the following year in the Sunday newspaper *Le Gaulois*, owned by Arthur Meyer (proprietor of the Grévin wax museum). The poem rests on the conceit that the scene it describes in minute detail over 2,100 lines—a seaside with a beach, bathers, a lighthouse, even a whole hillside with villas—has been captured in a microscopic photograph that the narrator is looking at through a Stanhope viewer. The "Stanhope," as it came to be known, was a popular tourist souvenir of the times. A decoratively embellished pen, pencil, or letter-opener, it would contain microscopic photographs viewed by looking though tiny peepholes containing a magnifying lens. While technically the poem exemplifies the figure of rhetoric known as ekphrasis, the principal theoretical transduction from visual experience to linguistic expression, it is in many ways the exact antithesis of Keats's "Ode on a Grecian Urn."

Ekphrasis usually serves as a unifying backdrop against which a narrative can be told about an artwork, with license taken in not following its original organization or *dispositio* (syntax). But the photograph in Roussel's poem is artless and authorless: it displays no aesthetic pathos or style and dispenses no overall judgment about truth or beauty. There is no original artistry to put in relief through the poem's own artistry: the photographic camera's work is automatic, impersonal, even inhuman, and so, at first, appears to be Roussel's rendering of it into metered verses. This automatism explains the poem's astounding length and utter lack of emplotment. For instance, a faraway group of four children takes up 103 lines, 38 lines being dedicated to the slight difference between the two bows in a little girl's hair. Here is a sample from a passage of 85 lines devoted to a boy throwing a stick to his dog:

> On the beach, a child is close to the water; he throws
> With quickness, almost with violence
> Some useless piece of wood . . .
> . . . precisely the piece of wood is leaving
> At this very moment the boy's right hand;
> It is a thin fragment of a plank with a crack
> At one end; somewhat closing on itself, the crack
> Is curved, describing a slight slope,
> But without spreading to a greater length (v. 449–59)[10]

This reads like mere forensic observation in verse form. There are no metaphors, no play with language, no explicit or implicit narrative, and no affects not directly present on the demeanor of the persons photographed. It is literature without poetics, verse without poetry, rhyme leached out of any lyricism. Hence it comes as little surprise that no critic—with the crucial exception of Foucault—ever bothered with it.

In the passage above, nonetheless, we might be intrigued by the expression, "curved, describing [*décrivant*] a slight slope," since it is a ballistic description in which *to describe* is itself used in the ballistic sense of tracing a geometrical trajectory in time. This suggests that the poem is surreptitiously wrestling with *temporal description* in spite of the medium of photography that might be thought to cancel it. The piece of wood is cracked: the crack not only occurred in the past, which it now indexes, it also occurred within duration and through causality: it took an event in time to crack it. It is as if the poem were displacing the ballistic temporality of the stick's throw, which we can never see since it exceeds the arrested poetic world of the photograph, onto the stick itself. More broadly, this might be the project of the poem as well: that of reinscribing onto the *description* of the photograph the (imaginary) temporality from which it was mechanically wrenched. It is striking that when we read the poem, everything in it cries out for duration and movement, everything pulses from the living network of relations and causality—neither of which can be directly attested. Moreover, since the term "describing" implicates both the scene and the observer, it raises a central question for the poem: If there is neither plot nor figural or metadiscursive level about the photograph, what modality of coverage does Roussel adopt to "describe" it? Since as a mimetic reproduction of the real the image has no artistic origin, and neither organizing subject matter nor dramatic focus, by which principle is it to be accounted for? As the poem deploys only simple deictics of location ("to the right," and "further away," and "behind the wave") the deeper into the image we get the more we lose our bearings, and the less able we are to situate the parts we have already visited and those we have not—indeed the less we "see" the photograph as a whole. These two issues—the paradoxical temporality of photography, and the translation of a holistic image into the speech chain—are compounded with a third: the optical nature of the conceit of the poem which varies visual scale in two opposite directions at once, the microscopic and the macroscopic.

This double pull is crucial because it unsettles the optical grain and opens up a mobile POV that circumvents temporal arrest and progressively installs the describing agency within, or at least in proximal relation to, the scene described. Hence our linear reading of the poem, while it corresponds to scanning this or that portion of the two-dimensional photograph, nonetheless renders the space into which (and not at which)[11] we are looking, three-dimensional. This fantasy of a three-dimensional journey within photography's temporal immobility has historically motivated a series of optical devices such as the stereoscope, the cinema itself, and 3-D films, and more recently, "bullet time" (pioneered by *The Matrix*). In bullet time, one instant of time unfolds into a haptic volume with seemingly infinite viewpoints and circuits of entry, enacting as if a secondary temporality akin to that which Roussel's poem seeks out. Indeed, the poem's lines are like POV "bullets" entering and traversing the volume of photographic arrest, reconstructing via a hybrid of ballistics and ekphrasis the motion of wind, clouds, waves, objects, animals, and people—the entire kinesthetic matrix of the real and of actual perception. "La Vue," then, reinvents poetic writing at the brink where the discourse needed to render fully the photograph of a complex scene must envision itself as a form of imaginary cinema. The very title of the poem underscores this possibility. While "La Vue," may be translated as "A Scene," and also means "The Sense of Sight" in French, the proper translation is surely "Film," since it was the term of art for "a movie" and one that Roussel used in *Solus Locus* as we have just seen. That this one word *vue* denotes all at once a visual scene, the sense of sight, and a movie projection, stresses the permeability Roussel was inspired to imagine between the otherwise separate realms of object, subject, and technical mediation.[12]

We know that Roussel was fascinated by perspective: he loved to watch the same play several times, insisting on having the same seat to study slight viewpoint-invariant differences from one performance to the next.[13] As for cinema, during the years 1902–3 George Méliès considerably expanded the narrative and aesthetic capabilities of filmmaking by shooting *The Trip to the Moon*. It is a complex thirty-scene movie that, while still shot *tableau* style at ninety degrees, includes scenery painted using trompe-l'oeil perspective and sets staggered in depth. *The Man with a Rubber Head* also uses multiple exposures together with a forward tracking shot of a face producing a fantastic effect of scale enlargement. Roussel's poem comprises both techniques: multiple tableaus with perspectival effects and dynamic scale shifts.

"La Vue" opens on a framing scene, with the poet holding the Stanhope pen up to a window in order to light up the microphotograph. When the poem ends, we are returned to this framing scene: "brightness / Decreases within the glass and everything darkens" (v. 2041–42). Such initial lighting up and final darkening certainly evokes a movie screening. The shift from the poet's room to the photographed seaside launches the movement of simultaneous opposite scales—macro and micro—soon reprised within the poem itself, when we go from the boy at the edge of the sea (more or less equivalent to a LS), to the stick he holds (MS), then the configuration of the crack in the stick (ECU), all of which suggests a remarkably mobile magnification. In another passage, Roussel describes a sailboat, far in the distance, partly obscured by the plume of smoke from a closer and larger yacht, and adds that the two sisters sitting in it wear the same earrings (v. 302–42). Factual questions abound. The sisters would have to be identical twins (otherwise, how does Roussel know they are sisters?), each showing one earring clearly unobstructed (otherwise, how can Roussel establish their absolute similarity?). Of course, it is technically absurd: the microphotograph is a quarter of an inch in diameter, and the Stanhope lens' magnification, the scope of the scene, and the granularity of the paper all preclude the satellite-photo grade resolution necessary for making such an affirmation. Another scale shift is even more fantastic: on the hillside opposite the beach (VLS) is a road among villas on which rolls a carriage (LS) in which rides a man (MS) holding a cane whose handle (CU) is shaped like a human head the tip of whose tongue peers from its ivory lips between two of the man's fingers (ECU) (v. 1175–301). Even on panoramic daguerreotypes, whose silver compound density allowed for the greatest detail magnification, such a feat would seem impossible. Is Roussel then sticking his tongue out at us, mocking our desire for hyperrealist reproduction technologies? Or is he inviting us, with these imaginary zooming effects, to forego verisimilitude—for indeed there is neither photograph nor observer, but only *text*—so that we can experience and enjoy the poetics of volume and zoom, or the brink of movement and gesture within a photographic image? And does not this labile voluminousness of the work of the imagination after photography, with its constant suggestion of other possible angles of sight—what John Sallis has keenly proposed to be imagination's *laterality*[14]—render the imaginary cinematographic?

Key junctures of "La Vue" involve those moments when the "line rendering" of the flat photographic space swivels on a disturbing evocation of volume. For example, toward the end of the poem, a child decides to verify what he was (and we were) given to see and looks through a telescope to ascertain whether the beach is "the way he figured it with his naked eye" (v. 1456). Roussel invites us to trust the child, and

> To follow . . . through the air in our mind [*en pensée*]
> The straight and fictive line [*la ligne toute droite et fictive*] that is supposed
> To be described [*décrite*] by his eyebeam [*rayon visuel*] (v. 1457–59)

Such a passage creates a cascading stereoscopy. First, we are invited to look at the child, but also to *imagine* what he sees the way he sees it. But then the terms used (thought, fictive, described, visual) apply to the very poem that we are reading, since they invite us not only to "see" what it describes, but also to see ourselves imagining this scene. Perhaps with these terms Roussel even means to theorize his own poem, from the inside out as it were, letting it produce its own poetics. After all, this passage recalls Mallarmé's "mesmerizing fiction of a continuous rail" stressing what biking and reading—a kinesthetic and a supposedly disembodied activity—have in common. But this passage is striking for yet another reason: it makes plain a key process of transition between two shots in cinema that was only theorized as such in the 1920s: the Kuleshov effect via the implicit eyeline match. The Kuleshov effect stipulates that if in shot 1 character A looks in direction x at something which is off frame, and if shot 2 contains object O, then spectators will conclude that A is looking at O from direction x. The suturing of shot/countershot works through a similar eyeline match. Since in 1917, another poet, Pierre Reverdy, gives a precise account of what Lev Kuleshov had not yet theorized, perhaps it should be renamed the Roussel-Reverdy-Kuleshov effect?[15] In any case, to return to the poem, what is at the end of the eyebeam that we follow in our mind turns out to be a lighthouse. We are thus "looking" at a boy's eyebeam itself looking at an apparatus that projects light-beams, back at him and at us, like the projector of a movie theater. Perhaps, then, we might propose that what Roussel is rendering rather than a photograph, is a short film of a seascape, or a beach, or bathers, or boats—or else, a synthesis of all such "*vues,*" which were favored as a genre in early cinema.

But this cannot be the case either, since the poem painstakingly brackets any inkling of visual animation or automorphism, the very miracle about which all early spectators marveled. So Roussel's poem focuses on a specific paradox: how nodes of instantaneity—the stick flying off a hand still suspended—foreground the necessary involvement of photography with suspended motion. Early photographs contain blurry spots because long exposures recorded things moving in time.[16] Only high-speed photography, as Tom Gunning recently noted, could create perfect stills, and only very closely spaced perfect stills could decompose (chronophotography) and recompose movement (cinema).[17] So, in a direct, causal way, it is *because* of the absolute arrest depicted in "La Vue," that cinema is possible. Roussel's narrator indicates that the photograph he holds up in his pen is "fugitive and not very stable" (*fugitive et peu stable*) (v. 26), so we might say that "La Vue" describes properly neither a photograph, nor a composite of photographs, nor a movie made of photographs, but precisely their differential poetics, what I would call the "photo-cinematic difference."

While early cinema was regularly called "animated photography," the photo-cinematic difference proceeds from a reciprocal action of cinema *upon* photography. Roussel's poem strongly suggests that photography itself acquired a potential imaginary animation after the emergence of cinema. As Tom Gunning and André Gaudreault have shown, "the cinema of attraction" fetishized the very act of animating a still by slowly cranking the image into motion—it cinematized photography. Using the term "dephotographing"—invented by poet Henri Michaux to name this putting-into-motion of the still image—we might call this early film practice *dephotographing monstration*.[18] One of its perceptual corollaries is that with cinema comes a new photographic imaginary: the photo as latent film. In other words, postcinematic photography no longer indexes only *negatively* the field of duration it was excerpted from. Hence, the Barthesian "ça-a-été" (this happened), defining traditional photography as indexical entropy (loss of animation, context, time) is countered in postcinematic photography by an imaginary potential for a new mode of animation that Barthes himself acknowledges: "[a photograph] enlivens me and I enliven it [*je l'anime et elle m'anime*]. . . . The attraction that makes [a photograph] exist: animation." He connects this animating potential directly to writing and poetry and, albeit negatively, cinema:

> What I like in the end, is the relationship of the image to writing, which is a very difficult relationship, but because of that provides real creative joys, the way poets used to love to work on difficult problems of versification. Today, the equivalent, is to find a relation between a text and images. I must say also that if I chose photography, it is somewhat *against* the cinema.[19]

Let us return now to the boy and his stick. Rather, let us note that Roussel returns three times to the very moment when the stick is leaving the boy's hand. It is as if the most ballistic and cinematic part of the photo-scape acted as its hinge, the organizational center for the description. Roussel's depiction goes nearly 360 degrees, bending the two-dimensional conceit into a three-dimensional imaginary panorama, before stumbling on a group of beachgoers intently looking at the boy: "The four spectators, transfixed [*figés*], seem to wait / From the jetty's edge, on top, for the result / Of its [the stick's] next plunge" (v. 2038–40). The spectators are absorbed—literally, they are "frozen," and thus as if twice immobilized, while the stick suddenly acquires contrastively more mobility since it is being thrown *again*, as if a different throw from the one we witnessed (or rather did not) earlier. This anamorphic flickering of cinema within the field of photography recalls another jetty—Chris Marker's film, *La Jetée*, in the course of which only the blink of an eye "moves" automorphically. Oddly enough, these four spectators, ten lines earlier, are only three: " . . . the great sincerity / Of the interest that holds them in place intensifies / In the gaze of each of these three" (v. 2028–30). Thus while this group of observers is also mentioned twice, and almost thrown into temporality like the stick, a fourth observer has surreptitiously joined them. Is it not the reader herself—caught in the web of eyelines, sucked into the imaginarily unfolded space of photo-cinematic writing, in the same way as the hero of Argentine writer Bioy Casares's 1940 story becomes the living prey of Dr. Morel's automatic three-dimensional cinema (itself, curiously, also set in motion by waves)?[20]

Eyelines, beams, jetty, trajectory, continuity, visuality, fiction, mind's eye: these are the terms of the poetics of photo-cinematic difference of "La Vue," and they are all contained in the largest passage about the boy looking through the telescope:

> To follow . . . through the air in our mind [*en pensée*]
> The straight and fictive line [*la ligne toute droite et fictive*] that is supposed
> To be described [*décrite*] by his eyebeam [*rayon visuel*]
> We arrive, via a continuous trajectory [*trajet continuel*]
> To the other side; the view [*la vue*] is stopped
> Far to the right, by a long jetty [*une longe jetée*] (v. 1457–62)

The fact that this passage cites the very title and arrested condition of the poem, "the view is stopped" (*la vue est arrêtée*) confirms that it acts as a kind of hinge for the poem. I mean to say that this is where the photo-cinematic staging of the poem can also be read as its textual poetics, where the "straight and fictive line" is both eyesight and verse, where the "long jetty" figures at once on the (fictive) photo and on the real paper of the page—a 2,100-verse-long straight and fictive jetty.

The manuscript of the poem reveals that Roussel wrote it in a very curious way. He found all the end-rhymes first, putting a few words in each line as a loose scenario for the poem. Epic poets and verse dramaturges have often laid out portions of their end-rhyme scheme, to be sure, but probably not the whole end-rhyme strip all at once. By deciding on end-words while the verses themselves remain hollow, unfilled dummies, Roussel repudiates the romantic organic model that sees a continuum in regress between verse, rhythm, voice, and soul. The first draft of Roussel's poem presents a curiously apoetic language of blanks, arrhythmia, and malaproprisms ("devient grandi" is "becomes grown"):

la photographie
très petite si l'on se fie
au verre dont le morceau
dépoli au verso
devient grandi quand l'oeil s'approche[21]

Roussel composes as if in slow motion, minding only the jetty of rhymes, or better, the rhyme-track, leaving the page blank where later text is to be interspliced. Without proposing anachronistically that Roussel may be directly thinking about film tracks and splicing here, it is noteworthy that he approaches poetic (and later novelistic) composition as the material construction of a strip of text.

I consider "La Vue" to be cinepoetic because the photo-cinematic difference that emanates from the ambivalence of its "description," both discursive and kinetic, directly informs a metacommentary of the poem upon itself. Hence poetry, for Roussel, remakes itself at the contact of photo-cinematic processes and the kinesthetic sensorium. In the following passage, the kinetics of visual description melds with a reflection on the materiality of writing—the book as paper and lines and as "volume":

. . . a man consults
A voluminous [*volumineux*] guide opened on his knees;
He pinches in his fingers, away from himself, by two of its ends
A map stretched flat, attached to the book [*tenant au livre*],
Undone and unfolded [*défaite et déployée*] entirely; he devotes himself
Complacently to queries over places
Seeking to deepen points, out of curiosity [*approfondir des points, en curieux*] (v. 1835–40)

The text unfolds as if it were a scene of the unfolding of the book's three-dimensionality, within a sensorial spectrum that recalls Mallarmé's notion of the book's voluminousness. In the same way that "tenant au livre" is polysemic—meaning both "materially attached to the book" and "concerning the book" (an oblique reference to Mallarmé's "Quant au livre"?)—the verb *approfondir* means "to deepen" both materially and abstractly. The passage continues:

> He seeks in the surroundings a good itinerary,
> Dreaming of a tour that would distract him [*Rêvant de faire un tour afin de se distraire*];
> He is not used to it and cannot find his bearings
> In this countryside that he wants to see [*qu'il tient à voir*]; a coast
> Stands out on the solid new map;
> Gulfs and thin capes can be seen; a river
> Whose course is very tortuous, sinuous,
> Comes out, shy at first, from a mountainous place;
> It curves and angles about, undulates,
> Comes near several villages, moving forward, backward [*avance, recule*], (v. 1841–50)

It is remarkable how easily the whole passage—in Roussel's fashion, it is a single sentence—lends itself to a *découpage* into a sequence of discrete camera shots. The sequence would go:

1. MS: man sitting
2. LS in countershot: pan on landscape
3. MCU: man unfolding a map
4. CU low angle: dreamy face scanning surrounding landscape
5. ECU over-the-shoulder low angle: following river on map
6. LS pan superimposed on 5 [or helicopter shot]: river snaking among villages

While this technical know-how exceeds the common practices of film production in 1902, it is not beyond what was imaginable or even technically contemplated. The one-reel *Histoire d'un crime* (France, 1901, dir. F. Zecca) had seven "tableaus" in LS and MLS linked by dissolves—including a dream scene with a split-screen. Movies were thus already legible as complex articulations of eclectic shots linked by sudden changes of scene and scale.[22] Moreover, composite illustrations with photographs of different scales and shapes, linked by a loose narrative of advertising, entertainment, or tourism, were common. The two other "epic" poems that accompanied "La Vue" in a single volume published by Roussel in 1904 described such illustrations: a hotel letterhead and the sticker for a mineral-water bottle, both melding landscapes and words.

In the passage above, the "sinuous, tortuous," river "undulates" and "moves forward, backward," in a movement that echoes the scanning focus of the poem ranging all over the photograph. The question of the poem's focal movement seems directly addressed by the "description" in the form of a metacommentary, or rather, *superimposed exegetic layer*:

> L'homme s'adonne avec prévoyance à l'étude
> Persévérante et sans aléa d'un tracé;
> Un chemin par lequel il n'est jamais passé
> Lui semblant hasardeux, scabreux, il le précise.
>
> [The man applies himself with foresight to the study,
> Persevering and nonrandom, of a tracing;
> A way through which he had never passed
> Seeming to him chancy, tricky, he sharpens it.]
> (v. 1834–61)

This is exactly the recipe of the "metagram technique" Roussel revealed in *How I Wrote Some of My Books*. In it he describes the method of writing he used to generate his narratives: by positing an opening sentence, then a closing sentence that differs from it by only a few letters, and then narratively joining together these two extremities. Here the man's narrative itinerary is similarly mapped out and scripted in advance, "traced" like the rhyme-track of the poem. The emphasis on lines, beams, and jetties on the one hand—that is, what is straight—is thus counterbalanced by another emphasis on the sinuous, the river, the trace, which are irregular curves. The straight line in mathematics is one-dimensional, and in literature it corresponds to prose—from Latin *proversus*, meaning straight (text). The curve is two-dimensional, and it corresponds to verse—Latin *versus*, turning (text). "La Vue," by zooming into the space of the photo opens a three-dimensional fictive space, and the poem's progression or "tracing" within that space flickers at the brink of four-dimensional automorphosis.

Roussel appears to reflect on the poem's dimensional unfolding in an earlier episode concerning a girl flying a kite, which is described as "oscillating, unstable, worried, turned / Toward silence" (v. 815–16). This anxious metacommentary asks explicitly whether the kite/poem might not be "in distress, slanting, monstrously flat [*monstrueusement plat*]" (v. 820). The word "flat" here refers both to the photograph and the poem, perhaps reflecting Roussel's anxiety that both lack, respectively, sensorial depth and profundity. The analogy is accentuated by the fact that the kite is made of paper with black lines:

Upon itself it sports, to make it prettier, lines [*raies*]
Dark on a white, clear background . . .
. . .
Each line, following the larger contour,
Reproduces it, shorter and flimsier
The more one nears the center
. . .
A paper tail makes soft movements,
Undulations . . .
. . .
A black line [*fil*] seemingly unbreakable, tense,
And by which the horizon is as if split [*fendu*]
Comes down from the kite which it holds firmly, passing
Inflexible, alone, rigid, through space;
When one's gaze, persistently, follows it
Downward, to reach its goal, it leads—
With its rigid line [*ligne rigide*] which at times shines
In the sun—to a little girl (v. 821–38)

The verse, "each line, following a larger contour," suggests a kind of concentric filling-in of visual scenes by the poem, following the outside limits of the snapshot. Occasionally, a felicitous verse occurs so "its rigid line . . . at times shines." But more generally this metapoetics of the kite opens a space of intermedial encounter *between* the text and its double, the imaginary photograph. For here, the kite's string, like the crack in the stick, is the poem's line now inscribed upon the visual scene itself—the text superimposed on the photo as it were like a long line. It is very possible that Roussel is aware of this cross-medial metacinepoetics when he writes:

. . . it is around a stick
That the string [*fil*] she holds in reserve is rolled [*s'enroule*],
Forming in midsection a large ball;
It constantly entangles itself, lengthwise, crosswise,
Its passages [*passages*] each time layered over;
It traces [*trace*] and forms with itself diamonds
Almost all imperfect and shifty, strange;
Some, better defined, more privileged,
By chance arranged themselves nicely, regularly;
But at other places, everything is entangled and entwined. (v. 844–53)

While the kite's two-dimensionality reflects the poem's design or plan and its paper support, the line reeled around a stick seems to put the poem in motion, within an experiential volume, and explicitly within time, as a filmstrip. For "its passages each time layered over," clearly correspond to reading or scanning within the epistemology of the reeling/unreeling of the moving image. In combining the straight and the curved—an analogy adrift between prose and poem, and poetry and cinema—our reading encounters possibilities for "entanglement," as well as occasional jewels when, "[the line] traces and forms with itself diamonds." Another later episode makes explicit the connection between reeling/unreeling and the book a man carries under his arm:

> A ribbon to mark—if not the true passage [*passage*]
> The paragraph or the line [*ligne*]—at least the page
> Where one is [*où l'on est*], juts out from the leaves, light, wagging [*ballant*],
> And hangs aimless and turned toward the void, rolling
> On itself [*s'enroulant*], now that nothing prevents it from doing so. (v. 1381–85)

Roussel's words invite us to read this wagging ribbon (an echo of the dog's tail "full of exuberant animation"; v. 472–73) as the poem's progressive movement, curling upon itself, its rhyme-track rolled around "the void" of its seemingly pointless "description," in fact a new poetics of photo-cinematic difference. This centripetal motion might include a direct reference to the film stock—regularly called "*ruban*" by early French filmmakers—symbolically sticking out from the "rigid lines" of the page, curling into the brave new space that extends from the book—and ambiguously *away* from it—toward new modes of cinepoetic writing.

One of the consequences of such a cinepoetic reading of Roussel's "La Vue" concerns a notion that plays an important role in film theory and cinema history: Alexandre Astruc's "caméra-stylo." Published in *L'écran français* in March 1948, Astruc's piece argued that, in the cinema of the afterwar, filmmakers would be claiming for themselves the same status of author that writers had enjoyed for so long. It is usually considered a declaration of independence for cinema from the elder muse of literature, as well as a first inkling that cinema would rival literature in the reconstructed French (and European) cultural landscape, by no longer relying on adaptation as its default source for narratives. François Truffaut's famous January 1954 manifesto "A Certain Tendency in French Cinema," which launched the "*politique des auteurs*" and gave rise to the auteurism movement, was a direct continuation of Astruc's piece. The paradox of auteurism, of course, is that by claiming the status of literary authors for themselves, filmmakers reinforced rather than undermined the authority of literature.

Moreover, by positing literature as a monolith, implicitly impervious to other media like cinema, Astruc and Truffaut bracketed the long history of cinema's permeation of literature. In other words, the strategic efficacy of Astruc's "camera-pen" rested on forgetting the cinepoetics of such works as Roussel's "La Vue" and its "pen-camera." In fact, given Truffaut's and other New Wave filmmakers' return to literary adaptation in the early 1960s, we may question whether the true target was not—rather than classical literature—the literary avant-garde's experiments with cine-literature in the early 1950s that threatened the integrity and continuity of cinema itself. Alain Robbe-Grillet's 1955 novel *Le Voyeur*, for instance—notably inspired by Roussel's "La Vue," and one of the key works of the New Novel—is but one instance of the "pen-camera" at work. Yet the critical reception of Robbe-Grillet's work, as pioneering the hybridizing of literature and cinema in fiction, also contributed further to obscuring the cinepoetic experiments that had taken place before its publication.

In many ways, that is the thrust of Michel Foucault's reading of "La Vue," in his beautiful 1963 monograph titled simply *Raymond Roussel*—his only book devoted to a writer.[23] It is in and around this book that Foucault began developing the influential notion of *dispositif* (apparatus), which culminated in the power/knowledge phase of his thought in the 1970s. The notion of *dispositif* ultimately offered to critical theory a crucial operational synthesis of the Marxian opposition between infrastructure and ideology—that is, between material conditions, including implemented technology, and discursive formations. I would like to suggest that Foucault's *dispositif* bears unmistakable traces of the cinepoetics of "La Vue," in how it meshes language with the technical dispositions of the cinema apparatus.

If Foucault planned that *Raymond Roussel* would come out on the very same day as his *Birth of the Clinic: An Archaeology of the Medical Gaze*, it was to acknowledge their entwinement. Both books tackle the same epistemic movement within the same conceptual constellation: death, formerly exterior and opposite to life, has in modernity become lodged into the living. The corollary is that the visible loses its legibility in favor of language, now alone capable of disentangling what separates death from life, and the visible from the invisible. After that, certainly, the projects differ in their aims. *Birth of the Clinic* affirms that "considered in its overall layout [*disposition d'ensemble*], the clinic appears . . . as a new outline of the perceptible and enunciable,"[24] and through this new *disposition-dispositif*

Foucault announces his archaeological method as a reform in the field of intellectual history. As for the Roussel book, it undertakes both to explain why Roussel divulged his metagrammatic method in *How I Wrote Some of My Books*, and to theorize (and perhaps exorcize privately for Foucault) the link between Roussel's praxis of language and his suicide.

What the two books share, then, is an investigation of how the interface of language and the visible devolves from an epistemology running deeper and more historically than any pathology. For Foucault, the secret of Roussel's metagram process and of his suicide is ultimately hidden in plain sight: "The process consists in purifying discourse of all the false coincidences of 'inspiration,' of fantasy, of the pen running on by itself, in order to confront the unbearable evidence that language comes to us from the depth of a perfectly clear night [that] is impossible to master."[25] It is hard not to read between the lines Foucault's own archaeological project—remapping discursive regimes through a merging of language and death. With his "machinery of language,"[26] Roussel sought that toward which history was inchoately moving: the disappearance of man in the sense of the anthropos question at the core of the humanities, as he famously declared in *Words and Things*.

But this is where "La Vue" poses a major problem. Foucault indicated in an interview that he discovered Roussel by chancing upon "La Vue" in 1961, having never heard of its author, and that since then the poem has always occupied a privileged place in his thought.[27] However, *Raymond Roussel* focuses on Roussel's metagram process, which was not applied in "La Vue," making the poem something of a bad object to be dismantled in order to demonstrate the superior logic (for Foucault's purpose) of the later *Impressions of Africa* and *How I Wrote Some of My Books*. Since Foucault posits that "All of Roussel's devices . . . are . . . an image of the process itself,"[28] the camera-pen of "La Vue" raises the specter of the exception. Foucault thus strives to prove that "La Vue" belongs to a bygone epistemic moment (a crucial kind of move in his archaeological enterprise): "Since *La Vue* the configuration of language has changed. It was a linear language that spread slowly beyond itself, carrying, in a regular flow, things to be seen. Now language is arranged [*disposé*] in a circle within itself, hiding what it has to show, flowing at a dizzying speed toward an invisible void."[29] Foucault opposes the *slow, flat, linear flow of the affirmed visible* in "La Vue" to the *fast, voluminous, concentric, flow of invisibility* in the novels. A single photograph on the one hand, Chris Marker's circular photo-film *La Jetée* on the other? We could also read the contrast as that between the moment when the film-strip passes in front of the lens (*défilement*) that projects it, and is thus straight, and when it unreels or reels back on itself, invisible and curved (*déroulement/enroulement*). The technical matrix out of which Foucault figuratively works fits the cinema apparatus quite well. "La Vue" is indeed problematic precisely in bringing technology and tropes in close contact. He deals with the problem in various stages. First, he reduces the poem "La Vue" to its pen-camera, then he makes this device into a pure trope: "*How I Wrote Certain of My Books* can be likened to the lens of *La Vue*: a minuscule surface that must be penetrated by looking through it in order to make visible a whole dimension disproportionate to it."[30] Then he disregards its robust technological materiality, that is, its cinepoetics: "Although access to it is through a glass lens or a vignette on a label or a letterhead, it's not to stress the mediation of an apparatus (instrument) between the eyes and what it sees."[31] Foucault is then free to operate the final reduction of the material components of Roussel's cinepoetics into pure language: "It is the pen of *La Vue*, and none other, that will write the works using the process, because it *is* the process, or to say it more precisely, its *rebus*: a machine to show the reproduction of things, inserted within an instrument for language."[32] By italicizing "rebus" (an emphasis omitted by the translator), Foucault stresses that language ultimately organizes the visible, so that even a stringent optical setup as in "La Vue" can be discounted, thus remaining within the "circle" of language. Thus, standing on its head Roussel's own comment that he wanted to rewrite "La Vue" in *Nouvelles Impressions d'Afrique*, Foucault ends up inserting "an ontological crack" in the pen-camera's lens, from then on preventing Roussel from "seeing things arranged [*se disposer*] of their own accord into alexandrine verses."[33] Language alone is left, and the agency from the visible world and its instrument is evacuated.

For all this, and because he knows "La Vue" very well, Foucault describes the poem in remarkably precise terms that go against the reduction of its *dispositif* to pure language. Keenly, he locates in what I have referred to as the ambivalent "description" of the poem, "an equivocal gyration (half-inspection, half-parade) where everything appears still, both eyes and landscape, but where without frame of reference, or objective, or motor, they never stop moving, each in relation to the other."[34] This image of *relative* rotation recalls at once the panoramas of the fin de siècle, such as Piasetsky's Trans-Siberian rolling panorama or the *cinéorama*, a filmic panorama of a hot-air balloon ascent, but also the concentric structure of Bantham's *panopticon*, unmistakably Rousselian in how it was also "arranged [*disposé*] in a circle within itself."[35] Yet in spite of this intuition of Rousselian cinepoetics in which processes of kinesthesia, optics, voluminous sensations, and photo-cinematic referentiality organize language rather than the reverse—and his *Raymond Roussel* in many passages confirms this deep permeation—Foucault seems particularly intent on neutering the possible agency of moving image media.

Only a few months after the publication of *Raymond Roussel*, in a review of several works of fiction by New Novel writers, Foucault notes of Claude Ollier's *Été indien* that the movements it contains, "are prolonged, echoed, displaced or frozen by photos, fixed sights ("*des vues fixes*"), and fragments of film."[36] He adds, "[The gaze] detach[es] [things] from themselves virtually within their thickness, to make them enter in the composition of a film that does not exist yet and whose scenario has not been chosen. It is such undecided 'sights' ['*vues*'] that remain 'options' that, between the things they no longer are and the film that not yet exists, form with language the texture/plot ['*trame*'] of this book."[37] Not only does Foucault allow that virtual cinema and writing can mesh into the new literary texture that I call cinepoetic, but his insistence on using the obsolete term "*vue*" in quotes shows that he must have been well aware of that meshing while writing his book on Roussel.[38] By seeking, not always successfully, to evacuate the *dispositional* robustness of the cinema apparatus in Roussel's poetry, while at the very same time sketching the *dispositif* in *Birth of the Clinic*, Foucault invites us nonetheless to see cinepoetry as a kind of photo negative out of which was developed the positive hybrid construct of the *dispositif*, at once discourse and its other.

CHAPTER THREE

Le Film surnaturel

Cocteau's Immersive Writing

Jean Cocteau, born the same year as Abel Gance (1889), was among the first poets to take note of cinema and experiment with ways of integrating it into writing, before even turning to filmmaking per se. His signal cinepoetic contribution was to reinterpret bodily experiencing through elements of the cinematographic apparatus. Famously maligned by Breton for his flamboyance and flair as a rival pioneer in the new spirit of the postwar, Cocteau continues to be short-changed by recent film historians who downplay his keen interest in cinema and filmic thought.[1]

Cocteau, so the common approach to his work goes, was a writer and poet who progressively turned toward filmmaking in the 1930s and 1940s. His career would thus neatly replicate the teleology of the muses within a postmodern articulation of modernity. Yet that narrative does not work since his filmmaking career began in earnest in 1925 with the lost *Cocteau fait du cinéma*[2]—an homage to Chaplin. Together with Apollinaire, Blaise Cendrars, and Max Jacob, he was among the presurrealist poets experimenting with the cinematic permeation of poetic writing already during World War I. So clear was this cinepoetic undercurrent for Cocteau that he describes his first important novel, published in 1923, thus: "Cinema should unfold as a psychology without text. I try, with *Thomas* [*l'imposteur*] to unfold a text without psychology [*de dérouler un texte sans psychologie*]."[3] Cocteau uses, by coincidence it would appear, the very verb on which Mallarmé's note on cinema and text hinges. He rejected at first the actual integration of text and moving images, writing of a film in

1919: "Events succeed and run into each other, superimposed, banning the text."[4] But he later made conspicuous use of writing in his first film, *Blood of a Poet* (1930), both through intertitles, voice-over, and as part of staging. The cinepoetics of Cocteau complements that of Mallarmé, in that both saw in cinema a medium making deep connections among embodiment, the arts, writing, and meaning. Yet while for the latter embodiment was largely an aesthetic question—he takes dancing, biking, and sailing as oblique refractions of art making—for Cocteau, the body provoked a host of much more urgent personal and pathological questions.

Larry Schehr is right in warning critics against pathologizing Cocteau, in particular from the queer angle of his study.[5] Yet both biographically and artistically, Cocteau came of age during the Great War that punctured modernity's utopianism and led to or amplified a host of altered perceptual and bodily experiences, many of which he underwent first hand: illness, depression, opium use and abuse, hyperesthesia, queer sensibility, homosexuality, and probably PTSD after his tour at the front in 1916. Rather than through values of normalcy, we must approach Cocteau as involved in the new altered sensorium that Abel Gance, Jules Romains, and Jean Epstein explored after 1918, in which injury, trauma, and fatigue were legitimate and creative bodily states, "other healths" as Epstein dubbed them, indexing altered modernity.

In the attention of Cocteau to a host of visual and nonvisual sensations, in his choices as a writer and a multimedia artist, in his relations to his own body and in his thoughts about embodiment, we can recognize specific filmic components. Christian Rolot notes that Cocteau never said much about the possible influence on his work of his friends at Editions de la Sirène, Louis Delluc and Jean Epstein, or for that matter of other filmmakers of the French narrative avant-garde, such as Germaine Dulac or Marcel L'Herbier.[6] The reason is likely that Cocteau appears to have developed his idiosyncratic cinematic taste very early on, before their work became established. The usual narratives around Cocteau's early career center on pathological events, from the suicide of his father to his association with Diaghilev's Ballets Russes, his liaison with Raymond Radiguet, or the opium addiction after Radiguet's sudden death. This chapter will be approaching Cocteau less through biographical data than through the sensorial motifs and perceptual constructs that run underneath a good deal of his works. I agree with Williams that Cocteau was a "profoundly materialist artist" in that he foregrounded the complex nature of the link between his own self-mystery and artistic activity—that is "the organic link between a creator and his creation," which other artists tend to naturalize, transfigure, or conceal.[7] Such a link, I propose, involves just as much the conspicuous mise-en-scène of the self that Cocteau has claimed and his critics berated, than other aspects of cinematic production having to do with body, affect, and perception, or involving the particulars of the cinema apparatus. It is in this embodied and material layer that cinepoetry must ultimately be located as a kind of metapoetics informing all at once his writings and some of his later film output.

In May 1917, when he wrote the libretto of *Parade* as a collaboration with Diaghilev, Picasso, and Satie, Cocteau insisted on rendering the flicker of film projection: "The little girl quivers . . . like the images of a film," he explicitly wrote.[8] By transducing into a child's body a loud, hypnotic, and parasitical mechanical phenomenon, Cocteau intimates that movies trigger poly-sensorial experiences—visual, as well as aural, haptic, and sensorimotor. The quivering, of course, points to Chaplin's Tramp protagonist, whose spastic gait similarly registered the rhythmic imprint of film projectors. It is paradigmatic of Cocteau's poetic attention that it drifted toward such side-effects of the cinema apparatus rather than the more conspicuous aspects of animation, motion, or CU. The 1916 preface to his underappreciated autofiction *Le Potomak*, written in 1913–14, invokes other secondary attributes of the apparatus: "The rays of the cinematograph, this sheaf of moonlight laden with actors and landscapes which we cannot see, delivers them, in cross section, against the screen."[9] Rather than considering a movie as the projection of two-dimensional moving images on a two-dimensional screen, Cocteau takes cinema to generate a three-dimensional light cone bisected by a plane—in accord with the geometrical program of conical sections. This bisected cone is not so much valued for being phenomenologically correct (although it is), but for representing the volumetric elongation of 2-D images stretching to infinity until a plane lends them repose. This conic model is far from marginal. It figures in Bergson's philosophy—where the present is the punctual intersection of the cone of past images and the cone of virtual futures—as well as in Deleuze's "plane of immanence," indebted to both Spinoza's monism and Jean Epstein "unified plane," itself linked to the screen.[10]

For Cocteau, the cone of light matters very much because it is film's primary automorphosis, the initial locus of its "matter," in a literal way it is its *medium*. He writes in 1917: "The conical image, blooming and illegible, of this white horse of cinema, unbound by the sheer obstacle of a wall for our human eyes."[11] The "white horse of cinema" brings to mind the bet of Leland Stanford concerning how many legs a galloping horse rests on the ground simultaneously, since this is what led Muybridge to develop chronophotography in 1878. As for the idea that the "image cone" blooms, it refers both to films of accelerated vegetal growth and to the automorphic visual plasma of the cone of projection that human vision cannot disentangle. Cocteau says as much in 1924: "The ray of the cinematograph knits images into a form our eyes cannot read. A flat surface must cut through it. Then our eyes can decipher [the images] and rejoice."[12] In both instances, the conical flow of images inaugurates a regime of meaning that contrasts with reading (a text), via the foundational cinepoetic homology /page⇔screen/. Hence the cone of projection marks the material difference between the order of meaning of cinema and of text, and conversely it suggests that texts themselves may be cross-sections within a dynamic continuum.

That difference is staged in several poems about the light cone of the projector, in the collection *Embarcadères* from 1916 in which cinema is omnipresent. Titled "La Jeune Fille rayonnante" (The beaming maiden, or The maiden made of beams),[13] one poem transforms the automorphic cloud of images into a woman, ostensibly to follow her fate from projector to screen. She is envisaged first as an already aged modern Fate clicking her knitting needles—"old electricity / is knitting"—the Fate that spins the diegetic time-space of the movie, and perhaps a reference to Mallarmé's muse, Loïe Fuller, who was the "*Fée de l'électricité*" at the 1900 Paris World Fair where Cocteau saw her dance.[14] In two other poems in the collection women are associated with cinema because of bodily extremes. In "Carmagnole," a tomboy film star that is probably Pearl White is said to be "boxing, galloping, leaping on a train,"[15] while in "Annonciation" the figure of the Virgin Mary seemingly "turns" into honey or smoke via a double meaning: "Tourne le film comme un miel," meaning either "Shoot the movie like some honey," or "The movie turns like some honey."[16] The female body seems to be at issue here, either as excessively physical and sexual or, at the other pole, excessively immaterial and asexual, transparent and malleable. In both cases, female embodiment inhabits the extremes of automorphism. In "La jeune Fille rayonnante," the old cone/crone electricity produces a man, a black man who "déplonge

Figure 17. The poet *deplunging* from the mirror in Cocteau's *Le Sang d'un poète* (1930). © Pierre Bergé, courtesy of Comité Cocteau.

entre les crocodiles" (undives from among crocodiles).[17] (Figure 17). The crucial image for Cocteau's oeuvre of the poet unplunging out of the mirror in *Le sang d'un poète* (1930) has its origins in this very poem. Or rather, the poem is a cross-medium relay since the image comes from further back, from the Lumières's cinema of attraction: already in 1896 (when Cocteau was seven) children jumping into the sea were shown in reverse motion, "unplunging" skyward. Let us note, then, the deep resonance of this trick technique for Cocteau, especially in connection with the automorphic medium of water, and the mutation of the old crone into the black man in the poem, before he himself reverts to:

cette
jeune fille rayonnante
elle traverse d'un seul jet la tabagie
et
s'applique en riant
sans la moindre honte
face au public
contre le mur blafard

après   elle sort
dans le vide

caché
là haut
dans son petit phare
le rémouleur des silences[18]

It is important to reproduce the text as a *visual poem*, since Cocteau uses the flat indented space to represent the vertical screen against which the maiden "applies herself"—in another double entendre at once plainly material (the beams are applied to the screen) and vaguely obscene and murderous, since she applies herself arduously, facing the public naked, or at least vulnerable, before being disappeared. As we return full circle to the origin, the projectionist is now male, and the strident metallic sound from the projector returns as well, as if it were knives, thrown at the maiden perhaps, or used as surgical tools to produce the alternating series of gender shifts—female-male-female-male.[19]

The cone of projection encompasses the limbo mysteries of life and death, and sexuality or sexing, and the automorphic virtuality of syntax, precisely through words that acquire a second meaning, a new malleability through the cinema apparatus: *tourner, rayonner, déplonger, appliquer.* For Cocteau, the embodied experience of (distracted) movie viewing directly informs a new cinepoetic reserve of meaning in language and writing. Another poem, titled "Pipe," begins:

Dans les coulisses du vide au cinématographe
D'où sortent les voleurs, les bateaux, les lions
Et les rayons peuplés, le peuple des rayons,
Confondent leur hiéroglyphe

[In the backstage void of the cinematograph
From which come robbers, ships, lions
And the peopled rays, the people of the rays,
Mix up their hieroglyph][20]

This new reserve of meaning—here linked to a chiasmus that makes the light cone come alive and community life a matter of projected beams—also has its source in the void, the "behind the scenes" of the screen, an imaginary cavern of presence, which is in fact nothing at all, that is, death. In another poem, titled "Lune" (Moon), Cocteau writes, "Open window   insomnia / shadows of the American cinematograph / with opera glasses one can make out craters / of a dead planet."[21] In a way, Cocteau extends the thought of early commentators who thought that cinema preserves life against death, by seeing it as the realm of a life after death, at once a distant world (Africa or the Moon) and the dark corners in any theater with an impossible space behind or around the screen. The poem "La Lumière droite" (Straight light), addresses this multiple existential bifurcation:

> Dans le faisceau de rayons livides
> Il y a des personnages qui vivent
> . . .
> Nous sommes un beau film projeté
> Par le soleil et par la lune
> Et la nuit nous continuons à vivre sans
> être vus
> Comme les cow-boys et les détectives
> À droite et à gauche de l'écran[22]

The cone of projection is a secondary existential realm in which we experience characters as genuinely having a life; and conversely, our own dream-life goes on in a space that is as paradoxically ungraspable as the off-screen space in a movie. As a parenthesis, few filmmakers or chroniclers of cinema were even aware of the weight of off-screen space in the late 1910s. It is no exaggeration to say that notions of "other world" or "nether world" or "dream-world" in Cocteau are undissociable from cinema's "beam of livid rays." The light cone generates a number of objects, figures, and formal echoes in several of Cocteau's films, plays, and novels: from the megaphone and the gramophone pavilion in *Parade*, to automobile lights sweeping through the night in *Les Enfants terribles*. The 1917 poem "Madame," mentions "a cone/cornet of darkness" (*un cornet de ténèbres*) alive with "the blue silence of American films," while on the face of the actors "one sees a thought being born / in their eyes like glass vessels [*pareil aux cornues*]."[23] The conical motif here mobilizes both sight and sound, and extends metonymically to hornlike shapes—*cornet*, *cornue*—both near homophones of the word "cone." Embodied and distracted or dysfunctional movie viewing disclosed to Cocteau the cone of projection as a mysterious correlate to the kinesthetic and synesthetic imaginary of cinema, and also as a new form on meaning and even *writing*, as the title to his collection of writings on cinema attest: *Le Cinématographe*.

I have insisted on the automorphic nature of the cone as a fluid cloud—very much visible in smoke-filled theaters—because light and smoke provide an immersive *material* correlate to the visual and imaginary immersion into the screen. In other words, for Cocteau, the experience of movie viewing was embodied because, perhaps more than other viewers, he felt himself literally *immersed*, that is, sliding into another fluid medium. This hyperaesthetic immersive sensorium was related to two specific films that Cocteau must have seen around 1913–14, at the same time he began to take opium.[24] In the summer of 1914, right before the war erupted, *The Scott Expedition to the South Pole*, also titled *Eternal Silence* (*L'Éternel silence*, echoed in Cocteau's *L'Éternel retour*) was shown on Parisian screens. This first footage of the Antarctic, reviewed by Colette, could be said to be "posthumous" since it communicated to the living images of (world famous) people who had died. With it, cinema literally brought something back from death:

> . . . a final gesture of goodbye
> is engulfed empty screen
> a white quiver
> where Captain Scott and his friends
> return to die
> long ago
> every night
> in a shroud Veronica esquimo cinematograph[25]

Then Cocteau adds:

> this supernatural film opens a hope
> of discoveries
> worth our while

This poem belongs to a sequence title "Escape Attempt," from *Le Cap de Bonne-Espérance* published in 1915, the first significant collection of poems Cocteau produced—after his Parisian phase of dandy juvenilia. What is supernatural about this film is that in it cinema holds life in abeyance in an interspace and intertime as white as the page. Cocteau's obsession with snow, as both a white expanse and the stuff of deadly projectiles (to recall the snowball thrown by Dargelos at Paul in the opening scene of the 1923 novel *Les Enfants terribles,* reprised in the film *Blood of a Poet*) has to do with its indexing of the common potentiality of page and screen. I believe this is the source of Cocteau's fascination with cinepoetry as an *intermedium.* When Jacques is about to die of a cocaine ("snow") overdose in *Le Grand Écart* (The great divide), he feels he is becoming "the man of snow"[26]—an equally apt description of Paul lying half-dead on the snow after being hit by Dargelos's snowball, or of Scott's eternal "return to die / long ago / every night" on the screen.[27] Snow and ice clearly have a privileged correlation with the photo-cinematic difference since *freeze* frame and *moving* images (as Gide understood in his "Treatise of Narcissus") metaphorize the change of state from solid to moving water.

Accordingly, Cocteau is also mesmerized by the underwater medium, and in particular one of the first films shot under water and released in 1914: John Ernest and George Williamson's *Thirty Leagues Under the Sea*—a title winking at Jules Verne. Through a device that happens to be conical, "an observation chamber with a large funnel-shaped glass window," the brothers filmed the marine life of the Bahamas at a depth of a hundred and fifty feet.[28] Early films inspired by Jules Verne had produced as theatrical simulacrum the sensation of being underwater, sometimes using aquariums in superimpression.[29] Now, cinema had penetrated a new world—or interworld—to discover a new spectrum of sensations of moving and living underwater. Cocteau indeed makes of this film an emblem of his entire aesthetic project: "We were free and sought nothing more than to lower within our human and inhuman night the bell the Williamsons were the first to lower down the deep."[30] In a 1916 poem he refers more succinctly to "Périscope Williamson" as a shorthand.[31] Whereas Freud famously described the Ego as emerging from the drying up of the marshes of the Id, Cocteau's aim is converse: a Rimbaldian descent into—and literally the filming in a low-angle shot (*plongée*) of—the liquid underworld of consciousness. Such underwater imagery pervades Cocteau's early writings. "I float within myself," Jacques asserts throughout *Le Grand Écart,*[32] and this "I" immersed in the self ultimately sheds his envelope: "Perhaps, this diver [*ce scaphandrier*] that can't breathe within the human body wanted to take it off."[33] Water and cinema are linked from the very opening words of the novel: "Jacques Forestier cried quickly. The cinematograph . . . drew tears from him."[34]

Cocteau's first fully realized book, *Le Potomak*, sections of which date from 1913, already equates existential anxiety with the diving-suit-like envelope of the self: "Stupefaction at being myself, at having to die. / I open my diving suit [*scaphandre*] a little."[35] Named after the real *body of water*, the "potomak"—with a k—turns out to be an imaginary, semitransparent, and amphibian fish kept in an aquarium that eats gloves (the hand's envelope) and mandrake roots (because they are anthropomorphic). It is a fluid body or embodiment as fluidity: "My confused life and the coherence of my dreams make me a relative of this Potomak. The same fluid courses through us," Cocteau writes.[36]

Behind the "oceanic feeling" of the underwater world that sensorially connotes the weightlessness of opium, and beyond the Thule myth of the snowy land of the dead, what is at play in this aqueous sensorium is the amphibology of volume and surface, screen and page, skin surface and corporeality. The cinematic imaginary for Cocteau provides a multidimensional key: the 4-D of dynamic immersion and automorphosis, the 2-D of boundaries that disclose the imaginary—skin, screen, mirror, page—and the passage through cones of projection or porous surfaces, like the suddenly watery visual image (mirror) in *Blood of a Poet*. It is in cinepoetry's sensorial multidimensionality that we find an explanation for the striking presence of an Ubuesque comic strip titled *Les Eugènes* within *Le Potomak*[37] (Figure 18). Drawn by Cocteau with a keen understanding of line drawing and comic book continuity, the Eugènes are male and female comics figures invented around 1915 ostensibly to spoof French war jingoism: "eugène" means "of good birth," and has connotations of eugenics for Cocteau, since the plot revolves around the cannibalistic ingestion by the Eugènes of the Mortimers, Anglo-Saxon characters blending British and German traits (although the name comes from a town in Normandy—Mortemer, meaning "dead sea"). Accounting for the genesis of the comic strip, the narrator advances a curious ethics: "As soon as a figure is inscribed [*inscrite*], we become responsible for it."[38] This responsibility amounts to "free[ing] it from its flat prison,"[39] since "the Eugène communicated to me their wish to move in three dimensions."[40] This rhetoric of space-time dimensions, which is part of the avant-garde's conceptual panoply, is clearly cinepoetic for Cocteau.[41] The comic strip of the Eugènes, then, serves as an exploration of the page as a writing space pregnant with other dimensions—volume and time—informed by cinema. Let us recall that Cocteau initially sought to make an animated film in lieu of *Blood of a Poet*, thus showing the continuity between the comic strip and the filmstrip. The narrator of *Le Potomak* confesses that the Eugènes "became the cornerstone of my sensibility,"[42] while their dimensional fluidity was also "horrific," because of how they "execute mutations" (*exécutent les mues*). The pun is that their mutations are a form of execution, so that Cocteau's cinepoetic experiments with dimensions and corporeality, seeking for

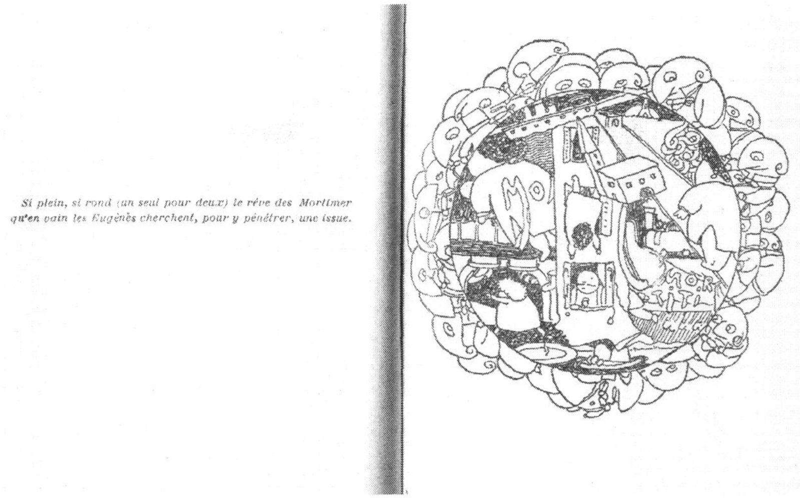

Figure 18. Cinematic "iris" dream scene from "Les Eugènes," the comic strip in Jean Cocteau's *Le Potomak* (1916). © Pierre Bergé, courtesy of Comité Cocteau.

instance "to discover the unrevealed dimension where the drama is played during the trip from the lamp to the wall" is not devoid of anxiety or indeed trauma.[43]

Cocteau appears to struggle with remaining in his place, socially, bodily, artistically, and, I would add, within the materiality of writing. The *Potomak*'s narrator declares, "Where a wall forces philosophers and scientists to stop meticulously, there a poet begins."[44] Social partitions, the separation between the arts, the material limits of writing, even the limit of the skin, are all in question in Cocteau's dimensional imaginary. Stepping outside the frame or the text can be figured as dangerously walking through walls—like a ghost. The title of Cocteau's first novel, *Thomas l'imposteur*, contains the formula by which one becomes a ghost since Thomas means "twin," and an "impostor" is someone assuming another's position. The hero of *Thomas* crosses some kind of wall within himself in order to reach his ghostly twin. When he does, the novel ends: "In himself, fiction and reality were but one. Guillaume Thomas was dead."[45] Let us recall that already for Villiers and Mallarmé, the cinema involved a new form of ghostliness. A 1915 poem of Cocteau confirms such an implication: the original version of a line, "une jeunesse de fantômes" (a youth of phantoms) was corrected to read "une jeunesse de films" (a youth of films).[46] The poem refers to the posthumous footage of Captain Scott waving his ghostly goodbye.

The motifs of doubles, twins, self-mirroring, and self-splitting, ubiquitous in Cocteau's oeuvre, are often linked to the optical expansion or projection of a surface into a volume. At the end of *Le Potomak*, a traveler looking out from the window of a train, observes, "Between the evening, then, and himself, is interposed a confusing partition," because

> against the glass . . . there is still a third image: himself
> And, behind him, the door,
> and behind the door another door,
> and another glass,
> and behind these aquariums another river and other factories
> . . .
> His double scrutinizes him barely . . .
> Planes [*les plans*] shift and change places[47]

Freud's own experience of the uncanny also occurred on a train, but with feelings of aggression rather than Cocteau's visions of an expanded self. The flat likenesses of himself reflected on the windows open up to the voluminousness of the outside world seen through them, as both sides of the train tracks rush by, creating ghostly doubles that roam a semitransparent interdimensional realm of refraction and wateriness.[48]

Les Enfants Terribles provides another dramatic translation of doubling, reflection, and ghostly cinematic dimension. The bedroom of siblings Paul and Lise was "a shell where they lived, washed, dressed, as two limbs of one body."[49] When Paul cannot sleep, Lise wants to "hypnotize him," although it is she who falls asleep: "sleep swept over [*balayait*] her efforts with broad black rays turning like those of automobiles on the snow."[50] The cone of cinematic projection haunts the snow at the border of sleep, where the two twins separate. While Paul, who is ill, is examined by the doctor, Lise experiences a vertiginous state of in-betweenness metaphorically rendered by shadowy projections of headlights against the ceiling: "This misprision of a room suspended in the void was enhanced by the slightly alive mirror that represented an immobile ghost between the window ledge and the ground. From time to time an automobile swept over the whole thing with a broad black ray."[51] The black rays do not feel like shadows sweeping, but like a black light entwined within white light, and coming from the sinister realm of "the left."

This returns us to the movie flicker. For when a movie flickers at low projection speeds (films were often projected at 16–20 fps during the silent era), the spectator can perceive the stroboscopic alternation of light and dark. The black ray of death and darkness sweeps as though from the backstage of the movie. This is what transpires in the early climactic scene of the novel *Les Enfants terribles* when Dargelos is about to throw the snow-covered rock at Paul: "The snow flew, crashing against the capes, constellating the walls. Here and there, between two darks, you could see the detail of a red face, open mouth, a hand pointing at a target."[52] These two sentences are composed as a virtual shot-by-shot storyboard. The French for "between two darks," by which Cocteau means the black capes worn by two schoolboys, is the odd "entre deux nuits" (between two nights). This recalls "the human and inhuman night" cinema allows us to discover. It also denotes two vertical masks inserted on the lens of a camera to reduce it to a slit. But most certainly it refers to the intermittent flicker of black rays and white rays in the filmic image at slow speed. Hit by the stony blow, Paul is about to lose consciousness in the snow when he glimpses Dargelos, who appears as if "under a supernatural lighting," an echo of the virtual "supernatural film," which the Scott expedition's *outre-tombe* footage evoked for Cocteau.

Between the cross-media experiments of *Le Potomak* in 1913–14, and its narrative translation in the 1922 *Thomas l'imposteur*, Cocteau, like Thomas, went to the front. He was part of a mobile nurse unit, and as his biographer Williams indicates, the record is sparse regarding what he did in the trenches.[53] What is certain is that he risked his life in several missions and subsequently cared for severely wounded soldiers. It was often the experience of war (and possibly PTSD) among poets who were soldiers or survivors that drew them toward cinema, perhaps because the flickering intermittence of spectatorial immersion presents perceptual echoes with the syncope of shock.

The connection of cinema and trauma is plain in one of Cocteau's most important early poem, "Visite," from *Le Discours du grand sommeil* (The discourse on the big sleep), drafted between 1916 and 1918. In this poem, two voices, once again two twins, talk to each other across the separate realms of life and death. "I have a great sad piece of news to tell you," one twin tells the other. "I am dead." *The Discourse* is dedicated to one of Cocteau's lovers, Jean Le Roy, killed at the front in April 1918; his death left Cocteau, in his own word, "amputated."[54] But while the two twins may represent Cocteau's phantasm of Le Roy talking to him, they appear to correspond also to poetry and cinema declaring their interdimensional affinities across media and material practices: "I talk to you, I touch you. Relief [*le relief*] is good. . . . Each of us is a bottle that impresses a different form to the same water. . . . I am us. You are I."[55] The old chestnut of lyricism—Hugo's apostrophe to his reader, "ah fool! you who think that I am not you"[56]—now acquires an intermedial hue, where "the poetry of cinema" and "the cinema of poetry" deal with different impresses of the same material. Poetry's materiality, as in Mallarmé, unfolds from page to volume: "Life only shows you a small area of a page folded on itself many, many times. . . . Poetry resembles death."[57] It does so because poetry unfolds its page in the same intermittence, interregion, and interdimension as cinema: "The same strip of photos unfolds our actions [*Un même ruban de clichés déroule nos actes*]. But you, a wall cuts the ray and frees you. You can be seen moving in your landscapes. Our ray goes through walls. Nothing stops it. We live abloom in the void."[58] The voice that speaks is that of poetry, telling its twin cinema that, "the same strip of photos unfolds our actions," as though poetry too is driven by the automatic motion linking its images. But, as language, it does not find release and expression through a cross-sectional projection on a surface, since its "ray goes through" it. While Cocteau's "supernatural film" thus affirms that the kind of cinema poetry is transcends the apparatus, it nonetheless overcomes poetry's regime of purity and exception by rethinking it as essentially entwined with the cinematic sensorium. With Cocteau, in other words, poetry ceases to be able wholly to define itself autonomously and must acknowledge instead that as a "supernatural" version of cinema, it is now inherently cinepoetic.

PART TWO

Telepresence of the Marvelous

Cinepoetic Theories in the 1920s

CHAPTER FOUR

Jean Epstein's Invention of Cinepoetry

Because it is so complex, this language [of cinema] is also incredibly subtle. All the details simultaneously pronounced outside of words trigger words at their very root, and even before words, those feelings that preceded them.
—JEAN EPSTEIN, "Langue d'or," *Écrits*, 1922[1]

POETRY AND PSYCHOPHYSIOLOGY FROM SEGALEN TO EPSTEIN

The hyperesthesia experienced by Cocteau during the spectacle of image projection and Foucault's passion for Roussel's "La Vue" at the time he was writing *Birth of the Clinic* hint at intersections between cinepoetics and medicine. Already in the 1890s, Jules-Étienne Marey as a trained physiologist and Albert Londe as an assistant to the psychiatrist Émile Charcot had improved Muybridge's chronophotography and, for the former, experimented with protofilms, with the aim of analyzing bodies in motion and the inner movements coursing through the body: blood or unconscious muscular impulses. Early cinema, as Jonathan Crary has suggested and Rae Beth Gordon shown, reveled in the display of bodily phenomena bridging the normal and the pathological such as hypnosis, somnambulism, mesmerism, dreaming, attention/distraction states, and ghost apparitions.[2] The cinema of attractions dovetailed with such pathological states by placing viewers' attention at the focus of early screenings, manipulating perceptual expectations through slow motion, reverse motion, stop-action, composite effects, and other editing tricks.

Poets were surprisingly mindful of the interconnection between cinema and the physiology of attention. (History even winks at it since the recipient of Arthur Rimbaud's famed 1871 "Lettre du voyant," Paul Demenÿ, was the brother of George Demenÿ, who conducted the first experiments in synthesizing chronophotography for his boss, Marey.) The best example is probably Jules Romains, who studied medicine in 1918–19 and published under his original name, Louis Farigoule, a monograph on extraretinal vision (optical stimulation in other parts of the body). He did so at the NRF, which published his "cinematographic fable" *Donogoo-Tonka* the same year.[3] We might also recall that André Breton and Louis Aragon worked in psychiatric medicine during the years 1916–18, when both young poets experimented with cinepoetry.

But two other poets should be considered the precursors of the psychophysiological origins of cinepoetry: Victor Segalen and Jean Epstein. As early as 1897, the former had collaborated on medical experiments with a brand new imaging technology—x-rays—before devoting his MD thesis to normal and pathological perception in literature. Titled *L'observation médicale chez les écrivains naturalistes* (Medical observation of the work of naturalist writers) and written in 1899, the year he mentions cinema in a letter to his parents, it posits that symbolism and naturalism had both been shaped by the reflection of writers, and especially poets, on perceptual experience. He showed the thick thesis to his neighbor in Brittany, the poet Saint-Pol-Roux, who would have been fascinated by it and forwarded it to *Le Mercure de France*'s editor Remy de Gourmont. Gourmont, who had written on cinema in 1897, suggested that Segalen develop one chapter around synesthesia. In 1902 "The Synesthesias of the Symbolist School" appeared in *Le Mercure*.

By focusing on multisensory perception in poetry, Segalen's essay provides a direct link between the attention to phenomena in late symbolism and the post-1917 Esprit Nouveau cinepoetics of Jean Epstein, who had received medical training as well. Segalen describes synesthesia as a sensation inducing a secondary sensory pathway—classically, a sound triggering a color sensation—and argues against explaining the phenomenon as either pure cognitive association or pure physiological resonance between the senses, the two rivaling medical etiologies of the time. For him, the synesthesic experience consists of a "subjective reaction" linking two sensations that display "the same affective energy."[4] Synesthesias involve equally sensation, affect and thought. The evidence Segalen adduces is not the least bit experimental, however, but entirely literary. Under the guise of medical science, he propounds a new theory of embodied poetics.

It is the influential poetic notion of "correspondences" from Baudelaire's eponymous sonnet that is at stake, and which Segalen wrenches from Baudelaire's Swedenborgian mysticism to place it in the modern sensorium affected by technology. Synesthesiae do not result from Swedenborg's *harmonia mundi*, but instead from the contamination of technologies. Following the opinion of poet and theorician Gustave Kahn,[5] Segalen argues for instance that Rimbaud's "Vowels"—the other great modern sonnet on synesthesia—was written with Charles Cros's poetics in mind, since Cros was "haunted by photographing colors."[6] Given Segalen's interest in new technologies of imaging, perception, and reproduction, this invocation of Cros and photography is far from trivial. The latter had envisioned cinema's automorphosis in an 1872 tale predating the invention of chronophotography. Optical technology is thus deeply nested within modern poetry's turn toward multisensory phenomena. And behind explicit mentions of this or that device, technology appears to play a much more subjacent and epistemic role. Segalen writes, "Out of the barrenness of lines and curves, of diagrams and abstractions of Space, there comes a procession of new Images, a sustained, ordered, coherent series of *Literary Figures* whose sole raison d'être is not their beauty and novelty, but their answer to actual modes of associated Thoughts."[7] This passage ostensibly about Joris-Karl Huysmans's writing encapsulates a new poetics based on a new kind of figure attempting to reproduce the very sequentiality of an "association d'idées" (thought associations). Throughout *Les Synesthésies*, Segalen insists that the poetic image should no longer be considered as a discrete picture, but rather as part of a series of percepts and imaginary representations correlated to what happens in embodied perception. This recalls Mallarmé's chronophotopoetic model, as well as his emphasis on both sequentiality or "succession" and simultaneity in the preface of *Un Coup de dés* and *Le Livre*. Segalen's suggestion that symbolist poetry developed a new type of literary figure based on *the serial synthesis of perceptions* fits the broad cinematic episteme of his other writings.[8] In the wake of the emergence of cinema, poets and thinkers like the phenomenologist Edmund Husserl were suddenly struck by the centrality of the moving flow of images in both imaginary and cognitive processes.[9] Countering Max Nordau's influential critique of symbolism as degenerate sensualism, Segalen locates synesthesias within normal embodied cognition: "Sensorial correlations . . . seem to us . . . normal and adequate to the Eternal Procession of Ideas, to this great law that makes Analysis succeed chaos, and Synthesis succeed analysis."[10] The melding of analysis and synthesis, I would argue, refers equally to Hegel's dialectics (or at least Hegelianism) than to the analysis and synthesis of serial photography that was surely part of Segalen's knowledge of imaging technology. The new analytic/synthetic figures Segalen terms "Synesthesia-Figures."[11] This coinage anchors the presumed "artificiality" of rhetoric (another of Nordaux's critiques) to sensory life, connecting language directly to the body. Following this cue, we might think of other figures like *energeia* and *ekphrasis* not as erudite exercises in visual transcription, but as psychophysiological correlates that render the intensity, potentiality, and temporality that come with experiencing an image. Segalen ends up subsuming under the serial synaesthesia-figure other figures of rhetoric essential to poetry: prosopopoeia, apostrophe, onomatopeia, repetition, metaphor, even paraphasia (using one word in place of another). Concluding that the "Synesthesia-Figure," represents a "sensorial evolution," that inaugurates "new Functions of the mind,"[12] Segalen celebrates both his faith in scientific Progress and his utopian hope that poetry might be called upon to collaborate with it. Largely forgotten by subsequent avant-gardes, Segalen's essay—and the interest of de Gourmont and Saint-Pol-Roux—shows that turn-of-the-century poets were already shifting their model of creative imagination from the subjective realm of rhetoric and "abstractions of Space" to that of the body interacting with its newly technologized sensorium.

EPSTEIN'S CINEPOETRY

Only fifteen years later, Jean Epstein would pick up exactly where Segalen had left off. Born in 1897 in Warsaw, Jean Epstein attended medical school in Lyon toward the end of World War I, while serving as secretary to Auguste Lumière. Between 1917 and 1922, during which time he befriended Blaise Cendrars and Abel Gance, he wrote sometimes explicit homoerotic poetry, and also one of the best books of twentieth-century poetry criticism. In the early 1920s he gravitated toward cinema, shooting a biographical documentary on Louis Pasteur in 1922, followed by an adaptation of Balzac's tale "The Red Inn" for Pathé. Directing full features in the 1920s and documentaries in the 1930s, Epstein also wrote abundantly on cinema until his death in 1953. His theory of *photogénie* forms the core of what has become known as the first French film avant-garde, French impressionist, or the French narrative avant-garde.[13]

In 1921, at the as-yet-uncertain juncture between his medical, poetic, and filmic avocations, Epstein fashioned an original theory of poetry expounded in *La Poésie d'aujourd'hui, un nouvel état d'intelligence* (Today's poetry: A new mindset), and a series of essays published in *L'Esprit nouveau* under the title "Le Phénomène littéraire." The same year, he published *Bonjour cinéma*, a work all at once lyrical, essayistic, and illustrated that is paradigmatic of cinepoetry.[14] Like Segalen and Romains, Epstein considers that within the realm of technological modernity the really new poetics is informed by sensory experience—including synesthesia.[15] His 1928 film on several tales of Edgar A. Poe, *La Chute de la maison Usher*, may be regarded as a manifesto combining cinema, synesthesia, and symbolism. What motivates Segalen and Epstein is, however, quite different. The former interiorized the turn-of-the-century fears of entropy, general depletion, and cultural loss and ultimately preserved the rule of the normal over the pathological. The latter, coming to maturity as a queer half-Jew during World War I, embraced the inner manifold (Segalen's *divers*) that he found in both his subconscious and the cinema apparatus, suspending the normative boundaries between high art and mass culture, and the normal and pathological. More so than Segalen and Romains, and in this only comparable to Benjamin (who, however, may well have been influenced by him), Epstein set out to reform poetic theory entirely. He did so on the basis of three interlocking phenomena defining modernity: fatigue and the subconscious; mass culture and technology; and aesthetic determinism.

Before examining his work, let us tarry a little on the enormous obstacle Epstein set out to circumvent: the sheer difficulty of making technology or modernity relevant to poetic theory. Two recent examples will help us make this idea more tangible. In 2007, Mutlu Konuk Blasing outlined a new theory of lyricism based on each poet's experience of "coming to language"—that is, learning its workings and entering into its circuits of sociality.[16] She takes poetry and language, in this model, to exceed humanist concerns and traditional hermeneutics because the language the poem employs and indeed "re-members" as "an inhuman code," always precedes the discursive subject.[17] The psychic and perceptual experience of facing this otherness of language seems pertinent to reopen lyric theory, yet it also remains at an individual and a-historical level. One chapter titled "Pound's Soundtrack" cites a line of Pound, "thin film of images," without reference to the cinema apparatus or technology.[18] It becomes clear that the otherness of language and poetry is predetermined to have no essential components that are embodied, prosthetic, or historico-technological. Of course, this brings humanism right back through the rear door, restoring lyricism to a pure species of voicing in a regime of pure technological amnesia. Another recent and equally fine book, by Nicolas Castin, invokes phenomenology and psychoanalysis in attempting to recenter sensible experience within modern French poetry criticism. Yet here too, sophisticated phenomenological analyses of sound and sensation are limited to "immersion within the natural world," that exclude de jure our everyday technologically mediated experiences from the realm of poetry.[19] What Blasing's and Castin's otherwise keen, well-researched, and admirable works ultimately testify to is the sheer difficulty Epstein overcame in confronting technology and the body as forces shaping poetry on an equal ontological footing as subjectivity and the force of language.

Epstein begins his theory from the radical immanence of lived experience and modern sensibility—those daily sensations and affects resonating with the mass networks, systems, rhythms, and possibilities of the city, and triggered by new work, entertainment, transportation, and collective arrangements. In the companion essay to *La Poésie d'aujourd'hui*, he provides his general conceptual model: "Civilization allows man to develop a larger area of contact with the world; it multiplies pathways of absorption."[20] Modernization is no loss, as in Nordau or Freud's *Civilization and its Discontent,* but a broadening of the field of experience, an extension of sensibility connoted by skin as interface—at once a metaphor and a body praxis. This sensorial enhancement should be confused neither with Marinetti's warlike male cyborg nor with eugenic fantasies, since Epstein notes presciently how "evolution has already been used complacently for too many purposes."[21] It results instead from fatigue and the means of counterfatigue that mass culture and the cinema initiated.

Rather than pulp culture aping high art, he asserts the opposite: it is poetry's turn to take its cue from what he nonpejoratively calls "subliterature"—pulp sentimental and adventure fiction, and by extension serials and melodramatic movies. A Copernican revolution has occurred, and now the features of pulp culture's homeopathic remedy to fatigue must be carefully studied by artists. First, it is hegemonic because there is no end to the fatigue of the working masses—an oblique acknowledgment that the hegemony comes indeed from capitalist modes of production. It is also hyperlogical, driven by a happy-end finalism, featuring Manichean morals and perfect justice, and it is anti-intellectual in substituting to reflection effortless sentimentality and emotional intensity. Thinkers indebted to Marx (such as Breton and Adorno) rightly denounce the anaesthetic effect of mass culture upon the modern masses. But Epstein takes the step they skip in recognizing that the working masses need tangible ways of coping with the exhaustion of body and mind: "The masses have not enough strength for, all at once, living their disappointments and considering them, that is to say, reliving them, without compensation."[22] But this is just what revolutionary cadres would have them do. Epstein bestows dignity on workers also by affirming that the fatigue of poets and artists is of the exact same nature as theirs. Yet he has a novel concept of fatigue. Rather than following contemporary psychologists like Théodore Ribot and Albert Deschamps who see fatigue as a lack—asthenia or anaesthesis[23]—Epstein makes it a paradoxical *excess*. Fatigue is a state of hyperstimulated restlessness; an inchoate bodily potential that, excited by the repetition of dulled stimuli, seeks expression. This idea echoes energetic models such as de Gourmont's pre-Freudian theory of sexuality as electrical current (1903): "art hooks itself like a shunt upon the genital current."[24] Hyperexcitation also acts as an anesthetic on memory, which, following Proust and Baudelaire, Epstein considers a potent and potential emotional reserve. Despite surface similarities with Freud, however, Epstein's model rejects a transcendental unconscious in favor of the "subconscious," denouncing psychoanalysis as bourgeois detective fiction, probably in part because of Freud's heteronormative family romance. His views are in fact resolutely nonnormative, since he insists in conclusion that "health does not exist: there are several healths [*plusieurs santés*]."[25]

Contrary to producers of mass culture who adroitly conceal mastery of the psychophysiology of fatigue, modern poetry's task consists of objectifying it and deriving creative means of counterfatigue. Epstein focuses especially on two objectifying features of modern poetry derived from pulp aesthetics: approximation and schematization. "Approximation is a lack of exactitude which implies: nonchalance, laziness, ignorance, or fatigue," while "the schema is a willful simplification," he summarizes.[26] He mentions Apollinaire's near-rhymes whose coloration matters more than exact match, and Cocteau's metaphor, "I was an ox then," a dense schematic simile triggering a process of unpacking that revives the reader's sensibility.[27] Such "approximation by excess," he asserts, forms "the caricatural, deforming, antiphotographic part of all art."[28] With this comment, he rejects mimetic theories of art because their purported realism implies that reality is given, when it must instead be disclosed and amplified—an idea in line with the deepest intuitions of late symbolism. He condemns posed or composed photography, praising instead spontaneous photography: "The snapshot, the only mode of sincere photography, becomes the privileged mode in literature."[29]

Rather than technologies of reproduction, photography and cinema are, for him, technologies of *presentation* or *disclosure* whose surprises, accidents, and schematics exemplify the ways in which writing can reanimate the sensibility of writers and readers. This is how cinema is tangentially introduced in the book, with Epstein celebrating "a series of mobile details" in a poetry collection by André Salmon, or Cendrars's 1919 *Le Film de la fin du monde*, a poem-scenario we will examine in Chapter 7.[30] But Epstein quickly sketches a network of deep correspondences involving cinema and literature, for instance a direct analogy between the suggestively imprecise nature of memories, rendered by the past perfect (*l'imparfait*), most notably in Proust, and gauzy or greasy lens shots[31]—a rather striking homology: /past perfect mode⇔fuzzy lens/.

The book culminates in a detailed section actually listing the features of modern poetry through their homological relation to cinema, thus making *La Poésie d'aujourd'hui* the first extensive cinepoetic manifesto. Epstein states boldly, "Cinema saturates modern literature . . . modern literature and cinema are equally enemies of theater. . . . In order to shoulder each other, the emerging literature and cinema must overlap [*superposer*] their aesthetics."[32] The term "*superposer*" pointedly denotes the superimposition of two takes in a dissolve or a composite shot.[33] Before going through the catalog of analogical features he proposes between cinema and poetry, we need to analyze the four interrelated notions that ground this analogical matrix. Such an analysis is warranted both because of the complex system of Epstein's intermedia theory and because André Breton relies heavily on it for his *Manifesto of Surrealism*.

THE SUBCONSCIOUS, COENAESTHESIS, "THE UNIQUE PLANE," AND *PHOTOGÉNIE*

For Epstein the nexus of the modern embodied self is the subconscious (*le subconscient*). While Freud's unconscious and preconscious alike house variously repressed ego *narratives*, Epstein's subconscious is the realm of affects and sensorial intensities preceding emotions and language, and best expressed in *poetry*. He notes that Cocteau and Paul-Jean Toulet conduct "grammatical suicides," when affects overflow their syntax, while Proust's digressions take their time in tracing every last ramification of affects poetically.[34] Thus potential poetic meaning remains steeped in the affect and sensory layer, "the physiological face of the subconscious," which Epstein defines with the medical term: "coenaesthesis" (*coenesthésie*).[35] It encompasses what current perception studies refer to as "interoception," sensations of the workings of the body such as ingestion, digestion, excretion, breathing, blood circulation, muscular-skeletal motion, and other visceral sensations connected to pain and sexual excitation.[36]

Coenaesthesis certainly does not belong to the "high" mimetic tradition of ars poetica. It devolves from the "lower" sensibility rescued by psychophysiological research, and contemporary with the cinema episteme and movie spectatorship. Epstein's coenaesthesis also belongs to the framework of *photogénie*, a key term in the French film avant-garde of the 1920s that he made synonymous with his theory of cinema. Photogénie denotes filmic images in their automorphic quality per se. On the one hand, the screen of automorphic images mediates the profilmic world and its embodied others in their Lucretian plethora of sentience ("behind" the screen) and, on the other hand, embodied and imaginarily active spectators ("before" the screen). Photogénie is the automorphic space of encounter—at once imaginary and real—between complex motions of all things on screen and complex bodily affects within spectators. For Epstein, only cinema has the power to make subjects and the world meet through the phenomenal truth they share: automorphosis. So-called mediated experience is thus (potentially) more "real" than unmediated experience.

This is at once a romantic and an antiromantic stance. In suggesting a fusion of subject and object, Epstein's photogénie echoes the Kantian dream of the exterior material manifold fitted to the interior realm of the human—what Kant calls the schema.[37] Informing the "literary absolute" from the Iena romantics onward, this fantasy is certainly present in Epstein. Yet it is also resolutely antiromantic on three counts. First, photogénie takes technological *mediation* to be sine qua non; second, it short-circuits the dream of an *immaterial* fusion in the realm of the intellect by placing world and self in an utterly material relation;[38] and finally, this aesthetics eschews actuality—the *kairos* of complete fusion—in favor of virtuality, an experience that unfolds and resonates into further experiences via a poetics of becoming.

Epstein's techno-romanticism rejects a priori distinctions between the mind, the material world and body, and the (presumably ontologically neutral) function of instruments. This holism is what Epstein—in whom Gance saw a "young Spinoza"—calls "the unique plane" or "the unique intellectual plane," uniting bodies, minds, and objects with a clear Spinozist intent.[39] These ideas might strike us as anachronistically Deleuzean: surprisingly, the reverse is the case. Deleuze was among the rare thinkers familiar with Epstein's writings, and his "plane of immanence" is indebted to *Poésie d'aujourd'hui*.[40] Epstein envisions the plane as a surface akin to the skin's "area of contact with the world," and characterizes cinema as "the theater of the skin," when close-ups disclose the tremulous subconscious of actor's bodies.[41] At once skin and screen, the "unique plane" is also implicitly the page of modern poetry with its "typographical emphasis that reaches to an optical overload with the superimposition [*superposition*] of text on picture."[42] The "unique plane" is thus a homological relation between signifying surfaces of body, book, and cinema: /unique plane⇔screen⇔skin⇔page/. Epstein makes it clear in a comment on a poem by Aragon: "Hence it appears clearly that modern literature affirms a single intellectual plane. Everything: thought and action, idea and sensation, today and tomorrow and yesterday, forecasts and certainties and memories, everything is projected together, side by side, on the same square of screen."[43] Epstein is careful to reject Simultaneism in favor of the *jet* or draft in progress: "the quick description . . . of modern letters can be explained with . . . a concern or capacity for noting only the variation in a tableau rather than its stable background."[44] Any totalizing or simultaneity occurs in the homological play of planes: "All the images [of poetry] project themselves on the same intellectual plane."[45] And again, this *projection* places cinema as poetry's new operational condition. This is what informs Epstein's catalog of two-way homologies between cinema and modernist poetry:

1. The aesthetics of proximity
2. The aesthetics of suggestion
3. The aesthetics of succession
4. The aesthetics of mental quickness
5. The aesthetics of sensuality

6. The aesthetics of metaphors
7. The aesthetics of the ephemeral

This conceptual matrix is innovative enough even today to go over it briefly. The first, "the aesthetics of proximity," places in correspondence the Griffithian close-up with a new form of condensed phrasing in poetry, both summarizing or virtualizing a longer sequence or development.[46] An example is Cendrars's line from *Nineteen Elastic Poems*: "I have electrical cheekbones at the end of my nerves."[47] Epstein glosses it through the experience of driving a convertible that telescopes the sensations of the driver's wind-whipped face, the prosthetic pathways between driver and machine, and the facial analogy / car front⇔human face/ placing electrical headlight where cheekbones are. This bodily proximity has erotic but also ethical implications foreshadowing Walter Benjamin's focus on auratic distance and perception in the age of film.[48]

The second homology, "the aesthetics of suggestion," is based on silent film's gestural ellipses: "On the screen the essential quality of a gesture is not to end."[49] The term "suggestion" comes out of Mallarmé's symbolist credo, "to paint, not the thing, but the effect it produces," which goes against the *ut pictura poesis* tradition: /film editing ellipses⇔virtual Mallarméan effects/. The next homology, "the aesthetics of succession," recalls Segalen's serial "Synesthesia-Figure," cinema's flicker, fatigue's intermittency, "when, a reflection, even short, appears chopped up [*découpée*] in pieces, in successive images":[50] /serial images in cinema⇔fragmented images in poetry/. Epstein sums up this new common condition of temporality: "Cinema and letters, everything moves."[51] The fourth homology, the "aesthetics of mental quickness" links the speed of mise-en-scène and fast edits with the frequency of images in poems of Rimbaud or Cendrars, both mediums seeking to render synchronically the flow of consciousness, again as Segalen had suggested: /editing rhythm of film⇔flow of images in poetry/. The fifth homology, "the aesthetics of sensuality," concerns the cinema apparatus's foregrounding of the body, both male and female, as its primary object, replacing abstract sentimentality and narrative emotions with the sheer corporeality of poetic affects. This sensuality is directly connected to the queer dimension of Epstein's own poetry, film work, and an unpublished essay on homosexuality. From Mallarmé to Cocteau and the psychophysiologist poets Romains, Segalen, and Epstein, it is clear that cinepoetry has

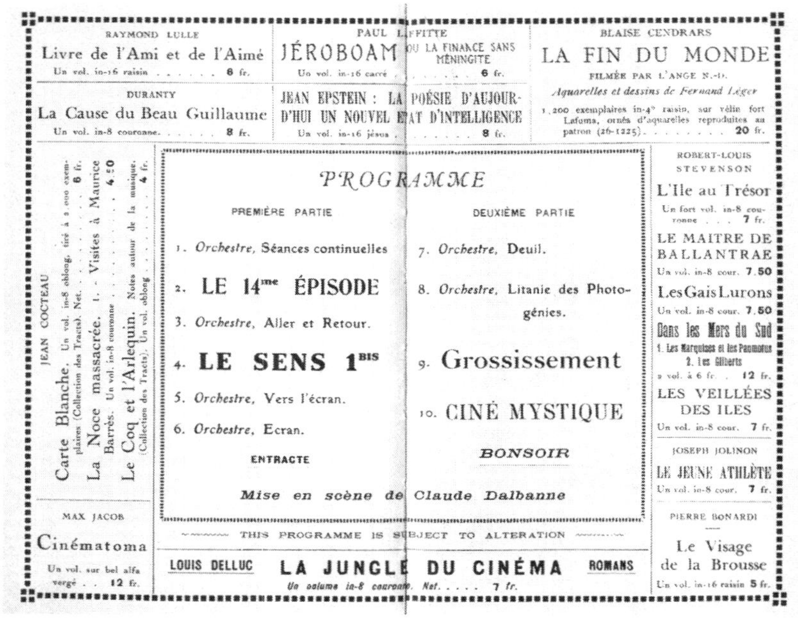

Figure 19. Table of contents in the form of a movie program, in Jean Epstein, *Bonjour cinéma* (1921).

much to do with a different emplacement of corporeality in aesthetics. The sixth homology, "the aesthetics of metaphors," is equally crucial and will be examined in a separate section below since it sheds light on Epstein's concepts of language. Epstein closes with "the aesthetics of the ephemeral," calling for images that are *modern* in Baudelaire's sense, that is, embracing the limitations of their historical and experiential situation. It is worth remembering that Epstein is writing at the time when film stock of flammable nitrate, absent efforts of preservation, made cinema the art of the "vanishing present" par excellence.

EPSTEIN'S EXPERIMENTS IN CINEPOETRY

I summarized these seven features through which *La Poésie d'aujourd'hui* culminates, as a full-blown manifesto of cinepoetry. But in fact these features are themselves short visual poems: the section on "the aesthetics of proximity" is written in free verse, both long and short, with two levels of indentation, thereby *performing* its homology, /montage with varying close-ups⇔varying lines of different semantic

Figure 20. Cover page of Jean Epstein, *Bonjour cinéma* (1921).

scale/. The section on "the aesthetics of suggestion" is written in running-line stanzas that gradually shift from explanatory prose to elliptical verse. Together with a critical program then, this is a list of virtual cinepoems, or even the movie program for a fuller theory/praxis of cinepoetry yet to come. The table of contents opening Epstein's following book, *Bonjour cinéma* (1921) is indeed labeled and laid-out as a "film program," in two parts with an intermission. Like a printed program it is accompanied with advertisements for other books from Éditions de la Sirène, which happen to include many cinepoetic works then available: *La Poésie d'aujourd'hui*, Cendrars's *La Fin du monde filmée par l'ange N.-D.* (*The End of the World Filmed by the Angel of Notre Dame*), Cocteau's *Carte Blanche*, and Louis Delluc's *La Jungle du Cinéma* (Figure 19). Such typographical visual cues are important in *Bonjour cinéma*, not least of which because they imply a collaboration with a book artist, Claude Dalbanne, duly listed as "metteur en scène" (stage director) on the TOC program. On the title page, the two *superimposed* title words are interlaced in such a way that their central letters "J" and "E" are on top of each other, forming both Jean Epstein's initials, J.E., and the most schematic of possible autobiographies, the single word "je" (Figure 20). It is in a way an autobiographical and theoretical cinepoem about how one falls in love with

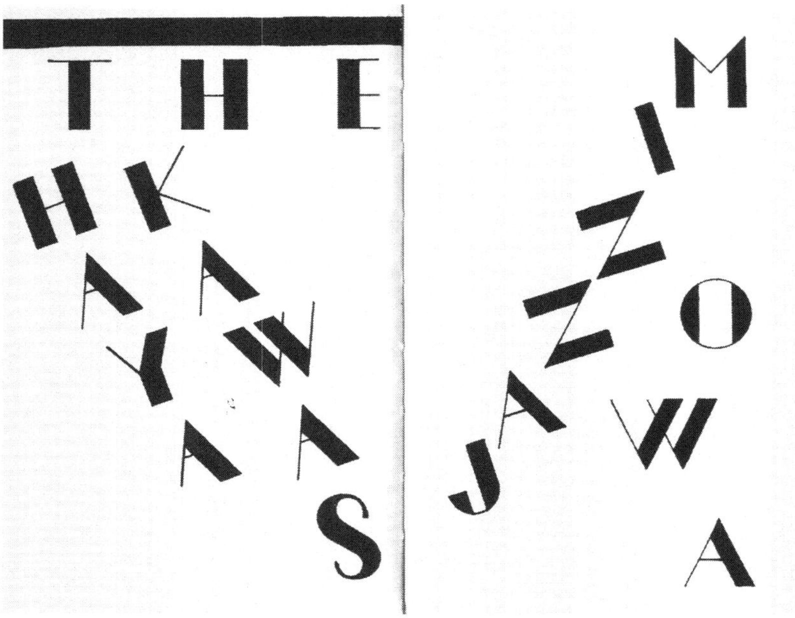

Figure 21. Opening pages of Jean Epstein, *Bonjour cinéma* (1921).

cinema. This is why the first pages after the TOC/program show the names of two of Epstein's favorite stars—Sessue Hayakawa and Alla Nazimova (Figure 21). Their names are projected into beams of letters that recall Apollinaire's *Calligrammes* (in particular "La pluie") and the light cone of Cocteau: they form new words, such as "JAZZ" when one "N" tilts into a "Z," or "THEM." We note that extra letters are added, such as the "J" and an inverted "S," and also that the names of the star form a rough triangle—a cone. It seems that the "THEM" forms a screen at the top of the page, while the "S" at the bottom, close to the reader, together with an inverted "A" on its right, would form the word "US." This cryptic calligram might well foreground the intercorporeal relation of photogénie between actors and spectators that Epstein develops in the book. It also enacts a homology Cocteau would have recognized: /mobile letters⇔signifying light beam/. The cover of the book itself stages a similar homology by making the very letters of the word "cinéma" stand for the projector and the light beam (Figure 22). If we have paid attention as *viewers*, even before entering the text sections of the book, we have had to enact a

Figure 22. Cover of Jean Epstein, *Bonjour cinéma* (1921).

para-semantic model of language, at once visual, kinesthetic, corporeal, and ethical.

The bulk of *Bonjour cinéma* is heteroclite: prose essays, left-justified free-verse sections (with the title at the end of the poem), visual poems, free-roaming letters, movie posters reproduced or invented, composite drawings (some with superimposed pictures), chronophotographs of Nazimova's face, cubist drawings of Chaplin's or Charles Ray's fragmented bodies, and in closing, the words "Merci" and "Bonsoir" printed on a film-stock background on two subsequent flip-book-like pages.[52] The work as a whole enacts a broad homology or allegorical relation between book and film cultures at large: /program, screenings, films, stars, posters, photos, frames, film stock, intertitles⇔reading, letters, autobiography, poems, book, pages, paper/. Two of Epstein's most important and most often commented-upon essays on cinema are included in the book: "Le sens 1bis (*The Senses b*)," which defines photogénie as the essence of cinema, and "Grossissement (*Magnification*)," a lyrical meditation on the power of short and mobile close-ups.[53] When the book was republished within Epstein's collected works in 1975, however, all the verse parts had been removed by the editors—ostensibly at the author's request (Epstein had died in 1953)—and the illustrations were grouped together and the typography normalized.[54] The cinepoem, in other words, was flattened and normalized into a prosaic essay in film theory. It is likely the marked homoeroticism of the verse sections that ultimately led to their excision, whether at Epstein's request or not. In any case, this excision suppressed crucial links within the history and development of cinepoetry. Take the very first verse section of the book:

> Next to a man
> I have walked on the snow
> right against his back
> with my eye on his coat
> He walked away in long strides
> without turning his head
> he was afraid he was cold
> at times he would hurry
> my supernatural cinema[55]

The reference is of course to the Scott expedition footage that so deeply struck the queer cinepoetic eye of both Colette and Cocteau. The last line directly cites Cocteau's: "this supernatural film opens a hope / of discoveries / worth our while." Hence in "Le Sens 1bis," when Epstein writes, "Cinema is supernatural by essence,"[56] the cinepoetic references to the Scott expedition footage via Cocteau's poem are no longer available, nor is the tender empathy toward Scott's vulnerable body. Among the excised verse sections, four are dedicated to male stars—Sessue Hayakawa, Charlie Chaplin, Charles Ray, and Douglas Fairbanks—and they focus on the spectatorial affects their filmic bodies trigger, as in this concluding passage on the Hayakawa section:

> He is precise acrobatic
> like a well wound spring
> and
> I love most of all
> at the edge of the screen
> when he expresses nothing
> but himself[57]

The cinepoetics Epstein limns out and enacts in his twin 1921 books *La Poésie d'aujourd'hui* and *Bonjour cinéma*, proposes strikingly different notions of poetry, cinema and thought, of spectatorship and readership, of authorship and ethics, than those of the film criticism of suspicion (Adorno, Baudry, Mulvey), or the figural failures in lyrical self-making (De Man, Friedrich, Barthes) that have dominated contemporary scholarship of the last thirty years in both poetry and film studies.

LANGUAGE, WRITING, AND POETRY AFTER CINEMA

The word is no longer the designation of anything precise, but on the contrary a kind of connector as universal as can be, used for linking the most distant images.

—JEAN EPSTEIN, *La Poésie d'aujourd'hui*

Epstein's conceptions of language are far from systematic in *La Poésie d'aujourd'hui* or *Bonjour cinéma*. When examined together with his articles and essays from the early 1920s, a more cogent picture emerges, furthering his fundamental insight that cinema reorganizes the economy of meaning in language, writing, and poetry. Since the famed lectures of the linguist Saussure were contemporary with Epstein's books, we can productively contrast their views on language. For Saussure, language is an *autonomous* system of signs that has three separate components: signifiers, which are the material face of signs (sounds or written marks); signifieds, the meaning(s) attached to each sign; and syntax that regulates each chain. The fact that language indexes or refers to the real world is unessential to Saussure's autonomous system. For Epstein, the indexical value of language comes first: "cinema is a language, and like all languages, it is animistic, that is, it lends the appearance of life to all the objects it designates."[58] Hence for Epstein the most important aspect of language is to create virtual replicas of all things so they can be put into social and imaginative play, and to do so they must feel real themselves.[59] This is very close to what Benjamin called "the mimetic faculty," ultimately crystallized into language. This replicating function of language, expressed variously by Cratylism, onomatopoeia, ekphrasis, and inner monologue, was fundamentally reshaped by the cinema apparatus. Epstein emphasizes the sheer materiality of its process: "Cinematographic language is prodigiously concrete, direct, brutal and alive."[60] There too his thought is precise: while it would be a mistake to see cinema's language as either a metaphor for or a language *other* than language, it would be equally wrong to consider it the *same* language we know. In silent movies, if we bracket intertitles and live commentary (which was no longer practiced by the mid-1920s, at least not in the cine-club where Epstein screened his films), we can say that the signifier and the signified were one and the same thing. A filmic shot meant exactly as much as what it showed, even—and that possibility is very present in Epstein's mind—even if we can see in it more than what it meant. The reason the close-up is central to Epstein's thought is that a face (again, in silent cinema) signifies only itself: its signifier *is* its signified. It is a motivated sign. What such a face-sign *refers to* is both part of the narrative of the film—hence it is discursive, language—and part of the subconscious behind the face, hence it is corporeal, coenesthetic, and affective. Before the talkies, there was a crucial balance between this double meaning layer of filmic signs.

Intertitles and intradiegetic printed words (handwritten letters, books, advertisements, signs), the only resources of natural language that could be relied upon in silent cinema,[61] often play a purely prosthetic role in early film theory. There is no doubt that cinematography and montage represent the two areas where Epstein's "motivated" cinema language should be located. Nonetheless, films of Delluc, Epstein, L'Herbier, and Dulac, conspicuously "photogenize" both intertitles and intradiegetic writing in a way that suggests that the cinegraphic imaginary was at play in them (Figure 23). Words were reanimated and transformed by filmic automorphosis and Epstein's kinetic letterings in *Bonjour cinéma* show that that mattered to him. Cinema was capable of making even *words* come alive in a concrete coenesthetic way, which is why Epstein describes them through an oddly animalistic trope when they "capture an emotion or, lower on the stem, the sensation at the very moment they enter into the resonating chamber of the intelligence."[62] Bee-words, we might say, gathering the pollen-affects of the flowers of rhetoric? But Epstein's metaphor itself feels filmic, as if out of the scientific footage of insects entering a trap he had extracted a new theoretical feature to understand language. Hence words are like butterflies whose most beautiful markings are only on their concealed side: "The most subtle thoughts are inscribed on the illegible underside of the most usual words," he writes.[63] These illegible filmlike prewords "in opposition to the words-in-freedom of Dadaist works,"[64] cannot be directly expressed because "the expression of a pure sensation can only consist of shouts."[65] The technique that allows their partial transcription Epstein calls "the play of intellectual intermittences," and it consists of the partial capture of these shouts by "withholding an emotion for an instant—long enough to write it down—from the control of the most reasoning, abstract, and perfected part of the intelligence."[66]

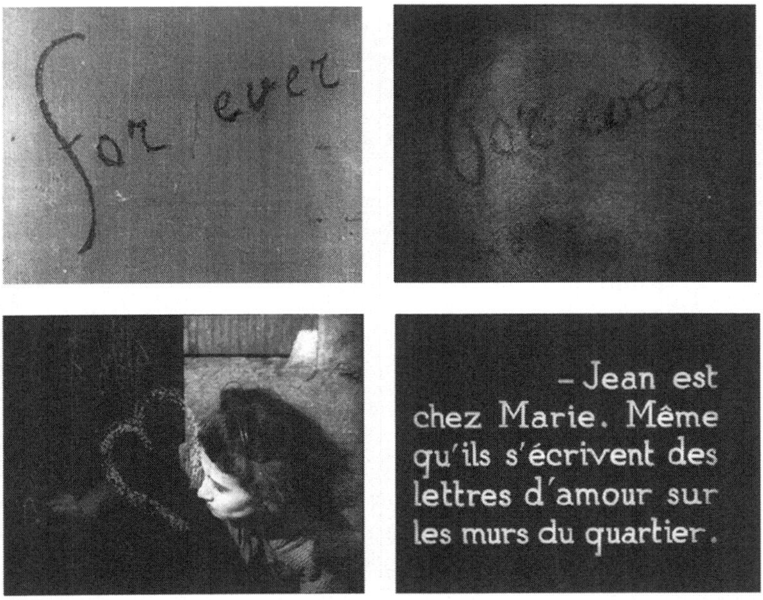

Figure 23. Stills from Jean Epstein, *Coeur fidèle* (1923). © Musée Gaumont.

There is a great deal of consistency here in Epstein's movie-infused intimations of another language within the concrete life of words. And it is worth exploring because it foreshadows automatic writing as well as linking cinema to Surrealism's focus on metaphor. The intermittence technique has two poles, the "sentence-thought," and the "association-thought." Epstein describes the first as "the thought of willed reflection [and] rational thought," which we use "to discuss within ourselves."[67] The second "oscillates between subconscious and conscious. . . . [I]t is no longer made of sentences, but, more often, of images, even images that are veritably visual."[68] To illustrate this "association-thought," he cites a cinepoem by Louis Aragon from 1918, "Chaplin mystique" (Mystical Chaplin), where fragmented utterances intermix with relatively random or loose images, both coming from Chaplin films and extrapolated from them. The intermittence technique then appears to result in a mode of writing that is partly cinematic and partly automatic.

In *La Poésie d'aujourd'hui* Epstein emphasizes the indifference of modern poets toward syntax[69] and punctuation,[70] in favor of the affective resonance of words: "Between the value of words in common speech and the value of these same words in literature, there is a dissociation, especially sharp since the vigorous change of direction by Symbolists and Mallarmé."[71] What drives such a dissociation is the sense that coenesthetic "living words" proceed from a cinema-like free flux, since they come in "an interrupted, quick flow, often incorrect like a conversation, halting, illogical like a dream, sudden, violent, childish here and two lines later senile, even drunk at times and, to sum it up, devoid of both grammar and order."[72] More than syntax, what matters is "spontaneous verbal rhythm,"[73] allowing the writer "to express more precisely his thought, to trace better with words its contours, wavy, illogical and mobile."[74] Epstein directly associates this variable speed of mobile, rhythmic, and flowing words to cinema: "The cinématographe allows a more precise observation of this phenomenon. Indeed, the film records and measures this speed of thought."[75] In a telling note, he adds, "The speed at which the films are shown must be taken into account. This speed varies according to the projectionist's fancy and the imperatives of the theater."[76] We stumble on a curiously extended cinepoetic homology: /rhythm of thought⇔poetic notation⇔film projection speed⇔projectionist's fancy/. Epstein's films are indeed remarkable and perhaps unique for modulating slow motion with barely perceptible speed shifts within the same film—*Finis Terrae* (1929) in particular.[77]

Epstein's semiautomatic "play of intellectual intermittences" involves another important component in his implicit theory of cinepoetic language: metaphor. It is in "the aesthetics of metaphor," the sixth section in the list of *La Poésie d'aujourd'hui* that Epstein makes one of his clearest cinepoetic statements: "Within five years we will write cinematographic poems: 150 meters long with 100 images linked by a thread [*fil*] that intelligence will follow."[78] This passage recalls quite strikingly Mallarmé's note from 1897: "a series of <imaginary mental written> images <linked b[y]> connected by a thread (*fil*)," as well as the "fil noir" (black thread) of the little girl's metapoetic kite in Roussel's "La Vue." Epstein devotes a separate and long chapter to metaphor in *La Poésie d'aujourd'hui*, "Metaphor-Thought and Inventive-Reasoning Among Modern Writers," that is especially noteworthy since in it he outlines a cinepoetic "surrealism" three years before Breton's manifesto.

Metaphor, for Epstein, designates the operation of free association in which one word or expression is semiautomatically joined with another through "the play of intellectual intermittences" to form a poetic image. Epstein, familiar with Greek, uses metaphor in the literal and dynamic sense of "moving across," thereby folding temporality and motion within the poetic image. Metaphoresis ultimately puts all interfaces of the "plane"—skin, screen, and page—in relation with each other: "Metaphor is a mode of comprehension, sudden comprehension, comprehension in motion. . . . A magnetizing force orients particles between the two poles of the comparison. An idea that one thought used up, empty and old, projected against another equally finished, and from the shock of their obsolescence a young spark is born. The image must be sudden or not be at all. This suddenness creates movement."[79] Epstein uses similes of electromagnetic force and sexual encounter, rejuvenation and birth, and chemical combustion and kinetics. This semantic range—on which I insist with a view to the next chapter on Surrealism—reappears in several passages, for instance in *Le Phénomène littéraire*: "[metaphors] join [*accolent*] words that are, one might say, not made to neighbor each other at all, but that neighbor each other all the same superbly; they couple up [*accouplent*] the most distant ideas, the most disparate, those with the most enmity, and the coupling occurs in a shock, a flash, a very violent explosion."[80] What takes precedence is the shock's visual display—again almost a film sequence in itself: "The metaphor rips [a] notion out of its lethargy, throws it full force like a ball/bullet [*balle*], against another notion, and from their instantaneous contact, falling back, unexpected, a thousand new significations will be born. The notion, as we can see at a glance, has acquired a brand new light; it shines, it still vibrates."[81] The visual shock of metaphoric revelation at the "association-thought" level in poetry compares to photogénie which Epstein defines thus: "I will call photogenic any aspect of things, beings and souls whose moral quality increases through cinematographic reproduction."[82] He adds a few pages below, "only the mobile and personal aspects of things, beings and souls."[83] In both cases then, a new relationship manifests itself; in poetry, through the suddenness of metaphor linking two words, notions, or sensations into one explosive cinematic visual image; in cinema, through the auratic and haptic quality that filmic automorphosis bestows on what it films. Poetic metaphor and photogénie each depends on medium specificity. Yet I would like to suggest that if Epstein called for "literature and cinema to superimpose theirs aesthetics,"[84] it was to find ways of combining the two: creating poetic metaphors animated by the imaginary haptic quality of photogénie's automorphism, and reciprocally, expanding photogénie's telepresent immediacy toward the marvelous energy of the sudden metaphor. That is the intermedial horizon of Epstein's cinepoetry.

Epstein never used the word cinepoetry. However, what he means by the words "surrealism" and "surreal," I claim, is this intermedial horizon of cinepoetry. In the chapter on metaphor-thought, Epstein illustrates his view that "metaphors used to be written by having reality pose as if for a village photographer; today metaphor is instantaneous,"[85] with a series of images:

> We write under fire. . . . [T]he shock of two men meeting through the four sides [of a pool table], a car accident, a telegraphic friendship. . . . Such a mad agitation pushes the limits of verisimilitude to the limits of the real. . . . What could not be lastingly true can be so for the time of a glance. Slow motion in cinema uncovers what ordinary cinema could not see; an intelligence on a faster pace also explores new lands. This is close to what Guillaume Apollinaire called surrealism—and the cinematographic comparison is his.[86]

Epstein's metaphoresis pointedly brings together instantaneous photography, film in slow motion, and Apollinaire's surrealism. As we know, the word "surrealism" was coined by Apollinaire in the preface of his 1917 play *The Breasts of Tiresias* where he writes, "When man tried to imitate walking, he created the wheel which does not resemble a leg. Hence he applied surrealism without knowing it."[87] Apollinaire means here that surrealism is a mode of metaphoric thought that rejects resemblance (mimesis), "to go back to nature itself, but without imitating it like photographers do," as he writes a few lines earlier. Yet Apollinaire does not mention cinema in the preface—although he does so in his 1917 talk, given a few months after the preface appeared—so that either Epstein was privy (through Cendrars?) to something Apollinaire said, or he telescoped the preface to *The Breasts of Tiresias* and the talk on "The New Spirit and the Poets." Still, in 1920–21, when Epstein wrote this, Breton had not yet made "surrealism" his proprietary word. It is significant that Epstein should have construed it as *cinema in poetry*. In 1923, he addressed the reciprocal intermedium—poetry in cinema—through the very same word:

> Poetry which might be thought of as an artifice of speech, a figure of style, a play of metaphor and antithesis, in short, a thing close to

> nothing, dons [in a film like Gance's *La Roue*] a bright incarnation. "Poetry is thus true and exists as really as the eye."
>
> Cinema is the most powerful means of poetry, the most real means of the unreal, of the "surreal" as Apollinaire would say.[88]

He returns to this antimimetic view of cinepoetic surrealism in the opening chapter (written in 1926) of *Le Cinéma vu de l'Etna* (The cinema seen from Etna): "The lens of the camera is an eye Apollinaire would have called surreal (without any relation to the surrealism of today), an eye endowed with inhuman analytical properties."[89]

By 1926, Epstein had renounced poetry as such to dedicate himself entirely to cinema. That same year, a young Spaniard wrote a letter to a friend that reads, "I'm committing to cinegraphy [*cinegrafía*)] I'm going to start helping Jean Epstein with mise-en-scène to learn the craft. Moreover, in parallel, I'll publish things related to cinema. Theory, scenarios, etc."[90] The letter is signed Luis Buñuel, who was to become for Breton the only true surrealist filmmaker.

Epstein held the word "surrealism" from 1921 onward—but we will see in the next chapter what Breton did to it—to be the appropriate name for the theory and practice of crossing the aesthetic, social, linguistic, and medium divides that had until then kept poetry and cinema separate. His keen and sophisticated understanding of how modernist poetry resulted from processes of convergence among modernity, embodiment, language, and cinema is the theoretical core of what I call cinepoetry in this study.

CHAPTER FIVE

Breton's Surrealism, or How to Sublimate Cinepoetry

At that time [in 1916], all we saw in cinema, whatever its kind, was a lyrical substance requiring massive random reshuffling [*une substance lyrique exigeant d'être brassée en masse et au hasard*].

—ANDRÉ BRETON, "As in a Wood," *Œuvres complètes*, 1951[1]

"In 1924," Gérard Durozoi writes, with a poke at Marx, "a specter haunted Paris—at any rate, the specter of Surrealism."[2] That specter haunts today's poetry studies in French, the criticism of international modernism and theories of the avant-garde, whether in writing, art, or film. André Breton was of course the main theoretician of Surrealism.[3] He might be more properly considered its scriptwriter and director since cinema, and even more so cinepoetry, have played a constitutive role in the orientation of the movement as well as in its formal and conceptual innovations, particularly automatic writing, associative leaps, the marvelous image, collagism, and the "exquisite corpse" game. Because that contribution was erased and silenced by Breton, we might say that Surrealism, in turns, was haunted by cinepoetry.

Specifically, Breton made four related moves: first, he recuperated cinepoetic writing's experimental thrust between 1917 and 1924 by bringing leading cinepoets into his movement; second, he campaigned against independent cinepoetic practitioners and theoreticians in the Paris world of letters; third, he decoupled cinepoetry from the cinema apparatus to reshape and sublimate it via the immateriality of the Freudian unconscious; and lastly, after 1925 he authorized or collaborated in limited cinepoetic experiments and a handful of films, but only when it was clear that his theory informed *them*, not the reverse. I should say that my aim is neither to reduce Surrealism to cinepoetry, nor to simplify the astounding productivity of ideas, practices, and participants that in the long run contributed to altering and expanding Breton's theoretical tenets. But I would like to set the record straight as to the part that poets like Cocteau, Cendrars, Soupault, Epstein, and Paul Dermée played in formulating an alternate surrealism, one whose conceptual and experiential matrix—cinepoetry—was largely co-opted by Breton.

THE LOST STEPS: EARLY BRETON AND CINEMA

Histories of the surrealist movement and biographies of Breton take note of the fascination cinema exerted on his late teens around 1916, against the background of widespread cinephilia at the height of World War I. These works also mention the narrow pantheon of movies that Breton officially condoned in the early 1920s: the serials of Feuillade and Pearl White, Murnau's *Nosferatu*, and a random and fragmented practice of movie viewing. Only two films were made under the surrealist imprimatur: Buñuel and Dalí's *Un Chien andalou* (1929) and *L'Âge d'or* (1930). Cinema scholars have recently dispelled such an arbitrary genealogy by examining these two films together with other contemporary avant-garde productions that, for one reason or another, Breton rejected.[4] These include Fernand Léger and Dudley Murphy's *Ballet mécanique* (1924), Duchamp's *Anemic Cinema* (1926), René Clair's *The Crazy Ray* (1924), and Man Ray's *The Return to Reason* (1923), *Emak Bakia, ciné-poème* (1926), and *L'Étoile de mer* (1928)—the latter based on a poem-scenario by Robert Desnos. Breton's investment in controlling the relationship between cinema and Surrealism has not, curiously, led scholars to reconsider the role of cinema within Breton's thought, even given the strongly visual methodologies of these scholars' work: for instance, the uncanny for Hal Foster, the optical unconscious for Rosalyn Krauss, phantasmagoria for Margaret Cohen, and collage for Elza Adamowicz. While their approaches tangentially touch upon the photo-cinematic apparatus—*Fantômas* (Cohen), photomontage (Adamowicz and Foster), chronophotography (Krauss)—all place psychoanalysis at the crux of surrealism and scarcely question its inaugural emplacement by Breton. In a recent monograph centered on visual art, Haim Finkelstein has decisively shown that a single aspect of the cinema apparatus—the film screen—can be shown to have profoundly shaped surrealist vision and art. Moreover, he writes, "The screen as a Surrealist paradigm rests on a theoretical basis whose ramifications are far too broad and rich to be confined to any single theoretical precept."[5] Surrealism's use of the cinema apparatus, it appears, diffracts psychoanalysis as a focus. This is even more the case when it comes to cinepoetry.

From his own account, Breton's interest for cinema follows a script of unrequited love. After a short juvenile infatuation, he demoted cinema to the role of mere catalyst, feeling more and more betrayed by the commercial and melodramatic nature of silent movies. The renewed focus on dramatic dialogue in the era of the talkies foreclosed even more thoroughly the promise of cinema as a means of collective expansion of desire and social mores. Briefly rekindled by the twin films of Buñuel and Dalí, his love decayed into melancholy for a lost object, until Breton confessed in 1951: "In life this age [the age of the cinema] exists—and . . . it passes."[6] Goodbye youthful vice.

In fact, cinema embroiled Breton in a much more complex sentimental education that involves homoeroticism. His early fascination with cinema in 1916 remained forever tied to his fascination for Jacques Vaché, a homosexual[7] with whom, exclusively it seems, he consumed the random serial and melodramatic fare of the Nantes theaters, in such an avid way two historians term it "cinephagous."[8] The same month that he met Vaché he wrote to Paul Valéry that he hoped to be "delivered from poetry's obsession," by finding "in cinema and the pages of newspapers . . . a Mythology."[9] So Breton turns to cinema and homoeroticism/bisexuality—whatever was the exact nature of his relationship with Vaché—at the very same time that he brackets poetry. Indeed, his interest in women in 1916–18 centered on film actresses, in particular Musidora (Jeanne Roques), who played Irma Vep in Feuillade's 1916 serial *Les Vampires*.[10] He wrote her a fervent letter after seeing her on stage in July 1917, calling her "a modern fairy adorably gifted for evil."[11] In her black bodysuit, Musidora coded a sexual continuum ranging from deadly seductress to dominatrix and lesbian, since it was public knowledge that she had had an extended affair with Colette.[12]

Breton's unspoken attraction to homosexuals resembles that of the novelistic hero of his one-time employer—Marcel Proust.[13] In his Proustian autobiographic text, *Nadja* (1928), he recounts attending "two or three times" a 1926 play titled *Les Détraquées* (The unhinged women) featuring two murderous lesbian schoolteachers. He was transfixed, he writes, by "what Solange and her partner are exactly prey to that they should become such superb beasts of prey."[14] The play had a mild *succès de scandale* because of its lesbian protagonists, albeit presenting "the worst possible view of lesbians," according to a historian of homosexuality.[15] His "boundless admiration" for this play, he adds, was such that he considered that it "loses almost everything in not being *seen*, or at least in every intervention of the protagonists not being mimed." Is Breton being coy about this trashy play's kitschy and criminal pseudolesbian body language, or else is he genuinely aroused? In a preceding passage he confesses his phantasm of encountering a naked woman "in a wood" (*dans un bois*), exactly as he once did, he adds, in the Electric-Palace movie theater he calls "a place of debauchery."[16] Let us recall that his adieu to cinema was titled "As in a Wood" ("Comme dans un bois"). Is Breton staging a false confession in *Nadja*? After all, the piece in which he writes about Vaché, after his death, that "[his] existence . . . is . . . almost all that still ties me to a life all too foreseeable with its daily problems," is titled "A Disdainful Confession." The piece ends with a citation of one of Vaché's last letters to him: "What a film I would play in!—With mad automobiles, you understand, bridges that crumble, and uppercase hands crawling on the screen toward some random precious document!—useless and priceless!"[17]

My point here is simple. Breton well knew that *Les Détraquées* featured lesbians, that Vaché and Musidora were homosexuals, that *Nadja*'s readers would conclude that he too must have sought "debauchery" in the Electric-Palace, and thus that he went to movie theaters as places of cruising. Yet such gender fluidity and sexual freedom in the war years, with their close association with cinema, were featured the better to be rejected *en bloc* by the "mad love" doctrine of serial monogamous heterosexuality that *Nadja* professes. Whatever else might be said of the contrast between Buñuel and Dalì's *Un Chien Andalou* (1929) and Cocteau's *Blood of a Poet* (1930)—which Breton never even addressed in his lifelong contempt for Cocteau—it is plain that the former is a heterosexual narrative within a tight Oedipal frame, while the latter deals with a full range of queer experiences—homoeroticism, voyeurism, sadomasochism, hermaphroditism, cross-dressing (the famous Barbette), even Cocteau's own lover (Jean Desbordes).[18] Breton reviled Cocteau for complicated and unfair reasons, not least of which was that he associated the latter's queer sexuality with fluidly interartistic pursuits.[19] Breton's heteronormative turn, I propose, parallels his progressive development of a rhetoric of purity that purged both queerness and cinema from writing, and returned him to both poetry and hetero-seriality.

It is crucial, in this context, to understand the sudden spread of cinepoetry during the relaunching of the French avant-garde around 1916–17. Pierre-Albert Birot's interart journal *SIC* (after the Latin "thus"), subtitled *Sounds, Ideas, Colors*, signaled the first stirrings of a new avant-garde in January 1916. Within a few months, Apollinaire declared in an interview with Birot in *SIC* that "the epic poet will express himself with cinema." In the same issue, Birot calls for integrating "cinematographic projections" in the new theater.[20] In December 1916, Max Jacob wrote a "Petite chronique cinématographique" for Ozenfant's journal *L'Élan*.[21] *SIC* was a key forum for all the future Dadaist/surrealist poets—Drieu la Rochelle, Paul Dermée, Philippe Soupault, Tristan Tzara, Louis Aragon, Raymond Radiguet, and Francis Picabia—since it made them known to a broad public and to each other.[22] It was in *SIC* that Philippe Soupault published "Indifference, A Cinematographic Poem"—the first explicit cinepoem in 1918. His contributions to the journal in 1917–18 focus heavily on cinepoetry and include pieces titled "Note on Cinema," "Cinematographic Poem," and two series of "Animated Photographs," composed of six poems.[23] His innovation—a direct response to Apollinaire's November 1917 call in "The New Spirit and the Poets"—opened the floodgates to dozens of cinepoetic works that followed over the next few years.[24]

Well informed and well connected, Breton surely noticed this proliferation of cinepoetry. He had published one of his first poems in May 1917 in *Nord-Sud* at that time led by Apollinaire and Reverdy with an agenda close to cubist painting. But even *Nord-Sud* included cinepoetry in 1917–18: a poem of Apollinaire entitled "Before the Cinema," Aragon's "Charlot mystique," and notes by Max Jacob on cinema and theater and by Pierre Reverdy on film montage. A rift was soon created between *SIC* and *Nord-Sud*, in part because of a hoax poem mocking Birot that Fraenkel and Breton wrote and sent to *SIC* under the signature of Cocteau.[25] In 1917, Breton wrote his first collage poem, "Forêt Noire" (Black forest), accentuating his drift toward visual poetry, under the joint influence of Mallarmé—whose republished *Un Coup de dés* had profoundly struck Reverdy and Apollinaire—and cubist collage. He also moved closer to Reverdy's poetics after the disappointing "nullity of thought"[26] of Apollinaire's talk "The New Spirit and the Poets," whose accompanying poem readings Breton himself had been in charge of selecting.[27] Commentators focus on the Germanophobia and weak reflection on lyricism in

Apollinaire's talk as causes of Breton's disillusionment. But the aesthetic thrust of Apollinaire's program placed cinema at the forefront of new means of surprise in poetry. In a 1923 talk, Breton faults Apollinaire for mistaking "the new lyricism" with a call toward "mechanism" (*machinisme*) and "the phonograph." Breton does not explicitly name cinema because he reserves it for another use, a few lines below, that of revealing the "burlesque of modern life" in the films of "Mack Senett, that are what the cinema has yet offered us that is the most mysterious."[28] Rather than discounting cinema out of hand, Breton intimates that poets ought to keep their distance from filmmaking or overt cinepoetics so movies can remain a "mysterious" reserve of inspiration. This shows he was wrestling with just how much and what kind of distance poetry should retain vis-à-vis cinema.

The first strategy used by Breton was to invoke cinema metaphorically, as it relates to visual art. This is what he does in the first text formulating the poetics of what he does not yet name Surrealism. In the catalog for the May 1921 Max Ernst exhibition he vaunts

> . . . the marvelous faculty, without leaving the field of our experience, of reaching two distant [*distantes*] realities and, from their juxtaposition [*rapprochement*], generating a spark [*étincelle*] . . .
>
> . . . We know today, thanks to cinema, how to make a locomotive *arrive* upon a painting. The more we generalize the use of slow motion [*ralentisseur*] and accelerating devices, the more we get used to seeing oaks unfold and antelopes fly, the more we foresee with extreme emotion what might be these local times we hear about . . .
>
> . . . [Ernst] projects for our eyes the most captivating [*captivant*] film in the world . . .[29]

Breton's formulations revel in distance and movement, in light, electricity, and time, and they climax in cinema—but only *metaphorically*. A month before Breton's text was written, in April 1921, Epstein's *La Poésie d'aujourd'hui* was published. In his chapter on "Metaphor-Thought" we read the following:

> An idea thought to be used up, empty and old, projected against another just as finished; and from the shock of their decrepitudes a young spark [*étincelle*] is born. . . . Such juxtapositions [*rapprochements*] are not a simple game. . . .
>
> . . . the slow motion device [*ralentisseur*] of cinema uncovers what ordinary cinema could not see. . . . This is close to what Guillaume Apollinaire called surrealism, and the cinematographic comparison is his.
>
> . . . Analogy crosses distances [*distances*] and species.[30]

The similarity between the five pivotal and rather improbable terms—*étincelle, rapprochement, ralentisseur, distance/distantes, cinématographe/film*—is beyond coincidence. Epstein's very first piece on cinema, published in February 1921, in *Le Promenoir*, a short-lived Lyon journal, had defined *photogénie* in similar terms: "Until now I have never seen photogénie lasting a whole minute. We must recognize that it is a spark and an intermittence."[31] Breton had cited the word "surrealism" prior to Epstein in January 1920, to describe the "spontaneous creations" of images, referring back to Apollinaire's contrast between the leg and the wheel in the 1917 preface to *The Breasts of Tiresias*.[32] By November 1922, he specifies his new usage of the word: "to designate a certain psychic automatism corresponding rather closely to the dream state."[33] My conjecture is that the leap from Breton's poetics of the image in the wake of Reverdy, and his new conception of surrealism as an automatic process of metaphorization, borrows from and reacts to Epstein's formulations of "surrealism" as cinepoetry.

Breton also borrowed from another cinepoet propounding automatism: Paul Dermée. In the inaugural issue of *L'Esprit Nouveau* in October 1920, Dermée published "Découverte du lyrisme" (Discovery of lyricism), a piece connecting lyricism, automatism, dream, Freud, cinema, and surrealism:

> This background activity that became autonomous and functions blindly without the use of conscious will, this is what we call "automatism" [*automatisme*].
>
> We dream, kaleidoscope of images, sensations and emotions function. The film unfolds, varied and captivating [*captivant*] and the whole richness of inner life traverses consciousness as a broad current: our soul fills up with a spontaneous melody, it is the lyrical flux that sings!
>
> As for images, they must be handled with great care, by preventing them from giving objects an existence in the exterior world. For nothing must make the reader come out of his deep self. Thus no images realizable through plastic means: only their *surrealism* [surréalisme].[34]

Breton's catalogue text on Ernst uses the very same expression—"captivating film"—as metaphor for the automatic psychic process. Beyond the highly likely borrowings from Epstein and Dermée, Breton's tack is significant for reducing cinema's materiality as an apparatus into a metaphorical ingredient for "cinephagous" writing—a "lyrical substance" to be distilled by the poetic psyche.[35]

CINEMA IN SURREALISM: FROM AUTOMATIC WRITING TO THE *MANIFESTO OF SURREALISM*

Together with vying with cinepoets for the control of Apollinaire's legacy concept of "surrealism," Breton also co-opted the most innovative cinepoets. Philippe Soupault, who by his own account went to the movies almost daily,[36] had been steadily publishing "cinematographic poems" in late 1918, in both *SIC* and the journal *Le Film*.[37] Louis Aragon also published an important piece on cinema in *Le Film* the same year and reviewed cinepoetic works by Hillel-Erlanger and Louis Delluc. Thus two of the "three musketeers" (as the tight Breton-Aragon-Soupault trio became known) were contributing to the journal of the theoretician of the *photogénie* movement, Louis Delluc. In spring 1919, Breton wanted to conduct a joint experiment with automatic writing and chose to work with Philippe Soupault: the result was *The Magnetic Fields*, purporting to document the uncensored productions of the unconscious in writing. To explain his choice of Soupault, Breton pointed to the latter's "gift of gratuitousness," but also to his capacity to evoke "threatening beings and confounding situations."[38] It appears that Breton had made up his mind to find in the unconscious a particular kind of automatic production involving threats and confusions.

Soupault disclosed in 1925 that the model underlying *The Magnetic Fields* was the teamwork of the authors of the thirty-two *Fantômas* novellas, Pierre Souvestre and Marcel Allain. In 1911, Souvestre and Allain were, Soupault writes, "dictating 14 hours a day," which led their work to "obey an absolute automatism."[39] Both teams followed a similar modus operandi, starting with a bare crime story outline and writing alternatively in each other's presence for several days on end.[40] The key differences were the generic frame—narrative for Souvestre and Allain, poetic for Soupault and Breton—and the recording technology: a dictating machine for the former, pencils for the latter. Most poets and artists were enthused by the five-episode serial *Fantômas* directed by Louis Feuillade (it ran from May 1913 to August 1914 when the war was declared) because they had read the novellas previously and suddenly their pulp textual imaginary was confronted by another imaginary: that of the screen. By going back to the original mode of production of *Fantômas* in *writing*, Breton was in essence reestablishing the hierarchy of media with which cinepoetry had broken.[41]

Francis Lacassin points out that the *Fantômas* texts abound in objects becoming agents of crime in a peculiarly "surrealist" vein: "letters whose text disappears . . . a razor moved by an invisible force striking a victim's throat . . . a pearl necklace coming to life to strangle its owner . . . a handgun that shoots by itself."[42] Such illusionism harks back to Georges Méliès and Émile Cohl, directly linking the semiautomatism of the authors of *Fantômas* with the automorphic agency of filmic objects in early cinema. As for the place of movie serials in *The Magnetic Fields*, Finkelstein notes that the first section's title, "La glace sans tain" (Two-way mirror) is a figural screen and, we might add, in the register of serials titles.[43] A few paragraphs into the *The Magnetic Fields*, Soupault writes of "cheap dream manufactures" right before mentioning the "magnificent cinema in which the acting parts were held by former friends."[44] This passage intimates that Soupault at least may have been contemplating cinepoetic or filmic projects for the surrealist group. Breton's emendations and corrections of the text of Soupault suggest that *his* ambitions were just the opposite: he covered over the more salient scenario aspects, mixing abstract and concrete terms, breaking action continuity, and quickly varying times, locales, speakers, and sentence types.[45] In short, he de-cinepoeticized Soupault's contribution.

There is an important precedent to *The Magnetic Fields* that may explain why Breton opted for a collective project. Shortly before Breton and Soupault set out to work in May and June 1919,[46] a cryptic ad appeared in the April issue of a journal for soldiers, *Le Crapouillot*: "This episode will be shown on *no screen* from the 1st to the 15th of April"[47] (Figure 24). The prank announces a new serial-like novella to be written by several authors as if it were a film. Titled "L'Homme sans tête" (The headless man), it epitomizes the virtual condition of cinepoetry that Benjamin Fondane would define in 1928 as that of "unshootable scenarios." The title may point back to Apollinaire's 1914 project of a pantomime-with-films titled, "The Eyeless, Noseless, and Earless Man,"[48] and it certainly may have been on Ernst's mind when he titled his 1933 collage novel *La Femme 100 têtes*, which can be translated as *The Woman with a Hundred Heads* and (phonetically) *The Headless Woman*. Subtitled "roman-cinéma," "The Headless Man" was written as a pastiche in installments without continuity by nine collaborators among whom was Drieu la Rochelle, then a close friend of Aragon and a sympathizer of Dada.[49] Pearl White—another fetish film star for the surrealists—appears as the perennial victim of the Headless Man, who proves to be Charlie Chaplin—the good guy gone bad. Drieu's episode[50] shows stylistic similarities with automatic writing:

> The bus was going at a vertiginous speed. Night fell. Through the fogged-up windows the riders thrown against one another, as the bus shook along, saw fantastic landscapes unfold looking nothing like those of Parisian boulevards. . . . When Pearl White woke up, the bus had as if run aground on a deserted field. Thousands of empty cans were the only presence in these indecipherable lands.[51]

Compare with the opening lines of *The Magnetic Fields*: "Prisoners of drops of rain, we are but perpetual animals. We are running through noiseless cities, and magical billboards do not touch us anymore. What is the use of these grand and fragile enthusiasms, these dried-up leaps of joy?"[52] The first passage maintains a filmlike continuity and includes random elements very comparable to, albeit less arbitrary than, those of the second. Breton and Soupault may well have been aware of "L'Homme sans tête," either via Aragon, who was so well informed of the genesis of *The Magnetic Fields* that it is largely through his testimony that we know its history, or through *Le Crapouillot* directly, since until August 1919, Breton served as an officer of the medical corps of the air force where the journal was distributed. Certainly "L'Homme sans tête" may be counted as cinepoetic, semiautomatic, and collaborative in the manner of an exquisite corpse.

We find among Breton's own automatic works a 1924 piece that demonstrates that he was programmatically engaged in a dismissal of cinepoetry. Ostensibly, the piece presents itself as a dream narrative from the automatic collection, *Soluble Fish* II.[53] It begins with the narrator, Breton—Breton *as* Breton—interrupting his reading of a book, leaving his house, and finding himself in front of a movie theater. A uniformed crier entices him to come in to peep at "la belle Noisette des Blancheurs" (The beautiful hazelnut of whitenesses). The theater is smoky, and the movie about a Russian noblewoman whose adopted son decapitates flowers and birds bores him. He gets up and goes toward the back of the theater, decorated with a huge Dragon's mouth. Pushing a curtain aside he walks into a room carpeted so as to resemble a tongue, and sits on a stool to "put his thoughts in order." I will withhold the end of the dream for now to point out four distinct moments: first, Breton puts a book down; second, he enters a movie theater under a peepshow pretense; third, he turns

Figure 24. Ad and title of the collective cine-novel published in *Le Crapouillot*, April 1919.

away from the screen; and fourth, he enters into a grottolike mouth, which subsumes the first three moments: the language of the book—*la langue*—the eroticized mouth, the close-up of cinema, and suggests yet another aspect, the unconscious, which Victor Hugo called "la bouche d'ombre" (the shadowy mouth). If there is something singularly didactic about this supposedly automatic text, this might be due to the fact that Breton meant *Soluble Fish* to be the literary evidence for Surrealism: indeed, the *Manifesto of Surrealism* of 1924 was originally written as preface to *Soluble Fish*, before Breton let it stand on its own.

The dream continues: Breton sits on a stool and brings "a small phosphorescent mirror" in front of his right eye, while holding in his other hand "the pencil which I use off and on to write down the main contradictions I record between my desires and reality"—a singularly realist statement for a dream! The account concludes, "The cinema [*le cinéma*] was but a wide field of distant poppies; the grotto in which a blue laugh burst from time to time seemed to me the locked bedroom in which my most beautiful mistresses had had their throats slit. I held up the mirror that was now opaque and threw it to the ground where it broke with the sound of a mechanical nightingale, in a mechanical forest."[54] The narrative presents the movie theater as a place of mystery not because of, but *in spite* of the screen and movie. Yet after turning his back to the screen in an anticinematic gesture, the narrator walks through the back wall as if it were itself a kind of immersive screen. The dragon's mouth on whose tongue he walks displays the sensorium of the close-up and partakes of the digestive effect of absorption into the screen exemplified by early attractions films like *The Big Swallow*. And again, though the narrator has his back turned to the screen, when he holds the mirror up to his eye, is the "blue laugh" not perhaps the reflection of a close-up on the screen? The text, in any case, centers on the fate of this "phosphorescent mirror" that both substitutes and stands for the silver screen of cinema. The mirror "cautiously brought near my right eye," with a pencil (the minimal technological tool of the *Magnetic Fields*) in the other hand, is endowed with a pointed polyvalence: it is at once mini-screen, camera, and page. Yet this compound of cinema and writing becomes opaque. It is a mere automaton, a machine in a "mechanical forest" that produces a false lyricism. In other words, "le cinéma"—both this movie theater and "cinema" in general—robs us blind, just like in that other wood of "As in a Wood," an expression that means indeed to be at the mercy of robbers ("se faire voler comme dans un bois"). The shattering of the opaque mirror stages a definitive renouncement of the dream's cinepoetic homology /page⇔screen⇔camera/, ostensibly in favor of the lyrical forest of the unconscious—the true "mirror" of the soul. A little too transparently, Breton rejects cinepoetry even more so than cinema, implicitly to return to the book whose reading he suspended in this unproductive journey through *le cinéma*.

It makes sense that this piece was meant to accompany the *Manifesto of Surrealism*, since that work too evinces cinepoetry—the "surrealism" of Dermée, Goll, and Epstein—the better to evict it quite methodically. Breton's narrative in the *Manifesto* regarding how he was led to formulate Surrealism begins with several contradictions. He indicates that the sentence, "There is a man cut in two by the window" (*Il y a un homme coupé en deux par la fenêtre*), distinctly *heard* in half-sleep, led him to theorize a new kind of image.[55] Yet in 1921 he had offered a different version: "A man has a window that passes through the middle of his body" (*Un homme a une fenêtre qui lui passe par le milieu du corps*).[56] Breton admits he does not remember the words exactly, and that it was "accompanied by the weak visual representation of a walking man bissected at midriff by a window," Breton hypothesizing that "it was simply a straightening up in space of a man leaning from a window. But this window having followed the man moving, I realized I was dealing with a rather rare type of image."[57] Both the verbal and auditory image have thus vanished, while only the visual image remained—even though Breton considers it merely ancillary. Significantly, he gives a distinct firmness and clarity to the presumably "faint" image and *animates* it in two ways. The ninety-degree rotation he describes is in fact a camera movement—it's called a canted shot—and then the man starts walking, as if in front of the imaginary camera that has just rotated. It resembles a gag from Chaplin, Keaton, or Senett: MCU on a man seemingly at his window, before a cant and a slight back-tracking show us that, in reality, the man is walking with the window encircling his body like a life preserver. Whether this is an actual film shot that Breton saw matters little: the point is that the first surrealist image is deployed through the cinematic imaginary.

In explaining the genesis of *The Magnetic Fields* in his *Manifesto*, Breton insisted that whatever is not "pure" in automatic writing is due to "suggestions coming from the outside world," and that both he and Soupault gave the name of "Surrealism" to this "pure mode of expression."[58] He then explains the emergence of the surrealist image:

> It is from the linkage [*rapprochement*], as it were fortuitous, of two terms that a particular light springs forth, *the light of the image* [*lumière de l'image*]. . . . The beauty of the image depends on the spark obtained; it thus depends on the difference of potential between the two conductors . . . the two terms are not deduced one from the other by *foreseeing* the production of the spark . . . they are the simultaneous product of the activity I call surrealist, reason limiting itself to acknowledging the luminous phenomenon [*phénomène lumineux*].[59]

This passage too recycles key terms and concepts of Epstein's cinepoetry. Besides the linkage and the spark, we can mention the electro-magnetic metaphor and deduction. Epstein wrote in *La Poésie d'aujourd'hui*, "A magnetic force guides the dust particles between the two pole-words of the comparison," and "The middle terms of the deduction have been cut away."[60] While Breton rejects "the principle of associations of ideas,"[61] which Epstein embraces through his "association-thought," both mean the same thing: automatic associations not controlled by reason. The very definition of Breton's Surrealism as "pure psychic automatism through which we propose to express verbally, in writing, or by any other way, the actual functioning of thought,"[62] again echoes formulations of Epstein regarding thought, "Truth will be the exact reproduction of thought,"[63] and the psyche: "Not only does the modern spirit let itself be invaded by vegetative life, but better yet, it goes out to meet it, leans over its rumblings, touches it, scrutinizes it, interrogates it, awaiting from it much marvels."[64] Like Epstein, Breton emphasizes the refusal of logic and shows the boundary between normalcy and madness to be porous. Both writers quote from or mention Rimbaud, Apollinaire, Aragon, Soupault, and Proust, although they also have diverging lists: Epstein cites De Gourmont, Mallarmé, Cocteau, Cendrars, Salmon, and Canudo, while Breton cites Freud, Lautréamont, Reverdy, Saint-Pol-Roux, Desnos, and Hegel. All of Epstein's authors (apart from Rimbaud) had written on cinema or were cinepoets, while this is the case of only two poets in Breton's exclusive list: Robert Desnos and Saint-Pol-Roux.

We must conclude that the *Manifesto* reduces cinepoetry by extracting from it "the light of the image" while dispensing with screen and movies; by retaining the filmic "spark" of metaphor but jettisoning Epstein's cinepoetic theory; and by sublimating the technologically mediated adventure of cinepoetry into a neoromantic search for raw images springing apparatus-free out of the unconscious. Breton's modus operandi is sublimation rather than complete erasure, for as he reviews potential catalysts of surrealism, Breton relents: "Photography? I have no objections. Cinema? Hurrah for dark theaters."[65] So long, that is, as the poet turns away from the screen to seek mad love with female spectators, or to dream uncinematic dreams on the negative screen of the unconscious.

In the closing paragraph of the *First Manifesto* we read, "Surrealism is the 'invisible ray' [*le rayon invisible*] that will allow us one day to best our opponents."[66] Are not these opponents cinepoets like Cocteau, fascinated with the filmic cone of projection? The *Manifesto* was written in spring 1924 as René Clair—who orbited around the surrealist group—was finishing the editing of a film to be released in February 1925. Before it was titled *Le Rayon de la mort* (The death ray), and finally *Paris qui dort* (Paris asleep; released in the United States as *The Crazy Ray*), its original title was *Le Rayon invisible*.[67] A lyrical science-fiction film about a mad scientist whose invention freezes all the inhabitants of Paris, it references an early film of Abel Gance on a similar subject, *La Folie du Dr Tube* (1915).[68] After the release of *Paris qui dort*, in 1925, Clair directly addressed the relationship of cinema to surrealism, keenly noting that "cinematographic technique runs the risk of losing a large part of the purity of this 'pure psychic automatism.' . . . Yet cinema and surrealism are far from being foreign to one another."[69] Breton's citation of Clair's film title was likely meant to side with the villain, who freezes cinema back into photography (against the grain of Roussel's unfreezing photography into cinema). Breton revisits this inverted photo-cinematic difference in *Mad Love* (1937) by illustrating his call for "convulsive beauty" with a photo of Man Ray, *L'Explosante fixe* (The standstill burst), depicting a blurred flamenco dancer in a flurry of garments. Breton explains that the marvel of convulsion would be lost "if it was conceived as motion rather than as the precise expiring of this motion itself," and thus he affirms the importance "of the reciprocal relation linking the object seen in its motion and in its repose."[70] Writing and imagination alone, he implies, must provide the convulsiveness of the image—not cinema.[71]

ANDRÉ BRETON, SAINT-POL-ROUX, ABEL GANCE

SURREALISM . . . SUPERNATURALISM . . . cf. also the IDEOREALISM of Saint-Pol-Roux.

—ANDRÉ BRETON, 1924

Call the [cinema] apparatus the ideorealizer.

—SAINT-POL-ROUX, ca. 1925

. . . some strange matter, a kind of luminous and sensitive plate of mind-states, a photograph perhaps of sensibility . . . whence conversion of everything into images, trances, for inward materialization, x-ray, cinema . . .

—ABEL GANCE, ca. 1913[72]

Divesting surrealism of its cinepoetic antecedents was the thorny theoretical problem Breton faced in his conception of the *Manifesto*. His solution would be to invoke a half-forgotten symbolist poet, Saint-Pol-Roux, in order to sublimate the material aspects of cinema into an apparatus-less poetics of the marvelous image. However, it turns out that Saint-Pol-Roux, at that very time, was working on his own theory of cinepoetry.

Breton's improbable yet central invocation of Saint-Pol-Roux in *The Manifesto of Surrealism* has never been convincingly elucidated. Aged sixty-three in 1924, Saint-Pol-Roux typified the lyrical-mystical branch of symbolism, less influential than the language-centered poetics of Mallarmé (who admired him very much nonetheless). A church-going poet still writing in the florid style of 1895, Saint-Pol-Roux would appear at odds with surrealism's anticlericalism, search for novelty, and Marxist penchants. Why did Breton dedicate his first major poetry collection in 1923 to him and subsequently visit him in Brittany in September 1923, before organizing a disastrous banquet in his honor in Paris in 1925, with attendees unsure if the intent was celebration, provocation, or mockery?

In a text published just before Saint-Pol-Roux's arrival in Paris, Breton celebrated "the extreme purity of his attitude" entirely dedicated to the "unforeseen and sudden" power of the image. Calling him "the master of the image," Breton adds that "it is through the force of images that, as time goes on, *true* revolutions could be accomplished."[73] Breton cites two passages by Saint-Pol-Roux that display a rapid fire of hyperbolic similes and neologisms ("la changeance" [changingness]) and belong to the more stilted and manufactured side of Saint-Pol-Roux's style. Breton made a habit of positioning himself as heir apparent to leading writers: he was in short turns very close to Valéry, Proust, Apollinaire, and Reverdy. Saint-Pol-Roux never was, indeed refused to be, in that class, and Breton professed to admire him for that reason. Was the latter trying to lift the former—or to extract the last drop of dynastic capital from an unsung originator of symbolism?

Saint-Pol-Roux's vatic diction, part of the revival of dramatic poetry in the 1890s (Maeterlinck was a close friend), would seem out of joint with the postwar Esprit Nouveau. The distance is tantamount to that which separates Hegel's *Aesthetics*—which Saint-Pol-Roux mentions in an 1891 interview with Huret—from the *Phenomenology of Spirit,* which profoundly changed French thought after 1928.[74] In a sense, Breton's romantic reconciliation of the real and the ideal lay smack in-between these two Hegelian moments. In a prophetic 1913 article, Saint-Pol-Roux had articulated the continuity between the first "ideaist" (*idéiste*) symbolist wave of the 1880s (Mallarmé) focused on the absolute, the second "ideorealist" (*idéoréaliste*) generation (himself) around 1900 seeking to reunite the absolute and the world, and lastly the new "supernaturalist" poets of the afterwar (from Cendrars to Breton) who sought a grand synthesis through the total transfiguration of the world.[75] It is in part this clearly Hegelian schema of evolution that attracted Breton: Surrealism would be the dialectical sublation of fifty years of poetics. However, for the Saint-Pol-Roux of that period, this sublation was not Surrealism at all—it was cinema.

While Saint-Pol-Roux never abandoned the romantic goal of reunifying language and things, words and world, body and mind, he turned toward technology as agent for this synthesis. Gérard Macé has exhumed Saint-Pol-Roux's copious notes on technology from the 1920s and 1930s, ranging from mechanization to automobiles, and biology to quantum physics. Technologies of light, speed, and the physics of high energy especially—as already noted by Jarry, Segalen, and Mallarmé—carried the highest fantasmatic poetic potential. Scattered across hundred of pages, Macé saw that Saint-Pol-Roux had used cinema as a privileged mediation capable of enacting this techno-poetic utopia, and he regrouped these notes under a recurring draft title: *Cinéma vivant* (Live cinema). A patchwork of "critical poems" and essays, *Cinéma vivant* amounts to a cinepoetic summa comparable in scope but not in detail to Epstein's cinepoetics. The core idea is that actual cinema will ultimately be perfected into an instrument of enlightenment, spiritual illumination, even quantic alteration of the body.[76] To the human project cinema literally brings a new light, a new spatial and visual ubiquity: "The law of cinema is the sun."[77] This is what he calls "live cinema" and—quite surprisingly since we are in the 1920s—"television" (*télévision*) and "televiewing" (*télévisionner*).[78]

Saint-Pol-Roux had coined the term "Ideoreality" (*idéoréalité*) in the 1890s, a poetic concept condensing Hegel's equation of reality and ideality, and romantic mysticism à la Novalis. Then suddenly cinema offered itself as an apparatus perfectly suited for making ideas real: the new personas and worlds that symbolist theater had *mimicked* and *suggested* could now be *created* in "live cinema" by using light and electricity, considered as material agents of the cosmos. This connection might strike us as naïve. However, as thinkers like Vilém Flusser and Patrick Maynard remind us, photography's beginning as "sun-writing" and heliogravure surreptitiously reinscribed solar myths within photographic technology.[79] The cosmogony of lighting and optics in the wake of cinema might explain for instance the revival of solar mythopoieia in the writings of Georges Bataille, Raymond Queneau, and Francis Ponge, and in the films of Germaine Dulac and Abel Gance.

For Saint-Pol-Roux, modernity transformed the key metaphor of Idealism—Plato's cave—into the material apparatus of cinema so that, he wrote, we might "call the [cinema] apparatus the ideorealizer [*l'idéoréalisateur*]."[80] In a crucial move, Saint-Pol-Roux brackets cinema's contemporaneous capacities of *reproduction* to point to a more archetypal and holistic cinema *producing* reality: "Present cinema is Plato's Shadows. The Sun is on the surface [*dessus*], that is, outside. It must be within [*dedans*]. All the cinematographic wretchedness is here. . . . Present cinema is the dark chamber. Future cinema will be the bright chamber [*chambre ardente*]."[81] This archetypal cinema conforms to the same desire for being enveloped by the cinematic image that fuels immersive media, what Bolter and Grusin call "the logic of transparent immediacy" of virtual reality.[82] Saint-Pol-Roux points to the architecture of immersion when he writes, "The screen or rather the set will be horizontal for vertical productions,"[83] and ultimately "Future cinema will have no screen—its realms constituting the universal empire."[84]

But Saint-Pol-Roux also extends toward ontology the astonishment of early cinema commentators by considering filmic likenesses not as *replicas* of the self but as new personas, new beings: "Future cinema will increase with its beings the traditional number of beings. . . . Through the means of these double, triple, hundredfold phantasms, Man will no longer die."[85] Edgar Morin in the 1950s considered this kind of magical doubling one of the crucial components of the cinematic imaginary. Saint-Pol-Roux writes in the aftermath of World War I when the *lumen naturale* of Progress had been eclipsed by *dis-aster.* The poet lost his only son, Coeladan, in the war, and writes, "Wasn't the 1914–1918 war like a precursor human catastrophe unsettling the anterior balance?"[86] Perhaps his loss informs the radical immateriality of future humanity in Saint-Pol-Roux's live cinema: "The child is an invention from before mirrors (the motto of Live Cinema)."[87] This striking formula substitutes filmic reproduction to sexual reproduction in order to conceive (of) disembodied "supercreations":[88]

> Films must be supercreations [*surcréations*] . . . in order to leave the screen and go into space. It is tomorrow's magic, which will add Mystery to Life by way of an ideoreal material. These characters added to Humanity will supplement [*suppléeront à*] Humanity, they will speak to the people, guide it and if need be fight for it upon interpopular [*interpopulaires*] saharas, messengers or suns of man, who stayed home. . . . Posthistory [*la posthistoire*] is about to begin.[89]

For Saint-Pol-Roux, cinema's "avatars" will supplement body and history, in a Derridian sense. They will provide the "ideoreal material" enacting posthistory as augmented reality for the continuation of humanism through other means.[90]

This live cinema relates directly to poetry through the dimensional sensorium of writing that we examined in Mallarmé. Saint-Pol-Roux writes, "Cinema will lead from line to surface and from surface to volume."[91] Recall that Segalen's *Synesthésie-Figure* used the work of Saint-Pol-Roux to exemplify the shift of poetic language from punctual denotation to serial sensorial experience. Saint-Pol-Roux thus envisions a cinematic metamateriality of the mind itself: "I believe in an 'abstract substance' of phantasms that will occupy a place in space without displacing air."[92] The focus on sensorial immersion and expansion progressively effaces the apparatus, "cinema will go from screenism [*écranisme*] to plasticism [*plasticisme*],"[93] leading to a metamorphosis of the image: "In the cinema until now the image was reflected; it will become crystallized."[94] The project of live cinema aims to overcome the apparatus in order to link poetry and enactment: "Poetry means action,"[95] Saint-Pol-Roux writes, in a way that connects Rimbaud to Breton, specifying that "words are forces."[96] The cinematic imaginary ultimately plays the role of transducing the apparatus into writing: "The sky is the least understood screen. . . . God had worlds for alphabetical letters, and he must have written with them on the page of the sky this unique poem that indefinitely unfolds [*se déroule*] upon our eyes that look without seeing."[97] For Saint-Pol-Roux, the sun "developed" the earth like a film after the last glacial era, under the poetic scenario written by the "Verbal cinema" of the divine.[98] So it appears that cinema instills to language a superior ideorealizing power. In 1910, he had described "some written volumes having the virtue of developing themselves within the world's sensibility and acquiring an actual, positive volume."[99] These words are deliberately chosen: "virtue" (*vertu*) has the sense of potentiality, "develop" (*développer*) is a photo-chemical term, and of course "volume" carries the triple sense of space, scroll, and book that we encountered in Mallarmé. An unpublished work of Saint-Pol-Roux written at the same time as his notes on cinema, *La Repoétique* (The repoetics) or *La Res poetica* (The res poetica), includes a section titled "Images and Word [*cinema*]," one of its passages imagining "a tree of poetry in the shape of an image-lyre [*lyre imagière*]," whose "flesh gradually affirms itself in a lyricism aggregated for the inexhaustible radiance [*rayonnement*] of the huddled idea." This "luminous lyre" is directly equated with "cinema."[100] A second passage brings all these cinepoetic elements together:

> Poetry, read by our eyes, bestows on us a soul. . . . The inner monster unfurls [*se déploie*] into a spectacle. To the limited result of reading, sound adds the vibrations of an animal plasticity [*plasticité*], even as matter is an exclusively spiritual subject. Through this revelation of energy, we go from egg to eagle, to schema or else to snake. The schema of writing self-dimensionalizes [*s'endimensionne*] into a solid,

> the ghost is humanized. The sign acquires a solid mass. Nails draw hollow and salient points and inflate the structure, even the architecture. An unknown nature makes itself known.Through the miracle of voice and agglomerated technique of sonorous light, the poem is festooned with flesh or decorated with matter. Inner geometry has received consolidating elements on its lines, blooming into a plenitude in space.[101]

The "vibrations of an animal plasticity" clearly point to automorphic images, while the "self-dimensionaliz[ing]," of writing by which the "sign acquires a solid mass" aptly describes the quasi-alchemical dream that underlies cinepoetry: language acquiring empirical substance and shape, and becoming an agency in movement. A mythical source shapes this passage: the fable of Amphion, mentioned throughout *Cinéma vivant*.[102] By the sheer play of his lyre, Amphion both built the blocks of stone and erected the walls of Thebes—in a kind of filmic reverse of the toppling of the walls of Jericho by trumpet. Mythic sound begets solidity, vibrations transform into matter, poetry acquires the malleability of a true lyrical substance. In the end, cinepoetic substance must remain virtual—"Poetry, above all potential"[103]—and he gives it a name explicitly paralleling the quanta of physics: "cinephanta."[104] The smallest units of cinepoetic virtuality. Such an analogy, /quanta in physics⇔cinephanta in cinepoetry/, comes close to the discipline invented by his friend Alfred Jarry: "pataphysics, the imaginary science of exceptions."

It seems to me that the "abstract substance" and "luminous lyre" of Saint-Pol-Roux's *Cinéma vivant* overcome the bothersome materiality of the apparatus, in just the way Breton was trying to circumvent cinepoetry when defining Surrealism: by making movies into a "lyrical substance" that could feed the poetic "light of the image" emanating from the unconscious. That is what Breton's equation of "Ideorealism" and "Surrealism" in the *Manifesto* plainly suggests.[105] Did Saint-Pol-Roux discuss his "ideorealizer" cinema with Breton in September 1923 when they saw each other in Brittany? Macé dates Saint-Pol-Roux's *Cinéma vivant* notes from roughly 1925 to 1930 on the basis of the movies he cites: Abel Gance's *La Roue* (1923) and *Napoléon* (1927), Walter Rüttman's *Symphony of a Great City* (1927), and Eisenstein's *Potemkin* (1925).[106] Yet he was already clearly a cinephile in the mid-1910s since he mentions Mary Pickford and Charlot, whose films were released around 1915.[107] It is even likely that he followed cinema from the beginnings of the Film d'Art, since he refers to the biblical episode in which Balthazar saw the words "Mane Thecel Phares" printing themselves on a wall.[108] In unpublished manuscript notes, Saint-Pol-Roux explains further that "the first screening took place at Nebuchadnezzar's palace. One night, there could be read on the palace wall that served as a screen for luminous letters from before the Lumière Brothers: Mane Thecel Phares. The film projector was none other than the prophet Daniel . . . there were lions like in the new film by Gina Manès."[109] This scene appears in Léonce Perret's famed 1911 *Festin de Balthazar,* which so impressed Marcel Proust and Raymond Roussel. Saint-Pol-Roux may also have been familiar with the writings of Epstein (whom he does not cite) since he coined the word "cinégénie" as a clear offshoot of photogénie.[110]

The planned dedication of *Cinéma vivant* was to Abel Gance.[111] We find in Gance's autobiographical notes, published in 1930, a cosmogony of light and the fourth dimension similar to Saint-Pol-Roux's in its sublimating of thought and the language of poetry through cinema. Gance was a technical thinker and inventor, the mainstream appeal of whose movies was anathema to Breton: Artaud was expelled from Breton's surrealist movement in 1926 over his role as Marat in Gance's *Napoléon* (1927)—a movie generally decried on the left as a panegyric to a dictator. Breton revised his opinion of Gance in the early 1950s, when the latter developed with the help of Nelly Kaplan a new process of *Polyvision* based on the triple screen of *Napoléon.* Breton went to the premiere and was bowled over by the show, writing soon after, "I have known—since my youth—that Abel Gance, if given free rein, was the only one capable of making us go 'through the screen' (the way one says 'through the looking glass')."[112] The homage implies that Breton had been much more aware and admiring of Gance's movies than he had let on during the high auto-da-fe period of his movement. Indeed, Breton's attitude toward the relationship of cinema and poetry changed somewhat suddenly with the end of silent cinema. In a questionnaire about the talkies from 1930, he writes, "The fusion of poetry and cinema took place a long time ago. The only fear is that it ceases."[113] While Breton addresses here poetry *in* cinema rather than cinema *in* poetry, I can't help hearing an implicit acknowledgment that Epstein's 1921 call for "the superimposition of poetry and cinema" had been carried out, perhaps in Breton's mind by Surrealism itself. But if cinepoetry no longer seems to count among Breton's "opponents," it is because the talkies, as much as the polarization of European politics in the 1930s, had removed cinepoetry from the active literary arena. Subsequent comments by Breton show his willingness to delve into particulars: "Cinema has in common with poetry that it proposes to represent the successive situations of life. Contrary to [poetry] it must, in addition, account for their linkage."[114] This remark from 1938 shows that Breton had given a great deal of thought about narrative and/or matching continuity in cinema. Nonetheless, by defining continuity as the mark of medium difference, Breton also reasserts his decision to delete instances of cinepoetic continuity from *The Magnetic Fields*.

In 1928, Aragon and Breton cowrote "The Treasure of the Jesuits"—a play that was to include onstage projections of old Musidora serials—as part of a benefit for a screen actor. The text freely waxes poetic about cinema: "There never was anything at once more realist and more poetic than the serial [*ciné-feuilleton*]." It also associates cinema and life on the existential level of Saint-Pol-Roux and Gance: "Life, this impossible film to follow"; and "what was the province of the screen has been transferred to life."[115] By 1928, Surrealism was sufficiently established, and cinepoetry seemed to have sufficiently lost its earlier utopianism and some of its more incisive practitioners—Epstein was now dedicated to cinema alone—that Breton relented and recognized the overarching cinepoetic homology he had always embraced: /cinema⇔life/.

CHAPTER SIX

Doing Filmic Things with Words

On Chaplin

"THEIR CHARLIE AND OUR *CHARLOT*"

A survey of Dada sympathizers in Breton and Aragon's journal *Littérature* ranked the popularity of world personalities in 1921. After Breton and Aragon (noblesse oblige), the most popular personality—ahead of Rimbaud, Vaché, Ducasse, and the likes of Dante, Marx, and Jesus—was Charlie Chaplin.[1] The poetry avant-garde of 1916–28 was so transfixed by Charlot (Chaplin's Gallicized name) that it is no overstatement to say that cinepoetry rode to prominence on the Little Tramp's tattered coattails.

Chaplin's movies arrived in France in 1915, in the thick of the "War to End All Wars," which had turned into the worst carnage modernity had experienced. It was while on leave from the front that Cendrars discovered Chaplin in 1915, as did Léger and Apollinaire in 1916 at the urging of Max Jacob.[2] Cendrars would lose his right forearm, Léger was almost killed by gas, and Apollinaire was hit in the head by shrapnel. The reception of Charlot by avant-garde poets and artists was heavily colored by injuries and war experience, even before the release of the 1918 *Charlot soldat* (*Shoulder Arms*), a movie preparing the US public for war involvement. In previous films, the Tramp's jerky gait, his frail but ultimately invulnerable body, his wild swings between mirth and sorrow against stark urban scapes, all had already seemed to echo the psychosomatic shocks of trench warfare. Prewar crime serials like Feuillade's *Fantômas*, while breaching with mystery every bourgeois façade, reassured spectators that rational agents (whether good or evil) choreographed the world. Chaplin's movies, often shot on location, and progressing with random gags and unforeseen reversals, refracted the waywardness of an underclass wrestling with a somatic and uncontrollable present. Against both war and social destitution, the Tramp triumphed—before his next fall.

French poets recognized in Charlot the shadow of *poètes maudits*—ill-starred bohemians like Gérard de Nerval, Paul Verlaine, and Tristan Corbière—combined with Chaplin's history-making status, comparable only to Hugo or Byron. Independent and wealthy (he had cocreated United Artists studios), socially conscious and siding with the underdog, Chaplin the artist of cinema offered a tantalizing paradigm for a new poetic persona in modernity. If "the crossroad of magic and materialism was hexed," as Theodor Adorno warned Walter Benjamin, another Chaplin admirer, Charlot's filmic embodiment seemed to poets a way to lift the hex.

Chaplin magically appeared everywhere in the French cultural landscape: in 1916 a literary critic at the *Mercure de France* marveled, not without annoyance, at the ubiquitous cardboard cutouts of *Charlot* at the entrances of Parisian theaters.[3] Cendrars quipped after the war that Chaplin must have been the decisive factor of allied victory since, banned in Germany, he was the only real difference between the two symmetrical camps.[4] In *Shoulder Arms*, Chaplin plays a soldier single-handedly capturing thirteen enemy soldiers. Asked how he did it, he answers: "I surrounded them." Poetic retorts such as this inspired Tzara and Breton to pull a hoax in 1919: in order to attract a large public to their second Dada evening, they announced that Chaplin would come and publicly convert to Dada. People materialized by the hundreds.[5]

Chaplin's appearance coincided with the war's disruption of French film production, which never regained world leadership.[6] The sudden availability of the films of Griffith, de Mille, and Chaplin, whose artfulness and dynamic continuity struck French critics and filmmakers alike, enjoined art and budding film journals to retheorize cinema. Charlot was the nexus of these French efforts. A 1922 article in *Le Crapouillot*, "Leur Charlie et notre Charlot" (Their Charlie and our Charlot), explicitly contrasts Chaplin, as an American mass product, to Charlot as the theoretical core of a new French aesthetics.[7] In 1921, as part of his effort to define photogénie, Louis Delluc published the first critical book on Chaplin in any language, declaring, "Chaplin is a painter like Villon was a poet. He is *himself*, under the

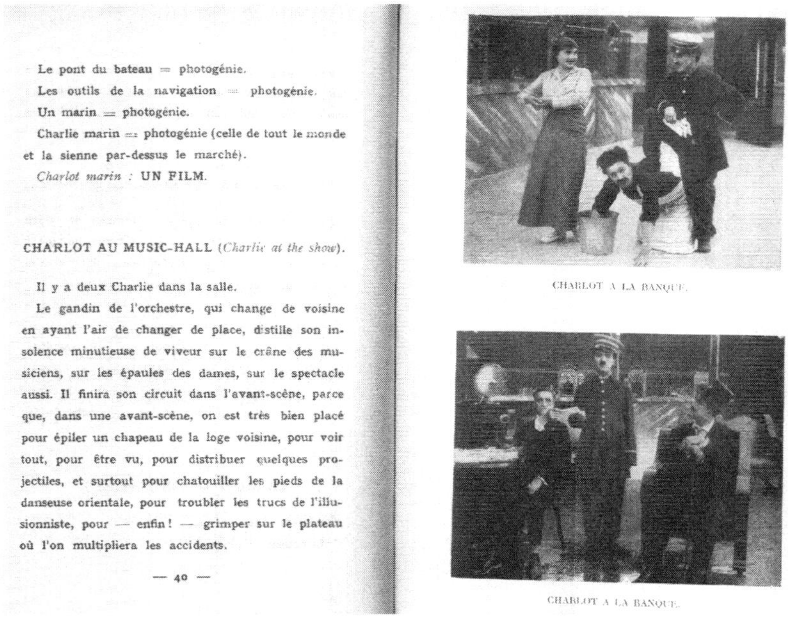

Le pont du bateau = photogénie.

Les outils de la navigation = photogénie.

Un marin = photogénie.

Charlie marin = photogénie (celle de tout le monde et la sienne par-dessus le marché).

Charlot marin : UN FILM.

CHARLOT AU MUSIC-HALL (*Charlie at the show*).

Il y a deux Charlie dans la salle.

Le gandin de l'orchestre, qui change de voisine en ayant l'air de changer de place, distille son insolence minutieuse de viveur sur le crâne des musiciens, sur les épaules des dames, sur le spectacle aussi. Il finira son circuit dans l'avant-scène, parce que, dans une avant-scène, on est très bien placé pour épiler un chapeau de la loge voisine, pour voir tout, pour être vu, pour distribuer quelques projectiles, et surtout pour chatouiller les pieds de la danseuse orientale, pour troubler les trucs de l'illusionniste, pour — enfin ! — grimper sur le plateau où l'on multipliera les accidents.

— 40 —

CHARLOT A LA BANQUE.

CHARLOT A LA BANQUE.

Figure 25. Facing pages from Louis Delluc, *Charlot* (1920).

most convenient form: *photogénie*”[8] (Figure 25). Delluc and Epstein's photogénie foregrounds Chaplin's innovative filmic persona as an integral part of a new philosophy of filmmaking. To reflect this novelty, the French propounders of photogénie crafted a new kind of discourse on cinema that combined criticism and poetry. Thus Chaplin transformed not only French cinema and the budding film theory in France, but also the forms of writing *on* cinema: this is in part what attracted poets.

Take Cocteau's first significant piece on cinema, from 1919, about an episode in *Shoulder Arms*. He writes, “Charlot camouflaged as a tree goes scouting. He is found out. He runs away, pursued by a formidable enemy. The scramble of the small tree jumping about, playing hide-and-seek in the forest with the big Wotan, is epic.”[9] The quick notational language seeks less to describe than to mobilize the reader's visual memory. Yet nested in this episode there is also a new corporeal imaginary. In the movie, Chaplin's protagonist in tree costume approaches, undetected, a group of bivouacking enemy soldiers. The camouflage is so successful that a German soldier nearly chops his arm for firewood. Hence, though invulnerable as a scout, he becomes vulnerable as a *tree*. As he flees in tree costume, the opposition is reversed: he becomes invulnerable when he stops (tree) and shot at when he moves (human). The ontological flickering only ends when he crawls through a large pipe to escape his pursuers, leaving behind an afterbirth-like tree slough, as he is rehumanized.[10]

Such a sequence crisscrosses a complex set of oppositions between human and inanimate, body and image, safety and harm, even war and play. Chaplin's face preposterously sticking out of the trunk presents a curious facial hybridity—a modern-day Daphne suspended between life and death, carnival and entombment. Through such scenes in Chaplin, poets took note of cinema's ontological porosity. *A Dog's Life*, for which Philippe Soupault wrote one of the first pieces of "synthetic criticism,"[11] presents a similar sequence. Charlot, penniless, is bounced out of a bar. Brought toward the camera in the grip of the huge bartender, we see him turn into a kind of puppet stripped of free will, both as an act of passive resistance and a way to minimize bodily injury. The comic tenor of the scene comes from our progressive realization that only in behaving like an object can he retain a shred of agency. In 1916, a journalist describes Charlot's embodiment as "le rebondissement fait homme" (bouncing made human), and poet André Salmon characterizes Chaplin as "a kind of live object, quick, mobile, black and white," noting, "this was new."[12] An unsigned note in *Le Crapouillot* in 1918 analyzes Chaplin's singularity as "making the human being (reasonable and thinking!) into a sort of mechanical automaton [*fantoche*]."[13] The defensive reification of Charlot's body—tree, marionette, ball, automaton—at a time when war stripped everyone of their humanity, contributed to poets seeing objects on screen as endowed with a new "personality," as Epstein puts it.[14]

AUTOMATIC RIDING

I have only recounted what I saw on the screen, respecting as much as possible the marvelous poetry that animates Charlot. . . . I have let my pen ride by listening to the dictation [*dictée*] of my memory.

—PHILIPPE SOUPAULT, *Charlot* (1930)

In a philosophical piece titled "On Decor" (1918), Louis Aragon theorized such "superhuman" characteristics of Chaplin as deploying an "inversion of all values" with a clear Nietzschean accent. It was published in Delluc's journal *Le Film*, where Aragon had also published his first poem, "Charlot sentimental," a few months earlier. Another poem, "Charlot mystique" appeared soon after in Reverdy's journal *Nord-Sud*.[15] Aragon's text opens on "a wall lyrically decorated with posters" and a bar "whose window bears uppercase letters of unreadable and marvelous words," both exemplifying the "obsessive beauty of commercial signage," which also informed his early novels such as *Anicet* (1921) and *Paris Peasant* (1924). Like Proust, Roussel, and Saint-Pol-Roux, he mentions the "Mane Thecel Phares" scene from Perret's *Beshazzar's Feast* with its "fascination for hieroglyphs on walls [that] an Angel traced . . . at the end of a feast." Aragon was clearly approaching cinema from the viewpoint of the cinegraphic imaginary. He links, for instance, the way the extreme close-up makes simple objects strange, to a child's incantation of a word emptying it of all meaning until it becomes "a touching and aimless part of speech." This is a rather sophisticated homology between cinema and language: /ECU on objects⇔lexeme stripped of denotation/. In a different vein as Saint-Pol-Roux, but with the same ontological efficacy, he invokes Chaplin as the first filmmaker exploiting the transformative power of cinema: "The décor, whose elements Charlot gathers around his character, participates intimately in the action. . . . Décor is the very vision of the world according to Charlot, through the discovery of the laws of mechanics haunting the hero to such an extent that, by an inversion of all values, each inanimate object becomes a living thing for him, and each person a dummy to be cranked."[16] Philippe Soupault in 1918 also pointed out that the cinema "upends all natural laws," and places "a new servant . . . at the disposal of [the poet's] imagination."[17] Aragon's "cranked dummy" refers to a scene in *The Rink*, in which Chaplin cranks up his nemesis with his cane, sending him skating away as if he were an automaton (Figure 26). Such "automatic riding" also points to the cranking of the camera—and by extension, the automatic unfolding of filmic spaces and diegetic continuity within the imaginary of the viewer. In other words, the filmic space (*le décor*), so tightly constructed around Chaplin's choreographed acrobatics as to be a direct emanation of his body, becomes the imaginary stage on which the eyes of the viewer ride automatically, perhaps distractedly. Cinepoetry aims to find more lasting practices and forms for such an automatic riding experience that is not unrelated to enactive vision.[18]

Figure 26. Chaplin in *The Rink* "winding up" a gent.

If we follow Aragon's distinction between "Chaplin" (the filmmaker) and the "hero" (the diegetic Tramp), then "Charlot" acts as an intermediary or floating figure between the actual and imaginary. Cinepoets tend to refer to Charlot as both poet and poem, object and agent, if not all at once filmmaker, filmed persona, and film. This protean fluidity of roles is central to cinepoetry. Aragon concludes his essay by pointedly conflating Charlot's automatic riding across ontological categories to the poetry of Mallarmé:

> When, in front of the screen devoid of projections, under the light of the projector alone, will we feel this indomitable virginity,
> *The white solicitation of our canvas!*
> O, purity, purity![19]

The verse is from Mallarmé's poem "Salut," which celebrates the virtuality of the page not yet written but also the call and agency already emanating from it. By insisting that the screen remain as blank as a Mallarméan page /lit screen⇔white canvas⇔blank page/

Aragon relates Charlot's "inversion of all values" to the virtual cinema of cinepoetry. The mock advertisement for *L'Homme sans tête,* played by a literary avatar of Chaplin—"this film will be shown on no screen"—as well as Aragon's "screen devoid of projections," are apt mottoes for cinepoetry.

I pun as automatic riding the convergence of several components in Aragon's text. (1) The postwar spectatorial affect of Charlot's riding out contingencies, as an object among objects nonetheless retaining a modicum of agency, especially in sequences where objects acquire in return an *automatic* agency (the car to which Charlot on skates is hitched; an escalator he rides; a rotating table on which he leans; an electrical fan with which he duels, and so on). (2) The self-mirroring of the cinema apparatus into such forms of embodiment: commentators have oft discussed the mimetic relation between the Tramp's somatic gestures and the flicker of the apparatus or machinery in general.[20] (3) The porosity between ontological opposites in cinema as noted by two of the three musketeers of surrealism, Aragon and Soupault, informing the genesis of *automatic writing.* (4) Cinepoems resulting directly from attempts to *transduce* Chaplin's reciprocal contamination of and by the mechanical world, so that, to cite Alain and Odette Virmaux, "in order to evoke such or such film by Chaplin, their critical commentary willfully turned into poems."[21] (5) The imprint of technology on the corporeal subconscious (rather than the unconscious) as the cinepoetic root of lowercase surrealism.

IVAN GOLL'S "KINO-POEM"

Chaplin and automatic riding are at the heart of an early cinepoems by Ivan Goll. During the 1924 controversy over ownership of the word "surrealism," Breton's most vocal opponents were Ivan Goll and Paul Dermée who, like Epstein, defined surrealism via cinema.[22] In the 1924 journal provocatively titled *Surrealism* that he launched, Goll contributed a short essay, "An Example of Surrealism: Cinema." It is a disappointing text not so much because of its bland main proposal—that the final rapid edit sequence of Élie falling from the mountain in Gance's *La Roue* "is what I deem surrealist in it"—but because Goll omits his own strikingly cinepoetic experiments as examples of surrealism.[23] These include his first collection of poems, *Films*, written in German and published in 1914, and "Die Chaplinade, Kinodichtung," of 1920 ("The Chaplinade, Cinepoem"), translated into French in 1923 as "La Chaplinade, ou Charlot poète, poème cinématographique."[24] That the latter was a perfect example of cinepoetic surrealism did not escape a keen reviewer at the NRF who mused, "When Jean Epstein wrote his very scientific book about today's poetry, did he suspect that Ivan Goll would prove him right so thoroughly?"[25]

Goll's poem-scenario cites short vignettes from Chaplin movies to launch a semiautomatic poetic narrative that alternates dialogue and monologue in free verse with short prose indications of mise-en-scène. It begins with Charlot coming to life from a movie poster, wandering through the city and countryside, triggering various events including a revolution, until, begged by the billposter afraid of losing his job, he steps back into the flat poster. The plot, circular almost by default, conceals a rich cinepoetic interleafing between media. The book is a French translation of a German text, illustrated by four lithographs of Léger, themselves derived from articulated Chaplin puppets Léger crafted for a stop-action film that never materialized, though the puppets appear at the beginning and end of the 1924 *Ballet mécanique* which he codirected with Dudley Murphy (Figure 27). In other words, both the lithographs and the text enfold similar mediun crossovers that inform their virtuality.

Near the beginning, the billposter takes Charlot "by the collar," and puts him back *on* the wall, where "he stays glued." Soon after, however, Charlot "rips the poster and leaves the wall," in a way that subtly contrasts with his coming to life *out* of the image the first time.[26] This difference activates cinepoetry's *elliptical patching*, whereby the reader "fills in" diegetical or experiential gaps via imaginary filmic continuity. We might, for instance, envision live-actor Charlot against the wall progressively covered over by poster Charlot in MCU through a dissolve (ca. 1920s) or through a crawling bottom-to-top mutation effect in digital cinema (ca. 2000). Echoing this play of flatness and volume, in the following scene Goll has words print themselves autonomously "on the screen, in large red letters." Both the patching and the invocation of credits/intertitles contribute to mobilizing the perceptual memory of the cinema apparatus in the reader, absent any direct cue. Cinepoetry enacts two distinct perceptual/cognitive processes—film viewing and reading—interacting and cross-pollenizing. Soon, all the posters of Chaplin come to life, and "a thousand Charlots pour into the streets, in all the known costumes" of his films.[27] Reprising the coming-to-life films of Méliès, this multiplication is also

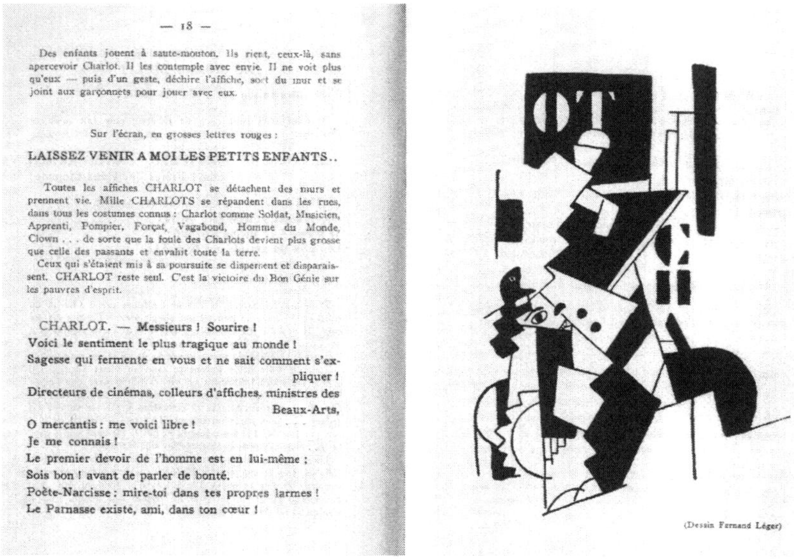

— 18 —

Des enfants jouent à saute-mouton. Ils rient, ceux-là, sans apercevoir Charlot. Il les contemple avec envie. Il ne voit plus qu'eux — puis d'un geste, déchire l'affiche, sort du mur et se joint aux garçonnets pour jouer avec eux.

Sur l'écran, en grosses lettres rouges :

LAISSEZ VENIR A MOI LES PETITS ENFANTS..

Toutes les affiches CHARLOT se détachent des murs et prennent vie. Mille CHARLOTS se répandent dans les rues, dans tous les costumes connus : Charlot comme Soldat, Musicien, Apprenti, Pompier, Forçat, Vagabond, Homme du Monde, Clown . . . de sorte que la foule des Charlots devient plus grosse que celle des passants et envahit toute la terre.

Ceux qui s'étaient mis à sa poursuite se dispersent et disparaissent. CHARLOT reste seul. C'est la victoire du Bon Génie sur les pauvres d'esprit.

CHARLOT. — **Messieurs ! Sourire !**
Voici le sentiment le plus tragique au monde !
Sagesse qui fermente en vous et ne sait comment s'expliquer !
Directeurs de cinémas, colleurs d'affiches, ministres des Beaux-Arts,
O mercantis : me voici libre !
Je me connais !
Le premier devoir de l'homme est en lui-même ;
Sois bon ! avant de parler de bonté.
Poète-Narcisse : mire-toi dans tes propres larmes !
Le Parnasse existe, ami, dans ton cœur !

Figure 27. Facing pages from Ivan Goll, *La Chaplinade, poème cinématographique*, in *Le Nouvel Orphée* (1923), print by Fernand Léger.

a singularly imaginary enactment of the thousands of film frames and dozens of films containing little Chaplin replicas, differently dressed, and as if each going their own way. Goll opts to follow a single Charlot, but after he murders an old woman and flees, he again "multiplies quickly: we can see suddenly twenty, fifty Charlots."[28] A few pages later, we are back to single Charlot, this time "pursued by fifty gendarmes."[29] Such automatic riding in the cinepoem has little to do with the automatic writing of Surrealism. Rather than plumbing the unconscious it refracts the perceptual subconscious, the interaction of sight and kinesthesia with coenesthetic affects of fragmentation and flight. Where Goll's poetic art lies is in folding back the cross-medium experiment into the sensorium and diegesis of the poem, for instance when Charlot writes a "poem which appears in large letters on the screen"—a poem-within-the-cine*poem*—before using a field glass to see a faraway cow "shown on the screen," an imaginary eyeline-match within the cinepoem.[30] It is as if poetic genius had been let loose into a film-within-the-poem, since poems seemingly write themselves on a menu or the bark of a tree,[31] becoming part and parcel of the automorphic realm. Simultaneously, specific episodes and films of early cinema up to Chaplin are indexed in quick referential flashes to maintain a certain level of filmic memory stimuli.[32]

The visual disposition of the illustrated text also reinforces the various levels of the cinematic imaginary deployed:

> CHARLOT, monologue.—**To be inspired means: thinking nothing!**
>
> **Waiting for a sunrise to inundate you like shampoo**
>
> **Cut the guy wires of the brain!**
>
> . . .
>
> He takes up the field glass and looks at the Alps. Snowy peaks. Glaciers. Ravines. Streams. Chamois that scrapes the sky. Giant film.[33]

The four distinct fonts, with Mallarmé's *Un Coup de dés* as likely prototype, each have their own function. The uppercase is used for both the names of characters and the writing printed on the screen /uppercase⇔extradigetic/. The regular lowercase corresponds to staging didascalia. The two other fonts are purely cinepoetic in that they have no clear function within the putative film. Charlot's free-associating monologue in boldface can have no analog in a silent movie since it is spoken in loose and quick verse. It might instantiate the distracted inner speech of a movie viewer—again, a form of automatic riding. As for the smaller regular font ostensibly didascalic as well, it becomes free indirect discourse, since the status of the utterance "giant film" is wholly uncertain: Who "speaks" that description? Goll? The cinepoet-within-the-text? The imaginary "director" of the cinepoem? Or the new "inner lyricism," Chaplin ventriloquizes in us as a reviewer of A *Dog's Life* for *Le Crapouillot* in 1918 puts it.[34] In 1925, chronicler Henry Poulaille, seeing in Chaplin the master of "a new writing," asked, "But if we speak better thanks to images, of what use will grammatical sciences [such as literature] be?"[35] The amphibology of scenario writing—writing all at once *after*, *for*, and *within* the cinema—concretely opens up a parallel technological imaginary to that of traditional poetry. While Chaplin's Tramp cinema relies very little on language (rare intertitles and dialogues, spare plot), poets followed its reverberations as deep as they could envision for it a new poetics of language. Journalist Paul Fierens wrote in 1924, "Charlot, a poet? Very well. . . . Poet, so long as he doesn't think he is. . . . Poetry in a pure, vacant state attracts us like the abyss. Do we know why?"[36] Chaplin was a trigger of cinepoetry precisely because poets could not answer that question.

Another cinepoetic book on Charlot cultivates a different linkage between automatic riding and automatic writing. Titled *Charlot*, and written in 1931 by Philippe Soupault himself, the coinventor of automatic writing, it is a lyrical text in prose that purports to be the imaginary biography of Charlot—resolutely not Chaplin. Rather than adopting a scenario form like Goll's cinepoem, the text is a prose narrative in short paragraphs, mixing dialogue and free indirect discourse, remixing and montaging Chaplin's films into a kind of virtual metafilm of the life of Charlot. What is immediately noticeable is that it would make little sense to think of such metafilm for any other actor than Charlot (or perhaps Keaton). The preface indicates that Soupault, who had been excluded from the surrealist movement in 1926, approached its composition as a continuation of his presurrealist cinematographic poems. He proposes to extract "the essential of Charlot, I mean, the poetry that flows in his veins," and explains that "Charlot is, in fact, a poet in the purest sense [*sens le plus pur*] of the word. If his life, black and white, is so moving, it is because it feeds at the very sources of poetry. . . . [I]t is not a biography that I should have written, but a poem."[37] Here we are, Charlot is all at once poetry itself, a poet, and a (virtual) poem. Soupault then compares the mode of composition of his not-quite-poem to automatic writing: "I have only recounted what I saw on the screen, respecting as much as possible the marvelous poetry that animates Charlot. . . . I have let my pen ride [*laissé courir ma plume*] by listening to the dictation [*dictée*] of my memory."[38] The language unmistakably echoes Breton's definition of surrealism in the *Manifesto of Surrealism*, with its "pure psychic automatism" unveiled through the "dictation of thought." Only it is not the unconscious but the productivity of the cinematic imaginary devolving from watching Chaplin's films that is at play in the writing of Soupault's prosaic cinepoem. We must read his pointed reference to "dictation" in the form of spectatorial automatic riding as a final rejoinder to Breton's evacuation of cinepoetics from automatic writing.

ARRHYTHMIA: CHARLOT AS HOUSEFLY

Charlot is the antiromantic poet because his goals are not lofty and universal but base and immediate. To the free and soaring imagination of nature in romanticism, he opposes the buzzing imaginary of hunger in the slums. He is a gadfly whose cane often serves to sting, a pestering housefly cheap eateries cannot get rid of. In Goll's *Chaplinade*, the first thing Charlot does after coming off the poster is to brush his teeth with water from the gutter, a clear signal he is paradox incarnate, an oxymoron at once hygienic and abject.[39] Referring back to early Chaplin (Keystone) films, Epstein notes, "At that time, Charlot was often drunk and always rude. He was not very honest, nor courageous, nor skillful. He was angry, devious and sensual."[40] In other words, he was a parasite.

This abject and parasitic dimension was no doubt linked with the xenophobia and anti-Semitism many foreign-born Jewish cinepoets (such as Epstein, Goll, and Fondane) experienced in 1920s France. Let us recall that chief among the questions that Chaplin's persona aroused was whether he was a Jew.[41] The other question was whether he was a communist, as the House Un-American Activities Committee decided in 1952 when they barred him from reentry in the United States. As he arrived for asylum in France, Guy Debord and three other dissident *lettrists* rushed a press conference, throwing leaflets calling Chaplin, among other things, "a fascist insect"—another oxymoron.[42] But the parasitical/insectlike nature of Chaplin goes beyond prejudice: for writers at least, it touches upon the somatic novelty of cinepoetics itself. In Soupault's book, when Charlot is still in infancy, he stares at "discrete insects hurrying toward an obscure task."[43] Is it because Charlot registers the failures of the sociobiological model of community, the human hive where each and all should have a function and derive benefits? In an international collection on Chaplin published in 1924, poet Francis Ponge contributed a curious piece titled "Le Sérieux défait" (Seriousness undone). Its second stanza reads:

> Ladies and Gentlemen, the face of the fly is serious. This animal scurries and flies as it pleases and hurriedly. Then it suddenly alters its goals; where it goes next is unpredictable: it is said that this insect is duped by chance. It cannot be approached. On the other hand, however, it comes, and touches you often and where it wants; or else, from farther away, it turns toward you only the face it wants. Batted away, it flees, but returns a thousand times through a thousand ways to land on the batter. We laugh at ease. We say it's comical.
>
> Thinking a bit we might also say that people gaze at flies.[44]

Charlot wears black, and Chaplin is rather small statured, moving with jerky and angular motions. Certainly the analogy hinges on his kinetic silhouette and gait, and especially the way he descends upon social situations with unpredictable results. My point here is that the fly's flight and Chaplin's gait and goals are equally semiautomatic and semi-improvised, their arrival is equally unwanted and generally causes mayhem. To the rhythms of social life and fictive narratives, Charlot brings a constant counterpoint, an unforeseeable arrhythmia. Soupault writes:

> [Charlot's] gait makes him lose sight of immediate necessities. He stumbles, hesitates, falls, and this vacillation, making him suddenly turn around, amuses those who see him, the innumerable spectators of his bumbling ways.
> Automatism.[45]

The mention of "a thousand times" in Ponge and "innumerable" in Soupault, as well as the cloning motif in Goll, point to a important aspect of cinepoetry's proper mode of signification: it relies on the multiplication or even bursting forth of images, the proliferation of modes of vision, and the various rhythms editing imparts on a movie. Blaise Cendrars, in *L'ABC du cinéma,* makes this connection plain: "A hundred worlds, a thousand movements, a million dramas simultaneously enter the field of this eye which cinema has bestowed on humanity. And this eye is more marvelous, if arbitrarily, than the faceted eye of the housefly."[46] Charlot's body, with its Protean capacity for becoming a thing, incarnates through the housefly's arrhythmic flight and multifaceted gaze, what Jean Epstein calls "one of the rarest qualities of the cinematographic eye, *that of being an eye outside the eye*, that of *escaping the tyrannical egocentrism* of our personal vision."[47] This cinema eye is thus metasubjective, multiple, and potential. It recalls the mythical character of Argus—the giant with a hundred eyes—through whom Alfred Jarry redefined poetry as multiple and potential, by envisioning it through "a unique work made of all possible works offered to all the eyes encircling the Argus-like lighthouse at the periphery of our spherical skulls; [while in other types of poetry], the ratio of the verbal sentence to all the meanings that may be found in it is constant; in the latter it varies infinitely."[48] Jarry suggests in 1894 that a new form of meaning in poetry correlates with an alteration of faculties brought about by new technologies of surround vision. In 1903, Jarry relates this circular sight to another mythological figure, Ixion, who is tortured on a wheel: "Let us note that Ixion's eyes are turned outward, and thus reflect the world, in the same manner as the lenses of a Lumière cinématographe."[49] In another text of 1897, Jarry compares the speed of a conversation between two hashish eaters, "because of the number of images," with "*accommodating* . . . to the flicker of a cinématographe [*un tremblement de cinématographe*]."[50] What Jarry intimates in his references to multiplied sights and the cinema is the sheer shock of optical mobility and, equally so, the human perceptual-cognitive capacity to adapt to it.

We encounter these twin ideas in two early cinepoetic texts of Henri Michaux, one involving experiments with flies, and the second about Chaplin. In a short 1922 essay cryptically titled "The Autonomy of the Development of the Faculties, Nervous Centers, Image Associations . . . and the Vase," Michaux conjectures that the plasticity of mental faculties explains how new technologies of vision alter cognition and the sensorium.[51] While referring to Epstein's "Le Phénomène littéraire" in passing,[52] he adduces two examples of physiological plasticity: the "vase," in which the lower bodies of certain Chinese children were supposedly kept to stunt growth, and the fruit-fly larva whose head was constrained by biologists in order to produce teratological outgrowths. For Michaux the advent of cinema represents a comparable neoplastic outgrowth in human faculties. He ascribes the beginning of this historical process of sensorial adaptation to the early nineteenth century:

> The Broca center for speech, for spoken and heard speech, this center is inside, in the vase! (Perhaps another appendage, mid-19th century, romanticism, printed photography, extension of the virtual image [*image virtuelle*]).
>
> And now, there is a new appendage. Grown by cinema:
>
> 3,000 images for 10 lines of text, and 300,000 gestures for one written page.
>
> Predominance, prodigious development of the visual image and predominance upon it of the MIMING IMAGE, the miming intelligence[53]

It is the fly-eye of cinema that inspires Michaux's explicitly cinepoetic homology /3,000 images⇔10 lines of text/. The micromovements that constitute the automorphic texture of cinema further increase the equation to /300,000 gestures⇔1 written page/, so "the extension of the virtual image" into writing is another definition of cinepoetry. The cinepoem he wrote in 1924, "Notre frère Charlie" (Our brother Charlie), suggests that such virtual images in writing relate explicitly to the embodiment of Chaplin and form a new idiom in modernist poetry. Not only does Charlot embody "the modern soul" that "Picasso, Tzara, Freud, [and] Satie," indirectly express,[54] he "installs" this soul within a mason or a policeman as a kind of graft: "Mason, policeman, he fits all professions—and in there [*là-dedans*], he is a modern soul." This protean and larval ubiquity gives Charlot the power to synthesize and transcend various modern poetry movements: "The Unanimists claim him. He would be one of theirs. He would also be a Dadaist, a reaction against romantic sensibility, a subject of psychoanalysis, a classic, a primitive."[55] In short, Charlot is a new body with the new sensibility of "an actor of the subconscious" that informs a new kind of writing with which Michaux experiments by weaving together in a prose poem episodes from Chaplin's films and theoretical ideas about poetry and art.

As Laurent Guido has shown in his interdisciplinary study of rhythm, Chaplin's films raised the problem of gauging and reconciling Charlot's embodied "inner rhythm," with the "exterior rhythm" of cinema, that is, montage.[56] The editorial of the special 1924 issue of *Le disque vert* considers that Chaplin was "the creator of cinematographic rhythm."[57] Mallarmé's influential notions of rhythm, formalized by Gustave Kahn in his 1897 "Essay on Free Verse," already makes of poetry's rhythm an extension of the embodied psyche of the poet. It became obvious to many cinepoets of the interwar such as Jean Epstein that, through rhythm, Chaplin and cinema were providing perceptual correlates and a brand-new field of experimentation to ideas of rhythm of Mallarmé and symbolism that had seemed limited to language. For example, for Blaise Cendras, cinema provides language with a new sensorial and rhythmic texture:

> The real no longer makes any sense. Any signification. Everything is rhythm, speech, life.
>
> . . .
>
> Alphabet. Letter. ABC. Segue and close-up.
>
> . . . a race of new humans will emerge. Their language will be cinema.[58]

The plasticity of this new sensorium-driven language appears to relate, for several cinepoets, to the effects of war trauma. But there was no doubt for many of them that cinema and poetry together had the potential and the duty to reveal this new layer of human experience. In a 1933 text on "La Vieillesse précoce du cinéma" (The precocious old age of cinema), Artaud denounces the insufficiencies of extant cinema, calling on filmmakers to "further its experiment, to offer us not only certain rhythms of everyday life, such as the ear or eye can recognize, but obscure and slow encounters with what hides under things, or the crushed, trampled, loosened or thickened images of what swarms within the depths of the mind."[59] This reserve of larval images unfolds halfway between cinema and poetry since "its poetry is found not beyond but on the nether-side of images,"[60] a formulation akin to Michaux's "virtual image." The one genre of film singled out by Artaud as giving a true sense of the rhythmic/imagistic potential of cinema is comedy, implicitly that of Chaplin: "I am not speaking of the arrangement of rhythms imposed on the appearance of real objects but life scanned according to its own rhythm. I think that humor in cinema comes, in part, from the steadfastness of a base rhythm [*rythme de fond*] on which may be woven (in comic films) all the fantasies of a more or less irregular and vehement movement."[61] We hear marked echoes of the preface to *Un coup de dés*, built, according to Mallarmé around a "leitmotiv" upon which are grafted "accessory motifs."[62] Chaplin again dovetails with Mallarmé. Artaud concludes on a note of virtuality that echoes Mallarmé, Michaux and Jarry: "The kind of poetry, then, which cannot emerge from all this is a potential poetry [*poésie éventuelle*], the poetry of what could be, and it is not from cinema that we can expect [it]."[63] Not from cinema directly, but from cinepoetry's cultivating all at once Mallarmé's "multiple significations," Michaux's "virtual image," and Jarry's and Artaud's new poetry taking up the possibilities of cinema as its own potential. Artaud himself would experiment with this new mode of writing in a form that seemed ideally suited: the scenario—the "unshootable scenario" of Fondane, that is. As for Chaplin and the fly, each resurfaces at intervals within subsequent developments of cinepoetry.

PART THREE

Cinepoetry and Postwar Trauma Cultures

CHAPTER SEVEN

The Poem-Scenario in the Interwar (1917–1928)

The decoupage as well as the few technical indications given in the text of these three cine-poems should be taken but as distant allusions to cinegraphic realization; they were only meant to collaborate in the creation of a temporary state of mind that memory consumes in the act of reading.

—BENJAMIN FONDANE, "2x2," *Écrits pour le cinéma*, 1928[1]

BLAISE CENDRARS: TRAUMA AND REVERSE MOTION

After two amputations of portions of his right arm, Cendrars fell into a depression in 1916, with rare bright spots at the movies. In a poem of that year dedicated to Erik Satie, he wrote: "Theme: Orchestra conductor CHARLIE CHAPLIN keeps time [*bat la mesure*]."[2] The keeping of time, finding a new life rhythm, mulling over how to reverse or at least counter the entropy and trauma of war were broad cultural preoccupations. On September 1, 1917, in the space of one night, so he assures us, with his left hand retrained to write, he composed "Le Film de la fin du monde" (The film of the end of the world).[3] In a letter to Cocteau written on the heels of this epiphanic night—his thirtieth birthday—he calls this text "[a] lyrical fugue of 50 pages!"[4] It was the first poem written explicitly in the form of a scenario that was expressly *not* meant to be filmed, as a manuscript note to his companion Raymone indicates: "For Raymone/ this film/which will never be/ shot/Blaise Cendrars."[5] "Le Film de la fin du monde" was published in the first postarmistice issue of *Le Mercure de France* in December 1918, alongside Apollinaire's "The New Spirit and the Poets," inviting poets to collaborate with cinema. Symptomatically, one of the first articles on shellshock or PTSD, "La Peur du danger chez le soldat" (The Soldier's Fear of Danger), appeared in the very same issue.

Cendrars had envisioned cinepoetry as such as early as 1912 when he was in New York. Dated April–May 1912, and titled (in original English) "New York in Flashlight," a short text came on the heels of the completion of *Easter in New York*, the book that comforted the poet in his career and after which he switched his name from Sauser to Cendrars.[6] "I have entered in treatment with the cinematograph," the text begins. In clipped almost telegraphic style, Cendrars explains why he uses "a camera [*un appareil*] . . . especially at night when I've worked on a poem and the rimes don't come." Both the camera with which he shoots and the films he watches bring poetry back to sheer materiality: "No metaphysics. No abstraction." Together with other mechanical agents of accelerated sensation, such as the metro and the phonograph, cinema revolutionizes the imaginary of writing:

> I bought a gramophone. To economize. I record on sympathetic disks the speech of people dialoging in the street. No more imagination costs. My novels are dictated by a speaking machine which, at times, raises its voice to shout the headlines of a newspaper. It advertises me. I have tons of readers. I know how to combine the marvels of the modern world. I invented an apparatus which, activated by the wheels of express trains, unfolds its transparent films [*déroule ses films transparents*], thereby disentangling, for bored commuters, the tangle of telegraphic news sputtered by a gramophone.[7]

The tone of messianic claim that recalls Rimbaud's hallucinatory *Illuminations* is mixed with a certain ironic bravura. Cendrars mentions "Villiers" and "my laboratory" so that it is clear he has *L'Ève future* in mind. In a letter about this new project he writes, "This book . . . begins the functioning of the machine. . . . I am ready to send impressions, films, cinematographic insights [*aperçus cinématographiques*] of the life of a large American city."[8] "New York in Flashlight" might serve as a form of advertisement for a new cinepoetic project that would include poetic reportages in the form of both telegraphic texts and actual footage. In one of his typically unverifiable claims, Cendrars represented that he shot documentary films for Pathé in 1912, for a collection called "La nature chez elle" (Nature at home).[9] Regardless, Cendrars converted to a cinepoetics much earlier than previously thought, and from the start he considered that the cinema apparatus had a therapeutic potential: "The film purrs. Images are raining. The brain is engorged with rain . . . cinema is my hydrotherapy."[10]

If we skip Cendrars's other wild claims—that he shot a film in Italy in 1916—his first documented involvement in cinema dates from 1917–19 when he was a stagehand working with Abel Gance in the Nice studios of Le Film d'Art. He played a soldier in a cameo role in the closing sequence of Gance's antiwar movie *J'Accuse* (1919) in which ghost soldiers played by actual *gueules cassées* ("broken mugs," or disfigured soldiers) get up from their graves to come and ask the living why they had died.[11] Gance himself had been badly gassed at the front in 1917. So in the years 1917–19 Cendrars was renewing in several ways the originary theme of cinema transforming the dead back into the living that has accompanied the development of cinepoetry from Mallarmé and Roussel onward.

That is the central motif of *La Fin du monde filmée par l'ange N.-D.* (*The End of the World Filmed by the Angel of Notre Dame*), published as a book in 1919 with illustrations by Fernand Léger. It is an elliptical narrative in fifty-five numbered paragraphs of a few lines (Figure 28). Each paragraph is at once a concise prose poem written in the quick rhythm of "New York in Flashlight," or *L'ABC du cinéma*, and a virtual shot sequence playing loose with the homologies /prose poem⇔shot sequence/ and /book⇔film/. A satire, it recounts how God as CEO of the cosmic corporation seeks new markets for mass death now that World War I is over. He goes to planet Mars to present his "best war films,"[12] but the fragile bubblelike creatures, bursting when faced with such orgy of murder, throw him out. God then plans an ultimate film that would make biblical prophecies of the end of the world come true. But it is not the cataclysmic devastation by an asteroid that Camille Flammarion had envisaged in his 1893 *La Fin du monde* (The end of the world)—a novel using a form of interplanetary cinema to communicate with Mars, which Cendrars had certainly read, and which Gance adapted in 1930 with Jean Epstein as assistant director. Instead, the end of the world is simply the end of time: time's arrow just reversing itself and the cosmos devolving back to original chaos. Civilization regresses, humans disappear, the world freezes, and animals face devolution and vanish. As all life is about to disappear entirely, however, the film apparatus malfunctions. God's projectionist Abin (a compound of Abel and Cain), who had not been mentioned and had remained as if off-screen, accidentally causes the apparatus to wind the wrong way, thus projecting the film *backward*. The reversal of evolutionary time in an imaginary movie is thus itself reversed thanks to film. Time is rebooted, animals evolve again, and we are quickly back to the present.

Why is Cendrars staging such an odd contrivance as a double filmic reversion? The answer, it seems to me, has everything to do with traumatic temporality. What trauma does is to compulsively pull the subject backward to a past present, which shock has both erased and burnt

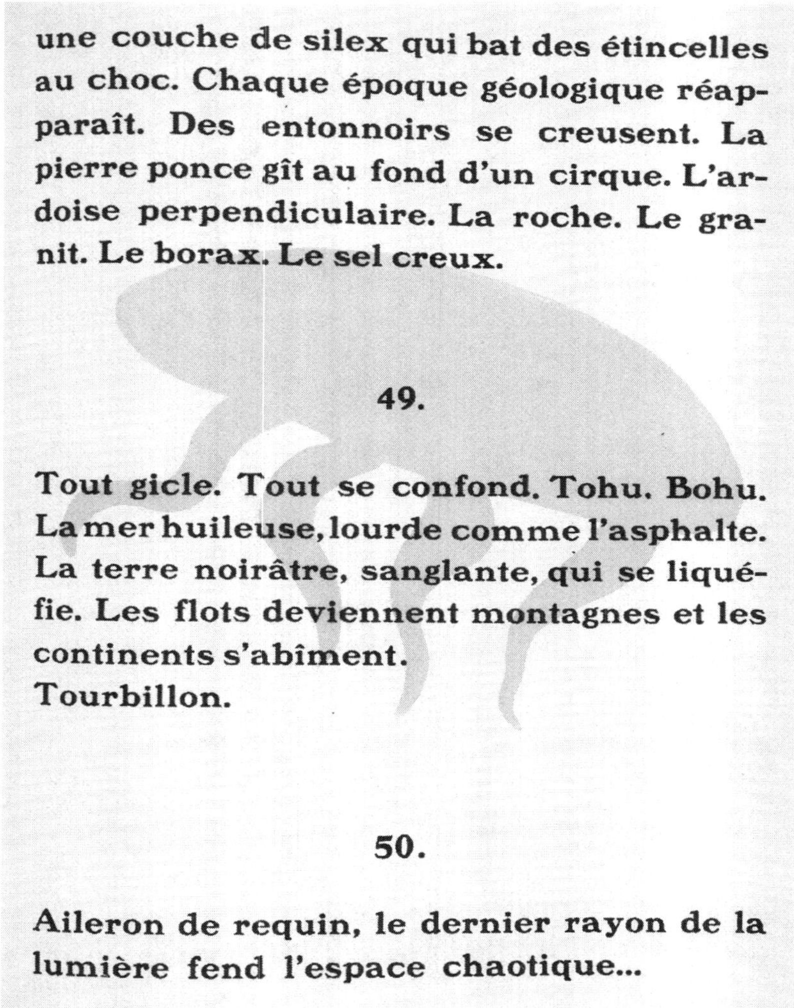

une couche de silex qui bat des étincelles au choc. Chaque époque géologique réapparaît. Des entonnoirs se creusent. La pierre ponce gît au fond d'un cirque. L'ardoise perpendiculaire. La roche. Le granit. Le borax. Le sel creux.

49.

Tout gicle. Tout se confond. Tohu. Bohu. La mer huileuse, lourde comme l'asphalte. La terre noirâtre, sanglante, qui se liquéfie. Les flots deviennent montagnes et les continents s'abîment.
Tourbillon.

50.

Aileron de requin, le dernier rayon de la lumière fend l'espace chaotique...

Figure 28. A page from Blaise Cendrars, *La fin du monde filmée par l'ange N.-D.* (1919), illustrated by Fernand Léger. Courtesy of the Beinecke Rare Books and Manuscript Library.

into the perceptual apparatus. Freud was wrestling with just such ideas in *Beyond the Pleasure Principle*, which he was writing in the late war years as well. Bergson's linear and vitalist duration no longer made much sense to those suffering from PTSD. On the one hand, reversal enacts the desire to return to the origin, that is, to the time before trauma, finding an egress out of the frozen present and reopening time. It lunges toward both past and future. On the other hand, trauma compels a return to its originary site—its past that will not pass because it was not lived—as though in such returns it could solve and dissolve itself, restarting time. What is striking in Cendrars's poem-scenario is that cinema is all at once the technology that gives form and perhaps facilitates trauma's temporal reversal, and yet, as itself a reversible technology, cinema also homeopathically assists in *presenting*—making present—and thus undoing the backward pull of trauma.[13] Through cinema, we might say that the postwar inaugurates a new view of temporality not as unidirectional anymore, but going forward only as a *double reverse motion*—doubly mediated by the cinema apparatus.

The End of the World Filmed by the Angel of Notre Dame indicts the institutions of capital, religion, and science that fueled the war—the same critique leveled by Dada and Surrealism. Yet rather than bracketing trauma as does Surrealism—though Breton and Aragon experienced it vicariously, working in a psychiatric hospital for soldiers in 1917—Cendrars innovates a cinepoetic scenario that can serve as a countertraumatic aesthetics. This project transpires through most of Cendrars's writing in 1917–18. For instance, in the autobiographical piece "J'ai tué" (I Have Killed) (February 1918), Cendrars gives a dense, halting, and kaleidoscopic account of a battle climaxing in the narrator killing a German soldier. It begins with a shadowy general using "probability calculus" to plan his next carnage—a figure very much similar to the calculating businessman-God. When the barrage of artillery launches the offensive, we are plainly at the end of the world:

> The curtain is ripped. Everything bursts, cracks, explodes all at once. A general conflagration. . . . Against the glow of assaults the crazed profiles of bending men, an index finger on a signpost, a horse gone mad. The flicker of an eyelid. A magnesium eye-wink. A quick instantaneous photo. Everything disappears. We glimpsed at the phosphorescent sea of trenches and black holes. We pile in the parallel furrows for the assault, mad, hollow, haggard, wet, exhausted and harassed.[14]

The sensory overload has a stroboscopic and mechanical quality: it is as if each disjointed image was burnt on the eye that had become a photographic plate, while the soldiers are cameralike recording machines. At the climax of the *The End of the World*, on the brink of the void, we find the same optical impress: "A dark eye shuts down over all that was," until "the last ray of light darts through space filled with chaos."[15] Cosmic genesis, war, cinema, and trauma, all converge in the same flickering effect for Cendrars. And again, albeit now in a destructive key, trauma and cinema impel new forms of sense and language, for instance when explosions imprint themselves deep inside the body: "Apocalyptic mouth, open pocket, from which flow inarticulate words, as huge as drunk whales. It links up, forms sentences, takes on meaning, intensifies. It gets more defined. You can perceive a particular ternary rhythm, a proper cadence, like a human accent."[16] Cendrars's piece explains how a poet-soldier can commit murder when transformed into a bare automaton of pure matter: "Water, air, fire, electricity, radiography, acoustics, ballistics, mathematics, metallurgy, lighting, travels, the table, family, universal history are this uniform which I wear."[17] The automatic language of techno-perceptual impress overrides the poet's reasoned pacifism and invokes cinema as a better sensorial and semantic framework for self-understanding. This is what "L'ABC du cinéma," written a few months before "J'ai tué," makes clear: "Cinema. The whirling of movements in space. Everything falls. The sun falls. We fall after it. Like a chameleon the human spirit camouflages itself by camouflaging the universe."[18] Cinema's "camouflage" provides a zone of safety from chaos, from the *dis-aster* of the disappearance of the *lumen naturale* from the livable cosmos. If "the sun falls," it's because the "magnesium eye-wink" of explosions replaces "the sun [that] has been dissolved" as Cendrars writes in *The End of the World*.[19] As in Saint-Pol-Roux mourning the death of his son in World War I, "live cinema" provides an ontological camouflage as a new form of working-through: "Automatism. Psychism. New commodities. Machines. And it is the machine that recreates and displaces the sense of orientation and in the end discovers the sources of sensibility . . . a million dramas enter simultaneously into the field of this eye bestowed on man by cinema."[20] Rather than a pat declaration of simultaneism, this passage proposes that the imaginary polyvalence of cinema can help us splice, reedit, and reunify experience once fragmented by stroboscopic trauma. Cinema is prosthetic and therapeutic. *The End of the World* climaxes when:

> 51.
>
> In his [projection] booth, Abin, the employee manipulating the lantern, puts the apparatus on fire [*met le feu à l'appareil*]. A fuse blows. A spring breaks. And the film unfolds vertiginously backward [*à rebours*].[21]

Titled "A rebours" (Backwards), this chapter follows a longer one, "Cinéma accélé, cinéma ralenti" (Fast forward cinema, slow-motion cinema) (Plate 3). Until that point in the poem-scenario Cendrars has kept filmic indications tacit at best: in these two culminating chapters, the apparatus moves to the foreground. We should note that Abin's action is pointedly unclear: the French "met le feu à l'appareil" translates both as "activates the apparatus" and "puts the apparatus on fire." The very next section begins, "The last ray of the sun puts the oily sea on fire" (*met le feu à la mer huileuse*), and just as pointedly it sustains the ambiguity, halfway between the literal and the figural, between the technical and the imaginary.

Reverse motion plays an important figural role in Cendrars's reconstruction of the postwar sensorium—and it may also directly reflect his amputation and thus the experience of writing with his other hand, reversing the movement of the writing hand across the page. In *L'Eubage, aux antipodes de l'unité* (L'Eubage: The antipodes of unity), a 1917 tale mixing poetry, philosophy, and science fiction, he invents "the Sponge of Darkness," an oxymoronic and alchemical antitrauma substance: "The most simple primal sample, the most elemental in a family of reverse-beings [*êtres à rebours*], unqualifiable and inadmissible, at the Antipodes of Unity."[22] Reverse motion, a unique technological feature of cinema becomes, via the cinepoetic imaginary, a tangible device for psycho-sensorial repair.

Mary Ann Doane has noted that while early film played with "reversing filmic temporality," on the whole "mainstream film has worked historically to familiarize temporal irreversibility."[23] This is certainly true overall, yet Epstein's or Cocteau's influential use of reverse motion in *Finis Terrae* (1928) and *The Blood of a Poet* (1930) complicates this opposition. Postwar mainstream film construction—increasing techniques like flashback, overlapping cut, and parallel editing, and broadening the use of shot/*reverse*-shot—intensified minute reversible idioms *within* global irreversibility at the diegetic level. Cinepoetic works appear to register this change by focusing on reversibility both as an imaginary therapy to actual trauma, and a new technologically mediated generic marker for poetry, since reversibility clearly exceeded the Aristotelian definition of narrative (diegesis) as having minimally a beginning, a middle, and an end. Cinematic reversibility allows narratives to become something else—to tend toward poetry without becoming poem. That, also, is the crux of cinepoetry.

CANUDO: TRAUMA AS FILM STILLS

Canudo was probably the first poet paid to write movie scenarios (for Italian producers) around 1910, a job subcontracted to him by Gabriele d'Annunzio, who was later handsomely paid for his script for Giovanni Pastrone's 1914 *Cabiria.*[24] In 1911, d'Annunzio wrote a scenario in free verse on the motif of the painting coming to life: *L'Homme qui a volé la Joconde* (The man who stole the Mona Lisa).[25] It tells of a painter named Jean-Joseph Vermeer who is so in love with a portrait of a woman that he loses his sight. After an alchemist restores it, Vermeer realizes that the portrait has lost its attraction, so "he grasps . . . a sharp tool; and blinds himself horribly. He renews on himself the desperate act of Oedipus."[26] The alchemist concocts an elixir with blood and pours it on the painting in order to "animate" it:

> The figure suddenly has relief. It is like an instant incarnation. She jumps out of the canvas. She lives for a few moments. Then dissolves.
> On the canvas, the image is erased.
> Nothing is left of the apparition.[27]

I cite from this poem-scenario to contrast its prewar futurist kitsch—moving images ultimately figuring a by-product of painting—with Canudo's poem-decoupage of war trauma, *L'Autre aile* (The other wing) from 1924. A key figure in the Italian and French literary and filmic avant-gardes, Canudo wrote poetry, novels, and scenarios, and he began theorizing cinema in 1908, before launching the journal *Montjoie!* in 1913. His thoughts on cinema as art were germinal for the whole French film avant-garde and cine-club movement and informed the work of several cinepoets.[28]

The best way to describe *L'Autre aile* is as a work in several layers or tracks. The long subtitle reads: "A visual novel, followed by the original novel, illustrated by the most beautiful photographs from the film, a Dal production movie." Indeed, the film adaptation directed by Henri Andréani was shot the same year (Figure 29). The first seventy-nine pages of the book contain a decoupage of the film in 299 shots, including forty-two boxed intertitles, accompanied by seventeen production stills. The last seventy-seven pages (with separate page numbers) reproduce the original 1922 novel, initially serialized in *Le Figaro* in December 1920, much closer to the end of the war.[29] *L'Autre aile* is then all at once feuilleton, novel, poem-decoupage, photo-novel, and film. In the preface to the original novel, Canudo alludes to "Graphiques de poèmes visuels" (visual poem graphs), as a model for this narrative:

> The Plastic Arts are going deeper toward the discovery of formal play, through this astounding voluminous writing [*écriture de volumes*] that is called Cubist; they pass on the scepter of evocation of linear writings [*écritures linéaires*] to this other human invention that is Photography, pushed to its most powerful degree of perfection by the Cinématographe.[30]

Even before the poem-decoupage version was written, the novel was already conceived as cinepoetic, in the singularly same terms used by Mallarmé: writing volume through cinema.

The plot concerns the trauma of a painter, Hélène, who witnessed the plane crash of her lover, Reymat. This traumatic sight leaves her "looking straight ahead, her eyes empty, haggard, like a somnambulist."[31] The presence of the sun in her line of sight at the time of the accident accentuates the photographic quality of the images "burnt" into her visual memory. Before crashing, Reymat's plane had been "flying in loops, falling in corkscrews, playing on one wing in the splendid sky."[32] The cinematic fluidity of airplane flight—especially looping—is directly opposed to the photographic fixity of the traumatic image.[33] Hélène's collection of paintings echoes d'Annunzio's prewar aesthetics, with items such as "the sheet of Veronica, with, in the middle, the effigy of Christ . . . a large reproduction of Moreau's Salomé, with the bloody severed head of John the Baptist. Images of headless bodies [corps sans tête]."[34] Canudo was wounded while serving in the French army during the war (dying of his wounds in 1923) and his account of combat in a 1916 poem closely conforms to the kaleidoscopic renderings of Cendrars.[35] The headless bodies of symbolist painting acquire a different valence with the war as context and likely partake of a persistent traumatic motif with "L'Homme sans tête," or Cendrars's narrator beheading of a German soldier in "J'ai tué." Compulsively painting the haunting image of her lover's plane crash, Hélène too has "lost her head." She resolves to begin piloting airplanes herself, and on her maiden voyage she exults with suicidal enthusiasm: "To the sun! Do not change direction. It burns like a great fire. I see a man's face burning in the middle of the sun."[36] It is noteworthy that neither the paintings nor what are obvious composite shots with superimposition of Robert's face in MCU appear in the original novel.

Soon an accomplished pilot, Hélène struggles with the scene and space of her trauma, pitting the frozen sight and its death drive

Figure 29. Still from Henri Andréani, *L'Autre aile* (1924).

compulsion to the possibility of a renewed fluidity. This tension progressively unfreezes the photograph of death: "Hélène suddenly has an extremely confused and quick vision of the machine of the pilot Reymat burning in space."[37] The still image is on the verge of *animation*: the trauma photograph of death is about to acquire the automorphic liveliness of film. While her paintings always had the same vantage point on the accident, her flying opens new angles, restoring fluidity to the space of her trauma. She soon falls in love with another pilot, as desire literally motivates her imagination of movement: "She sees herself taking her first flight, accompanied in space by Robert, flying together on the paths of light."[38] Robert, however, is marked by his own traumatic memories of World War I, which he shares with his friend, a mechanic, and which likely echo Canudo's own memories: "They see themselves, both, in the war, in a trench, without shelter, under fire, pressed in each other's arms during a bombing."[39] Robert was Reymat's protégé and his desire for Hélène is tainted with his own traumatic guilt: he has a vision of "The image of Hélène gliding in her machine, flying in her plane which breaks apart a few feet from the ground."[40] Canudo's text is remarkable in its detailed descriptions of how Hélène heals progressively by beginning *to edit the film of her trauma* in substituting Robert to Reymat: "Then she sees again the burning plane with the image of Reymat. She sees Robert . . . climbing in his machine, then falling down. She sees again the burning plane with the image of Robert."[41] Canudo expresses her growing control over traumatic memory through her capacity to manipulate virtual dissolves.

The melodramatic conceit climaxes in an air show that includes a mock duel exercise between Robert and his mechanic friend. This explicitly conflates war trauma with cinema, since the duel is filmed both from the ground and the air: "The machine guns can be seen sporting recording cameras."[42] But it is as if the reproducibility of actual cinema technology was a threat to the imaginary countertraumatic cinema, by reinforcing trauma's repetition compulsion: as a result, it seems, Robert's plane suddenly catches on fire and crashes. But Robert is only slightly hurt. In the final scene, Hélène's trauma dissipates—indeed becomes a *filmic dissolve*. In her vision, "the head of the pilot Reymat vanishes progressively. . . . The image of Reymat's plane comes back, nebulously, without any human face on it."[43] The novel version deemphasizes the head shot dissolve as the mark of loosening the traumatic hold, focusing instead on the metaphor behind the title. Hélène tells Robert, "And you see it. The other wing . . . The one that was burnt . . . It is reborn."[44] The rhetoric of trauma has shifted from amputation and regrowth in the novel to the animation of a photograph and film editing in the scenario.

The melodrama, I would argue, is entirely subsidiary to the cinepoetics of trauma that underlies *L'Autre aile*. Both the protagonists and the airplane setting thinly veil Canudo's interest in psychodynamism, perceptual therapy, and the techno-cognitive cinepoetics of modernity. However, neither the novel nor the film (which is lost but garnered no critical attention) are able to bracket the melodrama sufficiently. Only the "formal play" of the poem-decoupage succeeds because its "écriture en volumes," relying equally on text, boxed text, stills, and our perceptual filling-in, enacts a cinematic imaginary that is meant to be of the same order as Hélène's countertraumatic working-through. Behind a disingenuously melodramatic façade, in the poem-decoupage Canudo develops several cinepoetic homologies at once: /cinema apparatus⇔psychological apparatus/, /multimedia film decoupage⇔imaginary enactment/, and /poetic writing in volumes⇔airplane flight⇔virtual enactment therapy/.

APPOLINAIRE AND DESNOS: THE SCENARIO-WITHIN-THE-SCENARIO

Other interwar scenarios by poets similarly bracket the narrative to explore the cinepoetic virtuality of reversibility, looping, and circularity, as if metadiscursively, or better, as if they were *transcursive* effects of the cinema apparatus on writing. Canudo expressly calls in the preface to *L'Autre aile* for "more cursive and essential . . . rhythmic arts . . . leaving behind discourse and narration."[45] This is the case with the scenario cowritten by Apollinaire and André Billy in 1917, *La Bréhatine,* which they sold to a producer though the film was never shot. On the surface, it is a *drame Breton*, a popular film genre in the postwar about the frontierlike region of Brittany untouched by modernity. Raymond, a Parisian novelist, visits a lighthouse whose keeper Aline (from Bréhat, thus a Bréathine) tells him that her lover Yvon abandoned her. Raymond writes a novel based on them, also titled *La Bréhatine*, that is serialized in newspapers. After a chance encounter with Yvon, who has become a lowlife, Raymond concocts an ending in which Yvon had become a murderer and was executed, following which Aline throws herself off the lighthouse. When "real-life" Aline, who has followed what she recognizes as her own life in the newspapers, learns the fate of Yvon, she throws herself in the sea. Learning of her planned suicide from a letter she sends him, Raymond goes remorsefully in search of Yvon, and the two grieving men travel to Brittany to pay homage to Aline's tragic love. Up at the lighthouse, Yvon takes out Aline's ring to kiss it, the ring slips, and Yvon falls to his death trying to catch it. This final fall likely involves a reminiscence of Hoffman's "The Sandman," which ends similarly in an accidental fall after a *faux-geste* or *geste manqué* (a failed act).[46]

We can recognize formal markers of cinepoetic constructs, notably the homology /lighthouse⇔film projector/ (cf. Roussel's "La Vue") and the interleafing of media with the dramatic action: oral narrative, novel, newspaper, letters, and *in fine* film. Film manifests itself as medium in a similar manner as Cendrars's reverse motion marking the apparatus. But instead of a given technological attribute, the scenario enacts a formal play on the very nature of a film scenario: prolepsis. Raymond's novel scripts the death of both Aline and Yvon in just the way Apollinaire and Billy script the fate of Raymond. This prolepsis undermines Plato's mimesis as the essence of art, since the script *precedes* what it describes, to an equal degree the death of the former lovers scripted *in* the film by Raymond, and the film itself scripted by Apollinaire and Billy. With this new proleptic device that is the scenario, art need no longer follow reality, it can very literally generate it. Having given her account to Raymond, Aline reads its fictional ending in the newspapers, and internalizes the scene so powerfully that she enacts it. Apollinaire indicates that Raymond read about the suicide-for-love of an American woman over Niagara Falls in the newspapers—possibly a real piece of news Apollinaire or Billy too read. Facts, news accounts, and the proleptic scenario form fold into each other. Apollinaire and Billy render this entwinement cinematically. They devise a sequence in which on Raymond's hand in CU, as it is writing the fictional story of Yvon, we see superimposed scenes of Yvon's imagined actions, then Aline's reactions when she reads them. In other words, we are watching a film *adaptation* of Raymond's novel, but before or as it is being written, and these scenes acquire a peculiar liminal status. *La Bréhatine* as scenario uses both the device of the scenario-within-the-scenario (Raymond's novel), *and* that of the film-within-the-film (the superimposed shots), while presenting itself as an unimpressive text in short numbered paragraphs and simple and flat language. Written during World War I, it has clear echoes of the traumatology of Cendrars's and Canudo's scenarios. Aline is haunted by the imaginary sight of Yvon being guillotined, and "like an automaton" she walks to the sea and throws herself in.[47] When she first learns that Yvon has become a murderer, she falls unconscious. As she wakes, she sees that the lighthouse reflects her traumatic syncope: "The lighthouse, profiled in white against the night that has fallen. It is not lit."[48] The lighthouse-cinema homology has been expanded to /lighthouse⇔cinema apparatus⇔psychic apparatus/. Behind such a small but highly visual and scenic detail, we also recognize the insistent figure of cinepoetry, in the *blank screen* or *impossible projection*—like that of Aragon's "Le décor," and Mallarmé's "Salut," of "L'Homme sans tête," or Fondane's virtual films. As in Canudo, the melodrama matters only because it provides an affective horizon against which a formal poetics of exploration of the cinema apparatus in writing can take place.

The thinning of the melodramatic conceit is even more acute in Robert Desnos's 1925 scenario "Midi à quatorze heure" (Noon at two o'clock), subtitled "An essay in the modern marvelous."[49] The decoupage is in 161 numbered sections/stanzas of 1–2 lines each with almost no shooting indications. It uses a triangular melodrama to produce a cinepoem about guilt as a form of sensorial haunting. The unnamed man in a couple drowns soon after another unnamed man arrives for a visit and begins an affair with the first man's female partner.[50] The accidental drowning causes "Circular ripples," on the river, a shot that recurs rhythmically twice more in short succession from the viewpoint of the lovers, then of a peasant witnessing the drowning form afar. The proverb behind the title, "to seek noon at two o'clock," means complicating things uselessly, yet the scenario is utterly simple. The rhythmic ripples evoke another proverb, "to make waves," yet neither the death nor the two surviving lovers make any wave at all. Taking the proverbs at face value, however, we see that they signal a dysfunction of time and space, and perhaps language as well. Indeed, the scenario is suddenly overtaken by a compulsive motif: the multiplication of circular and spherical objects: "The setting sun perfectly circular," "Their eyes in the foreground. Circular pupils," "The moon perfectly circular." Soon, round plates, round napkin rings, the round door handle, the hoop of a boy, and so on, place the couple in a state of paranoid siege. A "cricketlike ball" appears on the stairs and, self-propelled, leaves through the door to the garden. The ball grows to cannonball size, and continues coming to the house, moving about, standing on the dead man's chair at the dinner table, then disappearing again, as mute as the memory of the Albatross of Coleridge. As it keeps growing, the ball undertakes a long circuit through the countryside, a town and the beach. When it ultimately returns, it has become so large that it crushes the house with the lovers in it, leaving but "a large funnel-shaped hole."

Clearly, the scenario has no interest in its narrative, melodrama or unrounded characters. It does, however, attempt to graft on the fiction film an abstract or geometrical cinema à la Walter Rüttman or Oskar Fischinger. From the metonymic ripples that resulted from the man's death, Desnos extracts a general metaphor—circle is death—and literally lets it loose on the narrative. The curious homology he deploys links the intensity of affects of guilt, loss, persecution, even paranoid hallucination, to the size of a geometrical shape. Or rather, it is not the size per se that matters, but the growth itself, as an autonomous process on screen, the automorphism of affects concretized out of the two lovers' bodies, as if the "fruit" of their love was nothing but a malign growth. Instrumental to this process of biomorphic materialization of something immaterial is, again, the very genre of the scenario. Desnos, in a way, pathologizes the generic specificity of the scenario that aims at materializing itself as a film as if it were inhabited by a mad inner plasticity. This calls to mind movies such as Méliès's 1901 *The Man With a Rubber Head*, expressly connecting filmic automorphism with uncontrolled bodily growth. Behind his deceptively simple story, Desnos establishes a complex homology that presents a deep cinepoetics of film history: /neurotic autonomy of affect⇔prolepsis of the scenario⇔bodily growth⇔automorphic images of cinema/. *Midi à quatorze heure*, indeed . . .

ARTAUD'S UNCANNY CINEPOETRY

Antonin Artaud has the unique distinction among poets of having come to cinema as an actor.[51] He played in over twenty films from 1917 to 1935, never as the main protagonist. Although Cendrars, Cocteau and Buñuel acted on screen, they did so as already published and established writers acting either as directors or cameo. Artaud's cinepoetics is enmeshed with a central existential questioning that concerns the play of identity, meaning and even incarnation between a "real" self and fictive film characters. He reflected on various aspects of the cinema apparatus in conjunction with this ever spiraling questioning. Desnos's scenario showed the close family resemblance between cinepoetry, the scenario form and paranoia: in all cases, what is imagined is imagined not in the traditional mode of *make-believe* exterior or parasitical to reality, but in a new mode of *making-real* fundamentally shaped by cinema's automatic self-presentation threatening to become uncontrolled.

Among the many scenarios Artaud penned and planned, the most intriguing is "Les Dix-huit secondes" (Eighteen seconds), written in 1924–25.[52] Taking place entirely in the mind of an actor standing at a street corner, the action lasts eighteen seconds of diegetic time, "although it will take one or two hours of projection on the screen."[53] On the brink of gaining worldwide stardom, and thus finally obtaining the woman he loves, an actor is afflicted with a sudden mental condition: he can no longer put his thoughts into words—he no longer even masters his own thoughts. After eighteen seconds of inner turmoil, he shoots himself. In response to a 1923 questionnaire on cinema by René Clair, Artaud had called for "fantasmagorical films, poetic films in the thick, philosophical sense of the word—psychic films."[54] Certainly "Les Dix-huit secondes" is meant to be just that. But then Artaud adds, "In cinema the actor is but a living sign. . . . This is why [actors] do not exist."[55] What inspires this comment?

Artaud's first role on screen was that of a strangler in Claude Autant-Lara's 1923 *Faits divers*, a thirty-minute film that, he hoped, would open for him the doors of the movie world. It did—but perhaps at a heavy price. Artaud was typecast and railroaded into playing protagonists that were mad, criminal, guilt-ridden, murderers or murdered. His best know roles are the confessor of Jeanne d'Arc in Dreyer's 1927 *La passion de Jeanne d'Arc* and Marat in Gance's *Napoléon* (1927)—two protagonists respectively famous for assisting in murder and being murdered (Figure 30). He played a treacherous secretary in L'Herbier's *L'Argent* (1928), a knife-sharpening angel in Fritz Lang's *Liliom* (1933), a gang leader, even Savonarola, the fifteenth-century monk crusading for moral purity who was tortured and burnt at the stake. In 1927, as Jean Epstein made plans to shoot *The Fall of the House of Usher*, Artaud lobbied Gance to help him pressure Epstein into giving him the role of Roderick: "If I don't have this character in my skin, no one does. I enact him [*je le réalise*] physically and psychically. My life is that of Usher and his sinister shack. I have stench in the soul of my nerves and I suffer from it. . . . I think like Usher, all my writings prove it."[56] The identification is extreme. Rather than "entering into the skin" of the character, as French language puts it, the character is already in his, and he enacts him fully, with the verb "réaliser" meaning "to direct," as if Artaud had already made his own mental film with Roderick: little surprise then that Epstein found him too hyper for the role when

Figure 30. Antonin Artaud looking treacherous in Marcel L'Herbier, *L'Argent* (1928). © Musée Gaumont, courtesy of Marie-Ange L'Herbier.

he had him try for it. Jean-Paul Morel rightly depathologizes such typecasting in the industry, yet it seems that in Artaud's case the frustrating inability of securing a main role had particularly deep resonances.[57]

In the first of his famous self-defining 1923 letters to NRF editor Jacques Rivière, Artaud writes:

> I suffer from a frightful disease of the mind. My thought abandons me at every turn. From the simple fact of thinking to the exterior fact of its materialization into words. Through words, the form of sentences, the inner direction of thought, simple reactions of the mind, I am constantly chasing after my intellectual being.[58]

Compare this to segments from "Les Dix-huit secondes":

> He has been struck with a bizarre illness. He has become incapable of reaching his own thought; he kept his entire lucidity, but to any thought presenting itself to him, he cannot give it an exterior form, that is, translate it into appropriate gestures and words.
>
> The necessary words elude him, do not come when summoned; he is reduced to seeing unfold [*défiler*] within himself nothing but images, an excess of contradictory images that have little to do with one another.[59]

The unemployed actor in the scenario suffers from the same disease as Artaud the writer. The actor's disease extends to language (including gestures), exposing him to an uncontrollable and unedited inner film. Can we deduce anything of the striking resemblance between the writer and the actor? We might posit that Artaud came up with a compromise formation to address the difficulties of wanting both to act and write: cinepoetry. A fictional letter from Artaud's first published book of poetry, *L'Ombilic des limbes (The Umbilicus of Limbo),* also written in 1924–25, shows that he places cinepoetry exactly halfway between writing and acting:

> Dear Sir,
>
> Don't you think that now would be a good time to try to join together Cinema and the intimate reality of the brain. [*sic*] I am including excerpts from a scenario that I would like you to publish. You will see that its mental plan, its inner conception gives it a place within written language.
>
> . . . I am not telling a story but simply stringing along [*égrène*] images. . . . I am attempting to strike at surreality [*surréalité*], to make it give up the ghost, exhale its marvelous venom . . .[60]

The piece referred to in the letter appears to be "Paul les oiseaux ou la place de l'amour" (Paul the birds or the place of love)" from 1925. It is a stage-play with Donatello, Brunelleschi, Ucello, André Masson, and Artaud himself, who is "about to deliver [*en gésine*], and is set on the other side of all mental windows, and who spares no effort to think himself elsewhere than here."[61] Rather than the windows of Cocteau's *Le Potomak* that multiply "takes" on the self, here we have darkened windows, caches obscuring parts of the image, placing the self off-screen, out of the field of his own vision. Further on Artaud writes:

> It is a problem that came to the mind of Antonin Artaud, but Antonin Artaud does not need a problem, he is already stumped by his own thought and, among other things, by having encountered himself within himself, and found himself a bad actor, for instance, yesterday, at the movies, in *Surcouf*, not to have also this larva of Petit Paul come and eat his own tongue within himself.[62]

The resemblance of the "real" letter to the "virtual" scenario thus turns out to be connected to a "real" failure as an actor. In the film *Surcouf* (1924 or 1925), Artaud plays the minor role of a traitor. In a crucial sequence that he found important enough to describe to Génica Athanasiou in minute detail,[63] a CU on his face at the top of a tower cuts to a MS of his gesticulations, then another cut to a CU of his face on the ground writhing in agony. The grammar of continuity invites viewers to *imagine* the fall or leap that takes place out of sight, off-screen—in this case an ellipsis that spells out Artaud's own death. We are dealing with a series of gaps, leaps, and syncopes between media, moments, and modes of expression. Artaud the writer writes a scenario in which a film actor has the same illness as his, then another scenario in which a character named Artaud hates his filmic likeness. Artaud writes a letter to no one in which his illness, and perhaps its cure, is found in both "written language" and automatic "images." It seems that cinepoetics is involved anywhere and anytime Artaud encounters a failure of vision, language, or identity. Let us turn to a brief analysis of "Les Dix-huit secondes."

It begins with an ECU on the watch of the actor at his street corner, and explains the conceit of eighteen seconds representing a much denser mental duration: "The spectator will see unfold [*se dérouler*] the images that, at a given time, will begin going through [*défiler*] the man's mind."[64] This is perhaps the first time that the tacit homology that runs through the cinepoetics of Mallarmé to Epstein and Breton, /train of thoughts⇔montage of shots/, is made so explicit. Artaud saw himself as the actor of this virtual film,[65] so we can surmise that its cinepoetics—in the silent era, where words appear on screen alternating with images—served to bridge the cognitive failures of writing and the expressive failures of acting. During the initial sequences of the scenario, we differentiate a flashback at the psychiatrist's, visions that the man has, and superimpressions of nature shots as correlated to them. But unlike most other scenario decoupages carefully separating diegesis and didascalia, Artaud's quickly blurs the diegetic, the extradiegetic, and the biographical: "Oh, to be anything! To be this miserable hunchback street seller who hocks his newspapers at night . . . to be truly the master of one's own mind, at last, to think!"[66] Is the actor *saying* this? Can this be *written* on an intertitle card in free indirect discourse? Is this an *example* of what the protagonist is thinking or some kind of scenic *indication* Artaud provides ostensibly from his own vantage point as scriptwriter, outside the plot? The scenario provides a truly bizarre answer: the plot immediately aligns itself with the hunchback street seller, and the POV of the actor/protagonist simply disappears, only to reemerge somehow in the street seller, like the transbody leap in Spike Jonze's 1999 *Becoming John Malkovich*.

The scenario accelerates into a vertiginous stereoscopy: the street seller, who "truly possesses his own mind," and "can hope to conquer the world" (how is Artaud envisioning to represent this on screen?), meets a woman who happens to be the actor's lover, but then the street seller is found insane and institutionalized. Although Artaud punctuates the text with "Vision of the street seller [*vision du camelot*] . . . ," "Vision of the woman . . . " "Vision of the man . . . ," we have lost any sense of a diegetic arc with a stable protagonist—an essential condition in drama and novel alike. The hunchback is soon freed, chosen as king, whereupon his inability to think returns, he falls asleep, dreaming of himself as king, who is on stage, and happens to be playing a hunchback opposite "his" real-life mistress. I put "his" in quote because it is impossible to tell whether it refers to the king, the hunchback, the actor, or Artaud casting himself into the scenario from the outside. We have landed in a "multiple world" postmodern film (such as *The Matrix* or *Dark City*), but all within a single individual's psyche. Plays of dissociation and misrecognition, betrayals and existential leaps multiply until finally, "the two characters [king and hunchback] fuse into each other on screen."[67] With a final quick-edit sequence, all the previous scenes are sampled in a *reverse* zipback and we are returned to the street corner, where the actor shoots himself.

It is striking that the moment of *identification* of the king with the hunchback, and the indication "on screen," should signal the spiraling of the actor—who is neither and both—toward death. Danger does not come just from the dissociative force of the apparatus but also from its power *to collapse and suture identities*, such as actor-Artaud playing a traitor who dies off-screen. The cycles of avatars, caused by a new POV coming from the outside to graft itself on the previous one, delays the deadly moment of identification—thus also the return of Artaud's dreaded incapacity to think. The apparatus provides the poison of dissociation, but it is a remedy to the worse poison of identification. The final quick edit flashback may quote from Abel Gance's *La Roue*, which came out in 1923, pointing to the same scene of Élie's fall with a life zipback that Goll cited as an instance of "surrealism."

Needless to say, Artaud's scenario is unshootable. Not because it leaves narrative behind to enact a schizoid spiral, but because, compared to Desnos's for instance, it is remarkably devoid of visual decoupage. This is surprising since Artaud's theoretical texts on cinema embrace Epstein's photogénie, insisting that cinema shows "the human skin of things" and bestows on objects "a meaning and life that is proper to them," with close-ups making "leaves, a bottle, a hand, etc., live with a quasi animal life."[68] Yet, Artaud's commitment is also to the functioning of thought as such, which took him very close to Breton. Artaud writes of his own 1927 scenario, *The Seashell and the Clergyman* that "it restitutes the pure working of the mind,"[69] a near-quote of Breton's *Manifesto* defining Surrealism as "pure psychic automatism." Breton's endeavor to sublimate cinema and cinepoetics may have undercut Artaud's explorations of poetic scenarios during the time he was welcome in the Surrealist movement.[70] Artaud's fictive letter seeking "to strike at surreality" (*attenter à la surréalité*), with cinema may have aimed to merge Breton's psychic Surrealism and Epstein's surreal cinepoetics, through a kind of transgressive hybrid since the French *attenter* is reserved for acts of utter transgression.[71]

Artaud's scenario, in the end, illustrates the ambiguous power of cinepoetry. As an intermedial practice allowing writing to dream itself as a kind of cinema; conversely, transforming movie experiencing into opaque words and unthinkable ideas, it can become the opposite of Saint-Pol-Roux's ideorealizer: an uncanny derealizer and disembodier. In this case, Artaud's paradoxical homology would make poetry and cinema communicate through their sheer excess: /unlimited bodily identifications through labile POVs in cinema⇔unlimited bodily dissociations through the stasis of words in poetry/.

ROLLAND AND HILLEL-ERLANGER: THE TECHNOPOETIC UNCONSCIOUS

Artaud is ambivalent about whether the apparatus adds to or reveals something of the human mind. The "physical drunkenness" spectators feel at the "rotation of images," he writes in 1927, comes from a "kind of virtual power in images [*puissance virtuelle des images*] [that] seeks within the mind heretofore unused possibilities."[72] In 1933, he insisted that a new cinema could still disclose, "obscure and slow-motion encounters with what hides under things, or the crushed, trampled, distended or thickened images of what crawls in the underworld of the mind."[73]

Two cinepoets, Irène Hillel-Erlanger and Romain Rolland, located the poetic disclosure of the nonconscious at the very boundary between the human and cinematic technology. Yet rather than new psychic phenomena, what this boundary revealed was more prosaic: war, trauma and political power. A poet and translator, Hillel-Erlanger launched in 1915 with her partner and lover, the filmmaker Germaine Dulac, the first woman-owned film production company in the history of cinema: *Films DH*. Hillel-Erlanger wrote short treatments for a number of Dulac's films, including *Les Soeurs enemies* (Enemy sisters) (1917)—her first scenario—and *La Belle Dame Sans Merci* (1920). While her early poetry in 1909 consisted of rhymed pastoral odes, by 1919 she was publishing in Breton and Aragon's review *Littérature* a free-verse cinepoem in honor of Pearl White the American actress of *The Perils of Pauline* and *The Exploits of Elaine*, combined in a French serial: *Les Mystères de New York*[74] (Figure 31).

In 1919 Hillel-Erlanger wrote and published *Voyages en kaléïdoscope* (Trips through the kaleidoscope). A loose narrative of clipped sentences in an irregular layout, it strongly resembles visual poetry, and compares with Pierre Reverdy's *Le Voleur de Talan* (1917), which is subtitled "roman poétique." In the short foreword Hillel-Erlanger writes, "this is not a novel."[75] The text is almost devoid of omniscient narration, and consists mostly of letters, newspaper articles, phone calls, accounts of films, or poetic sequences tangential to the narrative. Michel Carrouges provides an alchemical reading of the work in *Les Machines célibataires*, but glosses over the pivotal role of cinema.[76] Hillel-Erlanger's "kaleidoscope" is an explicitly filmlike apparatus invented by scientist Joël Joze, convinced that "the Universe, such as our eyes take it to be, differs completely in its true form. We see and can see only what is in ourselves."[77] Two semimythical enemy sisters, Véra and Grâce, vie for the love of Joze and the monopoly of his invention. Véra incarnates reality and pleasure, and is compared to Loïe Fuller,[78] while Grâce represents the Keatsian accord of Truth and Beauty. Joze invented his Kaléidoscope with the aim of:

> . . . capturing on the pupils of every living being, the images of all visible things, in order to condense them, to compress them . . . and to obtain, thanks to a surprising and vertiginous process, a chemical synthesis; so that these images, projected on a screen, might instantly appear as ANIMATED METAPHORS.[79]

This "sort of Cinématographe"[80] functions as a metacinema in (1) recording the neuro-optical images, not only of humans, but of all living things, (2) distilling them into new composites, and (3) proposing a cinepoetic language of moving metaphors. Artaud's introduction to *The Seashell and The Clergyman* scenario, which Dulac directed, expresses a similar idea:

“ Par amour ”

fantaisie musicale et variations
sur le
Nom
de
PEARL WHITE

Nom *joli-*,
-ment ajusté à cette exquise héroïne de la
vie américaine vue à travers le Ciné-feuilleton
« Vie américaine » 1919
comme
« Vie parisienne » 1865.
(*Cora* — Pearl — *White*)
Celle-ci : Paris par Triple prisme scintillant *(Meilhac-Halévy-Offenbach)*
Celle-là : rose de lapidaire taillée à facettes
et
Pearl White
nous entraîne dans un New-York féerie
le Tube de Radium
et quelques choses analogues tenant lieu de
baguette magique

PEARL
actuelle acrobatique
rieuse verveuse nerveuse (et de sang-froid)
sachet cachet
rêve d'amour et revolver
boxe bouquets
joyau gingembre et jiu-jitsu

ÉCRAN
Pearl *parait*
d'abord
Son Elégance :
divinement chaussée

Figure 31. Irène Hillel-Erlanger, “Par Amour” published in *Littérature*, 1919.

> The aim is not to find in visual language an equivalent of written language . . . but rather to make the very essence of language publish itself [*faire publier l'essence du langage*] and to transport action on a plane where translation is useless and this action would act almost intuitively on the brain.[81]

Artaud and Hillel-Erlanger's Joze share with Saint-Pol-Roux and other cinepoets and artists (such as Duchamp[82]) the idea of enacting through the cinema apparatus a more primal and, paradoxically *less mediated*, layer of meaning circumventing the tired logos. A cinepoetics of hypermediacy. Joze's kaleidoscope relies on what Andrea Goulet has theorized as the late nineteenth-century belief in the "optogram," the photolike inscription of an image in the eye, especially of a dead person.[83] Joze extends optography to the animal realm and moving images, correlating it to life rather than to photography's deathly fixity. The synthesis of the kaleidoscope's footage suggests a method of collective dreaming of the real that combines science with Unanimism, since to function properly the kaleidoscope requires a democratically diverse collective.[84]

The narrative opens on a malfunction of the kaleidoscope, recounted in a newspaper article. In front of gathered dignitaries, the apparatus hooked to Joze's mind fails to project images and the screen remains blank with "nothing but the sheath of electrical rays illuminating the white screen."[85] Through his letters to Véra who pushes him toward commercialism and political power, we learn that the malfunction is imputable to his love for this Salomé-like woman. While remaining convinced that "the screen was not empty!"[86] he spirals into an unaccountably acute psychic breakdown with "quasi-epileptic" reactions.[87] He flees the theater and wanders the streets aimlessly in a paranoid state, hallucinating:

> . . . dejected persons . . . withered and deaf-mute . . . shriveled . . . atrophied . . . reflected and multiplied . . . in a mirror . . . and this strident voice . . . in my ear . . . constantly shouting
> "The screen! The screeeen! Not empty!"[88]

Joze is rescued by Grâce who displays none of the outwardly sexuality of Véra, and suggests that a child should operate the kaleidoscope to purge it. Joze recruits Gilly, his thirteen-year-old boy apprentice, charging him with "writing down our projections and your running comments [*boniments*]."[89] What renders Gilly pure is, of course, his love of Charlot.[90] Successfully operating the kaleidoscope, Gilly transfigures persons into filmic objects and metaphors, through the same kind of ontological shift between the animate and the inanimate that Aragon had analyzed in "On Décor," through Chaplin.

Véra and Grâce incarnate the two poles of a raging debate in filmmaking circles of the late 1910s and 1920s. It pitted existing cinema, "the commercial expansion of the Kaleidoscope" as instrument of "vanity" and "lucre" associated with Véra, against "pure" cinema, that of "Parabolas," which "put light in the foreground not lucre"[91] in the words of Grâce. As both strong characters, they also reflect the new woman of post–World War I enjoying a new social capital, while men traversed a deep crisis of masculinity (this theme is present in films jointly made by Dulac and Hillel-Erlanger). In the climactic scene of the novel, as Véra bends Joze to her will by making him play the Kaleidoscope in order to visualize his desires for her and for power, the apparatus suddenly "unfolds in reverse"[92]—as in Cendrars's and Artaud's cinepoems. Grâce then arrives to challenge Véra, leading not to a melodramatic catfight, but a cosmic battle resembling the cinematic descriptions of combat by Cendrars: "Conflagration Detonation Millions of bombs Billions of incendiary grenades." It is plainly a panegyric for the dead of World War I:

> . . . Victims
> thousands and thousands
> incinerated
> asphyxiated
> torn to pieces
> —children—women—men—.[93]

After the destruction of the commercial Kaleidoscope, Joze finds himself in recovery, free of the apparatus, if perhaps not of trauma. As for the place of the "good" cinema in *Voyages en kaléïdoscope*, diegetically it is represented by the comic films based on the collective psyche that Gilly channels. The haunting mantra, "the screen was not empty," aside from traumatic amnesia and the blanking out of commercial cinema, is a variation on the *empty screen* as marker of cinepoetry, so the good cinema may well be that which remains virtual. We will examine in Chapter 10 the five "films" on paper that represent the essential cinepoetics of the book on the margins of its narrative.

The motif of the machine falling into the wrong hands conflates two disparate concepts: technology is innocent for the very reason that it is inhuman (Gilly), and technology is dangerous because it summons something very human which cannot be controlled (Véra). This dilemma is played out in Romain Rolland's 1921 *La Révolte des machines ou la pensée déchaînée* (The revolt of machines or the mind unbound), a film scenario illustrated with beautiful woodcuts by Frans Masereel[94] (Figure 32). It too revolves around an inventor, the "Master of Machines" Martin Pilon, known by his employees as Marteau Pilon—meaning die-casting press—and by his enemies as Pilon Marteau, which means "Pilon nutcase." He incarnates the ambiguity of scientific genius possessed of an "energetic and abrupt mien . . . brusque and awkward gestures. . . . An enormously concentrated violence," causing him to be "charged with subconscious electricity."[95] Married to Félicité, he lusts for La Belle Hortense, "a comedian . . . queen of fashion . . . of the Republic of Machines: one of its indispensable pieces of furniture."[96] The struggle between glam power and truth is here too staged as a love triangle. Ridiculed by the public, and ignored by La Belle Hortense, Pilon's demonstration in the Hall of Machines turns aggressive. Using his "machine to read thoughts," which projects images on a screen, he shows that the mind of the President of the Republic is empty: "the screen stays blank (with a few floating vibrations)."[97] The emblem of the cinepoem is also here an occasion for technology to speak truth to power. But someone places the camera-machine in "the form of an eye at the end of an extensible elephant's trunk," on the back of Pilon's head, and his disdain for everyone and his passion for the "actress" are projected for all to see.[98] Mad with humiliation, "he loses control of himself; and his subconscious begins to take over. It is the beginning of 'The Revolt of the Machines.'"[99] The rest of the plot is predictable: propelled by Pilon's subconscious anger, the machines destroy the world, until a young innocent couple (the flapper Aviette, and Pilon's assistant Rominet) restores the promise of a new Golden Age. In the last paragraph a chastened Pilon is seen drawing new peaceful machines.

The climactic moment is worth returning to. The world is unified into a single Republic headed by a mindless President, so power rests with the mechanocratic Pilon. World War I is clearly the context: Europe's mindless political class controlled by the military-industrial complex. Apart from Rominet mischievously placing the camera on Pilon's head, all humans appear to be on automatic pilot. By contrast, the machines themselves—rather "the machine people"[100]—display volition and fantasy: a moving walkway dances, a tube farts in the face of an admiral.[101] Setting out to destroy the world, they do so with

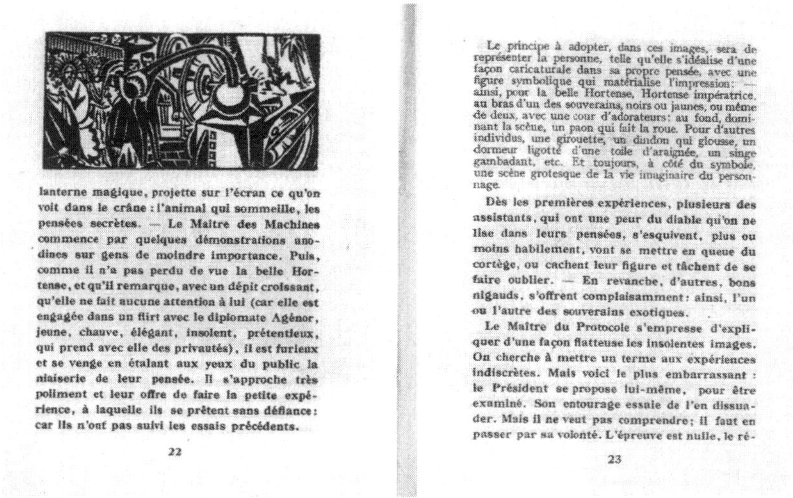

lanterne magique, projette sur l'écran ce qu'on voit dans le crâne : l'animal qui sommeille, les pensées secrètes. — Le Maitre des Machines commence par quelques démonstrations anodines sur gens de moindre importance. Puis, comme il n'a pas perdu de vue la belle Hortense, et qu'il remarque, avec un dépit croissant, qu'elle ne fait aucune attention à lui (car elle est engagée dans un flirt avec le diplomate Agénor, jeune, chauve, élégant, insolent, prétentieux, qui prend avec elle des privautés), il est furieux et se venge en étalant aux yeux du public la niaiserie de leur pensée. Il s'approche très poliment et leur offre de faire la petite expérience, à laquelle ils se prêtent sans défiance : car ils n'ont pas suivi les essais précédents.

22

Le principe à adopter, dans ces images, sera de représenter la personne, telle qu'elle s'idéalise d'une façon caricaturale dans sa propre pensée, avec une figure symbolique qui matérialise l'impression: — ainsi, pour la belle Hortense, Hortense impératrice, au bras d'un des souverains, noirs ou jaunes, ou même de deux, avec une cour d'adorateurs: au fond, dominant la scène, un paon qui fait la roue. Pour d'autres individus, une girouette, un dindon qui glousse, un dormeur ligotté d'une toile d'araignée, un singe gambadant, etc. Et toujours, à côté du symbole, une scène grotesque de la vie imaginaire du personnage.

Dès les premières expériences, plusieurs des assistants, qui ont une peur du diable qu'on ne lise dans leurs pensées, s'esquivent, plus ou moins habilement, vont se mettre en queue du cortège, ou cachent leur figure et tâchent de se faire oublier. — En revanche, d'autres, bons nigauds, s'offrent complaisamment : ainsi, l'un ou l'autre des souverains exotiques.

Le Maître du Protocole s'empresse d'expliquer d'une façon flatteuse les insolentes images. On cherche à mettre un terme aux expériences indiscrètes. Mais voici le plus embarrassant : le Président se propose lui-même, pour être examiné. Son entourage essaie de l'en dissuader. Mais il ne veut pas comprendre; il faut en passer par sa volonté. L'épreuve est nulle, le ré-

23

Figure 32. Facing pages showing the mind-camera, from Romain Rolland and Frans Masereel, *La Révolte des machines ou la pensée déchaînée* (1921).

relish, not anger. When tanks are sent to cut down the rebel machines, the two groups "sniff under each other's tail. They exchange marks of affection,"[102] and no combat occurs. Technology is depicted as what reveals human savagery, amplifies and implements its drives, while remaining neutral, like a domestic animal. The point of the satire is not that humans are becoming machines—they already are—but that machines are dangerously vulnerable to being contaminated by destructive human drives. Both Hillel-Erlanger and Rolland associate this destructive power with a certain kind of sexuality that is amplified and distorted by cinematic machines.

Rolland and Mazereel's book clearly has the cinema industry in mind, or rather, the role of cinema in shaping mainstream culture and the public sphere through the star system: this is what la Belle Hortense embodies. Rolland's play with the space of the page and Masereel's imaginary film stills thus deploy their cinepoetics as a political alternative to film industry products. Their narrative ends on a utopian note that may itself be open to critique—particularly with regard to what exactly is so fearful about film-mediated sexuality—yet in pointing out the neutral character of technologies such as cinema they occupy a midway position between technophobes and technophiles. In so doing, Hillel-Erlanger, Rolland, and Masereel, together with the likes of Goll and Gance—all of them among the most outspoken pacifists of the interwar—show that cinepoetic experimentations tend to reflect both a profound seduction by the apparatus but also a measured lucidity toward some of its more catastrophic promises.

CHAPTER EIGHT

Reembodied Writing

Lettrism and Kinesthetic Scripts (1946–1959)

I believe that from here on published scenarios . . . could circulate independently of films like plays in print.

—ISIDORE ISOU, "Préface," in Maurice Lemaître's *Le Film est déjà commencé?* 1951[1]

LIBERTY, TOTALITY, VIRTUALITY: POETRY AND CINEMA IN THE POSTWAR RECONSTRUCTION

The disintegration of France in 1940, the Occupation and the collaboration leading to the deportation of Jews, then the Liberation—each would seem to have further eroded the ideal of a techno-social utopia that had largely inspired the high days of cinepoetry in the 1920s. Marked by purges of collaborators, the return of survivors from the camps, penury, the penumbra of the Cold War, and the reinvention of national unity, the mid-1940s was a period of forced lucidity and sheer realism that repressed the traumatic experiences of war to make way for the future. This resulted in a trauma culture rechanneling repressed violence, for instance in the bloody state repression of independence movements in Algeria in 1945 and Madagascar in 1947, in which tens of thousands died with seemingly little reaction in France. The experience of defeat and the Occupation left paradoxical marks on poets and writers. Jean-Paul Sartre, Samuel Beckett, Georges Bataille, and Raymond Queneau, for instance, point to the Occupation as an uncanny period of pregnant temporality—a time outside of time, both a suspension of and dissociation from History. It is against such a dystopic background, in contrast to the driving utopia of the 1920s, that cinepoetry arose again, more multiform than before and even more thoroughly steeped in reverberations of trauma than after World War I.

The respective cultural fate of poetry and cinema were, in the postwar, proportionally inverse. Cinema never was more popular. With the arrival of the vast Hollywood backlist, 424 million tickets were sold in France in 1947, a record unsurpassed to this day.[2] While the thirst for entertainment, the limited fare of the Occupation, and the material difficulties of the postwar may, in themselves, explain this enthusiasm, there are less obvious factors at play. Cut from History by the media veil of German Occupation, the French were busy making up for lost time, reliving the years 1940–45, and learning about American culture, of which they often knew very little.[3] Going to the movies was a remedy to the wartime fracture in cultural time and space. As for poetry, its relative popularity during the years of resistance made way to a sense of stagnation in part due the large segments of the art and intellectual avant-garde having sought refuge outside of France during the war. Marie-Claire Bancquart speaks of a general "occultation of poetry" in 1947.[4] Surrealist faithful Benjamin Péret's 1945 pamphlet, "The Dishonor of Poets," denounced the propagandistic pseudolyricism of the poetry from the Resistance whose writers, he claimed, stopped "to be poets in order to become advertising agents" writing at the "poetic level of pharmaceutical advertising." Rather ironically, the iconic image of Fantômas with his foot on Paris that the whole avant-garde had so cherished and reproduced was originally . . . a pharmaceutical ad.[5] To this backward-looking verse poetry at the service of the state Péret opposed "a poetry understood as the total liberation of the human spirit,"[6] in keeping with Breton's surrealist emancipation. The nature of "total liberation" was indeed the crux of postwar debates in France as in its colonies. Like Péret, literary thinkers like Blanchot and Bataille also sought to place poetry's capacity to embrace the totality of experience at the center of philosophical reconstruction. Sartre virulently dismissed this claim of poets and thinkers in his 1947 *What Is Literature?* condoning only a realist approach to language and political commitment. Introducing his newly launched journal *Les Temps Modernes*, Sartre advocated for a collective commitment broadening the narrow view of the bourgeois self: "I shall call this conception 'totalitarian'" he writes, explaining that, within the collective, the individual will be "totally committed and totally free."[7] Bataille, in an article in *Critique*—a journal he launched in 1946 in part as an alternative to *Les Temps Modernes*—pointed to poetry's more encompassing totality, noting that "the exigency of poetry pries it wide open," no matter what "emptiest intentions" it harbors, because "this is the condition of its freedom."[8] For Bataille, poetry's totality confronts a more confounding totality—the wholly-other (*tout-autre*) of experience. Such thoughts echo in the new developments in cinepoetry that often took place in conjunction with extreme experiences of survival, trauma, and psychophysiological injury.

In contrast to the precarious situation of poetry in the postwar, the groundwork for the reconstruction of French cinema had begun under Vichy, with filmmakers connected to cinepoetry in the 1920s becoming key players. In 1943, the first national film school (IDHEC) was created, largely through independent efforts by Marcel L'Herbier. In the very first days of the Liberation in August 1944, Jean Painlevé was appointed to the newly formed position of director-general of Cinema. In October 1944, Philippe Erlanger, the son of Irène Hillel-Erlanger, made plans for the first Cannes Film Festival that would open in 1946.[9] L'Herbier, we recall, had gone the farthest in embedding words on the screen—a cinepoetics *in* cinema, we might say—while Painlevé, known for his scientific films, had shot the avant-garde short *Metusaleh* in 1927, a film featuring Artaud, with a script by Ivan Goll.[10] The Liberation also witnessed a resurgence of the cine-club, a hybrid cultural and political structure launched by Canudo and Dulac in the 1920s. The Cinémathèque of Langlois, which continued its preservation work during the war, enlarged its holdings to one hundred thousand films by 1946, making the history of cinema available for the rebirth of the French film industry. All this directly led to the creation of the Institut de Filmologie in 1946, the most important scientific structure for the study of cinema up to that date, with Jean Epstein, Roland Barthes, and Edgar Morin among its early contributors.[11]

This extraordinary emphasis on cinema toward the end of the war was not lost on writers and thinkers. Between 1942 and 1950—with a peak in the years 1946–47—there was an avalanche of books on the theory and history of film, by André Malraux, Jean Epstein, Georges Sadoul, Léon Moussinac, Alexandre Arnoux, Gilbert Cohen-Séat, André Cayatte, François Mauriac, Marcel L'Herbier, Jean Charansol, Pierre Artis, and many more. In the same period, books based on films or original scenarios were published in major presses by Jean Giraudoux in 1942 and 1944, Pierre Mac Orlan in 1945, Cocteau in 1946 and 1947, Georges Bernanos in 1948. Sartre, Bataille and Boris Vian each penned several scenarios between 1943 and 1950. While established writers had often disguised or marginalized their work in cinema in the interwar, after 1942 cinema became a recognized avenue for major writers and intellectuals: this total liberation from the strictures of high literature directly led to the reemergence of cinepoetics in the New Novel of the late 1950s as we saw with Robbe-Grillet's reading of Roussel.

"TOTAL CINEMA"

The currency of the word "total" should make us pause since it is a spillover from the idea of "total warfare" (von Clausewitz's expression), the new kind of conflict fought by totalitarian states that translated into the Cold War in 1947. The enrolling of film industries in the United States and Britain for the war effort hastened cinema's new status as a cultural totalizer. Hence Gilbert Cohen-Séat's theory of *filmologie* in 1945 took cinema to be a rational correlate to society as a whole, and thus could be studied as such. Cinema was considered central and capable of remobilizing other forms of culture as well. In a conference at IDHEC in March 1945, Maurice Merleau-Ponty (Sartre's coeditor at *Les Temps Modernes)* presented his existential phenomenology to film students as a new holism. Since living and thought derive from perception, he asserted, so should all intellectual endeavors, and filmmakers should "apply to filmic perception all that has been said about perception in general."[12] After addressing technical questions (montage, track integration, dialogues, and so on), Merleau-Ponty turned to the question of holism, arguing that film demands attention to its totality as a multimedia form: "The distribution of silences and dialogue thus constitutes, beyond sound metrics and visual metrics, a more complex metrics overlaying its priorities on those of the two previous ones."[13] This more complex metrics is not only akin to the rhythm of a poetic form—a central argument of prewar cinégraphie—but to an apparatus:

> The problem we encounter here, aesthetics encountered it in poetry or the novel. . . . A poem always alludes to things or ideas. And yet the function of the pure novel or pure poetry is not to signify such facts, ideas or things, for then the poem could be exactly translated into prose, and the novel would lose nothing in being summarized. . . . [T]he art of poetry does not consist in didactically describing things or exposing ideas, but in creating a machine of language which, in an almost infallible way, puts the reader in agreement with the poet.[14]

Somewhat circularly, Merleau-Ponty proposes that a film should be like a poem since as "a machine of language," a poem is already an apparatus. This mechanized view of poetry devolves in part from Paul Valéry's newly coined "poetics" which he had defined in 1938 as "the comparative analysis of the mechanism [*mécanisme*] (that is, what we can, through a *figure*, call thus) of the act of the writer."[15] As the mediating apparatus through which "philosophy and cinema are in agreement,"[16] poetry was de facto transformed into "a certain sort of instrument" in the words of Sartre's *What Is Literature?*[17] Hence both Sartre and Merleau-Ponty stamped poetry as being like cinema in order to instrumentalize it for the program of social totality that prose and philosophy were better suited to implement.[18]

In 1946, in Bataille's journal *Critique*, André Bazin published one of his most famous essays, "The Myth of Total Cinema." Arguing against Georges Sadoul, Bazin claims that cinema is not the result of technical innovations in the base infrastructure (the Marxist viewpoint), but is instead an "idealist phenomenon" resulting from genius "bricoleurs" pursuing an idea that, he notes, was prefigured by "Villiers's *The Eve of the Future*."[19] Poets are the precursors of these early bricoleurs whose "imagination identifies the cinematographic idea with a total and integral representation of reality; it envisions from the start the rendering of a perfect illusion of the outside world with sound, color, and relief."[20] Although Bazin does not privilege poetry here, his essay was directly inspired by a book that does and which he fails to mention.

Published in 1944 by future science-fiction author René Barjavel, *Cinéma total, essai sur les formes futures du cinéma* (Total cinema: Essay on the future forms of cinema) placed poetry front and center. It starts from the very premise of Bazin: "[The evolution of cinema] will come to a close when it will be able to present to us protagonists in relief and color, and perhaps with odors; when these protagonists will free themselves from the screen and the darkness of theaters to take a walk in public squares and in everyone's apartment."[21] Barjavel credits a 1927 text of Jean Epstein with this notion of an expanded cinema to come, and he goes on to prophesize that total cinema will be able "to put in motion chatty ghosts, absolutely similar to living beings."[22] In his peripatetic notion of cinema, Barjavel echoes ideas of Saint-Pol-Roux such as the fusion of "radio, cinema and television."[23] He foresees "pay-per-view" ("receptors equiped with counters"),[24]videotapes and DVDs ("a show of several hours will be preserved in a small volume, disk, or reel"),[25] movie rental chains ("the neighborhood cinematheque"),[26] even a holographic home projector ("total cinema, briefly imprisoned in a receptor and its screen . . . will project a virtual image [*image virtuelle*] . . . somewhere in space between floor and ceiling").[27] Such total cinema will ultimately change society itself since "Machines will do everything for man. Even choose," and Barjavel adds, "In this way he will become a part within a passive, female mass, which a few men, masters of the world, themselves slave to fate, will process and shape. The individual will be erased, will melt into the collective flesh and soul."[28] This revival of Unanimism with a dark Orwellian and misogynistic twist connects explicitly with totalitarianism: "The USSR and Germany have shown us what role cinema could play in the education of the citizen. . . . He will no longer be able to escape total propaganda."[29] Barjavel is unsentimental in his deflationary acceptance of the new agency of technology, although he indicates that "sensibilities and the senses" might become new channels for interclass solidarity[30] in counterbalancing the power of "state cinema." But while paying heed to politics, Barjavel's focus is the imagination of cinepoetry: he invites "poets" "to imagine" imperceptible noises—"a tree growing," "the song of water in a fish's ear"[31]—as ways to show what a total immersive environment will be. Thus

> [Cinema] reaches poetry. Total cinema is the means to express genius.[32]
>
> Relief will give total cinema its ultimate possibilities, surpassing the maddest imaginations of surrealists.
>
> . . .
>
> The more the vocabulary of cinema, a vocabulary of sounds, images, colors, volumes will be enriched, the more the film auteur [*auteur*] will submit it to a rigorous syntax. Not for the sake of a flat realism, but to lead the crowd, using the material appearances of truth, straight into the heart of poetry.[33]

Like Merleau-Ponty, Barjavel construes cinema as a technology of mass control, and likely inspired by Epstein, as an instrument of mass invention and poetry.[34] His reference to the "auteur" comes as a surprise since only with Truffaut's 1959 manifesto, "The Politics of *Auteurs*," did it gain theoretical currency. Jean Giraudoux used the word in the preface to his 1942 book, *Le Film de la Duchesse de Langeais*, where it is applied specifically to film directors who write their own scenarios.[35] Barjavel echoes Giraudoux by offering to replace "metteur en scène" (*director*) and "metteur en film" (*filmmaker*) "by the simple term 'auteur,'"[36] granted the radical technical transfiguration of literature:

> The principal means of expression for moribund Old France was literature. That of tomorrow's mechanical civilization will be cinema. Machines for visual recording, as well as transforming, emitting, and receiving devices, will replace the pen [*stylographe*]. As soon as cinema will enter the home, and the preservation of film will be guaranteed and its replaying [*relecture*] frequent, thinkers will no longer want to express themselves with dry sentences. They will accompany them with images, sounds, colors, volumes. They will give form to what their predecessors were reduced to suggesting.[37]

The symbolist aesthetics of Saint-Pol-Roux appears to be reinvoked here in fusing literature within cinema in an experimental cinepoetics, implicitly leaving behind the Vichy regime's antiquarian politics.

Bazin clearly knew Barjavel's book. Several key passages of his essay are close paraphrases, such as Bazin's conclusion that "Cinema has not yet been invented!"[38] a quasi citation of Barjavel's "Cinema does not yet exist."[39] More damningly, Bazin cites the same obscure film historian as Barjavel—G. Potonniée—making the same point about the evolution of stereoscopy into precinema, and the contingent invention of the phenakistiscope by Plateau.[40] The main difference is that Bazin, like Sartre, has no use for poetry.

Overall then, cinepoetry was all at once recalled, reinvented and evacuated in the years following the Liberation. On the left, Sartre and Merleau-Ponty argued for social totality by recuperating poetry's holism and the cinematic imaginary for the benefit of prosaic and filmic engagement. On the Christian-democrat side, Bazin took over Barjavel's cinepoetic "cinema total" in the name of greater realism. Despite such elisions, cinepoetry remained an active matrix for innovation in the postwar, albeit in a more dystopian register. We will examine specific instances of renewed cinepoetics among poets who worked with Alain Resnais, then in the inception of lettrism by Isidore Isou, Maurice Lemaître, and Gabriel Pomerand, and finally among several writers in the broad wake of Surrealism.

JEAN CAYROL'S LAZAREAN CINEPOETICS

Deported to Mathausen-Gusen as a political prisoner in 1942, Cayrol returned to France to become a central figure in the literary world. His novels focused on the psychological alienation of the survivor and directly inspired the New Novel, while as literary director of Le Seuil in the mid-1950s, he encouraged and published Francophone literature and launched the influential journal *Tel Quel*. In 1946 he published *Poèmes de la nuit et du brouillard* (Poems of night and fog), written during and in the aftermath of his internment. The title reappropriates for the poet-survivor the cynical poetic label the Nazi regime invented for prisoners it sought to "disappear," and complicates Adorno's dyspeptic maxim that "to write poetry after Auschwitz is barbaric,"[41] since poetry written in the camps shows the categories of survivor and poet to be mutually nonexclusive. When Alain Resnais was invited to make a documentary on the tenth anniversary of the liberation of the camps, he accepted on condition that Cayrol would write the script, and he chose a title echoing Cayrol's book title: *Night and Fog*. A well-established but not well-known documentary filmmaker, Resnais was faced with the challenge of finding a way to break through the repressed memory of the camps while avoiding the still-taboo issue of the French role in carrying out deportations. After 1948, following some initial interest in the general French public leading to the production of a couple of documentary movies, concentration camps and the experience of deportation, as well as the return of deportees, had all but vanished from national consciousness.

Resnais's 1956 *Night and Fog* has acquired a paradigmatic status for the conundrum of representing the Shoah and its traumatic memory on film. Most critics have focused on the issue of visual representation, even though, as Joshua Hirsch recently pointed out, Resnais was committed to an egalitarian interart effort between a filmmaker (Resnais), a poet (Cayrol), and a musician (Hanns Eisler) requiring attention to all three media: the visual, the word, and music.[42] I want to extend this interart insight by looking at specifically ethical valences that a cinepoetic reading of the film through Cayrol's words might offer. Hirsch theorizes two stages in the spectatorial reception of films on the Holocaust. In the first, raw footage is received as document, attenuating its traumatic aspect,[43] while in the second, images are manipulated so as "to invoke a posttraumatic historical consciousness," which includes, as "exemplified by *Night and Fog*, attempts to produce in the spectator a traumatic afterimage, an image that formally repeats the shock of the original encounters with atrocity—both the original eyewitnessing of the atrocities themselves, and the subsequent cinematic encounter with the images of atrocity."[44] For Hirsch, mimesis and antimimesis are key to the second phase of posttraumatic cinema that he characterizes as formalistic through its interferences in the narrative flow, such as making the apparatus conspicuous, addressing the reader, or disordering temporality. "We call it modernism," states Hirsch, adducing that such filmic modernism proceeds from a similar "posttraumatic narration" as that which marked the "French impressionist film movement"[45] in the wake of World War I. For Hirsch, posttraumatic cinema proceeds from a similar "crisis of representation"[46] as the New Novel "where no suturing edit provides an escape from the camera's melancholy, walking stare at the remnants of atrocity."[47] This "walking stare"—enacted by long tracking shots[48]—makes, he claims, the narration falter as if "in that faltering suddenly [the narration] became aware of itself, of the entire apparatus supporting its activity."[49] Ostensibly then, undoing the seamlessness of narrative devices shocks the spectator, precipitates a cognitive crisis, and insures maximum spectatorial adhesion to the traumatic images as "a form of historical knowledge."[50]

This view of *Night and Fog* leaves a number of questions unattended. Is the maximum transmission of trauma by forcibly placing viewers, in Merleau-Ponty's words "in agreement" with the film, not problematically coercive? Whose trauma is at play—that of "eyewitnesses" or victims and survivors? Moreover, the status of the "crisis of representation" is unclear: Is it an aesthetic and political decision by the filmmaking team, or a compromise formation improvised at the limits of representability, which succeeds only through its modernist "faltering"? Finally, is trauma a cognitive crisis, more than a corporeal, affective, and perceptual reconfiguration, and in the latter case, is narrative still its optimal form? While I very much admire Hirsch's work, his approach seems to me to reinscribe two versions of the Shoah's unrepresentability. On the one hand, because cinema must fail to represent the victims' trauma as such, it is left with perpetrating in its stead a vicarious trauma on viewers, and on the other hand other mediums such as poetry (pace Adorno) are considered too obscenely aesthetic and sensorial to do justice to the victims of the Shoah, while canonical modernist narrative techniques are not. I will argue that consideration of Cayrol's text, in how it interposes its cinepoetic virtuality between the images and the spectator, allows for a nonvicarious and ethical redeployment of victims' trauma that alleviates some—of course not all—of the problems of representation.

Cayrol's 1946 *Poèmes de la nuit et du brouillard* explicitly addresses the question of the terms under which poetry and language survive extermination: "des poètes aux gestes lents / des souffrances dans la lettre / la poussière veut renaître" (out of slowly gesturing poets / out of the pain in the letter / dust wants to be reborn).[51] In another poem,

Cayrol writes of the poet that, "il revient de si loin il brûle encore" (he comes back from so far away he is still burning),[52] and so hot are his "flames" that "aucune main ne peut s'en approcher" (no hand can come near him).[53] Critics have rightly taken the scenario of *Night and Fog* to task for mentioning the word "Jewish" but once. Nonetheless, this thematic of "flame," "burning," and "dust" coinciding with the poet's body suggests an internalization or corporeal introjection of the by-products of the crematory ovens in which mostly Jewish victims were killed. Is this form of internalization ethical or traumatic, and does it carry over to the cinepoetics of the narration in *Night and Fog?* I will try to answer these questions by closely reading the film script together with two essays of Cayrol: "From Death to Life," a 1949 reflection on trauma's warping of the sensorium and of aesthetics, and *Le Droit de Regard* (The right of inspection), coauthored with Claude Durand in 1963.

Cayrol's 1949 essay, "De la mort à la vie" (From death to life), examines how posttraumatic experience opens a new sensorium and a new organization of perception that can meld with—and find aesthetic resonances in—interplays of writing and cinema.[54] Cayrol's radical account provides a complex existential phenomenology of the trauma survivor's lived experience. It begins in familiar territory with the survivor's solitude[55] and sense of subpersonhood[56] caused by a dissociated state of half-life[57] stemming from having "exhausted in the camp all the possibilities of dying."[58] In this postmortem living, the unsteady world out of focus[59] does not cohere[60] and is traversed with phobias, violent bursts of anger, rage, and fear.[61] The survivor can follow no existential project,[62] needs others but fears polluting them,[63] since he considers his own affection and eroticism as parasitic,[64] having essentially let others down by surviving.[65]

While fitting general accounts of PTSD in accord with trauma theory,[66] these symptoms are not approached as abnormal by Cayrol, since he sees no possible return to normalcy. They amount instead to a new reality, which Cayrol calls a "Lazarean milieu,"[67] and is not just individual since it has problematically seeped within "the European and even the world psyche."[68] This milieu reshapes the sensorium of art, informing for instance a "Lazarean painting" consisting of "the constant repetition of the same formulae, a hypnotic state of forms and volumes, color tension, and the panic world of objects"[69] that evokes artists such as Christian Dotremont and George Dubuffet. Thus rather than a crisis of representation, the sensibility informed by survival and for which "the emotional shock remains more powerful than ever,"[70] is properly a transfiguration of *aisthesis*, the sensory domain as well as the domain of artistic perception.

The new "Lazarean work"[71] that emerges out of the blunting of the logos in experience finds homeopathic resonances in cinema. Cayrol's descriptions seem indeed to imply an uncontrollable cinematic gaze:

> . . . beings, landscapes present themselves as if 'veiled' like a photographic plate . . . [The survivor] does not know how to 'frame,' he does not succeed in shooting them under the right lighting.[72]

> A face infinitely multiplies within the survivor's gaze. His reflexes having been annihilated [the survivor] cannot choose one *instant* in the face; its transformation is unstoppable and illogical.[73]

In focusing on the face, the mobility of shots and the new power emanating from objects and landscapes within posttraumatic perception, Cayrol intriguingly echoes Epstein's articulation of *photogénie* as similarly focused on faces and objects rendered sentient by the apparatus:

> Since we have returned, the survivor muses—who has found his face, who has been capable of reentering his own features, who has not undergone operations of the face?[74]

> The point is not to express the truth of an action or feeling, but rather to draw around such action or such feeling an *aura*, to bestow on them an unimaginable luster, the resonance of crystal whose ring would be prolonged for pleasure.[75]

> . . . this is why the Lazarean hero seems surrounded by a diffuse light, a kind of halo which makes him appear more distant than he is. Reality as a whole becomes iridescent around his face.[76]

> . . . objects which are a part of his fragile patrimony have a presence, which often the living do not have for him. . . . The world of objects thus plays an attentive and detailed role in the Lazarean novel. It has its duration, its affect, its passions, its reticence and, in the midst of solitude, it might become the way out, the opening toward the world of others, its 'eye.'[77]

I quote at length because the convergences are so strong that it retrospectively raises the possibility that the entire photogénie movement may well partake of the Lazarean aesthetics of survivorship. In both Lazarean vision and photogénie, faces become iridescent and new, the gaze closes in on the face as space relations are altered, and objects appear to absorb an excess of human qualities. Surface stylistic differences exist—photogénie seems more eroticized, the Lazarean novel seems more angst-ridden—but the overall relation to a sensorium marked by the signal possibilities of cinema contemporary to it and in the wake of collective trauma appears to be the same.

In the 1963 book *Le Droit de regard*—whose *bandeau publicitaire* argues "For an ars poetica of cinema"—Cayrol and Durand directly link Lazarean aisthesis to the encounter between poetry, cinema and history. "We are," they write, "like beings excluded from the simple ability to feel, to hear, to taste, to transmit or to have access [to the real]," and this state of "victims of a disaster in body and soul" (*sinistrés de corps et d'âme*) is the situation of "the generation of the Spanish civil war, of the concentration camps, of the Algerian war."[78] It is this state of "survivorship" (*survivance*),[79] Cayrol and Durand assert, that the new cinema such as Agnès Varda's *Cléo de 5 à 7* addresses.[80] Such works reprocess trauma via the Lazarean aisthesis by recognizing the new order of imagination—the imaginary—for which cinema is foundational: "The imagination could thus be defined as the perception or apprehension of the real through this parallel universe submitted to it by cinema, and whose reading cadence (the rhythm of montage) would no longer be the time of seeing one image, too quickly, but the *time of vision* necessary to double up this image."[81] This crucial doubling up, similar to that which we encountered in Cocteau, echoes the "doubling of the Lazarean being" that forced him "to live on two distinct planes nonetheless connected through an invisible thread."[82] Cayrol and Durand intimate that a new cinema allowing spectators to deploy their cinematic imaginary through or besides the actual images has the potential to engage and reconfigure trauma, then no longer conceptualized only through dysfunction. This parallel or virtual work that cinema might do has the poem as model: "Cinema can reorganize this fragmented perception that we have of our world into a homogenous whole that is invented, tightly held together, and that would find again the coherence of the poem."[83] In contradistinction with Merleau-Ponty's invocation of poetry's rhetoric of forcible holism, however, Cayrol and Durand insist on a form of coherence distinct from the politically suspicious "totalscope"[84] of narrative commercial cinema. What they call for is a freer relation between images and language, indeed the undoing of the fascinating hold of cinematic images: "Language never ceases to be a combatant: from the moment someone speaks, he engages the film. Only speech can reactualize a situation. Text must be given back its leading role, which is not to explicate or repeat, but to be free speech, freeing images from detention. Speech is hence *in exile* with respect to images."[85] The Lazarean condition clearly echoes in the word "detention," and the cinema they envisage exploits the gap or better, the *discrepancy* between images and text. At the same time, the poetic language that "doubles up" the image is not the traditional, sovereign poetry, but poetry from the "parallel universe" of cinematic imagination. It is cinepoetic.

That cinepoetic discrepancy of Cayrol's posttraumatic aisthesis invites us to alter accounts of *Night and Fog* such as Hirsch's by looking closely at the work of the text. According to Hirsch, the opening sequence of the film functions as a liminal "trap": it brings the viewer into the camp via a tracking shot of a countryside abruptly showing the same countryside but from behind the barbwire. The text, however, "free[s] images from detention" by underlining the trap through anaphora:

> Même un paysage tranquille; même une prairie avec des vols de corbeaux, des moissons et des feux d'herbes; même une route où passent des voitures, des paysans, des couples; même un village pour vacances, avec une foire et un clocher, peuvent conduire tout simplement à un camp de concentration.
>
> [Even a peaceful landscape, even a field with flying crows, harvests, and burning hay, even a road where cars, peasants, and couples pass by, even a vacation village with a fair and a steeple, may casually lead to a concentration camp.][86]

The anaphora plays a dual role here. Because its rhythm is hypnotic, it mimetically pulls the viewer into the sequence. The French text reinforces this anaphoric effect with words beginning with the plosive /p/: "paysage," "prairie," "passent," "paysans," the awkward "pour vacances," (instead of "de vacances") "peuvent," contrasting with the more deceptive series in /k/: "corbeaux," "couples," "clocher," "conduire," "camp." But this didactic gesture also prepares and deflects the shock of shifting from outside to inside the camp: it works more as a Brechtian device of distanciation than identification. One paragraph later, as Hirsch indicates, Cayrol mentions the "camera" and "our [step]" resounding in the camp, undoing the illusion of a transparent observer. For Hirsch this serves to "open [spectators] to the traumatizing potential of the images without having to resort to the defenses of numbing, denial, or premature mastery."[87] But Cayrol's emphasis on the corporeal location in the camp of the voice that speaks and especially of the crew that films, may serve the exact opposite purpose: to mobilize an ethical imagination. Cayrol's text aims to evince sensorial, perceptual, and intersubjective reactions in the spectator alternatively forcing and *forestalling* identification with the locus of images. That oscillation is crucial. Narrated by the distinctively heady voice of Michel Bouquet, softly upbeat in its melody, Cayrol's text precludes a stable mimetic relation with the vicarious trauma the shots and montage tend to elicit. Not only does the text work independently of images, it often goes against their pathos, breaking their spell with irony, *affirming* rather than *dramatizing* the corporeal practices of detention that they index.[88] The subtle but almost constant rift between the filmic images and the text (as well as between them and the music) generates less a cognitive crisis than a *surplus* of experience. This surplus partakes of the inherent virtuality of cinepoetics which uses text to remain "beneath not beyond images" to cite Artaud. "In a short film at least, speech does not have to be set to the time of the images. It brings a human time, the order or the disorder of memory," Cayrol and Durand write.[89] Cayrol's script is not pursuing a strategy of crisis making or confrontation with the unimaginable: it deftly modulates the distance and the cognitive-affective place from which spectators "focus" their attention, ever so slightly pushing and pulling spectators in and out of the images, keeping their framework of reception unstable and incomplete.

By alternating between various rhetorical voices—ironic pastoral, mock documentary, flat historical, accusatory, lyrical, pedagogic, and militant—the commentary keeps spectators aloft in the discursive space, preventing the arrest of fascinated shock, emphasizing the "human time" of viewing through the parallel universe the text elicits against the images. At times, the syntax Cayrol uses closely follows some of Epstein's cinepoetic categories such as schematism: "Closed and locked trains, the deported piled a hundred per wagon, neither daylight nor night, hunger, thirst, asphyxia, madness."[90] The parallel construction acts here as a substitute edit of short clauses standing for missing or impossible or indeed overly traumatic film fragments. In so doing, the project of *Night and Fog* reveals itself to be the diverting of visual experience away from fascination, and toward memory and the imaginary, though the text—and the voice and music.[91]

It is worth noting that the sentence cited above has no main verb and thus no grammatical subject. The ethical imaginary of *Night and Fog* results in large part from unstable pronominal shifts between detainees, the filmmaking crew and viewers. Before the internees and victims are referred to, necessitating a problematic "they,"[92] Cayrol points to "our [steps]."[93] Diegetically, the steps might be those of the film crew. Yet Cayrol was not among them; he was, however, among the detainees. In the voice-over, the "our" is also that of viewers imaginarily stepping into the camp. This unstable identification is key to eschewing any preordained position that might render the victims of the Shoah as others—as "they." At the same time, Cayrol's personalization of the victims—"Burger, German worker, Stern, Jewish student of Amsterdam, Schmulzki, retailer in Cracow, Annette, high school student in Bordeaux"[94]—combats the depersonalizing aim of extermination camps, and allows for multiple viewer identification: German, French, Polish, men, women, Jews, non-Jews, young and old. Cayrol suspends a radical differentiation between "them" and "us" as persons, but also as noncontemporaries, yet without undermining the historical logic that led to the creation of the camps and the "final solution."

While allowing for such partial and fleeting identifications, Cayrol is careful to follow the historical sequencing that led to extermination, and from which nonsurvivor viewers are de facto excluded. I disagree here with Hirsch's association of *Night and Fog* with the New Novel as forming a "new historiography" of "hypersubjective and fragmented inscriptions of time."[95] For, although the script uses deictics to render the distance between viewers and victims porous, the linear temporality of internment is strictly respected. After mentioning the creation of the camps in 1933,[96] Cayrol crosscuts between three linear progressions: first, the historical development of extermination policies, second, the fate of prisoners from capture to gassing or survival, and third, our filmic tour of a camp today, going from outside to inside and following its floor plan all the way to the ovens. What stitches these heterochronic sequences together is both the movement of pronouns and an ethics of history.

After the initial "our," a seemingly less personal "*on* (both 'we' and 'one')" walks the tracks into the camp.[97] Inside, the "on" first becomes the depersonalized victim, "the humiliated person"[98] who is introduced to the rules of the camp requiring a three meter distance between the S.S. and the prisoners: "*On lui parle à trois mètres,*"[99] the French reads, and the "*on*" should be translated all at once as "they," "one," and "we." Hence while the "*nous*" immediately reappears didactically—"This reality of the camps . . . it is in vain that we, in turn [*à notre tour, nous*], try to uncover its remnants"[100]—the "*on*" of the camp returns in counterpoint: "[*on*] slept three in a bunk." Rather than for some modernist formalism, Cayrol harnesses pronominal shifts as an ethics, an affirmation of intersubjectivity and solidarity above all else. His 1949 text had clearly spelled out the fundamental question of this ethics: "What is the meaning of the death of the other?"[101]

The cinepoetics of Cayrol transforms the "*on*" into an ethical pronoun of substitution that discloses the virtual film that constantly doubles up the emptiness of *Night and Fog*'s shots where all we see is the past erased—images without people. Describing a night in the camps, Cayrol begins with the effort required so that "*on*" today "imagine this night interrupted with shouts."[102] In the very next sentence, in the morning, the "we"-"*on*" has imperceptibly become the "*on*"-"they" of victims: "Woken with sticks, *on* scramble, *on* look for *our* stolen stuff."[103] As pronoun of substitutability between first- and third-person, "on" serves to confront the range of our possible actions as spectators. We might be the "*on*" that finds shreds of humanity where it is eclipsed: "*On* gives up some of one's food. *On* creates networks of support."[104] But "*on*" can equally shift into the architects of the final solution: "*On* orders boxes of zyklon gas."[105] "*On*" even shifts in the same sentence from victims, to writer/spectator, to perpetrator: "With the bodies . . . but *on* can no longer say anything . . . with the bodies *on* wants to make soap."[106] By contrast, Cayrol usually reserves the "*nous*" for us, today, alive, tempted with political indecision that may lead to further genocides. In the penultimate paragraph Cayrol suggests that this smug "*nous*" harbors actors of the "final solution" both in actuality and in potentiality.

While Cayrol's Lazarean text points to the failure of language alone in providing an account of the horror of the Nazi killing factories, *Night and Fog* does not expose traumatic images in order to butt against the unrepresentable or unimaginable. It mobilizes a cinepoetics of discrepancy between images and text in order to document evidence of extermination while also creating an ethical imperative to imagine—in the dual sense of envisioning what took place in undocumented History, and folding any excess into a community (merely symbolized by the allied arts of the film) capable of envisaging a future without genocide. Poetry alone, or cinema alone are incapable of addressing the Lazarean condition. In this, Adorno agreed with Cayrol when, in 1966, the former amended his statement on poetry after Auschwitz:

> . . . it may have been wrong to say that after Auschwitz you could no longer write poems. But it is not wrong to raise the less cultural question whether after Auschwitz you can go on living—especially whether one who escaped by accident, one who by rights should have been killed, may go on living . . . his own existence since has been *imaginary*, an emanation of the insane wish of a man killed twenty years earlier.[107]

Adorno's shifts in referents—from poets to everyone then on to "one" (the survivor) to "his" (referring to Adorno himself)—underline the same ethical fluidity as Cayrol's. Postwar cinepoetry devolves from this new mode of "imaginary" existence that alters the autonomy of language in no small part because of the resonances between survivorship and cinema.

The post–World War I cinepoetics of Cendrars and Epstein appealed to cinema's homeopathy for rebooting poetic language toward utopia. Cayrol's cinepoetics, belonging to the ethos of high reconstruction and the looming shadow of the Algerian war, is far less sanguine. In spite of its affirmation of the efficacy of language and poetry, the text of *Night and Fog* transfigures some of Epstein's aesthetic categories of cinepoetic language, notably those of schematism, thought-association, and proximity. Cayrol's description of the camps develops a new figure of rhetoric, which, following Deleuze, we might call the "x-whatever." For Deleuze, cinema's ubiquitous gaze—specifically that of Neorealist films in the immediate postwar—enacts a time-image of "any-space-whatever," that is, shots unmoored from narration in locales not introduced through continuity editing. A camp, for Cayrol, is located in any-site-whatever and detains anyone-whatever.[108] There is neither grid, nor narrative, nor any reference point: indexical singularity—here, now, this woman, my life—has vanished into the *negative schematism* of anything-whatever. This regime contaminates everything including language. Hence rules are arbitrary, maxims are random,[109] and in factories cheerfully bearing women's first names, forced female laborers in fact die.[110] A "spoonful," which is the very definition of next to nothing, becomes life itself, one more day of survival. The built world and objects also undergo a complete inversion into the "x-whatever." A death camp includes a zoo;[111] hospitals manufacture death; bandaging becomes food.[112] The aesthetics of proximity (close-up) and thought-association of Epstein have become the *negative proximity* to miniature foods and objects, while faces of survivors are the antithesis to the enhanced photogénie of faces in close-up. As for the marvel of thought-association it has become the nightmare of *free association-whatever.* All these features, derived from the concentrationary aporia, may be seen as informing the whole range of post–World War II cinepoetry in very direct ways.

CINE-LETTRISM: A JEWISH AVANT-GARDE AFTER THE SHOAH

At the very dawn of Liberation and following a different set of concerns, Isidore Isou and the group of lettrists had devised a radical approach to poetry and cinema starting from a situation very similar to the "x-whatever" of Cayrol's essay on the camps. In more radical ways than Cayrol, they tried transmuting the Lazarean condition which, for their new generation—and especially those among them who were Jewish—was simply an unacceptable legacy.

Literary criticism at large has remained indifferent to lettrism. Although he single-handedly restarted the poetry avant-garde in the postwar, Jean-Isidore Isou (pseudonym of Isidore Goldstein) has largely remained a footnote in the history of his disciple Guy Debord's movement: Situationism. Lettrism was the first major alternative to Surrealism, it directly informed Situationism (after all, originally named *L'Internationale lettriste*), COBRA, and postwar concrete and sound poetry. A recent and otherwise excellent book by Tom McDonough on Debord's wake, subtitled "Reinventing the Language of Contestation in Postwar France, 1945–1968," does not even mention Isou once, although his 1949 book *Traité d'économie nucléaire, le soulèvement de la jeunesse* (Treatise of nuclear economy: On youth uprising), was the first clear inkling of what culminated in the May 1968 student revolt that is the focus of McDonough's book.[113] Debord himself, writing with Gil Wolman after their 1952 break with Isou, paid homage to lettrism's "optimism of invention" standing as a "refusal" to the postwar status quo, especially through its "affirmation going beyond refusal."[114] The two dissident lettrists specify the three exemplary means that Isou and his friend Maurice Lemaître invented: "poetry reduced to letters, metagraphic narratives, cinema without images."[115] All three forms, I argue, arose as an anamnesis of interwar cinepoetry which Isou and Lemaître were very much aware of and which lettrism, in central ways, tried to reinvent otherwise. Symptomatically, Isou's break with Debord resulted from a profound disagreement over the central pseudoheroic figure of interwar cinepoetry: Charlie Chaplin.[116]

The forceful irruption of Isidore Isou upon the cultural Parisian scene in 1946 has been recounted by Jean-Paul Curtay and Greil Marcus.[117] A Jewish refugee from Rumania born Isidore Goldstein in 1925, Isou arrived in Paris in 1945 with a suitcase full of manuscripts written between 1942 and 1944. Unable to interest Gallimard in his writings, Isou and his friend Gabriel Pomerand crashed a presentation by Michel Leiris of a Tzara play in 1946, shouting that they wanted lettrist poetry not warmed-over Dada. After the newspapers reported on the new "trend" (of which no one had ever heard), Gallimard offered to publish his theoretical essay, *Introduction à une nouvelle poésie et une nouvelle musique* (Introduction to a new poetry and a new music) (which includes twenty lettrist poems and one "symphony") together with an autobiographical novel entitled *L'Agrégation d'un nom et d'un messie* (Aggregation of a name and a messiah), both coming out in 1947. This rather meteoric rise to fame recalls that of Dada in many respects. Tristan Tzara too was an exiled Rumanian Jew (pseudonym of Samuel Rosenstock), and when he and Breton decided to make a splash in 1919 they contrived a show whose headline was the purported "conversion" to Dadaism of none other than Charlie Chaplin. Breton's leveraging of scandal to acquire cultural capital was the clear model for Isou—even though his animosity toward Breton prevented him from ever acknowledging this debt.

Isou's lettrism rested on a rather simple cyclical view of history, placing the poetics of the letter at the apex of a century of preoccupations by poets with different parts of speech, and naming Isou himself as messiah bringing about this epochal change. Let us examine the curious rationales at play behind these two ideas. The main philosophical impetus behind lettrism is that *creation* drives humanity, rather than sex (Freud), death (Heidegger), or dialectical materialism (Marx). Creation has two major poles or tendencies: "*amplique*" (a neologism) and "*ciselant*," two terms that may be rendered as "amplific" and "chiseling." In the amplific phase, new creations abound and multiply quickly around a productive and collective new sensibility (for example, romanticism). In the chiseling phase, makers refine the amplific, developing subtle variations: "The prototypes of the amplific were lyrical poets with a tumultuous breath and a respiration of ground-shaking volume. The chiseling poets show aspects of an inspiration by nuance."[118] Isou underlines with contrasting breathing metaphors the "centrifugal" expansiveness of the amplific and the "centripetal" contraction of the chiseling.[119] Hugo, on the one hand, Mallarmé, on the other. While the two tendencies mix, the macroscopic history of poetry is amplific "from Homer to Hugo" with a focus on the "contents" of the poem, and becomes chiseling from Baudelaire to Isou, with more attention spent on the "means of expression" of poetry.[120] Isou, however, speaking of himself in the messianic third person, signals a restart of the amplific: "Evolving along the deepening of poetry, traveling through the necessary narrowing of the material, *the poem* (Baudelaire), *the sentence* (Verlaine) and its destruction (Rimbaud), *the word* (Mallarmé) and its devaluation (Tzara), Isidore Isou is bringing THE LETTER."[121] Maurice Lemaître seconds the importance of Mallarmé's view of language for lettrism: "If Mallarmé was able to tell Degas 'Poetry is not made with ideas but with words,' we must be able to launch our motto by paraphrasing the latter: poetry is not made with words, but with letters."[122]

This focus on the letter leads in several directions. Since lettrism does not appear at first to be animated by an overarching program or social exigency, it is hard to shake the impression that the self-promotion of lettrism amounts to a purely artificial form of vanguardism: after the defiguration of the word, well, now the letter. Automatic innovation. But we might point to the nuclear age as powerfully foregrounding the constituents of matter (atoms, particles) to explain why poets deepened their attention to the constituents of speech, in France and elsewhere, if we think of Robert Ducan's attention to the color of vowels or Charles Olson's theory of projective verse.[123] In this regard, lettrism announces the critical turn toward the signifier that became synonymous with French theory in the 1960s. One crucial difference between lettrism and Derrida's 1963 affirmation of *différance* (a difference of one silent letter with "*différence*") is lettrism's emphasis on the "live display" of poems[124]—whether through readings or in association with music, or as "pictorial vision" in Lemaître's *metagraphics*, a mixture of letter art, body art, and visual poetry. Lettrists favored the contingent process of production and communication in the present, in clear contrast to Derrida's theoretical critique of phono-centrism and presence.

The pseudonym Isou /IZU/ deftly combines the French onomatopeic youth movement, zazou /ZAZU/, with the Romanian word for Jesus, Isus /IZUS/. This very fusion of words points the cult of the letter in lettrism toward the syncretism of the Greek Gematria and the Jewish Kabbalah, both of which invest individual letters with a demiurgic power. Isou's messianism makes such syncretism explicit:

> . . . Christianity was at its beginning a sect within a religion, later to become a true religion, standing alone, independent. To play within poetry the role played by Jesus within Judaism, that is the intention of Isou, that is, to break a branch off and make it into a tree. Isouism, the Christian form of poetic Judaism.[125]

This Judeo-Christian syncretism is essential to understanding the genesis of the movement. For instance, Marcus characterizes lettrism as "a secret utopia accessible to anyone capable of recognizing it," and he illustrates his comment with the following passage from Gabriel Pomerand's 1950 book *Saint ghetto des prêts* (Saint ghetto of the loans; a play on homophones prés/prêts): "Saint germain des prés is a ghetto. Everyone there wears a yellow star over his heart . . . Saint germain des prés is a mirror of heaven."[126] Marcus does not gloss this provocative excerpt, nor does he mention that Pomerand and Isou are Jewish or that one of the practices of the Zazous of Saint-Germain-des-Prés in wartime was to wear a yellow star, often with the word "Zazou" printed in the middle.[127] Lettrism itself sprung out from the chance encounter of Isou with Pomerand in 1945 in a canteen for Jewish refugee orphans: Pomerand's mother had been deported to Auschwitz.[128] Although Isou progressively elided Judaic aspects of the movement as non-Jews joined in, another Jew, Maurice Lemaître (pseudonym of Moïse Bismuth), became central to the group in 1949. Lemaître was a fifteen-year-old yellow-star wearer the day of the *Rafle du Vél d'hiv*, when the French police rounded up thirty thousand Jews in Paris. By pure luck (he was in the bathroom), he was not picked up. Alain-Alcide Sudre considers that that event shaped a good deal of Lemaître's lettrism.[129] In his autobiographical novel *L'Agrégation d'un nom et d'un messie*, Isou indicates that to find his way through war-torn Europe from Rumania to Paris, he was obliged "to pass" as a survivor from Auschwitz. He also states that his hometown, Botosani, suffered a pogrom during which Jewish properties were attacked and burned, his parent's apartment being spared only because it was located atop a pharmacy owned by a non-Jew.

The "aggregation" in Isou's title should be read as contrasting with, even retorting to, the defensive call of "integration" and "assimilation" of Jews in postwar Europe as a solution to what Sartre termed "the Jewish Question." Isou's novel argues for a different and *affirmative* Jewish embodiment and persona exemplified by Isou himself:

> . . . the man aggregated in this novel is ALIVE, REAL.
>
> . . .
>
> From this kind of man ([Robespierre, Casanova, Amiel, Alexander the Great, Socrates, Saint-Just, Cellini, Pico della Mirandola]), the author seeks inspiration while trying to create Isou, an example of the Successful-Complete man. A balanced hero, sure of his own possibilities of representation.
>
> . . .
>
> A value of vitality, of a living being, and not of a phantasm molded by the imagination, allows this integration.[130]

This emphasis on the question of self-creation must be replaced in the traumatic context of survival among a European Jewish generation barely out of its teens. Isidore Goldstein, a central European Jew who managed to cross Europe in 1945 and elude the Shoah, chose for himself another persona named Jean-Isidore Isou who affirms his right to exist by reconstructing a kind of historical necessity for his being and survival. The novel's preface is titled: "For the accumulation of a perfect, successful, and living persona [*personnage . . . vivant*]."[131] There is something uncanny and tragic, but also immensely transgressive in a way that may elude our historical consciousness after the creation of the state of Israel, about a Jewish refugee arriving in France in 1945, untouched by the Shoah, and claiming vociferously a new "persona" endowed with the right to be both "alive" and "successful." It is as if a living and self-affirmed Jew was not only an exception in post-1945 Europe, but somehow an aberration and an impossibility. A section title in the novel elucidates Isou's project of enacting "the Christian form of poetic Judaism," as partly Jewish militancy and partly grandstanding chutzpah. It is titled:

> Theoretical Carcass V
> Notes Toward the Judeification of France
> Bills to Be Posted on Parisian Streets 1947[132]

To Sartre's well-intentioned *Anti-Semite and Jew* (1946), aiming to erase anti-Semitism by emptying Jewishness of any positive content in the name of a classless society that erases all distinctions, Isou retorts that Sartre's book still functions in the logic of the "Ghetto . . . to which, one day, others will come to set fire, under other (this time, incendiary!) pretexts."[133] For Isou, the proper answer to the deportation of French Jews should not be a reinforcement of the (Gentile) notion that Jews are deviations from an existential norm, which would only prepare the next genocide. "You mumble to each other 'they will no longer dare!' . . . But already they are egging on the carnage, they are preparing the great slaughterhouses,"[134] Isou writes, addressing Jews who accepted Sartre's argument—such as Claude Lanzmann in the 1950s.[135] Instead, and much more radically, Isou inverts Sartre's dissolution of Jewishness by calling for the "judeification of France": "I am countering, in France, all of Catholic literature and philosophy beginning with Joinville and ending in Péguy, Maritain, Claudel, with a Judaic literature and philosophy."[136] There is certainly a troubling automatism in such gestures of supremacy. By calling for a "lettrist dictatorship"[137] and the judeification of France, and even proposing to post bills to this effect, Isou mimics troublingly in negative Vichy's attempt at purging Jewishness from France. Moreover, by affirming a "successful-complete man" who is Jewish, Isou echoes Alexandre Kojève's deliriously influential lectures on Hegel (published in 1947 at Gallimard by Raymond Queneau) heralding "the end of the historical evolution of Man" brought about by the completion of Euro-Christian philosophical thought. Even by substituting Judaism to Kojève's Euro-Christianity, Isou ends up emulating Kojève's posthistorical fantasy:

> And thus Judaism will naturally impose itself—to France and the World—like a fundamental given of consciousness, like the last curve of accomplishment.
>
> And the reign of Jews, of all men being Jews, will be realized—according to the ancient prescriptions purified—into a concrete and real art.[138]

Such an apology for Jewishness, at times sarcastic, at other times dead serious—Isou speaks of "the courage I have learned among Zionists"[139]—confirms that lettrism cannot be severed from the immediate wake of the Shoah. The youthful narcissism and outrageous posturing that Isou and Lemaître displayed was most likely a strategy for repudiating survivor's guilt and affirming the right to be young, creative, Jewish, and alive in post-Shoah Europe. Among Isou's early poems, two address the Shoah directly: "Shouts For 5,000,000 Slaughtered Jews," and "The War," a polyvocal poem in four movements. Both poems follow Isou's principles in doing away with syntax and focusing on the texture of words, the *spoken letters* that make them come alive as sonorous bodies in the intersubjective space of the present. Lettrism claims to invent a transnational metalanguage[140] by phonetically hybridizing words of different languages, as in this excerpt from "Shouts For 5,000,000 Slaughtered Jews":

crescendo jusqu'au hurlement (crescendo all the way to a howl)
ioudn VEÌNÌN boudn loudn KLEININ
schoudn guéinîn FAIERE guysn REININ
taîère leînin schpisn zoudn heînin
IOUDN IOUDN schmisn moundn meînin[141]

We can detect Germanic words such as KLEININ=kleinen, "small," REININ=reinen, "pure," next to IOUDN=Juden, "Jews." Other possible references include Russian (leînin=Lenin?), perhaps English (FAIERE=fire?) and French (taîère=tailleur), as well as Yiddish (schpisn; schmisn). Obliquely, the European diaspora is under the mounting threat of a pogrom ("Juden! Juden!") through racist connotations in words like "pure" and "tailor."[142] The resonance of single words that have become monstrously hypersignifying takes the place of narrative: "GUERINGUE" (Göring); "Auschwitz – schwitz – schwitz."[143] Portions of this poem are inserted within the longer symphonic "The War" that bursts with similar hyperwords—"HAÏL HITLER";[144] "WARSCHAOU";[145] SALJUIF / SALE JUIF / PARIII."[146] Only by reading aloud do certain words or connections appear. Hence in "Shouts" we read:

Mathousenne
MOGHILOW!
MOGHILOOW!
Galgal – Raîwensguergue[147]

The references to the concentration camps of Mathausen and Moghilow (or Mogilev, in Transnitria, Eastern Romania, where the first gassing by automotive exhaust took place in 1941) are clear. Behind "Raîwensguergue" we might read Ravensbrück as well—the "ravens' bridge" (Rabensbrück) transformed into a "raven's maw." The presence of the Hebrew word "galgal" ("wheel/chariot") in this series poses a problem, until we note the phonetic connection between Moghilow and Hebrew "megillah," a scroll, which shares the same root ("galal," something round or turning) as "galgal," and may have suggested the reduplicated Romance-sounding "guergue" ("maw, throat," as in Gargantua). The absence of syntax invites such contamination of layered meaning through phonetic similarities precisely at the level of letters.

Isou explains that "the goal of lettrist poetry is to realize new broadcasts [*émissions*] and substances for other creations," and he specifies that "Isouian creation must be Mallarméan," that is, rest upon the "edifying construction of a given material."[148] When Isou theorizes this "material" dimension of lettrism he refers to Mallarmé's dual attention to poetry's rhythm in time (music) and in space (the page), and also insists on the "virtuality" or "potentiality" of lettrist poetics: "An utterance is a treasure bearing characteristic mirrors open to all virtualities."[149] It is no surprise then that, like Canudo synthesizing the arts and time and the arts of space through film, Isou should gravitate toward cinema as a model. He ends the preface to his poem "La Guerre, première symphonie lettriste" (The war, first lettric symphony), with the following plea: "One must feel in front of "The War" as in front of the first cinematographic reels of the Lumière Brothers, of Marey or of Méliès. And already recognize what later will be carried under the name of an Eisenstein, a Carné, a Wyler."[150] Cinema is not just a metaphor here, but an imaginary framework toward which lettrists would gradually turn in order to revive the "palpable flesh" of words. By insisting that the letter "is conscious of itself,"[151] lettrists hoped to inject cinema's automorphosis into the very materiality of poetic language—both visually and orally—in order to make language consubstantial with reality again. Although they invented their own mode of cinepoetry, this dream of the automorphic letter fully motivated (signifier=signified) reprises the cinepoetics of Mallarmé and Saint-Pol-Roux, as well as the dream of Kabbalists such as twelfth-century Abraham Abulafia for whom letters could directly reshape the real.

In 1950, consequently, Isou began the ad hoc shooting of a movie, *Traité de bave et d'éternité* (Treatise of spittle and eternity), which became the talk of the 1951 Cannes Film Festival where it premiered.[152] As with poetry, his aim was to decompose cinema into its basic constituents, and to do so he made use of five techniques. First, the very stuff of the film is culled from the dead: rushes found in the garbage of labs and of the Ministry of War's Services cinématographiques, found footage, and random leaders recycled. Isou's dearth of financial means was total—more so than Italian neorealist and New Wave filmmakers—and necessity became an aesthetic component. Second, Isou invents "the chiseled image" (*l'image ciselée*) by inscribing some of the frames by hand with scratches, drawings, graffito, and invented letters (Figure 33). For Devaux this pioneering "palimpsest-cinema"

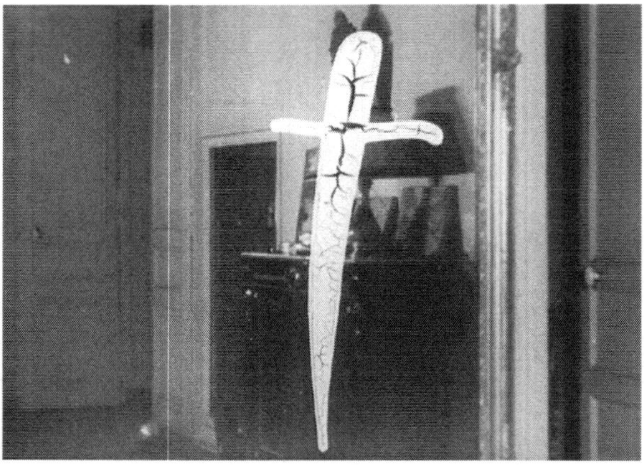

Figure 33. Lettrism on film: an invented "letter" scratched on the film itself by Isou, *Traité de bave et d'éternité* (1951).

complicates the preeminence of writing by "overlaying . . . several layers of 'graphein.'"[153] Third, the editing desynchronizes the image- and soundtrack, making sound autonomous, and Isou calls this "montage discrépant" (discrepant editing). On a 1951 poster announcing a projection of the film, he claims to show "a scenario that introduces the imaginary [*l'imaginaire*] to cinema. We say: 'Daniel turned around' and we don't see him turn around; we systematically act against photography, within the invisible."[154] Such discrepancy renders systematic the gaps between the image track and the sound track that Artaud and Cayrol and Durand had tried theorizing. Fourth, there is no narrative, apart from vignettes of generic love stories in the soundtrack about a certain Daniel, while we see mostly Isou walking the streets of Saint-Germain. No clear boundaries exist between the documentary and the fictive, or the diegetic and extradiegetic: voices speak about the film as if retrospectively; credits play in the middle; segments are repeated; photos of the likes of Cendrars and Cocteau appear randomly; lettrist poems and choruses interrupt the voice-overs, and so on. Finally, during the Cannes showing, because he had had no time to edit the film beyond the first part, after a few minutes the screen became blank, then the projector light was turned off, so spectators remained in pitch darkness while Isou let the soundtrack roll. Devaux recounts the scandalized reactions of some of the critics and spectators, while others were enthralled, notably a seventeen-year-old named Guy-Ernest Debord (who is often credited with the blank screen innovation for his 1952 *Howling in Favor of Sade*). The blank screen marks cinepoetry since Mallarmé onward, especially for Aragon, who writes that the blank screen could generate as a provocation "the purity that attract spittle [*crachat*]."[155]

But Isou's cinema of the "imaginary" straddling writing and film is more than provocation: by superimposing filmic images with lettrist signs it reincorporates language, *literally reprojecting it onto* the new reality of postwar Paris. In this, Isou expanded post–World War I cinepoetry in a parallel yet new direction. It is noteworthy that his 1953 essay "Esthétique du cinéma" (Esthetics of the cinema) shows great familiarity with most of the producers of interwar cinepoetry, and indeed with the very notion of cinepoetry. He conjectures for instance that, "If an Apollinaire or a Breton had wanted to make films, they would have been the René Clair and the Buñuel of cinema."[156] In a note on the same page, Isou refers to Desnos's scenario for *L'Etoile de mer* (1928), shot by Man Ray, and Artaud's scenario for *La Coquille et le clergyman* (1927), shot by Dulac. He also refers to fellow Rumanian Benjamin Fondane[157]—who used the term "ciné-poème" invented by Man Ray—as well as to theoreticians and cinepoets of French Impressionism: Gance (whose book *Prism* he cites);[158] Canudo;[159] Delluc;[160] Dulac;[161] and Epstein.[162] Commenting on his own "chiseling" of the film stock with marks that he calls "hypergraphic" or "metagraphic," as if *materially* "superimposing" poetry on film (as Epstein had suggested!), he articulates an explicit cinepoetic theory: "The chiseling will offer the world its Baudelaire, its Mallarmé, its Apollinaire, its Tzara, without mentioning its lettrists and metagraphists."[163] Cinema becomes a new medium of poetry not metaphorically—as in Cocteau's "poetry of cinema"—but literally, as a *new support for poetic inscriptions*: "The scenario that develops in and of itself without concerns for the image, discovers its original frame within the chiseling film. The beautiful and coherent sentences, through their inactive independence, manifest themselves in their primary cinematographic formula."[164] Isou's film aesthetics largely centers on the "*bande-parole*" (speech-track) or "*bande-scénario*" (script-track),[165] rather than on the image-track. Perhaps that inversion of the teleology of mediums is the most definitely cinepoetic aspect of lettrism: the chiseling of the film stock places the act of writing as such both *on* and *in* the automorphic images of cinema.

Together with his friend Maurice Lemaître, Isou went even farther in transforming cinema by regrafting writing on its apparatus. The occasion was Lemaître's 1952 book, *Le Film est déjà commencé?* (The film has already started?), which presented itself not as a "novelization" of the eponymous film which had come out the year before, but (as the back jacket states) as "the first attempt at breaking the normal frame of cinematographic exhibition."[166] The main section of the book is divided into three columns representing on facing pages the soundtrack in one full page (with twenty-six voices and voice-over reflections on the film), and on the facing page the corresponding image-track and events in the theater (Figure 34). The image-track contains found footage, scratches, leaders, painted frames, composite shots, and random messages. The "in-the-theater" column describes how the manager, the personnel, and actors organize a disruption that spills over from the lobby into the auditorium, where other actors playing spectators start another commotion. In their respective prefaces, Isou and Lemaître echo each other in announcing the evolution of cinema by redefining the cinematic spectacle as an apparatus involving not just the film, the screen, and the projector, but active spectators and the space of the auditorium, the personnel of the theater, modifications brought to the screen and the film stock, even written material associated with the film (the book is itself subtitled "Séance de cinéma" [A movie show]). Lemaître renames this expanded form of cinema "syncinema." Isou sees Lemaître's project as enacting "cinema's living aesthetic relief (expanded to its surroundings),"[167] so that it becomes "une plasto-prose tridimensionnelle" (a tridimensional plastic prose).[168] Such statements uncannily ring with echoes of Saint-Pol-Roux's living cinema and expanded screen which the lettrists, however, could not know at the time. Both Isou and Lemaître specifically argue in favor of a cinepoetic textuality. Lemaître writes, "For the first time in the history of cinema a film will be as interesting to *read* as to *see*."[169] In order to imagine the film, Lemaître suggests that the reader "refer back to the visual memory of preceding cinematographic works,"[170] which might point directly to Fondane's cine-poem (see the epigraph of Chapter 4). While both cinepoets explicitly vie with the famous triple screen Abel Gance invented for his Napoleon in 1927,[171] their expansion of cinema covers the entire field of what we mean today by cinema apparatus. Indeed, Lemaître was among the first to use the term "apparatus" in connection with cinema when he wrote of "the apparatus of the new screen" (*le dispositif du nouvel écran*).[172] Lemaître progressively transformed the cinema

Le film est déjà commencé?

Organisation d'une Séance de Cinéma

SON

NÉANT

> *Les diverses nuances avec lesquelles le son du film est* ***dit*** *n'ont pas été notées si elles ont été résolues dans le film lui-même.*
>
> *Le problème de la* ***voix*** *est trop complexe pour être abordé ici. Des comédiens sont devenus célèbres par leur voix, dans le film sonore. Alors que l'avènement du parlant en a réduit d'autres au chômage.*
>
> *Mais Lemaître, qui a horreur de sa voix, croit à l'indéfinie perfectibilité de l'homme, et améliore sans cesse celle-ci. Une telle création dans le* ***son*** *du cinéma ne peut que s'accompagner d'une création parallèle dans le domaine de l'****expression*** *de ce son.*

IMAGE

NÉANT

SALLE

Un écran portatif de couleur rose sera installé devant l'entrée du cinéma aux néons tous éteints, dès que la nuit se sera allongée sur le boulevard. Une heure avant la séance et jusqu'à celle-ci, un opérateur impassible y projettera des classiques du film : « Intolérance de Griffith », par exemple. Sur le trottoir, devant la salle seront écrits en lettres énormes, d'un blanc yaourt, les mots : *« Ici, à 20 h. 30, séance de cinéma »* avec une flèche dont la pointe sera dirigée vers la caisse. Au dessus de cette caisse, sur le fronton, une gigantesque affiche, sans aucune illustration, indiquera le titre du film : *« Le Film est déjà commencé »*. De chaque côté du hall d'entrée, sur les murs, des photos sous verre représenteront :

a) **Un baiser (gros plan), les vedettes important peu.**

On recouvrira l'image de motifs abstraits en mouvement... (p. 145)

(Négatif)

— 105 —

IMAGE

Néant

" Ce film est dédié à Jean Isidore Isou qui reste pour moi, envers et contre tous, celui qui viendra. "

Sept plans négatifs pris dans n'importe quel film.

SALLE

raient qu'à leur attirer des ennuis, sans leur donner de satisfaction d'ordre matériel.

Ils sortiront en discutant tandis que viendra sur la scène l'auteur du film. Maurice LEMAITRE commencera à lire une longue défense de son film, entrecoupé par les huées des figurants. L'opérateur de la salle, tenant dans ses mains de la pellicule en vrac, fera irruption à côté de l'auteur et, l'accusant d'avoir fait un film en contradiction avec ses propres idées, se mettra à déchirer cette pellicule. Un autre personnage, se présentant comme le producteur du film se précipitera sur lui, essayant de sauver le maximum de pellicule. Ils sortirons tous en criant.

Silence

Les figurants demanderont à grands cris qu'on éteigne la lumière, ce que l'on fera. Ils pousseront alors un "ah !" de satisfaction. On rallumera aussitôt cette lumière, accueillie par des hurlements. On n'en tiendra pas compte pendant un certain temps, puis on éteindra définitivement les lampes de la salle.

8

Figure 34. Two sets of facing pages from Maurice Lemaître, *Le Film est déjà commencé?* (1952), showing the three tracks corresponding to sound, image, and audience.

apparatus into a set of conceptual features that included little, and in some cases, no actual film material. He called these, "imaginary films," and in so doing reached from the cinema side the very outside edge of cinepoetry on the writing side. Both Isou and Lemaître, for financial and aesthetic reasons, turned to "hypergraphic" printed works that mix text, invented letters, drawings and photographs. In 1965, Lemaître published the book *Au-delà du déclic* (Beyond the shutter's click) as a work of "cine-hypergraphics"—a virtual film on paper, with words, hypersigns, photos and illustrations—and in 1970, he shot a film that shows nothing but the pages of that book, an innovation usually associated with Marcel Brodthaers.[173] One of the more recent works Lemaître published is the 2005 *Écran total, roman-film* (Total screen, film-novel), which harks back both to the cine-novels of the 1920s and 1930s, and to the notion of "total cinema" in the afterwar (Figure 35).

The third main lettrist, Gabriel Pomerand, was a true zazou: nomadic, semiasocial, and close to the underworld. In 1953, he codirected a documentary titled *La Peau du milieu* (The underworld's skin) on the tattoos of ex-cons and veterans in Parisian working-class neighborhoods. This establishes a direct connection between lettrism's hypergraphic body performances, the tattoos of the underworld, and the driving homology of cinepoetry /page⇔skin⇔screen/. In 1950, Pomerand published *Saint ghetto des prêts*, a series of forty-seven plates of black-and-white pictograms (*rébus*) with their equivalent in plain French on the facing page (Figure 36). Like Lemaître's *Au-delà du déclic* it oscillates between visual and graphic media. The text was first written as a long prose poem, which was turned into visual rebuses, the poem being then laid-out and cut—sometimes midword—according to how many pictograms would fit on its facing page. While Isou's lettrist cinema was nonsynchronic, Pomerand's work favors a radical synchronicity, to the detriment of the organic integrity of verse or meaning units. This jarring mode of rhythmic cut, akin to how Godard nibbled the beginning and ends of the shots of *Breathless* (1959), is inherently filmic. As for its content, *Saint ghetto des prêts* tells of a disjointed and at times semiautomatic journey through the locales, mores, and personalities of Saint-Germain-des-Prés. It adopts the same rather repellent tone of constant vituperation found in so many works of lettrism—an ostensibly mixture of antiseduction, anticommercialism, and rebellion without a cause, that insured its failure and skids toward paranoia.[174] It opens on a rant against Cocteau, then against a "pederast" (perhaps Cocteau[175])

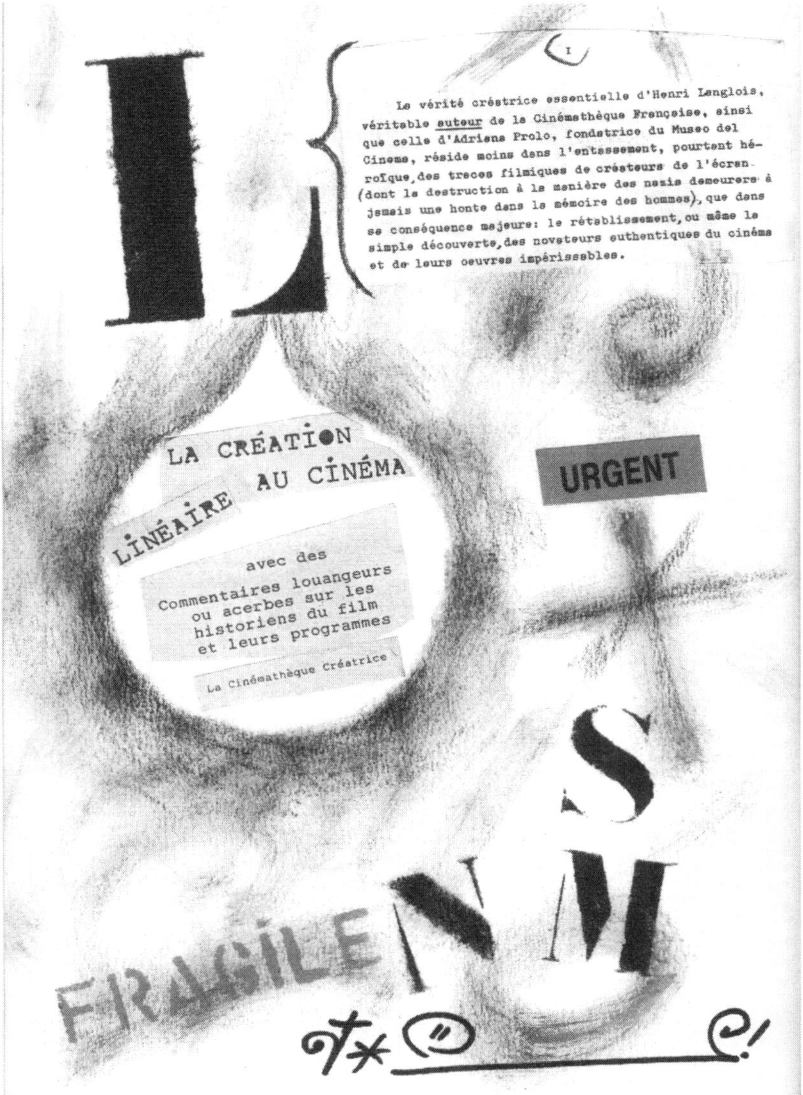

Figure 35. A page of Maurice Lemaître, *Écran total, roman-film* (2005).

trying to pick up the narrator, before stating that women come to the neighborhood to get raped.[176] We are far from Boris Vian's touristy *Manual of Saint-Germain-des-Prés* published in 1949—against which Pomerand explicitly rants.[177] Lest the reader lose faith, however, Pomerand confesses he suffers from "psychoanalytical burps" and that "we are a generation whose men, having been in too many long lines [*ayant trop fait la queue*] during the recent war, have lost it today [*l'on perdue ce jourd'hui*]."[178] "Queue," of course, also means "cock." We begin to suspect that the narrative of cynical ambulation hides a palimpsestic story possibly linked to war traumas. Hence a pictogram of a snake slivers over a page early on,[179] and surreptitiously reappears much later as the Seine, sprawled over the entire page, looking strikingly like a snake's skeleton sprawled across Paris.[180] A mother and daughter silhouette (Pomerand's mother died in Auschwitz) ominously underlies a page about a future police roundup. While the pictograms are black on white at first, they progressively shift and end white on black—as if the cinepoem had undergone an inversion, ending in a film negative of itself. Simultaneously, the small rows of crosses and stars of David that stand for a word Pomerand does not care to parse into rebuses, grow larger and more numerous until they cover the final image. Like Isou, Pomerand's rhetoric disturbingly echoes fascist and Nazi politics, calling for instance for "the hanging of onomatopoeic poets"[181] and razing Saint-Germain-des-Prés like the Nazis did a seedy Marseille neighborhood where Pomerand lived.[182]

Midway through the book the narrative morphs into a film, when Pomerand compares Saint-Germain-des-Prés and Hollywood because of American cinema's romanticizing of the Latin Quarter. "Any film is a singular marvel,"[183] he begins enthusiastically, before finding Lazarean echoes to the sense of living in a film since the "individualized heroes of the screen"[184] end up as "shadows unfaithful to the canvas."[185] Ultimately, Saint-Germain proves to be nothing but "decors" of "cardboard and papier-mâché mansions, where puppets, activated by fragile strings, throw water and urine on the heads of sleepwalkers who come visiting."[186] *Saint ghetto des prêts*'s cinepoetics is no imaginary utopia induced by cinema's automorphosis, but a post-traumatic dystopia that detects filmic fakery underneath the reality principle itself. This being said, Pomerand cites abundantly from the hidden tradition of cinepoetry: Cocteau, but also Mallarmé,[187] Alexandre Astruc (who coined the "camera-pen" expression), Claude

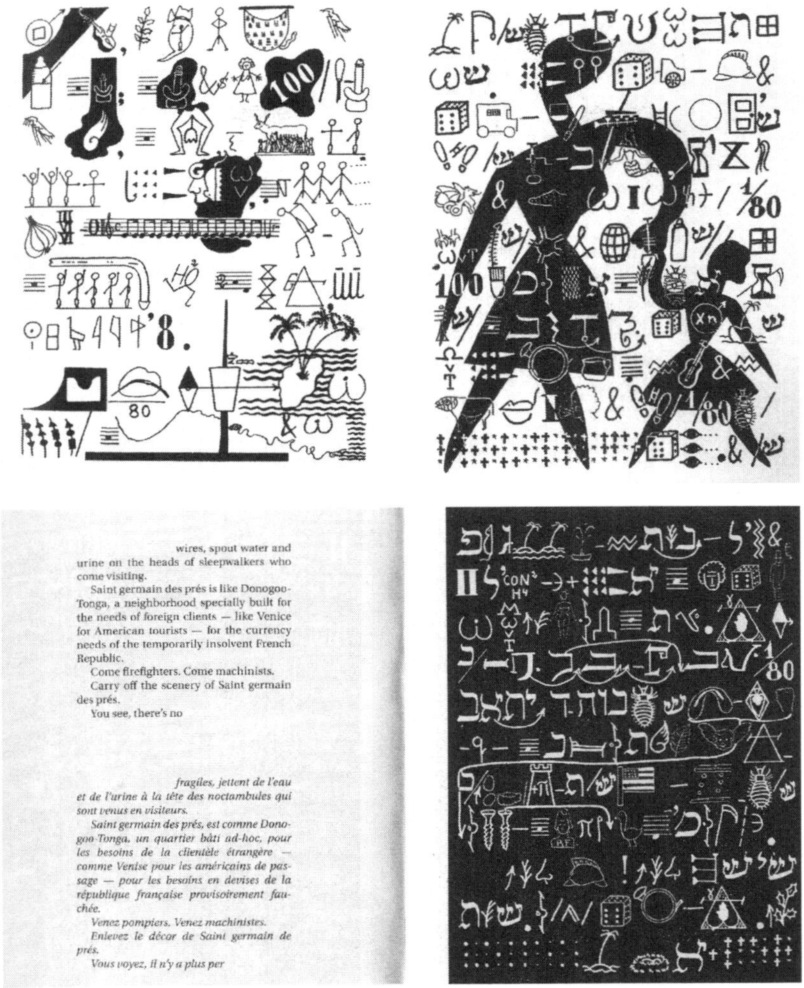

Figure 36. Pages from Gabriel Pomerand, *Saint ghetto des prêts* (1950). Courtesy of Ugly Duckling Press.

Mauriac (who wrote a book on cinema published in 1954),[188] and most importantly one of the first imaginary films published in book form, Romains's 1919 *Donogoo-Tonka*, to which Pomerand refers as "Donogoo-Tonga."[189] *Saint ghetto des prêts* nonetheless ends on a kind of undoing of the cinepoetic imaginary, via the removal of the stage props of Saint-Germain as if they were as factitious as those of

Donogoo-Tonka. This leaves nothing but, "a dog howling to death in the solitude of an empty desert,"[190] a Cynic survivor in a desert of graves.

Through the lettrism of Isou, Lemaître, and Pomerand, experimental practices of cinepoetry were at once revived and redirected. While interwar cinepoetry came to a grinding halt after the arrival of the talkies and the retheatricalizing of cinema, lettrist cinepoetics by contrast revalued the vital mediation of voice and direct speech. Sound cinema, with its perceptual holism integrating human voices and language to the visual universe of film, offered a new prosthetic avenue for resuturing poetic voice to a postwar reality from which it had been wrenched by historical trauma. With its main practitioners Jewish and intimately touched by the destruction of European Jews, lettrism developed a cinepoetics resonating with posttraumatic affects that exploded, expanded, and thus defined, the cinema apparatus as such. Ultimately lettrists used the sensorium of film to return language back to lived experience, through a new intermedium of images and text: hypergraphics, the "total screen" of expanded cinema, imaginary films, live body art, and so forth. Lemaître in particular used his seminaked body as a screen to project one of his films with pictographic letters.[191] Such a holistic performing of the driving homology of cinepoetry, /page⇔skin⇔screen/, was less meant to remedy the dissociations between language, writing, and the embodied subject brought about by the disasters of World War II, than to dramatize its new historical nexus.

MIND, BODY, AND LINE: MICHAUX'S CINEPOETIC GRAPHS

For poetry after the war, only Francis Ponge has had a role comparable to that of Henri Michaux in crafting an influential alternative to the poetry of Surrealism—a movement both poets first embraced then abandoned in the 1920s. While Ponge's work remained marginal until the language turn of the 1960s, Michaux's became paradigmatic for young poets seeking new directions bypassing Resistance poetry after 1946. Both poets opened their poetics to silent cinema and Chaplin's automatic riding in a way that Breton always resisted: this difference may be constitutive of the waning of Surrealism in the postwar period while the work of Michaux and Ponge rose to preeminence among poets, theoreticians, and philosophers.[192] Already in 1925, Michaux had taken Breton's automatism to task for being too limited when he foretold that "automatism will be taken farther. We'll see whole pages of onomatopoeias, syntactic cavalcades, medleys of several languages"—the very program of lettrism.[193] In this piece, titled "Surrealism," Michaux explicitly favors Epstein's *La Poésie d'aujourd'hui* over and beyond Breton's theory. Cinema—via Epstein's cinepoetics—shaped Michaux's writing into an imaginary medium combining language, the automatic burlesque of Chaplin, and drug-assisted psychodynamic investigations of perception and sensations.

Two recent critics, Maurice Mourier and Raymond Bellour, have proposed detailed mappings of the place of cinema in Michaux's writings.[194] For Mourier, who notes the broad appeal of cinema to the generation of poets born around 1900, Michaux recognized in the moving image a "psychedelic" revelator of his own sensibility akin to other drugs (mescaline, hashish, LSD) he tested on himself.[195] Many prose poems of Michaux, Mourier points out, emulate film techniques, especially the comic slapstick genre of Chaplin, Keaton and the Marx Brothers. He also argues that cinema's dynamism constitutes the common denominator of Michaux's movement-centered work in both writing and painting. Animation films by the Disney studios, Tex Avery, and Norman McLaren, he conjectures, would have especially suited Michaux's fascination with metamorphosis.[196] Bellour too retraces Michaux's encounter with cinema, by examining his scenario for a film shot in 1963 by Éric Duvivier, *Images d'un visionnaire* (Images by a visionary).[197] He advances a chronological framework for the permeation of cinema in Michaux's oeuvre. After the early texts of 1923–25 on cinema's plasticity and Chaplin, Michaux invoked cinema as a metaphor for the process of "thought-imagination." We might formulate this shift as the homology /moving image apparatus⇔psychodynamic imagination/ extending to /film editing⇔thought construction/. In a second period in the 1950s, as Michaux reflected on painting and drawing, the production of images became central and Bellour suggests a new analogy at play around questions of visualization: /images in the mind⇔film in the camera/.[198] A final period is represented by a short 1982 text, "Une foule sortie de l'ombre" (A crowd coming out of the shadows), which relates how Michaux's sensorial enjoyment of an unidentified film was cut short by a painful migraine.[199] For both Bellour and Mourier this last episode emblematizes several instances in Michaux's writings when cinema encroaches upon and dissolves the sense of self and reality—paradoxically, more so than drugs. The fine analyses of both critics, however, take it for granted that poetry and cinema remain *separate practices and mediums*. I would like to argue the opposite: that Michaux's work affirms the constitutive contamination of writing by cinema, and does so specifically in the wake of World War II.

I showed how Michaux's reflection on cinema in the 1920s was indebted not only to Epstein's notions of fatigue and coenesthesis, as Bellour has pointed out, but to Epstein's formulation of cinepoetry.[200] Yet, significantly, it is during World War II that Michaux returned to cinema as a theoretical framework for renewing his writing practice. In a 1942 piece titled "Idées transversales" (Transversal ideas), he weaves together "war neurasthenia," the problem of tracking the "fugitive ghosts" of his thought, and "short films."[201] A few pages earlier, he mentions the case of a London fireman who, flung six stories upward after an explosion and landing with only mild injuries, stated that his flight had been one of the best moments in his life.[202] Michaux comments that such an out-of-body suspension of the "frame"[203] of everyday life has become common for him. War amplified his kinesthetic sensibility at a moment when film returned among his preoccupations, especially after 1946 when cinema saturated French cultural reconstruction. Subsequently, and here is my main point, Michaux will prove simply *unable* to write down his psychedelic experiences without having recourse to a lexicon of "unfolding" (*déroulement*), "film," and "screen."[204] I insist that such references should not be read as *metaphorical* but cognitive and experiential. More so perhaps than any other poet of his generation, Michaux understood that cinema was now equiprimordial with, and embedded in, perception.

In the 1942 piece cited above the topic following cinema is "human [neuroplasticity]"[205] and Michaux clearly links the two via automorphosis. Certainly the term "automorphosis" fits Michaux's oeuvre like no other: movements, tremors, metamorphoses, turbulences, waves, semiliquid flows, visual and auditory mirages, circuits of duration, and sentient creaturely figures (animal or homunculus-like) traversing perception—all are omnipresent in his writings. Virtually all of Michaux's titles are synonymous with automorphosis: *Darkness Moves, The Far-Off Inside, Apparitions, The Space Within, Passages, Life in the Folds, Emergences-Resurgences, The Turbulent Infinite, Movements, Repose in Shattering*, and so on. Here is a passage from *The Turbulent Infinite*: "More than libidinous scenes, the rising piracy of objects fascinates me, confounds me, a poem of swarming, of larvae, of floods, of tropical exuberances, indefinite like the sea, exalting but much more so and, like it, knowing no boundaries, no durable appeasement, an immense orgiastic respiration."[206] Invoking a full register of immanent forces including sex, decomposition, reproduction, catastrophes, the ocean, vegetal growth, and breathing, almost indistinguishable from Epstein's formulations of coenesthesis, the would-be poem tackles what might be termed Michaux's *automorphic sublime*: natural forces passing through, resonating within, and at times overwhelming the body's sensorial potentialities.

Throughout the 1950s, Michaux increasingly described the kinetic hallucinations of mescaline as a hybrid phenomenon of technology and perception, as in this passage of *Miserable Miracle* deploying both retinal persistence and chronophotographic synthesis:

> The successive generations of a body, the successive generations of a figure (geometrical or natural) take place in successive discharges, with a complete pause after each, or after each series, followed by an almost immediate restart, the process going at such a speed that it is almost instantaneous. . . . Whatever occurs in this space, you have all the time to witness the spectacle. With your new time, with your minutes of three thousand instants, you will not be overwhelmed, with your subdivided attention you will never be outdone.[207]

This passage is much more technological than similar accounts of psychodynamic perception in Baudelaire and Valéry. Recall that in 1923 Michaux had written of the "3,000 images for 10 lines of text"[208] that cinema produces. The "three thousand instants" of this 1956 piece refer just as directly to the frame-per-second frequency of the projecting apparatus.

To trigger and mobilize cinematic automorphosis, Michaux often resorts to looking at photographs in order to "dephotograph" them into "visions of the inner cinema,"[209] sometimes by constructing composites of two photographs.[210] This animation of photography (or reanimation, since de-photographing points to movement and cinema as originary) focuses on two types of images: landscapes and bodies, especially faces, the two categories favored by Epstein's photogénie. Michaux's project is then to reinject photogénie into the dead "punctum" of photography (to use Barthes's term). Michaux selects women's faces, and occasionally naked female bodies, to generate a tremulous network of affects—"microperceptions" and "micropleasures" (*microjouissances*)[211]—and foster a sense of "imaginary communion" with the other through the sensation of "touching human radiance," leading to the impression that "the photograph breathes."[212] Yet it may be less a romantic communion that Michaux seeks in such faces than the photogenic experience of the deep embedding of technology in contemporary perception: "as if you constantly formed within yourself a fluid face, ideally plastic and malleable, that would transform itself according to ideas and impressions, automatically, in an instantaneous synthesis, all day long and as though cinematographically."[213] Here the perceptual subconscious becomes a ghostly cinematic face, another twin figure, and reflects all the affects that enter the self. This places the poet not in the active position of movie director but as a passive spectator to inner filmic shocks:

> . . . the "liberated" images go on and will go on for three hours, quick, astounding film that slows down at times, becomes still, stops . . . film from which I occasionally drop out to flow into depths from which I cannot easily emerge . . .[214]

> Victimized by the image, by this forcible cinema, that has neither rhyme nor reason, he [the subject] would want to eschew this bazaar of random images no longer allowing him to follow anything and that hack him with infinite infinitesimal jolts . . . metamorphoses more than films, kaleidoscopes more than films, and, above all, discharges.[215]

Michaux's fine-grained cinepoetic spectrum does not hinge on an active/passive opposition. As his early statement on surrealism suggests, his abiding interest is for zones extending between active and passive, between will and automatism. Indeed, this might be the central ambition of Michaux's cinepoetry: substituting for Breton's automatic writing—a mere subterfuge of "pure psychic automatism" since it is tainted with *willful* edits—a less theoretical and more experiential form of psychodynamic notation, what he describes as "the basic phenomenon," that of "thoughts in the nascent state, thoughts in freedom,"[216] this last phrase having Marinetti's "words in freedom" as intertext. That Michaux kept Breton in mind is plain: his 1967 scientific notation of different hallucination speeds ("a," "b," "c") clearly mirrors Breton's in *The Magnetic Fields* (speeds v, v', v'', v''', v'''').[217] By recasting the opposition between will and automatism, and perception and technology, Michaux aimed at a new relation between writing and images merging Breton's Surrealism with the cinepoetic surrealism of Epstein, Dermée, and Goll.

After the war, Michaux launched a graphic oeuvre of ink drawings and paintings, attesting to the growing pressure of visual representation on his thought. Commentators tend to see it as decisive break with his prose poetry. The framework of cinepoetry allows us to gauge the shift in a new light, since it is fully in line with the cinepoetic attempts of Mallarmé and Segalen to combine film and visual written systems (Chinese ideograms), according to aesthetic and epistemological intuitions of recording traces that Jules-Étienne Marey had envisioned. Evoking the "endless screw . . . peppered with images and words . . . the flow . . . that stops only with [life ending]," Michaux adds that, "a scroll, a kakemono, would have accounted for it better than a book, on the condition it could be unfolded, or a volume with a single page endlessly unfurled."[218] His drawings display a family resemblance with the anthropomorphic figures of Émile Cohl's animation films, and his seismographic notations of the inner flux of hallucinations are often comprised of words (Figure 37). Indeed, they appear to result from words being written too rapidly and transformed into squiggles, when the poet "could still follow words, but meaning would not follow suit."[219] Moreover, at times, he hallucinated images *of* writing, "reflections instantly visualized into written or even printed letters."[220]

These encounters between image and language come, for Michaux, with a strong perception that some kind of imaginary screen or interface is at play. "Images, this means placing a screen,"[221] Michaux states succinctly. Photographs, for instance, are explicitly envisioned as an imaginary support for writing and image to melt into each other: "This face is moving, in fluid movements, admirable screen where inscriptions of feelings inscribe and undo themselves and where new inscriptions indefatigably return."[222] Such polyvalent screens, reminiscent of Cocteau's bisected cinepoetics, sample but also sever the three-dimensional flux: "By writing down the word, I decapitated myself from the vision and its meaning, leaving the word alone, a useless witness."[223] Words are snapshots or stills orphaned from the moving matrix of visionary experience, which they index only like shooting stills index a film. This is why images represent "the enemy of poetry" since they force the poet "to write by enumeration," and disrupt the mechanics of writing: "The [inner] word workshops take a beating and many useful weirs fall."[224]

Such failures at the interface between image and language inform Michaux's famous statement about drawing: "It is precisely, to the contrary, for having freed me from words, these tiresome partners, that the drawings are spritely and joyous. . . . Hence I see them, a new language turning its back on verbal language, as *liberators*."[225] He

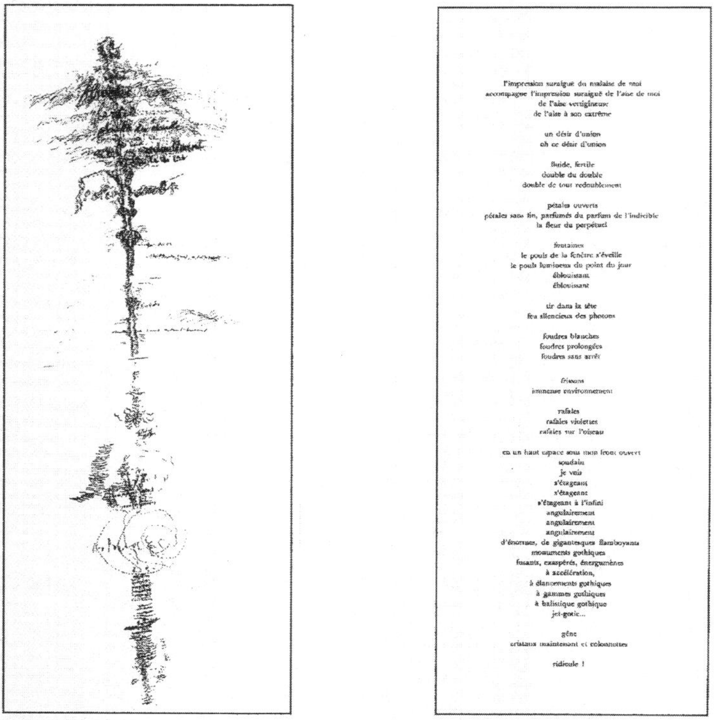

Figure 37. Henri Michaux, *Paix dans les brisements* (1951), visual juxtaposition of the hand-drawn cinematic text and its print transliteration. © Éditions Gallimard.

refers here to his anthropomorphic-ideographic ink drawings born both from his "kinetic desire" and from his wish for a "Direct writing at last for the unreeling [*dévidement*] of forms / for the solace and the disencumbering of images."[226] Drawing thus represents a mutated, cinepoetic form of writing. Michaux strikingly describes the inception of his drawings as a cinematic experiment in 1951:

> . . . lying on my bed . . . I would animate one or two or three shapes, but always one faster, one more favored, one more diabolically fast than the others. . . . I would infuse it with an unbelievable mobility, of which I was its double and its motor, although I was immobile and lazy. I would *turn its power on* [*je la mettais sous tension*], while I remained the despair or disdain of active people.[227]

Through drawing, Michaux became the film director of his automorphic perceptions by doing away with words and the cinematic screen—"this vibrating sheet, torn, flapping noiselessly, where a world was unfolding [*se déroulait*]."[228] To do so, he chose one of the several automorphic footages running in his head, and turns his electrical gaze toward it to start a process of editing. On a more pedestrian basis, this choice between several channels might well refract TV, operated remotely.[229]

Still, cinepoetic writing insistently resurfaces in Michaux's drawings—through the hand-drawn line. When he writes, "a line for the pleasure of being line," it isn't clear whether it is a line of verse, line drawing, or indeed the sheer pleasure of tracing by hand.[230] Halfway between one and two dimensions, the line reduces the cinema apparatus to a rhythmic and musical thread: "Music, which it is impossible to project as such, on an exterior screen via visible material indices, when you listen to it, forces you to follow it along interior trajectories."[231] This virtual pattern of abstract musical graphs harks back to the Symbolist modelization of music, notably Mallarmé's preface to *A Throw of the Dice*. The graphic line becomes a polyvalent medium through which temporality, tracing, and visualization complement the arbitrariness of written words:

> . . . I had wanted to draw the moments which, end to end, make up a life, to offer for viewing the inner sentence, the wordless sentence, a sinuous thread that ceaselessly unreels [*se déroule*] and, at one's most intimate, accompanies everything that occurs inside as outside. . . . [I wanted to draw . . .] what shows itself when, at night, is replayed (shortened and soundless) the exposed film that captured the day.
>
> Cinematic drawing.
>
> My own film was little more than one line or two or three encountering here and there a few others. . . . [Other people] were not concerned with unfolding [*déroulement*]. Cinema had not been born for very long.[232]

In this statement, cinema serves as graphic hyperlanguage—"wordless sentence"—whose characteristics are insistently cinematic: montage, exposure, splicing, and unfolding. At the core of this multisensory experience is the homology between the celluloid ribbon and the graphic line: /film reel⇔hypermedium line⇔graphic trace/.

Breton's automatism teetered in between two theoretical amphibologies in its avoidance of cinema: first, it is based on a sentence "heard" but forgotten, recalled as a perfect visual equivalent, from which a second sentence is derived that has exemplary status ("there is a man cut in two by a window"); and second, it is a Freudian theory of poetic language that places the spontaneity of the mental image at its center while bracketing the automorphic role of cinema. In his aesthetics of the unconscious, Breton makes no allowances for the perceptual subconscious, technology-driven neuroplasticity, or the psychodynamic interspace between image and language. Via the explicit inspiration of Epstein's thought on cinema, Michaux's oeuvre tackled all these blindspots by lodging cinepoetics at the very core of his polysensorial and multimedia aesthetics.

DUPREY'S ACINEPOETICS

Another poet who sought to recast surrealist automatism in the 1940s and 1950s through cinepoetic and coenesthetic experiences was Jean-Pierre Duprey (1930–59), whom Breton considered in 1950 the new postwar voice of Surrealism. He grew up during World War II in Rouen, a city strategically located on the Channel, and this may have exacerbated what the editor of his collected works describes as possible early schizophrenia. In 1944, at age fourteen, following an intense pre–D-day bombardment by allied forces that destroyed parts of Rouen, he participated in search and rescue operations, noting that he "spent the day assembling whole dead people from bits and pieces in order to bury them."[233] Such an experience might explain in part the mimetic fascination of his first poems toward Rimbaud, like himself a precocious poet thrown into war and encountering the war dead (cf. "Le Dormeur du val"). In 1959, at the height of the Algerian war, he pissed on the flame of the Unknown Soldier under the Arc de Triomphe. Badly beaten by the police, he was subsequently thrown into a psychiatric hospital, committing suicide shortly after his release.

Duprey's first mature work was titled *Derrière son double* (Behind one's double), a surrealist poem-play consciously permeated by the works of both Artaud (*The Theater and Its Double*) and Jarry. The "double" in the title may well be a recognition by Duprey of his compulsion to imitate poets of the surrealist pantheon. The play of Jarry that Duprey most closely echoes is *L'Autre Alceste* (The other Alceste) (1896), in which doubling is both a narrative and a sensorial leitmotif. As we have seen throughout this study, cinema's automorphic likenesses revived myths of mirroring, dissociation, doubling, possession and ghosts, all of which dovetail with Cocteau's and Cayrol's

Lazarean sensibility of war trauma. Given this focus on vision, it isn't surprising that Duprey's poetry should be rife with optical imagery: eyes, gaze and blindness, visual doubling, doppelgangers, and especially reversions of sight from outward to inward. In *L'Ombre sagittaire* (The Sagittarian shadow) (1949) for instance, he writes of "my shadow, projected on my back," while he is carrying "a photograph of the void (slightly out of focus however)."[234] This sense of having only a backside implies a defect in either one's faciality or the frontality of the visible world: "seen from the back because the FRONT no longer exists.[235] Michaux, by contrast, sees his own double as a vis-à-vis: "I was standing in front, electrically alert, myself as if doubled."[236] Duprey's doublings, I argue, evoke a sense of disincarnation, which Jean Cayrol defined the same year, 1949, in the posttraumatic purview of the Lazarean perception as "the doubling of the Lazarean soul"[237] caused by the difficulty of "reentering one's own [facial] features."[238]

Derrière son double opens on a section titled "De l'invisible de l'oeil au regard de la bouche" (Of the invisible character of the eye with regard to the mouth), which reorganizes the relation between organs of vision and language, thus images and words. That new relation generates two oddly named characters: "Mouth-Thunderbolt-Eye" and "Say-It-All-Eye."[239] It is in such figures of sight diverted into apertures opening toward the inner body space of language that cinepoetic elements arise:

> The reality of a void appeared on the screen whitened with bone powder . . . [240]
>
> The pierced eye floods eternity. I tell you: a wall of whiteness will combat the black wall; between the two: the lightning-crook, light-darkness.[241]
>
> . . . razor blades that had cut up light in ribbons of flaccid mirrors[242]

Such tropes of death, injury, and blank sight bespeak a palimpsestic cinematic apparatus at once self-injurious, embodied, and dystopic. We might offer as an homology for this combination of stricture and failure: /masochistic haptic introspection⇔defective cinema apparatus/. Other poem-plays of 1949 complement this dysfunctional inner cinema with specific references. We find, for instance, a spellbinding film reel—"a shadow-catching silk wheel"[243]—virtual films on "an imaginary screen,"[244] "images succeeding each other on a white wall,"[245] a "silent actor"[246] or a "film without actors,"[247] and film projections that break down or freeze: “break your mirror on which your image appears to me like a sound-projection (indeed, you speak to yourself from afar) from the magic ice lantern (it stills shadows, freezes flames).”[248] In just about every reference to cinema, Duprey injects an element that undercuts, resists, or dismantles the apparatus. Even his single reference to a film, Feuillade’s serial *Fantômas,* is defaced into *Fantômate* by compounding it with automaton (automate).[249] It is as though for Duprey cinema was not to be sublimated into poetry, as per Breton, but put under ostentatious erasure: /surrealist poetics⇔~~cinema apparatus~~/. Hence we find expressions that refer dystopically to cinepoetry, such as “window-pane pages with dead ink,”[250] or a passage inventing “within the circle of a fast-turning wheel, a large book with images where were told in different ways—as if traced by the ink-stained legs of the centipede spider—the story of God having become a carp.”[251] This passage appears to combine several excerpts from Jarry that refer to cinema.[252] Another passage invokes the hypothetical reception of Duprey’s own poem-plays as a curious form of deflated cinepoetry:

> . . . Mister H, his trip occurring in reverse or not at all, could only communicate the last scene of the last act to us, a scene reduced to its minimum which is a single word—without precedent in the play—that we could see tracing itself again on the screen decorated with two ears of half-donkeys that amount to a whole one; in the mouth (toothed according to the number and signs of the alphabet) of invented actors; and in the eyes of readers. . . . And the Word of the play inscribed itself on the locked door of sire H’s apartment, and thus we could read, in four letters devoid of particular signification, the word: FIN [THE END].[253]

Behind the ostensible “play” Duprey camouflages the cinema apparatus—obliquely referenced through the “screen,” the upper case word “FIN,” and a likely reference to Buñuel’s *Un Chien andalou.*[254] As for the figure of self-traced writing, while it usually signals the self-discovery of a poet’s cinepoetic imaginary, here it points more to its self-curtailing, its unwriting by anticipation as it were. Duprey was sufficiently interested in cinema to write a scenario for a six-minute film (now lost) by Georges Goldfayn and Jindrich Heisler in 1952. In it, a phone conversation is followed by several scenes that use similar graphic and visual matches as those used by Buñuel and Dalí in *Un Chien andalou* and *L’Âge d’or*: for instance, a shot of an egg cuts to that of a (round) door handle, then an oval head.[255] With mentions of a "vampire," a gloved hand, and "a head covered with a stocking,"[256] Duprey seems to reminisce on silent movie serials à la Musidora. A line of dialogue at the beginning of the script reads: "Allo . . . before the end [*la fin*], would you like an example of velocity in the animal realm?"[257] The script ends with the word "FIN" preceded by the ominous line: "Each word that is turned off [*s'éteint*] is a precursor of death."[258] Duprey's cinephilia might reveal itself here since "FIN," signaling the violent arrest of film-viewing's automorphic pleasure when it appears on screen, or more precisely, *when it too vanishes*, connotes death. Part of Duprey's film script was adapted from his last work, titled *La Fin et les moyens* (The end and the means).[259] He asked his wife to take it to the post office and mail it to Breton. While she was out he hung himself.

The cinepoetics of Duprey remains a paradox not only in its bracketing of the explicit apparatus, but in its anachronistic view of poetic imagery and technology. His poetry echoes the Symbolist register of the 1890s with animals, natural elements, the human body, characters from fairy tales, and ageless artifacts (mirrors, blades, furniture). There are no overt references to current history or modern technology beyond firearms, umbrellas, bicycles, telephones and undifferentiated "machines"[260]—that is the horizon of the 1890s. No planes, cars, trains, tanks, television, power plants, and so on.[261] We might thus speak of a retro or blocked cinepoetics in comparison to Saint-Pol-Roux's whose symbolism was very much coextensive with contemporary technics. For all this, Duprey's stifled cinepoetics might not be unrelated to lettrism in seeking to renew poetic language through the quasi-sentient materiality of letters. In the long passage on camouflaged cinema cited above, we recall that the narrator oddly refers to "FIN" as a word of "four letters," as if one belonged to a different realm or had not yet become visible. Duprey's poetry generalizes such orthographic paraphasia, modeled partly on Jarry's distorsions of words such as "externité" (externity) for "éternité" (eternity), or "merdre" (shrit) for "merde" (shit), and partly on surrealist games of letter substitutions (as in Desnos's Rrose Sélavy). My sense is that Duprey's letter manipulations deeply inform his writing, so that what he calls "the alphabet-lighthouse with 26 glimmers,"[262] doubles writing with the automorphosis of cinematic experience. Shortly after uttering, "I am closing the window-panes [*vitres*]," a character adds, "I am still vitral [*vitral*] (another would say vital [*vital*])."[263] Duprey unfolds an imaginary experience that conflates "vital" and "vitre," a vital window. Meanwhile, the word keeps hybridizing autonomously into a "vithral armor" (*Armure Vithrale*) behind which "your Double will welcome you."[264] Neither game nor grand theory as in lettrism, such word mutilations or letter-tumors have a troubling automatic aspect. Hence the word "profondeur" (depths) loses part of its ending and embeds an eye, "profondoeil" (deepeye),[265] perhaps via the expression "fond de l'oeil" (back of the eye). Such splicings suggest the homology: /superimpression⇔telescoped words/. The word "eau-de-vie" (brandy, lit. water of life) becomes a polyvalent formula, "O-de-vie" (the egg, the circle, and the zero of life).[266] Duprey indeed has a peculiar visual fascination for words like "Œil" (eye) and "Œuf" (egg) that he capitalizes to emphasize the spliced letters. He invents a word and a character, "L'Orrye,"[267] a howling female ghost who summons the horizon of death, or rather its "*Horifond*" (horidepth or horridzone),[268] beneath which we hear the word "horreur (horror)," as in "*il est Orr-heure*" ("it is Horro'clock"),[269] as well as *l'oreille*—the ear. Most letter mutations in Duprey's poetry involve death, depth, doubling, vision and movement, and an occult agency. The teratological autonomy of the "alphabet-lighthouse" and the concomitant dissimulation of cinema point to a general homology in Duprey's work: /cinema automorphosis⇔poetry with mutant words/. The book of Duprey from which come these examples is *The Sagittarian Shadow*. In the French, *L'Ombre Sagittaire*, it is difficult not to hear stereophonically, "*l'ombre s'agitait*" as well as "*les ombres s'agitèrent,*" both "the shadow was moving" and "the shadows were moving." Yet neither sentence—both blatant and anachronistic palimpsests of cinema—is really heard. Only their self-erased double, their dyslexic echo.

RODANSKI'S CINEMASK

A book, a succession of shots to be framed within the white space delimited by the screen of the page.

As I approach everything that is pure, a veil spreads before me. It ranges from the celluloid of films to the most complicated forms of the mind.[270]

Jean-Pierre Duprey and Stanislas Rodanski (born Bernard Glücksmann in 1927) have uncanny resemblances: they orbited around Surrealism after the war (which marked both deeply), developed obsessive identifications with Surrealist figures (particularly Jacques Vaché for Rodanski), were haunted by suicide and incarcerated in psychiatric hospitals, became close friends of Surrealist painter Jacques Hérold, and belonged to a small semisecret group of writers in the late 1940s and 1950s calling themselves *The Black Generation* (with Alain Jouffroy, Jean-Pierre Faye, and lettrist François Dufrêne).[271] There are two notable differences between them. Rodanski was Jewish and at seventeen, in November 1944, he was caught and deported to the working camp of Mannheim, from which he returned in May 1945.[272] Also, the apartment building in Lyon where he grew up, abutted a movie theater. In part because of what was avowedly an intense exposure—"The imaginary gangsters of quotidian cinema, the zombism of daily concerns, the ghosts, excessive use of cinema during puberty"[273]—he placed cinema at the center of his experience less as an ancillary medium for poetry than as the very platform of psychic life.

In the early 1950s, Rodanski wrote *La Victoire à l'ombre des ailes* (Victory in the shadow of wings), a title that echoes an Office of War Information radio program, *Wings to Victory* (1940–43). A first-person hybrid text combining a parody of B-series spy noirs and an autobiographical meditation with surrealist maxims, it could be compared to George Perec's similarly hybrid *W, or The Memory of Childhood* (1975). Tasked with delivering two tons of "torture gas" to a Pacific atoll, the spy-for-hire narrator relentlessly makes out with his girl, Rita. She is the Rita Hayworth of *Gilda* (1946), one of the "bad girls" in the star pantheon analyzed by Edgar Morin, after whose character one of two nuclear bombs dropped in 1946 on the Bikini atoll was nicknamed.[274] Rodanski's text thus partakes of a precise pre–Cold War moment of intertwining between war, film, the tropics, and sex: "bikini" soon became the new term for a two-piece bathing suit, no doubt because it was "explosive." Julien Gracq, a close friend of Rodanski, wrote a preface in 1975 that puzzles at the capacity of Rodanski's generation for "eliminating history," after having had "to face in childhood" the events of war in their "immeasurable dimension."[275] He goes on to point out that *Victory* was written "in a mode of tasteless and inauthentic theatricality that has the very affective tonality—the 'unhappy' tonality of our age, the age of cinema."[276] Gracq gets the "affective tonality" of cinema right but misreads as "inauthentic theatricality" the homeopathic and Lazarean dimension of cinepoetics linked to postwar trauma.

On the very first page of *La Victoire*, we read:

> A film reminded me that I was going with the flow [*jouer le jeu*]. And the explanation relied of course on a misunderstanding all the way to untransferable sleep. The days were replaying *a film projected on my mind's screen/plot* [*trame*] until the end of the reel; there flowed in me unflinchingly from the middle of the adventure to the end of the world the feeling of being "doubled." Life begins each time like advertising footage [*métrage réclame*] for household items.[277]

We find in this passage Michaux's analogy, /recollecting daily events⇔replaying a movie/, complicated, however, by the dual meaning of "*trame*" as both screen and narrative plot, and sundered by the same overwhelming feeling of doubleness as in Duprey and Cayrol. Moreover, moving image advertisement is presented here as a new kind of prosthetics, part of the postwar reconstruction of the quotidian through household products which, for Kristin Ross, especially marked the Americanization of France in the 1950s.[278] In spite of its cheap picaresque, *Victory* is a Lazarean document in which distorted perception informs most of the cinematic plot elements:

> A naked woman had just gone out. Rita was kissing me, thinking herself another woman, as I play-acted the very woman she thought about. I quickly guessed these mortally cold lips; the game stopped when, waking up, I thought I was pretending.[279]

> It is once you cross the paradise of couples lost, found, harassed, interchanged that you arrive smack into cinema. The studio car ripped the quiet afternoon with its speed and howling siren. . . . It seemed we were cleaning up the text of the kidnapping scene of the testy star of the Unique[280]

> The thing is, the onion is composed of successive membranes [*pellicules*], membranes that are nothing but whose growth around imaginary axes represents the famous "something."[281]

> We are the actors paid to play in a porno movie, conducting our task earnestly, while deriving the legitimate satisfaction of a job well done, but with the kind of supreme detachment which conforms to the abstract requirements of the scenario.[282]

The main character-actor lives in a number of fluidly interconnected realms (recalling Artaud's *Les Dix-huit secondes*), none of which amounts to a firm reality: a film, the shooting of the film, and the text of the script. The layers of the onion point to pages ("papier oignon" is "onion paper"), but also to film ("pellicule" is "film stock") and to endless veils, none of which yields the Real, "the Unique," as anything but an effect of "imaginary axes." Even sex becomes the performance of a porno movie since the subject sees himself from outside—failing to adhere even to the reality or gender of his own body—satisfied only with the sense that he his dutifully following a scenario. Cayrol speaks of a sense of "double life" coming from the "parasitic love" of bare sex to which Lazarean subjects are condemned. Cayrol faults the star-system that "projects on our world the shadows of famous couples" in a kind of "*dictatorship*" linked to or echoing the sense of being "castrated" by the concentration camp experience.[283] While Morin concurs with Cayrol's film projection trope, he notes less judgmentally that the movie star "proposes a new ethics of individuality, which is that of modern leisure."[284] Leisure as respite from work, as Epstein saw, but also as an artificial reality from which to reconstruct the self in a posttraumatic world. Rodanski's cinepoetics of the actor combines traumatic self-loss and homeopathic self-reinvention. While Cayrol sees the Lazarean subject as an "astounding mime" due both to his "aptitude for doubling himself" and his "permanent state of disembodiment,"[285] Morin considers that "personality is a mask," adding that "the star provides the image and the model of this mask," that "allows us to make our voices heard."[286] That a sense of self can—in the traumatic aftermath of war and Rodanski's own internment—only come from cinema, is suggested by his 1948 collection of short autobiographical prose pieces, *Des Proies aux chimères* (From preys to chimeras). It presents the narrator's life as "the 'parenthesis' that exiles me" as a "bubble of void, iridescent with all that an actor defines by the effects he produces upon a group of the living [*viveurs*]."[287] The unusual term "*viveurs*" connotes a difference between the living and the narrator that likely has to do with the latter being a survivor, hence an actor, a mimic. The end of the text suggests that connection:

> Wisdom in the poses of fashion pictures: showing oneself an incognito CINEMASK of misfortunes.
>
> Translucent action and my eyes, my own eyes.
>
> . . .
>
> Shadowy zone to cross while exteriorizing oneself into appearance: film tricks [*truquage*].
>
> My beautiful film tricks[288]

What Rodanski later explicitly called "this devastating 'postwar' of the mind"[289] resonates with Lazarean strictures such as inhabiting a shadowy alternate world, or having a secondary face. Its general homology is: /mask of the star + film tricks ⇔ subjective space of the survivor/.

The postwar subject as film actor figures prominently in *La Victoire*, where the narrator's name automorphically prints itself on the wall of a cell in which he is locked: "LANCELO GLUCKSMANN." It is a combination of the tragic hero of the Round Table (with a –t– mysteriously dropped) and Rodanski's given name. It is as if Rodanski was able to "play the role of my life"[290] and identify one of his avatars with himself only inside the detention cell of an imaginary film-in-writing.

Definitively incarcerated in a psychiatric hospital after 1954, Rodanski describes his detention and surveillance in chilling terms, insisting both that he is "master of an unparalleled situation" and that he ignores "what the masters of the world want. What film . . . ," adding immediately: "In any case! I am through writing. Two hundred pages . . . and a heap of ashes."[291] He expressly associates his incarceration with his experience in the concentration camps: "in this country as much as in Germany, I have undergone the cruel experience of penitentiary systems."[292] A dream account he wrote in 1950 begins in a camp of deportation with the "two- or three-bed bunks I have known in Germany."[293] The dream account does not mention cinema, but Rodanski writes a secondary text interpreting this dream that invokes cinema at several crucial points.[294] The dream feels like "a series of optical relays" spaced by "the burst of a light with the white smoke of magnesium," with special effects of perspective, scale shifts, "slow motion," and the impression of "an image of cinema suddenly projected on nature." A part of the dream dealing with a train entering a tunnel suggests to Rodanski an animated cartoon he used to see as part of a "stock of films" from a high school he attended. The crucial scene shows a "phantom ride" in the turn-of-the-century lexicon—a subjective camera one-shot film taken at the front of a train—which enters a series of tunnels, each growing from a black spot to complete obscurity then full light again, in a variant of a Freudian *fort-da* game. He and his classmates, Rodanski notes, used to wonder whether this was the same tunnel every time. Rodanski provides two other versions of such cinematic *fort-da*. The first is from his childhood: "a clock used for the presentation of film images," in which "a photo stayed a while in a neon-blue frame," before being swallowed into the clock. The second occurred right after his temporary release from psychiatric internment in 1950, when he saw a series of sheets in the twilight as "a succession of planes/shots (*plans*)," which his "walking itself made concrete." It is as if even the return to freedom and the real was predicated on chronophotographic synthesis or cinematic montage as alone capable of fusing things together.

Such figures of *fort-da*, intermittency, and circularity hint at the question of temporal reversibility in Rodanski's evocations of cinema and in his cinepoetic meshing of realms of authoring, acting, and fiction. In his intellectual testament, the famous 1952 *Lettre au soleil noir* (Letter to the black sun), he associates the Yseult of the Round Table and the Justine of Sade to the erotic martyrology of the "films of Buñuel."[295] Characterizing the world as a "spectacle" he defines himself as "the virtuality I transfer to it—the ego" (*la virtualité que j'y transfère—le moi*). He glosses: "il me faut être comme personne de ce drame, jusqu'à la fin,"[296] a sentence that semantically flickers between opposite meanings of "*personne*" as "person" and "nobody": "I must be as if nobody/a person in this drama until the end." In a Duprey-like expression, he calls this postwar condition that of a "cinemask" (*cinémasque*), a person that cinema simultaneously helps to be someone, and keeps being nobody—that is, literally, a mask, or again, *persona* in Latin.

Rodanski's writing traverses several historical epochs indexed by cinema as if to reach a kind of standing virtuality of the cinematic past which alone can constitute the present. After reading Yseult through Buñuel, he similarly deciphers John Ford's westerns through Shakespeare, and ultimately identifies Ford's classic hero as "the gunslinger more or less dreamed of throughout the surrealist adventure."[297] The earlier incarnation of this gunslinger would have been Rio Jim, played by William Hart in the Thomas Ince films that the surrealists relished. It is to these westerns that the last letter of Jacques Vaché, who served at the front, refers before his suicide in 1919.[298] This common fascination with the figure of the gunslinger is part of why Rodanski wrote of Vaché: "he is my 'imaginary interlocutor' in the solitude of my cell."[299] From one war to another, the traumatic cinemask reappears, and the virtuality of cinepoetics with it.

With Isou, Michaux, Duprey, and Rodanski, the cinepoetics of the Liberation remained indebted to the "surrealist adventure" and its surreptitious love affair with cinema, while recouping the homeopathic practices of post–World War I cinepoetry in dealing with trauma. We can nonetheless detect a dual tendency in this new cinepoetry of the 1950s. On the one hand, a fantasmatic return to the utopian conditions of 1916–17 when cinepoetry emerged, a period to which the maturity of cinema history from the purview of the new generation suddenly gave much more relief. This backward glance also lifted the standing injunction against cinema (and cinepoetry) that Breton had reiterated in 1951. On the other hand, the new self-awareness that the 1950s were deeply permeated by film and movie culture deflated, in a way, the thrust of experimental cinepoetry and especially its aesthetico-social utopian potential. Yet cinepoetry proved again the intermedium of choice to undertake the partial reconstruction of subjects, especially survivors, and begin addressing the radical gap between damaged experience and language.

Plate 1. Blaise Cendrars and Sonia Terk-Delaunay, "La Prose du transsibérien et de la petite Jehanne de France," 1913 (detail).

Plate 2. Intertitles and intratitles from Marcel L'Herbier's 1920 *L'Homme du large*. © Musée Gaumont.

Plate 3a. Page from the chapter "Cinéma accéléré et cinéma ralenti," in Blaise Cendrars, *La fin du monde filmée par l'ange N.-D.* (1919), illustrated by Fernand Léger. Courtesy of the Beinecke Rare Books and Manuscript Library.

28.

L'homme mort et les animaux domestiques détruits, réapparaissent les espèces et les genres qui avaient été chassés. Les mers se repeuplent des baleines et la surface de la terre est envahie par une végétation énorme.

29.

On voit les champs en friche verdir et fleurir furieusement. Une végétation audacieuse s'épanouit. Les graminées deviennent ligneuses ; les herbes folles, hautes et fortes, durcissent. La ciguë est légumineuse. Des arbustes apparaissent, poussent. Les bois s'étendent, et l'on voit les plaines d'Europe s'assombrir, se recouvrir uniformément d'apalachine.

Plate 3b. Page from the chapter "Cinéma accéléré et cinéma ralenti," in Blaise Cendrars, *La fin du monde filmée par l'ange N.-D.* (1919), illustrated by Fernand Léger. Courtesy of the Beinecke Rare Books and Manuscript Library.

difficile d'évaluer la hauteur, restait fixée sur la rétine : grand portail de feu fermé sur la nuit :

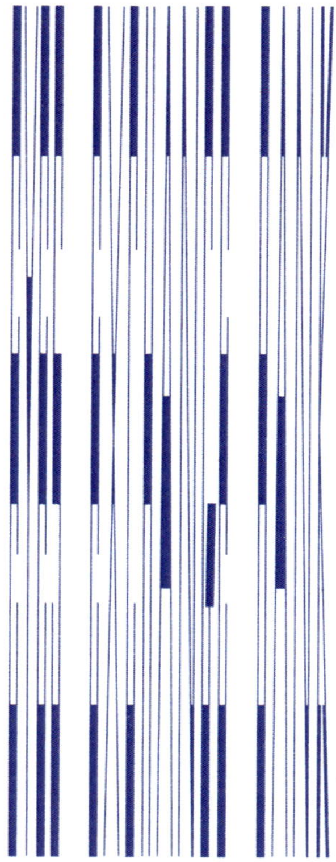

Il fallait pour comprendre, pour percevoir d'un seul coup toute l'image, faire concourir les lignes de hauteur au même

120

Plate 4. Anamorphosis in Maurice Roche, *Compact* (1966). © Éditions Le Seuil.

J'imaginais — machinalement — une réalisation pour le piano de cette glissade, ce couperet sonore

(sur la partition : ligne oblique descendante, de gauche à droite ;

sur le clavier : exécution de droite à gauche.

De sorte que, si les deux lignes se coupent en leur milieu dans l'espace,

le décalage dans le temps

entre la lecture et l'exécution a pour effet de supprimer le point d'insertion.)

, le choc à retardement

contre le choc. il se formait un angle obtus = « trait » oblique et « tenue » du *si*). (déchirant, déchirant l'étoffe d'un bruit blanc — dans la trame duquel Il se tissait un signal d'alerte — tocsin ?

Vous seriez traversé de plaintes confuses taillées dans un agglomérat d'injures de vociférations de menaces. « … il ne se rappelle « pas ? Et le coup qui lui a fait perdre la mémoire ? Non plus ? « Pourtant ça doit frapper ! » Je me faisais sonner les cloches… sonorité changeante, des harmoniques diverses apparaissant et disparaissant subitement… « Il n'est pas né amnésique de « parents amnésiques, etc. »

Plate 5. Double page from Maurice Roche, *Compact* (1966).

rubans d'informations) : « … années lumière calculées en « (quelques) secondes… »

(et se lance dans une suite d'exclamations gutturales progressivement accélérées et renforcées jusqu'à)

« … FLASH / BANG ! PIKA / DON ! « coup / lueur ! … obnubilation du jour par l'éclair même… »

(un hurlement)

J'avais, « descendu » par un coup sur la nuque cette fois, dérapé le long de mon court gémissement et, perdu le fil juste à ce moment, Il passait — voiture lancée à grande vitesse — un bruit tranchant : (à peu près du *fa*

au

si ———— ; je

me retrouvai quelques lignes plus bas que moi.

7. AU CINEMA
7. AT THE MOVIES
7. IM KINO

les mots se dégagent
the words break off, free
Wörter lösen sich

du temps comme l'éclaircie
of time as in a clearing
von der Zeit wie die Helle

couple d'amoureux au cinéma 1
lovers at the movies 1
Liebespaar im Kino 1

déplacer nuages
to move all the clouds
Wolken versetzen

versus déplacer montagnes
versus moving a mountain
gegen Berge versetzen

couple d'amoureux au cinéma 2 (photographie aux infrarouges)
lovers at the movies 2 (infrared photography)
Liebespaar im Kino 2 (Infrarot-Aufnahme)

la douceur permise
a softness allows
erlaubte Wohltat

Plate 6. A page from David Lespiau, *Ouija Board* (2008). © Éditions Héros-limite.

PART FOUR

Cinema's Print Culture in Poetry

CHAPTER NINE

Postlyricism and the Movie Program

From Jarry to Alferi

Consider this passage from a long 1914 poem by Max Jacob: "Printemps et cinématographe mêlés" (Spring and the cinematograph intermixed):

> Buds are as bitter as a hospital bed
> And you can see the lawn through a crystal.
> . . .
> And hazel trees without lilac
> Will be a support for honeysuckle,
> Tonight I am going to the movies [*au cinéma*].
>
> To the thoughtful theater of François de Curel
> Let us prefer the natural colors of the movies [*le Ciné*].
>
> With a music that is absurd
> We will see a parade of Kurds
> The son of the banker Capulet
> Madly in love with Juliet
> And if the story is too dumb
> The props won't be so ugly.[1]

This cinepoem "intermixes" spring and film—the green "lawn" seen through a "crystal" lens. Images of growth, from trees and flowers to birds and insects do not point to the pastoral ode of romanticism: they suggest instead the automorphic images of cinema. Jacob—living in Paris, across the street form the Val-de-Grâce military hospital—deploys a *poetics of splicing* that collates fragmentary sights of nature in the Latin Quarter and references to a medley of movies and movie genres, as an alternative to the tropes and metaphors of lyricism.

A typical movie program around 1914 would comprise several short *actualités* (newsreels), several short slapstick, chase or trick films, and one or two multireel features adapted from literature or history, or serial pulp crime fiction. This explains the reference to a Kurdish parade abruptly juxtaposed with an adaptation of *Romeo and Juliet*, and further on in the poem allusions to Sherlock Holmes, the visit of the King of England to Italy, a detective feature, and a play by Molière. For Jacob, the seemingly random conflation of genres, geographic spaces, styles and tones in a movie program is in fact in tune with the patchwork of "natural colors" of spring, and represents a truer and more popular form of theater than that of playwright François de Curel.[2]

The heteroclite nature of the film program informs Jacob's apology for cinema over theater in an essay from 1918. For him cinema shows that "a king on screen is but a squire with decorations," and by celebrating the scientist and the gangster equally, it becomes "the living epithalamium of the wedding of all human forces with all others." The new sense of totality, hand in hand with social leveling, places everything in relation with everything else. Concluding that, "The cinematograph realizes the unreal"—a proposal close to Saint-Pol-Roux's "ideorealizer" notion of cinema—Jacob explains that "all the splendors of the world are juxtaposed (*rapprochées*) so as to generate powerful effects." The movie program, in its randomized juxtapositions of the real and the unreal, the documentary and the fictional, not only showed the whole gamut of filmic genres available, it also presented a radical prototype of montage that could not yet be achieved within a single movie.[3]

THE PROBLEM OF PROSE POEM COLLECTIONS

Jacob and Reverdy both revived the prose poem after 1915, competing intensely with each other to define the form anew.[4] Reverdy invoked the "high" model of Rimbaud's *Illuminations* to craft introspective collages of images, while Jacob sought a synthesis of personal anecdote, popular culture, and gnomic humor. Reverdy's 1920 prose collection title *Flaques de verre* (Glass puddles) declares its focus on the visual by obliquely referring to Rimbaud's *Illuminations'* initial title—*Painted Plates* (original English)—that is, slides for a magic lantern painted on glass plates, or *plaques de verre*. As for Jacob, his 1917 prose collection *Le Cornet à dés* (The dice cup) winks at Mallarmé's *A Throw of the Dice*, by welcoming elements of chance in the heterogeneity of voice, discourse, and tone of the collection. It contains two poems on Feuillade's *Fantômas*, another titled "The Cinematograph," and several concerning popular and serial novels. While both immersed in cinema, the two collections develop a different prose cinepoetics: Reverdy's poems center on collaged images and tend toward homogeneity, /prose poem⇔montage of film images/, while Jacob favors the more macroscopic scale of the film program: /prose poem collection⇔sampling from disparate films/.[5]

How prose poems may alter the function of poetry collections is a question Walter Benjamin tackles indirectly in thinking about the structure of *Les Fleurs du mal*, Baudelaire's verse poems. In "On Some Motifs in Baudelaire," Benjamin argues that if there is a "secret architecture in [*Les Fleurs du mal*]," it is to be found in Baudelaire's shock-experiences of modernity (*Erlebnis*) that foreclosed the poet's introspective experience (*Erfahrung*), whose cultivation had been the traditional conceit of the lyric.[6] Benjamin characterizes "the plan at work in the composition [of the collection]" as a kind of grid to be filled: "Blank spaces hovered before him, and into these [Baudelaire] inserted his poems."[7] Benjamin then famously equates this process of filling-up with various shock-experiences: the chance exchange of gaze in a crowd, taking a snapshot, viewing a film, factory assembly work, and gambling.[8] For Benjamin, we might say, *Les Fleurs du mal* represents the last lyric work of modernity because the impossibility of making recollections of shock-experiences cohere has become the structuring (postlyrical) principle of a collection of verse. Yet, it is oddly from the preface of Baudelaire's *prose* poem collection, *Le Speen de Paris*—a work of postlyricism as such, and about which Benjamin says almost nothing—that he derives "the decisive, unmistakable experience,"[9] of Baudelaire's life, which forms the "hidden figure" that organizes *Les Fleurs du mal*: "the crowd . . . imprinted on his creativity."[10]

Benjamin elides Baudelaire's prose poetics because he wishes to locate prose modernism in a spectrum having Proust at one pole, and newspapers at the other. Proust's novel exemplifies the "effort it took to restore the figure of the storyteller" through involuntary memory,[11] which Benjamin triangulates through Bergson and Freud's memory trace, so as to make it the equivalent in prose of Baudelaire's "secret architecture" in verse. Benjamin's other prose model, the newspaper, represents the antithesis of both Baudelaire's verse and Proust's prose:

> If it were the intention of the press to have the reader assimilate the information it supplies as part of his own experience, it would not achieve its purpose. But its intention is just the opposite, and it is achieved: to isolate events from the realm in which they could affect the experience of the reader. The principles of journalistic information (newness, brevity, clarity, and above all, lack of connection between the individual news items) contribute as much to this as the layout of the pages and the style of writing[12]

These principles of "newness, brevity, clarity, and above all, lack of connection" are precisely those of the prose poems of *Le Spleen de Paris*. In the part of the preface that Benjamin does not cite, Baudelaire argues that, "We can cut where we want; I, my daydreaming, you the manuscript, the reader his reading: for I do not suspend the latter's reticent will to the interminable thread of a superfluous plot." And he adds, "Hack it in many fragments, and you will see that each can exist on its own"—exactly like newspaper articles.[13] So Benjamin transfers back to *Les Fleurs du mal* the random and antinarrative structure of Baudelaire's prose poem collection, as well as the optical shock-experiences it foregrounds. My point is that Reverdy and Jacob, in reinventing the prose poem, went back to Baudelaire's prose collection and reinterpreted its principle of random sampling of optical experiences with the cinema in mind, and in the case of Jacob, the film program as such.

Dominique Combe has proposed that French poets after Mallarmé, from Valéry to Breton and Bonnefoy, were committed to what he calls "a rhetoric of genres," whereby poetry can only define itself as the pure opposite of narrative.[14] Combe sees it is as a category mistake since, whereas a narrative organizes acts of language at a deep cognitive level, poetry is merely a genre resting on fluid conventions—not a linguistic structure. The prose poem hence occupies a vexed and liminal place in much poetic theory. On the one hand it shows poetry and narrative not to be antinomic, while on the other hand it brings attention to small differences that might reinforce the presumed opposition. Benjamin's hesitancy to confront *Le Spleen de Paris* suggests that he had not overcome the rhetoric of genres, thus preventing him from seeing the prose poems of Jacob and other pre-Dada cinepoets as a new assemblage poetics refracting both Baudelaire's panoramic sampling and the generic diversity of movie programs.

Film exhibition practices in France have a complex and varied history that still remains only partially known. Itinerant and fairground exhibition programs in the early years of cinema presented hybrid shows of live acts, musical numbers, oral commentary, and one-reel films of miscellaneous genres. The rise of movie palaces with set show schedules (ca. 1905) and of the more highbrow multireel feature (ca. 1910) reorganized exhibition practices. The first salient feature for my purpose was the exhibitors' imperative after 1910 to manage audience interest by way of "sequencing principles" (order of film genres) and "measures to either prevent or encourage links between successive films" including by editing the films directly.[15] Nico de Klerk insists, however, that such control was illusory, in the face of spectators' potential to make their own associations. We may then assume that, besides the automorphic imaginary, spectator poets like Jacob reframed the question of the relationship between poems through an imaginary of linkage and accidental refractions derived from associations between heteroclite films in early cinema. A case in point is Jacob's friend Alfred Jarry.

JARRY'S PROSE CINEPOEMS

As Maria Tortajada has shown and as we have seen, Jarry was among the earliest poets to have been fascinated by the cinema apparatus: he mentions *le cinématographe* from 1897 onward in five different texts.[16] In *Gestes et opinions du Docteur Faustroll* (Exploits and opinions of Doctor Faustroll pataphysician) written in 1898, Jarry explains the function of an imaginary machine in the chapter titled "Clinamen." The name comes from Lucretius' atomism in which clinamen denotes the random swerve of an atom in the constantly moving cosmos. Jarry describes his Clinamen as a "Painting Machine" that rotates on itself, "blowing" on the "canvas of the walls a succession of fundamental colors."[17] Maria Tortajada has keenly noted the cinematic character of the machine. I would like to expand upon her insight, and consider the short titled prose texts embedded in the "Clinamen" chapter as transposing an early film program into cinepoems.

The number of texts in the 1898 "Clinamen"—thirteen—fits well with a movie program: screenings featured from ten to twenty shorts between 1896 and 1901.[18] Moreover, the overall register of Jarry's titles echoes that of one-reel films in contemporary catalogues—sometimes quite strikingly:

JARRY'S "CLINAMEN" (1898)	FILMS FROM 1896–1901
"Nabuchodonosor changé en bête"	

(Nebuchadnezzar Changed Into a Beast)	
"Le Fleuve et la prairie" (The River and the Meadow)	*Baignade dans le torrent* (Méliès, 1897) (Swimming in A Stream)
"Vers la croix" (To The Cross)	*Le Chemin de croix* (Lumière, 1898) (Way of the Cross)
"Dieu défend à Adam et Ève de toucher l'arbre du bien et du mal. L'Ange Lucifer s'enfuit" (God Forbidding Adam and Eve From Touching the Tree of Good and Evil. Lucifer Flees)	
"Amour" (Love)	*Idylle* (Gaumont, 1898) (Idyll)
"Le Bouffon" (The Buffoon)	*Tom Old Boots* (Méliès, 1896)
"'Plus loin! Plus loin!' crie Dieu aux résignés" (Farther! Farther! God Shouts To The Resigned)	
"La peur fait le silence" (Fear Falls Silent)	*Un horrible cauchemar* (1901) (A Horrible Nighmare)
"Aux enfers" (In Hell)	*La damnation de Faust* (Méliès, 1898) (The Damnation of Faust)
"De Bethléem aux oliviers" (From Bethlehem to The Olive Garden)	*La Crèche à Bethléem* (1898) (The Manger in Bethleem)
Le Jardin des oliviers (1898) (The Olive Garden)	
"Simple sorcière" (Simple Witch)	*Chez la sorcière* (Méliès, 1901) (The Witch's House)
"Sortant de sa félicité, Dieu crée les mondes"	

(Leaving His Felicity God Creates
The Worlds)

"Les Médecins et l'amant" (The Doctors and the Lover)[19]	*Le Malade imaginaire* (Méliès, 1898) (The Imaginary Invalid)

With the exception of titles referring to the Old Testament, the thematic similarity is plain, more so than the exact title or date of the films (titles tended to vary, and film companies pilfered each other's treatment and titles). The one-reel films on the New Testament are from *La vie et la passion de Jésus Christ* (France, 1898, dir. G. Hadot, Lumière cat. #933–945) which was sold in thirteen episodes that exhibitors could buy and project individually or rearrange in their programs. This is just what Jarry appears to do, in both "showing" the Road to the Cross before the Olive Garden, and conflating into one text the films on Bethlehem and The Olive Garden. A clear reference to cinema comes from textual indications in the first embedded text, "Nebuchadnezzar Changed into a Beast," which concerns an episode from *The Book of Revelation* (Daniel 4). Describing the palace of the king, Jarry writes that "the architecture, resulting from all these flames, is quite animated and moving (*animée et mouvante*), but too Romantic!"[20] A mention of the moon in quasi close-up might refer to another famous 1898 Méliès film, *La Lune à un mètre* (The astronomer's dream). This prose cinepoem is highly visual and kinetic, featuring vivid colors and a "metamorphosis." This would seem to point doubly to the films of Méliès, specifically in 1898, since his use of hand-painted color stencils,[21] and his development that year of a new genre of trick films called "scène à transformation" (transformation film), gave him a leg up on the competition. These films used scale shifts (with long axial dolly shots), caches, stop action, and multiple exposures to show such scenes as human limbs being severed, moving, or dancing freely before reuniting with their bodies.

The second prose cinepoem is much shorter, a bucolic scene anthropomorphizing a male river, a female meadow and a child-island, and it may be based on a number of sundry shorts showing rivers and bathers. Its sequencing exemplifies the jarring "lack of connection" of both prose poem collections and film programs. This effect is repeated by the third cinepoem which renders the crucifixion as an infernal scene that recalls paintings by Hieronymus Bosch, with a whirling Pierrot and devils with "legs of acrobats," such as are found in Méliès's *Cakewalk infernal*

(1903) and Edison's earlier *Skeleton Dance, Marionettes* (1898). The other cinepoems tend to cultivate the neomedieval grotesque vein of Méliès tricks, such as "Farther! Farther! God Shouts to the Resigned":

> The mountain is red, the sun and the sky. A finger points upward. Rocks spring forth, the uncontested mountaintop is not in sight. Some bodies that have not reached it roll back down, head first. One body falls backward on his hands, letting go of his guitar. The other is waiting, walking backward, near his bottles. One body lies on the road, letting his eyes go on with the ascension. The finger still points, and the sun is waiting to be obeyed before disappearing.[22]

Jarry focuses on movements typical of the cinema of attractions (spurting, rolling, falling, walking, disappearing), and crafts visual and nonnarrative textual fragments with a dynamic ekphrastic character, set within the firm boundaries of a typical *tableau* film. The autonomous eyes suggest at the very least a form of immersion of the gaze in a film. Cinema is the perfect illustration of 'pataphysics [*sic*], which Jarry defines as "the science of those beings and contraptions [*engins*], either present or future, together with the Power of their Use (*discipulus*)."[23] Jarry uses the Latin form of "disciple" for its original meaning of "handling" and "manipulating." Méliès's manipulations of reality through the cinema apparatus would have qualified as 'pataphysical in Jarry's eyes, especially since 'pataphysics approaches "objects as described through their virtuality [*virtualité*]."[24] We have shown in the introduction how Mallarméan ideas of virtuality, potentiality and latency open up connections between language and vision that cinepoetics explored so as, in Jarry's own words, "to describe a universe that we can see and perhaps that we should see in place of the traditional one."[25] In another 1898 text, linked to the Faustroll cycle, Jarry offers a 'pataphysical explanation of the Time-Machine (of Wells) ostensibly relying on the theory of duration of his own high-school philosophy teacher—Henri Bergson:

> The way into the Past consists of the perception of the reversibility of phenomena. We will see the apple bouncing upward from ground to tree, or the dead man wake up, and the ball return into the canon. This *visual* aspect of succession is well known to be theoretically obtainable by going faster than light, then continuing to move outward at a constant speed equal to light. The Machine, on the contrary, will transport the Explorer with all his senses to the very heart of Duration rather than into a hunt for images preserved by Space.[26]

This semisatirical mash of Wells, physics, and Bergson conceals Jarry's reliance on the exclusive sensorium of cinema: reverse motion—the signature of early film—and "the *visual* aspect of succession," that is, automorphosis as such. For Jarry, the new sensorial apparatus of cinema commands a new order of poetic images exceeding static iconicity and traditional pictoriality toward the self-unfolding of the image.

The earliest expression of Jarry's cinepoetics is found in his first poetry collection, *Les Minutes de sable mémorial* (The minutes of memorial sand) of 1894, which mixes prose, verse and dialogue pieces, together with hieratic woodblock prints. First published in June 1893, Jarry's liminal poem, "Lieds Funèbres" (Funereal lieder), opens with images projected on a white screen through a *succession* of magic lantern plates. The first line reads: "On the completely white screen [*l'écran blanc*] of the great tragic sky, the black centipedes of funerals pass by [*défilent*], like glass plates in a monotonous magic lantern."[27] The stroboscopic effect from the decomposition of movement into "centipedes" or "mille-pattes" (as if anticipating Balà's famous 1911 painting of a dog with stroboscopic legs!) and the implicit desire to hasten and diversify the images of "dead" poetry, point both back to Marey's experiments with walking and running and may well reflect Uzanne's account of Edison's *Kinetograph* in *Le Figaro* in April 1893. It is also quite likely that in high school in 1892, he attended with his friend and future poet Léon-Paul Fargue, the Musée Grévin shows of Émile Reynaud, whose sequential projection of hand-painted gelatin plates represents the earliest kind of nonphotographic cinema show.[28]

Jarry's prose cinepoetics opens an oblique path between his ideas on physics, philosophy, and pulp entertainment. In 1903, Jarry published "Opinion of a Man Cut in Pieces," a burlesque dialogue about the dangers of the automobile for pedestrians, taking place between the narrator and a man "divided in disparate fragments."[29] That the man is still alive and seems unconcerned suggests the plot of Feuillade's film, *Le Bon Écraseur* (Run over by a nice driver) (1906), in which a drunken man falls asleep on the pavement and has his legs cutoff at midthigh by a passing taxicab. The man wakes up, sits on the road, and wags one of his legs at the off-screen car. Fortunately, the cab's fare is a doctor who gets off and calmly reattaches the legs, the man walking away unperturbed. The film was sufficiently famous that the journal *L'Illustration* wrote an article with lavish photographs. There are a number of precedents to this film, in British cinema particularly, such as Cecil Hepworth, *How It Feels to Be Run Over* (1900) and W. R. Booth, *Cab Accident* (1903), with similar, if less finely executed, special effects. Jarry's journalistic piece clearly refers to this specific subgenre of trick films. Taken together, Jarry's indirect evocations of the cinema to come (1894), a random movie program (1898), and a "run-over by automobile" film (1903) demonstrate the depth and scope of his cinepoetic thought.

"ALMOST CINEMA": SEGALEN'S PROSE *BONIMENTS*

In a letter of 1913, following publication of *Stelae*, his collection of visual prose poetry, Victor Segalen confided that he had wanted to invent "a new literary genre" with poems written in *versets* (short rhythmic prose stanzas) presented as derived from Chinese sources.[30] He adds that the book "can still be called a collection of prose poems, although the rectangle containing them frames rather harshly this otherwise elastic genre." He continues by referencing the project he had begun in 1912, *Peintures* (Paintings), which would be published in 1916:

> *Paintings* will have no established name. . . . If I had to give it one, I could find no other than "Running Commentary [*Boniments*]," or "Parade on the stage-fair." . . . A crowd, spectators to amaze, and large canvases with bright colors . . . to be commented upon, "to show off" [*faire voir*]. Here, since it is literature, there are no canvases, and words alone must not only summon the image but become image [*faire l'image*]. . . . Verbal phantasmagorias . . . [31]

The conceit of *Stelae* is that the layout of the poems invokes and retains something of steles of rock actually sitting on the ground in China: they present themselves, in Charles Peirce's semiotics, as "indexes" materially tied to what they refer to. With *Peintures* written as running prose, the semiotic relation of indexicality is imaginary and virtual: no painting "exists" except through the performing of words. While this is in some sense the basic condition of fictive writing in general, I argue that Segalen's emphasis on "becom[ing] image," involves the same rejection as Jarry's renouncing "the hunt for images preserved in Space," in order to develop a new prose cinepoetics. In other words, the prose poem approached as static and indexical stele has made way to the becoming-image of an imaginary painting—with the crucial addition of the *boniment.*

The year 1913 marks an important shift in the standardized presentation of movies in theaters. Early cinema until then had relied on diversified and sensational elements (for instance, a heteroclit program with narration, music, and folley artist, interspersed with live acts), what historians have called "a system of monstrative attractions." Around 1913, the movie show began centering on longer fiction films with more complex plots and edits, giving rise to a new filmic regime based on "a system of narrative integration."[32] One consequence was the somewhat abrupt disappearance in France of the lecturer-commentator, whose role had been to assist the audience in the reception of filmic images. The commentator's spectrum of discourses and performances included explanation, punctuation, mimics, side-jokes, shadows, and so on, aiming both to entertain, channel, and even discipline the audience.[33] The commentator was named in French "*bonimenteur*," "*bonisseur*," and "*conférencier*," and his (it was almost always a man) more or less improvised verbal performance was consistently referred to as "*boniment*."[34] In the new poems of *Paintings*, set on a stage and describing Chinese paintings, Segalen insists that "everything must be secondary to the fundamental attitude: a Commentary [*Boniment*]."[35] Both the preface and the prose pieces themselves leave little doubt that Segalen offered these paintings, like those of Jarry's Clinamen, as thin palimpsests for movies.

Although some of the paintings are flat panels juxtaposed to create a large picture, most are scroll-paintings, "unrolled [*déroulées*] from top to bottom."[36] For the filmmaker Eisenstein such scrolls were the direct predecessors of movies.[37] After characterizing the book's pieces as "spoken Paintings," that are "not suited for interruptions,"[38] Segalen invites readers to open themselves to a particular state of attentiveness: "This is a reciprocal work: on my side, a kind of parade, a monstration [*une montre*], a *boniment* . . . [and] a *certain* attention, a *certain* acceptance from you."[39] The focus on attention evokes the quasi-hypnotic trance that Jules Romains had explained in his 1911 essay on movie spectatorship. Segalen continues, "Let yourself be surprised by this, which is not a book, but something said, a call, an evocation, a *spectacle*. And you will quickly agree that to see [*voir*] . . . means to participate in the Painter's gesture; it means *to move* [*se mouvoir*] into the depicted space . . . I unroll [*déroule*] the first of these Paintings."[40] Segalen's preface prepares its audience to read his pieces cinepoetically, using the phonetic embedding of "voir" within "mouvoir," to focus the "spectacle" on the kinetic process of "unfolding" represented by one verb springing out of the other. He also urges readers not to ask themselves "whether the drawn protagonists have *one* dimension in space, or two or three . . . "[41]—which suggests just the kind of transdimensional leap (from 2-D text to 3-D film) that marks the cinepoetic imaginary.

The pieces themselves follow no particular order, and present in jarring juxtaposition humorous, vaudeville and dramatic prose poems, precisely with the randomness of a movie program. As in Jarry's case, the similarities between Segalen's titles and films by Méliès, are quite striking:

SEGALEN'S *PEINTURES*	FILMS BY MÉLIÈS
"Cinq génies aveugles" (Five Blind Genies)	*Les Deux Aveugles* (1900) (The Two Blindmen)
	Le Génie du feu (1908) (The Fire Genie)
"Eventail Volant" (1904) (The Flying Fan)	*Le Merveilleux Eventail vivant* (The Marvelous Living Fan)
	La Femme volante (1902) (The Flying Woman)
"Peinture vivante" (Living Painting)	*Peinture animée* (1903) (Animated Painting)
	Le Portrait spirite (1903) (Magical Portrait)
"La Flamme amante" (The Flame Lover)	*La Flamme merveilleuse* (1903) (The Marvelous Flame)
	La Danse du feu (1899) (The Fire Dance)

We should note that all these films belong to the first period of early cinema (1895–1908) in contradistinction to the shift toward narrative movies (1908–13), and the onset of the "studio system" mode of production with intertitles and tighter continuity after 1913. References in the text evoke the filmic world of Méliès as well, such as its "smoke and mirror" apparatuses: "What is being readied is mobile and mechanical. A kind of / THEATRICAL GESTICULATION / . . . the machine is as shoddy as the infernal apparition and fires and flames and smokes around the genie."[42] Méliès's made abundant use of fire, flame and smoke, for instance in the *Cake-walk infernal* in which hellish demons (often in blackface) appear and disappear in a flash of smoke. In Segalen's "Flamme amante," a flame progressively transforms into a woman

Figure 38. "Scène à transformation" film showing an inanimate object (a playing card) coming to life, from Georges Méliès, *Les cartes vivantes* (1905).

and back into a flame,[43] recalling a well-worn Méliès trick of successive dissolves played forward and backward to show a metamorphosis, then its undoing (Figure 38). A "machinic apotheosis" described in another section of the book shows a water-powered machine animating musical flying puppets for a whole night, and it resembles hybrid exhibitions of film, puppetry, and songs on phonograph, in turn-of-the-century fairgrounds.[44] Segalen's anachronism suggests that what motivates *Peintures*, in part, is the celebration of early exhibition venues and formats now lost and normalized. His entropic fears that Maori, Tahitian, and Chinese cultures were losing their specificity extended to Europe's waning diversity of mass cultural practices.

Segalen's cinepoetics in *Paintings* has philosophical, programmatic, and intuitive aspects.[45] In 1913, while planning his expedition to China, he mentions taking along a stereoscopic still camera and a projector, with a view to giving paying lectures with still projections upon his return. He summarizes these plans as: "conferences; projections; almost cinema."[46] Returning to France in the midst of the war, he reworked *Paintings* throughout 1915 but makes no further references to cinema. There is little question, however, that the screen and the materiality of film reveal themselves in *Peintures* beneath "the twelve large leaves of a screen [*écran*] higher than a man with his hand raised"[47]—roughly the scale of a movie screen—and the "enveloping and continuous painting . . . two-thousand yards long [*deux mille pas*],"[48] which is comparable in length to multireel films ca. 1913.[49] The *bonimenteur* repeatedly and hypnotically exhorts the spectator/reader to "unroll without discontinuity from right to left," "unroll, unroll," "unroll slowly."[50] This places the reader in the position of the film operator responsible for and capable of varying the speed of the projection: /reading a prose poem⇔hand-cranking a film/. Implicitly, this allows reverse motion—again, the unmistakable "signature" of early cinema—to become part of the self-enacted imaginary of the reader, for instance, when a painter is said to "rise up like the wind in a reversed fall [*chute inversée*],"[51] or when a whole "parade" (a favored film genre in early newsreels) is shown backward: "here all the characters are in motion and walk hastily. . . . You could even force the Parades to walk backward and rivers to swallow back their source."[52] Other perceptual and sensorial motifs belonging to cinema proper include a zoom-in combined with a moving POV: "In this isometric space, without the fear of being crushed by the foreground, freed from the 'point of view,' taking our size to the farthest reaches, we can . . . take part [in the Feast]."[53] This plunge into a pictorial space freed from POV seems difficult to reconcile with noncinematic thought. The poem "Eventail volant" (Flying fan), ostensibly a painting on a fan, describes in quickly succeeding near-dissolves, several fuzzy and fragmented images of wings, eyes, and pagoda, before lingering on a monk's living eyes and rotten body, ultimately settling on his face: "Here is a surprised face staring at you; so magically and deeply that it is about to adhere to your face and become *your face*."[54] Only the close-up, with its virtual protrusion into the viewer's perceptual space, generates such a fantasmatic sensation of adhesion. Compare with Epstein's description of the CU in 1921: "When a character is going to meet another, I want to go along with him, not behind him or in front of him or by his side, but in him. I would like to look through his eyes and see his hand reach from under me as if it were my own."[55] In this same poem, the *bonimenteur* exhorts the operator to "fan some more, fan," instructing the reader that the painting must be "spread out with one sharp flick of thumb and index finger," although it is useless to "count the number of ivory blades."[56] Mallarmé used the fan both as a writing surface and as an analogy to the material virtuality of the book; here, Segalen appears to refract the cinema apparatus quite directly by focusing on its flickering effect, recalling also the para-cinematic technology of the mutoscope or flip-book.[57]

In "Quatre peintures dioramiques pour les néoménies des saisons" (Four dioramic paintings for the neomenies of the seasons), the spectator is invited to "enter" a cave then lift her gaze: "look up from the bottom of this immense tank of which you are the pivot," the *bonimenteur* says.[58] The high angle reveals a portion of the sky where the first moon of each season can be seen: the spectator is invited to turn ninety-degrees at a time (each turn replete with embedded stories) in a 360-degree dioramic view. Yet before the circle is complete, a new poem-painting fades in, "The Ring of Immortals," of which the narrator had offered a glance fifty pages earlier from a different POV.[59] We begin to suspect that the set of paintings forms an overall immersive space made of prose cinepoems connected to one another. Such a virtual dioramic or surround cinema eschews the paralysis that Foucault detected in Roussel's "La Vue," because the absence of clear suturing and definite ordering on one hand, and the reader's active participation and optical involvement on the other hand, contribute to maintaining Segalen a degree of virtuality to ekphastic immersion.

The apparent "lack of connection" among films in a movie program comes with the possibility that new connections can be made. Similarly, the lack of overt transitions in *Peintures*—yet the suggestion that interpenetrations are possible—opens the prose cinepoems to one another, at the reader's fancy. There is a deeper philosophical concern at play in such open-endedness. In Segalen's view of the universe, only *the unending possibility of alternate order* can vouchsafe cosmic and human diversity and keep entropy at bay. This potentiality redefines postlyric subjectivity along the model of an open-ended film archive out of which "these Paintings for too long enfolded [*pliées*] at the bottom of myself,"[60] can be reprojected by the reader-operator in any number of new ways, with any number of new boniments. Taken together, the prose cinepoems of *Peintures* mobilize the film program as a tool against entropy.[61]

In "On Some Motifs in Baudelaire," Benjamin wrestles with the place of photography in Baudelaire's poetics, since he directly associates it with the snapshot, while conjecturing that if Baudelaire disapproved of the daguerreotype it was because it destroyed the aura. Benjamin's approach is paradoxical in that he looks at photography as a process—*the photograph* in its reproducibility—rather than a product: a mass of *photographs*. Even the snapshot is singularized: "With regard to countless movement of switching, inserting, pressing, and the like, the 'snapping' by the photographer had the greatest consequences."[62] This retraining of the human sensorium through the snapshot leads, for Benjamin, straight to cinema as another singularized process. Yet "a mass of photographic images," as Sheryl Krueger has shown, occupies the center of "Mademoiselle Bistouri (Miss Scalpel)," a prose poem by Baudelaire that she reads as an implicit theory of prose poetry.[63] Philippe Ortel has confirmed the influence of books or series of photographs as new models for the prose poems for Baudelaire and Rimbaud, on an equal footing with photography as a process.[64]

This brings us back to Segalen. While he prepared the manuscript of *Paintings* for publication in 1916, the photographs of his expedition to China were published in scholarly articles and were circulating in sinological milieux (the Académie des Inscriptions et Belles-Lettres in Paris, and the Royal Asiatic Society in London and Shanghai), often accompanied by an explanatory text he wrote.[65] From 1914 onward it is his photographic work in China that propelled his budding career as a sinologist. Giving an account of his May 1917 conference in Shangai, he writes that "the projections worked very well" and that they amounted not to "a mundane chat or a cinema," but a scholarly exposé.[66] Hence from 1913 to 1917, he describes his own lecturing with photographic projections in reference to "cinema," while writing and publishing *Peintures* as a book of prose poems envisioned as a running *boniment* on highly kinetic pictures. These actual and imaginary performances mark the range of his cinepoetics: texts that open the punctum of still images through the filmic imaginary, shirk narrative closure, yet remain an "almost cinema."

POETIC EXPANSIONS OF THE MOVIE PROGRAM

The movie program of poets involves not just imaginary films (and other live acts or attractions), but a more or less implicit or virtual space of performance, and also a text that puts that space in motion, in play and in time. This constitutes a secondary apparatus distinct from the primary apparatus of cinema (projector, screen, and viewer). In 1918, poet and budding filmmaker Marcel L'Herbier released a film and a lavish booklet with the same long title: *Rose-France, cantilène héroïque en noir et blanc composé et visualisé par Marcel L'Herbier* (Rose-France, heroic cantilena in black-and-white composed and visualized by Marcel L'Herbier).[67] The booklet opens with a "Programme" section (in lieu of a table contents). It lists "unpublished impressions" by the likes of Georgette Leblanc-Maeterlinck, "a summary of the film," "stills of the actors," and "suggestions for illustrating and defending a French conception of the cinema." Quotes in verse are decorated with symbolist imagery (peacocks and grapes). Alain Carou has retraced the history of such "brochure-programs," which developed in the hinge period 1907–14, before progressively disappearing together with the *bonimenteur* during World War I. Starting around 1911, under the impulsion of multireel movies, such programs contained a full summary of the film from four to eight pages, up to fifteen pages in 1914.[68] Since projections halls were dark, these programs raise questions of how and when spectatorial and reading practices intermixed, and whether they were coordinated with live commentary or intertitles. Also, spectators are often directly addressed by the program text, thus integrating them within the "program" as it were—yet either before or after the performance. Carou indicates that after 1915, the pulp novelization of films—part of Epstein's "subliterature"—produced by the publishing industry (rather than film companies) took over this ancillary market, sometimes publishing adaptations before the film itself came out. L'Herbier's booklet demonstrates that the "brochure-program" format was not necessarily ancillary: it could have its *own* program, sometimes with a manifesto-like quality. If we look at the discursive structure of one of the earliest manifestoes of the new French avant-garde, Apollinaire's 1913 "The Futurist Antitradition," we recognize under its heterogeneous lists and sublists a program of future steps (among which is inventing "phonocinematography") not unlike a brochure-program, even including a list of "roles" with both villains and heroes.[69]

Irène Hillel-Erlanger's *Voyages en kaleïdoscope* (1919) includes a long section titled "Journal-Program [*programme-journal*] of the Great Kaleidoscope Trips," that embeds such a "brochure-program" within the poetic scenario. The program is authored by Gilly, the apprentice of Joël Joze who invented the "Kaléïdo," the latter asking him to "write down, casually, the way we talk, our [future] projections and your *boniments.* With that we will have enough to print a Journal-Program."[70] Hillel-Erlanger, who was herself a scenarist for Germaine Dulac, recycles the direct address to spectators as a prominent feature of this section, inventing five Dada-like "movies" that combine prose, free-verse typography, and drawings by Van Dongen. The proleptic aspect of the brochure-program is emphasized by repeated publicity interruptions within each "summary":

> (Note from the Manager: The limited space at our disposal in this program forces us to provide only an abstract of our Visions, compressed Trips. The rest will be on the Screen.)[71]

> (The Manager reminds the public that luxuriant and suggestive details are amply provided on the screen. Uninterrupted shows day and night.)[72]

The movie program as ancillary text merely *announcing* to its *readers* the fictive "films" to come, curiously shifts to present the last film as if directly *enacted* on screen for its *viewers*. Hence what reads like the summary of the fifth and last film suddenly gives way to several lines of ellipses and the mention, "(5 minutes of interruption: power outage),"[73] as if the movie show had been "live" and the ellipses represented the darkened screen. The undetectable difference between telling (as summary) and showing (as film) demonstrates the slipperiness between the various layers of fictive texts and ekphrastic performances. The fifth film is about a telephone whose battery has died: the film's plot contaminates its own performance, it seems, which in turn suspends the program after it has mysteriously shifted from "text" to "projection."

The plots of the five films largely defy summary because they veer into a form of *boniment* to the viewers/readers, becoming themselves poetic performances of a uniquely virtual kind, all at once filmic, textual, and verbal. For instance, the third film is titled "Alphabet"[74] and begins: "Public / you see here / the Imprimerie nationale (or another [printing press])." It invites us to consider the shapes and materiality of metal case letters as mediated by cinema: "These thin or smeared characters / in a wink of an eye / the Kaleido lends them / human bodies." While we readers/viewers are busy thinking through the polysemy of "characters" as linking letters to people, Hillel-Erlanger brings us right back on the page—not quite her page, but that of the fictional film program we are reading: "Public / when you read this chapbook / will you be angry? transported? / by Characters evil or good?" Clearly, it is not the voice of the fictive Manager addressing the would-be viewers of his films that speaks, nor that of Gilly who seems confident of his art, but that of Hillel-Erlanger, wondering whether the cinepoetic program will in fact cohere in the eyes of her readers/viewers.

In slipping into metadiscourse in this (new) way, Hillel-Erlanger is taking advantage of the reciprocal embedding of textual and visual media that the program-brochure deploys. The Kaleidoscope, the narrator reminds us in the program-brochure, functions by "a transformation that operates" on newsreels, largely through the free association of metaphors which the operator, Gilly, directly *impresses* onto the footage. This presumably nonconscious process, described as "another way of seeing,"[75] consists of Gilly's imagination refracting other movies, particularly those of Chaplin.[76] Of course, this process resembles the transformation by a skilled scriptwriter of a simple treatment into a series of scenes that can be both shot and assembled into a movie. We indeed find resemblances between Gilly's work and Hillel-Erlanger's own scriptwriting. In a short treatment for a film project by Dulac, "La Chienne jalouse de Colette" (Colette's jealous bitch, or The bitch jealous of Colette), slyly presented as being about Colette's relationship to animals, Hillel-Erlanger notes the need to develop "a double atmosphere" with "original notations on animal psychology," that climaxes in a "talking cure with Lady [the dog]."[77] This parallel figural register wherein dogs would become understandable to film viewers as both dogs and more than dogs, is just the metaphorical level at which Gilly works for his scripts and *boniments.*

The genre of the program-brochure allows Hillel-Erlanger to give a specifically cinepoetic form to the intermediary space where textuality undergoes radical transformation in order to fit the requirements of a treatment, a scenario, and finally a shooting script. It isn't clear who among her readers recognized the centrality of the program-brochure in her book. Louis Aragon gave a short and cryptic review of it in *Littérature* 9 (November 1919), which carefully manages to avoid referring to cinema, the imaginary films of Gilly, nonconscious processes or the connections between them. Hillel-Erlanger's uncanny cinepoetic metadiscourse qua program-brochure may nonetheless have become an inspiration for other surrealists. Georges Ribemont-Dessaignes, for instance, wrote a number of program-brochures and film novelizations for money, and was a steady presence in both French Dada and Surrealism.[78] Sadly, the disappearance of the program-brochure from the movie and material culture archive has rendered the essential cross-medium component of the cinepoetics of *Voyages en kaléïdoscope* all too opaque.

While the opacity of Hillel-Erlanger's prose cinepoems is due to our historical amnesia, other poets rendered the program-brochure opaque as a strategy for innovation. This is the case of the Canadian Marcel Dugas and his 1916 *Psyché au cinéma* (Psyche at the movies), a collection of nine long semiautobiographical prose poems. On the basis of Dugas's ironic backward look at his youth in the poems, his commentator Claude Filteau has suggested that we approach them as experiments with movie culture as a catalyst for the recovery of personal memory images in a process akin to psychoanalysis.[79] The French word "*psyché*," lends itself to such a reading since it denotes all at once the Greek life principle, the mythical heroine, and the post-Freudian psychological realm. Dugas invokes "*psyché*" also in its common usage of a full-length pivoting mirror, thus firming up the classical analogy: /textual cinema⇔self-reflection/.

According to Filteau, in the original 1915 layout, each poem displayed a similar peritext: (1) a generic title based on the word "shower" ("Quick Showers," "Frivolous Showers," "Dying Showers," and so on); (2) an explanatory footnote beginning with "In favor of . . . "; and (3) the title of the piece. For instance:

> LUKE-WARM SHOWERS (*)
> A Man of Order
> [text of first page of poem]
> [bottom of page:]
> (*) In favor of a voluptuous and ironic cinema, flowering with light sarcasms, flying around virgins that are mobile, caressing, and fluid like the water of a lake or mirrors.

We are left to wonder how the intriguing label, "*Douches . . .*" (Showers), designates a subgenre of cinema in writing. As *Psyché au cinéma* is explicitly—via the myth of Psyche and Cupid—concerned with love, and more obliquely with sex ("volupté," and "perversité" reappear insistently), we might for instance look into early "blue movies," a spectrum of films ranging from salacious *pochade* to staged voyeurism and hardcore pornography, in which taking baths served as the classical alibi for female nakedness.[80] We could also think about movies with thematic showers, such as *Saved by a Shower* (US, 1915, dir. Allen Curtis) or Fernand Zecca's 1902 *La Douche imprévue* (Unforeseen shower), yet neither kind of movie gives much of a hermeneutical hold on Dugas's framing.

Specific movie genres are referred in the poems. "On the Little Hats" (subtitled "Frivolous Showers") seems congruent with "quick-change" and "shadowgraphic" vaudeville acts by famous *chapeaugraphists* like Leopoldo Fregoli, featured on films of the Lumière (*Chapeaux à transformation*) (1897) and Méliès (*Dix chapeaux en soixante secondes*) (1896).[81] Another poem titled "He Was a Little Boy . . . " ("Quick Showers") cites literary children characters such as Alphonse Daudet's *Le Petit Chose* and Jules Renard's *Poil-de-Carotte*, next to a certain "Jack." The reference is almost certainly to Chaplin's 1915 *The Kid* played by child-actor Jack Coogan, the poem providing an imaginary life of Jack comparable to Soupault's 1930 *Charlot*. A third poem is an homage to Racine's "Phèdre" ("Burning showers"), and while no filmic adaptation of the play was made by 1916, Camille de Morlhon shot Racine's *Britannicus* in

1912, and Dugas may have tried envisioning sequences for a similar adaptation. For such an anti-Aristotelian medley of genres—comic, tragic-comic, tragic, bucolic (other poems resemble touristic newsreels of Paris and Italy)—no capacious form other than the movie program seems suitable.

The label "Showers," may well be a motivated metaphor for poetry's *permeation* by film, or cinepoetry's *immersive* imaginary—note the liquid register. In Paul Dermée's *Films, contes, soliloques, duodrames* (Films, tales, soliloquies, duodramas) (1919), mixing prose with quasi-verse cinepoems, figures of immersion are as central as in Romains' text on cinema of 1911 or Cocteau's cinepoetry. In Dermée's "Cosmogony," we read for instance:

> I remember my dives in the sea of
> Alise when I was a deep-sea diver for
> unforeseen beasts
> . . .
> Oh the weight of this whole
> column of water on my
> shoulders and on my heart
> . . .
> One by one my thoughts leave me and
> rise to the surface with the chains of
> air bubbles
> . . .
> All this plays back as a film in my me-
> Mory.[82]

Dermée's poetics proceeds from the broad analogy: /immersive sensorium of cinema⇔poetic sensorium of memory/. The dedication for Dugas's collection reads: "To mirages still floating, to the figures of my youth brought back before me, and that I have drunk again (*rebues*), with closed eyelids, in the night of reality's appearance."[83] The cinepoetic virtuality indicated by the "figures" projected behind "closed" eyes mobilizes a different water imagery—floatation rather than immersion, drinking rather than swimming. The sentence hinges on the very rare word "*rebues*," an uncanny echo of "*revues*" (seen again), which the syntagm "*figures . . . que j'ai* [ ]" would seem to require. This gesture of resistance to the immersive sensorium of cinema is central to Dugas's project, in that it implies a return to a romantic notion of the imagination and of reality, not far from Segalen's liminal "almost cinema." Exhortations to himself makes this clear:

> . . . imagine [this lesson of realism]—build with your mind, your sensibility and your bitterness an existence you barely know . . .[84]

> Be incoherent, be incoherent! And to tease nature, give to yourself, in imagination, the comedy of total perversity.[85]

Other cinepoets bracket the imagination the better to probe the prosthetic imaginary of film. But Dugas insists on another lyrical motif, voice: "I still listen, in my imagination, to the singing syllables alive on their lips . . . I drink their laughter."[86] As in the dedication, drinking substitutes to visual representation—active absorption or *in*-spiration undoes passive absorption in filmic images. Hence Phèdre, "shudders from the kiss that her delirious imagination created for an instant," and she is left to "drink the face of Hippolyte who flees to avoid her embrace."[87] In the brief coda to the collection, the self reflected and mediated by cinema is invited to drink poison:

> In a moment, ô Psyche, the proprietor of the cinema will come to tell me that you are dead. Drink this bitter beverage that my cruelty has distilled: it is your hemlock!
>
> . . .
>
> I will keep the memory of your eyes glazed over in which a sea seems to have become stopped.[88]

The label "Showers" thus points to a kind of decontamination from cinema's absorptive power to return to the unmediated sourcing of imagination within reality. A chastened Orpheus, the poet vows "not to blaspheme before reality anymore,"[89] choosing, "the night of reality's appearance" over the Eurydice-like night of cinema.

Cinematic elements nonetheless creep into this narrative of conversion away from cinema: for instance, the freeze-frame that arrests immersion within the eyes of dying Psyche-cinema. In "Paroles à la morte" (Words to the dead woman), the second of two poems in "Dying Showers" the poet entreats a female ghost to go back to the realm of the dead. Through her intercession, the narrator revives a second ghost, whose "imaginary remains" he thought had vanished. This ghost is a fatherly figure, a "dear old man" the savage whippings at whose hands the narrator recollects troublingly as acts of "love."[90] In the end, the narrator fully introjects this male ghost: "I felt him slip into me, he again inhabited my heart, head and senses. . . . He lived again in me, and me in him."[91] Such magic fusion with a double—here a paternal imago—partakes of the imaginary of doubling Edgar Morin argues cinema revived and transfigured: "The stars live on our substance, and we on theirs.

[They are] ectoplasmic secretions of our substance."[92] Dugas's narrator thanks the intercession of the female ghost by offering to "drink the imaginary blood,"[93] dripping from her "caved-in chest"[94]—a sensational image that can hardly sustain its dynamism.

Dugas's *Psyché au cinéma* is a paradoxical cinepoem that is perhaps seeking to reconvert the cinematic imaginary back into pure imagination. Yet to invert the immersive pull of cinema, Dugas deploys a purgative rhetoric that remains marked by the filmic gaze. While only the movie program appears to bring unity to the disparity of its mysterious genre, "douche," we might wonder if under the odd "rebues" of the dedication we should not also read "rebus." In this case, Dugas might be pitting an age-old form of visual decipherment against the effortless shower of images streaming from the screen.

PIERRE ALFERI: THE CINEPOETICS OF TV

The disappearance of the heteroclite movie program was among the early signs of the industrial uniformization of silent cinema. Perhaps the last ditch cinepoetic piece refracting the film program is a poem titled "L'escalier aux cent marches," by Benjamin Péret, from his aptly named backward-looking collection *De derrière les fagots* (From deep in the cellar) (1934). It is made of the title of a hundred mostly obscure films, and reads as a random program, a wild transect through the history of cinema. Already during the 1930s, and even more so in the aftermath of World War II producers firmed up their control of movie exhibition practices and imposed the fixed one- or two-feature format with newsreels (or in France, one short-feature and one long-feature). It was round this time that television arrived.

The variety of TV offerings led to a major revival of both the program matrix and the program in print, within a new major stricture: the seven-day TV program. The logic of time slots, audience share and advertiser control—although it was less salient in 1970s state-monopolized French TV than in corporate TV markets in the United States—imparted to the weekly program a calculated cyclical nature that dampened the possibilities of variations and unforeseen connections. So powerful was this new program matrix that in both French and English, synonymous with "a broadcast" (*une émission*), each showing became "a program" (*un programme*).

In 1994, poet Pierre Alferi (born 1962) published *Kub or*, a collection of verse poems accompanied with photos by Suzanne Doppelt

au lieu de moquer marquise
me font vos yeux beaux mourir
penser images seconde
arrangement d'étourneaux
qui vont à la ligne haute
tension battre le flip-book
et revoir le mouvement

cinéma

Figure 39. First page and first photograph from Pierre Alferi and Suzanne Doppelt, *Kub or* (1997), emphasizing cinema and screen.

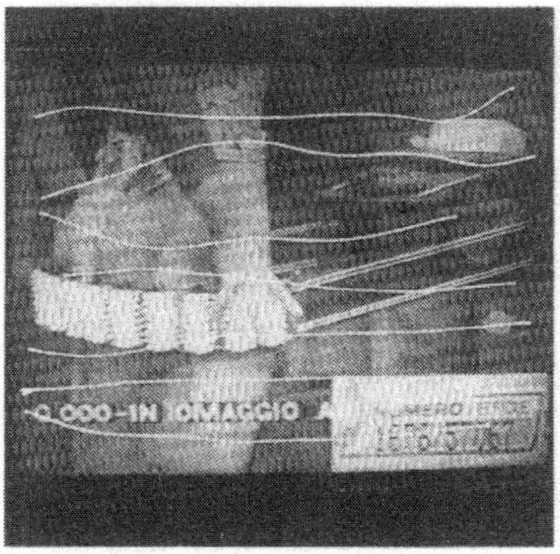

victime d'interférences

Figure 40. A bouillon cube box

(Figure 39). It is entirely structured around the number seven: seven sections of seven poems of seven lines of seven syllables, with seven photos. The poems have the same square format and size as the photos. "Kub or" is the trademarked name of a bouillon cube that comes in a gold foil wrapper (Figure 40). Since Mallarmé is mentioned, the small cube might allude to *A Throw of the Dice*, in which The Big Dipper's seven stars broken into groups of four and three suggest the two opposite faces of the transparent die of the cosmos (opposite faces of a die always amount to seven). The trademarked name also evokes Blaise Cendrars's 1924 collection of poems *Kodak*, the only major collection originally titled after a brand name, especially since it was changed to *Documentaires* after the Kodak Corp. threatened to sue. Cendrars's book remixed pulp novels by his friend Maurice Le Rouge, and the notion of remix is at the heart of *Kub or* as well.[95]

What Alferi and Doppelt's book indeed remixes first, more than any of these works per se, is their common transformation of an operational device—whether dice or camera—into a poetic form and a new mode of poetic meaning. In what ways, we wonder, is a bouillon cube such a device? Here is the opening poem:

instead of mocking marquise
make me your lovely eyes die
think images per second
arrangements of starlings
that go to the high voltage

wire [*ligne*] to shake the flip-book
and view the motion again

cinema[96]

The clipped, dense, elliptical syntax and absence of prosody (even in French) disorient the reader, until the title-coda reveals the poem to function as a kind of riddle. That this is not a lyrical work, and that we should only consider the verse as pro forma, are confirmed by an important theoretical essay Alferi coauthored with Olivier Cadiot in 1995, titled "La Mécanique lyrique" (The mechanics of the lyric).[97] In it, the two authors call on poetry to expand beyond verse and lyricism by considering other kinds of text and discourse, as well as material objects, as having an inherent structural potential usable to create new poetic forms. A bouillon cube, for instance. Before returning to the opening poem, let us jump to the last poem of the book since it is on the bouillon cube and its position as coda might help us solve the general riddle of the poetic form:

before plunging a kub
or maggi one puts oneself in
a state of ebullition
ah it's so ah this is really ah
absorbing these words tampon
periods/periodical [*périodique*] to unfold
quick another a last one quick

envoi[98]

The "envoi" is a stanza ending an ode by either addressing the poem's recipient or commenting back on the work as if from outside. The "*envoi*" poem, we suspect, sets up an analogy between the reading of the poems in the collection and the dissolution of a bouillon cube. How? To find out, we can start almost anywhere. For instance, we could imagine that we readers act as boiling water, letting the poems of *Kub or* release their dense meanings, so that we can absorb and enjoy them—as our own poetic soup. Is that what Alferi and Doppelt possibly have in mind? Let us read on into the poem and explain the strange exclamations. For the linguist George Lakoff, cross-cultural metaphors of the body heating up, boiling, or filling up with steam, have to do with affects of pressure seeking release (anger, sexual drive, bodily need).[99] The fourth and seventh lines of the poem indeed alter their speech register under the pressure of satisfaction and addiction respectively, as though the poem were a strong intoxicant. So the poetic soup we drink is both pleasurable and addictive. But Alferi organizes a second apposite analogy in "*envoi,*" between words and tampons, both having the ostensible ability to absorb periodical secretions. This invites a rather grotesque synthesis: bouillon cube poetics results from words being sponged up into a compact form that we are then invited to "unfold" into an infusion and . . . ingest. What rescues this process from grossness is its monumental literary antecedent: Proust's spongy *madeleine*. Permeated with a tisane made by and thus marked by his grandmother, the madeleine unfolds the past like so many tiny Japanese folded papers, Proust adds, progressively inflating into recognizable scenes.

Proust's clearly automorphic process points to moving images. Similarly, I believe that *Kub or* transforms the *madeleine*, via the tampon, into the cultural bouillon of the TV set and the TV program. Unlike Proust's, Alferi's project does not consist of a lyrical recovery of the stratified ego—the pronoun "I" is mentioned only once in *Kub or*, and it is overheard from a passer-by. It is almost the opposite: an assessment of how the cultural past of moving images informs contemporary forms of subjectivity and aesthetics. The bouillon cube and the tampon function as allegorical objects, but they are likely to be recollections of ads seen on TV in the 1970s, and whose unforeseen linkage—feats of liquid absorbency and flowerlike unfolding for the tampon; feats of dissolution and flavor density for the bouillon cube—Alferi harnesses as a reversible model for the writing and reading of his postlyrical cinepoems.

In tampon ads from the 1970s onward, the tampon-qua-flower unfolded through special effects—time-lapse and accelerated motion—exactly like the flowers and crystals that so fascinated the filmmakers and cinepoets of photogénie. This connection explains, I think, why *Kub or*'s first poem addresses not television but its antecedents: cinema and an ancillary product, the flip-book. The poem's opening lines cite a well-known comic scene from Molière's *Le Bourgeois gentilhomme* (Act I, scene 3) in which The Bourgeois's philosophy master offers variations on the sentence "Beautiful marquise, your lovely eyes make me die for love," including "make me your lovely eyes die, beautiful marquise, for love," which Alferi cites. The next line of Alferi's poem, "think images per second," seems to suggest that cinema's unfolding images somehow replace the resequencing possibilities of *prosaic* syntax. The explanation comes from the lines that follow, "starlings / that go to the high voltage wire," which, more literally translated include the phrase: "starlings / that go to the next line [*vont à la ligne*]." This refers to line breaks, the ultimate criterion of verse. In the same scene of *Le Bourgeois gentilhomme*, the Philosophy Master instructs The Bourgeois that since language is divided into verse and prose, either you do one or the other. The Bourgeois then exclaims, full of self-admiration, that this means he has been "making prose" for forty years unbeknownst to him! A true "scatterbrain" this bourgeois—which is just the figurative sense of "étourneaux" (starlings). Alferi's intent in the liminal poem "*cinema*" becomes clear. Poetry should not be as scatterbrain as Molière's Bourgeois in thinking that line breaks a poem make. If the poet can "think images per second," he can make a poem out of cultural sediments, the quick succession of moving images, and the principle of montage, thus echoing Mallarmé's injunction of a hundred years earlier: "Why not go straight to the cinématographe?"

Alferi seems very aware that his project is a throwback to another era. The poem "*newspaper*"[100] opens with, "that is all and for prose / there is no longer prayer" which alludes to a well-known line of Apollinaire's 1913 poem "Zone": "That is poetry this morning and for prose there are newspapers." But Alferi's revisiting of the "New Spirit" of pre–World War I poetry eschews newspapers to point instead to precinema antecedents. The poem "*pigeon*" mentions "Muybridge";[101] "*vacancière*" (female vacationer) compares a woman sunning herself on the beach to "the victim of a silent film" who is "tied across the rails" like stunt actress Helen Holmes in *The Hazards of Helen* (US, 1914–17, Dirs. J. P. McGowan and James Davis);[102] "*cinema*" mentions the flip-book; "*small screen*" spoofs the 8 o'clock news on TV;[103] "*boy at his window*" refers to the Japanese anime *Akira* (Japan, 1988, dir. Katsuhiro Otomo);[104] and "*x film*" describes the experience of peeking at a partially scrambled porn movie on early French cable.[105] *Kub or* can be read through the respective filter of each of these moments in the technology of moving images. Like chronophotography, it slices continuity into verses of equal *temporal* length /heptosyllables⇔chronophotographic frame/. Each poem is a hectic episode with its own riddle as in a crime serial installment /poem⇔serial episode/. With its square poems and square photos located at the same place on the page, *Kub or* also resembles a flip-book, especially a flip-book on a circular ring (a mutoscope) with no beginning nor end since the book lacks pagination, and "*preface*" is the seventh poem /poem collection⇔mutoscope/. Finally, like a film viewed through a TV scrambler, we get slices or portions of images, the rest being left out to our imagination: /poem⇔scrambled TV program/.

Cinepoetic processes are at play across poems even when they do not thematize the moving image. A poem describes a male worker on the phone in "an office facing the street," then a woman having her hair done in a salon.[106] Only the title-coda, "*rdc (ground floor),*" reveals what the poem was up to: walking down the street, the poet peers into open windows and sutures these sights in an automatic montage, fostering the homology /pedestrian vision⇔editing table/. This psychic editing is a crucial element in another poem titled "*billboards*":

> more than by the preaching in
> four by three mute benetton
> we are convinced by this
> single legend a deal
> voice-activated reclining
> bed not illustrated
> in a metro stairway
>
> *billboards*[107]

Here we are faced with two billboards from the metro. One promotes the sweaters Benetton, with multicultural models and pseudoaltruistic globalism. The other is an ad for a cheap voice-activated bed. The handsome Benetton ad, selling the youth and health of its models, needs no tagline, no words—it is "mute"—and speaks for itself. The ad for the bed, however, aimed at the elderly and the sick, is "not illustrated," because a reclining bed is a sad sight. It has only text, in shouting letters one supposes, a "single legend a deal." Alferi contrasts the two functions of advertising: fantasy mimesis (be just like them), and material necessity (get our cheap product). Image on the one hand, text on the other—like the photos and texts of *Kub or.* Yet both billboards are framed by the pedestrian experience of their discovery, through walking the passages and stairways of the subway. Alferi surreptitiously generates a kind of cinema-in-walking that becomes a cinema-in-reading when we behold one poem after another, slowing down its "images per second" to let its packed language unfold in slow(er) motion. In "*mallarmé's umbrella,*"[108] Alferi describes the umbrella's "rib lines [*lignes*] / that unfold are read refold [*se déploient lues se reploient*]," in an homage to Mallarmé's cinepoetics of "unfolding," and to Ponge's "Le Dispositif Lautréamont/Maldoror" (The Lautréamont/Maldoror apparatus), which introduced the notion of *dispositif* in modern poetry via the umbrella.[109] In fact the seven enigmatic photos of Doppelt at the center of the book—each with a line of caption that, taken together, may form a ghostly fiftieth seven-line poem—these photos implement to the letter Mallarmé's very idea that cinema's "unfolding" will alter the relationship of "images and text."

Doppelt's first photo is a still from a "Kub or" TV ad, and the genealogy of precinema and cinema in *Kub or* is ultimately sublated into television—the cubical *gold* standard of global contemporary culture and experience. In the poem "*preface*,"[110] which makes plain the book structure of "seven times seven times seven times seven" and calls it a "grunge idea" (*idée grunge*), television is explicitly the (dis)organizing principle behind that idea. The poems are described as shaped

> into hard cubes of nearly
> anything at all actually like on
> TV almost as good [an idea]
> as to compress trash [*ordure*]

Cubic TV sets compact trash culture the way the poems of *Kub or* compact the poet's grunge experience. This rhetoric of compaction points straight to the cubic sculptures of the artist César, who pioneered the artistic use of the trash compactor in the 1960s. He compacted a car offered by the Vicomtesse de Noailles—the financial backer of Cocteau's *Le Sang d'un poète*, and Buñuel and Dalí's *Un Chien andalou*. César became such a successful figure, in large part through his appearances on TV, that the French Oscars were named after him when they debuted in 1976. The very necessity for such heavily televised awards rests almost entirely in the ceremony itself, reminding TV viewers of the genealogical continuity between cinema and TV.

In the moving images compacted in *Kub or* there is a similar slippage from TV back to cinema, as if the latter was the true *or dur* (hard gold) of the *ordure* (trash) of TV culture. In 2003 Alferi published *Cinépoèmes*, a DVD in which words flicker on the screen against excerpts of B-series films or digitalized video backgrounds. Such transmediation across poetry, cinema history, TV and digital video, forms a kind of tesseract, an imaginary hypercube in four dimensions that has accompanied the virtual threshold of cinepoetry (the poem "*preface*," mentions "seven times seven times seven times seven"—an hypercube of seven). From 1965 to the mid-2000—most of Alferi's life—a single publication has led the circulation of all weeklies in France: *Télé 7 jours* (the equivalent of *TV Guide*). Structured around the TV cycle of weekly programs, such weeklies—which are called "périodiques"—represent the last remnant of the movie program in the digital era.

CHAPTER TEN

Cine-Verse

Decoupage Poetics and Filmic Implicature

As mentioned in the Introduction, an overwhelming number of concepts from cognitive linguistics and pragmatics were derived from cinema without much questioning as to the possibly nonheuristic nature of such epistemological transfers. While "frame," "script," "scenario," "flashback," "flash-forward," "projection," and "viewpoint," are undoubtedly marked by cinema, less-transparent terms likes "deixis," "trajector," "landscape," "scalarity," "blending," "edgework," or "radiant ignition," belong to the same kinetic-visual episteme as that which fostered the development of precinema and cinema.[1] There are two significant problems with using such notions unawares of their techno-perceptual legacy. First, it naturalizes and neutralizes the historical strata and the networks of usage which inform their theoretical currency in the neurosciences. The term "scenario" for example has an eminently traceable history that would show its meaning evolve out of theater to adapt to the new demands of cinema, progressively reaching broader cognitive and linguistic contexts (war, politics, the everyday, and forecasting) from about the 1910s to the present. It is therefore not a feature or datum of mind so much as a cultural item with a bundled history which adapted to yet a new context in sciences of mind. The second issue with this lack of historical consciousness is that cognitive studies will likely gloss over artifacts or actions that display a self-awareness of the linkages between cognitive/perceptual processes and cinematic experiences and notions. The two texts under examination in this chapter, André Beucler's *Un Suicide* (1925) and Pierre Chenal's *Drames sur celluloïd*

(1929), fall under this last category: they both use the scenario form while reflecting on it in a variety of ways ranging from intellectual inquiry to sheer irony.

The reason to include these works in the present book is that they are both written in verse—or rather, in short lines with end breaks resembling verse. Indeed, this form defies categorization and calls into question the dichotomy taken for granted (not just by Molière's master of philosophy and his student) between verse and prose. Moreover, both works lack prosody and rely only minimally on established poetics, which differentiates them for instance from Cendrars's voice-centered recutting of Maurice Le Rouge's prose into the blank verse of *Documentaries*, or the image-driven collage-poems of Dada and Surrealism. These works deploy a new form and economy of blank verse poetry that we might call *cine-verse*. Its distinctive feature is that it has little to do with meter or rhythm, that is, sound, nor with an authorial subjectivity—the "poet" whose voice in the present resounds in the poem. Instead, cine-verse signals a mode of immersive and mediated meaning-making that requires the reader to engage with processes of reading that have to do with the prospective dimension of the scenario form. Rather than being based on the poet as a vocal presence in lyrical verse, the poetics of cine-verse relies on the reader as the agent unfolding the imaginary potentiality of the text through its virtual filmic pragmatics and her viewing experiences.

ANDRÉ BEUCLER'S *UN SUICIDE* : DECOUPAGE POETICS

Throughout the 1920s and 1930s, Gaston Gallimard, the head of *La Nouvelle Revue Française* (*NRF*)—the premiere institution of French literary publishing—sought to capitalize on the growth of subliterature and cinema to offset losses in sales of "high" literature.[2] In the 1920s, he published film journals, and in the 1930s launched film production companies and financed the (unsuccessful) *Madame Bovary* adaptation of Renoir.[3] In 1925, he started a new collection called *Cinario*, ostensibly attempting to carve out a new hybrid literary niche: *cin*(nema and scen)*ario*. Since it was a commercial move, it comes as no surprised that the hybridity was rather fluidly couched, embracing all at once novels that were written to be adapted to the screen, novelizations of existing movies, and ancillary texts like brochure-programs or even *boniments*.[4] Gallimard advertised the future collaboration of well-known writers, screenwriters and film critics such as Georges Duhamel, Pierre Mac-Orlan, Joseph Kessel, Alexandre Arnoux, and Pierre Bost. In reality, the collection floundered after four books, two of which were published in parallel with movie adaptations released at roughly the same time.[5]

André Beucler wrote *Un Suicide* (A suicide) in 1925 as a literary project whose main interest is the difference it crafts with an actual film. The text was conceived neither as a script ready to shoot, nor a narrative to be ultimately adapted to the screen, but as an entirely new genre of work: a text to be read *in lieu of* or *as if it were* a film. Here is the beginning:[6]

> Fall
> Towards the end of the day.
> Water . . .
> A place on the Seine somewhere.
> Rings on water, reflections, images . . .
> of a familiar locale in Paris.
> On the bank, a man sitting;
> His face is tormented.
> He looks at the play on water
> Of a thousand moving roofs of the City.
> The moon . . . the embankment . . . a tramway . . .
> The face of this man.
> He gets up with an effort and starts walking.
> We see his back for a moment.
> the sad and desert neighborhoods,
> the rare pedestrians,
> the clouds swirling around the moon
> give an idea of his solitude.
> The man, seen from the back.
> Here he is in front of his door.
> He goes in—the building is harsh—
> and harsh is the concierge
> who does not even greet his tenant.
> He glances at the mailbox,
> but there is no letter for him.
>
> | He never received any letters |
> |---|

The text flows uninterrupted along one hundred and twenty-three pages with only rare breaks made of one line or two, an intertitle box, or three stars marking something like a longer fade to black (Figure 41). The passage above serves as an establishing sequence

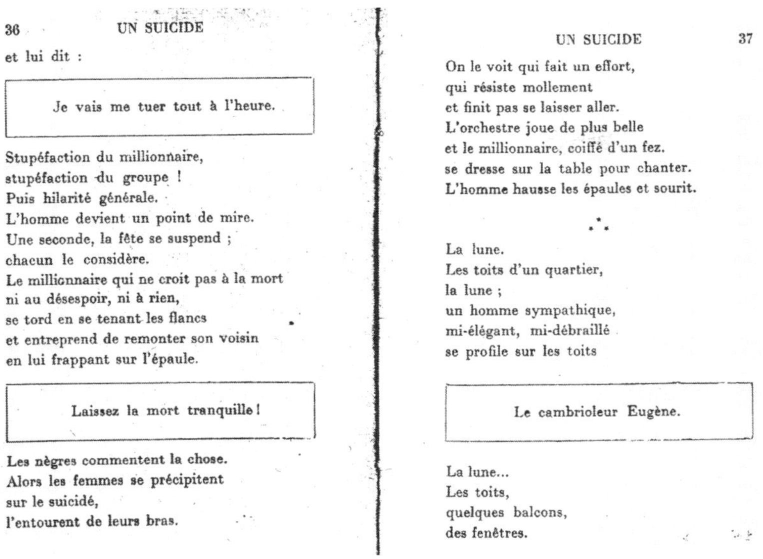

36 UN SUICIDE

et lui dit :

Je vais me tuer tout à l'heure.

Stupéfaction du millionnaire,
stupéfaction du groupe !
Puis hilarité générale.
L'homme devient un point de mire.
Une seconde, la fête se suspend ;
chacun le considère.
Le millionnaire qui ne croit pas à la mort
ni au désespoir, ni à rien,
se tord en se tenant les flancs
et entreprend de remonter son voisin
en lui frappant sur l'épaule.

Laissez la mort tranquille !

Les nègres commentent la chose.
Alors les femmes se précipitent
sur le suicidé,
l'entourent de leurs bras.

UN SUICIDE 37

On le voit qui fait un effort,
qui résiste mollement
et finit pas se laisser aller.
L'orchestre joue de plus belle
et le millionnaire, coiffé d'un fez,
se dresse sur la table pour chanter.
L'homme hausse les épaules et sourit.

∴

La lune.
Les toits d'un quartier,
la lune ;
un homme sympathique,
mi-élégant, mi-débraillé
se profile sur les toits

Le cambrioleur Eugène.

La lune...
Les toits,
quelques balcons,
des fenêtres.

Figure 41. Facing pages from André Beucler, *Un Suicide* (1925) showing the cine-verse with intertitle box.

for the film-book, and through it we can gauge an immediate difference with scenarios by Apollinaire and Cendrars in that each line or few lines tries to evoke a specific shot: /film shot⇔line(s) with a break/. The box contains intertitles mimetically rendered and aims at facilitating the reader's textual envisioning,[7] by foregrounding only the use of the written word within the apparatus that the Cinario seeks to displace. At the same time, the lines "Rings of water, reflections . . . images / of a familiar locale in Paris. / On the bank a man sitting" keenly describe the position of a film viewer: someone sitting and seeing moving images. What's more, by showing us first what he sees then himself, Beucler both adapts the Kuleshov effect to writing and invites us to identify with him in our literary imagination. It is this bi-directionality—pulling at once toward cinema and text, not necessarily in opposite directions—that makes cine-verse fascinating.

The intertitle, "He never received any letters," contrasts with the first twenty-first lines in two major ways. First, its tense belongs to the regular narrative past instead of the "technical" present of the rest of the scenario. Second, it is redundant, since the images have already showed us the empty mailbox. Such features invite us to characterize the writing of *Un Suicide* as paradoxical: its heavily visual, material, and event-driven narrative provides no temporal perspective other than the unfolding of the narrative itself, and it leaves little room outside of intertitles for abstract or introspective discourse. At the same time, the absence of technical indications leaves its possible adapter a free hand in how to transform the text into an actual script.

This paradox discloses what I call the *decoupage poetics* of *Un Suicide* . While foregoing overt shooting indications, the Cinario deploys a remarkable technicality at the subjacent level and in part through inconsistencies of textual formatting and plot organization. Capitalization, for instance, follows at times the poetic tradition of starting each verse with a capital (lines 9–10), at other times the grammatical rule of capitalizing only the first word of a sentence (lines 5–6), or it disappears altogether (lines 15–18). This inconsistency at the very beginning of the text reinforces our growing sense as readers that the /line⇔shot/ equivalency cannot be sustained, and that we are dealing neither with poetry nor prose, neither with a scenario, nor with a text uncontaminated by the film apparatus. While line 12, "The face of this man," corresponds to a strongly indexical fixed CU shot, line 24, "He glances at the mailbox," would command a double shot with an eyeline match between a slight high-angle MCU of the man and a slight low-angle ECU of the inside of the mailbox. In lines 21–23, "He goes in—the building is harsh— / and harsh is the concierge / who does not even greet his tenant," employs a rhetorical chiasmus to denote a shot/countershot. Decoupage is barely suggested and goes in and out of textual focus as it were.

At the narrative level, Beucler's text recounts a triangular melodrama about an unnamed lonely man saved from suicide by meeting the kept woman of a millionaire. As in other poem-scenarios, its content is principally meant to further its form. The plot of *Un Suicide* progresses through a single device: the uncanny proliferation of revolvers in the flat of the suicidal protagonist. While he is out—after having sold his belongings, keeping only a razor, a revolver and an ashtray—his flat is broken into by Eugène (the only named character in the book). As Eugène puts down his own revolver next to the suicide weapon, a shot goes off and he flees, leaving the revolver behind. Meanwhile, the protagonist spends his last dime in a nightclub. A millionaire befriends him and invites him to spend the night in his apartment where he meets and falls in love with the millionaire's mistress. Realizing their feelings are mutual, the jealous millionaire gives the suicidal man a revolver and reminds him of his decision. The protagonist goes home to kill himself, finds the extra revolver on the mantle next to his, and while he puzzles over this miraculous doubling, he adds the revolver the millionaire had given him, overtaken by uncanniness:

> He counts the three weapons, touches them
> one after the other, notices
> that six of them can be seen when counting
> those that are in the mirror.[8]

Beucler renders this uncanny moment by overlaying this scene of vision, reflection and hallucination, with three enjambments that, as a rule, the text does not use otherwise. The "flatter" cine-verses should read:

> *He counts the three weapons,
> touches them one after the other,
> notices that six of them can be seen
> when counting those that are in the mirror

The multiplication of revolvers (a fourth will be added),[9] acts as a kind of rhyming structure both egging him on to kill himself, yet dissuading him from doing so because of the fantastic nature of those appearances. This uncanny proliferation dovetails with the compulsive repetition of parts of the opening sequence when he goes home, finds his mailbox empty, and contemplates the revolver. This sequence takes place in the narrative proper,[10] but also through morbid daydreaming.[11] Movie viewers would likely take such heavy recurrences to be excessive, yet in Beucler's cine-verse repetition is needed to remobilize the quasi-filmic memory of readers, absent actual image filling up their perceptual horizon.

The cinepoetic decoupage must then craft within a textual economy both equivalents of and compensations for the perceptual intensity deployed by filmic images and edits (indicated in a regular scenario). At the level of editing, for instance, Beucler makes use of the two-room crosscut by staging a discussion between the hero's flat and his neighbor across a wall.[12] A passage introduced by a line of dots (the only one in the book) contains a quick edit sequence of disparate shots that presents a zip-back crosscut summary of the narrative up to this point.[13] Quick crosscuts are indeed easily translatable to writing, for instance when the hero plays the piano in the woman's room: "He keeps playing furiously. / His hands. / His eyes. / The woman's eyes. / The man's hands."[14] Note that this is simultaneously a chiasmus and a shot/countershot. Other easily rendered effects include graphic matches, as when the smoke of his cigarette "mixes" with the smoke of a poster showing an ocean liner; and composite effects—a champagne bottle rotating "by itself" and changing into a woman's face.[15] An eyeline match, however, causes textual ripples. When a limousine drives by the protagonist, Beucler writes, "but one [*on*] had the time to see / inside / within the intimacy created by the ceiling light."[16] This unmotivated POV shot (no important character is in the limo) risks throwing readers off the main plot: this is why Beucler uses the past tense, removing the shot from the protagonist's narrative present which we are following. Only in a couple of fades does Beucler allow the apparatus to reveal itself, as it might in an actual movie: "And the shadow of the screen covered him up,"[17] and, "Then he becomes smaller and smaller / on the screen / and is swallowed by darkness."[18]

Rare shooting suggestions concern the scale of shots from ECUs, as we have seen, to VLSs, such as the final shot showing the train receding "to the farthest reach of the screen."[19] There are a few dramatic pans until the end, when we see the protagonist in MCU alone in his train compartment, then smiling to what the camera reveals to be the woman sitting across from him.[20] No precise camera work is intimated (such as angles, tilts, and so forth) apart from a single shot showing the man "going up the stairs / whose stairwell rotates on the screen."[21] Such a shot suggests a rare handheld camera for cinema ca. 1925. These mentions of the screen are nonetheless remarkable: they signal the enormous challenge of conveying casually in writing certain visual relationship having to do with the compositional role of the frame in the organization of space. As for playacting, it is foregrounded in a single puzzling scene:

> He takes the weapon,
> looks at the young woman,
> —their eyes—
> and explains to her with gestures
> that between the tip of a revolver
> and his temple which he points to,
> there is now but a woman,
> and that this woman,
> is her.[22]

Needless to say, Beucler writes, "She did not understand," any more than we would, presented with this wrongheaded screen mimicry likely meant to palliate too many intertitles.

Beucler's cine-verse thus embed a variety of precise film techniques within what is at first glance unsophisticated flat-footed writing. As we have seen in other cinepoetic scenarios, formal features—such as the magical multiplication of revolvers, the repetitions of the man's routine—take over the melodramatic structure, which holds little interest. The protagonist is presented as a complete blank slate, living in a small flat with no apparent job, lover or friends (apart from his kind next-door neighbor), and seemingly devoid of desires, interests, and life projects. He incarnates the dehumanized consciousness of the modern "City," whose anonymous dwellers belong to no community, and whose dwellings Beucler connotes as a "spiral prison,"[23] when referring to the building's stairwell. Suicide is the logical last revolt against such modern urban dehumanization. The fascination with guns—"he touches it and caresses it"[24]—and their sheer multiplication—"he touches them one after the other"[25] points to a phallic theme, curiously echoed when he falls in love with the woman:

> Something got lodged
> between the instant when he decided
> to die,
> and that at which he was going to pull the trigger.[26]

Like the English "to lodge," the French "se loger" in this context refers to bullets. This passage set in the past tense with a plus-perfect hypothetical eschews the present tense, defies filmic representation, and thus goes against the logic of the Cinario. This may well characterize the outer limits of cine-verse's hybridity. The anomalous passage continues:

> It is a woman—
> and not a woman like any other—
> but a woman who seems
> so lazy, so indifferent, so amorphous,
> that she is already in a still sensible domain,
> something like death.[27]

It is not just love qua bullet but the woman's prehensile and deadly eroticism—octopus- or jellyfish-like—that enters him, substituting to his own death and perhaps preempting suicide. This moment of homeopathic wounding leads the protagonist to an anxious dream sequence that takes place in hallways similar to Dulac's 1928 adaptation of Artaud's *The Seashell and the Clergyman*. In the dream, the man is offered guns at every turn, by random persons and invisible hands coming out of walls (as Cocteau would stage twenty years later in *La Belle et la bête*). When, still in the dream, he decides to shoot himself, the woman appears, takes the gun away, and vanishes. From then on, every time he tries to kill himself invisible hands take his gun away. If modern urban life disempowers the protagonist to the point of suicide, love comes not as salvation, but as the further spoliation of the ultimate power to end it all. The woman is thus partly a personification of the City—*La Ville* is feminine—and in the well-worn tradition of Baudelaire both are indeed prostitutes. The end of *Un Suicide* shows the couple fleeing from the City by train. Only by escaping from the social roles of urban anonymity—a theme reprised by Poetic realist cinema—can man and woman become free to develop a true identity and a shared history.

The challenge of devising an overall interpretation integrating the original cine-verse form of *Un Suicide*, its subjacent filmicity, its melodramatic economy, centered on the fantastic psychoanalytical motif of gun multiplication, and the putative experience of its reading, suggests that we look toward the capacious framework of cognitive poetics. As outlined by Reuven Tsur and Peter Stockwell, cognitive poetics ultimately aims to create models of what happens to an embodied reader undergoing the complex experience of reading a literary text.[28] In their ongoing elaboration of workable models, these cognitive scholars rely on several key premises. First, they insist, reading a literary text does not mean merely decoding it as if it were a specialized message, but experiencing it perceptually and differentially as a striking figure against the ground of our normal perception. A literary text, they assert, proposes to draw our attention to, and thereby refresh our modes of ordinary perception of space, time, movement, situations, and so on. This is in line with the principle of defamiliarization of Russian Formalism, although cognitive poetics requires specifying a *positive* content to such altered perceptual experience. Second, cognitive poetics seeks to identify mental structures that are cross-cultural universals and bring them to bear on the reader's understanding of a text. These structures, both Tsur and Rockwell contend, are multidimensional and involve linguistic grain (how we categorize and focus on salient aspects), virtual enactment (how we rely on general schemas to process a situation), and action sequencing (how we modify schemas and move from one to another). Within these general premises, cognitive critics deploy dizzying and often divergent arrays of analytical terms and notions for modeling the working of embodied mind structures, with the even farther perspective of relating them to the biology of the brain.

A book such as *Un Suicide*, complicates these premises in several ways. The scenario template, to begin with, preorganizes the perceptual world of the reader according to the broad possibilities of moviemaking (ca. 1925), in a way that disrupts any neat opposition between a "natural" perception and a "literary" one. Tsur writes, "Cognitive poetics conceives of literary devices as of adaptation devices originally developed for survival in the physical and social environment, and eventually turned to aesthetic ends."[29] He distinguishes "normal cognitive processes," from "modification or disturbances of these processes," and finally "their reorganization according to different principles" in the literary text.[30] The cinepoetics of Beucler's cine-verse strains this model. On the one hand, it fits in that cinepoetics can be though of as another device of cognitive alteration between so-called native and literary modes of cognition. We would then be dealing with two layers of alteration of normal cognition, one cinematic and the other poetic. On the other hand, such a model does not work since the reader does not perceive *Un Suicide* as the normal world "disturbed." To the contrary: apart from the few (albeit crucial) exceptions we have pointed out, cine-verse can very well be received as a transparent decoupage of perceptual experience by an average reader familiar, unbeknownst to her, with moving images. This transparency is precisely the reason why literary scholars have taken no notice of the book. Yet more problematic, the central gist of cognitive poetics—that aesthetic effects proceed from perceptual norm disturbance—does not consider the possibility that so-called normal perceptual experience might already be layered with a host of other active kinds of disturbances such as technology habituation, which themselves may be taken up as topic for literature.

The motif of suicide represents what cognitive critics call a "script," that is, an organized set of ordered context-dependent notions, which Stockwell explains as "a socioculturally defined mental protocol for negotiating a situation."[31] Thus the script KILLING ONESELF involves minimally a means of ending one's life, a cause (psychological distress, communal rejection, or an ethical or rational decision), a time and a place, and perhaps a ritual for carrying through the act. Stockwell compares scripts in cognition to how a "frame" in the visual field acts as "the context brought by viewers to disparate objects."[32] The protagonist of *Un Suicide* follows the script by securing the place, emptying it (ritual), and securing the means (revolver): the only thing missing is the time—somehow he cannot settle on the moment. If the script has the form CAUSE+DECISION+MEANS TO ACT+ACT= SUICIDE, the hero fails to undertake the decisive step. The intrusion of the second and third guns does not so much disturb the script, which is already suspended, as repeat its middle term, pushing further back the final step: DECISION+MEANS TO ACT+MEANS TO ACT+MEANS TO ACT . . . This stuttering in the cognitive script is equivalent to a dysfunction in the cinematic apparatus: the broken freeze-frame, an arrest on the same image. In a way, it is this dysfunction of the film apparatus that reveals to the protagonist the cognitive scenario he is engaged in and, by the same token, extricates him from it.

It is difficult to gauge to what extent this might be the very focus of Beucler's Cinario, that is, that cinema and cognitive processes reflect each other. Certainly, the cinema apparatus functions today as a powerful default model for cognitive psychology and the philosophy of mind which both seem entirely unaware of working out of the homology: /mental processes⇔film techniques/. For instance, Daniel Denett lauds Antonio Damasio for asking not only the question of "how the brain 'generates the movie in the brain,'" that is, the mind, but for tackling the question of how a subjectivity emerges from it in terms of "how the brain 'generates the *appearance* of an owner and observer for the movie *within the movie*."[33] Neither Denett nor Damasio problematize their conceptual reliance on a historical technology of perception to model the mind.

This blind spot also bears on the debate about "the modernity thesis" (see my Introduction), gauging to what extent technology has transformed regimes of perception in modernity. To recap, film historians have split into two polarized camps over this question, with Gunning favoring limited but actual (although not necessarily hard-wired) changes in such regimes, while Bordwell takes the longer evolutionary view that such alterations must be minimal and are much less determinant than mutations in film stylistics and conventions of movie production. I stated in the Introduction that we have today so very little access to precinematic perception and cognition, and that we are so thoroughly permeated with moving images, that Bordwell's evolutionary argument is woefully unverifiable. I would like to shore up this claim by arguing that, in fact, the evolutionary record suggests that Gunning must be right. At stake is the very tight coevolution of neural faculties with motion, motion perception, and vision. Neuro-physiologist Rodolfo Llinás has proposed as "irrefutable" that "a nervous system is only necessary for multicellular creatures (not cell colonies) that can orchestrate and express active movement."[34] This means that, evolutionarily speaking, motricity is directly linked to, and informs, neural development because of the need to centralize predictive functions regarding the relation of an organism's movement with its milieu and with other organism and objects in motion.[35] The relation between neural and motor functions is so tight that Llinás writes, "*that which we call thinking is the evolutionary internalization of movement.*"[36] This process of internalization explains both higher organisms' reliance on teleception (remote sensing allowing more time for position prediction) and the development of language. Llinás contributes an original view to the emergence of language, by stating that its prerequisite lies in "the nervous system's capacity to generate the premotor imagery required to abstract the properties of things from the things themselves."[37] This is a profound remark. It means that the human mind produced "images" as nonmotor correlations (rather than reflexes that are motor correlations) to aspects of things, so as to make them distinct from things themselves, and mentally manipulable. Only by sensing that a gesture or sound could be separated from its action-reaction context could the human mind give it a unique value: this is what we call meaning. Llinás asserts that such a neural modeling of motor perceptions, as distinct from these perceptions, must preexist for language itself to arise. This view is very close to Epstein's notion that cinematic language because of its indexical animism, discloses something new about what language does transparently. Artaud concurs in a 1927 article on cinema where he writes, "The question is not to find in visual language an equivalence of written language . . . but to objectify the very essence of language."[38]

While cognitive scientists do so merely heuristically, cinepoets explicitly link the mind, language and cinema for reasons that may have to do with the very nature of perception and cognition. This suggests that the two camps of "the modernity thesis" might meet. Cinema did not alter regimes of perception in the prosthetic sense of adding brand new faculties to it that were not "in" the brain before. It did so by focusing on and disclosing to our conscious attention the central role of motor perception within cognitive processes, language and the imaginary. This does not mean that we should regard Beucler's cross-medium work as a cognitive document, however. It is steeped in the technical horizon of filmmaking conventions ca. 1925, and its focus on handguns, for instance, should be contextualized within the new currency of such weapons and the crisis of masculinity in the wake of World War I. Nonetheless, one of the unstated aims of cine-verse as a postlyrical hybrid of literature, motor perception and the cinematic imaginary, was to isolate processes of embodied cognition. A 1925 debate on the relationship between the scenario and literary writing wrestled with very similar issues. Beucler contributed to this debate a short essay entitled "The Cinematographic Poem," which confirms his ambition in *Un Suicide* to overlay poetic, linguistic, and cognitive processes: "A film is a verb or a substantive. I am proposing SIGNS addressed first of all to the expectations of the eye, then, before they settle at the bottom of reason, to the thousand intermediary flights that so perfectly imitate, within the association of ideas, the spectacle devoid of cracks and logic that is the visible world."[39] Beucler's dense formulation is not easy to gloss, but it does suggest that the "thousand intermediary flights" of the eye should inform what he calls "poems of the visual" that may not be ideally represented by films, but by "SIGNS" closer to the cine-verse of the Cinario. At least, Beucler is very much aware that our involvement in reality, which he tropes as "the white pages of daylight," has much to learn from the light the encounter of cinema and poetry throws on the functioning of our embodied cognition.

CINEPOETIC IMPLICATURE IN PIERRE CHENAL'S *DRAMES SUR CELLULOÏD*

A debate on the scenario as a possible literary form took place in 1925, in two special issues of the journal *Les Cahiers du mois*. The first offered six literary scenarios—including Desnos's "Midnight at Two o'clock,"—and the second contributed theoretical reflections by writers and critics. Even those who opposed such cinepoetic experiments understood the novelty of the attempt. André Desson points out, "These are not scenarios ready to be filmed . . . the goal, in writing them, was not that they should be." He hastens to define this "written cinema," as "an adjacent art—adjacent to cinema, not to literature."[40] Other critics felt, on the contrary, that the scenario had the potential to become a new form of poetic writing. Maurice Betz writes of Louis Delluc's recently published scenarios, *Drames de cinéma*: "The literary scenario is too new a means for us to discern its dangers and problems. It seems to me supple and seductive because, in a way less unilateral and subjective than inner monologue, it allows for the translation of the first draft of certain ideas and certain poetic themes."[41] Betz suggests that the scenario form can provide both a cognitive account and a terrain for poetry that are freer than the more arbitrary conventions of inner monologue. Another commentator, writing about Romains's *Donogoo-Tonka*, also insists on the perceptual transparence of the scenario-form, noting the filmic competence of readers: "The emotion that is provoked tends to shift from being an inner emotion to being a visual, imaginative, and relatively outer emotion . . . since the habit of cinema is ingrained."[42] In all these cases, the narrative fabric seems pushed to the background by the literary scenario that focuses instead on mobilizing the cinematic cognition and imaginary of the reader as its primary material.

Most of the scenarios in the first issue are written in cine-verse according to various decoupage poetics. Here is one example by Jacques Bonjean:

> Anne laughs.
> We see the deck of a fishing boat.
> Faceless men
> effortfully
> lift on board
> a heavy net.[43]

This full paragraph/stanza establishes two levels of equivalences: /line⇔shot/ and /paragraph-stanza⇔sequence/. Yet the connection between Anne's face and the fishermen loading their catch could be either a shot/countershot or some other kind of cut between two shots (a MCU and a LS) or a play of foreground and background within a single shot: /paragraph-stanza⇔shot/. Bonjean weaves shooting techniques into his cine-verse sometimes explicitly (superimpressions in particular), but more often, like Beucler, more subjacently. In one scene, however, an explicit superimpression takes on a theoretical quality for cine-verse:

> He begins to read
> . . .
> Only his face is visible:
> his eyes that endeavor to follow the lines,
> his lips that form the sound of syllables.
>
> The spirit of the letter is superimposed
> on that of the reader.
>
> Written characters dance,
> having been provided with feet, and legs
> . . .
>
> The characters gather
> So as to form words:
> Don't listen to slanderers . . .
> The truth . . .

Is that I have entered into . . .

a wonderful marriage . . .[44]

The scenario stages automorphic lettering to mirror the cognitive process of reading cine-verse, which involves folding words and moving images together. This radicalizes—but *in writing*—similar plays of automorphic lettering that Feuillade and L'Herbier had carried out in their movies. No longer are "the spirit" and "the letter" separated, cine-verse poets hope: they can now fuse in "[the mind] of the reader." The cine-verse scenario tries conversely to mimic through its spatial and visual form the cognitive processes whereby words can unfold specific components of the cinematic imaginary. One of the editors of the two issues, François Berge, singles out the cine-verse form of Cendrars's *The Film of the End of the World* as instrumental to this cognitive enactment by admiring, "the swaying between the long paragraphs and the others shorter—often very short—one word. With nothing but his instinct for indents and paragraphs [*alinéas*], Cendrars succeed in hypnotizing his spectators. For he does so without any poetic sophistication, or any literary art."[45] By insisting that Cendrars's scenario was not aiming for literary innovation, Berge seeks to reinforce the idea that the cine-verse aims at a perceptually and cognitively objective translation of the cinematic imaginary. The claims of commentators and cinepoets regarding the cognitive transparence of cine-verse, however wishful or exaggerated they may be, draw attention to the unique capacity of moving images to disclose otherwise hidden dimensions of language ranging from pragmatics to semantics. Film has too often, and mistakenly, been reduced to an unproblematic variety of text. But the reciprocal promises a much better yield, and we might ask whether understanding text, today, might not benefit from the economy of meaning that seems native to film.

I would like to approach Pierre Chenal's *Drames sur celluloïd* from this perspective by looking at how its twenty-four scenarios, most of them in cine-verse stanzas, enfold filmic elements within the semantic function of written language. Presenting itself as a film program in two parts with an intermission, the book was published at the very end of the high cinepoetic experimentation when sound cinema arrived in 1929. One scenario onomatopoeically titled "BA-BE-BI-BO-BU," features an "*Épatant-Parlant-Palace*" or "Topnotch Talking Theater," and pokes fun at the infantilizing talkies, whose sound is "horribly scratchy" when not desynchronized altogether (the canary barks and the dog tweets), and whose dialogues are ridiculous hybrids of high theater and boulevard lingo: "Exasperated am I! Break everything break!" utters the puzzlingly off-screen voice of the protector of a kept woman generically called "Girl."[46] Although most scenarios of Chenal are in a comic vein, almost all of them center on the cognitive and perceptual affordances of the cinema apparatus. Take for instance "Article de Paris" (Item from Paris), which is a visual cinepoem:

A baby at the center of a spiral

A cobra is feeding it –

coiled around [it]

20 YEARS

LATER . . .

Coiled around nothing –

the cobra adjusts its pair of glasses:

in his three-piece snake-suit – a gigolo smiles

Since there is no overt reference to cinema we could opt to read this short treatment as a pseudo-Aesopian epigram for modern era parents: if you're a snake sooner or later your child will show himself to be of the same stripe. A semantic analysis would thus connect animal lore, anthropomorphic figurality, and the economy of the moral tale, noting in passing that "snake with glasses" is a synonym for cobra in French, and that the text takes on the visual aspect of the Greek letter χ after which the chiasmus is named. Bringing cinema to bear on the interpretation of the text changes its semantic and pragmatic valences. In suggesting a LS, the first line now has a referential content it would seem to lack otherwise, since semantically speaking the first three lines should be equivalent to: "A baby is fed by a cobra coiled around it." With cinema as their pragmatic horizon, the first three lines evoke: (1) LS on baby in spiral (not recognized as a snake); (2) CU on cobra head feeding baby's mouth; (3) MCU showing cobra body wrapped around baby. There is now a visual organization and a progression in cognitive spotlighting. The actual film that might result could be an animated cartoon whose visual pleasure centers on the morphing (à la

Émile Cohl) of a snake and a baby into a human-snake hybrid, perhaps via the motif of the snake swallowing a baby who keeps growing inside of it—a recurrent motif in cartoon animation. I insist that the difference between a cinematic and noncinematic reading of this poem is not just one of semantic context or visual representation, but of a different cognitive register and perceptual load. The "spiral" and the chiasmic repetition of "coiled around [it]" and "coiled around nothing," also evoke the self-referential imagery of the filmstrip as a snake (as in early posters),[47] an analogy that probably rests on the sensorial impression of envelopment and swallowing by filmic immersion.

The cinematic reading of the poem taps into a range of potential meanings that is not explicit in the text, although its context of poem-scenario suggests that such potential meanings should be seen as more than related to the text. Adapting a word that the linguist Grice coined in the 1960s, I would like to call this potential meaning of passages in a scenario text linked to the cinema apparatus, *cinepoetic implicature*. For Grice, implicature is the difference between what an utterance says explicitly and what it implicitly conveys. My use of implicature, while less strict, aims to expand the semantics of scenario-texts, especially very condensed versions such as Chenal's, toward implied meanings that refract broad movie-viewing experiences. The very economy of the scenario-text consists in inviting these cognitive and perceptual haloes, sometimes aided by oblique or direct references to filmmaking techniques, to inform the reading. The originality of Chenal is that he points to a number of cinema effects in order to make sensible the cinepoetic implicature of his own scenario-texts.

Let us look at a few examples. The first scenario-text, entitled "Couleurs sans danger" (Colors without danger), stages a de-stratification of the filmic image in its first stanza:

> A man in color arrives running
> in front of a whitewashed wall
> He runs so fast that the colors
> detach from him—and leave the frame[48]

Meeting a smartly dressed man who is only a "shadow" against the wall, the runner "points at his double in color / who rejoins him—penetrates him—and recolors him." As the runner gesticulates, "The color of his gloves is trailing [*a du retard sur*] their motion." Then it rains and the colors wash off the runner who becomes "absolutely white." More than the theme of doubling, certainly present, it is the perceptual layering of moving images through the cinematic apparatus that is at the center of the scenario-text. Chenal, I argue, is placing *en abîme* within the plot of the scenario-text itself, the way implied cinepoetic significance "trails" explicit meaning. This implied significance gives all its sensorial grain to the bare-bone animation film that the text merely indexes, perhaps depending on the filmic saturation of the reader's imaginary. Chenal's *Drames sur celluloïd* are not short scenarios written in order to be realized into films: they are cinepoems, written as if the films already existed. The function of the word "celluloid" in the title is to make imaginary films paradoxically more tangible.

Several scenario-texts revolve around this tacit tangibility. In "Air connu . . . " (Well-known song . . .), the doubles of a wife and her husband's male secretary symbolically kill the husband's double and have an affair, while the three "real" protagonists are picnicking. Germaine Dulac's 1927 *The Smiling Madame Beudet* may be referred to since the eponymous character of that film has an imaginary fling with a tennis player who comes to life out of a magazine photograph, after which they both throw the husband's double out of the window. In Chenal's piece the real and fantasy plots unfold in parallel, and end with the husband dismembered and put back together in the fantasy plot, a nod to Méliès's well-known trick dismemberment films. The function of doubling in the imaginary film serves again of cognitive and imaginative facilitation ("mise en abyme") for "visualizing" the scenario itself. Similarly, in "Summer Hour," a man cuts off his shadow while his fiancée's reflection tarries in the mirror. They kiss only as doubles: first from within a piece of paper on which the man draws them both and, after the woman cuts out a replacement shadow in umbrella silk, as shadow and ersatz shadow. "Drame au cinéma (Drama at the cinema)," takes place in a movie theater where the projectionist blows on the light-cone, which disrupts the film projected, causing the filmic world to spillover into the audience world, in a kind of comic variation on Cocteau's poetics of the light-cone. All in all, Chenal's scenarios cannily mirror the replicating function of the cinema apparatus the better to activate our cinematic imaginary in reading them. Implicature here works by amplifying the processes of automorphosis and metamorphosis. Although the twenty-four scenarios of *Drames sur celluloïd* feature occasional references to film shooting, editing, and projection techniques—slow- and accelerated motion and close-ups—the kinesthesia of moving images generally informs their implicature.

"Mort d'un chameau" (Death of a Camel), for instance, in which an explorer in the desert causes various transformations of a tree, a

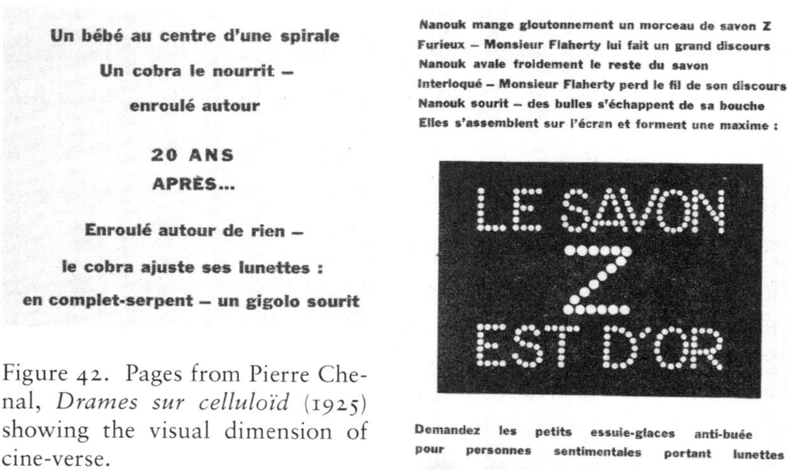

Un bébé au centre d'une spirale
Un cobra le nourrit –
enroulé autour

20 ANS
APRÈS...

Enroulé autour de rien –
le cobra ajuste ses lunettes :
en complet-serpent – un gigolo sourit

Nanouk mange gloutonnement un morceau de savon Z
Furieux – Monsieur Flaherty lui fait un grand discours
Nanouk avale froidement le reste du savon
Interloqué – Monsieur Flaherty perd le fil de son discours
Nanouk sourit – des bulles s'échappent de sa bouche
Elles s'assemblent sur l'écran et forment une maxime :

LE SAVON
Z
EST D'OR

Demandez les petits essuie-glaces anti-buée
pour personnes sentimentales portant lunettes

Figure 42. Pages from Pierre Chenal, *Drames sur celluloïd* (1925) showing the visual dimension of cine-verse.

camel, bottles of liquor, fire, and a balloon, relies on the metamorphic films of Émile Cohl and Windsor McKay as implicature: the reader must recall these prefilms into her reading experience to fulfill the potential of the scenario-text. Automorphic letters appear in "Le Grand Soir" (Big night), in which a poet dreams that the aluminum letters of a shop-sign double and triple, then detach themselves, "fall in slow-motion,"[49] and pursue him. The word they form, *Opticien* (Optician), might well rearrange, with an extra –é– into *Poéticien* (Poetician). Automorphic print is featured in "Projet de film" (Film project), in which the books of a scriptwriter (who has sloughed his skin like a snake) move by themselves and fall out of a window in "low angle shots of the best kind,"[50] before he shakes a dice cup from which spring the protagonists of a scenario-within-the-scenario. The automatic riding of this scenario thus involves quite remarkably imaginary texts coming to life within the imaginary filmic world in order to generate randomly further imaginary filmic worlds! Other pieces also feature complex and reciprocal embeddings of film and writing. "Entr'acte" (Intermission), for instance, stages an ad for "soap Z" in which the filmmaker Flaherty remonstrates Nanook (from his 1921 *Nanook of the North*) for eating soap (Figure 42). But Nanook defiantly keeps eating the soap until bubbles come out of his mouth that slowly form the letters of the slogan: "Soap Z is gold."[51] Here the automorphic letter serves as enactment of the cinepoem, and critique of commercialism and colonial ethnology all at once.

The reciprocal enfolding of writing, automorphosis, and cinema reaches an ironic climax in the penultimate scenario-text, "Entreprise d'aventure" (Adventure business). It begins with a hand that writes on a card in ECU, "the name of its owner . . . Pierre Chenal."[52] Chenal qua protagonist has come to talk to a film producer. There is a cut and a man enters the office of the producer and forces him with a gun to read "his 24 scenarios"—the very number of scenario-texts of *Drames sur celluloïd*. The first text begins, "A man in color arrives running / . . . ,"[53] which reproduces the first lines of "Couleurs sans danger." The cinepoetic implicature goes full circle here by embedding and mirroring the full film program of *Drames* within one of its scenarios. Chenal-qua-protagonist falls asleep and dreams, and the office metamorphoses into a room with dials and electrical machines in which robots riding on magnetic chairs select books to be made into films (in this case *Daphnis and Chloe*). We then tour "Cinepolis," a Metropolis-like world where various large halls contain thousands of extras, couples, and handkerchief-waving ingénues all waiting to take part in a shoot. Smaller halls have robots transforming books into scripts. In the Hall of Adapters, *Daphnis and Chloe* becomes "transparent," before the chain-production process sends it to the Hall of Mixers where stories are mixed together (in one mixing machine are: Kipling's *Captains Courageous*, Conrad's *Typhoon*, and Poe's *The Narrative of Arthur Gordon Pym*). The satire of a movie industry unwilling to take risks on original scenarios and ever reprising and recombining the same stories could not be clearer. The scenario ends on a vengeful note. Upon waking to find that the producer has died of apoplexy, Chenal qua protagonist drinks twenty-four glasses of the latter's brandy. Real-life Chenal then concludes his book with an ultimate scenario-text about a scriptwriter looking—not surprisingly, in vain—for an actual producer.

Beucler and Chenal pushed the scenario the farthest in the direction of a new cinepoetic genre of writing. They retro-adapted from cinema decoupage and movie-viewing experiences respectively, to create a new modality of textual meaning that took the form of a post-lyrical line: the cine-verse. Yet the poor reception of these works may be among the reasons that both authors became filmmakers in the 1930s. Beucler worked in Germany with UFA on multinational films, including *Adieu les beaux jours* (Germany/France, 1933) with Brigitte Helm and Jean Gabin (now lost). As for Chenal, his adaptation of a novel by Marcel Aymé, *Rue sans nom* (France, 1934), was the first film to which the expression "Poetic Realism" was applied (the term was coined by Jean Paulhan in a 1929 review of that same novel). For both of them, nonetheless—as for Cocteau—it is worth bracketing the model of the writer-turned-filmmaker to assess instead their imaginary cinemas as a separate practice from both their writing and their filmmaking careers.

PART FIVE

Skin, Screen, Page

Cinepoetry's Historical Imaginary

CHAPTER ELEVEN

Max Jeanne's *Western*

Eschatological Sarcasm in the Postcolony

procession of shadows
empty gestures
silent cinema
of an entire people adrift
still wearing at its ankle
the age-old ball and chain of slavery

—MAX JEANNE, *Western*[1]

Critics who have pondered the changed relationship of literature and cinema in post–World War II French culture generally point toward Alain Resnais's influence on new novelists such as Jean Cayrol, Marguerite Duras, and Alain Robbe-Grillet as a turning point.[2] I have tried to show that the broader cultural landscape after 1943, including the new cinema-inflected theory of the imaginary of Sartre and echoes from interwar cinepoetry in the lettrist avant-garde and among other poets, played a significant role that has been overlooked. Here I would like to suggest that Resnais's undoubtedly crucial reframing of the exchanges between writing and film intersects with the cinepoetic imaginary. Indeed, Resnais himself, as Clerc noted, states that his concern is with "the imaginary" rather than "memory"—a word with which his work is almost invariably saddled.[3]

Resnais opens *Hiroshima mon amour* (1959) by inserting an unsettling distance between the images we see and the voices we hear. On the screen in MCU, two bodies whose heads are not visible writhe in pleasure or pain, their skin covered in droplets that appear to be either sweat or fallout ashes—love or the atomic bomb. We hear the off-screen voices of Emmanuelle Riva and Eiji Okada engaging in a strangely poetic dialogue about Hiroshima. While in Melville's *Le Silence de la mer* (1947), the off-screen voice is received as post facto narration, as is also the case for the posthumous voice in Wilder's *Sunset Boulevard* (1950), Resnais's film leaves it unclear whether either the images or the voices coincide in any filmic "present." This ambiguity marks *Hiroshima mon amour* with a past that does not pass but compulsively repeats itself or loops back, preempting and precluding a simple chronological present—presumably a distinctive symptom of postmodern temporality.

Skin and touch are the film's privileged site and sensory modality. The thick-grained film stock Resnais selected for his opening shot brings attention both to the film as a kind of skin (*la pellicule*), and to skin as a sensitive plate capable of registering both amorous contact and deadly contamination. We recall that Epstein's "theater of the skin" was informed by an affect-driven conception of the "unified plane" of perception and cognition across literature and cinema. We might similarly propose that the two voices of *Elle* and *Il*, the French woman and the Japanese man, rather than being considered off-screen might be attributed to their skin. Or rather skins, since the opening shot shows that they have a slightly different hue pointedly marking racial difference. Hence the movie opens on the "antislick" terrain of interracial and intercultural promiscuity.[4] Laura Marks has recently argued that experimental intercultural cinema and video translate exclusions from the Eurocentric cultural archive into a skin-deep retention of experiences, memories, and corporeal affects as a new and virtual core for transported identities.[5] Migration and displacement, she argues, reconfigure the memory of the senses. For Marks, intercultural cinema is haptic and centers on embodied practices because it recognizes the potential of filmic experience to stimulate, reevoke and transform the sensate memory of intercultural subjects. Within this sensorium of displacement, tactility may be especially crucial since effects of distance and proximity, dislodgment and desired contact, belong to the somatic register of haptics and touch.

Hiroshima mon amour likewise emblematizes the damaged historical sensorium through skin and touch. The skin fragment of a Hiroshima victim floating in serum in the Atomic museum—half-dead skin—connects with the slap "He" gives "Her" to revive her own half-dead skin envelope and shock her into reintegrating her bodily present. The corporeal experiences screened out by her trauma correspond to the social humiliation of having her hair shorn in public for sleeping with a German soldier, the memories of her German lover's body, and her bruising her fingers and face raw against the basement walls in which her parents locked her until her hair grew back. A very similar bodily register appears already in Resnais's *Night and Fog*: skin fragments removed by Nazi doctors and stitched into a lampshade, and the marks of fingernails of victims of the Shoah on the ceiling of the shower room where they were gassed. Through these oblique and nonassimilable correspondences, Resnais anchors the haptic and skin as the site of a posttraumatic imaginary after 1945.

The focus on the tactile sensorium correlates with a new relationship between text and images as well. Maurice Lemaître asserts in 1960 that Resnais and other new filmmakers derived it from the lettrists' "discrepant" cinema of desynchronized image track and soundtrack.[6] Whether this is in fact the case or not, Resnais asked Marguerite Duras to write the script for *Hiroshima mon amour* "as if you were commenting on the images of a film already made," and Duras's 1960 book contains pieces written both before and after the film, undoing any clear relation of precedence.[7] This alters Resnais's status as a film *auteur*—the oddly literary moniker Truffaut invoked to emancipate filmmakers from literature in 1959—and places him in the earlier cinepoetic *auteur* category that Giraudoux and Barjavel theorized in the 1940s to signal an immanently historical fusion of literature and cinema. The three cinepoetic narratives we will examine below, written between 1966 and 1978, belong to this first *auteur* tradition: all are informed by skin-deep experiences or figures of the haptic skin redeployed through imaginary cinema-in-writing in order to address collective catastrophes and racial genocides.

The seemingly "new" relationship between language and moving images inaugurated by the cinema of Resnais and other Left Bank filmmakers such as Agnès Varda and Chris Marker on the one hand, and by the New Novel's deep permeation by cinema and Robbe-Grillet's 1961 coinage of the "cinenovel" genre on the other hand, have tended to relegate previous cinepoetic works either into oblivion or into the heap of politically innocuous modernist experiments.[8] Yet Resnais himself is steeped into this earlier interart and pulp modernism. In the 1950s he made plans for a new adaptation of Souvestre and Allain's *Fantômas*, and until 1967 he sought to adapt Harry Dickson comics, tracking down its Belgian author Jean Ray and enlisting in turn Boris Vian, Frederic de Towarnicki, and Pierre Klast to write or edit four different versions of the scenario.[9] Hence he approaches the collaborative work between text and image within its historical continuum. The 1960 book version of *Hiroshima mon amour* was

Figure 43. First double page of Marguerite Duras, *Hiroshima mon amour* (1960, original edition). © Éditions Gallimard.

illustrated with thirty shooting stills (suppressed from subsequent editions), and one extra photographic montage next to the title page: a photo of Resnais superimposed with a miniature portrait of Duras in insert (Figure 43). I read it as suggesting the centrality of the theme of forbidden *collaboration*—between France and Germany, between the French girl and the enemy boy, between the Western woman and the Asian man, French and Japanese cinemas, and in the continuous collaboration between writing and the cinematic imaginary. Two of the texts in part V—Maurice Roche's *Compact* and Max Jeanne's *Western*—make direct references to *Hiroshima mon amour*, and both *Compact* and our third text, Nelly Kaplan's *Le Collier de ptyx*, refer to Nazi concentration camps, while *Western* tackles the genocide of slavery. Far from marking some kind of postmodern break, these three texts explicitly make links with and renew the earlier cinepoetic experiments that also inform Resnais's interart cinema.

In 1978, Guadeloupean writer Max Jeanne published a book-length visual poem entitled *Western* and subtitled *Ciné-poème guadeloupéen* (Guadaloupean cine-poem). This is only the third use of this generic term after the film *Emak Bakia*, subtitled *Cine-Poem* (France, 1926, dir. Man Ray) and Benjamin Fondane's 1928 chapbook *Trois scénarii, ciné-poèmes* (Three scenarios, Cine-poems), illustrated with two photos of Man Ray.[10] *Western* is a postcolonial satire restaging as a western movie the colonization of the Caribbean and the deportation of African slaves. To contextualize its reliance on cinema, we will take a quick look at Léon-Gontran Damas's 1956 *Black-Label*,[11] which Jeanne had certainly in mind.

Sometimes referred to as the Holy Spirit in the trinity of negritude—with Léopold Sédar Senghor (the African father) and Aimé Césaire (the chosen Caribbean son)—Damas was a mulatto from French Guyana who lived in Paris in the 1930s, served in the French army during the war, and became a representative of Guyana to the French parliament and a UNESCO diplomat, before teaching in US universities in the 1970s. *Black-Label* is a long poem in four parts whose title telescopes a whisky brand, addiction, and oblivion, with racial stigmatization in France's white society. A self-professed "Afro-Amerindian"[12] also of white ancestry—"Three rivers flow in my veins"[13]—Damas suffered also from not quite fitting the "black label" within the pan-Africanist movement of the 1950s. This doubly injurious too black but not-black-enough condition informs the melancholy of the poem voicing the poet's "compressed desires,"[14] keeping him from "intensely drawing pleasure / from all the little nothings which make up a euphemistically creole soul."[15] These "little nothings" (*petits riens*) composing the metis self are all but unimportant, since they have to do with choosing and being chosen as object of sexual desire.

Black-Label attempts to dispel "the taut taboos"[16] stifling desire through an anamnesis of the history of Guyana and the poet's own sexual history. Self-love, for Damas, implies the free possibility of loving another "whose image is forever in ONE / WOMAN glimpsed in the Island with the thousand and one flowers."[17] This hybrid of Baudelairean *passante* and female archetype is the missing half of the androgynous union he names "Elydé":

> I call ELYDÉ two beings fused into one only
> ever alone
> despite the very first scene
> which a still puzzled cheek remembers[18]

It is through the memory of skin contact that a "first scene" is brought back to view—a scene that is explicitly cinematic: "and here is ELYDÉ / and suddenly awakened again there unfolds [*se déroule*] the film of the recreated dream."[19] This "film" appears to center on the sexual attraction that "Ketty," a white woman, "blonde / beautiful / and naked"[20] felt for him, and which he immediately reciprocated, forming an Elydé "of you and of me who already were / but one beautiful unsatisfied desire."[21] The third part of the poem, however, explains why the poet rejected this incarnation of Elydé:

> Breaking the fear which made us mute
> You told me
>
> —I LAUGH AT CHANCE BUT NOT AT FATE
> that unfolds [*déroule*] as it will the film
> and everything is here tonight that recalls
> out of a past life
> the coarse perfume of the day
> when despite the interdiction
>
> WAS HANGED THIS MORNING
> AT DAWN A NEGRO GUILTY
> OF HAVING WANTED TO CROSS
> THE LINE[22]

White racist institutions that policed the crossing of the line by non-white males, and punished it by death, get in the way of the black poet having sex with a white woman. This appears to be the tenor of the compulsive film, since Damas repeats the lines of page 46, "and suddenly awakened again there unfolds [*se déroule*] the film of the recreated dream," a few lines before voicing his hopes

> To be among those who never stopped being
> a memory that suddenly recovers at last
> the thread of the drama interrupted
> by the heavy rattle of chains[23]

The film, whose soundtrack echoes with the din of the slaver's chains, supplants the "thread" (*le fil*) of Caribbean history and sends his life into the compulsive loop of arrested personal history. Rather than the film, he wishes for the song of community to unfold:

> it means letting the *palabre* unfold itself [*se dérouler*]
> it means delivering the message
> it means singing the poem for dancing[24]

The alternative is suicide, like this image of a woman who hanged herself, symptomatically "after having piled it all / rolled it all up [*tout enroulé*] / packed it all / wrapped it all up."[25] Postcolonial identity becomes a question of cautiously negotiating the cinepoetics of unfolding as a way of freeing the sensorium from the phantasm of subaltern "impotence."[26] The compulsive movie of self-castration can only come to an end through a different script breaking colonial laws of miscegenation—these "taut taboos," that also translate as "hard-on taboos" (*tabous bien bandés*).[27] Before the early 1960s and the release of movies such as *Bridge to the Sun* (France/US, 1961, dir. Étienne Perrier), *One Potato, Two Potato* (US, 1964, dir. Larry Peerce), *A Patch of Blue* (US, 1965, dir. Guy Green) and *My Baby Is Black* (France., *Les Lâches vivent d'espoir*, 1965, dir. Claude Bernard-Aubert), interracial romance movies between a white woman and a "colored man" always reinscribed the taboo by staging bitter or broken love, or death. *Hiroshima mon amour*, released three years after *Black-Label*, remains problematically liminal since male lead Eiji Okada had only a ventriloquized agency, even though it broke the taboo of interracial sex on screen.[28]

Less confessional than *Black-Label*, *Western* generalizes and collectivizes the convergence of racial trauma and cinema that Damas initiated, in order to recast the compulsive looping of racism that has shaped Caribbean history. The western's structural racism against Native Americans, and its commercial focus on cattle—and Jeanne figures slaves through both—prove bitingly apt at recounting the deportation and enslavement of Africans and their descendants. The cine-poem unfolds chronologically in chapters, interspersed with drawings by Michel Rovela, stylistically reminiscent of Wilfredo Lam's angular masks and biomorphically tortured figures. *Western* is very spare: pages with a single unrhymed verse section alternate with pages floating their texts on the blank page—often parodies of official warnings, legal language, and film industry lingo. This last category is the largest and includes film credits, dialogues, entry tickets, advisory language, and modified movie titles, such as *Muroroa mon amour* (Muroroa my love),[29] spoofing Resnais's and Duras's film, which was shot while France was preparing its own nuclear testing in the Algerian desert (testing at the Muroroa atoll began only in 1966).

The book's title page reads:

WESTERN
Ciné-Poème

You are asked to leave
Your heart
And your anger
In the lockers
Please

This poem must be presented
Upon any request

The facing page echoes this disempowering message with a collage depicting the severed head of a black woman, supported by two thin hands, her mouth open in speech, floating above a crowd of men who walk toward the viewer, ambiguously either coming to work or marching toward an uprising. This severed head serves as a symbol for Guadeloupe (a feminine toponym) but also likely refers to Césaire's 1948 collection *Soleil cou coupé* (Sun severed head), a title citing the last line of Apollinaire's 1913 poem "Zone," itself reprising the theme of headlessness that permeates cinepoetry.

The imaginary of damaged embodiment is strongly foregrounded by Jeanne's early retelling, under the title "In black and white / The slave trade," of a Creole pun that revolves around how Columbus "discovered" (*dékouvê*) Guadeloupe and did not "cover" (*kouwé*)[30] her up again, leaving it/her naked after this rapelike initial encounter. While both Césaire's *Notebook of a Return to the Native Land* (1947) and Damas's *Black-Label* (1956) interweave the history of slavery with a personal confession and a redemptive call toward collective unification, Jeanne eschews both the personal and redemptive aspects. *Western* stages a racist film without any hint at a happy ending. The question *Western* asks of its reader, therefore, is what to do with its author's refusal to engage in any redemptive or revolutionary hope. The answer that I will limn out derives from the eschatological potential of cinepoetry on the one hand, and *Western*'s unwavering focus on sarcasm, that is, quite literally *flesh* (Gr. *sarkhos*) on the other hand.

The original inspiration for Jeanne's use of cinema is the notion that recorded history functions as a selective discursive construction analogous to editing: "And how many cuts / how many fuzzy shots / in the film of your History / Guadeloupe."[31] Colonial history was crafted by French political discourse as an "official cut" that controls spectatorial reactions. Cinema theoreticians of the 1970s such as Debord, Metz, Baudry, and Mulvey promoted the view of the apparatus as a tool of discursive power and subjective production.[32] Jeanne's cinepoem echoes the thrust of such ideology critique by making the history of the Caribbean "a Franco-Spanish co-production," in which "sweat, blood and tears" are played by "the Guadeloupean people," and the film-stock technology is "Sangcolor"—"bloodcolor" but also "colorless"—while the shooting received "technical assistance" from "the CIA."[33] Apparatus theory is reprojected as historical amnesia through a pun on "tourner," both "to shoot" and "to turn": "SILENCE / On tourne / la page" ("SILENCE / Action, let's turn / Another leaf").[34] Every film released in France from World War II to 1981 was subject to censorship: films and published scenarios both bear a "*visa de contrôle*" or "*visa ministériel*" number indicating that they have been "*visé*" (viewed) by political authorities. Thus Duras's scenario for Resnais's film *Hiroshima mon amour* bears at the end of the printed credits: "visa ministériel n°29.890."[35] As a send-up, Jeanne adds at the end of his credits: "Visa sans contrôle 000971."[36] This suggests that cinema in poetry directly results from the political impossibility (in 1978) of shooting an actual film denouncing France's responsibility for slavery and its continued political control of the Caribbean: /cinepoem⇔unauthorized film/. At the same time, this "uncontrolled visa" introduces a metapolitical vista of justice as an ethical and cinematic perspective on history. Evoking the arrest and deportation of independence militants in May 1967, Jeanne writes, "And again / Under the lens of the sun [*sous l'objectif du soleil*] / the same film in slow-motion."[37] Only the sun looks on—at once as lens *and* as objective purview—on France's continued denial of historical justice and of Guadeloupe's political independence.

This metapolitical purview of *theatro mundi* is restaged in the poem in the guise of a movie theater, whose audience is segregated by Jim Crow laws—"Balcony: whites only / Orchestra: colored people (Balcon: Whites only / Orchestre: Coloured-people)"[38]—and in which the movie played is history itself:

> Because of the exceptional length of the film
> Five centuries
> There will be one projection only
> The island will not be taken in again
> [*L'île ne se laissera plus embobiner*][39]

The single projection deprives Guadeloupe of any opportunity of "replaying" its own history, all at once pointing to and suppressing a unique affordance of the apparatus. Yet, once the film has been shown to all, Guadeloupe will not be taken in again; the word "embobiner" conveying all at once "to con," "to reel in" like a fish, and "to rewind" (*rembobiner*) a film reel.[40] The theater also features films-within-the-film, such as *Gone with the Wind* (1939), translated into French as *Autant en emporte le vent*, cannily punned by Jeanne as the slave trade: *"autant en import-exporte le vent"* (Imported-exported by the wind).[41] Jeanne's movie theater is on the verge of transforming itself into a mainstay of Hollywood films: the courtroom drama. This is, I argue, a crucial possibility in Jeanne's cinepoem, one that is pointedly featured before being foreclosed. A three-page section has Jeanne's own "poem / handcuffed / brought before French tribunals" although no justice is to be expected from the "French high court of injustice" (*palais d'injustice français*).[42] Instead, the film replays the historical condemnations of Toussaint Louverture, Angela Davis and George Jackson.[43] Though this nightmare tribunal, like that in Genet's *Les Nègres* (1956), perversely condemns the victim again, I argue that it nonetheless points to the horizon of eschatological justice, Jeanne reminding us that meanwhile the Guadeloupean people have been left with "no role other / than that of extra [*figurant*] / in the film of [its] own History."[44] Damas's compulsive film has become generalized in the face of a denied hearing: "And every day the scenario begins again / And the show goes on [*Et le cinéma continue*]."[45]

Western culminates in the recognition of the traumatic blanks whereby actual events are left out of the France-controlled edit of History:

> Caribbean island
> bloody stump of land
> amputated of its sun of speech
> and of its History
> and unable yet to write its true name
> upon the white expanse/beach [*plage blanche*] of TIME[46]

We are returned to Guadeloupean embodiment defined throughout the cinepoem by compulsive amputation: "my poem / already armless [*manchot*] / before even being,"[47] or "my poem embalms / their bodies abandoned to putrefaction."[48] These bodies are the reason for the "never healed scar / of the colonial yoke,"[49] since the wounding, amputations and hangings sanctioned by the French law of the *Code noir*[50] were never redressed in a court of law. The cinepoem ends with a parody of the western comic books *Lucky Luke* by Belgian artist Morris, which invariably closes with the good cowboy riding into the sunset, singing: "I'm a poor lonesome cowboy so far away from home." Jeanne amends the song to: "I am a poor lonesome / Jim-crow-boy / far from Rum / and a long long way / from Africa."[51] Jeanne's sarcasm would fall flat, however, if we failed to read in the "white expanse" of time the "white page" (*page blanche*) of his own cinepoem, and to note how the blank spaces left by montaged history mirror the blank expanse of his own sparse pages. Jeanne's cinepoetics is one of blanks between traumatic-filmic and textual-historical representations: "Screen of my days / White page of my nights [*page blanche de mes nuits*]."[52] The cinepoem cannot rewrite history other than by making visible the blanks in the record, inviting us to reconsider the "one-time" projection of the heavily edited film of history seen in daytime against the background of its full version, the imaginary *cinéma-vérité* of history.

There are several clues that the work of the cinepoem consists in undoing its own inability "yet to write [Guadeloupe's] true name,"[53] or rather that this "yet" is not a function of time's arrow, of a future of justice, but rather opens a new dimension of temporality that precisely involves a partial *rembobinage* or rereeling of history.[54] For instance, his poem progresses chronologically in five periods, from 1493 to 1971—an end-point curiously foreshadowed by the visa number: 000971. In replacing the Christian millenary by a triple zero, Jeanne points toward another scale of time obliterated by the Christian calendar. Devoid of origin point, the Caribbean past holds the key to a new order of nontelic temporality. Indeed, if we now look into the cinepoem we find intriguing echoes to the "not yet" on which it ends:

> CARDINAL POINTS OF TIME
> of theater
> consciousness
> I am a consciousness
> quartered
> alive
> upon the parallels of the World
> and I decipher the Space
> of the Poem
> like an illfinite [*un malfini*]
> [deciphers] the parchment of the Sea
> with always in my memory
> this island's name
> that echoes like an oracle

This section on page 66 appears to come as a surreptitious continuation of the one on page 136 (cited above), since the blank page/beach is here a temporal theater with "cardinal points" that can be deciphered and theorized, and the island's unwritable name can at least be heard. In (mis)quoting Levis-Strauss's title as "Tristes topiques" (Sad topics).[55] Jeanne implicitly invokes structural anthropology as agent in the undoing of Western teleology. The neologism "malfini" points toward a nonfinite system of thought that refracts the constitutive amputations of Caribbean subjectivity, perhaps allowing for the development of a new oracular faculty and the decipherment of "the parchment of the Sea." The term "malfini" also suggests that time is not either finite or infinite—the theological conceit of Western temporality—but *illfinite*, inviting strange loops and returns.

Our reading is thus not meant to end with the poem's own endpoint. Reading certain sections in reverse order—projecting the film backward as it were—may yield an answer to the question of the island's name.

> Images become fuzzy
> in my memory
> pages
> and pages, white,
> cover the bed of my silent Poem
> like an abandoned *Carbet*
> and alone
> there still shouts
> at the four cardinal points
> of Time
> the echo of an ancient name
> the old Samba
> our uncle
> the Caribbean wind

This is on page 26, yet it seems to be a direct continuation of the enigma of page 136 partially resolved by page 66. Played in reverse, like Cendrars's *La Fin du monde filmée par l'ange N.-D.*, Jeanne's cinepoem *Western* lets the possible originary "name" of the island christened Guadeloupe be heard: it may lie in the word *Carbet*, which means a shack, in the sense of "big house" in the Carib tongue. It may even be close to the root word *Carib* itself designating the people of the archipelago. Hence the cinepoem written in French becomes "silent" while the soundtrack fills up with echoes of ancient voices and languages. If we move backward again we read on page 12: "Subtitled in creole / Postsynchronization: the griots." Indeed "postsynchronization"—at once synchronous and post facto—might be another way of characterizing the "illfinite" temporality of the film that Jeanne proposes we imagine. The alternative is the arrow of colonial-consumerist time punned by the line: "In a few moments / our pogrom will resume"[56] where "pogrom" and "program" become troublingly interchangeable terms.

Cinepoetry in its illfinite practice in Jeanne's work—especially with reference to the curtailed court scene—might be contributing an original solution to the conundrum of eschatology, the realm of justice and ends in Western thought. As Derrida noted in his deconstructive reading of Levinas's *Totality and Infinity*, the problem with eschatology and metaphysical thought is that they entail leaving the historical plane behind and, in effect, unchallenged.[57] Jeanne's cinepoetics, however, crafts a virtual filmic purview that resists deploying an extrahistorical eschatology: on the contrary, the full unedited version of the film of history is made of the same stuff as censored or illfinite history. For the cinepoem, justice can only be "in" history, albeit as an imaginary potential, and even if the cutout scenes cannot be found in the archive. This represents a kind of negative eschatology fostering no redemptive belief in redress yet committed to the potential witnessing of all events left out of the historical record.[58] This tacit negative eschatology, I believe, fuels the sarcastic energy of the cinepoem and empowers the cinepoet's work as political and emancipating.

Jeanne's cinepoem ultimately aims to provide a new theoretical framework for countering the denial of redress as well as colonial amnesia. It gives palpable form to the political overdetermination of the historical record (censorship and editing), it accounts for the structurally compulsive trauma in sociohistorically damaged populations (filmic loops), and it designates a mode of metahistorical witnessing (the imaginary film) from which purview other temporalities and readings are possible (reverse motion and remix). The source of this negative eschatology of cinepoetics is the genre of the western as a whole, which, for Jeanne, represents nothing short of the metahistory of slavery in the Western hemisphere unconsciously replaying itself through cinema.

CHAPTER TWELVE

Maurice Roche's *Compact*

Word-Tracks and the Body Apparatus

Reflected in the dark chamber of the brain—according to the proportions of the head, while conserving its own dimensions intact—the interior of a giant thaumatoscope formed itself.

—ROCHE, *Compact*[1]

While Pomerand's film *La Peau du milieu* (1953), documents the tattoos of the waning underworld, in Ray Bradbury's *The Illustrated Man* (1951), scenes tattooed on a man's skin predict the future. This framing device serves to link eighteen different stories that Bradbury published between 1947 and 1950—the first years of the Cold War. The future is radically grim, and the Illustrated Man wants none of it: "I'd like to burn them off. I've tried sandpaper, acid, a knife."[2] Each of the stories comes to life like a miniature film on the skin of the Illustrated Man: "at night I can feel them, the pictures, like ants, crawling on my skin. Then I know they're doing what they have to do."[3] But what is the future doing through this literary conceit—animating itself as moving pictures on human skin?

At about the same time as Bradbury, lettrists like Maurice Lemaître were also dislodging moving images from the cinema apparatus:

> A man will come on the stage and rip the screen, going through it. (From there on, the projection will unfold on the tatters of the screen, on the curtains, on objects and protagonists placed on the stage).[4]

On December 8, 1964, Lemaître literally became the Illustrated Man when, as a performance, he offered his body as medium for writing, painting, and collage to a group of artist friends: the resulting photographs formed for Lemaître a "cine-hypergraphy," which he published as a book in 1965, *Au-delà du déclic*, before shooting the pages as a film in the 1970s.[5] Epstein's cinematic "theater of the skin" had now become the skin *as* movie theater.

Compact (1966)—the first literary work of Maurice Roche (1924–97)—is ostensibly a narrative focusing on the dragon tattoo of a dying blind Japanese man.[6] Formally, it is a very challenging text in irregular visual poetic fragments belonging to eight voices, each set in a distinct locale and perhaps time period, with its own verbal tense and pronominal case, and each represented by a different ink color (Plate 4). The book makes little sense if we lose sight for a minute of its historical intermedia horizon: the exteriorization of writing on the skin through the cinema apparatus.

A voice in black ink opens the book, in the future tense and singular "you" form, emanating from the bodily "Mnemopolis" of the dying man lying in a room. It corresponds to his unconscious memories. It segues with a voice in red ink in the present third person form "*on* (one)" located in a room in Tahiti whose walls are covered with maps of major cities. Then comes a green first-person narrative voice, that of the conscious dying man describing his aural surroundings in Paris and recounting an attempt to have sex with an inflatable doll. A blue omniscient narratorial voice punctuates these three with distant reflections (we learn later that the voice is "set" in new York), and a fifth, also omniscient voice in purple describes objects located on the dying man's night table—a clock, a miniature atomic mushroom, a 3-D model of an earthquake, a small casket—which all have to do with Japan and a Noh play. The sixth voice in yellow is the direct discourse of a Japanese doctor who seeks to enter a *compact* to care for the dying man until his death, in exchange for his tattooed skin which he will add to his macabre yakuza tattoo collection. In an interview, Roche indicated that the motif of the tattooed skin is all at once "comic," "sad," and "polemical," and he specified its self-referentiality: "You give someone a contract for his skin exactly as you'd give a contract for a book. The clauses are identical."[7] The doctor's mock pidgin French sends up postwar film stereotypes of the calculating and cruel Japanese male, while, as in *Hiroshima mon amour*, it deprives the Japanese male's voice of full agency. At the same time, Roche's yellow voice deconstructs any pretense of "race blindness" since the doctor harbors racist commercial plans to sell reproductions of the skins he collects. With these objects, Roche has the doctor say, anyone can "make love with the back of beautiful Scandinavian man [*sic*], his back transformed by tattoo into a precious woman of color / Honorable blind man may easily, since he is blind, imagine a black woman."[8] Winking at Diderot (who thought that blindness enhances imagination) Roche collages races—the image of a black woman tattooed on Scandinavian skin—while denouncing the racial hierarchy that locates blackness always "against" whiteness, as a mere tattoo on it, a fetish image—a figment: "figments of their imagination—indeed, everything and anything except me," as Ellison famously wrote.[9]

The penultimate voice to appear, in the future tense and conditional mood, is a you-plural or polite form (*vous*), printed white on a black strip. It might be the photo negative of the voice in black, since both are "you" forms. It is described as the voice of "a prophecy in reverse,"[10] and has a similar metahistorical and eschatological dimension as Jeanne's *Western*. This voice makes several references to the Shoah: "You would forget this dreamed-up place to reach death (but you would have on the forearm, near the wrist, a tattoo: a number) . . . ," and "N.N. Stadt (Unimaginable amnesia. IHR, WENN IHR EINGETRETEN . . .) where you would have known the Kultur of the cadaver, on a land which is impossible to cleanse from now on."[11] The motto atop concentration camp doorways is also cited: "ARBEIT MACHT FREI."[12] An ironic reference, "*Das Sein zum Tode* pills,"[13] links Heidegger's "Being-for-Death" and Germany's chemical industry of mass death.[14] Midway through the narrative, the doctor brands the dying man with the Japanese ideogram for "pain," when he appears to refuse the Faustian compact. We also learn that the doctor is interested in "skins of the badly burnt victims of Hiroshima,"[15] which suggests that he covets the dragon tattoo on the man's back perhaps as much as the tattooed concentration camp number on his arm. The eighth and final voice is beige-brown and first-person plural—the multilingual voice of the corporate radio present spouting commercials and reports of war. It is the voice that closes the book by ventriloquizing (perhaps in an ad) a couple celebrating the New Year in a typical Parisian underground nightclub or "caveau." This last word literally means "funeral crypt," and the nightclub is located in the "Impasse des Catacombes" (Cul-de-sac of the catacombs).[16] The book thus ends in a traumatic impasse, the same dead space with which it opened, since "catacomb" literally means "lying down below," the very situation of the blind voice that begins the book. As this cursory description of *Compact* makes plain, the incredibly complex apparatus it deploys opens up a host of narrative, literary, poetic, racial, historical, and visual questions.

Close to Philippe Sollers and the team of the journal *Tel Quel* in the early 1960s, Roche was among the founding editorial members (with Jacques Roubaud, Jean Paris, and Jean-Pierre Faye) of the journal *Change* that resulted from a philosophical split from *Tel Quel* in 1968. The theme of the inaugural issue of *Change* was "Montage," and contributors (including Maurice Roche) explored the formal possibilities of a broader conception of montage expanded to various artistic, cultural and ideological productions. "We live in montage societies," the editors state in the introduction to the issue.[17] The central inspiration was Eisenstein, and the editors cite from his 1938 *Non-Indifferent Nature*: "We are discovering that cinematographic montage is only a particular case of the general principle of montage."[18] *Compact* clearly belongs to such expanded montage works, and its polyvocal construction echoes Bakhtin's *Rabelais* and James Joyce's *Finnegans Wake*—two fetish montage-centered texts among the *Tel Quel* and *Change* writers—but also points to the innovative multi-POV narration introduced by Kurosawa in his 1950 *Rashomon*.[19] Indeed, it is Jean-Louis Baudry, the pioneer of film apparatus theory, who notes that *Compact* radically alters the classic structure of the narratological voice: " We will never know—it may be the essence of poetic experience—whether it is the power of the [reader's] inner voice on the text or, on the contrary, the intimations which [the text], with its contents, its meaning, its typographical arrangement suggests to [the inner voice], which prevail over the other."[20] Roche explicitly states that he envisioned his following book *Circus* as "a montage in the cinematographic sense."[21] The green first-person voice of *Compact*, which is the closest to an authorial voice, states: "I had reached the point of mentally making an approximate montage (with possible disorder and some lacunae)."[22] The single instance of the word "compact" in the text is also in the green voice and describes an apparatus self-referentially: "I could move through the sliced-up universe with this compact device [*appareil compact*] broadcasting sections of faraway mental cities."[23] While the general conceit of blindness connects this apparatus with a radio,[24] *Compact* deploys a textuality that both recycles strategies used by previous cinepoets and pushes them in new directions of poly-sensorial immersion and textual materiality.

Trained as a musician, Roche composed the orchestral music for Henri Pichette's 1947 poetic play, *Les Épiphanies*, staged by Gérard Philippe and Maria Casarès. Pichette had been a journalist at the front during the war, and his work reverberates with postwar and Cold War angst. Especially in his later play *Nucléa* (1952), which used a white screen as its background, there is evidence of his abiding aesthetic interest for cinema.[25] Roche's first book was a monograph on vocal composer Claudio Monteverdi, and the conceit of blindness in *Compact* serves to foreground aural rather than visual perception and to adopt a polyvocal rather than monochord practice of writing. This being said, *Compact*'s sonic focus bears not directly on musical form (structure and score), but on the corporeal experience of the ways in which sound discloses motile space. Hence the blue voice draws a mental map of Upper Manhattan based on the chimes of the various public clocks,[26] while the green voice is constantly absorbed by/into the loud goings-on of the neighbor of his apartment.[27] The text also visually renders the experience of sound in motion: the passing of a fire truck generates four line breaks,[28] the decomposition of stereophonic hearing through one ear and then the other is rendered with white spaces between "left" and "right,"[29] and the Doppler effect of a passing car is made visible by means of increasing indents on the page.[30] The green voice points to the visual translation of the aural: "I was patiently sculpting a musical totem that I elongated in space until I made it transparent."[31] The formal conundrum of *Compact* lies in Roche's decision to translate through purely *visual* means—color changes, irregular layouts, symbols, drawings and non-Latin writing systems including sarcastically mock Braille (it is not in relief!)—the imaginary suspension of sight.

Roche attacks our visual experience of the page from the inside, as it were. The tattoo theme approached through the visceral phobia of skin removal, the episode of branding, and an abscess that plagues the red "*on*" voice with which we readers may identify,[32] all evince haptic sensations of the page as if it were living skin. Roche shows on a right-hand page of the book a small drawing of a ripped black page.[33] When the reader turns the actual page a similar drawing of the ripped page is found, but now it is only a black contour line around an odd grey on which is written in red ink: "One wrote what follows in sympathetic ink." The grey turns out to be the ripped black page of the reverse bleeding through, since it is printed at exactly the same place on both side of the physical page.[34] Two *representations* of a page match to reveal the page itself as not a mere surface but a 3-D object, a violation of the presupposed invisibility of the page. Roche's ingenious device serves to remind us of its two-sidedness and materiality in the same way that Mallarmé's famous blanks brings our reading back to its surface. The tattooed skin and the two-sided page thus invite us to imagine corporeal space as the underside of the skin—"sympathetic ink" fused with the sympathetic nervous system. While a key feature of the postmodern is the visual flattening out of depth into an all-surface, Roche's emphasis on blindness and tactility aims at reattaching surfaces to their tremulous depths—Epstein's coenesthesis.

Blindness in *Compact* does not aim to negate sight—which would only reaffirm the logocentric metaphysics of light—but to bring back vision and voice into a fluid and haptic space. In one of the most striking visual effects of the book, an illustration that looks like a barcode proves to be anamorphic words, which, by putting the book aslant, the reader deciphers as "Eyes Exchange Bank."[35] The page must be moved in space in order to "exchange" the usual perpendicular axis of reading for a more productive one (Plate 5). Roche also invokes retinal persistence on two occasions,[36] as if to "tattoo" the image on the eye's material surface, proving the eye to be a photo-organic apparatus requiring a "screen,"[37] and a "dark chamber,"[38] not an immaterial perspective on all things. Hence, if *Compact* enrolls the cinema apparatus in the first place it is in order to deconstruct any premise of omniscient POV in the narrative—rather than to undo vision itself.

The reembodiment of the eye in Roche is a countershock to the fate of the human body's devaluation in World War II: this is the central historical association of the book.[39] Roche's interview cited above associates the fate of the writer and that of the tattooed protagonist through the homology, /book to be written⇔skin to be flayed/. Rather than an instance of vicarious trauma, I read this as a philosophical engagement of writing with the history of mass victims. Like *Hiroshima mon amour*, *Compact* attempts to reframe and rebuild historical consciousness and embodied subjectivity in the wake of the Shoah and Hiroshima. Roche attempts this via the carnival of narrative heteroglossia and humor, on the one hand, and by rematerializing writing and the book as an embodied form of cinepoetics.

Compact foregrounds postwar corporeal culture through a remarkable performance of bodily and gender deconstruction narrated by the Japanese doctor. With "lanterns" projected on his body, a man on a stage (the doctor's former secretary) appears to be a naked woman,[40] before the "rays of the projectors"[41] draw a harlequin suit on him, which in turn disappears to reveal him again as a naked woman whose sexual attributes and accessories—"genitals, thong, breasts, buttocks"—subsequently remove themselves, showing the body in a man's suit which, however, is nothing but a "tattoo."[42] Next to him is what appears to be a beautiful redheaded woman, also naked, whose body is similarly made of "projections from magic lanterns,"[43] which, under the man's commands, are turned off one after the other to reveal her true body: she is an armless, legless, eyeless, toothless, and bald "trunk-woman," with a pacemaker and an artificial heart.[44] The man places neon teeth in her mouth ("a radiant smile!")[45] as well as two artificial eyes in her empty eye sockets: they are capable of motion and produce a "blinding gaze."[46] Such cascading (dis)embodiments relate both to Artaud's scenario of transmigration via different bodies, and to Chenal's scenarios of compulsive doublings. Cinema and moving images more generally mediate any direct presentation of bodies: the artificial eyes of the trunk-woman directly reference the emergence of the cinematic imaginary in literature, since Villiers's Hadali in *L'Ève future* is similarly fitted with artificial eyes. The purpose of this grotesque and macabre corporeal striptease is critique: the trunk-woman is on loan from a Boston laboratory that uses her for testing new prostheses—an uncomfortable reminder of the currency of eugenics in the twentieth century, from the Tuskegee Syphilis Study to Nazi torture in the name of medical experiments. This performance of biopower's entanglement with the society of the spectacle (Debord's book came out one year after *Compact*) informs the plot, for example the blind man's infatuation with an inflatable doll.

But conversely, *Compact*'s reliance on technologies of visual mediation assists us readers in rematerializing the book, writing, poetry, and the body all at once. An impressive array of cinematic techniques is referred to in *Compact*, from "super-impression,"[47] "extreme close up," "pull-back reveal [dolly shot]" "off-screen voice,"[48] "lap dissolve,"[49] "leaving the frame,"[50] "filmstrip,"[51] "reverse projection,"[52] "Technicolor,"[53] "screen,"[54] "slow-motion,"[55] "pan,"[56] "animated cartoon,"[57] and "framing."[58] Because of its antiocular and poly-sensorial premises, *Compact* resists any simple equivalence /book⇔film/ and instead settles on a more polyvalent homology: /sightless voice⇔words in mind/on skin⇔visual strip of text/. In this working homology, both automorphosis and the imaginary prove crucial. The verb "to imagine" and its derived forms recurs twenty times in *Compact*, and I would argue that in the expression "networks of imaginary movements"[59] we find the core of Roche's cinepoetics. Or better, phonocinepoetics since its model apparatus might be a hybrid of tape recorder and projector, encoding a voice that projects itself into a strip of text: "I feel the magnetic tape . . . unreeling and reeling again in me," so that "a ribbon of spoken wo / rds lifts itself up" and the "voice-strip [*pellicule de voix*] detaches itself"[60] until "the text of the magnetic tape . . . leaving the frame [*le champ*], had sunk into a wall of the rooftop studio."[61] A few pages earlier, the layout of the book made visible this mobile strip of text, first through capitals with vertical lines around them,[62] then with ticker-tape street signs in a cartouche.[63] The you-plural voice of History, in a negative black highlight strip that most resembles a physical film, then takes over,[64] immediately attending to words in their materiality: "You would, thickly, cut out diluted words. / You / would want to coagulate his speech."[65] During the gender-bending performance, different channels render the visual and aural dimension of words: "each text projected in neat typography / on a screen stage left was also broadcast through a / stereophonic process within the theater."[66] *Compact* ends in the green first-person voice, when the written compact between the doctor and the blind man—the author and its blind reader—is torn: "he crushes words until they are reduced to the crackling of dried up ink . . . the echo of sentences coiled around each other [*entortillées*]."[67] This figure represents an equivalent in the sound cinema era to the ribbon sticking out of Roussel's book to suggest the virtual cinepoetic protrusion of the text into our living sphere.

Cinema figures most explicitly in the purple voice's description of miniature artifacts through a long dolly shot going from one artifact to the other. The voice then switches to a series of sung voices, first coming out of a gramophone, then from a Kyogen play. Kyogen, a form of farcical theater interspersed in Noh performances, means literally "mad speech" and includes a main character or *shite*, often reappearing as a ghost, and a chorus of generally eight voices, the *ado*, which may inform the octovocal structure of *Compact*. The first object described on a shelf next to a bed is a Swiss clock nonetheless "made in Japan" after a "US patent" as if to redefine the "universal time"[68] of post–World War II. The second object is a miniature garden around a temple in front of which is a "casket in which lays an effigy in a gold kimono."[69] This is a vignette from Japan's pre-Meji era, evoking Shogunic stories of unfelicitous love ending in death. The third object is a tiny 3-D model of a Tokyo earthquake showing a pie-slice of earth with a copper wire figuring the complex trajectory of the shock wave.[70] This model represents probably the 1923 Tokyo earthquake in the aftermath of which Japan embraced the machine era to reconstruct itself as a fully modern state.[71] The fourth object is a lamp shaped like the atomic mushroom marking both Japan's end as a military power and the world's entrance into the nuclear age. All four objects are tacit emblems of the book's negative cinepoetics: they excerpt an event from its duration to freeze its form: the clock seems stopped at midnight;[72] the casket contains a saintly body undecomposed; and both the copper wire and the atomic lamp freeze a historical cataclysm at its climax. Such frozen instants correspond to the photo-cinematic difference we have examined in Roussel's poem, evoking in negative the durational experience of cinema, although here these objects' arrest is three-dimensional, like that of the book or transparent page.

Roche describes the Kyogen play as if it were a hybrid of film, vocal narration, and text:

> *SUBSTITUTE FOR THE OLD MAN*
>
> a character
> whose
> mobile lines
> might constitute
> other vocables[73]
>
> *WHAT'S THE USE OF TURNING OFF . . .*
>
> . . .
> the lit lantern
> in place of the blind old man whose
> shadow impressed on the ground
> has now crossed time[74]

This last stanza refers to atomic shadow traces of volatilized humans that *Hiroshima mon amour* also alludes to, and which for Akira Mizuta Lippit exemplifies a new regime of postwar visibility/invisibility:[75]

> . . . two steps of a thres-
> hold: an oblong trace is
> contoured against their
> shape, molding a relief,
> the movement.
>
> legend:
>
> "shadow of a person
> volatilized by the
> lightning strike of the
> atomic bomb"[76]

Compact reoriginates cinepoetry by cycling its imaginary apparatus through the new regime of human visibility/invisibility in the wake of the atomic bomb, and the new regime of corporeal culture in the wake of the Shoah. Both the shadow trace of a person volatilized and the tattooed skin of a dying man (who may in fact incarnate the emblematic victim of both the Shoah and Hiroshima) point to the biocinematic "avisuality," which Lippit has defined as linking 1945 to 1895, the year of "emergence of three new *phenomenologies of the inside*: psychoanalysis, x-rays, and cinema."[77] For Lippit, avisuality marks the cinema apparatus (we recall Mallarmé's allusion to the human "ghost" transformed into "pure light") but also leads to a mode of "sightless vision" that Paul Virilio theorized as constituting the end of cinema and the rise of the posthuman "vision machine." Roche's cinepoetics in *Compact* similarly enfolds sightlessness within historical visuality, dislodging language from its metaphysical exteriority to matter (as logos), and forcing its encounter with damaged embodiment, i.e, on the terrain of corporeality. This is why the page becomes skin (and screen) and the text becomes a strip of mobile signs.

Roche fetishizes the skull, which recurs as a visual symbol throughout *Compact*. Yet it is not merely as a *memento mori* that it figures prominently, but as a part of the cinepoetic apparatus, as a virtual reversible camera both filming ("dark chamber of the brain")[78] and projecting, as in Michaux. Commenting on the presence of the skull in *Compact*, Roche said that it took "the form of a hidden figure (calligram), rather like in certain films when one image is replaced by another—say, by an advertisement. The spectactor/reader doesn't see the image but [the image] makes its impact subliminally."[79] In the case of *Compact*, a number of such hidden figures come straight out of the history of cinepoetry. The use of colored inks was pioneered by Cendrars's and Delaunay's 1913 simultaneist poem *La Prose du transsibérien*, and there is a neosimultaneism at play in Roche's text: "In a tempo of reading, at the same instant but at different times, at the same hour but not at the same moment, events unfold (that we don't know or which we don't remember)."[80] Raymond Roussel also originally intended to print *Nouvelles impressions d'Afrique* (1931) in colored inks in lieu of its seven levels of parentheses. Blindness, artificial vision and second sight run through cinepoetry from Mallarmé's "fiction of a blindingly continuous rail," to Michaux's drug-induced visions and lettrists' essays and experiments on screen-less and image-less cinema. Even the visual representation of sound was tackled by Antonin Artaud, who comments on his 1931 scenario, "La Révolte du boucher" (The butcher's revolt):

> . . . it will be seen that this is a talking film insofar as the words spoken are placed there only to make images rebound. Voices are placed *in space* like objects. And it is on a visual plane that we must, if I may say so, *accept* them.
>
> . . .
>
> Sounds, voices, images, interruptions of images, all this belongs to the same objective world where it is above all movement that counts.
>
> And it is the eye that ultimately picks up and underlines the residue of all these movements.[81]

Compact remains among the most daring attempts of (phono)cinepoetics. It singlehandedly manages to draw resonances from a great deal of the hidden history of cinepoetry, particularly its involvement with homologies between bodies, the imaginary apparatus, and the text, while resolutely inhabiting the post–World War II historico-epistemological horizon. Its defiantly complex structure requires cinepoetics to become intelligible and tangible—indeed intelligible in its imaginary haptic, textual, and sonic spatiality.

CHAPTER THIRTEEN

Nelly Kaplan's *Le Collier de ptyx*

Mallarmé as Political McGuffin

Three musical notes resound, after which a sentence appears on the TV screen:
A THROW OF THE DICE WILL NEVER ABOLISH CHANCE.
—NELLY KAPLAN, *Le Collier de ptyx, ciné-roman*, 1971[1]

Thanks to [Nelly Kaplan], cinema may, one day, become surrealist.
—ANDRÉ BRETON, *Oeuvres* 4: 1449; 1957

One constant of cinepoetry as an avant-garde practice is a paradoxically rear-guard attention to the cinematic imaginary long after mass culture and contemporaneous thought have taken it for granted. Saint-Pol-Roux's anachronistic revival of symbolism through a utopian reappraisal of the film apparatus in the 1920s, or Michaux's amplifications of the sensorium of silent cinema in his post World War II explorations of psychedelic drugs, exemplify a peculiar form of decoupling technology from progress in poetic practice and theory. This resistance devolves certainly from the nonlinear temporality of the cinema apparatus itself—its unique capacity to offer flashbacks and flash forwards, loops, shifts, repetitions, crosscuts, and altered duration, not as arbitrary artifices but as reflections of the dynamics of our actual experience and thus of our historicity.

The work of Nelly Kaplan illustrates the waywardness of cinepoetic practice with respect to artistic currency. A poet, novelist, and filmmaker of Jewish-Russian ancestry, she was born in Argentina in 1931 and moved to Paris in 1953. Imbued equally with cinema and high Surrealism, she met both André Breton and Abel Gance (becoming the latter's assistant in 1955) and was partly responsible for their rapprochement. After making documentaries on Gustave Moreau, André Masson, and Pablo Picasso in the 1960s, she directed several fiction films in the 1970s articulating a post–New Wave feminism and eroticism, in particular in a movie released in the United States under the titles *A Very Curious Girl* or *Dirty Mary* (*La Fiancée du pirate*, France, 1969).[2] In parallel, under the pseudonym of Belen, Kaplan has published novels and collections of poetry linking Surrealism and the *real maravilloso* of South American magical realism. Susan Suleiman has characterized her subversively feminist rereading of Surrealism as animated by a "raunchy black humor."[3]

Both magic realism and black humor inform the "cine-novel," which Kaplan published in 1971, *Le Collier de ptyx*. A poetic scenario taking place in South America, it enrolls Mallarmé's invented word "*ptyx*" (from his famous "Sonnet in –yx"), as a postcolonial and anti-totalitarian MacGuffin within a virtual noir movie. The book's two liminal citations from Mallarmé's sonnet and Pierre Mabille's 1940 *Mirror of the Marvelous* place Kaplan's scenario at the transhistorical intersection of symbolism, Surrealism, and magical realism.[4] While Kaplan cites Mallarmé's hapax "ptyx" to revive symbolist poetry's yearning for a signifier capable of generating its own ideoreality, her mention of Mabille's "revolutionary animus" aiming to impose "the power of desire over the laws of the universe,"[5] has a broader, markedly political valence. In South America, the early 1970s were a period of increasingly bloody repression at the hand of dictatorships supported by the United States. Kaplan's project consists in tapping popular detective cinema to mount a poetic offensive against totalitarianism in the name of surrealist ideals of absolute freedom.

The plot combines romance and mystery against a noir backdrop centered on a MacGuffin (a term for a gratuitous object coveted by all parties, popularized by Hitchcock)—in this case, a necklace made of Mallarmé's poetic substance, ptyx. An antique dealer (Stéphane Ducasse) meets a mysterious woman on a rainy night (Ashby), and after they make love in a motel she disappears. Villains who track her subsequently show up at Ducasse's shop and threaten him, while he too searches for her. He finds images of Ashby in an old silent film and learns more about the mysterious necklace for which she is hounded. While investigating the lair of the villains he is supernaturally saved when he was about to be caught. Ashby reappears and disappears again, until a final showdown in a cemetery. When Ducasse's cat Maldoror falls asleep curled up on the ptyx necklace, he unwittingly saves the day. The necklace has the magical property of making the dreamer's dreams come true, and Maldoror's dreaming of the villains transformed into mice that catch on fire is realized.

The happy ending has Ashby, Ducasse, and Maldoror the cat leaving together in a car.

Underneath this stock plot, however, lie multiple layers of literary and political references. The necklace that Ashby sports,[6] as Ducasse finds out, proves to be "the keystone of the Yaquimba cosmogony,"[7] the Yaquimba being the first people of the current Republic of Caraiba who were exterminated by *conquistadores* through the treachery of their grand priest Niatep. The necklace had been under the latter's stewardship, but was taken by his daughter as she fled the colonizers. The names of the main protagonists evoke the canon of surrealism: Isidore Ducasse (alias The Count of Lautréamont) is the author of *The Maldoror Cantos*, and Ashby comes from "Devotion," a poem of Rimbaud's *Illuminations* that fascinated Breton and Kaplan, and includes the name "Léonie Aubois d'Ashby."[8] As for Ducasse's first name, Stéphane, it points to Mallarmé: indeed, he is presented as a literary critic who wrote a book on *Igitur or The Problem of the Time Chamber in Mallarmé,*[9] and often uses dice to decide what to do. Kaplan's odd splicing of Lautréamont and Mallarmé in 1971 would receive a few years later a theoretical justification in Julia Kristeva's 1974 *A Revolution in Poetic Language*, whose subtitle in French reads, *L'avant-garde à la fin du 19ème siècle, Lautréamont et Mallarmé.*

Although the Yaquimba is an imaginary indigenous tribe, this rare name turns out to be that of Julio Yaquimba, a Guambiano Indian who organized indigenous resistance against landowners in 1910s and 1920s Colombia.[10] Because the name of the arch-villain is Hernán Duvalier—a conflation of conquistador Hernán Cortez and Haiti's dictator François Duvalier—we can ascribe a broad anticolonial and antitotalitarian intent to Kaplan's nomenclature. The name of the evil priest, Niatep, discloses a third spatial and historical dimension of *Le Collier*, since it is that of Pétain—the architect of France's collaborationist policies during the Occupation—written backward. The other villain's name, Werner von Mengele, directly links Nazi Germany and the Americas, since it combines the names of Werner von Braun, a member of the SS and the creator of the V2 rocket program before working for the Pentagon on ICBM's and at NASA, and of Josef Mengele, whose eugenic experimentations tortured and killed thousands at Auschwitz, and who fled to Argentina where he was semiofficially hidden by the government until his natural death. Describing the necklace of ptyx as "having the fabulous power of making reality and dream interpenetrate,"[11] Kaplan pits the poetic antecedents of Surrealism against the Spanish and French colonization of South America and the Caribbean, World War II and Nazism, and the dictatorships of the South American hemisphere sanctioned by US containment policies—all of which touch on her Jewish, Argentinian, and French heritage. Intermittent signs of insurrection on the street, in schools, convents, and barracks, are reported in radio and TV broadcasts throughout the cine-novel, for instance when Duvalier fears, "a revolt . . . on my plantations."[12] By combining the Haitian Revolution and the Spartakist Uprising with South American Marxist movements that lead notably to Salvador Allende coming to power in Chile in 1970, Kaplan embeds Surrealism within the potential aspirations of all revolutions.

That cinema lends itself to a new mode of synoptic vision of history, in which distinct periods refract each other in new ways, was Griffith's signal innovation in his 1916 *Intolerance*. While using classic crosscuts to alternate between simultaneous actions within each of four periods, Griffith invented a cross-historical edit, as it were, presenting historical consciousness as a montage across four narratives belonging to these four different geohistorical situations. Kaplan's scenario, though it also relies on classic crosscuts, nonetheless finds another macroscopic solution to transhistorical linkage—*polyvision*, an idea of Abel Gance which Kaplan combined with Breton's theory of the surrealist image. But before addressing these two questions, let us examine how the strictures of the scenario and the imaginary of the apparatus shape *Le Collier*.

Singularly devoid of shooting indications beyond "exterior day" and "the camera shows," the text is less than a decoupage and something other than a mere treatment. For example, when Ducasse proves unable to change a tire on his car, Kaplan quips, "For him, the plowing hand is surely not worth the same as the writing hand."[13] This is a paraphrase from *A Season in Hell* where Rimbaud writes, "The writing hand is worth the same as the plowing hand." Yet since Kaplan does not specify a voice-over, it is not clear whether or how she planned to integrate this quip into the film, or whether she planned on making a film at all. Further on, after indicating "exterior day" the text adds "there are no projected shadows," and although it is full sun, "one distinctly hears the noise of strong rain, a stormy rain."[14] The first indication refers to the famous park scene in Resnais's *Last Year in Marienbad* (1958) in which conic trees project no shadows, while the discrepant soundtrack might cite Cocteau's *Blood of a Poet* (1930) in which off-screen shouts are heard when the poet goes through the mirror, or perhaps Isou's film. At this point in Kaplan's narrative, Ducasse is in fact dreaming although the text provides no didascalic indication, thus tricking readers in the same way movies routinely disorient viewers. Like Cocteau, Kaplan reveals her cinepoetic sensibility via the multiplication of light cones, from the establishing headlights of a car,[15] to a torchlight,[16] a spotlight,[17] and omnipresent "rays of light" streaming out of windows and doors.[18] Light projection informs the very nature of the McGuffin necklace since its twenty-eight stones "were born of the wedding of the remains of the night with the first rays of the sun"[19]—a figure of the *hierogamos*, or sacred wedding of opposites dear to Jung and Breton, extended to that between writing and cinema.

After their initial encounter, Ashby disappears from the diegetic world, becoming a specter in a secondary diegetic realm of images: dreams, film, and photographs. After she vanishes, Ducasse goes to a movie theater playing a silent film Ashby had circled in a newspaper: *The Trail of the Octopus*. This happens to be the film to which Breton refers twice in *Nadja*.[20] Kaplan reinvents the film as a scene in which Death dances with guests at a party, disguising itself as the opposite gender of each (perhaps a surreptitious critique of Breton's heteronormativity), killing each of them as the dance ends. Ashby is the last one alive, and as she is getting the upper hand on Death the film breaks.[21] This ploy recalls the breakage of the apparatus in Cendrars's *The Film of the End of the World*, as well as the malfunction of the projector in Hillel-Erlanger's *Voyages en kaléïdoscope*. Ducasse obtains the broken piece of film from the projectionist and tries tracking Ashby by contacting the film director, but the scene he saw was never included in the released film in which, according to the director, the last character, a woman, dies in the last scene.[22] This discrepancy between variants of a film points both to Kaplan's cinephilia—this is a common predicament in silent film historiography—and to the eschatological cinepoem of Jeanne in which a fuller account of untold history figures as an imaginary film.

With the broken film as his only clue, Ducasse finds a photo of Ashby on a tomb. Dead to the diegesis, she has, in a way, vanished into the apparatus itself, transporting us back to the beginning of cinema, where the "vanishing woman" act was a favorite trick of magician Méliès before he started his film company. Karen Beckman suggests that such spectacles of "vanishing women" can be understood to refract the social acceptance of women's disappearance, either through social or real death.[23] The political "disappearance" of political opponents in South American and Caribbean dictatorships was certainly on Kaplan's mind already in 1971. When Ducasse opens her tomb, he does not find her body. Instead, he is knocked unconscious when the villains throw him in. The gravedigger who rescues Ducasse provides him with a photo of the tomb, showing Ashby's photo on it (it too has disappeared). As in Chenal's *Drames sur celluloïd*, but within a political context, Ashby has become a media refraction, a photo-within-a-photo in a film-within-a-novel.

In a wink at *Alice in Wonderland*, Ducasse reaches Ashby's virtual realm by falling through a tree trunk and landing in a grotto: "The walls in rock crystal reflected images back and forth which, fusing with one another, created the mirage of new forms."[24] This kaleidoscopic realm of images holds a tapestry that turns into a photographic reproduction of the dictators:

> Ducasse discovers, running like a fresco at the bottom of the tapestry, a succession of shoes. . . . It is manifestly a photo. Ducasse pushes the curtain aside and discovers a life-size reproduction. . . . They are ALL here: Duvalier, Mengele, the three gorilla-mercenaries, the colonel du Béret, the judge Ponce, Mother Anastasia. . . . In the middle of the life-size photo Ducasse notices a handle. He realizes that the blown-up photo is glued on a double door astutely concealed.[25]

When he opens the door, all those figures appear "in flesh and blood."[26] Kaplan combines here the crime serial ploy of the hidden door—a leitmotiv in Feuillade's *Fantômas*—with the magical imaginary of photographic reproduction reversing back to the reality it displays. Other apparatuses of optical relay punctuate the narrative, from a panoramic scope[27] to a pair of "speaking glasses";[28] from visual framing devices such as doors, windows, and small apertures to image reproductions in drawings, billboards, signs, cards, and a message written in lipstick (reminiscent of Hitchcock's 1942 *Saboteur*) reproduced as illustration in the text. Moreover, the resolution of the plot revolves on a *symbolon*—literally an image cut in two and which Kaplan offers to the reader as a visual enigma. There is no better emblem of cinepoetry than this symbolon: it is an actual *image of (cut-off) words on the page*, diegetically figuring an "inscription guillotined by bad framing" in a color photograph of Ashby looking through the scope (Figure 44). By finding in a book titled *Panoramas and Viewpoints* the locale where the photo was taken, Ducasse is able to track down Ashby and actually sees her when he looks into the scope. Hence, as in Roussel's poem, the scope sutures the narrative so that the sliced-off letters ultimately produce a filmic eyeline match: /visual text⇔eyeline match⇔narrative splice/. Kaplan inserts in this geographical locale a sign reading "The Sublime Point." Georges Sebbag reads it as a direct quotation of André Breton's thesis, in *The Second Manifesto of Surrealism*, that "Everything leads us to believe that there exists a certain point in the mind from which life and death, the real and the imaginary, the past and the future, the communicable and the incommunicable, the high and the low stop to be perceived as contradictions."[29] If *Le Collier* can be considered a cinepoetic novel, it is insofar as it crystallizes the aesthetics of Kaplan as a reconciliation between poetry and cinema—a reconciliation she also brought about by personally orchestrating the historical reconciliation between her two lovers and mentors: Breton and Gance.

She had signaled this aesthetics in a short but crucial text of 1955, *Manifeste pour un art nouveau, la polyvision* (Manifesto for a new art: Polyvision), with a preface by Philippe Soupault—the inventor of "cinematographic poems" in 1918. A dense manifesto, *Polyvision* invokes all at once Surrealism, the stagnation of cinema (on the brink of its renewal by the New Wave), and the old dream of the fourth dimension that harks back to Jarry. It also mounts a strong feminist offensive against the sexism of the movies in the 1950s. The manifesto has its roots in Abel Gance's lifelong technical and philosophical pursuits of a new kind of multiscreen and stereophonic cinema, for which he patented "Cinerama" in 1926, and which he first applied in his 1927 *Napoléon*. While shooting the film, Gance experimented with newer techniques such as 3-D sequences and saturated superimpressions of "up to sixteen images on top of one another; I knew you wouldn't be able to see anything after the fifth image but they were in there . . . and so were their potential: like in music when you have fifty instruments."[30] Starting in 1947, Gance had been pushing his project for *The Divine Tragedy*, a Christian epic to be projected on several lateral screens simultaneously, each of which would show a different epoch, from the life of Christ to a nuclear apocalypse.[31] In 1952, the three-projector Cinerama, with stereophonic sound, was launched in the United States, followed by 3-D movies and the CinemaScope (invented by astronomer Henri Chrétien, a student of Camille Flammarion) in 1953. Gance had been advocating for

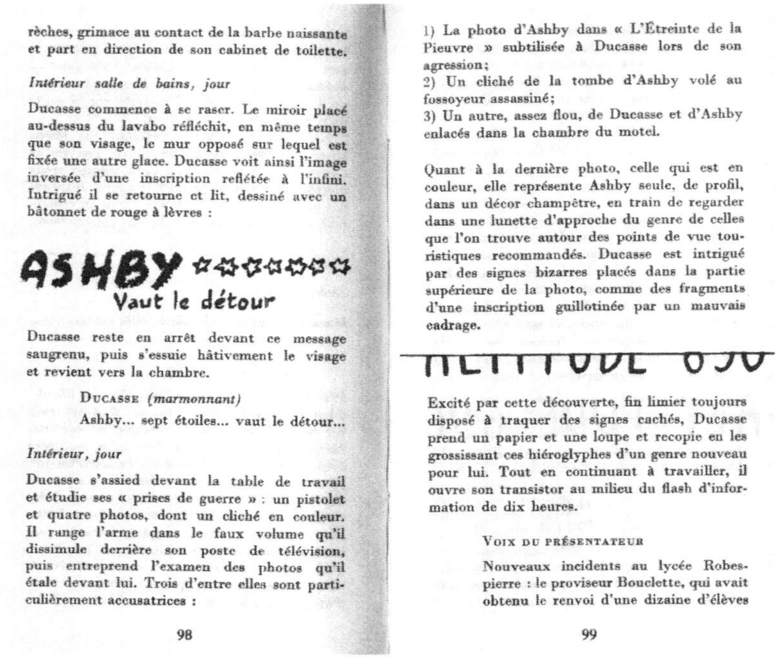

rèches, grimace au contact de la barbe naissante et part en direction de son cabinet de toilette.

Intérieur salle de bains, jour

Ducasse commence à se raser. Le miroir placé au-dessus du lavabo réfléchit, en même temps que son visage, le mur opposé sur lequel est fixée une autre glace. Ducasse voit ainsi l'image inversée d'une inscription reflétée à l'infini. Intrigué il se retourne et lit, dessiné avec un bâtonnet de rouge à lèvres :

ASHBY ✩✩✩✩✩✩✩
Vaut le détour

Ducasse reste en arrêt devant ce message saugrenu, puis s'essuie hâtivement le visage et revient vers la chambre.

DUCASSE *(marmonnant)*
Ashby... sept étoiles... vaut le détour...

Intérieur, jour

Ducasse s'assied devant la table de travail et étudie ses « prises de guerre » : un pistolet et quatre photos, dont un cliché en couleur. Il range l'arme dans le faux volume qu'il dissimule derrière son poste de télévision, puis entreprend l'examen des photos qu'il étale devant lui. Trois d'entre elles sont particulièrement accusatrices :

98

1) La photo d'Ashby dans « L'Étreinte de la Pieuvre » subtilisée à Ducasse lors de son agression;
2) Un cliché de la tombe d'Ashby volé au fossoyeur assassiné;
3) Un autre, assez flou, de Ducasse et d'Ashby enlacés dans la chambre du motel.

Quant à la dernière photo, celle qui est en couleur, elle représente Ashby seule, de profil, dans un décor champêtre, en train de regarder dans une lunette d'approche du genre de celles que l'on trouve autour des points de vue touristiques recommandés. Ducasse est intrigué par des signes bizarres placés dans la partie supérieure de la photo, comme des fragments d'une inscription guillotinée par un mauvais cadrage.

Excité par cette découverte, fin limier toujours disposé à traquer des signes cachés, Ducasse prend un papier et une loupe et recopie en les grossissant ces hiéroglyphes d'un genre nouveau pour lui. Tout en continuant à travailler, il ouvre son transistor au milieu du flash d'information de dix heures.

VOIX DU PRÉSENTATEUR
Nouveaux incidents au lycée Robespierre : le proviseur Bouclette, qui avait obtenu le renvoi d'une dizaine d'élèves

99

Figure 44. Visual play in Nelly Kaplan, *Le Collier de ptyx* (1971). © Éditions Jean-Jacques Pauvert.

such expansion of the screen and what he had called "perspectival sound" since the mid-1920s. During the Cannes Festival of 1953, he rendered a last homage to Jean Epstein, who had just died, and to the techno-poetic cinema both of them had been dreaming about for thirty years and that Hollywood had now implemented, albeit only to fight against the exponential rise of television.[32] Through the support of Nelly Kaplan's *Polyvision* manifesto on the one hand, and that of the burgeoning group at the *Cahiers du cinéma* and official interest in a homegrown version of American innovations on the other hand, Gance resurrected his triple-screen stereophonic film projects. Under the title "*Protérama*," Gance published his own manifesto for what he called "polygraphy" in 1953, proposing a new equation for multiscreen cinema: "Images add to themselves in vertical sequences; images multiply themselves in vertical alignments." This "euphoric intrusion into a kind of fourth dimension," he argues, would allow for a "true psychological relief, more important than the animated wax museum optical relief we are given," and leading to an encounter of "the real and the surreal."[33] Mere automorphism, in other words, was obsolete as cinema's principle, and surreality was invoked as its new prosthesis. In December 1956, Gance and Kaplan organized the *Magirama* show, a projection on three screens of several new films they had shot in 1956, together with remastered excerpts from *Napoléon*, and a film by Norman McLaren. The French intelligentsia—not just of cinema—from André Bazin to George Sadoul, and Jean-Luc Godard to André Breton, showed up to be awed by France's answer to Hollywood's recuperation of Gallic techniques. Breton celebrated *Magirama,* which, he wrote, "takes a decisive step toward this new *structure of time* that Paul Valéry, in his "Methods" of 1896, and Marcel Duchamp in 1912 and 1913 called for."[34] Godard was less enthused, Jean Mitry was critical (he was conducting his own triple-screen experiments with Pierre Boulez at the time), and *Magirama* soon vanished from the pages of *Cahiers du cinéma* as well as from the canon of film history.

Kaplan's *Polyvision* defines Gance's new cinema of "the fourth dimension" as "the exploded image" (*l'image éclatée*), and she too associates it with "poetic surrealism, the creator of multiple temporalities."[35] She rails against the "tridimensional asphyxia" of the times:

> There is but one art, the most marvelous of all since it assembles and condenses them all, possessing the richness and the poetry necessary to translate, reflect, and sublimate the movement and the becoming of the atomic era, in which never yet experienced speed, ubiquity, and sensations are becoming or will become an everyday element.
> This art is cinema.[36]

Apart from the "atomic era," the terms are strikingly similar to texts by Canudo and Epstein in the early 1920s. Kaplan's manifesto also takes on the "patriarchal system" of cinema perpetuated in genres such as westerns, noirs, musicals, mafia movies, and "little princess" films.[37] She also indicts existing cinema for its multiple "castrations" resulting from "capital and its blackmail," its various levels of "precensorship" and "postcensorship." She reaches conclusions similar to Gance's as to the imaginary resonance of polyvision: "The simultaneity of the vertical and horizontal unfolding of scenes will excite somnolent imagination and the associations of ideas buried in the viewers' subconscious [*subconscient*]."[38] We might then say that for Gance, Kaplan, and Breton alike, the merit of polyvision lays much less in its panoramic immersive qualities than its capacity to evince from spectators *a virtual cinema* springing from the interstices of absorption *between* lateral screens. It is indeed a cinema as close as possible to cinepoetry.

In the dénouement of *Le Collier de ptyx*, after the cat Maldoror causes the villains Duvalier and Mengele to burn by his sheer dreaming, the necklace dematerializes, and "bit by bit, as the necklace of ptyx is consumed in an ultrasonic whistle, it reappears, like an indelible tattoo, on the neck of Ashby."[39] Here again cinepoetry appears to imply direct impress on the skin, as in Jeanne and Roche, and for the same reason: the /skin⇔screen⇔page/ homology discloses a new understanding of the insurmountability of history, and a commitment to remobilize representational systems together with the body.[40] The circularity emblematized by the necklace also implicitly recapitulates the history of cinepoetry. Launched by Mallarmé's null word "ptyx"—mere ink on the page—Kaplan's McGuffin travels in reverse through the history of cinepoetry's entwinement with silent cinema, Gance and Surrealism, history and trauma. It ultimately reappears as a movie-mediated ink palimpsest tracing itself on imaginary skin—the mark of a poetic subject coming on the heels of the postcolony and the Shoah.

Conclusion

The Film to Come in Contemporary Poetry

THE "LANGUAGE TURN" TURNS TO PHOTOGRAPHY AND CINEMA

The period during which cinepoetry best understood itself as an aesthetic project coincides with the utopian ethos of the literary avant-garde in the cinephilic interwar, from 1918 until the arrival of sound in 1929 and 1930. At other times it remained just under the surface currents of poetics, whose directions and upheavals it continued to prompt or inflect. Starting in the 1980s, and even more strongly since the 1990s, cinepoetry has conspicuously reemerged within new experimental writing. This resurgence might be correlated to three loosely linked features: (1) a rejection of modernist poetic diction and/or the theory-inflected poetics of the 1970s that came out of it; (2) the proliferation of photographs published with poetry books; and (3) an approach to language mediated by pragmatic protocols—the poetics of the *dispositif.*

All three features have their roots in earlier transformations of poetry after the Liberation, when avant-garde poets turned again toward cinema as a realm of encounter between language, the lived world, and damaged experience. While this postwar overcoming of the symbolist-surrealist aesthetics may not be the avowed concern for post-1980s poets, their horizon of innovation both extends and exceeds the influential dismissal of poetry by Sartre's committed view of literature in 1947, and the apposite transfer of literature's center of gravity to prose. This transfer was most clear among writers of the

1950s and 1960s who adopted a compromise formation that Barthes called *écriture blanche*—"blank writing." It might be characterized as an apparent commitment to narrative that nonetheless relies on poetic devices at every turn to puncture prose's formal tendency toward "grand narratives" of moral edification, political thesis, or Bildungroman. Blank writing dovetailed with the New Novel that gazed sideways and stereoscopically at both cinema and poetry—as we have seen in the case of Cayrol and Robbe-Grillet, two of its pioneers.

Blank writing squeezed avant-garde poetic language in the 1960s and 1970s into an ever-tighter corner where linguistic theory and psychosexual intensification were leveraged as tools for social critique and hypothetical reader mobilization. This was the common animus of the key journals of the moment, *Tel Quel* and *Change*. Denis Roche emblematizes this precarious position in claiming that modernist poetry's ideals and formal research have increasingly become "inadmissible." He states in 1968, "Writing can only symbolize what it is in its functioning, within its 'society.' It must stick to that."[1] The "Preamble" to one of his last poetic "series"—Roche refutes the poem as a unit—and to which this excerpt belongs, ends on the word "immolating." Logically, perhaps too logically, Roche's poetry self-immolated in 1972 by stopping altogether, emulating Rimbaud's defection from symbolism a century before him.

Roche turned to or rather *converted* to photography. Through the photographic apparatus as a device of framing, indexicality, and material reference he reopened the articulation of language and direct experience that the *Tel Quel* group had largely sought to bracket.[2] Roche's momentous conversion has recently been reinterpreted by poetry theoreticians like Jean-Marie Gleize, Christophe Hanna, Jan Baetens, and Olivier Quintyn as paradigmatic for the changes that have affected experimental poetry since the 1970s.[3] These changes inform the three new overlapping directions mentioned above. First, post-1980s works of experimental poetry pushed aside questions of lyrical voice, diction, and poetic images that, in spite of differences, held together symbolism, Surrealism, blank writing, and *Tel Quel* within a fairly cohesive genealogy. Second, an increasingly polyvalent dialogue with photography and the inclusion of photographs alongside poetic texts have brought the visual and cultural spheres, as well as issues of technical reproducibility, to bear on the traditionally autonomous realm of poetry and text. Finally, a new theoretical nexus has rivaled the primacy of the lyrical construct (linking the voicing subject, mediating addressee, and world object) as an operational model of creation: the *dispositif.* Minimally, it involves writing a text through an operational process that reflects and combines social and material forces, technological contaminations of subjectivity and impersonal discursive fields—in lieu of the traditional subjective matrix. Alferi and Doppelt's *Kub or* is emblematic for this new *dispositif* poetics.

Commenting on Roche's 1980 book of photos and texts, *Dépôts de savoir & technique* (Deposits of know-how and technique), Quintyn has synthesized all three directions by formulating Roche's *dispositif* as "*a textual photomontage with a pseudocinematographic unfolding or dynamics*."[4] Roche's writings on photography (and the exclusive use of black-and-white in his photographic work) point insistently to the transition from photography to cinema, and represent yet another instance of the reversibility or retroversion that has accompanied cinepoetry since its beginnings.[5] Post-1970 experimental poetry marked by photography and the *dispositif* signals an important new chapter in the adventure of cinepoetry. We will take Quintyn's "pseudo" caveat to heart in how it implies simultaneously and paradoxically an acknowledgment and a deconstruction of the cinema apparatus as poetry's limit imaginary.

THE PHOTO-CINEMATIC DIFFERENCE AS POETICS OF "THE THWARTED FILM"

Roche's conversion has its own cultural logic. It is the culmination of the broad iconophilia of the second half of the nineteenth century that hastened the penetration of material images as models for poetic discourse, then as companion medium in poetry publications.[6] Baudelaire represents a kind of liminal case. Félicien Rops's famous engraving for the 1866 *Les Épaves* appears as a frontispiece, that is, outside of the text. In spite of his iconomania, Baudelaire remained a purist. By contrast, Édouard Manet's engravings for Mallarmé's 1870 translation of Poe's "The Raven," appear side by side with the poem. Subsequently, an important faction in symbolism, led by Jarry, de Gourmont and Mallarmé—all three pioneer cinephiles—favored the programmatic juxtaposition of images with literary texts. While the first two launched in 1894 the journal *L'Ymagier*, with woodblock reproductions and essays and poems, Mallarmé planned to illustrate *A Throw of the Dice* with engravings by Odilon Redon in 1897, and his close disciple Rodenbach was the first to integrate photographs in a work of literature in his 1892 *Bruges-la-morte.*

Photography and poetry are generally considered to have first cohabited under the aegis of Surrealism. Breton's 1928 *Nadja*, with photos by Jacques-André Boiffard, Raoul Ubac, and anonymous photographers, was followed by René Char's 1930 short collection of poems *Le Tombeau des secrets*, illustrated with portraits of his family, and Paul Éluard's 1935 poems *Facile* with erotic photos by Man Ray. But it is in fact Epstein's 1921 *Bonjour cinéma* that should claim primacy, influenced in part by internationalist journals such as *L'Esprit nouveau* that were richly illustrated with photographs. The proliferation of shooting stills in pulp adaptations of movies, such as in Canudo's 1923 *La Roue*, also opened the way for photo-literature in the interwar. Poetry books incorporating photographs are few and far between, however, during the 1930–70 period. Yet again, movie adaptations by established writers maintained a crucial continuity in quasi-cinepoetic practices. Hence, the book version of Jean Cocteau's 1948 *Blood of a Poet* with production stills took novelization out of its pulp domain to inscribe poetry, cinema, and photography within a new intermedium in book form (Figure 45). It directly prepared and informed Duras's 1960 book version of *Hiroshima mon amour.*[7]

By the time Robbe-Grillet published his vaunted cine-novels (in particular the 1974 *Glissements progressifs du plaisir*), what has been termed "photoliterature" had a long literary history. In 1976, Marie-Françoise Plissart and Benoît Peeters launched an important scenario project titled *Fugues* that was inspired by Italian photo-novellas and popular comics. Thus by the late 1970s, photoliterature represented an ideal new genre for skipping across all kinds of divides.[8] This likely explains the sudden irruption in the late 1970s of photographs in the published works of poets born after the war, such as Mathieu Bénézet and Emmanuel Hocquard. They were among the first to do so, quite significantly in two poetic works labeled as prose: Bénézet's 1979 *La Fin de l'homme, roman abandonné* (The end of man, an abandoned novel) and Hocquard's 1980 *Une Journée dans le détroit, récit* (A journey in the straits, narrative).[9] Both books pursue similar autobiographical projects of a new kind: prose serving as cover for a poetic subject seeking reconstruction out of his own use of language, rather than imposing a certain form of language based on preordained models of aesthetics and subjectivity.[10]

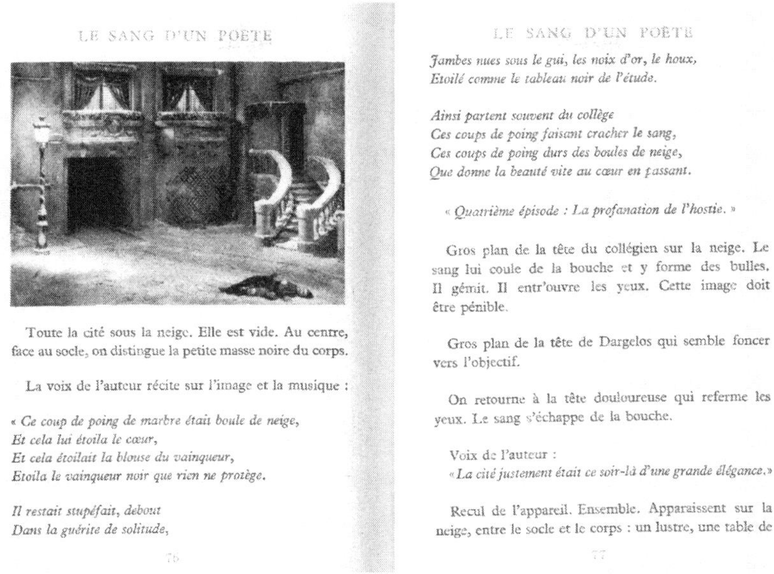

LE SANG D'UN POÈTE

Toute la cité sous la neige. Elle est vide. Au centre, face au socle, on distingue la petite masse noire du corps.

La voix de l'auteur récite sur l'image et la musique :

« Ce coup de poing de marbre était boule de neige,
Et cela lui étoila le cœur,
Et cela étoilait la blouse du vainqueur,
Etoila le vainqueur noir que rien ne protège.

Il restait stupéfait, debout
Dans la guérite de solitude,

76

LE SANG D'UN POÈTE

Jambes nues sous le gui, les noix d'or, le houx,
Etoilé comme le tableau noir de l'étude.

Ainsi partent souvent du collège
Ces coups de poing faisant cracher le sang,
Ces coups de poing durs des boules de neige,
Que donne la beauté vite au cœur en passant.

« *Quatrième épisode : La profanation de l'hostie.* »

Gros plan de la tête du collégien sur la neige. Le sang lui coule de la bouche et y forme des bulles. Il gémit. Il entr'ouvre les yeux. Cette image doit être pénible.

Gros plan de la tête de Dargelos qui semble foncer vers l'objectif.

On retourne à la tête douloureuse qui referme les yeux. Le sang s'échappe de la bouche.

Voix de l'auteur :
« *La cité justement était ce soir-là d'une grande élégance.* »

Recul de l'appareil. Ensemble. Apparaissent sur la neige, entre le socle et le corps : un lustre, une table de

77

Figure 45. Facing pages form Jean Cocteau's book adaptation, *Le Sang d'un poète* (1949). © Éditions du Rocher; © Pierre Bergé, courtesy of Comité Cocteau.

Opening on a single photo of an ageless Mediterranean fishing boat, Hocquard's four-part "narrative" blends childhood autobiography with an account of a fishing trip in the Straits of Gibraltar. Hocquard's work has been central to a development in post-1980's poetics that Jean-Marie Gleize has labeled "literal poetry." Keeping poetic diction and metaphor to the background, this new poetry investigates the minute workings of everyday grammar, lexicon, communication, and cognition, explicitly under the tutelage of Wittgenstein. Hence the first short section meditates on the impersonal pronoun of French in "Il fait du vent" (it is windy), through memories of a windy grass field with a scarecrow. The section concludes: "Il est le gardien des mots et de la grammaire," a maxim ambiguously translatable as "he [the scarecrow/the poet]/it [the very impersonal word 'il'] is the guardian of words and grammar."[11] Since Hocquard associates this particular memory with the prohibition of writing aslant, like the grass under the wind, for which he says he quickly compensated by stooping his posture, the section suggests an identification of the child-poet with the scarecrow buffeted by the winds of language, the rules of grammar, and the corporeal stakes of writing.

This deflating of the lyrical conceit of a birth to and through language leads to the second section, which can be read as a poetic program *in nuce*. A ruined cemetery near Valencia, with votive images and names falling to pieces—"Here and there bits of writing and of images of persons lie on the ground among old papers and rubble"[12]—suggests a poetics of found images and words united by a fragmentary principle. The word "straits" (*détroit*), Hocquard indicates, is placed in a dictionary "between *detritus* (used up by friction) and *destroy* [*détruire*]."[13] Thus the straits connotes a kind of negative space between two words, each of which denotes destructive fragmentation. Hocquard remarked while travelling in Greece that on the side of ferryboats is written the word "*metaphoros*," literally, "transport." Crossing the straits would seem all at once to involve a language game, a statement of fragmentary poetics, and a perilous *experience*—a word etymologically linked to the dangers of navigating too close to coasts. On the way to a fishing boat, Hocquard picks up pottery shards and broken glass, as if the realms of poetics and history were suddenly permeating his everyday experiences too, in the most concrete manner.

The fishing trip is a bust. Strong currents cause the young hired pilot to lose sight of his landmarks. Meanwhile, Hocquard feels a sudden panic at "the slippery points of reference in the mobile landscape," and hallucinates an end "to space as well as time," figured as "an immense pane of glass in the middle of the strait . . . a vertical, transparent and empty surface."[14] Is this the ghost of literal poetry, perhaps, which is precisely all about language's surface? Certainly, it is a very surprisingly grandiloquent "vision" in Hocquard's lucid and realist text. We might wonder whether what emerges out of this kinesthetic landscape is not a kind of ghostly cinema apparatus, another iteration in the long series of empty screens we have encountered. Ostensibly centered on the fishing trip, this second section of the book is titled "Shadow Theater." After the moment of nauseating vision, that title becomes clear: Hocquard interjects remembrances of a shadow theater from his childhood, which was performed once a year on Christmas eve and included hundreds of characters and backgrounds. One specific background, he recalls, was never used: "a sheet painted blue . . . " on which "by transparence paler stripes would appear with, in the middle, the shape of an octopus."[15] Neither

Leonardo's sensorial memory of a vulture, nor Kane's yearning for his lyrical rosebud, the octopus signals a lost apparatus (Breton's and Kaplan's reimagined film, *The Trail of the Octopus*?), a protocinema that informed Hocquard's sense of language and words as immersed and immersive fragments.

In the third section, Hocquard recalls that he learned to read with "a mobile alphabet" of red letters,[16] which he associates with small fish washed ashore,[17] and thousands of dead pink jellyfish,[18] insisting that from this association he concluded early on that "a word, a book would always be first an assemblage of letters" rather than "the meaning it carries to conjure an oppressing threat."[19] Hocquard's heightened sense of space and surfaces under an always very fluid light, echoing his readings of Lucretius and the pre-Socratics, compensates for fragmentation with an immersive mise-en-scène, struggling to mend meaning from isolated words, to suture poems from isolated lines.[20] The closing section exemplifies this holistic immersion as temporary relief from the tensile force of the components of language. It is a minimal scene in which he beholds a gauzy piece of fabric drying on a line, and "which moved only slightly and to which the Western light gave a pink hue."[21] As darkness fell, the outline of the village visible *through* this scrim progressively vanished so that "this fabric up in the air would offer as its only glimpse its own transparence."[22] The word "tissu" (fabric) is from Latin *texere*, as is the word "texte," and certainly this scene stages something like the waning of "oppressive" meaning from the twilit literal text. Yet if it is an allegory for literal poetry—as all-surface—the allegoresis is remarkably filmic, or rather a-filmic since it culminates only in an opaque but empty screen.

A Journey in the Straits evinces only a "pseudocinematographic" apparatus because it must remain pointedly inoperable. Its opening photograph and semitransparent screens, its shadow theater recalled from out of an automorphic landscape, its montage of memories—all are components that refuse to cohere into a stably immersive cinepoetics. I would argue nonetheless that its poetic condition of possibility implicitly associates the cinematic imaginary with the automorphic immersion of the fishlike "mobile letters" on which Hocquard insists as a primal scene. Hence, while it may be right to say that literal poetry busies itself with the gauzy surface of language, this does not mean that it abandons the Merleau-Pontyan depths of the lived world—on the contrary. Literal poetry aims to conduct an unceasing investigation of how, by what expressible rules, can the lived world properly finds its way into language across the straits that separates experience from writing. To do so, it couches the Wittgensteinian testing of linguistic situations as quasi-cinematic setups for projecting experience into words, with quasi-spectatorial rules for visualizing experience out of writing. For such a poetics, cinema no longer functions as poetry's limit or utopia. Yet it remains the paradigmatic protocol for imagining how the inner articulations of language fit patterns of embodied cognition and the converse.

Hocquard himself appears to have become progressively more aware of this underpinning of the literal poetry project. The title of his 1991 *Théorie des tables* (Theory of Tables) refers to his practice of placing objects on surfaces in order to view them—the Greek *theorein* meaning "to view." Thereby, poetry's minimal injunction becomes a kind of display *dispositif*: "Arrange [*dispose*] on a table / the words that describe the image / Question the words."[23] This amounts to *projecting* words and examining their projection to gauge what kind of image they appear to evoke. Such images explicitly include, "photographs / of a peninsula in the shape of a question," so that photography is not a neutral medium in the *dispositif* entwining language and vision, but the very heart of the question.[24] "Photography is omnipresent in the poem," Hocquard recognizes in his afterword, adding that, "the small and very meaningful pieces of ordinariness can be seen to connect to each other in a different way than through normative grammar."[25] The pseudocinematographic apparatus thus bestows an imaginary syntactic aura on fragments of the everyday that no grammatical rule holds together: /literal poetry's imaginary syntax⇔pseudocinematographic montage/. In 1996, with photographer Juliette Valéry, Hocquard published *Allô, Freddy*, a cine-novel that is discrepant in the lettrist sense since the scenario and the shooting photos appear in distinct sections, both shaped in irregular boxes (Figure 46). It is rigorously a pseudofilm, complete with a diegetic microfilm—a film-within-a-film reminiscent of Hitchcock's McGuffin in *North by Northwest*. It comments on itself that, "In any case this scenario isn't worth squat," while suggesting that, "The scenario was comprised of a number of mobile pieces," perhaps the immersed/immersive words in *Une Journée*.[26] Again, Hocquard's poetry flirts with, yet eschews cinepoetics.

Such a pseudocinema-in-writing culminates in a collaboration with painter and filmmaker Alexandre Delay in their book *Le Voyage*

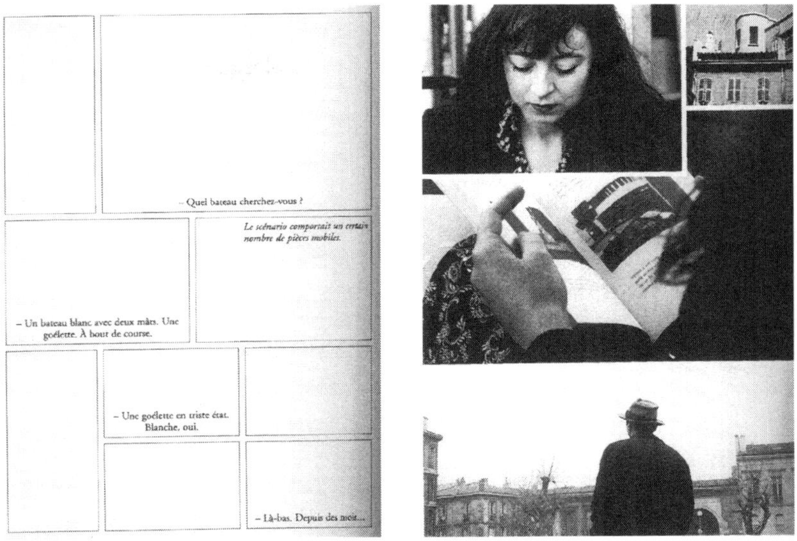

Figure 46. Two pages from Emmanuel Hocquard and Juliette Valéry's discrepant photo-novella, *Allô, Freddy?* (1996). © Éditions P.O.L.

à Reykjavik (The trip to Reykjavik) (1997). The book chronicles the making of a film that Hocquard quickly unravels: "I would like for our film to be neither an acted film [*film joué*] nor a nonacted film [*film non-joué*] but a thwarted film [*film déjoué*]."[27] Stills from this video shot in Iceland are reproduced, sometimes with words superimposed on maritime images—a striking return of Marcel L'Herbier's 1920 *L'Homme du large* that connected words floated on the screen with the sea. "We could also say that statements are floating propositions," Hocquard indicates at the beginning of his epistolary exchange with Delay as they plan the film.[28] The theoretical center of Hocquard's correspondence in *Le Voyage à Reykjavik* turns out to be his own account of *Une Journée*, which he invokes as the explicit model for the film. Ultimately, he calls "the circulation over a given space" and during "the time that you take to cross this space" in *Une Journée*, both a "mechanics," and "a *dispositif*."[29] Hocquard and Delay's thwarted film is expressly meant as a correlative to this mechanical *dispositif*, but in a way that leads to reexperiencing the book itself as a pseudocinematographic *dispositif*: "The advantage of video for us . . . is that it allows for moving images, images that progress the way one progresses through reading a book."[30] Hocquard's poetics is undoubtedly cinepoetic, but in a new way that expressly "thwarts" the prestige of cinema as a potential and teleological expansion of writing. At the same time, the cinematographic apparatus remains the overarching techno-cognitive model within which the encounter of language and image, as well as that of writing and experience, can be figured and imagined.

The photo-cinematic difference derived from our reading of Raymond Roussel's 1902 "La Vue," deployed poetry as the virtual film inherent to describing a photograph in the era of cinema. Roussel's cinepoem refracts the film apparatus' chronophotographic *synthesis*: /photography+poetry⇔virtual cinema/. Hocquard reverses the photo-cinematic difference by using writing to undo the cinematic character of our imaginary through an *analysis* of experience into photograph-like statements: /cinema⇔poetry+virtual chronophotographs/. Photographs no longer stand for frozen duration, as in the new context of mobile vision ca. 1900, but for momentary islands of slowed-down time and unlikely vantage points for beholding self-clarified propositions: "Photographs to shore up the whole," as Claude Royet-Journoud, the other main proponent of literal poetry, puts it in a recent book.[31]

Works similar to Hocquard's analytical and thwarted cinepoetics can be found among poets who enlarge the program of literal poetry, for instance, Suzanne Doppelt and Nathalie Quintane. Doppelt began as a photographer, collaborating with poets such as Alferi and Anne Portugal, before publishing books for which she authored both text and photos.[32] Her 2007 *Le Pré est vénéneux* (The meadow is poisonous) combines one-page prose sections, usually ending midsentence, with assemblages of two to nine photos, some of which are on a double-page with a caption (Figure 47). Rather than a set narrative, the book weaves a dynamic field of relations between the photos (of exteriors and close-ups of interiors), intertexts (Apollinaire's "Colchique," Rimbaud's poems, Ponge's 1971 *La Fabrique du pré* [The fabric of the meadow]), films (Resnais's 1953 *Statues also Die*; Cocteau's 1949 *Orpheus*), and enigmatic narrative fragments. Aptly, the initial guide to this "meadow" of texts and images is a familiar cinepoetic agent: the housefly. Its chronophotographic eye shows the field to be "composed of 1000 plots," and thanks to its fragmented optics, "The space is specified, intermittent, parts exist one at a time," while "fuzzy silhouettes and badly drawn facts moving about in the air,"

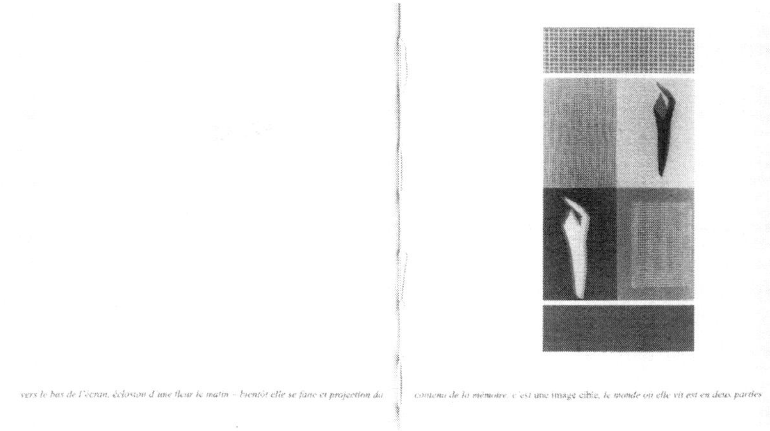

Figure 47. Facing pages from Suzanne Doppelt *Le Pré est vénéneux* (2007). © Éditions P.O.L.

form "a beautiful fantoscope."[33] In Doppelt's housefly gaze, "relief changes in front of one's eyes [*à vue d'oeil*], various matters circulate and combine with each other, flexible and convertible."[34] Unlike Epstein's camera-eye, Doppelt's fragmented poetics forms a chronophotographic fantoscope that never coheres nor seeks to remediate automorphosis.

One of Doppelt's photos recurs in several of her books: a roll of semitranslucent flypaper with flies stuck on it. While resembling a roll of film, it also figures the undoing of cinema, its profane expenditure. A similar photo by Jacques-André Boiffard had appeared in an issue of Georges Bataille's journal *Documents* in 1930, similarly undoing the photographic aura (Figure 48). *Le Pré* multiplies partial resemblances to cinema the better to distend any direct analogy with its text. Underneath the first photo the caption reads, "toward the bottom of the screen, the blooming of a flower"[35]—a reference to Dulac's accelerated films. Yet we are kept on a brink where, "scenes are outlined, images unfold, the meadow is kinetic,"[36] but purposefully *not* cinematographic. The book ends on two grids of twelve photos each, that is, twenty-four photos or one second of an impossible cinema since the photos are not sequential. "He hates movement that shifts the lines," Doppelt writes in another caption,[37] a modified quote of a verse from Baudelaire's sonnet "Beauty." Rather than Baudelaire's poem, however, this citation likely points to Marcel

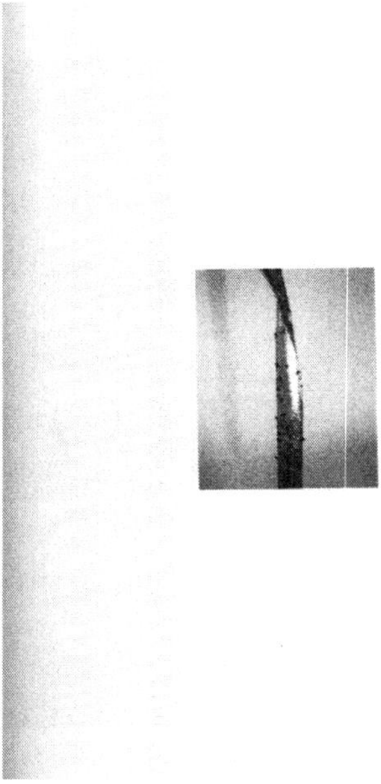

Figure 48. The fly-paper from Anne Portugal and Suzanne Doppelt, *Dans la reproduction en 2 parties égales des plantes et des animaux* (1999); (facing page) Suzanne Doppelt, *Le Pré est vénéneux* (2007); Suzanne Doppelt, *Totem* (2002). © Éditions P.O.L.

Broodthaers's 1973 book titled after the same verse: *Je hais le mouvement qui déplace les lignes.*[38] Broodthaers's anticinema cinema—he shot at least three films inspired by Baudelaire—aimed at altering and expanding the apparatus by using print, drawings and still shots to cultivate the contradiction between the movement and the static aspect of the image. A major figure in the turn of postmodern art toward expanded cinema, Broodthaers started as a cinepoet deeply influenced by Mallarmé's *A Throw of the Dice*, about which he made both a film and a book that translates words into visual black strips. In 1948, he published his first cinepoetic piece in *Le Surréalisme révolutionnaire*, "Project For a Film," which begins: "A fly has entered into / the still landscape."[39] Doppelt's housefly gaze suspends or delays the automorphic imaginary within cinepoetry in a manner comparable to Broodthaers with cinema itself.

In 1999, Nathalie Quintane published *Mortinsteinck*, subtitled *Le Livre du film* (The book of the film).[40] Like Hocquard and Delay's *Un Voyage à Reykjavik*, it is not a "novelization" of a film that Alexandre Gérard, Stéphane Bérard, and herself actually shot, but an attempt to find a new mode of writing at once ancillary and complementary to the film. Of the disparate texts of the book, she writes

elle mange les mêmes choses que nous mais l'huile la tue, il ne faut rien sous-estimer, même les mouches ont une rate. Elle aime le sang et beaucoup le lait, le poème d'un jésuite raconte sa noyade dans une jatte : blancheur et douceur du liquide, noirceur du corps et amertume de la mort. Elle va si souvent au lait qu'elle y demeure et après le repas, elle nettoie ses pattes selon 7 techniques

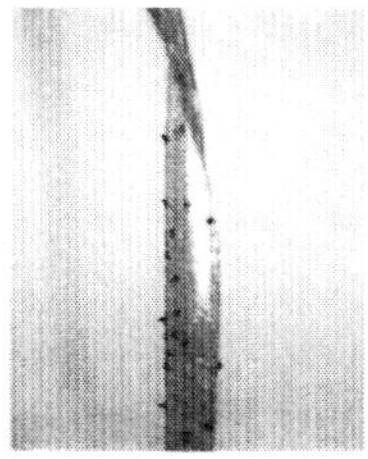

Comme l'homme l'animal est soumis à des rythmes et phases. La nuit la mouche à miel se pend à une tige par sa mandibule. Sa tête et ses antennes chutent sa fréquence respiratoire ralentit Mais cette torpeur se dissout avant l'aube à la même heure chaque jour sa pendule interne la réveille. Il en va de même pour la mouche drosophile dotée elle aussi du gène du temps la musca bovina ou pour la mouche bourreau. De son côté l'antilope s'éveille immédiatement après s'être endormie. Quant à celle qui enregistre les mouvements de l'ennemi on pourrait croire qu'il s'agit d'un avion mais c'est un modèle réduit de bateau petit navire mouche qui doit toujours rester éveillé. Les mouches sont puissantes au point de gagner des batailles d'empêcher notre âme d'agir et de manger notre corps. Et quand on veut célébrer un héros on le compare non pas à un lion mais à une mouche pour son ardeur son caractère intrépide la constance de ses assauts. Sa queue n'est pas une arme comme celle de la guêpe ou de l'abeille. Elle utilise sa bouche et sa trompe pour se nourrir attraper et attaquer. La dent qui sort du caillou réduit à la pointe pique sans douleur et boit le sang. Dans sa cellule en passe de devenir vampire Renfield les compte une à une tandis que le comte D met un pied hors de son embarcation. Elle possède d'autres caractéristiques : elle ne vole pas en silence mais fait un certain bruit différent de celui du moustique du taon ou de l'abeille et beaucoup plus mélodieux que celui de la guêpe. La nuit la tranquillise. Elle ne bourdonne pas se ramasse et ne bouge plus jusqu'à l'arrivée de la lumière.

that they are "texts without photo," because they concern "a sub-film [*sous-film*], a film underneath all others," and "because in order to be texts, they have had to rid themselves in one way or another of filmed images."[41] While *Mortinsteinck* alludes to twenty-two films (from Howard Hawks's 1944 *To Have and Have Not*, to the Coen brothers' 1998 *The Big Lebowski* and Duras's 1975 *India Song*) and contains half-a-dozen production stills, it pointedly falls short of remediating the photo-cinematic difference as a new poetics. And while structured around a scenario in forty numbered sequences, as if to gesture toward a possible cinepoetics as a relic of modernism, it disseminates these sequences throughout the book, appending to them numerous digressions, the better to break any immersive-like effect.

Quintane's "sub-film," Hocquard's "thwarted film," and Doppelt's "fantoscope," strain the overarching analogy of cinepoetry—/cinema⇔poetry/—by defamiliarizing all at once cinema, poetry, and their historical linkage. In so doing, they propose a new mode of encounter and interrelation between the two: the *dispositif*.

CINEPOETICS OF THE *DISPOSITIF*

Chapter 2 examined the paradoxical cinepoetics of Foucault's reading of Roussel's "La Vue" and suggested its place within the genealogy of the Foucauldian *dispositif*. The genealogical notion of the *dispositif* is twofold. On the one hand it refers to the cinematic apparatus (*le dispositif de base* or *l'appareil de base*) formulated in the orbit of *Tel Quel* by Marcelin Pleynet, Jean-Louis Baudry, and Gérard Leblanc in 1969–72, giving rise to the theory of the apparatus in film studies. On the other hand it refers to the apparatus that Foucault defined in the mid-1970s as a field of practices shaped by sociopolitical and discursive forces.[42] The thought of Pleynet, Baudry, and Foucault devolves in important ways from their readings of the mid-1960s, especially liminal poetic-novelistic works whose prismatic language and blank writing reverberates with the cinematic imaginary, such as Roche's *Compact*. Cinepoetry's hybrid construct of writing and virtual film apparatus, I have argued, precedes and informs both notions of the *dispositif*. Moreover, the ideological effects of the *dispositif de base* was defined with remarkable prescience as early as 1946 by Jean Epstein, in the last chapter of *L'Intelligence d'une machine* (A machine's intelligence) titled "Retour à une poésie pythagoricienne et platonique" (Return to Pythagorean and Platonic Poetry):

> The cinematograph is also an experimental *dispositif* that constructs, that is to say, that thinks, an image of the universe. . . . But it is only an idea, and an artificial idea, whose existence cannot be affirmed as other than ideological and artificial, a trick [*truquage*] in a way. Still, this trick is very close to the process whereby the human mind generally fabricates an ideal reality for itself.[43]

The main difference with apparatus theory from the 1970s is that the latter places machine and mind in parallel via the Freudian Unconscious rather than poetry and corporeality for Epstein.

Contemporary poetic theory has developed a new approach to the *dispositif* as the broad ecology of poetry in the age of conceptual art and digital media. However, neither cinepoetry nor the literary antecedents of the *dispositif* have yet figured in significant ways on this theoretical horizon. Christophe Hanna has provided the first extensive poetic theory of the *dispositif*, as presenting four features. It is (1) a set of heterogeneous semiotic objects, (2) each of which functions within its own semiotic modality, (3) while also refracting their specific modalities on each other, (4) all three features being activated by its readers/receivers.[44] Francis Ponge provides an illustration for Hanna, in how Ponge's writings combine phenomenological descriptions of objects and events with etymological accounts of words as well as moments in the history of rhetoric, in order to stage both a kind of phenomenology of language and a rhetoric of the real. Contextual displacement, code shifting, and the redeployment of textuality via linguistic pragmatics (real-world situations) are all key operational principles. Olivier Quintyn has usefully reinscribed the poetry *dispositif* within a continuum of practices that go from collage, to montage, reappropriation, and installation. Informed by Hanna's work, he defines the *dispositif* as "a construction using distinct ontological entities, in which this very distinction becomes a principle for the functioning and articulation of difference so as to produce a real and/or symbolic effect."[45] Certainly, this would fit the cinema apparatus as well as the corpus of cinepoetic practices we have analyzed throughout this study. Yet neither Hanna nor Quintyn consider that cinema and its imaginary effects on writing practices represent special paradigms within the emergence of the *dispositif*. We might put it even more forcefully: the theory of the *dispositif* pushes cinema and cinepoetry aside so conspicuously that we must ask whether they do not constitute its unthought. Hence the "pseudocinematograph" Quintyn intuitively posits as Roche's central *dispositif*, ends up being reduced to a "discursive . . . body" of photo and texts substituting for the "phenomenological body" of the friends documented in Roche's project.[46] This simplified opposition of discourse and phenomenology recycles a base antirealism equating the pseudo-cinematograph with a mere rejection of film's presence effect.

In practice, poetic *dispositifs* arise very often in conjunction with cinema and cinepoetic features. Here is one example. Within *Un Voyage à Reykjavik*, Hocquard and Delay insert a separate project-within-a-project titled "Le Canale: Synopsis." It recounts their creating of an optical illusion in the countryside, by shaping a trapezoid of dirt on the ground in such a way that, from a specific viewpoint, it will appear as a square in a photograph. In Italian, *le canale* means "the channel." Reproducing photos of the progressive making of the earthwork amid Wittgensteinian reflections on the ways in which what can be seen may or may not be affirmed in language and communicated, "Le Canale" interrogates the role of "anamorphosis" in the intermedium "image-language."[47] As "Le Canale" becomes a book, referring to "the channel" becomes more vexed since it may indifferently point to the conceptual project, the earthwork implementation or the book itself. Toward the end of the text, one of the authors points out to the other how early schoolbooks remain lifelong "grammar books—*dispositifs*. Everything that you will read, write, and think subsequently, you will do so by echoing this *dispositif*."[48] It is likely Hocquard who writes this about the recurring and operational memory of his grammar book with red mobile letters. A few lines later, one of them adds, "You say that this book is an echo of our film." It appears not only that in *Un Voyage à Reykjavik* cinema is the operational context for the multiple exchanges between mediums, but that cinepoetry—as the becoming-book of the film and the becoming-mobile of words—must be held (near) synonymous with *dispositif*.

Another example of cinepoetic unthought of the *dispositif* is poet Bernard Noël's 1988 *Journal du regard* (Journal of the gaze), a collection of poetic notes on vision dating from 1970 to 1982.[49] It provides an evolving account of a poet investigating zones of contact between language and visual arts, and technologies. The talkies were ruinous, Noël writes toward the beginning, because "Movies speak as if seeing was not enough. As if seeing was not already articulating."[50] This statement recognizes cinema only insofar as it integrates natural language, but it bemoans such mixed modalities. The work of poetry will then consist in cleansing the gaze from cinema's intermixture.

Noël expresses suspicions also toward photography[51] and television,[52] yet he assimilates these technologies directly to the human: we are a "dark chamber,"[53] our gaze is a "snapping in the box" (*mise en boîte*),[54] "the body contains in itself an archaic consciousness that is the lens of the dark chamber," and so on.[55]

This culminates in a curious text of 1978, "Une fois les dieux" (Once the gods), which describes in two parts a film project. First come the "ideas," then the "images," of what Noël presents as "The Film of a Gaze,"[56] in which no word is uttered, although there is a faint soundtrack. The film is a single take in subjective camera of a prisoner looking around his cell, scanning at one point a single graffito: "I once lived like the gods."[57] Insisting that, "the image is a viewpoint, and as soon as we behold it, we adopt this viewpoint," Noël aims to show that "confinement is the matter of the film (every gaze is a box), but, through the reduplication that denounces it, it is also its subject. / And its meaning."[58] The graffito echoes Hölderlin's verse on the disappearance of the gods, but connected here to the vanishing of a certain freedom of the gaze from the hold of the image similar to Merleau-Ponty's "machine of language" model of poetry. Further on in *Le Journal du regard*, Noël envisions in a 1980 note, "a conjunction of camera and computer allowing us to write visually with all the images of the world."[59] Hence it is via a singular updating of Saint-Pol-Roux's live cinema that he ultimately mitigates his notion of the image as confining the gaze. Symptomatically, Noël uses the word "*dispositif*" in a 1982 note about an installation of hundreds of small mirrors with slides projected on them, another analytical version of the photo-cinematic difference.[60] Cinema and cinepoetry are among the conditions of possibility of Noël's evolving investigation of vision, yet his articulation of the *dispositif* keeps them ultimately out of the frame of the gaze and out of the texture of the text. "The imaginary is an exit out of representation," he writes in concluding the "ideas" section of his film, "but it is also a detour to find it—elsewhere."[61] Imaginary cinema-in-writing precisely allows for the apparatus of representation to be escaped, displaced, and tested all at once—the very functions that Hanna ascribes to the *dispositif*.[62]

In a short preface to a 1992 collection of essays, Jean-Marie Gleize has defined literal poetry as a new mode of entry into the real through a kind of apophatic negation: rather than affirming or celebrating or describing the real, literal poetry entangles the very functioning of its language with it. It does not produce mimetic accounts of the real, it lets the real enter every aspect of poetics, every process of creation of the poem. The negation, for Gleize, bears specifically on the image, "not only this set of figures we call metaphors, or comparison, but the question of the image in general, of visual or imaginary representation—indeed the very possibility of representation."[63] This suspicion vis-à-vis the image and the imaginary comes in reaction to the romantic equation of poetry with the crafting of images and the manipulation of tropes which was reinforced by the mainstreaming of surrealist poetics. Gleize's anti-imagistic bias nonetheless explains why the ubiquitous presence of cinema in literal poetry—beginning with Danielle Collobert, one of its forerunners in the early 1970s, all the way to Gleize himself in the late 2000s—has taken so long to be theorized as such.[64]

The intersection of literal poetry with the newer practices of the *dispositif* has pushed any explicit cinepoetry further to the periphery. Cinepoetry is assimilated and rejected under the term "aesthetics" connoting formalist versions of modernism and stereotypes of symbolism as art for art's sake. In assessing the pioneering role of Denis Roche in the postimagistic mutations of poetry, Gleize speaks of "the passage from a conception of art dominated by formal-aesthetic models to an approach turned toward act, action, the contextualization of procedures and *dispositifs*."[65] Gleize goes on to define the *dispositif* in poetry in the wake of both Ponge and Roche as the preempting of poetic images in favor of clashing modes of prose (whether journalistic, essayistic, or autofictive). Photographs are acceptable complements to such "postpoetic" prose so long as they dispel their mimetic function to work in sets that destructure each image, with their compositions off balance or geometrical, the photo out of focus or unsteady.[66] This is tantamount to what we have called the photo-cinematic difference in poetry, and Gleize's inclusion of photographs with "postpoetry" unwittingly partakes of the broad cinepoetic episteme sketched in this study.[67]

In 1992, the same year he published his manifesto of literal poetry against images, Gleize published *Film à venir* (Film to come), a thin book in sparse verse sections without photographs that leans toward cinema as the kind of metaform or *dispositif*-matrix I have alluded to in the Introduction, regarding Quintane's *Grand ensemble*. In 2007, he published a second book under the same title that retains almost nothing of the first, and includes several photographs, a flyer, a map, and a page printed white on black. In 2001, he published a book titled *Television*.[68] It is around his 1999 book *Les chiens noirs de la prose* (The black dogs of prose) that both photography and the photo-cinematic difference initially enter Gleize's own rehauling of poetry. Under the title, "Straight Poetry Is Not Pure Poetry," he writes about "photography at the heart of all ruptures." Following sections point to a general deceleration of representation involving "slow-motion . . . film stocks, screens," and leading to the realization that: "Slow-motion is the true speed of the story [and/or] history [*de l'histoire*]." Among the shifting locales in the poem-narration one "looks like a movie theater."[69] While eschewing any analogy of the book with a film, *Les Chiens noirs* deploys in its writing a range of cinepoetic devices such as slow-motion, elliptical montage, and crosscutting. A spectral film that is either porn or experimental cinema or both, threatens to ingest its viewer at irregular intervals.[70] A letter makes quick connections between Lee Lew-Lee's *All Power to the People*, a 1995 documentary on Black Power, and early ethnic fiction films such as V. S. Van Dyke's 1928 *White Shadows on the South Seas* and 1931 *Tarzan the Ape-Man*, as well as F. W. Murnau's 1931 *Tabu*. On the back cover of the book Gleize gives a synopsis of the story: a man in a hotel room with the TV on is tormented by what "he imagines" (a singular return of the imaginative function in Gleize!) and by a "sentence and a few others whose meaning he does not understand." "What he wants," Gleize writes, "is to go out." This situation echoes both Noël's imaginary film of a prisoner's confining gaze and Maurice Roche's similarly confined voices in *Compact*—a work to which Gleize alludes in a key essay.[71] Noël writes of his imaginary film that "the film dramatizes the space of the gaze in order to make it perceptible. Space of the gaze, mental space, I think they are analogous and I refer the one back to the other. Their texture is invisible the way air is invisible to sight."[72] If for Gleize cinema represents a less and less implicit matrix for the poetics of the *dispositif* it is because it sustains analogical relations to the discontinuities and multimediality of a postpoetry practice. These analogies both continue and exceed the basic homology /cinema apparatus⇔cognitive functions/ that we have examined among photogénie thinkers like Epstein, and poets in their wake such as Artaud and Michaux.

As part of this new direction, in his later book, *Néon* (2004), Gleize describes a scene of automorphic writing that is squarely cinepoetic. A man in a room hallucinates lines of writing "to the left of the screen"[73]—and we recall that the left functioned as a kind of spectral cinepoetic margin for Cocteau:

> . . . he can read them one by one, as they are appearing. They come to the fore, they write themselves in front on the wall, right next to the screen where the waves turn with the half-rotten rag of algae, one by one, and erase themselves, one by one, another, another one . . . he sees these letters, one by one, they form words, black and green words . . . the burning green-silent rag of words drawn one by one up to the surface of the eyes, to the deep of the eyes, to the back of the head, in a clamor of great tide.

From Mallarmé's "words extinguishing themselves," to the burning "Mane Thecel Phares," printing themselves on screen for Proust and Saint-Pol-Roux, and from L'Herbier's shaped intertitles floated on the image frame in a marine-themed film, to Hocquard's primal watery words, cinepoets have reimagined the automorphic plasticity of writing through the fiery and watery fluidity and immersion of filmic images.

Unlike *Néon*, whose cinepoetic subdiscourse runs in the background, Gleize's *Le Film à venir, conversions* (The film to come, conversions) (2007) presents itself as a quasi film already on its first page, with the footage of a hospital room's lightbulb that slowly empties itself of light and melts: "At the end it drips and falls to the bottom of the screen."[74] The first page repeats several versions of this statement, blurring the potential film as it were: "It is within the interruptions of the projection of a film, in these cut-out zones in which ink spits appear, that the method of rotting the object imposes itself."[75] The very interruption of a flow of images is embedded in the flickering apparatus of cinema, so Gleize's *dispositif* for the apophatic production of writing by means of intervals within an imaginary film is inherently cinepoetic. To sustain this apophatic cinepoem, Gleize effects a number of "conversions" between modes of writing and types of films in order to multiply such intervals throughout the book. Hence he refers to a landscape "shot very close to the water's surface" at the conclusion of the story of Minik Wallace, an Inuit brought to New York in 1906 by Peary and soon abandoned there. Are we "seeing" what Minik Wallace saw when hunting in a kayak after his return to Greenland? Perhaps, since the film mentions "ferns," which grow in Southern Greenland. But then what about the hospital room and its melting lightbulb? Is it where Minik Wallace died of the flu in 1918, after his voluntary return to New York? Is this whole story to be read as an oblique allegory within Gleize's autobiographical project—one of the subdiscourses already present in *Néon*? That we do not know what film exactly we are supposed to imagine, or for what purpose and within what context, but can only glean clues from reading the text more closely, converting its components from one modality to another as we go, is precisely what makes us readers both the agent and patient, the viewer and director, of Gleize's apophatic cinepoetic *dispositif*. With *Le Film à venir, conversions*, cinepoetry shows itself to be a resilient and mutable matrix once again redeployed through the poetics of literality and the *dispositif*, reinjecting a new pragmatism of the image and the imagination, in spite of claims by Hocquard, Hanna and Gleize that these had to be extricated from contemporary poetry.

CINEPOETRY: THE DARK MATTER OF CONTEMPORARY POETICS

> The immobility of the person writing puts the world in motion.
>
> . . .
>
> The only "truth," movement. Movement, not rhythm.
>
> —CLAUDE ROYET-JOURNOUD[76]

Without reducing the complex poetics of the literal and the *dispositif* to it, we must recognize that the unthought of cinema and cinepoetry represents one of the major historical conditions of possibility for these new poetics. Gleize's title, *Le Film à venir, conversions*, in alluding to Maurice Blanchot's *The Book to Come*—which, with the latter's *The Space of Literature*, opened a new horizon in post-war theories of writing—may explicitly substitute cinema to the book as the limit-model of the procedures generating these new writing practices.[77] In the same way that the notion of the "book" for Blanchot derives from Mallarmé's commitment to a virtual oeuvre rather than actual published works (a virtual oeuvre we have shown to veer toward the cinepoetic in the last phase of Mallarmé's life), the notion of "cinema" for Gleize is rather more that of a force field inflected by the actual apparatus acting as its dark matter but never to be directly exploited to produce poetry.

However, among poets who are coming after Gleize, it would seem that this distinction between a potential and an actual cinepoetics is growing thinner. Let us briefly sample a few representatives in this very recent production.

Véronique Pittolo's 1992 *Montage* opens with a single line on its first page: "I have always wanted to be in cinema [*faire du cinéma*]."[78]

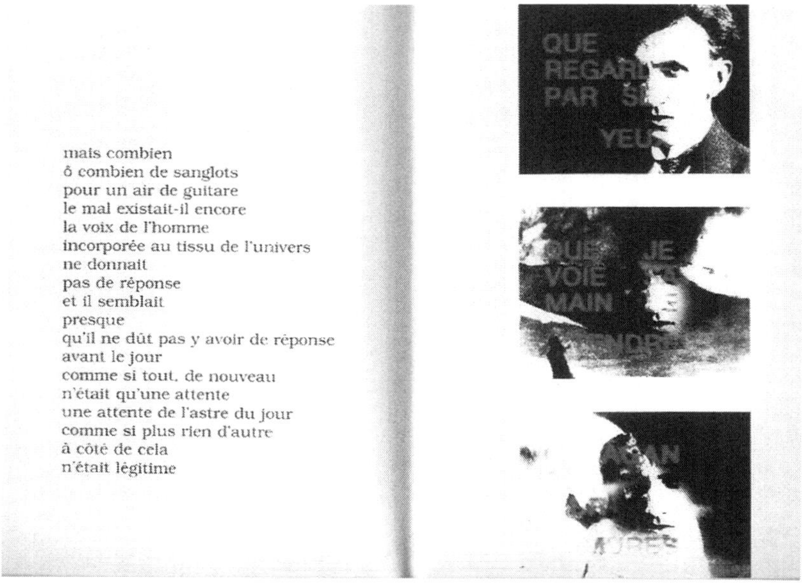

mais combien
ô combien de sanglots
pour un air de guitare
le mal existait-il encore
la voix de l'homme
incorporée au tissu de l'univers
ne donnait
pas de réponse
et il semblait
presque
qu'il ne dût pas y avoir de réponse
avant le jour
comme si tout, de nouveau
n'était qu'une attente
une attente de l'astre du jour
comme si plus rien d'autre
à côté de cela
n'était légitime

Figure 49. Facing pages (III: 132–33) of Jean-Luc Godard, *Histoire(s) de cinéma* (1998). © Éditions Gallimard.

The expression "faire du cinéma" is loose, meaning any profession related with the film industry—not necessarily directing. The book develops its narrator's profession of faith, as "cinema" gradually becomes a kind of autofiction process rather than cinema per se. The back cover tells us in summary: "he beholds his life on a film editing table" while also giving radio interviews to an interlocutor who then "intervenes in 'voice-over.'" The film editing table, which might be part of the polysemous use of "table" in Hocquard's *La Théorie des tables*, functions for Pittolo as a correlative to assembling words and texts into a book: /film editing table⇔text assembly/. In a following work, *Gary Cooper ne lisait pas de livres* (Gary Cooper did not read books), a title that makes plain the substitution of the "book" by "cinema," Pittolo moves even further toward an explicit cinepoetic *dispositif.* Entitling several poem sections in the book, "Shots of Protagonists," "Shots of Movies," and "Close-Up Shots," she reprises a central cinepoetic homology: /shot⇔poem/.[79]

One catalyst for this resurgence is very likely the books published by Jean-Luc Godard, first with the experimental poetry press P.O.L in 1996, then with the erstwhile publishing house for French literature, Gallimard in 1998 with *Histoire(s) de cinéma*.[80] While the novelization of films had, by the late 1990s, the antiquated feel of the New Wave-nouveau roman era—with self-novelizations by Robbet-Grillet and Marguerite Duras—Godard's books were decidedly freer in form and, indeed, more like antinovels, as attested by their revival of the cine-verse form (Figure 49). These well-advertised books may go a long way toward explaining a new diversification of cinepoetic works since the years 2000. Their cinepoetics is deployed more or less overtly, obliquely, or negatively.

For instance, Emmanuel Laugier's *Son corps flottant* (His floating body) (2000) makes no explicit reference to cinema, yet its long verse sequences tightly focused on the inner and outer experiences of a body in motion, deploy an automorphic sensorium that evinces the cinema apparatus as though from the back door. Taken among many other lines concerned with dilations of the body envelope, Laugier writes, "Everything leaks around my tissues / my accessories float and the color of my arms / pass into light": this could very well figure verbatim in Chenal's 1925 scenario of a walking man whose shadow and color fall behind, then catch up.[81] The tele-cinepotics of Alferi in *Kub or* made way in 2003 to digital video experiments that confirm his long-standing interest for cross-mediality: *Cinépoèmes & films parlants* (Cinepoems & talkies). Concurrently, he disseminated his cinepotics to other genres: the novel with *Le Cinéma des familles* (Family cinema) (1999), and poetic essays on B-movies, horror and fantastic films, *Des Enfants et des monstres* (Children and monsters) (2004), which includes an ode in verse to Lon Cheney.[82] His more recent digital video collaboration, *Ça commence à Séoul* (It begins in Seoul), is closer to expanded cinema art.[83] In 2007, Liliane Giraudon paid homage to artists, writers, and philosophers she admires in a collection of prose pieces, *Mes Bien-Aimé(e)s* (My beloved), illustrated with drawings and describing itself on the back cover as "Edited in successive scenes of an elementary cinemathon (closer to the magic lantern)." Neither filmmakers nor actors figure in the book, so cinema remains a purely ancillary metaframe invoked to assist readers in tackling its original form.[84] Halfway between oblique and overt cinepoetics, we find for instance David Lespiau's 2008 *Ouija Board*. It is made of short verse sections with interlinear translations in English and German printed in colored inks—like Cendrars's "Prose of the Transsiberian," and Roche's *Compact* (Plate 6).[85] With only two

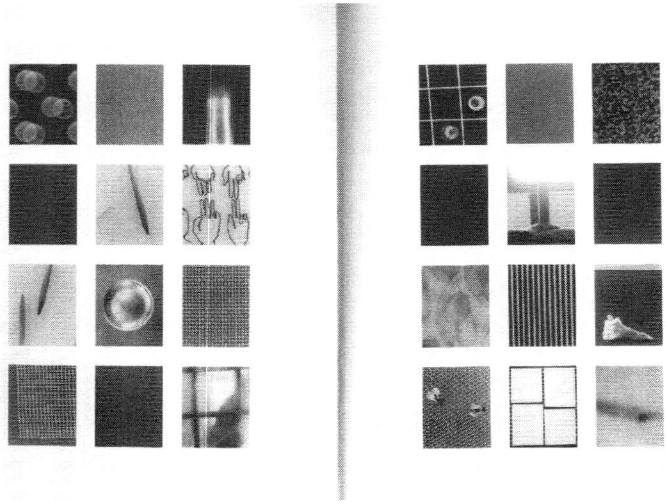

Figure 50. Twenty-four images, or one second of imaginary cinema. (Top) Double page from Suzanne Doppelt *Le Pré est vénéneux* (2007). © Éditions P.O.L. (Bottom) Cover of David Lespiau, *Ouija Board* (2008). © Éditions Héros-limite.

of eight sections devoted to cinema and film stars, it might be difficult to argue at first blush that cinepoetry is central to its multilingual *dispositif.* Yet a Ouija board, if nothing else, transforms writing into a kinetic activity in which letters have a relative autonomy. The book's cover by poet Tom Raworth shows twenty-four photographs—exactly one second of cinema. Suzanne Doppelt also uses twenty-four photos as an allusion to cinema at the close of *Le pré est vénéneux* (Figure 50).

By contrast, Jérôme Game, who is both an academic and a poet, has published overtly cinepoetic books such as *Corpse&Cinéma* in 2002, followed by a poetic mash-up of movies in 2007, *Flip-book*, while recently editing a collection on the new relations between text and image which includes an article by Nathalie Wourm on French video poetry (Figure 51).[86] His 2004 poem-book, *écrire à même les choses* (writing right against things), constructs a verse narration with "modulated lacunae" around a porn film that is ambiguously being either shot or screened, in order to explore the dynamics of perception. Michaux's cinepoetics is a clear inspiration since *Paix dans les brisements* (Peace in shattering) is twice alluded to.[87] Game's phenomenological attention—Husserl's injunction "to the things themselves," might be part of the project—comes with a curious crumbling of certain words that lose some of their letters (as in Duprey's poetry) as if to translate visual syncopes or sudden shifts in images. In Rémi Froger's 2008 free-verse sequence *Des Prises de vues* (Some photos/ film shots), a machine that is alternatively camera, projector, and VCR appears to take over when the narrator confesses, "I have lost my dictionary."[88] From this point on, although "the scenario seems acceptable."[89] words and letters become automorphic, "the distorsion of letters"[90] leading to "continuously unreeled letters . . . / with capitals for a better recording,"[91] until film and poetry merge. "He's shooting a film? / . . . / . . . where is the film?"[92] Froger seemingly asks himself, answering tangentially: "Black-and-white film in which he hid the secret of paradise / . . . / . . . I had signaled it, black on white."[93] This last expression appears to refer directly to Mallarmé's comment that writing, unlike the figures of constellations, takes place "black on white."[94] Froger also paraphrases the preface of "A Throw of the Dice," in a near definition of his own cinepoetics: "what I had to tell you the black spots on paper accelerate / accelerated articulations of things that rise and fall."[95] Froger's project appears to stumble on the very archaeology of early cinepoetry.

Figure 51. Cover of Jérôme Game, *Flip-book* (2007), written only on the right pages, with a list of the films shaping the text. © Éditions de l'Attente.

At the more overt end of the spectrum, a formalistic version of cinepoetry can be found in Jan Baetens, a theoretician of the text/image relation and also a poet who, in 2005, published a verse adaptation of a Jean-Luc Godard film of 1962: *Vivre sa vie, une novellisation en vers du film de Jean-Luc Godard* (To live her life, a verse novelization of a film by Jean-Luc Godard). Although the film's subtitle is *A Film in Twelve Scenes*, it counts fifteen sections, each sampling either a free or set poetic form, as if to disrupt classic models of uniform medium transposition.[96] Another willfully cinepoetic enterprise is by Joseph Mouton in 2007: *Delenda West*. His previous work, he tells us, sought to renew poetic writing through "rotational syntax," but *Delenda West* was written almost with the opposite realization that "life often falls very sloooooooooooowwwwwwwly into cinema."[97] A post-9/11 hybrid of poetic theory, porn, and auteur film, *Delenda*

West presents itself formally as a "general scenario," which Mouton defines as "the whole set of narrations and ways of telling that dominate today (and which I identify with HOLLYWWOD) literature, music, theater, and all the other arts fed by the Hollywood system."[98] One of its "commandments . . . you shall honor Good and Evil,"[99] reprises the exact terms of Epstein's 1921 observation that strict Manichean morals rules subliterature. In an afterword to the book, philosopher Patrice Ménaglier indicates that "hence poetry must create out of the poetic engine its exclusive object to fight on equal footing with the aging of language: [poetry] can avail itself of properly industrial means (Hollywood); the poet must subsequently become an industrialist."[100] In 1955, Epstein titled one of the chapters of his book *Esprit de cinéma* (Cinema's spirit), "Cine-Analysis or Poetry in Industrial Quantities," and in it he writes, "Plato, who exiled poets from his totalitarian city, would have a fortiori forbidden cinema as a high-yield poetry machine."[101] Only further study will reveal whether Mouton and other poets in the wake of the *dispositif* who are openly appealing to the cinema apparatus engage in a chance reinvention or willful recuperation of cinepoetry.

Dominique Fourcade's conundrum can serve as our last example. Committed, like Hocquard and Gleize, to the search for and valorization of the real on the condition of finding the right way to it through language alone, Fourcade published *Citizen Do* in 2008. He claims that "*Citizen Do* is not a book," because a true book has an inner dynamics that pulls the author along via, "A plot an opening [*sic*], a coherent action but whose direction is unforeseeable, whose only scenario is its inner unfolding [*déroulement*], from word to word a televisual word by word."[102] Sputtering along through "take 1" and "take 2,"[103] and alluding to the painter Poussin and the dancer Merce Cunningham as cryptically cinematic artists, "sensitive to the film of ultrathinness / on the supple surface of voice,"[104] the book fails as a book, by its own reckoning, *because* it fails as an auto-fictive film-text, overshadowed as it is by the cinematic perfection of Orson Welles's *Citizen Kane*. His 1988 book titled *Xbo* already opened with a narrator trying and failing to record moving images: "Ordinary day / I'm filming / The film stock is not impressed."[105]

Let us end, then, near where we began. Guillaume Apollinaire published a single verse poem about cinema under the ambiguous title: "Avant le cinéma," which can be read as "before cinema [existed]," or "before [going to] the movies." In simple and direct utterances the poem affirms that cinema has now become the major art, and it discusses its three names: "cinéma" for regular folks, "le ciné" for professionals of the industry, and "le cinématographe" for "old provincial professors" (like Mallarmé . . .). It was published twice, first in the literary journal *Nord-Sud* in April 1917, then in Delluc's journal *Le Film* in October 1918.[106] In the former the poem has no punctuation and the font is in double-spaced italics, so the fourteen verses float as if the page were a new medium, an imaginary screen. In the latter, the single-spaced poem in regular font is punctuated and framed by a floral motif, as was common on intertitle cards, and its aspect ratio is exactly that of a contemporary screen. Through its visual appearance alone, the former suggests the cinema apparatus as imaginary, while the second presents itself as one of its components, the intertitle. Such a duality, neatly accentuated by the twin publication in a literary and a film journal, bookends the field of experiments that is cinepoetry.

In a final oddity, the poem in *Nord-Sud* is listed in the table of content as "Après le cinéma," as if the typist was convinced that such a poem could only be written both once cinema existed, and after one went to the movies. This chance discrepancy can serve as a final state of affairs in that poetry today appears to be positioned all at once "before" another cinepoetry to come and "after" a cinepoetry that has not yet been fully disclosed.

NOTES

INTRODUCTION

1. Epstein, "Les Grands docteurs," *Écrits sur le cinéma*, 1:171 (henceforth *Écrits*, 1).

2. Blanchot, *L'Amitié*, 132. Blanchot refers to Duras's *Détruire dit-elle*; this citation is reproduced in Ropars-Wuillemier, *Écraniques*, 57.

3. Stam, *Companion to Literature and Film*.

4. See Gaudreault, "Variation sur une problématique."

5. I use "virtual" throughout this study in the sense of nonactualized, implied, and open experience in language, as in Mallarmé's uses of "virtuel" to describe his polysemic poetics, thus predating "virtual reality." See Lévy, *Becoming Virtual*. I am also inspired by the notion of "virtual agency" developed by Daniel Wegner's psychological critique of conscious will, summarized thus: "When people project action to imaginary agents, they create virtual agents, apparent sources of their own action. This process underlies spirit possession and dissociative identity disorder as well as the formation of the agent self." Wegner, *Illusion of Conscious Will*, chap. 7, "Virtual Agency," 221–70. Finally, I take the notion of image space in virtual reality, which Olivier Grau defines as "a multisensory interactive space of experience with a time frame," as congruent with the cinepoetic imaginary. Grau, *Virtual Art*, 7.

6. For instance, Jacob, *Cinématoma*; Némirovsky, *Films parlés*; Cendrars, *Films sans images*.

7. For instance, Guillaume Apollinaire's poem "Avant le cinéma," appears in *Nord-Sud* 2 and in *Le Film*, 17. See pages 373–74.

8. Trotter, *Cinema and Modernism*, 3.

9. Ivan Goll's 1920 poem *Die Chaplinade, Ein Kinodichtung* (The Chaplinade: A cinepoem) was subtitled in its French version "poème cinématographique," a subgenre Philippe Soupault appears to have first defined in 1918. Although Man Ray's 1926 film *Emak Bakia* used the subtitle "cinépoème," to mean a poemlike film, we have to wait until 1978 for poet Max Jeanne to give this same subtitle to his filmlike poem, *Western* (see Chapter 11).

10. Virmaux andVirmaux, *Un Genre nouveau*; Abel, *French Film Theory and Criticism* (henceforth *FFTC* 1). Many scholars also contributed essays on single poets: Mary-Ann Caws (on Cendrars), Maria Tortajada (on Jarry), Claude Mourier (on Michaux).

11. McCabe, *Cinematic Modernism*; Trotter, *Cinema and Modernism*; L. Marcus, *Tenth Muse*.

12. Colette, *Au Cinéma*, 33–34. Colette wrote her first scenario in 1917.

13. The "manifold" translates "le divers" and "diversité" in the sense given to these terms by Segalen, *Essai sur l'exotisme*, 53. The French words come from Segalen's friend de Gaultier who thus translates Kant's *Mannigfaltig* from *Critique of Pure Reason*; Gaultier, *De Kant à Nietzsche*, 102.

14. Quintane, *Grand ensemble*, 19–20. The words are repeated for half a page and end with the "A" of Arabic without a period.

15. See Chapter 7 for Cendrars's 1912 text on cinema. A 1913 letter by Cendrars refers to the poem as "la bande colorée" (the colored strip), with "bande" a common synonym for a movie. In March 1914, he titled one of his *Elastic Poems*, "Fantômas," and is credited with introducing Apollinaire to both the books and films. See Sidoti, "Genèse et dossier d'une polémique," 20, 138–39.

16. Canudo, *La Roue*. Hamp, *La Peine des hommes*.

17. Canudo, *La Roue*, 3–4.

18. 1908 is the year of Griffith's first adaptation of Tennison's poem "Enoch Arden." Iampolsky, *Memory of Tiresias*, 52.

19. Carou, *Le Cinéma français*, 45–77.

20. Ibid., 102–5.

21. Rostand, "Le Bois sacré." The financial arrangements of the Pathé brothers' adaptation of Rostand's play *Cyrano de Bergerac* (the film came out in 1909) were sufficiently public and noteworthy that George Bernard Shaw mentions them in a 1908 letter: DuKore, *Bernard Shaw and Cinema*, 2.

22. Henry Clouard, cited by Décaudin, *La Crise*, 247, n87.

23. Romains, *La Vie unanime*, 1982, 242.

24. Incidentally, the cinema was present in the thought of both Bergson (see Chapter 1) and Tarde. The process of imitation in Tarde has a clear technological basis. In the May 1895 preface to the second edition of *Les Lois de l'imitation* he characterizes imitation as "remote action . . . quasi-photographic reproduction of a cerebral snapshot [*cliché cérébral*] by the sensible plate of another brain" or "interspiritual photography" (Tarde, *Les Lois*, viii). In 1896, he published "Fragment d'histoire future," in which through the cinema and the phonograph a later civilization reconstructs the present. See Tarde, "Fragment d'histoire future," 612, 624, 653, for the references to "le cinématographe."

25. Romains, *La Vie*, 1982, 51.

26. Ibid., 12.

27. Abel, *Ciné*, 31.

28. Cf. Meusy, *Paris-Palaces*.

29. Romains, "Crowd at the Cinematograph," in Abel, *FFTC*, 1:53. Romains, "La Foule," 104.

30. Abel, *FFTC,* 1:53; Romains, "La Foule," 105.

31. Romains, "La Foule," 105.

32. Abel, *Ciné,* 171. For Abel the film united La Fontaine's fable with France's mascot (the rooster), as well as Pathé's red rooster trademark, to suggest that film was capable of combining popular literary and filmic cultures into a national and profitable spectacle.

33. Romains, *Donogoo-Tonka,* 57.

34. *Automorphosis* is a new term needed to denote the autonomous transformation of moving images. The words "animated (images)" or "animation" are too ambiguous, since they refer to nonphotographic cinema, and too mystical since "anima" means soul. "Moving images" is itself a misnomer when referring to film, since images "moved" in magic lanterns, moving panoramas, Phantasmagoria, optical toys, and so on. "Morphing" and transformism refer respectively to a film technique and a cabaret spectacle of quick-change. "Plastic" or "plasticity" are good fits since they etymologically point to malleability, yet they come with a built-in aesthetic connotation. The "cinema effect" or "phi-effect" insists too much on optical illusionism which is below the perceptual level. Finally, automorphosis occurs naturally: in the growth of living beings; in the autonomous malleability of streaming water, clouds, smoke, fire, fluids; in the (seemingly) autonomous motions of foliage and land cover under the wind; and in the motion of flocks or schools or crowds of animals or humans. Cinema is the first artificial form of automorphosis.

35. Romains, *La Vie,* 1982, 242.

36. Remy de Gourmont mentions Shakespeare, Mérimée, and Maupassant ("Epilogues: Cinématographe," 49), indicating that "cinema has solved the problem of the cheaper theaters" (ibid.), and he describes in tremulous terms a shot of the Zambezi Falls showing a bush "partially caught in a whirlpool [that] wavered constantly on the brink of the abyss; and its trembling, having come from such a distance away, inspired in me a strange emotion" (47). "Epilogues: Cinématographe," 124–27, translated in Abel, *FFTC,* 1:47–50. Canudo lists (in order) Poe, d'Annunzio, Aristophanes, Plautus, Vitruvius, Shakespeare, Racine, Corneille, Henry Becque, and Cézanne, and writes of film's "paroxystic convulsion of action" (*L'Usine aux images,* 24) as promising "a sixth expression of art" (ibid.) characterized as "*Sculpture developing in time*" (25) concluding on a Unanimist note that cinema is "a new joyous *unanimity* [nouvelle *unanimité* joyeuse]" (31, original emphasis). In a slightly different version in 1911, which adds Emerson and Nietzsche, Canudo describes cinema's automorphosis more precisely as "a series of visions and aspects tied in a vibrating sheath and seen like a living organism" (*une série de visions et d'aspects liés dans un faisceau vibrant et vu comme un organisme vivant*) (Canudo, *L'Usine aux images*, 33; Abel, *FFTC,* 1:59).

37. Décaudin, *La Crise,* 245. See previous note.

38. One example among many: poet Victor Segalen, accounting regularly for the money his parents gave him while he attended medical school, never once mentions cinema—understandably (although the category "various articles" appears often). Yet in a 1899 letter to his mother he writes

self-critically: "I spin [*je défile*] everything to you on a monotone. It's not a letter, it's a *cinématographe*. But it's all the more exact." This shows the implicit level at which he and perhaps his parents knew cinema firsthand. Segalen, *Correspondances*, 1:162 (letter dated March 13, 1899). Similar indications exist for many writers and could be collected: for instance, in 1911, Valery Larbaud was given tickets to a local cinema in La Flêche (Sarthe); see Grenier, *Ciné-roman*, 18.

39. Apollinaire wrote a short tale about a "snuff film" as early as 1905: "Un beau film," *Œuvres en prose*, 1:198–201. In 1911, he sought to consult scenarios (one-page treatments stapled with a few frames of the film) at the Bibliothèque nationale. He writes that the employee denied such items existed: "Why—this would be like having tapeworms in a library!" But Apollinaire was right: a trove of scenarios dating back to 1906 was found in the 1990s, demonstrating that the institution had long considered such writings part of the literary patrimony. Cf. Ramirez and Rollot, "Apollinaire et le désir de cinéma," 50–60. For the scenario *La Bréhatine*, see Chapter 7.

40. Apollinaire, *Œuvres complètes*, 2:944.

41. Virmaux, "La Tentation du cinéma," 257–74. Other collaborations: Cendrars and Abel Gance, Philippe Soupault and Walter Rüttmann, Robert Desnos and Man Ray, Jules Romains and Jacques Feyder, Benjamin Péret and Michel Zimbecca.

42. A good example would be Péret, "Pulchérie veut une auto, film," 17–23. Its amalgamation of slapstick, adventure, and oneirism forecloses the possibility of an actual shooting. Its subtitle, "film," suggests that it is enacted when and as it is read.

43. Cited in Ramirez, "Poésie et cinéma," 36.

44. A rare attempt is Abel, "Exploring the Discursive Field," 58–71.

45. Rancière, "Distribution of the Sensible," 7–45.

46. The terms "dissensus" and "police" are exactly opposite. See Rancière, *Politics and Esthetics*, 85, 89.

47. Pasolini defines the screenplay as "a structure that wants to be another structure," challenging the reader—in terms recalling Mallarmé—"to see the kineme in the grapheme, above all, and thus to think in images, reconstructing in his own head the film to which the screenplay alludes as a potential work" (Pasolini, "Screenplay," 192).

48. Ève Francis (ca. 1949), cited by Heu, *Le Temps du cinéma*, 192.

49. Brague notes that Baudelaire would know of Coleridge and the Iena Romantics via Poe and Victor Cousin, respectively (*L'Image vagabonde*, 45, n1). See Scott, *Pictorialist Poetics*, 12–14, for more on Cousin.

50. Baudelaire, *Œuvres complètes*, 2:627.

51. Lacoue-Labarthe and Nancy, *Literary Absolute*.

52. The intuition of Baudelaire's precinematic imaginary is found *in nuce* in several authors: Paul de Man's opposition of the static romantic symbol and Baudelaire's dynamic allegory (in "Rhetoric of Temporality"); Bazin's mention of Baudelaire in "Total Cinema"; and Cavell's *World Viewed*.

53. For the illuminating contrast between looking *at* and looking *into* (albeit language-dependent), see McGinn, *Power of Movies*, 20–40.

54. Baudelaire, *Œuvres,* 2:636–37.
55. Brague, *L'Image vagabonde*, 127.
56. Ibid., 133.
57. Baudelaire, *Œuvres complètes*, 1:432.
58. Ibid., 1:663–64.
59. Bazin, *Qu'est-ce que le cinéma?,* 22.
60. Ortel, *La Littérature.*
61. Lamartine, *Œuvres complètes*, 1:8.
62. The word is Valéry's, from a strange 1930 text, "La Photopoétique," *Œuvres*, 1:395. See also, Goulet's *Optiques.*
63. Friedrich, *Structure of Modern Poetry*, 8–9.
64. Cf. for instance, Casey, *Imagining*, 16–17; Kearney, *Wake of Imagination*, 185–87.
65. Iser, *Fictive and the Imaginary*, 185.
66. Cf. Huet, *Monstrous Imagination.*
67. Sallis, *Force of Imagination.*
68. Cf. Currie and Ravenscroft, *Recreative Minds*, who define imagination as "perspective-shifting," 9. Sallis, *Force of Imagination*, uses notions of "tractive" and "lateral" imagination throughout his book.
69. Kearney, *Wake of Imagination*, 13, 185; Sallis, *Force of Imagination*, "one wonders what remains today that is not thoroughly determined by the incessant flow of images," 81.
70. See Milner, *Fantasmagorie*; Gunning, "Phantasmagoria," 31–44; Warner, *Phantasmagoria.*
71. Poets range from Charles Nodier in the 1820s to Paul Valéry in the 1890s, including Lamartine, Hugo, Gautier, Baudelaire, Rimbaud, Nerval, Mallarmé, and Gide. The generic liminality of the term is present already in Goethe's early sketch for Faust, *Helena* (1827), subtitled *Klassische-Romantische Phantasmagorie, Zwischenspiel zu Faust.* Some markers: Rimbaud's "Je suis maître en fantasmagorie" in "Alchimie du verbe"; Baudelaire's account of Guy's sketching as "la fantasmagorie" in "Le Peintre de la vie moderne"; Des Esseintes's reference to "les dociles fantasmagories de ma cervelle," in *A Rebours* by Huysmans; and Valéry's cross-medium note: "Si on photographiait ce qu'ils 'pensent' – sentent – voient – entendent – on verrait quelle étrange et pauvre comédie! Toute l'intensité du sentiment n'y change rien. Le langage jette sur tout cela sa fantasmagorie d'abstractions" (*Œuvres*, 1:107).
72. See Sicard, *L'Année 1895.*
73. While "cinema as dream" is an omnipresent topos in film theory, from the 1920s to the 1970s, few critics have questioned what Freudian dream theory may owe to cinema—that is, whether dreamers' accounts might have descriptive components and dynamics not present before cinema. A recent collection scarcely raises that possibility, Bergstrom, *Endless Night.*
74. For the intersection of Husserlian phenomenology and Binswangerian psychoanalysis around the imagination, see Richir, *Phantasia.*
75. Cairns, *Conversations*, 78–80.
76. Iser concurs with this time frame, albeit without recourse to technology (Iser, *Fictive and the Imaginary*, 171).

77. " . . . mélange de sensible et d'imaginaire," Biran, *Journal*, 269.

78. The cyborg Hadaly explains the interregion between the world of artificial creatures and the human world: "The relational path through which the current flows between this doubled world is none other than . . . THE IMAGINARY [*L'IMAGINAIRE*]"; and Villiers's narrator carefully distinguishes the imagination as a faculty from the imaginary as a kind of matter: "this infinite substance, the Imaginary [*L'Imaginaire*]." Villiers de l'Isle-Adam, *L'Ève future*, 376 (book VI, chapter VI, "Figures in the Night").

79. Segalen, *Imaginaires*, 132.

80. Ibid., 50.

81. In an 1896 oneiric passage by Alfred Jarry, we encounter a similarly optical fusion of the face of a spectator with another face. The mythical Roboam first feels "a mask of white velvet weaving itself around my temples" (915), before realizing another face is in front of him and that "both our masks were fencing masks." As Roboam duels with the creature, his vision becomes "clouded as if a second cobweb had fallen on the eye-slits of my mask." The more the duel goes on, the more the enemy appears to be himself, until "I removed my false face . . . looking at the eye-slits which, like the eyes of my face, were closing, and had glued and fused shut their eyelashes" (916). This too seems to me derived from the haptic protrusion of an automorphic face on screen. Jarry, "L'Autre Alceste," *Œuvres*, 1:907–16.

82. Sartre, *L'Imaginaire,* 352–54. I am using the original French text because the English translation is an edited version.

83. Ibid., 250.

84. Ibid., 251; original emphasis.

85. Ibid., 146.

86. Ibid., 151.

87. Ibid., 163.

88. Ibid., 55.

89. Cf. Anderson and Anderson, "Myth of Persistence."

90. Sartre, *L'Imaginaire*, 259.

91. Jean Epstein may be glossing this very passage with a jab at Sartre when he opens his 1946 book on a "child" noticing this phenomenon of "bewitched wheels" on screen, adding that "it might happen that a twelve-year-old philosopher will heretofore be weary of a spectacle that paints the world with a capricious and perhaps falsifying brush" (*L'Intelligence d'une machine*, in *Écrits,* 1:255).

92. Sartre, *L'Imaginaire*, 260.

93. Ibid., 234.

94. Ibid., 232–33; my emphasis.

95. Sartre, "Apologie pour le cinéma," 390. For an analysis of this text, see my "Poire, plume Douve et bob." For the importance of cinema in Sartre's thought of the 1940s, see Connor, "Sartre and Cinema," especially a reference to the phi-effect in *Being and Nothingness* (1048).

96. Bachelard, *L'Air et les songes*, 7; emphasis in original.

97. Ibid., 8.

98. Ibid., 15.

99. Ibid., 16.

100. Ibid., 293.

101. Ibid., 294.

102. For Lacan's *imaginary* as an effect of image projection and reception, see the mind experiment with upside-down flowers in "La topique de l'imaginaire," in Lacan, *Séminaire,* 87–103, 143–47. Lacan's models of unconscious projection use optical cones and cross-section (reminiscent of Cocteau, see Chapter 3): cf. *Les quatre concepts fondamentaux,* 103–19. For the imaginary in Merleau-Ponty's 1945 *Phenomenology of Perception*, see Escoubas, "Merleau-Ponty et les métamorphoses."

103. Bachelard was a founding member of the directorial committee of the Association Française pour la Recherche Filmologique, see Lowry, *Filmology Movement*, 47.

104. Morin, *Cinema,* 203 (trans. slightly amended).

105. Ong, *Orality and Literacy.*

106. A broader study of the cinematicization of "the imaginary" would point to how Jean-Louis Baudry's apparatus theory relied on Lacan's influential concept of the imaginary, itself crucially worked out in the mirror stage as an act of spectatorship which, if my hunch is correct, he directly derived from a reinterpretation of Sartre's *The Imaginary.* Baudry cites Lacan's characterization of the imaginary as theater/film staging: "That he sustains himself as a 'subject' means that language allows him to consider himself the stagehand [*machiniste*] if not the director [*metteur en scène*] of the whole imaginary capture of which otherwise he would be but the puppet" (Baudry, *L'effet cinéma,* 25 n24).

107. Richard, *L'Univers imaginaire.*

108. Reynolds, *Symbolist Esthetics*, 84.

109. Ibid.

110. Christin, *L'image écrite*, 119.

111. Rancière, *Politics of Aesthetics,* 24.

112. Ibid., 22.

113. Ibid., 59.

114. Rancière, *Flesh of Words*, 3, 5.

115. Rancière, *Film Fables*, 11.

116. Rancière, *Future of the Image*, 47.

117. Deleuze, "How Jarry's Pataphysics," 74.

118. M. Hansen, "Benjamin and Cinema," 63.

119. Benjamin, "One-Way Street," 444–88, s.v. "Filling Station" (444), "Attested Auditor of Books" (456–57, on Mallarmé), "This Space for Rent" (476).

120. Perloff, *Radical Artifice*; Drucker, *Visible Word*; Bohn, *Modern Visual Poetry.* Liz Kotz has demonstrated how this new status of the word transformed American art in *Words to Be Looked At.*

121. Here are a few passages from Jules Romains, *La Vie unanime*:

> One evening someone in a room
> Will have read what I wrote,
> And the lamp will hold the words

Under the tip of its rays [*sous la pointe de ses rayons*]
Like a treasure beneath swords . . .
. . .
Someone up on a double-decker bus
Despite the jerking motion from the wheels
Will read my book; all the words
Will interpenetrate . . . [*entreront les uns dans les autres*] (39)
. . .
On the train . . .
The shock of the pistons will shake up the lines [*secoueront les vers*](40)

The odd comparison of words held under the projected light of the lamp like a treasure under swords refers to the clichéd passage of Ali Baba when thieves swear fealty by drawing their swords over the loot. In 1902, Ferdinand Zecca released *Ali Baba et les quarante voleurs*, which was subsequently restenciled and rereleased by Segundo de Chomón for Pathé in 1907. Abel, *Ciné,* 175.

122. Abel, *Ciné,* 259.

123. Fonds Saint-Pol-Roux, Bibliothèque littéraire Jacques Doucet, Ms 9823.8. See also Chapter 5.

124. Gauthier and Lacassin, *Louis Feuillade,* 81.

125. Butler, "Irma Vep, Vamp in the City," 213–14.

126. " . . . on the uniform surface of a person like any other have appeared, traced in an ink until then invisible, the characters that compose the word dear to the Greeks. . . . Instantly the words appear like *Mane, Thecel, Phares*. . . . [Everything] became as clear as a sentence which, devoid of sense so long as it was decomposed in letters randomly arranged, expresses, when the characters find themselves replaced in the proper order, a thought we will never forget" (Proust, *Sodome et Gomorrhe*, 1:15–16).

127. Bohn, *Modern Visual Poetry*, 130.

128. Crafton, *Émile Cohl,* 163, 364.

129. Cited in Boschetti, *La Poésie partout,* 180. We recall that in 1913 Apollinaire organized a Society of the Friends of Fantômas; his 1913 *Synthesis-Manifesto of the Futurist Anti-Tradition* mentions a new "Book or life capture or phonocinematography or wireless imagination" (Apollinaire, *Œuvres complètes en prose,* 2:938).

130. For intertitles and literature, see Sitney, *Modernist Montage.*

131. Albert-Birot, "Du Cinéma," 388; Epstein, *Écrits,* 1:148.

132. Reverdy, "Carrés," in *Plupart du temps,* 1:65–66. Cf. Isabelle Garron, "D'un Chicago corps 12," in Reverdy, *La Lucarne ovale*, 91–93. Reverdy published a short but forceful piece on cinema in his journal *Nord-Sud* in 1918 on which we will comment in Chapter 2.

133. Hubert, *Circonstances de la poésie.*

134. See Bordwell, *Poetics of Cinema*, 75–82.

135. Gunning, "Modernity and Cinema."

136. Ibid., 300.

137. Bordwell, *Poetics of Cinema,* 79.

138. " . . . the time required for the reading of a cinematographic image by an average spectator diminished in five years by thirty percent" [1928] (*Écrits,* 1:189).

139. Ong, *Orality and Literacy,* 17.

140. We should note that the computer metaphor of hard circuits versus software obscures the reality of the surprisingly rapid plasticity of neuro-perceptual reorganization. See Noë, *Action in Perception,* 226–27.

141. For Élie Faure, see "The Art of Cineplastics" [1922], in Abel, *FFTC,* 1:258–68, especially a comparison of the moving image with the shape-changing plume of a volcano (266); and Flinn, "Prescience of Élie Faure." For Sergei Eisenstein whose notion of "plasmaticness" refers both to animated film and to protoplasmic organisms, see *Eisenstein on Disney,* 69; for Epstein, see Chapter 4; and Bullot, "Photogénie plastique." Pasolini in 1965 describes the screenplay as a form of writing displaying "a magmatic grammar," Pasolini, "Screenplay," 191. In 1913, Henri-Martin Barzun, expanding Romains's Unanimism, called for a new poetry that would be "*plastic,* that is to say formed by plasma, by a living body, with dimensions other than just length, that is to say, *volumes, masses, depth.*" Barzun, "L'Art poétique."

142. See Malabou, *La Plasticité*; and Malabou, *La Plasticité au soir de l'écriture*, which links notions of plasticity and graphic trace.

143. Merleau-Ponty, *Visible and the Invisible*, chapter 4, "The Intertwining—The Chiasm," 130–54.

144. Maurice Merleau-Ponty, "Le Cinéma et la nouvelle psychologie." Merleau-Ponty writes, "The art of poetry does not consist of didactically describing or exposing ideas, but of creating a language machine which, almost infallibly, makes the reader agree with the poet" (941). Poetry, in this account, would seem diffracted through the film apparatus as a machine producing a commanding hypermediacy.

145. Morris, *Sense of Space,* 1, 7.

146. Ibid., 36, 42. Maurice Henry's 1949 *Philosophie et phénoménologie du corps*, based on Maine de Biran's analysis of the inner sense of the body, and independently of Merleau-Ponty, asserts the ontological primacy of sensory motion as well: "Sensation is always where it is, and this 'where' . . . becomes a spatial determination proper only on the condition of a real or possible movement of my gaze" (109).

147. Morris, *Sense of Space,* 114, 108, 116.

148. The housefly represents a curious thematic strand running through cinepoetry. A number of metaphoric aspects may be involved, among them: the free command of 3-D space; multifaceted eyes suggesting a simultaneist-chronophotographic vision; the plastic mystery of its larval metamorphosis (see Chapter 6 and Conclusion); writing troped through flies ("pattes de mouche" means tiny handwriting, "moucheter" means making small black marks).

149. Gibson, *Ecological Approach.*

150. Noë, *Action in Perception,* 29–30; original emphasis.

151. I refer to Martin Jay's *Downcast Eyes.*

152. “In the cinema each spectator becomes a big eye, as big as his/her person, an eye which does not content itself with its habitual functions but adds to them that of thought, smell, hearing, touch. All our senses become ocularized” (Supervielle, “Les lettres,” 183–84).

153. Noë, *Action in Perception*, 67.

154. For an antiecological attempt by an analytical philosopher to rethink this division, see McGinn, *Mindsight*.

155. Morin, *Le Cinéma*, 203.

156. Verschueren, *Understanding Pragmatics*, 9.

157. Bolter and Grusin, *Remediation;* Krauss, *Voyage on the North Sea*; for *intermédialité*, see the eponymous journal published by the Centre de Recherche sur l'Intermédialité of the University of Montreal.

158. Zielinski, *Deep Time*.

159. Kluitenberg, “Second Introduction,” 22.

160. Maurier, “Edison's Telephoscope.”

161. For Cros as writer and inventor, see Ortel, *La Littérature*, 69–74.

162. Cros, “Un Drame interastral.”

163. www.academie-sciences.fr/membres (April 12, 2009).

164. Cf. Sicard, “Passage de Vénus,” 53.

165. A close friend of Cros, cartoonist Émile Cohl, pioneered animation in 1907. See Crafton, *Émile Cohl*.

1. MALLARMÉ UNFOLDS THE *CINÉMATOGRAPHE*

1. “suite d'images <imaginaires mentales écrites> reliées p rattachées par un fil . . . ” (Mallarmé, *Œuvres complètes*, 1:1073).

2. This chapter section includes parts of Wall-Romana, “Mallarmé's Cinepoetics.”

3. *Le Livre* (not a title given by Mallarmé), published in 1957, was a 200-page sheaf of cryptic draft notes found after Mallarmé's death, on the aesthetics, mathematics, and economics of a new kind of public performance of poetry. See Mallarmé, *Le “Livre,”* and a new transcription in Mallarmé, *Œuvres*, 1:945–1060. The Paris World Fair was a high point for early cinema and para-cinematic inventions (Maréorama, and so on), and Mallarmé had written reports on previous World Fairs, such as the London Fair of 1872. See Toulet, “Le cinéma.”

4. This is *in nuce* in Andreas Huyssen's lowbrow versus highbrow great divide.

5. Valéry's work for Cecil Rhodes and Stevens's for Hartford insurances might explain their impulse towards a realm of “pure poetry” untouched by global capital. As a high-school English teacher and a socialist, Mallarmé had a different view.

6. See Dragonetti, *Un Fantôme dans le kiosque*; Shaw, *Performance in the Texts of Mallarmé*; Stafford, *Mallarmé and the Poetics of Everyday Life*; Zachmann, *Frameworks for Mallarmé*; Arnar, *Book as Instrument*.

7. The connection of Mallarmé and cinema was first explored by McCarren, “Mallarmé at the Movies.”

8. Marey and Dickson pioneered the filmstrip in the late 1880s, and Edison's Kinetoscope, patented in 1888, began commercial shows of peephole movies in 1894. But cinema results from exchanges among the likes of Jules-Étienne Marey, Thomas Edison, F. R. Dickson, Georges Demenÿ, and others in Germany, England, and elsewhere. As for animated images projected on a screen, Émile Reynaud's *Pantomimes lumineuses* accomplished the feat with hand-painted images on flexible gelatin inserted in fabric strip as early as in 1892. See Mannoni, *Great Art.*

9. Rittaud Huttinet and Rittaud Huttinet, *Dictionnaire des cinématographes,* 349–50.

10. The full program reads:

Poètes,

D'un geste, se conçoit, à l'heure—où prestige matériel évanoui, hélas!—en lumière pure se résout le fantôme humain, autrefois levé sur le pavois, de l'aède désigné quel, d'une présence réclamée dès lors, doit primer dans le respect et l'admiration, son front barré des unanimes palmes (Mallarmé, *Œuvres complètes,* 2:687).

[Poets,

It can be conceived through a gesture, now that—the material prestige having vanished, alas!—the human ghost resolves itself in pure light, yesteryear lifted on the shield, of the designated bard who, his presence called for as a result, must prevail through respect and admiration, his forehead lined with unanimous palms.]

By leaving it up to the reader to parse the text, allowing for "multiple comprehension" (Mallarmé, *Œuvres,* 1:428), Mallarmé emphatically demonstrates that his virtual poetics is de facto democratic, not monarchic (cf. the "*pavois*" used to hoist a new king). This is also a retort to critics like Lev Tolstoï and Max Nordau who attacked him as the leader of Symbolism, taken by them to be an elitist, obscurantist, decadent, even degenerate school. To Lloyd James Austin's suspicion that this is a pastiche, Bertrand Marchal has retorted that if so it was fully authorized by Mallarmé (*Œuvres,* 2:1742).

11. The posthuman is an epistemic privileging of information over substrate, prosthesis over embodiment, and mechanic simulation over consciousness (Hayles, *How We Became Posthuman,* 160–91). In May 1896 Mallarmé suggested that the bicycle disorders gender (pants giving female bicyclists "a dubious gender" [un sexe douteux],) but also humanness: "The human being does not with impunity come close to a mechanism and get mixed with it, without some loss" (l'être humain n'approche pas impunément d'un mécanisme et ne s'y mêle pas sans perte) (Mallarmé, *Œuvres,* 2:662). In March 1897, Robert de Souza countered accusations against Mallarmé's "personal syntax" by arguing that the poet must make "incessant improvisation" against "mechanical media (typewriter, etc.), rapid communication needs (telegraph, telephone, etc.)," which threaten to transform language into "a mechanical phenomenon." Marchal, *Mallarmé,* 441.

12. In the first week of January 1896 news came also of the discovery of Roentgen rays (x-rays). While it is possible that Mallarmé had x-rays in mind, its application in the radiography of the human body was not known

for several years. See Sicard and Lippit for connections between the x-rays and cinema.

13. Villiers de l'Isle-Adam, *L'Ève future*, 274, 284.

14. Ibid., 265.

15. Mallarmé, *Œuvres*, 2:51.

16. Ibid., 2:44.

17. In another eulogy of Verlaine Mallarmé refers to the afterlife as a shimmer reflected on spectators: "l'astre mûri des lendemains / Dont un scintillement argentera la foule" (the ripened star of tomorrows / Whose silver flickering will tint the crowd) (Mallarmé, *Œuvres*, 1:39).

18. It is crucial to note that the cinema apparatus reached the public sphere as an *imaginary apparatus* before it was actually implemented. The first account of it dates from June 1891—four and half years before the Cinématographe opened to the public. A. Vernier, "Causerie scientifique," 1. The "Kinetograph" is described as recording both images and sounds: "Mr. Edison has, as we see, combined two orders of observation; with the same apparatus he makes a picture, a mobile picture, in which life's movement is sequential, as it were, through separate impressions, sufficiently numerous to provide to the receiving retina the impression of continuity; at the same time he records sounds." The popular science journal *La Nature* described the Kinetoscope in 1894: Tissandier, "Le Kinétoscope d'Edison," 323–26.

19. Mallarmé, *Correspondance*, 94.

20. Uzanne, *Vingt jours*, 69–70.

21. Uzanne, "Une visite chez Edison," 1.

22. Meusy, *Paris-Palaces*, 20, 39.

23. For Arthur Meyer, see Mallarmé, *Correspondance*, 7:311–12; 8:140, 145. For Pierrot, see Mallarmé, "Mimique," *Œuvres*, 2:178.

24. Albert, "Théâtre de l'Oeuvre," 381.

25. In 1914, with Picabia, de Zayas, and Savinio, Apollinaire planned a pantomime with a "luminous screen" veiling the stage, and film "projections" shown against a "curtain," see Apollinaire, *A quelle heure un train partira-t-il pour Paris?* 6, 21. For Henri Rivière's multimedia shadow plays with electrical lighting and moving sets, culminating at the *Chat noir* in 1894–95, see Oberthür, *Henri Rivière*, 54–58 (my thanks to Fabienne Lécallier for this reference).

26. Mallarmé, *Correspondance*, 8:153.

27. Mannoni, *Great Art*, 466. In May 1897, Paul Nadar demonstrated his camera to the Musée Grévin board, which deemed it too noisy (Meusy, *Paris-Palaces*, 48, 74).

28. Huret, "Le Courrier des théâtres," 4.

29. Mallarmé, *Œuvres*, 2:697–702.

30. The first report of the *Cinématographe* in *Le Figaro*, in Huret's column, is post facto: "Giving the list of society figures who have be astonished by the invention of the Lumière is impossible: it would amount to reciting Paris's *Who's-Who* [*le Tout-Paris*]" ("Concerts et spectacles," 4). Other

reports on the Cinématographe followed on February 23, March 6, March 15, March 22, March 31, etc.

31. Clarétie, "La Vie à Paris," 3.

32. The editorial notes accompanying *Un Coup de dés* are reproduced in Berr, "La Vie littéraire," 3. For other notices, see Marchal, *Mallarmé*, 447–52.

33. Meusy, *Paris-Palaces*, 53–62. Remy de Gourmont wrote one of the very first literary essays on cinema at this occasion, "Le Bûcher," 558–63.

34. Mallarmé, *Correspondance*, 9:159–60, 173, 233.

35. Mallarmé, *Correspondance*, 9:224–25.

36. Mallarmé, *Œuvres*, 2:668, originally published in Ibels, "Enquête sur le roman illustré," 110. Both the *Mercure* and the 1945 *Pléiade* edition have "*remplacez la photographie* . . . " instead of "*employez la photographie*." This typo by the *Mercure* typesetter was corrected with the publication of the original letter (Mallarmé, *Correspondance*, 9:236). Ortel, *La Littérature*, 137–39, and McCarren are the only critic I know to have commented on Mallarmé's (uncorrected) statement on cinema, although Derrida cites it in full in *Dissemination* (see below).

37. Ibels, "Enquête sur le roman illustré," 101.

38. Mallarmé, *Œuvres*, 2:224.

39. Mallarmé, *Œuvres*, 1:392.

40. Passages from Mallarmé's note on cinema (June 1897):

. . . mais, si vous employez la photographie, que n'allez-vous droit au cinématographe, dont le déroulement remplacera, images et texte, maint volume, avantageusement.

[. . . but, if you use photography, why not go straight to the cinematograph, whose unfolding will replace, images and text, many a volume, advantageously.]

Passages from the two drafts of the preface of *Un Coup de dés* (spring 1897):

. . . mais si, pour quelque motif elle [la parole] requiert le papier, dépossédé de sa fonction originelle de montrer des images, alors ne doit-elle pas remplacer celles-ci à sa façon, idéalement et fictivement.

[. . . but if, for some reason it (speech) requires paper, devoid of its original function of showing images, then should it not replace them in its own way, ideally and fictionally.]

. . . or que dans un cas elle [la parole] requière la blancheur du papier, dépossédé celui-ci de sa fonction de surface ou présenter à l'oeil uniquement des images, alors la parole ne doit-elle pas remplacer celles-ci à sa façon, moins tangiblement par un texte ou littérairement. (Mallarmé, *Œuvres*, 1:403)

[. . . whereas it (speech) might in one case require the paper's whiteness, itself devoid of its function of surface or presenting to the eye solely images, then should not speech replace them in its own way, less tangibly by a text or literarily.]

41. Latour, *We Have Never Been Modern*, 6–11.

42. On epistemological intersections of artificial forces, cinematic devices, and somatic bodies, see Didi-Huberman, *Invention de l'hystérie*; Gordon, *Why the French Love Jerry Lewis;* Kittler, *Gramophone*; Massumi, *Parables;* Rutsky, *High Techné*; and Singer, *Melodrama and Modernity*.

43. Cf. Guido, *L'Âge du rythme*.

44. Mallarmé, *Œuvres*, 2:369.

45. Bergson, *Essai sur les données*, 146.

46. Ibid., 7.

47. Ibid., 1432.

48. Ibid., 720.

49. Ibid., 291.

50. Marey, *Le Mouvement*, 123.

51. Ibid., 137.

52. Ibid., 135.

53. Mannoni, *Great Art*, 320–63.

54. Dagognet, *Etienne-Jules Marey*, 65.

55. Ibid., 47.

56. Ibid., 102.

57. Bergson, *Œuvres*, 753.

58. On Zeno's paradox, see Doane, *Emergence of Cinematic Time*, 172–205; on visuomotor perception in film viewing, see Hochberg and Brooks, "Movies in the Mind's Eye." For Bergson and cinema, see Deleuze, *Cinema 1*, 1–11.

59. See Frizot, "Comment ça marche," for the human gait in the cinematic apparatus. Apollinaire's first definition of sur-realism is conceptualized as the transition from a poetics of walking to a poetics of the wheel (see discussion in Chapter 4).

60. For Fuller's contested rapport with her body as a lesbian, see Lista, *Loïe Fuller*, 53, 296, 300–2.

61. Mallarmé, *Œuvres*, 2:174–75.

62. Ibid., 2:163—the two words I indicate appear together in the preface to *Un Coup de dés*.

63. Ibid., 2:175–76.

64. Ibid., 2:171.

65. Ibid., 2:323.

66. Ibid., 2:163.

67. Ibid., 1:391.

68. Marey, *Le Mouvement*, 22.

69. See Zachmann, *Frameworks For Mallarmé*, with convergent analyses although not centered on cinema.

70. Villiers de L'Isle-Adam, *Contes cruels*, 8.

71. Ibid., 91. In "La Machine à gloire" (The glory machine), dedicated to Mallarmé, Villiers invents "*A pure machine proposed as a means to attain infallibly a purely intellectual goal*" (Villiers, *Contes*, 104; emphasis in original).

72. Crafton, *Émile Cohl*, 244; Meusy, *Paris-Palaces*, 72–73; Sadoul, *Lumière et Méliès*, 256.

73. Mallarmé, *Œuvres,* 1:391.
74. Ibid., 1:562.
75. Ibid., 2:233.
76. Ibid., 1:595.
77. For chronology and machinery, see Mallarmé, *Le "Livre,"* xx, xxi, 70, 91, 151; for language, see Derrida, "La Double séance"; for the democratic ritual, see Rancière, *Mallarmé.*
78. Mallarmé, *Œuvres,* 1:559, 614, 619.
79. Ibid., 1:618–19.
80. The filmic "séance" contrasts with live theater "représentation," Rittaud-Huttinet, *Dictionnaire* 350.
81. Mallarmé, *Œuvres,* 1:999.
82. Ibid., 1:392.
83. For Wagner, see Crary, *Suspension of Perception,* 2, 33–34; for Fuller, see Lista, *Loïe Fuller,* 156–59, 259; McCarren, *Dance Pathologies,* 157–59; and Iampolski, "La danse, le cinéma et un peu de physique"; for Mallarmé and electricity, which Richard mentions reluctantly (521), see Rancière, *Mallarmé,* 82–83.
84. Mallarmé, *Œuvres,* 1:173–74.
85. Ibid., 1:1046.
86. Ibid., 1:956.
87. Ibid., 1:958.
88. Meusy, *Paris-Palaces,* 42. The hand-painted film was rediscovered in 1996; see Mannoni, "Une féerie de 1896," 117–23. *Le Figaro* mentions that some of the thirty-two tableaus are "transformations," that is, films. Fouquier, "Les Théâtres," 3.
89. Mallarmé, *Œuvres,* 1:391.
90. Ibid., 1:606, 612, 622.
91. Ibid., 1:594.
92. The four-year séances at 1 franc per page per seat add up to the huge sum of 480,000 francs (Mallarmé, *Œuvres,* 2:1011–29). In its first six months the Lumière's *Cinématographe* brought in 1,060,805 francs (Mannoni, *Great Art,* 464), with between one and three venues; ticket price was 1 franc, one hour's wage for unskilled factory workers (Meusy, *Paris-Palaces,* 69).
93. Mallarmé, *Œuvres,* 1:165.
94. Rancière, *Mallarmé,* 62, 98–108.
95. Cited in Gorceix, *Maurice Maeterlinck,* 200, 248, 251.
96. Cited in Illouz, *Le Symbolisme,* 287.
97. Valéry, "Introduction à la méthode de Léonard de Vinci," 1:1193; Gide, *Le Traité du Narcisse,* 30.
98. Gide, *Traité,* 18.
99. Valéry, *Œuvres,* 1:1169.
100. Ibid., 1:1195.
101. Ibid., 1:1177.
102. Valéry, "Cinématographe," in *Œuvres complètes,* 2:1580–81.
103. Noguez, "Gide et le cinéma," 151–87.

104. Icart, *Abel Gance*, 15.

105. Ibid., 23–25.

106. Gance, *Prisme*, 107.

107. Jenkins, "Un Peu tard," 307.

108. One example is Raymond Bellour, in whose reflections on literature and cinema Mallarmé is omnipresent, cf. *L'Entre-Images 2;* and *L'Entre-Images, Photo, Cinéma, Vidéo.*

2. THE PEN-CAMERA

1. For the early influence of Mallarmé's *Un Coup de dés* on Duchamp before the poem was reprinted by the NRF in 1914, see Duchamp's 1913 notes reprinted in Nesbitt, *Their Common Sense*, 192–93.

2. Carrouges, *Les Machines célibataires.* Krauss's *Bachelors* provides a feminist retort.

3. Carrouges, *Les Machines célibataires*, 208, 24.

4. The notion of "robustness" comes from Hansen's *Embodying Technesis.* Hansen mounts a critique of poststructuralism's discourse on technology in which, he claims, "technology is stripped of its robust materiality in order to serve as *figure* for the impact of materiality on thinking" (20). While in broad agreement with Hansen, I think he reduces writing in the same manner as those he faults for reducing technology. Technology's robustness need not be "beyond writing": it is "in" writing as well.

5. See Rebourg, "Entre graphe et scope," 131–37; and Kitayama, "Raymond Roussel et le cinéma des origines," 1:183–207. In Roussel's *roulotte*, the large RV he built for himself and which he drove only through the park of his mansion, there was a movie projector.

6. Caradec, *Raymond Roussel*, 157.

7. Roussel, *Impressions d'Afrique*, 114–16.

8. Ibid., 116–18.

9. Passages with optical devices from *Locus Solus* (1914), are also cinematic, for instance when scientist Canterel muses on the mysterious contraption called *aqua-micans* that could "write in thin air bubbles arranged graphically" (89). Tableaux also form an ersatz film program in *Locus Solus,* 89–104.

10. Roussel, *La Vue.* The verse numbers refer to this work.

11. See note 53 in Chapter 1 for McGinn's distinction.

12. See Gunning, "Before Documentary."

13. Caradec, *Raymond Roussel*, 130–34.

14. Sallis, *Force of Imagination*, 110–11.

15. Fifteen years after Roussel, Pierre Reverdy gives a precise description of the eyeline match in "Le Cinématographe," 8. The eyeline match is dated around 1910–11 by David Bordwell, Janet Staiger, and Kristin Thompson, *Classical Hollywood Cinema*, 208.

16. Only recently was it discovered that on an early print by Nicéphore Niepce which was thought to be empty of people, thus foreshadowing Atget's depopulated urban photographs, there were indeed two blurry silhouettes on the sidewalk—a man having his shoes shined and the

shoe-shiner—visible only because, unlike all the other *passants*, they were partially immobile.

17. Gunning, "New Thresholds of Vision," 71–99.

18. See Michaux's use of "dephotographing" infra. Sartre writes, "We are, in a way, consciously *animating* the photo, lending it life to make it an image" (*L'Imaginaire*, 55; emphasis in original).

19. Barthes, *Œuvres complètes*, 5:804, 936.

20. Casares, *Invention of Morel*. Among early films of beach scenes, one is *Dogs Playing in the Surf* (US, 1898, Edison cat. # 1418).

21. Roussel, *La Vue*, 277.

22. Abel, *Ciné*, 97–101.

23. Foucault, *Raymond Roussel*.

24. Foucault, *Naissance de la Clinique*, xviii (translation modified).

25. Foucault, *Raymond Roussel*, 54; *Death and the Labyrinth*, 38, rectified.

26. Foucault, *Raymond Roussel*, 50; *Death and the Labyrinth*, 36.

27. Foucault, *Death and the Labyrinth*, 172–73.

28. Foucault, *Raymond Roussel*, 75; *Death and the Labyrinth*, 57.

29. Foucault, *Raymond Roussel*, 172; *Death and the Labyrinth*, 135.

30. Foucault, *Raymond Roussel*, 16; *Death and the Labyrinth*, 8.

31. Foucault, *Raymond Roussel*, 136; *Death and the Labyrinth*, 105, modified.

32. Foucault, *Raymond Roussel*, 115; *Death and the Labyrinth*, 148.

33. Foucault, *Raymond Roussel*, 176; *Death and the Labyrinth*, 138–39.

34. Foucault, *Raymond Roussel*, 141; *Death and the Labyrinth*, 109, modified.

35. Foucault, *Raymond Roussel*, 172; *Death and the Labyrinth*, 135.

36. Foucault, *Dits et Écrits*, 1:410.

37. Ibid.

38. Foucault's motive for the occultation of cinema in Roussel—not just in "La Vue"—has to do with his genealogy of a regime of "pure language," and the implicit notion that a return of cinema in the new novel takes place only *through* this pure language. As in Derrida's evacuation of the "imaginary," the targets are both the phenomenological school of criticism and the kind of alchemico-surrealist readings of Carrouges that insist on writing as transposition.

3. *LE FILM SURNATUREL*

1. Ramirez and Rolot, "Apollinaire et le désir de cinéma," insist that Cocteau was "ignorant of all things cinematographic" (50) until 1930. This is plainly untrue: cf. Azoury and Lalanne, *Cocteau et le cinéma, désordres*, 29. Note also that Apollinaire corrected Cocteau who called his own ballet *Parade* "a realistic ballet" (*ballet réaliste*), by writing that it enacted "a kind of sur-realism [*sur-réalisme*]," the first public use of the term. Albright, *Modernism and Music*, 320. Apollinaire, "Parade et l'esprit nouveau," 2:865–66. See also Williams, *Jean Cocteau*, 70–71.

2. See Nemer, "Cocteau s'amuse."

3. Cocteau, *Du Cinématographe*, 10.

4. Cocteau, *Carte Blanche*, 31.

5. Schehr, *French Gay Modernism*, 104.

6. Rolot, "Cocteau spectateur," 17.

7. Williams, *Jean Cocteau*, 13.

8. Nemer, "Cocteau s'amuse," 77.

9. Cocteau, *Le Potomak*, 16.

10. For Bergson and Deleuze, see Dumoncel, *Le Symbole d'Hécate*. For Epstein, see Chapter 4.

11. Rolot, "Textes inédits et retrouvés," 222.

12. Cocteau, *Le Secret professionnel*, 102.

13. Cocteau, *Œuvres poétiques complètes*, 148.

14. Williams, *Jean Cocteau*, 23–24.

15. Cocteau, *Œuvres poétiques complètes*, 142.

16. Ibid., 155.

17. Ibid., 148.

18. "this / young beaming maiden / she crosses in one go the tobacco smoke / and / applies herself laughing / without any shame / facing the audience /against the livid wall / after / she leaves / into the void / hidden / up there / in his little lighthouse / the blade grinder of silences" (Cocteau, *Œuvres poétiques completes*, 148).

19. This poem clearly foreshadows the gender-bending of *Le sang d'un poète*, and also its cathexis on the black male body (the angel) which, since it is shown in negative in the film, stands as a visual inversion of—or a filmic deplunging from—whiteness. (According to Williams, in 1915–16, Cocteau stayed among tirailleurs Sénégalais at the front, Williams, *Jean Cocteau*, 58–59.)

20. Cocteau, *Œuvres poétiques complètes*, 151.

21. Ibid., 145; spacing in original.

22. "In the beam of livid rays / Characters are living / . . . / We are a beautiful film projected / By the sun and moon / and at night we keep on living without / being seen / Like the cowboys and detectives / Right and left of the screen" (Cocteau, *Œuvres poétiques complètes*, 155).

23. Ibid., 160.

24. Williams, *Jean Cocteau*, 105.

25. Cocteau, *Œuvres poétiques*, 34–35.

26. Cocteau, *Œuvres complètes*, 1:90.

27. These lines were likely recalled by André Bazin's famous article title, "Mort tous les après-midi," about a bullfighting documentary whose text was written by poet Michel Leiris (translated in Margulis ed., *Rites of Realism*, 27-31).

28. Taves, "With Williamson Beneath the Sea," 54.

29. Trick submarine films include *A Visit of the Wreck of the Maine* (1898, Méliès, #147, 20 meters), *A Drama at the Bottom of the Sea* (1901, Pathé, #372, 20 meters), *The Tunnel Under the Channel* (1907, Méliès #936–950, 300 meters), *Two Thousand Miles Under the Sea* (Méliès, 1907, 265 meters).

Twenty Thousand Miles Under the Sea (1916, US, Stuart Paton) was the first film with actual underwater shots, cf. Taves, "Novels and Rediscovered Films," 30.

30. Cocteau, *Du Cinématographe*, 80.

31. Cocteau, *Œuvres poétiques*, 131.

32. Cocteau, *Œuvres complètes*, 1:103.

33. Ibid., 103, 88.

34. Ibid., 11.

35. Cocteau, *Le Potomak*, 60.

36. Ibid., 249.

37. It was striking enough that young Sartre and Paul Nizan refer to the *Potomak* and make their own spinoff in 1926, cf. Sartre, *Écrits de jeunesse*, 26–27.

38. Cocteau, *Le Potomak*, 68.

39. Ibid., 70.

40. Ibid., 71. Edwin Abbott's book *Flatland: A Romance of Many Dimensions* was published in 1884, and Cocteau may have read its translation into French.

41. Cf. Bohn, *Rise of Surrealism*.

42. Cocteau, *Le Potomak*, 69.

43. Ibid., 17. Between 1915 and 1917 Cocteau contemplated a project he titled *The Traveler to the Left* [*Le Voyageur vers la gauche*]. This curious title refers to the marginal space that comes before alphabetic writing and informs the directionality of visual images in the West: left to right. It is both the space of death ("left" is Lat. *sinister*), that of wandering away from the path (lit., perversion), and that of the pure virtuality of language before it is written and of the image before it is projected. Cf. Cocteau, *Le Coq et l'arlequin*, 60. In *Le Potomak* a synonym is "the backstage void" (*les coulisses de vide*) (17).

44. Cocteau, *Le Potomak*, 72.

45. Cocteau, *Œuvres complètes*, 1:184.

46. Cocteau, *Œuvres poétiques complètes*, 56, 1575.

47. Cocteau, *Le Potomak*, 335.

48. In *Potomak*, can we hear (in French) *Thomas*, even *peau-Thomas*, with perhaps the -ak of *Kodak*? Cocteau collaborated with Valentine Gross in May 1916 in creating, in his own words, "half-kodak half-fresco," works. Williams, *Jean Cocteau*, 64.

49. Cocteau, *Œuvres complètes*, 1:211.

50. Ibid., 1:212.

51. Ibid., 1:208.

52. Ibid., 1:195.

53. Williams indicates that Cocteau took opium and had sexual experiences with soldiers. Williams, *Jean Cocteau*, 59.

54. Williams, *Jean Cocteau*, 62.

55. Cocteau, *Œuvres poétiques complètes*, 444.

56. Hugo, preface to *Les Contemplations*, 1856.

57. Cocteau, *Œuvres poétiques*, 445.

58. Ibid., 444.

4. JEAN EPSTEIN'S INVENTION OF CINEPOETRY

1. Epstein, "Langue d'or," *Écrits,* 1:143.

2. Crary, *Suspension of Perception;* Gordon, *Why the French Love Jerry Lewis.*

3. Romains, *Donogoo-Tonka*; *La Vision extra-rétinienne et le sens paroptique.*

4. Segalen, *Les Synesthésies et l'école symboliste,* 25.

5. Gustave Kahn, a disciple of Mallarmé, theorized rhythm as the new poetic unit in free verse in the preface "Essai sur le vers libre," *Premiers poèmes.* With physiologist Charles Henry, he may have been the first to record poetry on a phonograph in the 1880s. A friend of Marey, Henry (who may be the bicyclist in a chronophotographic sequence of Marey, see Rabinbach, *Human Motor,* 114), is one of the links between artists and poets and precinema research. A theoretician of rhythm, Alphonse Chide, alludes in 1905 to Marey's attempts to record speech on his rotative chronophotographs (Quillier, *Courts métrages,* 16).

6. Segalen, *Synesthésies,* 27.

7. Ibid., 36.

8. Seriality is one form of "le divers" (diversity), in Segalen's *Essay on Exoticism.* By "exoticism" Segalen means the open-ended diversity of human experiences, not merely non-European culture. Its opposites are homogenization and (thermodynamic) entropy, both tending toward sameness. The Taoist saying, "Let us not try to suppress the steps that led to [the answer]" (Segalen, *Essai,* 76), points to the richer diversity of the serial process over the static product: "It is in order [to increase diversity] that I unfold [*déroule*] in a particular order certain thoughts I am trying to string together [*enchaîner*]" (ibid., 75). This note of 1911 is preceded in the text by another dating from 1909:

Even in philosophy, the subject, the meaning of ideas, have a lesser import than their succession [*enchaînement*], the pace at which they engage into one another [*engrènent*] and unfold [*se déroulent*], in short, their *play.* . . . The plotting of ideas is, in philosophy, equal to orchestral or pictorial dough (ibid., 63).

Segalen made the connection between seriality and diversity most clear in 1912:

Any series, any gradation, any comparison, generates variety and diversity. Separated, objects seemed vaguely similar, homogenous; united, they oppose each other or at least "exist," with all the more force in that matter, richer and more supple, has more means and more nuanced modalities (ibid., 80).

9. Husserl's 1901 *Logical Investigations* questions how objects coalesce in perception out of their "silhouettes" or "profiles" (*Abschattung,* lit. "adumbra"). As Dermot Moran puts it: "Husserl conceives of the object as the 'totality' or 'unity of the series' generated from thinking about the infinite sweep of profiles, *Abschattungen*" (Moran, *Essential Husserl,* 115). Husserl

first considered that we do not perceive the series as such, only the object, but later reversed himself (ibid., 131–32, 164). Merleau-Ponty expanded Husserl's serialism to the work of interpreting philosophy by proposing an intriguingly three-dimensional model of language as having both "frontal" and "lateral" meanings:

. . . what if the mediation changes the sense of the concepts it employs and even the sense of the problems; what if its conclusions are merely the results of a progression which was transformed into a "work" by the interruption—an interruption which is always premature—of a life's work? Then we could not define a philosopher's thought solely in term of what he has achieved; we would have to take into account what, until the very end of his thought, he was trying to think. Naturally words, which delimit and circumscribe this unthought, must attest to it. But then these words must be understood through their lateral implications as much as through their manifest or frontal meaning. We need what Husserl called 'a poetry of the history of philosophy' which is participation in an operative thought . . . (Merleau-Ponty, *Husserl at the Limits,* 5).

10. Segalen, *Synesthésies,* 49.

11. Ibid.

12. Ibid., 53.

13. See my *Jean Epstein.*

14. *La Poésie d'aujourd'hui, un nouvel état d'intelligence*; *Bonjour cinéma.* Since 1921, *Poésie d'aujourd'hui* has not been reprinted, and only brief excerpts are reproduced in the complete works: Epstein, *Écrits,* 1: 65–69. In English, excerpts are found in Stuart Liebman's PhD dissertation, *Jean Epstein's Early Film Theory.*

15. Epstein, *La Poésie,* 75, 101–3.

16. Blasing, *Lyric Poetry.*

17. Ibid., 9, 10.

18. Ibid., 157.

19. Castin, *Sens et sensible,* 19.

20. Epstein, "Le Phénomène littéraire," 43. It was serialized in *L'Esprit Nouveau* in 1921.

21. Epstein, *La Poésie,* 27.

22. Ibid., 12.

23. See Rabinach, *Human Motor,* chapter 6, "Mental fatigue, neurasthenia, and Civilization," 146–78.

24. Epstein, *La Poésie*, 32. Epstein's nervous pathways model resembles Freud's notion of innervation: "Emotion, on its way towards the genital sense which its mission is to awaken, encounters a center of resistance; it breaks down, coils on itself, yet settles there, and all other emotions of a similar kind passing through the same center, will have the same fate. . . . Aesthetic emotion, in its purest most disinterested form is but a deviation from genital emotion" (*Poésie d'aujourd'hui,* 32). For Walter Benjamin's model of innervation, see Miriam Hansen, "Benjamin and Cinema," 41–73; and for a possible influence of French film theoreticians' innervated notions on Benjamin, see my "Epstein's Photogénie as Corporeal Vision."

25. Ibid., 212.
26. Ibid., 48.
27. Ibid., 51.
28. Ibid., 53.
29. Ibid., 73.
30. Ibid., 74.
31. Ibid., 41.
32. Ibid., 170.
33. The movie lexicon was far from settled. Émile Vuillermoz uses "superpositions" (superimpositions) in an article on montage in 1920 (cited in Ghali, *L'Avant-garde cinématographique*, 184), while in 1929 "images superimpressionnées" (superimposed images) is used by Moussinac, *Panoramique du cinéma*, 60.
34. Epstein, *La Poésie*, 70.
35. Ibid., 83.
36. See Cameron, *Visceral Sensory Neuroscience*. For the identification of coenaesthesis with the sense of all the senses—Aristotle's "common sense"—see Heller-Roazen, *Inner Touch*. Coenaesthesis is not to be confused with synesthesia, though both involve the interrelation of the senses.
37. Bernard Stiegler has proposed that the Kantian schema is a kind of cinema in *Le Temps du cinéma et la question du mal-être*.
38. For Epstein's insistence that affects subtend logic, see *La Lyrosophie*, which attempts a deconstruction of the priority of logic over sensibility.
39. Gance, *Prisme*, 259.
40. See Gilles Deleuze's multiple references to Epstein in his two *Cinema* books.
41. Epstein, *La Poésie*, 171.
42. Ibid., 203.
43. Ibid., 145.
44. Ibid., 77.
45. Ibid., 209.
46. Ibid., 171.
47. Ibid., 58.
48. Epstein encapsulates the /screen⇔page⇔skin/ homology as: "projected on the screen, I land in the double space [*l'interligne*] of the lips," (ibid., 171). The close-up is not (just) scopophilic: it mobilizes an ethics of proximity and vulnerability close to that of Emmanuel Levinas. Curiously, Chaplin figures as a paragon of vulnerability for both Epstein and Levinas (in his 1934 *De l'Évasion*) while the key chapter in *Otherwise than Being, or Beyond Essence* is titled "Proximity," Epstein's first homology. A passage from Epstein's *Bonjour cinéma* reads:

The close-up alters drama through the impression of proximity. Pain is within reach. If I extend my arm, I touch you, intimacy. . . . I count the eyelashes of this suffering. I could have the taste of its tears. Never before had a face bent over mine this way. It comes to the closest, and I pursue it forehead against forehead. It isn't even true that there is air between us; I eat it. It [the face] is in me like a sacrament. Maximal visual acuity (Epstein, *Bonjour cinéma*, 104).

49. Ibid., 172.
50. Ibid., 193.
51. Ibid., 173.
52. See Sarah Keller, "Introduction," in *Jean Epstein: Critical Essays and New Translations* for the verse poetics of *Bonjour Cinéma.*
53. Jean Epstein "Magnification," and "The Senses 1 (b)," translated in Abel, *FFTC,* 1:235–41, and 1:241–46. For a recent book relying on both texts, see Casetti, *Eye of the Century,* 32–33, 44, 59, 65.
54. Epstein, *Écrits,* 1:102.
55. Epstein, *Bonjour cinéma,* 14.
56. Ibid., 43.
57. Ibid., 72.
58. Epstein, *Écrits,* 1:140.
59. See Pierre Lévy's point about language as a matrix of virtuality in *Becoming Virtual.* See also Rotman, *Becoming Besides Ourselves,* 13–31.
60. Epstein, *Écrits,* 1:127.
61. For nondeaf spectators, since, as producers quickly learned from outraged mail by lip-readers, deaf viewers had paradoxically access to the actors' filmed speech.
62. Epstein, *La Poésie,* 114.
63. Epstein, *Écrits,* 1:114.
64. Ibid.
65. Epstein, *La Poésie,* 115.
66. Ibid., 116.
67. Ibid., 101. Since Gourmont is a ubiquitous reference for Epstein, we may connect the "sentence-thought" to inner monologue, with which Gourmont experimented in his poetic novels, and which he associates explicitly with cinema in a book review of 1898. Of Émile Dujardin's *Les Lauriers sont coupés,* the first novel using inner monologue, de Gourmont writes: "This faculty of representing life to one's self, and just like a tableau, but an animated tableau [*tableau animé*] in which protagonists are walking, moving about in a thousand small gestures, he has used it in the most curious fashion in a novel that seems for literature an anticipated transposition of the cinématographe" (Gourmont, *Le Deuxième Livre des masques,* 74).
68. Ibid.
69. Ibid., 63.
70. Ibid., 98.
71. Ibid., 63.
72. Ibid., 70.
73. Ibid., 108.
74. Epstein, *Le Phénomène littéraire,* 52.
75. Ibid., 41.
76. Ibid.
77. I am grateful for the members of the Interdisciplinary Symposium on Jean Epstein organized by Sarah Keller and Jason Paul at the University of Chicago in 2007 for their collective discussion on this topic.
78. Epstein, *La Poésie,* 177.

79. Ibid., 131–32.
80. Epstein, *Le Phénomène littéraire,* 58.
81. Ibid.
82. Epstein, *Écrits,* 1:137.
83. Ibid., 1:140.
84. Epstein, *La Poésie,* 170.
85. Ibid., 134.
86. Ibid., 134–35.
87. Apollinaire, *L'Enchanteur pourrissant,* 94.
88. Epstein, *Écrits,* 1:141–42.
89. Ibid., 1:136.
90. Vidal, *Luis Buñuel,* 25.

5. BRETON'S SURREALISM, OR HOW TO SUBLIMATE CINEPOETRY

1. Breton, *Œuvres complètes*, 3:903.
2. Durozoi, *History of the Surrealist Movement*, 65.
3. I will capitalize Surrealism when referring to Breton's theory and movement, and use lowercase when it refers to the theories of surrealism of Apollinaire, Dermée, Goll, and Epstein.
4. For overviews, see Kuenzli, *Dada and Surrealism Film;* and Harper and Stone, *Unsilvered Screen.*
5. Finkelstein, *Screen in Surrealist Art*, 12.
6. Breton, *Œuvres,* 3:903.
7. Polizzoti notes that Breton defended Vaché against Théodore Fraenkel by saying Vaché was "all that I love." Polizzoti, *Revolution of the Mind*, 78, 639. Vaché was found dead of an opium overdose together with another man, both of them naked, in 1919. Polizzoti links Breton's homophobia to his love for Vaché (ibid., 89).
8. Béhar and Carassou, *Le Surréalisme*, 447.
9. Breton, *Œuvres complètes*, 1:1237.
10. Polizzoti mentions two other actresses, an "Alice" in Nantes, and Cyprian Giles, Adrienne Monnier's sister (Polizzoti, *Revolution of the Mind*, 49, 78).
11. Breton, *Œuvres,* 1:1745.
12. See Butler, "Irma Vep, Vamp in the City," 215; and Callahan, "Screening Musidora," 71.
13. Breton corrected (badly it seems) the proofs of *The Way of Guermantes* in 1920 (Polizzotti, *Revolution of the Mind,* 130–31).
14. Breton, *Œuvres,* 1:673.
15. Tamagne, *History of Homosexuality in Europe,* 197.
16. Breton, *Œuvres,* 1:668–69.
17. Ibid., 1:202. Breton leaves out Vaché's closing remark in he letter: "I've read the article (in *Film*) on cinema by L[ouis] A[ragon]." It refers to Aragon's important 1917 cinepoetic piece, "On Décor," published in *Le Film* (Abel, *FFTC*, 1:165–68). Vaché, *Lettres de guerre*, 24.

18. For Oedipal readings of *Un Chien andalou*, see Liebman, "*Un Chien Andalou*," 143–58; and Short, *Age of Gold*, 90–101. For Cocteau's *Blood of A Poet*, see Williams, *Jean Cocteau*, 142–51; and Azoury and Lalanne, *Cocteau et le cinéma*, 29–39.

19. See Williams, *Cocteau*, 76.

20. *SIC* 8/9/10 (October 1916), cited in Apollinaire, *Œuvres en prose*, 2:986.

21. Jacob, "Petite chronique cinématographique," 5.

22. Sanouillet, *Dada à Paris*, 51.

23. Soupault, "Indifférence, poème cinématographique" and "Note sur le cinéma," 1–2; "Photographies animées," 2; "Photographies animées," 1.

24. A partial list: Dermée, *Films, Duodramas, Soliloques, Contes* (Dermée cofounded both *Nord-Sud* with Pierre Reverdy in 1917 and *L'Esprit Nouveau* with Le Corbusier in 1920); Birot, *Cinéma, Drames, Poèmes*; Cocteau, *Carte blanche*; Jules Romains, Blaise Cendrars, Irène Hillel-Erlanger also published important poem-scenarios in 1918–19 (see Chapter 7); in 1920, Dermée's wife, Céline Arnauld launched her own short-lived journal *Projecteur* (Projector) and in 1923 the couple launched *Mouvement accéléré* (Accelerated motion). See Martin-Schmets, "Céline Arnauld," 171–82. Richard Abel ventures that *L'Esprit nouveau* relayed the waning interest of the Dada/Surrealist journal *Littérature* for cinema (Abel, *FFTC*, 1:216 n9).

25. Polizzoti, *Revolution of the Mind*, 57. It appears that Fraenkel and Breton also played a trick in 1917 on André Beucler (Sanouillet, *Dada à Paris*, 75 n74) also gravitating toward cinema (see Chapter 10).

26. Breton, *Œuvres*, 1:293.

27. See Apollinaire, *Œuvres en prose*, 2:1683–84.

28. Breton, *Œuvres*, 1:307.

29. Ibid., 1:246.

30. Epstein, *La Poésie*, 132, 135, 135.

31. Epstein, *Bonjour cinéma*, 94. See Abel, *FFTC*, 1:236; translation modified. The Max Ernst exhibition was reviewed in *Le Promenoir*'s third and last issue in May 1921. Breton, *Œuvres*, 1:1265 n4.

32. Breton, *Œuvres*, 1:239.

33. Ibid., 1:274.

34. Dermée, "Découverte du lyrisme," 29–37; quotes from 32, 34, and 37. Dermée also alludes to Freud and repression, 34.

35. In 1924, Picabia, Goll, and Dermée each engaged in a polemics with Breton about his appropriation of the word "surrealism." Marguerite Bonnet dismisses these recriminations on the basis that each of them "proposed a definition as broad as it is vague" (Breton, *Œuvres*, 1:1137). The articulation of a cinepoetic aesthetics allows us to consider Epstein's and Dermée's formulations to be in fact more focused than Breton's.

36. Soupault, *Les Cahiers du mois*, 179.

37. See Soupault, *Écrits de cinéma*, 23–25.

38. Breton, *Œuvres*, 1:128–29.

39. Soupault, "Observation présentée par M. Philippe Soupault," 8.

40. Polizzotti, *Revolution of the Mind*, 106.

41. See Azoury and Lalanne, *Fantômas*; and Gauthier and Lacassin, *Louis Feuillade,* for the cultural history of *Fantômas.* Breton later wrote with Aragon a "scenario" dedicated to Musidora, "Le Trésor des Jésuites," Breton, *Œuvres,* 1:994–1014.

42. Lacassin, *A la recherche de l'empire caché*, 125, 132.

43. Finkelstein, *Screen in Surrealist Art*, 106.

44. Breton *Œuvres,* 1:54, 1133.

45. Ibid., 1:1130–46.

46. Ibid., 1:xxxviii.

47. *Le Crapouillot* was a maverick journal for soldiers that turned to the arts as the war wore on (in part because of state censorship due to fears of mutiny). It published extensive issues on cinema and its relations to literature in 1920, 1921, and 1922. After 1920 *Le Crapouillot* took position against Dada. See Varagnac, "Dada," 8–9. In May 1920, the *Crapouillot* editor Jean Galtier-Boissière and his team engaged in a shouting match with Soupault during the Festival Dada evening, see Sanouillet, *Dada à Paris,* 154 n17.

48. This project alludes to *Fantômas* according to Bohn, *Apollinaire and the Faceless Man*, 63–64.

49. Sanouillet, *Dada à Paris,* 159.

50. Some episodes are unsigned, yet this one is recognizably Drieu's because the mention of "The burial of Jean Coqueteau" is yet another dig at Cocteau from the Breton clan to which he belonged.

51. Drieu La Rochelle, "L'Homme sans tête, 16.

52. Breton, *Œuvres,* 1:53.

53. Ibid., 1:534–35.

54. Ibid., 1:536.

55. Ibid., 1:325.

56. Ibid., 1:354 n1.

57. Ibid., 1:325.

58. Ibid., 1:327.

59. Ibid., 1:338.

60. Epstein, *La Poésie*, 131, 135.

61. Breton, *Œuvres,* 1:338.

62. Ibid., 1:328.

63. Epstein, *Poésie d'aujourd'hui,* 100.

64. Ibid., 156.

65. Breton, *Œuvres,* 1:345.

66. Ibid., 1:346.

67. See Ghali, *L'Avant-garde cinématographique*, 45 (citing Delluc); Delluc, *Louis Delluc*, 358; Abel, *French Cinema,* 26.

68. For a keen reading of the photo-cinematic difference in this film, see Conley, *Cartographic Cinema*, chapter 1, "Icarian Cinema: *Paris Qui Dort*," 23–39. Only passengers in a plane, the watchman at the top of the Eiffel Tower, and the scientist's daughter remain mobile, the latter sending an SOS over the radio received by the others. *Nadja*, written in 1927, ends on a newspaper account of a lost plane sending an SOS.

69. Clair, *Les Cahiers du mois*, 90.

70. Breton, *Œuvres,* 2:680.

71. I am indebted to Tom Gunning's exegesis of Breton's "convulsive beauty" in his "New Thresholds of Vision: Instantaneous Photography and the Early Cinema of the Lumière," in *Impossible Presence*, 71–99.

72. Breton, *Œuvres,* 1:327–28; Saint-Pol-Roux, *Cinéma vivant*, 24; Gance, *Prisme*, 70.

73. Breton, *Œuvres,* 1:900–901. An 1894 critical appraisal of Saint-Pol-Roux by Remy de Gourmont already saw in him "one of the most fecund and astonishing inventors of images and metaphors," cited by Hamot, "La Clef et la cithare," 73.

74. Saint-Pol-Roux, *De l'art magnifique*, 25. Both Villiers-de-L'Isle-Adam and Mallarmé were under the sway of what constitutes the second Hegelian moment in French thought, after that of Victor Cousin and Saint-Simonians between 1820 and 1840, and before the turn to the *Phenomenology of Spirit* in the late 1920s by Wahl, Bataille, and Queneau, and subsequent to Kojève, by Lacan et al.

75. Décaudin, *La Crise des valeurs,* 500–1.

76. Saint-Pol-Roux, *Cinéma,* 32.

77. Ibid., 77.

78. Ibid., 70, 114, 117.

79. Flusser, *Pour une philosophie*; Maynard, *Engine of Visualization*; Flusser, *Pour une philosophie.*

80. Saint-Pol-Roux, *Cinéma,* 24.

81. Ibid., 113.

82. Bolter and Grusin, *Remediation*, 21.

83. Saint-Pol-Roux, *Cinéma,* 111.

84. Ibid., 15.

85. Ibid.

86. Ibid., 39.

87. Ibid., 22.

88. A prose poem of Saint-Pol-Roux dated 1895, titled "The Stain-Glass Window Poet," recounts in terms similar to Breton's automatic text about the movie theater how the poet broke with the autoeroticism of the screen (he turns his back on "Onan's emblem") by breaking with his inkwell the female imago that the stain-glass window bears, from whose lips a medieval scroll unfurls with the words "I am the Truth": " . . . the window exploded into shards, the Image scattering in useless plates [*vaines lamelles*], its dislocated scroll at my feet" ("Le Poète au vitrail," cited in Briant, *Saint-Pol-Roux*, 178–79).

89. Saint-Pol-Roux, *Cinéma,* 118.

90. Saint-Pol-Roux wrote a "Petit traité de déshumanisme," which includes what looks like a sketchy film scenario titled "Osmose" (Osmosis) (*De l'art magnifique*, 86–101). In *Cinéma vivant*, the sublation of sexual reproduction is ambivalently sexist ("O, this fruit—the mouth of American women stars!" 78) and feminist, in seeing "the material fluid" of light as "the hystery of matter" (53), thus effacing any metaphysically dominant male spirit. Cinematic self-creation, surprisingly described as coming out of

"scientific masturbation" (81), is also a step toward the "hermaphrodite" (104), and ultimately broader sexual desires: " . . . cinema will be live. Until then we will be but *voyeurs*. Women's legs and breast are the coals of the future fire. Men should get the hell out. They behave like pimps. What is needed are wings: there are only fins" (114).

91. Saint-Pol-Roux, *Cinéma,* 62.

92. Ibid., 24.

93. Ibid., 80.

94. Ibid., 68.

95. Ibid., 69.

96. Ibid., 81.

97. Ibid., 67.

98. Ibid., 89.

99. Saint-Pol-Roux, *De l'Art*, 37.

100. Saint-Pol-Roux, *La Repoétique*, 18, 74, 75.

101. Ibid., 55.

102. Saint-Pol-Roux, *Cinéma*, 25, 28, 32, 62.

103. Saint-Pol-Roux, *De L'Art,* 15.

104. Saint-Pol-Roux, *Cinéma,* 112.

105. Breton, *Œuvres,* 1:328.

106. Saint-Pol-Roux, *Cinéma*, 51, 57, 119.

107. Ibid., 110.

108. Ibid., 27.

109. Fonds Saint-Pol-Roux, Ms 9823.8, Bibliothèque Littéraire Jacques Doucet.

110. Saint-Pol-Roux, *Cinéma*, 78–80.

111. *Cinéma vivant,* 119. There is record of one meeting between them in Brittany in 1936, when they discussed Gance's film adaptation of Saint-Pol-Roux's libretto for the opera, *Louise*. Gance, *Archives* no. 213.

112. Breton, *Œuvres,* 4:1072. Breton's appraisal of Polyvision reads literally: "making us pass to 'the other side of the screen'" (since *De l'autre côté du miroir* is the translation of Carroll's title into French), exactly what happened in Breton's automatic text of 1924.

113. Breton, *Œuvres,* 3:1099. Hubert dates Breton's response to 1930 (ibid., 1465–66).

114. Breton, *Œuvres,* 2:1262.

115. Breton, *Œuvres,* 1:995, 1022.

6. DOING FILMIC THINGS WITH WORDS

1. Breton and Aragon, "Liquidation," 1–5.

2. Poulaille, *Charles Chaplin*, 114. Cendrars, ever the mythomaniac, affirmed that he shared a room with Chaplin in London in 1911 (ibid.).

3. Dyssord, "En marge du cinéma," 668. See Meusy, *Paris-Palaces,* 424–26.

4. Cendrars, "Charlot et la guerre," 78.

5. Polizzotti, *Revolution of the Mind*, 127.

6. Abel, *FFTC,* 1:95–99.

7. Drésa, "Leur Charlie et notre Charlot," 17–18.

8. Delluc, *Charlot,* 8.

9. Cocteau, *Carte blanche,* 37–38.

10. Cf. Trotter, *Cinema and Modernism,* 194–95, for Bazin's reading of this sequence via Caillois's mimicry.

11. This is the name given by Aragon to film reviews which are pieces of writing in their own right and do not endeavor to describe the plot at all. Virmaux and Virmaux, *Les Surréalistes* 62.

12. Cited in Poulaille, *Charles Chaplin,* 119.

13. Anon., "Au cinéma," 8.

14. Louis Delluc notes regarding the drunk skit of *One A.M.,* that in the Karno troup objects were "played" by other actors: bearskin, collapsible bed, etc. Delluc, *Charlot,* 17.

15. Aragon, "Du décor," 8–10; Virmaux and Virmaux, *Les Surréalistes,* 105–11; "On Décor," in *Shadow,* 28–31; Abel, *FFTC,* 1:165–68.

16. Abel, *FFTC,* 1:167, translation modified ("*manivelle*" is not "starting-handle" but a "crank" with its dual camera/automotive meaning).

17. Soupault, *Écrits de cinéma,* 23.

18. Noë, *Action in Perception.*

19. Abel, *FFTC,* 1:168; translation modified to reemphasize Aragon's point that no film is projected. Interestingly, Breton and Aragon end their scenario "The Treasure of the Jesuits," on Musidora uttering a modified citation of Mallarmé: "The world should end on a beautiful café terrace," Mallarmé having said, "The world is made to end in a beautiful book." Breton, *Œuvres,* 1:1014.

20. David Trotter's notion of Chaplin's "hypermimesis" is one example, in *Cinema and Modernism,* 183, 198.

21. Virmaux and Virmaux, *Les Surréalistes et le cinéma,* 62.

22. See Marguerite Bonnet's account in Breton, *Œuvres,* 1:1331–38. See also Bertho, "Autour de la revue *Surréalisme,*" 24–51.

23. Goll, "Exemple de surréalisme," xi.

24. Goll [Tristan Torsi], *Films (Verse)*; Goll, *Die Chaplinade*; Goll, *Le Nouvel Orphée,* 10–41.

25. Fierens, *La Nouvelle revue française,* 126 (March 1, 1924), cited in Bertho, "Autour de la revue *Surréalisme,*" 28.

26. Goll, *La Chaplinade,* 17–18.

27. Ibid.

28. Ibid., 30.

29. Ibid., 34.

30. Ibid., 22.

31. Ibid.

32. The "bazars de la charité" (*Chaplinade* 12) point to the disastrous Paris fire of 1897 that almost engulfed cinema, while Charlot dressed as the "King of Heart" (11) refers to Méliès's trick films of images coming to life, such as the 1905 *Les Cartes vivantes,* where a Queen of Hearts comes to life. See Doane, *Emergence,* 108–12. Chaplin's films like *Soldier's Arms, The*

Vagabond, *Easy Street*, *The Fireman*, etc. (18) are cited and remixed: the billposter takes a collection for Charlot and flees with the money, as Chaplin's protagonist does to musicians in *The Vagabond*.

33. Ibid., 21.

34. Braga, "Un film de Charlot," 8. Tom Gunning indicates that Charles-Lucien Lépine and Segundo de Chomón's *Le Tour du monde d'un policier* (1906) contains binocular shots like that which Goll describes (personal communication).

35. Poulaille, "Charlie Chaplin écrivain," 56, 54.

36. Fierens, "Charlot Little Titch et la poésie," 71.

37. Soupault, *Charlot*, iv–v.

38. Ibid., iii–iv.

39. Goll, *Chaplinade*, 11.

40. Epstein, *Écrits*, 1:151.

41. For instance, Hanna Arendt and Albert Memmi thought so; see Desser and Friedman, *American Jewish Filmmakers*, 9. For Chaplin and Jewishness, see Lynn, *Charlie Chaplin and His Times*.

42. Marcus, *Lipstick Traces*, 340–43.

43. Soupault, *Charlot*, 7.

44. Ponge, "Le sérieux défait," 50.

45. Soupault, *Charlot*, 196.

46. Cendrars, *Tout autour*, 3:141.

47. Epstein, *Écrits*, 1:129.

48. Jarry, *Œuvres complètes*, 1:74.

49. Jarry, "La mécanique d'Ixion," 2:405.

50. Jarry, *Œuvres complètes*, 1:823 (*Les jours et les nuits*).

51. Michaux, *Œuvres complètes*, 1:9–15.

52. Ibid., 1, 11 n.

53. Ibid., 1, 11.

54. Michaux, *Œuvres*, 1:43.

55. Ibid.

56. Guido, *L'Âge du rythme*, 336–40.

57. Hellens, "Avant-propos," 50.

58. Cendrars, *Tout autour*, 3:142–44.

59. Artaud, *Œuvres complètes*, 3:97.

60. Artaud, *Œuvres*, 3:98.

61. Ibid., 3:99.

62. Walter Benjamin points to an article by Soupault on Chaplin that locates the latter's "poetry" as a "historical phenomenon," in its taking daily experience as material "to construct a film with a theme and variations." Benjamin, "Chaplin in Retrospect," 222–24.

63. Artaud, *Œuvres*, 3:99.

7. THE POEM-SCENARIO IN THE INTERWAR (1917–1928)

1. Fondane, *Écrits pour le cinéma*, 20.

2. Cendrars, "Musickissme," in *Complete Poems*, 91, 279.

3. Cendrars, "Le Film de la fin du monde," 419–30. It was retitled "La Fin du monde filmée par l'ange N.-D." in 1919 when it was published as a book (Cendrars, *Tout autour,* 3:361).

4. Cendrars, *Tout autour,* 7:359.

5. Ibid., 3:361.

6. Cendrars, *Inédits secrets*, 238–40. M. Cendrars, *Blaise Cendrars*, 221–25. See Cloët's detailed piece, "Blaise Cendrars ou le cinématypographe," *Revue polaire*, revue-polaire.com/spip.php?article53#nh87 (accessed 11/11/11).

7. M. Cendrars, *Blaise Cendrars*, 221.

8. Ibid., 225.

9. Cendrars, *Tout autour,* 6:508.

10. M. Cendrars, *Blaise Cendrars*, 221.

11. Cendrars, *Tout autour,* 3:x.

12. Ibid., 7:265.

13. Cf. Leys, *Trauma*, chapter 3, "Traumatic Cures: Shell Shock, Janet, and the Question of Memory," 83–119.

14. Cendrars, *Tout autour,* 3:19.

15. Ibid., 7:274, 276.

16. Ibid., 3:20.

17. Ibid., 3:22.

18. Ibid., 3:35.

19. Ibid., 7:274.

20. Ibid., 3:35.

21. Ibid., 3:277.

22. Ibid., 7:291.

23. Doane, *Emergence of Cinematic Time*, 27. Tom Gunning and André Gaudreault developed the concept of "cinema of attractions" for the first years of cinema during which the experience of the apparatus itself was central. Playing films backward to see the spectacle of laws of physics being broken was a major part of early film's appeal. Lumière shorts were often shot so as to be shown backward, such as *Ecriture à l'envers* [Reverse writing] (Lumière 1896, #42), or *Charcuterie mécanique* [Mechanical charcuterie] (Lumière 1896, #107), in which a pig enters a building while cold cuts come out the other end, the short being then reversed to show sausages turning back into a pig walking backward. Sadoul, *Lumière et Méliès,* 126–27.

24. See Antongini, *D'Annunzio*, 138; Gambacorti, *Storie di cinema e letteratura*, 271–315.

25. I quote and translate from the French version given in Janicot, *Anthologie du cinéma invisible*, 193–97.

26. Janicot, *Anthologie,* 193.

27. Ibid., 194.

28. Canudo is celebrated by Epstein and Dulac; he was a close friend of Apollinaire; his novel *Les Libérés. Mémoires d'un aliéniste* (1911) strongly influenced Cendrars's *Moravagine* (Cendrars, *Œuvres,* 7:xxvii).

29. Canudo, *L'Autre aile.* The novel, first serialized in *Le Figaro* in December 1920, was published in book form in 1922, made into a film in

1923—with the novel and the scenario republished together in 1924. [Since there are two sets of Arabic page numbers in the book, the second set is given as II, 5]. See Canudo, *L'Usine aux images*, 113–18.

30. Canudo, *L'Autre aile*, II, 5.

31. Ibid.

32. Ibid., II, 5.

33. Cocteau's 1915 poem "Les hangars" takes the huge airplane hangars at Billancourt as sensorially analogous to the space in American action movies, notably *The Lonedale Operator* (US, 1911, dir. D. W. Griffith), Cocteau, *Œuvres poétiques,* 55–59, n1575.

34. Ibid., 8.

35. Canudo, "L'Attaque dans l'orage," 14.

36. Canudo, *L'Autre aile*, 17.

37. Ibid., 26.

38. Ibid., 35.

39. Ibid., 42.

40. Ibid., 42–43.

41. Ibid., 56.

42. Ibid., 72, 74.

43. Ibid., 78–79.

44. Ibid., II, 76.

45. Ibid., II, 5.

46. Hitchcok's *Vertigo* follows a similar emplotment as *La Bréhatine*, with fiction preceding reality, a character's fictive death causes her diegetic death, and a fall due to a misprision.

47. Apollinaire and Billy, *La Bréhatine*, 79.

48. Ibid., 75.

49. Desnos, "Minuit à Quatorze heure, essai de merveilleux moderne," *Les Cahiers du mois, scénarios* 12, 1925, 106–13. Reprinted in Desnos, *Les Rayons et les ombres, cinéma*, 205–12.

50. The situation is partly autobiographical and partly inspired by Shelley—both his accidental drowning and that of his first wife Harriet, who committed suicide in the Serpentine of Hyde Park. Desnos mentions a project of scenario based on Trelawny's accounts of the aftermath of Shelley's death. Bibliothèque Littéraire Jacques Doucet, Fonds Robert Desnos, DSN 296.

51. Benjamin Fondane considers that cinema even preempted Artaud's theater career: "But read his manifesto: *The Theater and Its Double*; it seems [Artaud] is only looking for one thing: the lost path of cinema" (Fondane, *Écrits pour le cinéma*, 105).

52. Artaud, *Œuvres complètes,* 3:11–15.

53. Ibid., 11.

54. Ibid., 73.

55. Ibid., 74.

56. Ibid., 134–35.

57. Morel, "Artaud et le cinéma," 117–32.

58. Artaud, *Œuvres*, 69.

59. Artaud, *Œuvres,* 3:12; *Œuvres,* 101.

60. Ibid., 109.
61. Ibid., 105.
62. Ibid., 106.
63. Morel, "Artaud et le cinéma," 121.
64. Artaud, *Œuvres,* 3:11; *Œuvres,* 101.
65. Morel, "Artaud et le cinéma," 116.
66. Artaud, *Œuvres,* 3:12; *Œuvres,* 102.
67. Artaud, *Œuvres,* 3:15; *Œuvres,* 103.
68. Artaud, *Œuvres,* 3:80.
69. Ibid., 3:78.
70. Artaud wrote eight finished treatments/scenarios, and had half a dozen more projects in mind. Morel, *Artaud et le cinéma,* 116–18. The premiere of Germaine Dulac's adaptation of *The Seashell and the Clergyman* occasioned a clash between the Surrealists and the photogénie/cinégraphie group which made Artaud's collaboration with the latter more difficult. See Virmaux and Virmaux, *Artaud-Dulac.*
71. Breton in any case would have received it this way: in 1926, he excluded both Soupault and Artaud from the movement (with a final break for Artaud in 1929), purging two of its most gifted cinepoets.
72. Artaud, *Œuvres,* 3:80.
73. Ibid., 3:97.
74. The poem titled "Par amour" is reproduced in *Voyages en kaléidoscope* (137–41). Another visual poem of hers, "Tour du monde et coeur du monde" was published in Epstein's review *Le Promenoir* in 1921, and another Lucretian cinepoem, "Diaphragme," can be found in Dulac's archives.
75. Hillel-Erlanger, *Voyages en kaléïdoscope,* 13.
76. Carrouges, *Les Machines célibataires,* 165–79.
77. Ibid., 16.
78. Ibid., 17.
79. Ibid., 16.
80. Idem.
81. Artaud, *Œuvres complètes,* 3:22.
82. In notes dated 1914, Duchamp enisages a dictionary based on "films, shot in close-up, of parts of large objects," with "each film . . . the representation of a group of words in a sentence or separated so that this film takes on a new signification . . . and serves as basis for a kind of writing that would no longer have an alphabet or words but signs (films) now emancipated from the 'baby talk' of ordinary languages" (Duchamp, *Duchamp du signe,* 111).
83. Goulet, *Optiques,* Part III: "Villiers, Verne, and Claretie, Towards a Fin-de-Siècle Optogrammatology," 155–221.
84. It also resembles a world wide web in that, "The Speculator will be able to check the rise and fall [of stocks] . . . while the Journalist will have the joy of seeing the Earth transformed into a thousand pages devoured by the Public" (Hillel-Erlanger, *Voyages,* 17). Yet the "medley crowd" gives much better images than "a select and polished audience," which generates but "a bland and flabby agglomeration" of images (ibid., 88).
85. Ibid., 20.

86. Ibid., 23.
87. Ibid., 20.
88. Ibid., 36.
89. Ibid., 52.
90. Ibid., 53.
91. Ibid., 91.
92. Ibid., 104.
93. Ibid., 107.
94. Rolland, *La Révolte*. The book was self-published by Rolland and Masereel in 209 copies and Rolland never allowed it to be reprinted. The rights page reads: "For the adaptation [mise-en-scène], contact Frans Masereel, etc."
95. Rolland, *La Révolte,* 13.
96. Ibid., 14.
97. Ibid., 24.
98. Idem.
99. Ibid., 25.
100. Ibid., 18.
101. Ibid., 25.
102. Ibid., 42.

8. REEMBODIED WRITING

1. Isou, "Préface," 21 n.
2. Prédal, *50 ans de cinéma français*, 838.
3. The Blum-Byrnes accord opened France to Hollywood's war backlist of more than seven hundred films, flooding French screens over a two-year period and dwarfing the national production of one hundred sixty movies (Prédal *50 ans*, 40, 836).
4. Bancquart, "D'une intériorisation de la poésie," 20.
5. Péret, *Literary Debate,* 151. The masked man was originally holding a pillbox for a tanning pill with the motto: "pillules Paul pour personnes pâles"—hence the dark mask. Allain and Souvestre found it in the office of their publisher, airbrushed the pillbox and motto, and put a knife in his hand. See Lacassin, *A La recherche,* 142.
6. Péret, *Literary Debates*, 153.
7. Sartre, "Présentation," 34, 41.
8. Bataille, *Œuvres complètes*, 11:102.
9. Schwartz, *It's So French*, 59, 61. Erlanger's first attempt was curtailed by horrendous timing: it opened, September 1, 1939, the day Nazi troops invaded Poland.
10. Stills are reproduced in Bellows and McDougall, *Science Is Fiction*, 60–63. Painlevé is one of the nine collaborators of Ivan Goll's 1924 single-issue journal *Surrealism*.
11. See Lowry, *Filmology*, 16–28; Le Forestier, "Entre cinéisme et filmologie," 113–40.
12. Merleau-Ponty, "Le Cinéma," 937.

13. Ibid., 940.
14. Ibid., 941.
15. Valéry, "L'Enseignement de la poétique au Collège de France," in *Œuvres,* 1:1442.
16. Merleau-Ponty, "Le Cinéma," 943.
17. Sartre, *Qu'est-ce que la littérature?,* 18.
18. For Sartre's paradoxical translation of poetry into prose, see Guerlac, *Literary Polemics.*
19. Bazin, *Qu'est-ce que le cinéma,* 19, 23.
20. Ibid., 22.
21. Barjavel, *Le Cinéma total,* 9.
22. Ibid., 14.
23. Ibid., 60.
24. Ibid., 11.
25. Ibid., 64.
26. Ibid.
27. Ibid., 63.
28. Ibid., 11.
29. Ibid., 71.
30. Ibid., 104.
31. Ibid., 26.
32. Ibid., 15.
33. Ibid., 54.
34. Cf. Epstein, *Écrits,* 2, "Le Gros plan du son," 105–12; "Technique de poésie en quantité industrielle," 244–49.
35. Giraudoux, *Le Film de la Duchesse de Langeais.*
36. Barjavel, *Le Cinéma,* 91.
37. Ibid., 93.
38. Bazin, *Qu'est-ce que le cinéma?,* 23.
39. Barjavel, *Cinéma total,* 10.
40. Bazin's four-page article cites three texts, by Villiers-de-L'Isle-Adam, Paul Nadar, and "P. Potoniée [*sic*]." Barjavel in his 106 pages cites only from two texts by Jean Epstein and "Georges Potonniée" (19, 48). Why Bazin does not mention Barjavel's text probably has to do with the atmosphere of purge at the Liberation. Barjavel's publisher Robert Denoël was assassinated in 1945 for his ties with the German Occupation.
41. Adorno, *Prisms,* 34.
42. My discussion engages with Hirsch, *Afterimage,* chapter 2, "Night and Fog and the Origins of Posttraumatic Cinema," 28–62. Convergent with my reading is Debarati Sanyal, "Auschwitz as Allegory in Night and Fog," which deploys allegory as an ethical disclosure of vectors of complicity in the film.
43. Hirsch, *Afterimage,* 18–19.
44. Ibid., 19.
45. Ibid., 23.
46. Ibid., 15.
47. Ibid., 57.

48. Ibid., 56.
49. Ibid., 60.
50. Ibid., 62.
51. Cayrol, *Poèmes de la nuit et du brouillard*, 10.
52. Ibid., 14.
53. Idem.
54. Cayrol, "De La mort à la vie."
55. Ibid., 74.
56. Ibid., 64.
57. Ibid., 67.
58. Ibid., 78. Cayrol's language sounds Heideggerian when he mentions "the possibilities of dying." In *Being and Time*, death is referred to as "the possibility of the absolute impossibility of Dasein" (Heidegger, *Being and Time*, 294). Heidegger further specifies death as "that possibility which is one's ownmost, which is nonrelational, and which is not to be outstripped" (ibid.). Being a survivor opens another ontology of death in which the self has been radically *disowned* of death.
59. Ibid., 88.
60. Ibid., 94.
61. Ibid., 103–4.
62. Ibid., 89.
63. Ibid., 94.
64. Ibid., 84.
65. Ibid., 96.
66. Leys, *Trauma*, 230–33.
67. Cayrol, "De la mort à la vie," 69.
68. Ibid., 49.
69. Ibid., 53.
70. Ibid., 48.
71. Ibid., 60.
72. Ibid., 92.
73. Ibid., 94.
74. Ibid., 93.
75. Ibid., 98. Compare with Mallarmé's cinepoetic "lustre" in *La Musique et les lettres*, as well as Mallarmé's use of the verb *prolonger* in connection with Fuller's dancing (chapter 1).
76. Ibid., 107.
77. Ibid., 108.
78. Cayrol and Durand, *Le Droit de regard*, 13, 20. The book explicitly refers to the "Lazarus of the camps," 89.
79. Ibid., 21.
80. Ibid., 32.
81. Ibid., 24.
82. Cayrol, "De la mort à la vie," 67.
83. Cayrol and Durand, *Le Droit*, 4.
84. Ibid., 39.
85. Ibid., 20.

86. Cayrol, *Nuit et brouillard*, 17.
87. Hirsch, *Afterimage,* 61.
88. Bersani and Dutoit point out this discrepancy in *Arts of Impoverishment*, 183.
89. Cayrol and Durand, *Le Droit*, 33.
90. Cayrol, *Nuit et brouillard*, 20.
91. Emma Wilson draws attention to Resnais's insistence on the imagination, "Material Remains: Night and Fog," 93.
92. Ibid., 20.
93. Ibid., 18.
94. Ibid., 19.
95. Hirsch, *Afterimage*, 44.
96. Cayrol, *Nuit et brouillard*, 18.
97. Ibid., 21.
98. Ibid.
99. Ibid., 22.
100. Ibid., 23.
101. Cayrol, *Nuit et brouillard,* 96. This oblique question to Heidegger was also the source of the philosophy of another survivor, his student Emmanuel Levinas, whose ethics of ethics based on the other's death rather than my own deconstructs his master's philosophy and its moment of collaboration with Nazism.
102. Ibid., 24.
103. Ibid., 25.
104. Ibid., 32.
105. Ibid., 38.
106. Ibid., 39.
107. Adorno. *Negative Dialectics*, 363; my emphasis. For a reading of Adorno's passage as a reorigination of the lyrical "I" radically contaminated by guilt, see Noland, *Poetry at Stake*, 80–82.
108. Ibid., 25.
109. Ibid., 28.
110. Ibid., 26.
111. Ibid., 29.
112. Ibid., 31.
113. McDonough, *"Beautiful Language of My Century."* Isou, *Traité d'économie nucléaire.*
114. Debord, "Pourquoi le lettrisme?," 195.
115. Ibid.
116. See Debord, "Finis les pieds plats," *Œuvres*, 84–85.
117. Curtay, *La Poésie lettriste*, 11–16; Marcus *Lipstick Traces*, 246–51.
118. Isou, *Introduction à une nouvelle poésie*, 90.
119. Isou, *Introduction à une nouvelle poésie*, 91.
120. Ibid., 59.
121. Ibid., 53.
122. Cited in Schlatter, "Canailles, roman hypergraphique (1950)," in Lemaître, *Maurice Lemaître*, 120.

123. See Foster, *Understanding the Black Mountain Poets.*
124. Isou, *Introduction à une nouvelle poésie,* 293.
125. Ibid., 262 n1.
126. Marcus, *Lipstick*, 253.
127. Vinen, *Unfree French*, 139. "Zazou" was a youth movement that sprung during the Occupation. Zazous sported distinctive clothing (high slacks and short vests for men; striped sailor shirts and thick shoes for women), revered Jazz, partied against a background of bleakness and depravation, and occasionally mounted acts of symbolic resistance to the occupiers, and were hunted down by collaborationists.
128. Kasper, "Translator's Afterword," in Pomerand, *Saint ghetto des prêts*, 116.
129. Sudre, "Pensées sur l'oeuvre cinématographique," 57.
130. Isou, *L'Agrégation*, 16.
131. Ibid., 7.
132. Ibid., 422.
133. Ibid., 423.
134. Ibid., 413–14.
135. For the way Sartre's book—and Liberated France more generally—was responsible for Claude Lanzman's repressing his own Jewishness, and discovering in his own words a "Jewish positivity" only in 1952 in Israel, see Felman and Laub, *Crises*, 247.
136. Isou, *L'Agrégation*, 424.
137. Ignoring Lettrism's Jewish roots leads to such nonsensical statements as Greil Marcus's assertion that using the word "dictatorship" was "worse than the punk celebration of the swastika" (Marcus, *Lipstick Traces*, 252).
138. Isou, *L'Agrégation*, 428.
139. From a 2000 interview cited by Donguy, *Poésies*, 19.
140. Isou, *Introduction à une nouvelle poésie,* 175.
141. Ibid., 326.
142. For a critique of Heidegger's anti-Semitic exempla of tailors and cobblers, see Meschonnic, *Le Langage Heidegger.*
143. Ibid., 326–27.
144. Ibid., 369.
145. Ibid., "Warsaw," 381.
146. Ibid., "dirtyjew / dirty Jew / Pariiis," 389.
147. Ibid., 327.
148. Ibid., 52.
149. Ibid., 110, 163, 217, 49.
150. Ibid., 365.
151. Ibid., 294.
152. See Devaux, *Le Cinéma lettriste*, 39–67.
153. Devaux, *Le Cinéma lettriste,* 40.
154. Reproduced in Devaux, *Le Cinéma lettriste*, 60.
155. Abel, *FFTC,* 1:168.
156. Isou, *Esthétique du cinéma*, 109.
157. Ibid., 50.
158. Ibid., 110.

159. Ibid., 28, 110.
160. Ibid., 16, 66, 85, 110.
161. Ibid., 55, 56, 66, 85.
162. Ibid., 16, 76, 84, 85.
163. Ibid., 97.
164. Ibid., 103.
165. Ibid., 98.
166. Lemaître, *Le Film*.
167. Ibid., 25.
168. Ibid., 30.
169. Ibid., 55.
170. Ibid., 56.
171. Ibid., 16, 84.
172. Ibid., 127.
173. Devaux, *Le Cinéma lettriste*, 162.
174. Isou and Lemaître self-published dozens of pamphlets railing against established cultural figures from Breton and Tzara, Godard and Truffaut, to Duras, Jean-Louis Barrault, etc.
175. Cocteau supported Isou early on, especially at Cannes in 1951.
176. Pomerand, *Saint ghetto des prêts*, 9.
177. Pomerand, *Saint ghetto*, 24.
178. Ibid., 20, 22.
179. Ibid., 27.
180. Ibid., 57.
181. Ibid., 92.
182. Ibid., 90.
183. Ibid., 60.
184. Ibid., 58–60.
185. Ibid., 62.
186. Ibid., 104–6.
187. Ibid., 36.
188. Ibid., 50.
189. Ibid., 106.
190. Ibid., 108.
191. Devaux, *Le Cinéma lettriste*, 162.
192. The odd title of cinepoet Emmanuel Hocquard's compendium, *Ma haie*, seems to come from a text of Michaux, "Fin d'un domaine," stating that others "rest against my hedge [*ma haie*]," *Œuvres complètes,* 2:609.
193. Michaux, *Œuvres,* 2:61.
194. Mourier, "Michaux cinémane et cinématicien," 43–62.
195. Ibid., 47.
196. Ibid., 53.
197. Bellour, "Images du monde visionnaire, dossier du film," 3:1526–42.
198. Ibid., 3:1528–30.
199. Bellour thinks the film is Fritz Lang's *Mabuse* (1922), but it is very doubtful since Michaux writes that he did not know the filmmaker's name (ibid., 3:1308) and marvels that "they are making progress now at the movies."

200. Bellour, "Jean Epstein chez Henri Michaux," 432.
201. Michaux, *Œuvres,* 2:292.
202. Ibid., 2:286.
203. Ibid., 2:285.
204. In 1952 Michaux recalls a period when some people "would still not be interested in unfolding. The cinema had not been born very long ago" (*Œuvres,* 2:372). "Film" and "screen" respectively are mentioned throughout the 1950s: *Œuvres,* 2:371, 627, 642, 696, 711, 738, etc.; and *Œuvres,* 2:370, 620, 646, 723, 859, etc.
205. Ibid., 2:287.
206. Michaux, *Œuvres,* 2:868. See Max Loreau's chapter on Michaux in his *La peinture à l'œuvre et l'énigme du corps.* Loreau writes, "Though they are imported in an imaginary milieu, things are not passive; they mime, in the space within, the resistance of real things to the unreal and magical action of the mind set in its bubble. Thence comes the uncanny equivocation of Michaux's writings: they manipulate fictive objects that suddenly behave with the autonomy of real objects." (15).
207. Ibid., 2:680.
208. Michaux, *Œuvres,* 1:11.
209. Michaux, *Œuvres,* 2:709, 718. Instances of photos supporting hallucinations are numerous: *Œuvres,* 2:817–19, 830, 851, 879, 893, 947; *Œuvres,* 3:17, 49, 77–79, etc.
210. Michaux, *Œuvres,* 3:17.
211. Ibid., 2:997, 927.
212. Ibid., 2:948; *Œuvres,* 3:49.
213. Ibid., 2:321. Recent research in neurobiology shows areas of the brain wired for facial recognition: this may confirm Emmanuel Levinas's focus on the face as the deepest nexus of ethics.
214. Michaux, *Œuvres,* 2:926.
215. Ibid., 3:103.
216. Ibid., 2:999.
217. Ibid., 3:121, Breton, *Œuvres,* 1:1129.
218. Michaux, *Œuvres,* 2:1000.
219. Ibid., 3:124.
220. Ibid., 2:995.
221. Ibid., 2:62.
222. Ibid., 3:80.
223. Ibid., 3:18.
224. Ibid., 2:674.
225. Ibid., 2:599. In 1951, when this afterword to *Movements* was written, the word "*libérateurs*" would still be synonymous with the allied armies that freed France in 1944.
226. Ibid., 2:440–41.
227. Ibid., 2:599.
228. Ibid., 2:997.
229. In the 1950s Michaux knew musician Pierre Henry who worked for the new French TV (RTF) whose broadcasts developed from 1949 to

1953. See www.furious.com/perfect/pierrehenry.html (November 12, 2009). Henry wrote on Michaux: "Musique pour "Misérable miracle" d'Henri Michaux," 83–89.

230. Michaux, *Œuvres,* 2:362.

231. Ibid., 2:370.

232. Ibid., 2:371.

233. François Di Dio, "Biographie," in Duprey, *Œuvres completes,* 12.

234. Duprey, *Œuvres,* 103.

235. Ibid., 119.

236. Michaux, *Œuvres,* 2:997.

237. Cayrol, *Nuit et brouillard,* 67.

238. Ibid., 93.

239. Duprey, *Œuvres,* 131, 175.

240. Ibid., 33.

241. Ibid., 34–35.

242. Ibid., 40.

243. Ibid., 60.

244. Ibid., 76.

245. Ibid., 85.

246. Ibid., 60.

247. Ibid., 77.

248. Ibid., 88.

249. Ibid., 70.

250. Ibid., 105.

251. Ibid., 63.

252. "Lieds funèbres," Jarry, *Œuvres,* 1:174-77; "La Mécanique d'Ixion," Jarry, *Œuvres,* 2:405-7.

253. Ibid., 79.

254. In the film, a piano pulled by two priests sports two dead donkeys—an image Buñuel and Dalí came up with during their automatic script-writing sessions. See Short, *Age of Gold,* 64, 66.

255. Ibid., 246.

256. Ibid., 246–47.

257. Ibid., 245.

258. Ibid., 248.

259. See the note by Di Dio, in Duprey, *Œuvres,* 327–28.

260. "grand souffle de machine" (37), "une grande machine" (61), "machine-à-os" (69), "le Chœur-moteur" (99), "faux-masque à machinerie" (119), "machines-de-sang" (119), "membres mécaniques" (240), "machine au bloc de la mer" (249).

261. Even Duprey's thought about the four dimensions harks back to the turn of the century: "And, raising my head and, since it is inverted, looking underneath, I see, pupils within, the Pre-Primary Dimension traversing like a needle the glass-bridge of the three known dimensions" (102).

262. Ibid., 98.

263. Ibid., 127–28.

264. Ibid., 164.

265. Ibid., 177.
266. Ibid., 175.
267. Ibid., 93.
268. Ibid., 103.
269. Ibid., 108.
270. Rodanski, *Écrits*, 122, 324.
271. Wateau, *Bernard Noël*, 102.
272. François Di Dio and Jean-Pierre Goutier, "Repères biographiques," in Rodanski, *Écrits*, 11–12.
273. Rodanski, *Écrits*, 324.
274. Morin, *Stars*, 52.
275. Rodanski, *Écrits*, 26.
276. Julien Gracq, "Préface," in Rodanski, *Écrits*, 32–33. "The age of cinema" may be a direct quote of Breton's desultory comment that "that age passes."
277. Ibid., 51.
278. See Ross, *Fast Cars, Clean Bodies.*
279. Rodanski, *Écrits*, 56.
280. Ibid., 57–58.
281. Ibid., 77.
282. Ibid., 78.
283. Cayrol, "De la mort à la vie," 83–87. Cayrol's main explanation for this "parasitic love," however, is the absence of "God" and "creation" in sexuality.
284. Morin, *Stars*, 142.
285. Cayrol, "De la mort à la vie," 106.
286. Morin, *Stars*, 141.
287. Rodanski, *Écrits*, 188–89.
288. Ibid., 194.
289. Ibid., 330.
290. Ibid., 193.
291. Ibid., 360.
292. Ibid., 345.
293. Ibid., 307.
294. Ibid., 311–13.
295. Ibid., 322.
296. Ibid., 331.
297. Ibid., 335.
298. "I will be also a trapper, or a robber, or a gold-seeker, or a hunter, a miner, a prospector. Arizona Bar (whisky, gin and mixed)," cited by Breton, *Œuvres*, 1:202.
299. Rodanski, *Écrits*, 333.

9. POSTLYRICISM AND THE MOVIE PROGRAM

1. Jacob, "Printemps et cinématographe mêlés," 219.

2. Fiction films were often on colored film stocks until World War I, such as a multireel *Richard III* (US 1912) recently purchased by AFI. Other Shakespeare adaptations were:

Romeo and Juliet (US, 1911, dir. Barry O'Neill), *Giuletta e Romeo* (Italy, 1911, dir. Gerolamo Lo Savio), *Indian Romeo and Juliet* (US, 1912, dir. Laurence Trimble), www.unibas.ch/shine/linkstragromeowf.html (November 12, 2011). Military parade was a favorite genre of the early Lumière globe-trotting cameramen, such as *Défilé de l'infanterie turque* (Lumière #414, 1897), a genre revived during the patriotic wave of 1913 (Meusy, *Paris-Palaces*, 390–404). Contemporary Sherlock Holmes films include *Sherlock Holmes Solves the Sign of Four* (US, 1913), *A Study in Scarlet* (US, 1914, dir. George Pearson (I) and Francis Ford (II)), *Der Hund von Baskerville* (Germany, 1914, dir. Rudolf Meinert). An adaptation of Molière's *The Miser* came out in 1910 (FR, 1910, dir. André Calmettes). For Jacob's pioneering interest for cinema between 1907 and 1911, see Crafton, *Émile Cohl* 112.

3. Jacob, "Théâtre et cinéma," 9–12. This *rapprochement* in the film program is likely connected both to the definition of the poetic image by Reverdy (his one time disciple), to the cinepoetic image by Epstein and the surrealist image by Breton. Jacob has a clear sense of prosthetic automatism as well: "[the cinematograph] creates [the sensations that our time gives us of ourselves] in lieu of our lazy mind" (11).

4. Rothwell, "The 'Querelle du poème en prose,'" 51–66.

5. For the historical relationship between film program and montage, see Tsivian, "Some Historical Footnotes," 245–55.

6. Benjamin, "On Some Motifs in Baudelaire," 4:333. The "secret architecture" is an expression by Barbey d'Aurevilly who insists also in reading the poems "*in the order* in which the poet, who knows what he is doing, has arranged them." See Baudelaire, *Œuvres,* 1:798.

7. Benjamin, *Selected Writings*, 4:318.

8. Ibid., 4:324, 328–29.

9. Ibid., 4:343.

10. Ibid., 4:321.

11. Ibid., 4:316.

12. Ibid.

13. Baudelaire, *Œuvres,* 1:275.

14. Combe, *Poésie et récit.*

15. Klerk, "Program Formats," 534.

16. Tortajada, "Alfred Jarry," 101–13; Tortajada, "Machines cinématiques," 5–23; Tortajada, "L'Ombre projetée de la vitesse," 109–33.

17. Jarry, *Œuvres,* 1:714.

18. A few programs. From Meusy: Lumière 1897: 12 shorts (58); Biographe 1897: 12 shorts (62); Biograph 1898: 20 shorts (75); Lumière 1901: 22 shorts (98); from Abel's *Ciné*: Pathé 1905: 17 and 20 shorts (26).

19. Taken from the filmography from Sadoul, *Lumière et Méliès*; and McMahan, *Alice Guy Blaché.*

20. Jarry, *Œuvres,* 1:714. This episode of Nebuchadnezzar figures in several plates by William Blake (*Marriage of Heaven and Hell*, for instance) and since other titles have a Blakean Romantic resonance, it is possible that Jarry "adapts" Blake in his cinepoetic film program.

21. For the extremely varied and sustained use of color techniques in cinema before 1928, see Cherchai, *Silent Cinema*, 21–43.

22. Jarry, *Œuvres,* 1:717.

23. Ibid., 1:341.

24. Ibid., 1:669.

25. Ibid., 1:668.

26. Ibid., 1:394–95.

27. Ibid., 1:174.

28. Fargue wrote a disappointed meditation on cinema, "Ombres chinoises," in a collection titled *Lanterne magique*, that may recall a visit at Reynaud's. Fargue, "Ombres chinoises," 216–31.

29. Jarry, *Œuvres,* 2:465.

30. For a new edition and translation, see Segalen, *Stèles*. A companion volume of Chinese sources is available online only at www.steles.org.

31. Segalen, *Correspondance*, 2:73–74.

32. Châteauvert and Gaudreault, "Noises of Spectators," 184.

33. See Gaudreault and Albéra, "Apparition, disparition," 167–99. In Canada, World War I saw an increase in lecturer-commentators, see Lacasse, "Double Silence," 205–12.

34. Gaudreault and Albéra, "Apparition, disparition et escamotage," 191, 198.

35. Segalen, *Peintures*, 85.

36. Ibid., 9.

37. Cf. Ropars-Wuilleumier, *Le Texte divisé,* 84–85.

38. Ibid., 10.

39. Ibid., 12.

40. Ibid., 14.

41. Ibid., 10.

42. Ibid., 51.

43. Ibid., 38–39.

44. Ibid., 204–5.

45. Jules de Gaultier was among Segalen's oldest and closest friends. His Schopenhauer influenced phenomenology is avowedly cinematic:

> . . . on the one hand, a world object of knowledge, offered to the gaze [*regard*] and unfolding itself [*se déroulant*] before the mind's curiosity like a moving panorama [*panorama en mouvement*] . . . on the other hand, the subject of knowledge witnessing this spectacle, in the ego and outside the ego, through the optical apparatus [*appareil d'optique*] that compose the laws of phenomenal representation. (*De Kant à Nietszche*, 201)

46. Segalen, *Correspondance*, 2:269. His letters of September and October 1913 mention several cameras including a stereoscopic "*vérascope*" (209), future conferences with projections ("*ma mission terminée . . . je conférencie, je projectionne*") (231), and a photographic projector (242).

47. Ibid., 46.
48. Ibid., 188–89.
49. For example, *Les Misérables* (3,400 meters, 1913) or *Les Enfants du capitaine Grant* (1,770 meters, 1914). Abel, *Ciné,* 459, 462.
50. Ibid., 92, 94, 105.
51. Ibid., 84. In *Imaginaires*, a severed head rises and floats in the air, a favorite trick of Méliès (49).
52. Ibid., 91.
53. Ibid., 47.
54. Ibid., 35. See Segalen, *Imaginaires,* 50, for a similar scene.
55. Epstein, *Bonjour cinéma*, 98; Abel, *FFTC,* 1:237.
56. Ibid., 34.
57. The kineograph or mutoscope was invented in 1868 in England and its flip action (like a book) rivals the circular action of early Marey discs or the linear action of early Edison films, and inscribes the book as volume within early cinema apparatuses. An undated early mutoscope film from Marey may well alter the chronology of animation; Philipp Felsch, "Marey's Flip Book," www.vlp.mpiwg-berlin.mpg.de (Max Planck Institute) (accessed November 11, 2011).
58. Ibid., 71.
59. Ibid., 23.
60. Ibid., 217.
61. Segalen's *Essai sur l'exotisme* is a treatise on how diversity—"*le Divers*"—can prevent entropy (Western science and colonization) from erasing differences. The Second Law of thermodynamics announcing that all differences must, in the end, vanish is reinterpreted by Segalen as "The Kingdom of the Luke-Warm" (absolute average), which is also the end of time (88). Yet sheer plethora or extremes generate chaos that is another form of entropy (nondifference). So Segalen's diversity comes with a commitment to sequencing and seriality *only* if other series and sequences remain possible: "Any series, any gradation, any comparison generates variety and diversity. Separated, objects seem vaguely similar, homogenous" (80). The film program prevents both extremes: too much and not enough order.
62. Benjamin, *Selected Writings*, 4:328.
63. Krueger, "Surgical Imprecision," 66.
64. Ortel, *La Littérature*, 141–67.
65. Segalen, *Correspondance*, 2:831, 853, 856, 860, etc.
66. Ibid., 2:860.
67. For the film, see Abel, *French Cinema*, 302–5. The booklet is only available at the Bibliothèque Nationale de France (8–YF-2025).
68. Carou, "Récits-Programmes," 241.
69. Apollinaire, *Œuvres complètes en prose*, 2:937–39.
70. Hillel-Erlanger, *Voyages*, 52.
71. Ibid., 68.
72. Ibid., 74.
73. Ibid., 83.

74. Ibid., 75–76.
75. Ibid., 17.
76. Ibid., 53.
77. "La chienne jalouse de Colette," Fonds Dulac, Bibliothèque du Film, GD 638.
78. Carou, "Récits-Programmes," 242. In *Nadja*, Breton recollects a sequence from an episode of Duke Worne's *The Trail of the Octopus* (1919, released in France in 1921 under the title *The Grip of the Octopus*). In this sequence, a Chinese villain invades New York "with several million copies of himself"—a hyperbolic number since Breton is establishing that this film has "by far struck me the most." The fourth "film" on Hillel-Erlanger's program is titled "The Octopus." It denounces the tentacular grip of capital and the infernal replication of money: "Safes / choke-full, gorged / with Millions" (78). Since the passage of *Nadja* is involved with Breton's strategic reduction of cinema, I wonder whether there is not a reminiscence of Hillel-Erlanger at play. Breton includes a single photographic document on cinema in *Nadja*: a program-brochure from *The Trail of the Octopus*. Breton, *Œuvres*, 1:663, 665.
79. Filteau, "Marcel Dugas et le 'cinéma en prose,'" 29–45.
80. Usai, "Pornography," 525–26.
81. See Solomon, "'Twenty-Five Heads Under One Hat,'" 3–20.
82. Dermée, *Films, duodrames, soliloques, contes*, 55–59.
83. Dugas, *Psyché*, 9.
84. Ibid., 34.
85. Ibid., 40.
86. Ibid., 64.
87. Ibid., 57.
88. Ibid., 110.
89. Ibid., 101.
90. Ibid., 102.
91. Ibid.
92. Morin, *Les Stars*, 169. A short scientific and supernatural novella by Jules Lermina which is contemporaneous with the birth of cinema, *The Twice Dead Woman* (1895), deploys a similarly cinematic theory of projection-introjection of the dead. A man whose beloved has died revives her because his photographic memory becomes capable of projection: "visual memory is the projection outside of ourselves of a form stored in us," a friend of the lover explains, adding that it is "so real and alive . . . that you might be able to project it outside of yourself, with all the attributes of reality and life" (68–69). This is what the lover does in a kind of séance, during which the woman appear out of a "a wisp of vapor that seemed rooted in the chest" of the lover, so that "he was restituting, animating and vitalizing the beloved that he carried still alive within himself!" (Lermina, *La Deux Fois Morte*, 73).
93. Ibid., 103.
94. Ibid., 99.
95. A billboard with an ad for "bouillon *Kub*" appears in one original illustration for Cendrars's *War in the Luxemburg Gardens*. Cendrars, *Tout autour*, 1:106.

96. Alferi, *Kub or*, 1.
97. Alferi and Cadiot, "La Mécanique lyrique," 1:3–22.
98. Alferi, *Kub or*, 77.
99. Lakoff, *Women, Fire and Other Dangerous Things*.
100. Alferi, *Kubor*, 65.
101. Ibid., 56.
102. Ibid., 34.
103. Ibid., 11.
104. Ibid., 3.
105. Ibid., 6.
106. Ibid., 5.
107. Ibid., 26.
108. Ibid., 37.
109. The poetics of the unfolding umbrella also refers to an ironic text by Francis Ponge, "Le Dispositif Maldoror-Poésies" (The Maldoror-poems apparatus), couched in advertising language, that compares the use value of Isidore Ducasse within the postwar bourgeois library with an umbrella. Ponge, *Œuvres*, 1:633.
110. Alferi, *Kubor*, 7.

10. CINE-VERSE

1. Fauconnier, *Mental Spaces*.
2. See Andrew and Ungar, *Popular Front Paris*, 71–75.
3. Assouline, *Gaston Gallimard*, 171–89.
4. For the genesis of the *Cinario* collection, see Le Forestier, "*Le Roi de la pédale*," 259–77. Baetens, *La Novellisation*, 98–116.
5. See Le Forestier, "Le Roi de la pédale," released shortly before *Le Roi de la pédale* (FR, 1925, dir. Maurice Champreux); theatrical adaptations were also produced in 1925. The exact relationship betwen Boutet, *Gribiche*; and *Gribiche* (FR, 1925, dir. Jacques Feyder) has not yet been established.
6. Beucler, *Un Suicide*.
7. For a recent study, see Schwenger, *Fantasm and Fiction*.
8. Beucler, *Un Suicide*, 65.
9. Ibid., 74.
10. Ibid., 17, 24, 83.
11. Ibid., 27, 34, 51, 58, 97.
12. Ibid., 14.
13. Ibid., 30–31.
14. Ibid., 55.
15. Ibid., 45–46.
16. Ibid., 13.
17. Ibid., 14.
18. Ibid., 27.
19. Ibid., 123.
20. Ibid.
21. Ibid., 8.

22. Ibid., 93.
23. Ibid., 10.
24. Ibid., 24.
25. Ibid., 64.
26. Ibid., 75.
27. Ibid.
28. Tsur, *Towards a Theory*; and Stockwell, *Cognitive Poetics*.
29. Tsur, *Towards a Theory*, 43.
30. Ibid., 5.
31. Stockwell, *Cognitive Poetics*, 77; cf. also Tsur, *Towards a Theory*, 225–34.
32. Ibid.
33. Denett, *Sweet Dreams*, 144.
34. Llinás, *I of the Vortex*, 15.
35. Ibid., 23.
36. Ibid., 35.
37. Ibid., 228.
38. Artaud, "Cinéma et réalité," in *Œuvres complètes*, 3:22.
39. Beucler, "Le Poème cinématographique," 133–35.
40. Desson, "Qualité du cinema," 151.
41. Betz, "*Drames de cinéma*," 136.
42. Dausse, "En relisant *Donogoo-Tonka*," 137.
43. Bonjean, "Les Belles Noces dans la rue," 55.
44. Bonjean, "Les Belles Noces," 77.
45. Berge, "Connaissance de Cendrars," 139.
46. Chenal, *Drames sur celluloïd*, 117–20.
47. See Meusy, *Paris-Palaces*, 128. The Lumière short *L'arroseur arrosé* (1896, #99) implicitly links the snakelike watering hose with the filmstrip.
48. Chenal, *Drames*, 15.
49. Ibid., 61.
50. Ibid., 49.
51. Ibid., 73.
52. Ibid., 123.
53. Ibid., 124.

11. MAX JEANNE'S *WESTERN*

1. Jeanne, *Western*, 105.
2. Clerc, *Écrivains et cinéma*, 307–40; Jameson, *Postmodernism*; Higgins, *New Novel, New Wave*.
3. Clerc, *Écrivains et cinéma*, 311.
4. Renee Tajima uses "antislick" to denote an aesthetic counterideology signifying its own ethnic exclusion from Hollywood, in "Moving the Image: Asian American Independent Filmmaking 1970–1990," *Moving the Image*, 20. Cf. also Chapter 5 on Isou and the lettrists's practice of "*cinéma discrépant*," a material assault against the mimetic neutrality of the film stock in connection with the aftermath of the Shoah.

5. Marks, *Skin of the Film.*

6. Lemaître refers to New Wave/Left Bank filmmakers as "the tornado exhaled by those whom we secretly seduced (Marker, Godard, Resnais)." Lemaître, *Carnets d'un fanatique II*, 50.

7. Duras, *Hiroshima mon amour,* 107. See also Higgins, *New Wave, New Novel,* 43.

8. Marker's *Coréennes*, which combines photos (often in series) which he took in North Korea with a political and historical commentary, could be read as a cinepoetic narrative. Agnès Varda published very quickly book versions of her own films.

9. Lacassin, *A La Recherche,* 272–88; Torwanicki, *Les Aventures.*

10. Jeanne, *Western*; Fondane, *Trois Scénarii.*

11. Damas, *Black-label.*

12. Ibid., 84.

13. Ibid., 9.

14. Ibid., 65.

15. Ibid., 61.

16. Ibid., 84.

17. Ibid., 37.

18. Ibid., 44.

19. Ibid., 46.

20. Ibid., 40.

21. Ibid., 57.

22. Ibid., 58.

23. Ibid., 74.

24. Ibid., 75.

25. Ibid., 82.

26. Ibid., 46.

27. Ibid., 84.

28. From *Broken Blossoms, or The Yellow Man and the Girl* (US, 1919, dir. D. W. Griffith) to *The Bitter Tears of General Yen* (US, 1933, dir. Frank Capra) the "raced" man is played by a white man (Richard Barthelmess, Nils Asther). While *Hiroshima mon amour* breaks the taboo of interracial bodily contact on screen, Eiji Okada had to ventriloquize the French he did not speak.

29. Jeanne, *Western*, 113.

30. Ibid., 32.

31. Ibid., 26.

32. For a recent version of the hegemony of the apparatus, see Beller, *Cinematic Mode of Production.*

33. Jeanne, *Western*, 9–10.

34. Ibid., 29.

35. Duras, *Hiroshima*, iv.

36. Jeanne, *Western*, 10.

37. Ibid., 108.

38. Ibid., 8.

39. Ibid., 15.

40. For the Caribbean vacuum-cleaned and sucked dry by Europe's "fishing" expeditions, see Benítez-Rojo, *Repeating Island*, 5–6.
41. Jeanne, *Western*, 34.
42. Ibid., 109.
43. Ibid., 110–11.
44. Ibid., 137.
45. Ibid., 124.
46. Ibid., 136.
47. Ibid., 24.
48. Ibid., 56.
49. Ibid., 101.
50. Ibid., 35, 102, 243.
51. Ibid., 140.
52. Ibid., 125.
53. Ibid., 136.
54. For the work of the historian as "unwinding the spool in reverse," a metaphorical notion first developed by the Annales historian Marc Bloch, see Higgins, *New Novel,* 28.
55. Ibid., 103.
56. Ibid., 63.
57. Derrida, "Violence and Metaphysics," 79–194. See Crichtley, *Ethics of Deconstruction.*
58. For a similar sense of something beyond recognition in historical subjectivity, see Oliver, *Witnessing*; for the problem of exhibiting the unfinishedness of the historical past, see Wyschogrod, *Ethics of Remembering;* and Trouillot, *Silencing the Past.*

12. MAURICE ROCHE'S *COMPACT*

1. Roche, *Compact*, 93 (edition in color).
2. Bradbury, *Illustrated Man*, 3.
3. Ibid., 4.
4. Lemaître, *Le Film*, 165.
5. Lemaître, *Au-delà du déclic*; see Devaux, *Le Cinéma lettriste,* 162.
6. *Kwaidan* (Japan, 1964, dir. Kobayashi Masaki), released in France in 1965, features a blind monk battling a spirit every night, his skin covered with protective Buddhist text. See Lippit, *Atomic Light*,1–4, 115–19.
7. Hayman, "Interview with Maurice Roche," 67.
8. Roche, *Compact*, 147.
9. Ellison, *Invisible Man*, 3.
10. Roche, *Compact*, 111.
11. Ibid., 115.
12. Ibid., 128.
13. Ibid., 84.
14. Jean-Pierre Faye, codirector of *Change* with Roche, was responsible for the second Heidegger controversy in France when he published in

French the infamous Rectorate Speech of 1933. See Rockmore, *Heidegger and French Philosophy*, 154.

15. Ibid., 137.

16. Ibid., 163.

17. *Change* 1 (1968): 5. Roche's contribution is titled "Calques," 107–21. For Roche and *Change*, see Ffrench, *Time of Theory*, 117, 147.

18. *Change* 1: 41.

19. For the influence of Joyce on Roche, see Lernout and Van Mierlo, *Reception of James Joyce in Europe*, 398–99.

20. Baudry, "Compact sur *Compact*," 160.

21. Hayman, "Interview with Maurice Roche," 67.

22. Roche, *Compact*, 73.

23. Ibid., 142.

24. Ibid., 72.

25. The lettrists objected to what they perceived as Pichette's pseudovanguardist use of projector and screen in *Nucléa* (Devaux, *Cinéma lettriste,* 131). Pichette wrote a long text on Chaplin whom he defined as "a man whose perishable alphabets of the body are photographed in every detail" (Pichette, *Rond-Point*, 49). Pichette also wrote a long poem on a 1963 documentary film by Pierre Perrault and Michel Brault, "Préface à un film," *La Délirante* 7 (1967).

26. Roche, *Compact*, 18–19.

27. Ibid., 36, 45.

28. Ibid., 36.

29. Ibid., 80.

30. Ibid., 126.

31. Ibid., 39.

32. Ibid., 65.

33. Ibid., 105.

34. Ibid., 106.

35. Ibid., 120; in original English.

36. Ibid., 96, 121.

37. Ibid., 96, 122.

38. Ibid., 93, 121.

39. I disagree with readings of *Compact* as a text flattening history. Cf. Smith, "Fragments of Landscape, Scraps of Décor," 48–57. In a manifesto/advertising flyer inserted in his following book, *Circus*, Roche declares that *Compact* and *Circus* are, "Novel(s) containing all the attainments of past novels (thus of History)" (Roche, *Circus*, insert).

40. Roche, *Compact*, 88.

41. Ibid., 93.

42. Ibid., 118.

43. Ibid.

44. Ibid., 122–23.

45. Ibid., 123.

46. Ibid., 124.

47. Ibid., 27.
48. Ibid., 59.
49. Ibid., 66.
50. Ibid., 83.
51. Ibid., 81.
52. Ibid., 99.
53. Ibid., 116.
54. Ibid., 96, 120.
55. Ibid., 130.
56. Ibid., 142.
57. Ibid., 143.
58. Ibid., 154.
59. Ibid., 118.
60. Ibid., 80.
61. Ibid., 83.
62. Ibid., 71–86.
63. Ibid., 95–97.
64. Ibid., 111–61.
65. Ibid., 111.
66. Ibid., 122.
67. Ibid., 159.
68. Ibid., 26.
69. Ibid., 42.
70. Such a wire-mesh model is found in Cocteau's *Le sang d'un poète* (1930), in which the (severed) 3-D model of the head of the poet is projected in several shots.
71. See Burgin, *In/Different Spaces*, 115.
72. Roche, *Compact*, 26.
73. Ibid., 108.
74. Ibid., 125.
75. See Lippit, *Atomic Light*. A photo of human shadow trace is on page 86.
76. Roche, *Compact*, 59.
77. Lippit, *Atomic Light*, 5.
78. Roche, *Compact*, 93.
79. Hayman, "Interview," 72.
80. Roche, *Compact*, 26.
81. *Œuvres*, 3:47. In a letter, Artaud adds, "We should create a screen entirely talking and that would succeed in creating perspectives of sound in three dimensions, in the same way that the visual screen creates perspectives for the eye" (cited in Prieur, "La Machine à l'oeil buté," 111).

13. NELLY KAPLAN'S *LE COLLIER DE PTYX*

1. Kaplan, *Le Collier de ptyx*, 72–73.
2. See Richardson, *Surrealism and Cinema*, chapter 6, "Nelly Kaplan and Sexual Revenge," 93–106.

3. Suleiman, "Surrealist Black Humour," 9. http://www.surrealismcentre.ac.uk/papersofsurrealism/journal1/acrobat_files/Suleiman.pdf (accessed on October 3, 2009).

4. For Mabille's book influence on Alejo Carpentier's *el real maravilloso*, see for instance, Chamary, "Territorialization of the Imaginary in Latin America," 137.

5. Kaplan, *Le Collier*, 7.

6. Ibid., 21.

7. Ibid., 64.

8. Breton, *Œuvres,* 1:676. See Sebbag, *Le point sublime,* 15–37.

9. Kaplan, *Le Collier*, 51.

10. Albó, "Andean People in the Twentieth Century," 786.

11. Kaplan, *Le Collier*, 65.

12. Ibid., 81.

13. Ibid., 13–14.

14. Ibid., 26.

15. Ibid., 12.

16. Ibid., 16, 124.

17. Ibid., 84.

18. Ibid., 23, 76, 77, 91, 106.

19. Ibid., 65.

20. The title refers to Duke Worne's 1919 *The Trail of the Octopus*, a fifteen-episode "action-packed chapterplay"(www.loc.gov/rr/mopic/pickford/2003-archive.html). In *Nadja*, Breton refers to one of the episodes of *L'Étreinte de la pieuvre* as "the film which by far has struck me the most," erroneously calling it "the eighth and last episode" (*Œuvres,* 1:663), while the program reproduced in his book states "in 15 episodes" (ibid., 1:665). Breton goes back to the film at the end of *Nadja*, invoking "the disappearance of practically everything which is linked to *The Trail of the Octopus*" (ibid., 746). Programs for the third and fifth episode were in Breton's papers: www.geocities.com/surrealisme_in_nederlands/manuscrits/bretonmanus.html.

21. Ibid., 40–43.

22. Ibid., 44–50.

23. Beckman, *Vanishing Women*, 8–9.

24. Kaplan, *Le Collier*, 111.

25. Ibid., 112–13.

26. Ibid.

27. Ibid., 121.

28. Ibid., 99.

29. Breton, *Œuvres,* 1:783. Sebbag, *Le Point sublime*, 26.

30. *Archives d'un visionnaire, Abel Gance, Collection Nelly Kaplan* (Auction catalogue), Paris, 1993, n.p.

31. Icart, *Abel Gance*, 352–57.

32. Icart, *Abel Gance*, 359.

33. Cited in Icart, *Abel Gance*, 384–85.

34. Breton, *Œuvres,* 1:1072.

35. Kaplan, *Manifeste d'un art nouveau*, 28, 31, 17.
36. Ibid., 21.
37. Ibid., 22–25.
38. Ibid., 31.
39. Kaplan, *Le Collier*, 139.
40. Baudry, the initiator of apparatus theory, invokes Kaplan's polyvision to read through the transhistorical polyphony of Roche's *Compact*. See Baudry, "Compact sur compact," 167.

CONCLUSION

1. Roche, *La Poésie est inadmissible*, 437–38.
2. For an account of the failure of *Tel Quel* poetics, see Joan Brandt, *Geopoetics*.
3. See their respective essays in Magno and Gleize, *Denis Roche*.
4. Quintyn, "Clicks n'Cuts"; Magno and Gleize, *Denis Roche*, 289; emphasis in the original.
5. Roche has also published a number of pieces in *Les Cahiers du cinéma*. See Forest, "Mélancolies de l'histoire," 104–6.
6. Cf. Hamon, *Imageries;* and Ortel, *La Littérature*.
7. Cocteau, *Le Sang d'un poète*.
8. Robbe-Grillet, *Glissements progressifs du plaisir*. See Houppermans, "Alain Robbe-Grillet et le photoroman," 112–30. Meersxt and Peeters, *Fugues*. See Peeters and Plissart, "A La Recherche du roman-photo," 77–82.
9. Bénézet, *La Fin de l'homme*; Hocquard, *Une Journée*.
10. For links between Marcelin Pleynet and both Hocquard and Bénézet, see Russo, "Le Propre du temps," 167–77.
11. Hocquard, *Une journée*, 14.
12. Ibid., 22.
13. Ibid., 25.
14. Ibid., 37.
15. Ibid., 44.
16. Ibid., 55.
17. Ibid., 56.
18. Ibid., 58.
19. Ibid., 57.
20. Fetzer, "Emmanuel Hocquard," 137–47.
21. Hocquard, *Une journée*, 82.
22. Ibid., 84.
23. Hocquard, *Théorie des tables*, 32.
24. For photography in Hocquard, see Fetzer, *Emmanuel Hocquard*, 75–90.
25. Hocquard, *Théorie*, 57.
26. Hocquard, *Ma haie*, 310, 320.
27. Delay and Hocquard, *Le Voyage à Reykjavik*, 53. Marcel Mariën also published a book qua thwarted film: *Tout est possible, un film sans images*.
28. Delay and Hocquard, *Le Voyage*, 13.

29. Ibid., 18.
30. Ibid., 13.
31. Royet-Journoud, *Théorie des prepositions*, 56.
32. Alferi, *Kub or*; Portugal and Doppelt, *Dans la reproduction*; Doppelt, *Totem*; Doppelt, *Quelque chose cloche*; Doppelt, *Le Pré est vénéneux.*
33. Doppelt, *Le Pré*, 7.
34. Ibid., 23.
35. Ibid., 2.
36. Ibid., 23.
37. Ibid., 13.
38. Broodthaers, *Je hais le mouvement.*
39. *Marcel Broodthaers: Cinéma*, Exhibition catalogue, Barcelona: Fundació Antoni Tàpies, 1997, 276, 16. Broodthaers declared in an interview that the only advice Magritte gave him was "read Mallarmé and meditate on him," subsequent to which he says he was obsessed by *A Throw of the Dice* for "20 to 25 years" (ibid., 306, n13). For a discussion of Broodthaers's intermedium between cinema and the book, see Krauss, "*Voyage on the North Sea.*" See also Rancière, *L'Espace des mots.*
40. Quintane, *Mortinsteinck.*
41. Ibid., 103.
42. For the genealogy of the cinema apparatus, see Kirsten, "Genèse d'un concept et ses avatars," 8–16. For Foucault's apparatus, see Agemben, "*What Is an Apparatus?*"
43. Epstein, *Écrits,* 1:333–34.
44. Hanna, *Poésie action directe*, 67, 93–103.
45. Quintyn, *Dispositifs*, 26–27.
46. Ibid., 296–97.
47. Delay and Hocquard, *Le Voyage*, iii–iv.
48. Ibid., xxiv.
49. Noël, *Journal du regard.*
50. Noël, *Journal*, 12.
51. Ibid., 11.
52. Ibid., 16.
53. Ibid., 19.
54. Ibid., 22.
55. Ibid., 28.
56. Ibid., 40.
57. Ibid., 50.
58. Ibid., 41.
59. Ibid., 75.
60. Ibid., 93.
61. Ibid., 47.
62. Hanna writes of "displacement," "remediation," "reappropriation," and "testing." Hanna, *Poésie action directe,* 118–20.
63. Gleize, *A noir*, 15.
64. For Collobert's cinepoetry, see Wall-Romana, "Danielle Collobert's '*Aux environs d'un film,*'" 257–63.

65. Gleize, “J’écris, donc je photographie,” 17.
66. Gleize, “J’écris,” 18–19.
67. Ibid., 17.
68. Gleize, *Film à venir*; Gleize, *Télévision*; Gleize, *Film à venir, conversions.*
69. Gleize, *Les Chiens*, 16, 24, 26, 27.
70. Ibid., 28, 35, 61, 69.
71. Gleize, “Un métier d’ignorance,” in *A noir*, 106.
72. Noël, *Journal du regard*, 40.
73. Gleize, *Néon, actes et legends*, 26.
74. Gleize, *Film à venir, conversions*, 11.
75. Ibid.
76. Royet-Journoud, *La Poésie entière est préposition*, 9, 41.
77. While the title *Film à venir* refers to an announcement in the window of a theater that the next movie will soon be programmed—“Film to be announced,” *Le Film à venir* has a more prophetic dimension.
78. Pittolo, *Montage*, 7.
79. Pittolo, *Gary Cooper.*
80. Godard, *JLG/JLG*; Godard, *For Ever Mozart*; Godard, *Histoire(s) de cinéma.*
81. Laugier, *Son Corps flottant*, 107.
82. See Disson, “Comme au cinéma,” 257–63.
83. Alferi, *Cinépoèmes & films parlants*; Alferi, *Le Cinéma des familles*; Alferi, *Des Enfants et des monstres*; Alferi and Julien, *Ça Commence à Séoul.*
84. Giraudon and Chemin, *Mes bien-aimé(e)s.*
85. Lespiau, *Ouija Board.*
86. Game, *Corpse&Cinéma*; Game, *Flip-Book*; Wourm, “Poetry in Moving,” 101–19.
87. Game, *écrire à même les choses*, 34.
88. Froger, *Des prise de vues*, 20–21.
89. Frogier, *Des Prises*, 24.
90. Ibid., 36.
91. Ibid., 42.
92. Ibid., 49.
93. Ibid., 87.
94. Mallarmé, *Œuvres*, 2:215.
95. Ibid., 89. Mallarmé’s preface speaks of his poem’s “‘white [spaces]’” meant to “to accelerate and at times slow down movement,” while the intonation “rises or falls” (Mallarmé, *Œuvres*, 1:392–93).
96. Baetens, *Vivre sa vie.*
97. Mouton, *Delenda West*, 5, 7.
98. Ibid., 39.
99. Ibid., 62.
100. Ibid., 133.
101. Epstein, *Écrits*, 2:55.

102. Fourcade, *Citizen Do*, 15.
103. Ibid., 13.
104. Ibid., 107.
105. Fourcade, *Xbo*, 1.
106. Apollinaire, "Avant le cinéma."

BIBLIOGRAPHY

Abel, Richard. *The Ciné Goes to Town: French Cinema 1896–1914*. Berkeley: University of California Press, 1998.

———. "Exploring the Discursive Field of the Surrealist Scenario Text." In *Dada and Surrealist Film*, ed. Rudolf E. Kuenzli. Cambridge, MA: MIT Press, 1996.

———. *French Cinema: The First Wave 1915–1929*. Princeton, NJ: Princeton University Press, 1984.

———, ed. *French Film Theory and Criticism: A History/Anthology, Volume I: 1907–1939* and *Volume II: 1929–1939*. Princeton, NJ: Princeton University Press, 1988.

Adorno, Theodor W. *Negative Dialectics*. Trans. E. B. Ashton. New York: Continuum, 1973.

———. *Prisms*. Trans. Samuel and Sherry Weber. Cambridge, MA: MIT Press, 1997.

Agamben, Georgio. *Homo Sacer: Sovereign Power and Bare Life*. Trans. Daniel Heller-Roazen. Stanford: Stanford University Press, 1998.

———. *Infancy and History: Essays on the Destruction of Experience*. Trans. Liz Heron. London: Verso, 1993.

———. *"What Is an Apparatus?" and Other Essays*. Trans. David Kishik and Stefan Pedatella. Stanford: Stanford University Press, 2007.

Albert-Birot, Pierre. *Cinémas*. Paris: Jean-Michel Place, 1999.

———. "Du Cinéma." *SIC* 49–50 (October 1919): 388.

Albert, Henri. "Théâtre de l'Oeuvre." *Mercure de France* 56 (August 1894): 380–83.

Albó, Xavier. "Andean People in the Twentieth Century." In *The Cambridge History of the Native People of the Americas*, vol. 3, part 2: 765–870, ed. Bruce G. Trigger, Wilcomb E. Washburn, and Richard E. W. Adams. Cambridge: Cambridge University Press, 1999.

Albright, Daniel. *Modernism and Music: An Anthology of Sources*. Chicago: University of Chicago Press, 2004.

Alferi, Pierre. *Le Cinéma des familles*. Paris: POL, 1999.

———. *Cinépoèmes & films parlants*. Aubervilliers: Les Laboratoires d'Aubervilliers, 2003, DVD.

———. *Des Enfants et des monstres*. Paris: POL, 2004.

Alferi, Pierre, and Olivier Cadiot. "La Mécanique lyrique." *Revue de littérature générale* 1, 3–22. Paris: POL, 1995.

Alferi, Pierre, and Jacques Julien. *Ça Commence à Séoul*. Paris: POL, 2007. DVD.

Altieri, Charles. *The Particulars of Rapture: An Aesthetics of the Affects*. Ithaca, NY: Cornell University Press, 2003.

Altman, Rick. *The Sounds of Early Cinema*. Bloomington: Indiana University Press, 2001.

Anderson, Barbara, and Joseph Anderson. "The Myth of Persistence of Vision Revisited." *Journal of Film and Video* 45, no. 1 (spring 1993): 3–12.

Andrew, Dudley, and Steven Ungar. *Popular Front Paris and the Poetics of Culture*. Cambridge, MA: The Belknap Press, 2005.

d'Annunzio, Gabriele. "L'Homme qui vola la Joconde." In *Anthologie du cinéma invisible: 100 scénarios pour cent ans de cinéma*, ed. Christian Janicot, 193–97. Paris: Jean-Michel Place/Arte éditions, 1995.

Anon. *Archives d'un visionnaire, Abel Gance, Collection Nelly Kaplan* (Auction catalogue). Paris: 1993, n.p.

Anon. "Au cinéma." *Le Crapouillot* (September 1918).

Anon. *Histoire du surréalisme. Documents surréalistes*. Paris: Club des éditeurs, 1958.

Anon. "Notre feuilleton." *Le Crapouillot* (April 1, 1919): 8.

Antongini, Tommaso. *D'Annunzio*. Freeport: Books For Library Press, 1971.

Apollinaire, Guillaume. "Avant le cinéma." *Nord-Sud* 2 (April 1917): n.p.; *Le Film* 135–36 (October 21, 1918): 17.

———. *L'Enchanteur pourrissant suivi de Les mamelles de Tirésias et de Couleur de temps*. Paris: Gallimard/poésie, 1972.

———. *Œuvres en prose*, vol. 1. Paris: Gallimard, 1977.

———. *Œuvres en prose*, vol. 2. Paris: Gallimard, 1991.

———. *A quelle heure un train partira-t-il pour Paris?* Edited by Willard Bohn. Fontfroide: Bibliothèque artistique et littéraire, 1982.

Apollinaire, Guillaume, and André Billy. *La Bréhatine, Archives des lettres modernes* 126. Paris: Minard, 1971.

Aragon, Louis. "Charlot mystique." *Nord-Sud* 15 (May 1918): n.p.

———. "Charlot sentimental." *Le Film* 105 (March 18, 1918): 11.

———. "Du Décor." *Le Film* 131 (September 16, 1918): 8–10.

———. "Voyages en kaléidoscope." *Littérature* 9 (November 1919): 8.

Arnar, Anna. *The Book as Instrument: Stéphane Mallarmé, the Artist's Book, and the Transformation of Print Culture.* Cambridge, MA: MIT Press, 2011.

Artaud, Antonin. *Œuvres.* Paris: Quarto Gallimard, 2004.

———. *Œuvres complètes*, vol. 3. Paris: Gallimard, 1963.

———. *L'Ombilic des limbes.* Paris: Gallimard/poésie, 1968.

Assouline, Pierre. *Gaston Gallimard: A Half-Century of Publishing.* Trans. Harold J. Salemson. New York: HBJ, 1988.

Astruc, Alexandre. "The Birth of a New Avant-Garde: *La Caméra-Stylo.*" In *The New Wave*, ed. Peter Graham, 17–22. Garden City, NJ: Doubleday, 1968.

Aumont, Jacques, ed. *Jean Epstein. Cinéaste, poète, philosophe.* Paris: La Cinémathèque française, 1998.

Azoury, Philippe, and Jean-Marc Lalanne. *Cocteau et le cinéma, désordres.* Paris: Cahiers du cinéma, 2003.

———. *Fantômes, style moderne.* Paris: Éditions Centry Pompidou/Yellow Now, 2002.

Bachelard, Gaston. *L'Air et les songes, essai sur l'imagination du mouvement.* Paris: José Corti, 1943.

Baetens, Jan. *La Novellisation, du film au roman.* Brussels: Les Impressions nouvelles, 2008.

———. *Vivre sa vie, une novellisation en vers du film de Jean-Luc Godard.* Afterword by Sémir Badir. Brussels: Les Impressions nouvelles, 2005.

Bajac, Quentin, and Dominique Planchon-de Font-Réaulx, eds. *Le daguerréotype français. Un object photographique.* Paris: Editions de la réunion des musées nationaux, 2003.

Bancquart, Marie-Claire. "D'une intériorisation de la poésie." In *Poésie de langue française 1945–1960*, ed. Marie-Claire Blancquart. Paris: PUF, 1995.

Barbaras, Renaud. *Le tournant de l'expérience. Recherches sur la philosophie de Merleau-Ponty.* Paris: Vrin, 1998.

Barjavel, René. *Le Cinéma total, essai sur les formes futures du cinéma.* Paris: Robert Denoël, 1944.

Baroncelli, Jacques de. *Écrits sur le cinéma.* Paris: Institut Jean Vigo, 1995.

Barthes, Roland. *Œuvres complètes,* vol. 5. Paris: Seuil, 2002.

Barzun, Henri-Martin. "L'Art poétique d'un idéal nouveau." *Paris-Journal* (December 16, 1913): n.p.

Bataille, George. *Œuvres complètes*, vol. 11. Paris: Gallimard, 1988.

Baudelaire, Charles. *Œuvres complètes*, vol. 1. Paris: Gallimard, 1975.

———. *Œuvres complètes*, vol. 2. Paris : Gallimard, 1976.

Baudry, Jean-Louis. "Compact sur compact." *La violence, le chant, Maurice Roche*, 157–69. L'Isle-sur-la-Sorgue: Les voisins du zéro, 1994.

———. *L'effet cinéma*. Paris: Albatros, 1978.

Bazin, André. *Qu'est-ce que le cinéma?* Paris: Le Cerf, 1981.

Beckett, Samuel. *Film*. New York: Grove Press, 1969.

Beckman, Karen. *Vanishing Women: Magic, Film, and Feminism*. Durham, NC: Duke University Press, 2003.

Beller, Jonathan. *The Cinematic Mode of Production: Attention Economy and the Society of the Spectacle*. Hanover, NH: Darthmouth College Press, 2006.

Bellour, Raymond. "Le dépli des émotions." *Trafic* 43 (fall 2002): 93–128.

———. *L'Entre-Images, Photo, Cinéma, Vidéo*. Paris: La Différence, 2002.

———. *L'Entre-Images 2, Mots, Images*. Paris: POL, 1999.

———. "Jean Epstein chez Henri Michaux." In *Jeune, dure et pure! Une histoire du cinema d'avant-garde et experimental en France*, ed. Nicole Brenez and Christin Lebrat. Paris and Milan: La Cinémathèque française and Mazzotta, 2001.

Bellows, Masaki, and Marina McDougall, eds. *Science Is Fiction: The Films of Jean Painlevé*. Cambridge, MA: MIT Press, 2000.

Bénézet, Mathieu. *La Fin de l'homme, roman abandonné*, avec 8 photos de Jean-Louis Rabeux. Paris: Flammarion, 1979.

———. *Le roman de la langue*. Paris: UGE 10/18, 1977.

Benítez-Rojo, Antonio. *The Repeating Island: The Caribbean and the Post-modern Perspective*. 2d ed. Durham, NC: Duke University Press, 1996.

Benjamin, Walter. "Chaplin in Retrospect." In *Selected Writings, vol. 2:1, 1927–1930*, ed. Michael W. Jennings et al., 222–24. Cambridge, MA: The Belknap Press of Harvard University Press, 1999.

———. *Illuminations*. Trans. Harry Zohn. New York: Shocken Books, 1969.

———. "One-Way Street." In *Selected Writings, vol. 1, 1913–1926*, ed. Marcus Bullock and Michael W. Jennings, 444–88. Cambridge, MA: The Belknap Press of Harvard University Press, 1996.

———. *Reflections*. Trans. Edmund Jephcott. New York: Schocken Books, 1986.

———. *Selected Writings, vol. 4, 1938–1940*. Edited by Howard Eilan and Michael W. Jennings. Cambridge, MA: The Belknap Press of Harvard University Pres, 2003.

Benveniste, Emile. *Problèmes de linguistique générale*. Paris: Gallimard, 1974.

Berge, André. "Cinéma et littérature." In *L'Art cinématographique*, vol. 3. Paris: Alcan, 1927.

———. "Connaissance de Cendrars." *Scénarios. Les Cahiers du mois* 12 (1925): 139.

Bergson, Henri. *Œuvres complètes*. Paris: Gallimard, 1959.

Bergstrom, Janet, ed. *Endless Night: Cinema and Psychoanalysis, Parallel Histories*. Berkeley: University of California Press, 1999.

Berr, Émile. "La Vie littéraire." *Le Figaro* (April 27, 1897): 3.

Bersani, Leo. *The Death of Mallarmé*. Cambridge, MA: Cambridge University Press, 1982.

Bersani, Leo, and Ulysse Dutoit. *Arts of Impoverishment: Beckett, Rothko, Resnais*. Cambridge, MA: Harvard University Press, 1993.

Bertho, Jean. "Autour de la revue *Surréalisme*." *Surréalisme* 1, 24–51. Paris: Jean-Michel-Place, 2004.

Bertrand, Aloysius. *Gaspard de la nuit*. Paris: Poésie/Gallimard, 1980.

Beucler, André. "Le Poème cinématographique." *Cinéma, Les Cahiers du mois* 16–17 (1925): 133–35.

———. *Un Suicide*. Paris: Gallimard, 1925.

Betz, Maurice. "*Drames de cinema*." *Scénarios. Les Cahiers du mois* 12 (1925).

Biran, Maine de. *Journal*, vol. 2. Neufchâtel: La Baconnière, 1955 [1824].

Blanchard, Claude. "La naissance d'un film." *Le Crapouillot* (March 16, 1922): 11–13.

Blanchot, Maurice. *L'Amitié*. Paris: Gallimard, 1971.

———. *Le Livre à venir*. Paris: Gallimard, 1959.

Blasing, Mutlu Konuk. *Lyric Poetry: The Pain and the Pleasure of Words*. Princeton, NJ: Princeton University Press, 2007.

Bohn, Willard. *Apollinaire and the Faceless Man*. Teaneck, NJ: Fairleigh Dickinson University Press, 1993.

———. *Modern Visual Poetry*. Newark: University of Delaware Press, 2001.

———. *The Rise of Surrealism: Cubism, Dada, and the Pursuit of the Marvelous*. Buffalo: SUNY Press, 2002.

Bolter, Jay David, and Richard Grusin. *Remediation: Understanding New Media*. Cambridge, MA: MIT Press, 2000.

Bonjean, Jacques. "Les Belles Noces dans la rue, scénario nouveau sur un thème banal." *Scénarios. Les Cahiers du mois* 12 (1925).

Bordwell, David. *Poetics of Cinema*. New York: Routledge, 2008.

Bordwell, David, Janet Staiger, and Kristin Thompson. *The Classical Hollywood Cinema: Film Style & Mode of Production to 1960*. New York: Routledge, 1988.

Boschetti, Anna. *La Poésie partout, Apollinaire, Homme-époque (1898–1918)*. Paris: Seuil, 2001.

Boutet, Frédéric. *Gribiche*. Paris: NRF, 1925.

Bowie, Malcolm. *Mallarmé and the Art of Being Difficult*. Cambridge, MA: Cambridge University Press, 1978.

Bracken, Len. *Guy Debord Revolutionary: A Critical Biography*. Venice: Feral House, 1997.

Bradbury, Ray. *The Illustrated Man*. New York: Bantham Books, 1951.

Braga, Dominique. "Un film de Charlot: une vie de chien." *Le Crapouillot* (December 31, 1918): 8.

Brague, Rémy. *L'Image vagabonde, essai sur l'imaginaire baudelairien*. Paris: La Transparence, 2008.

Brandt, Joan. *Geopoetics: The Politics of Mimesis in Poststructuralist Poetry and Theory*. Stanford: Stanford University Press, 1997.

Brennan, Teresa. *The Transmission of Affect*. Ithaca, NY: Cornell University Press, 2004.

Breton, André. *L'Amour fou*. Paris: Gallimard, 1937.

———. "As in a Wood." In *The Shadow and its Shadow: Surrealist Writings on the Cinema*, ed. and trans. Paul Hammond. San Francisco: City Lights Books, 2000.

———. *Manifestes du surréalisme*. Paris: Jean-Jacques Pauvert, 1962.

———. *Nadja*. Paris: Gallimard, 1966 [1928].

———. *Œuvres complètes*, 1. Paris: Gallimard, 1988.

———. *Œuvres complètes*, 2. Paris: Gallimard, 1992.

———. *Œuvres complètes*, 3. Paris: Gallimard, 1999.

———. *Œuvres complètes*, 4. Paris: Gallimard, 2008.

Breton, André, and Louis Aragon. "Liquidation." *Littérature* 18 (March 1921): 1–5.

Breuer, Joseph, and Sigmund Freud. *Studies on Hysteria*. New York: Basic Books, 1998 [*SE* VII].

Briant, Théophile. *Saint-Pol-Roux*, Paris: Seghers, 1971.

Broodthaers, Marcel. *Je hais le mouvement qui déplace les lignes*. Brussels: Edition Hossmann Hamburg, 1973.

Bullot, Erik. "Photogénie plastique." In *La Plasticité*, ed. Catherine Malabou. Paris: Léo Scheer, 2000.

Buñuel, Luis. *An Unspeakable Betrayal: Selected Writings*. Trans. Garrett White. Berkeley: University of California Press, 2000.

Burgin, Victor. *In/Different Spaces: Place and Memory in Visual Culture*. Berkeley: University of California Press, 1996.

Butler, Judith. "Merleau-Ponty and the Touch of Malebranche." In *The Cambridge Companion to Merleau-Ponty*, ed. Taylor Carman and Mark Hansen, 181–205. Cambridge: Cambridge University Press, 2005.

Butler, Kristine J. "Irma Vep, Vamp in the City: Mapping the Criminal Feminine in Early French Serials." In *A Feminist Reader in Early Cinema*, ed. Jennifer M. Bean and Diane Negra, 195–220. Durham, NC: Duke University Press, 2002.

Byg, Barton. *Landscapes of Resistance: The German Films of Danièle Huillet and Jean-Marie Straub*. Berkeley: University of California Press, 1995.

Cairns, Dorion. *Conversations with Husserl and Fink*. La Hague: Nijhoff, 1976.

Callahan, Vicki. "Screening Musidora: Inscribing Indeterminacy in Film History." *Camera Obscura* 48, 16, no. 3 (2001): 59–81.

Cameron, Oliver G. *Visceral Sensory Neuroscience: Interoception*. Oxford: Oxford University Press, 2002.

Canudo, Ricciotto. "L'Attaque dans l'orage." *L'Élan* 9 (February 1916): 14.

———. *L'Autre aile, roman visuel*. Paris: Fasquelle, 1924.

———. *La Roue, roman, d'après le film d'Abel Gance*. Paris: Ferenczi, 1923.

———. "Triomphe du cinématographe." *Il Nuovo giornale* (November 25, 1908).

———. *L'Usine aux images*. Paris: Etienne Chiron, 1927; reprint, ed. Jean-Pierre Morel, Paris: Séguier/Arte, 1995.

Caradec, François. *Raymond Roussel 1877-1933*. Paris: Fayard, 1997.

Carou, Alain. *Le Cinéma français et les écrivains. Histoire d'une rencontre, 1906–1914*. Paris: Ecole nationale des Chartes/AFRHC, 2002.

———. "Récits-Programmes dans les salles de cinéma: un apprentissage du silence?" In *Le Muet a la parole: cinéma et performance à l'aube du XXè siècle*, ed. Giusy Pisano and Valérie Pozner, 237–58. Paris: AFRHC, 2005.

Carroll, Noël. "Einsenstein's Philosophy of Film." *Camera Obscura, Camera Lucida: Essays in Honor of Annette Michelson*. Edited by Richard Allen and Malcolm Turvey. Amsterdam: Amsterdam University Press, 2003.

Carrouges, Michel. *Les machines célibataires*. Paris: Arcanes, 1954.

Cartoux, Paul and Decoin, Henry. *Le Roi de la pédale*. Paris: NRF, 1925.

Casey, Edward. *Imagining: A Phenomenological Study*. Bloomington: Indiana University Press, 1976.

Casares, Adolfo Bioy. *The Invention of Morel*. Trans. Ruth L. C. Smith. New York: NYRB Classics, 2003.

Casetti, Francesco. *Eye of the Century: Film, Experiencing, Modernity*. Trans. Erin Larkin. New York: Columbia University Press, 2008.

Castin, Nicolas. *Sens et sensible en poésie moderne et contemporaine*. Paris: PUF, 1998.

Cavell, Stanley. *The World Viewed: Reflections on the Ontology of Film.* Enlarged edition. Cambridge, MA: Harvard University Press, 1979.

Caws, Mary-Ann. "Cinema in Poetry." In *The Inner Theater of Recent French Poetry,* 26–51. Princeton, NJ: Princeton University Press.

Cayrol, Jean. *Nuit et brouillard.* Paris: Librairie Arthème Fayard, 1997.

Cayrol, Jean, and Claude Durand. *Le droit de regard.* Paris: Seuil, 1963.

Cendrars, Blaise. *Aujourd'hui 1917–1929.* Paris: Denoël, 1987.

———. "Charlot et la guerre." *Le Disque vert* 4–5 (1924): 78.

———. *Complete Poems.* Trans. Ron Padgett. Berkeley: University of California Press, 1992.

———. "Le Film de la fin du monde." *Le Mercure de France* 491 (1 December 1918): 419–30.

———. *Films sans images.* Paris: Denoël, 1959.

———. *Tout autour d'aujourd'hui [Œuvres complètes],* vol. 3. Paris: Denoël, 2001.

———. *Tout autour d'aujourd'hui [Œuvres complètes],* vol. 6. Paris: Denoël, 2003.

———. *Tout autour d'aujourd'hui [Œuvres complètes],* vol. 7. Paris: Denoël, 2003.

Cendrars, Miriam. *Blaise Cendrars.* Paris: Balland, 1984.

Chamary, Amadyll. "The Territorialization of the Imaginary in Latin America: Self-Affirmation and Resistance to Metropolitan Paradigms." In *Magical Realism: Theory, History, Community*, ed. Lois Parkinson Zamora and Wendy B. Faris, 125–43. Durham, NC: Duke University Press, 1995.

"Charlot." *Le Crapouillot* (September 15, 1918): 8.

"Charlot (Charlie Chaplin)." *Disque vert* 4–5 (1924).

Châteauvert, Jean, and André Gaudreault. "The Noises of Spectators, or the Spectator as Additive to the Spectacle." In *The Sounds of Early Cinema*, ed. Richard Abel and Rick Altman, 183–91. Bloomington: Indiana University Press, 2001.

Chenal, Pierre. *Drames sur celluloïd.* Paris: Les Perspectives, 1929.

Cherchi, Paolo Usai. *Silent Cinema: An Introduction.* London: BFI, 2000.

Chion, Michel. *Un art sonore, le cinéma.* Paris: Cahiers du cinéma, 2003.

Christin, Anne-Marie. *L'image écrite ou la déraison graphique.* Paris: Flammarion, 1995.

Clair, René. *Les Cahiers du mois* 16–17 (1925): 90.

Clarétie, Jules. "La Vie à Paris." *Le Temps* (February 13, 1896): 3.

Clerc, Jeanne-Marie. *Écrivains et cinéma*. Paris: Presses Universitaires de Metz, 1985.

Cocteau, Jean. *Carte blanche*. Paris: Éditions de la Sirène, 1920.

———. *Du Cinématographe*. Paris: Belfond, 1973.

———. *Le Coq et l'arlequin*. Paris: Éditions de la Sirène, 1918

———. *Œuvres complètes*, vol. 1. Genève: Marguerat, 1946.

———. *Œuvres poétiques complètes*. Paris: Gallimard, 1999.

———. *Le Potomak, 1913–1914, précédé d'un Prospectus 1916*. Paris: Librairie Stock, 1924.

———. *Le Sang d'un poète*. Photographs by Sacha Mansour. Monaco: Éditions du Rocher, 1948.

———. *Le Secret professionnel*. Paris: Au Sans Pareil, 1925.

———. "Textes inédits et textes retrouvés." In *Le cinéma de Jean Cocteau* suivi de *Hommage à Jean Marais*, ed. Christian Rolot. Montpellier: CELF du XXème siècle, 1994.

Code, David J. "The Formal Rhythms of Mallarmé's Faun." *Representation* 86 (spring 2004): 73–119.

Colette. *Au Cinéma*. Paris: Flammarion, 1975.

Combe, Dominique. *Poésie et récit, une rhétorique des genres*. Paris: José Corti, 1989.

Conley, Tom. *Cartographic Cinema*. Minneapolis: University of Minnesota Press, 2007.

———. *Film Hieroglyphics: Ruptures in Classical Cinema*. Minneapolis: University of Minnesota Press, 1991.

Connor, J. D. "Sartre and Cinema: The Grammar of Commitment." *MLN* 116, no. 5 (December 2001): 1045–68.

Crafton, Donald. *Émile Cohl, Caricature, and Film*. Princeton, NJ: Princeton University Press, 1990.

Crary, Jonathan. *The Suspension of Perception*. Cambridge, MA: MIT Press, 1999.

Crichtley, Simon. *The Ethics of Deconstruction: Derrida and Levinas*. London: Blackwell, 1992.

Cros, Charles. "Un Drame interastral." *La Renaissance littéraire et artistique* 18 (August 24, 1872): 139–40.

Currie, Gregory, and Ian Ravenscroft. *Recreative Minds: Imagination in Philosophy and Psychology*. Oxford: Clarendon, 2002.

Curtay, Jean-Paul. *La poésie lettriste*. Paris: Seghers, 1974.

Dagognet, François. *Etienne-Jules Marey, la passion de la trace*. Paris: Hazan, 1987.

Damas, Léon-Gontran. *Black-Label, poèmes*. Paris: Gallimard, 1956.

Danius, Sara. *The Senses of Modernism: Technology, Perception, and Esthetics*. Ithaca, NY: Cornell University Press, 2002.

Dausse, Camille. "En relisant *Donogoo-Tonka*." *Scénarios. Les Cahiers du mois* 12 (1925): 137.

Debord, Guy. *Potlatch* (1954–1957). Paris: Gallimard, 1996.

———. "Pourquoi le lettrisme?" In *Œuvres*. Paris: Gallimard, 2006.

Décaudin, Michel. *La Crise des valeurs symbolistes, 20 ans de poésie française (1895–1914)*. Toulouse: Privat, 1960.

———. "De l'espace figuré à l'espace signifiant." In *Poésure et peintrie*. Paris: Réunion des musées nationaux, 1993.

Delay, Alexandre, and Emmanuel Hocquard. *Le Voyage à Reykjavik, Chronique*. Paris: POL, 1997.

Deleuze, Gilles. *Cinema 1: The Movement-Image*. Trans. Hugh Tomlinson and Barbara Habberjam. Minneapolis: University of Minnesota Press, 1986.

———. "How Jarry's Pataphysics Opened the Way for Phenomenology." In *Desert Islands and Other Texts, 1953–1974*, trans. Michael Taormina. Los Angeles: Semiotext(e), 2004.

———. "Le plus grand film irlandais ('Film' de Beckett)." In *Critique et clinique*. Paris: Minuit, 1993.

Delluc, Louis. *Charlot*. Paris: de Brunhoff, 1921.

———. *Ecrits cinématographiques*. 3 vols. Paris: Cinémathèque française, 1985.

De Man, Paul. *Blindness and Insight: Essays in the Rhetoric of Contemporary Criticism*. Edited by Wlad Godzich. Minnesota: University of Minnesota Press, 1983.

———. *The Rhetoric of Romanticism*. New York: Columbia University Press, 1984.

Denett, Daniel. *Sweet Dreams: Philosophical Obstacles to a Science of Consciousness*. Cambridge, MA: MIT Press, 2006.

Dermée, Paul. *Films, Duodrames, Soliloques, Contes*. Paris: Collection de l'Esprit Nouveau, 1920.

Derrida, Jacques. *La Dissémination*. Paris: Seuil, 1972.

———. "Violence and Metaphysics: An Essay on the Thought of Emmanuel Levinas." In *Writing and Difference*, trans. Alan Bass, 79–194. Chicago: University of Chicago Press, 1978.

Desnos, Robert. *Les Rayons et les ombres, cinéma*. Paris: Gallimard, 1992.

Desser, David, and Lester D. Friedman. *American Jewish Filmmakers*. Urbana-Champaign: University of Illinois Press, 2004.

Desson, André. "Qualité du cinéma." *Cinéma. Les Cahiers du mois*, 16–17 (1925): 151.

Devaux, Frédérique. *Le Cinéma lettriste*. Paris: Paris expérimental, 1992.

———. *Traité de bave et d'éternité de Isidore Isou*. Crisnée: Yellow Now. 1994.

Diderot, Denis. *Premières œuvres*. Paris: Editions sociales, 1972.

Didi-Huberman, Georges. *Invention de l'hystérie: Charcot et l'iconographie photographique de la Salpêtrière*. Paris: Macula, 1982.

Disson, Agnès. "Comme au cinéma, façonner des minutes réelles: Pierre Alferi." *Contemporary French and Francophone Studies* 9, no. 3 (September 2005): 257–63.

Doane, Mary Ann. *The Emergence of Cinematic Time: Modernity, Contingency, the Archive*. Cambridge, MA: Harvard University Press, 2002.

Donguy, Jacques. *Poésies expérimentales – zone numérique* 1953–2007. Paris: Les Presses du réel, 2007.

Doppelt, Suzanne. *Le Pré est vénéneux*. Paris: POL, 2007.

———. *Quelque chose cloche*. Paris: POL, 2004.

———. *Totem*. Paris: POL, 2002.

Dotoli, Giovanni. *Ricciotto Canudo ou le cinéma comme art*. Paris: Schéna-Didier érudition, 1999.

Dragonetti, Roger. *Un Fantôme dans le kiosque, Mallarmé et l'esthétique du quotidien*. Paris: Le Seuil, 1992.

Drésa. "Leur Charlie et notre Charlot." *Le Crapouillot* (May 16, 1922): 17–18.

Drieu La Rochelle, Pierre. "L'Homme sans tête, 9ème épisode." *Le Crapouillot* (August 1, 1919): 16.

Drucker, Johanna. *The Visible Word: Experimental Typography and Modern Art, 1909–1923*. Chicago: University of Chicago Press, 1996.

Duchamp, Marcel. *Duchamp du signe, écrits*. Paris: Flammarion, 1975.

Dugas, Marcel. *Psyché au cinéma*. Montréal: Triptyque, 1998.

Duhamel, Georges. *Scènes de la vie future*. Paris: Mille et une nuit, 2003.

DuKore, Bernard F. *Bernard Shaw and Cinema*. Carbondale: Southern Illinois University Press, 1997.

Dumoncel, Jean-Claude. *Le Symbole d'Hécate, philosophie deleuzienne et roman proustien*. Caen: Hyx, 1996.

Duprey, Jean-Pierre. *Œuvres complètes*. Paris: Christian Bourgois, 1990.

Duras, Marguerite. *Hiroshima mon amour: scénarios et dialogues*. Paris: Gallimard, 1960.

Durozoi, Gérard. *History of the Surrealist Movement.* Trans. Alison Anderson. Chicago: University of Chicago Press, 1997.

Dyssord, Jacques. "En marge du cinéma." *Mercure de France* 116 (August 1916): 664–73.

Eisenstein, Sergei. *Eisenstein on Disney.* Trans. Alan Upchurch, edited by Jay Leyda. Calcutta: Seagull Books, 1986.

———. *The Eisenstein Reader.* Edited by Richard Taylor, trans. Richard Taylor and William Powell. London: BFI, 1998.

Ellison, Ralph. *Invisible Man.* New York: Vintage, 1990.

Epstein, Jean. *Bonjour cinéma.* Paris: Éditions de la Sirène, 1921.

———. *Écrits sur le cinéma,* vol. 1. Paris: Seghers, 1974.

———. *Écrits sur le cinéma,* vol. 2. Paris: Seghers, 1975.

———. *La Lyrosophie.* Paris: Éditions de la Sirène, 1922.

———. "Le Phénomène littéraire." In *Jean Epstein: cinéaste, poète, philosope,* ed. Jacques Aumont, 39–84. Paris: La Cinémathèque française, 1998.

———. *La Poésie d'aujourd'hui, un nouvel état d'intelligence.* Paris: Éditions de la Sirène, 1921.

Escoubas, Eliane. "Merleau-Ponty et les métamorphoses de l'image-imaginaire-imagination." In *Les Dons de l'image,* ed. Alain Cambier, 293–304. Paris: L'Harmattan, 2003.

Everdell, William. *The First Moderns: Profiles in the Origin of Twentieth-Century Thought.* Chicago: University of Chicago Press, 1997.

Fargue, Léon-Paul. "Ombres chinoises." In *Lanterne magique,* 216–31. Marseille: Robert Laffont, 1943.

Fauconnier, Gilles. *Mental Spaces: Aspects of Meaning Construction in Natural Languages.* Cambridge: Cambridge University Press, 1994.

Faye, Jean-Pierre, et al. "Dialogue sur les enjeux." *Change* 24 (October 1975): 48–70.

———, et al. "Pour Danielle Collobert." *Change* 38 (October 1979): 42–70.

Feliu, José Ignacio Prado. *Mi(l) lente(s): Aparatos, espacios y cuerpos cinemáticos en la literatura hispánica y francesca.* Madrid: Ediciones Libertarias, 1998.

Felman, Shoshana, and Dori Laub. *Testimony: Crises of Witnessing in Literature, Psychoanalysis and History.* New York: Routledge, 1991.

Fetzer, Glenn. *Emmanuel Hocquard and the Poetics of Negative Modernity.* New York: Summa Publications, 2007.

———. *Palimpsests of the Real.* Amsterdam: Rodopi, 2004.

Ffrench, Patrick. *The Time of Theory: A History of Tel Quel (1960–1983).* Oxford: Clarendon Press, 1995.

Fierens, Paul. "Charlot Little Titch et la poésie." *Le Disque vert* 4–5 (1924): 71.

Filteau, Claude. "Marcel Dugas et le 'cinéma en prose.'" *Études françaises* 39, no. 3 (2003): 29–45.

Finkelstein, Haim. *The Screen in Surrealist Art and Thought*. Hampshire, England: Ashgate, 2007.

Flinn, Margaret. "The Prescience of Élie Faure." *SubStance* 34, no. 3 (2005): 47–61.

Flusser, Vilém. *Pour une philosophie de la photographie*. Trans. Jean Mouchard. Paris: Circé, 1993.

Fondane, Benjamin. *Écrits pour le cinéma, le muet et le parlant*. Edited by Michel Carassou. Paris: Plasma, 1984.

———. *Faux traité d'esthétique. Essai sur la crise de réalité*. Paris: Denoël, 1938.

———. *Trois Scénarii, ciné-poèmes*. Bruxelles: Documents internationaux de l'esprit nouveau, 1928.

Forest, Philippe. "Mélancolies de l'histoire." In *Denis Roche: l'un écrit, l'autre photographie*, ed. Luigi Magno and Jean-Marie Gleize, 104–6. Paris: ENS Éditions, 2007.

Foster, Edward Halsey. *Understanding the Black Mountain Poets*. Columbia: University of South Carolina Press, 1995.

Foucault, Michel. *Birth of the Clinic: An Archeology of Medical Perception*. Trans. A. M. Sheridan Smith. New York: Vintage, 1994.

———. *Death and the Labyrinth: The World of Raymond Roussel*. Trans. Charles Ruas. New York: Doubleday, 1986.

———. *Dits et Écrits*, vol. 1. Paris: Gallimard, 1994.

———. *Naissance de la Clinique*. Paris: PUF, 1963.

———. *Raymond Roussel*. Paris: Gallimard, 1963.

Fouquier, Henry. "Les Théâtres." *Le Figaro* (November 15, 1896): 3.

Fourcade, Dominique. *Citizen Do*. Paris: POL, 2008.

Friedrich, Hugo. *The Structure of Modern Poetry*. Evanston, IL: Northwestern University Press, 1974.

Frizot, Michel. "Comment ça marche: l'algorithme cinématographique." *Cinémathèque* 15 (1999): 15–27.

Froger, Rémi. *Des prise de vues*. Paris: POL, 2008.

Galison, Peter. *Einstein's Clocks, Poincaré's Maps: Empires of Time*. New York: W. W. Norton, 2003.

Galtier-Boissière, Jean. "Charlot." *Le Crapouillot* (February 1, 1920): 12–14.

———. "Premier épisode: Le phonographe enchanté. L'Homme sans tête ou

Les Mystères du Bar Javanais. Roman-cinéma." *Le Crapouillot* (April 1, 1919): 8.

Gambacorti, Irene. *Storie di cinema e letteratura: Verga, Gozzano, D'Annunzio.* Florence: Società Editrice Fiorentina, 2003.

Game, Jérôme. *Corpse&Cinéma.* Cambridge: CCCP Press, 2002.

———. *écrire à même les choses.* Paris: Inventaire/invention, 2006.

———. *Flip-Book.* Rennes: Éditions de l'attente, 2007 (+DVD).

Gance, Abel. *Archives d'un visionnaire.* Catalogue of the collection Nelly Kaplan sold at Drouot Richelieu, Wednesday, March 3, 1993. Paris: 1993.

———. *Prisme.* Paris: Gallimard, 1930.

Gaudreault, André. *Du littéraire au filmique.* Paris: Nota Bene, 1999.

———. "Variation sur une problématique." In *La Transécriture, pour une théorie de l'adaptation*, ed. André Gaudreault and Thierry Groensteen, 267–71. Quebec: Nota bene, 1998.

Gaudreault, André, and François Albéra. "Apparition, disparition et escamotage du 'bonimenteur' dans l'historiographie française du cinema." In *Le muet a la parole: Cinéma et performance à l'aube du XXe siècle*, ed. Giusy Pisano and Valérie Pozner, 167–99. Paris: AFRHC, 2005.

Gaultier, Jules. *De Kant à Nietzsche.* Paris: Mercure de France, 1900.

Gauthier, Christophe. *La Passion du cinéma: Cinéphiles, ciné-clubs et salles specialisées à Paris de 1920 a 1929.* Paris: AFRHC, 1999.

Gauthier, Patrice, and François Lacassin. *Louis Feuillade, maître du cinéma populaire.* Paris: Gallimard, 2006.

Gautier, Théophile. *Récits fantastiques.* Paris: GF-Flammarion, 1981.

Ghali, Noureddine. *L'Avant-garde cinématographique en France dans les années vingt.* Paris: Paris expérimental, 1995.

Gibson, J. J. *The Ecological Approach to Visual Perception.* Hillsdale, NJ: Lawrence Erlbaum, 1979.

Gide, André. *Traité du Narcisse.* Paris: Mermod, 1946.

Giraudon, Liliane, and Christophe Chemin. *Mes bien-aimé(e)s.* Paris: Inventaire/invention, 2007.

Giraudoux, Jean. *Le Film de la Duchesse de Langeais.* Paris: Bernard Grasset, 1942.

Godard, Jean-Luc. *For Ever Mozart.* Paris: POL, 1996.

———. *Histoire(s) de cinéma.* Paris: Gallimard, 1998.

———. *JLG/JLG.* Paris: POL, 1996.

Gleize, Jean-Marie. *Les Chiens noirs de la prose.* Paris: Le Seuil, 1999.

———. *Film à venir.* Crest: La Sétérée, 1992.

———. *Film à venir, conversions*. Paris: Le Seuil, 2007.

———. "J'écris, donc je photographie." In *Denis Roche: l'un écrit, l'autre photographie*, ed. Luigi Magno and Jean-Marie Gleize. Paris: ENS Éditions, 2007.

———. *Néon, actes et légendes*. Paris: Le Seuil, 2004.

———. *A noir. Poésie et littéralité*. Paris: Seuil, 1992.

———. *Télévision*. N.p.: Vice Versa, 2001.

———. *Le Théâtre du poème, vers Anne-Marie Albiach*. Paris: Belin, 1995.

Goll, Ivan. *Die Chaplinade, Kinodichtung*. Dresden-Berlin: Rudolf Kämmerer Verlag, 1920.

——— [Tristan Torsi]. *Films (Verse)*. Berlin-Charlottenburg: Verlag der expressionistischen Hefte, 1914.

———. *Le Nouvel Orphée*, Paris: Éditions de la Sirène, 1923.

Gorceix, Paul. *Maurice Maeterlinck, le symbolisme de la différence*. Saint-Pierre-Du-Mont: Eurédit, 2005.

Gordon, Rae Beth. *Why the French Love Jerry Lewis: From Cabaret to Early Cinema*. Stanford: Stanford University Press, 2001.

Goulet, Andrea. *Optiques: The Science of the Eye and Modern French Fiction*. Philadelphia, PA: University of Pennsylvania P 2006.

Gourmont, Remy de. "Le Bûcher." *Mercure de France* 90 (June 1897): 558–63.

———. *Le Deuxième Livre des masques*. Paris: Mercure de France, 1898.

———. "Epilogues: Cinématographe" (*Mercure de France*). (September 1, 1907): 124–27.

Grau, Olivier. *Virtual Art: From Illusion to Immersion*. Trans. Gloria Custance. Cambridge, MA: MIT Press, 2003.

Greene, Naomi. *The National Past in Postwar French Cinema*. Princeton, NJ: Princeton University Press, 1999.

Grenier, Roger. *Ciné-roman*. Paris: Gallimard, 1972.

Grice, Paul. *Studies in the Way of Words*. Cambridge, MA: Harvard University Press, 1989.

Guerlac, Suzanne. *Literary Polemics: Bataille, Sartre, Valéry, Breton*. Stanford: Stanford University Press, 1997.

Guido, Laurent. *L'Âge du rythme*. Lausanne: Payot, 2007.

Gunning, Tom. "Before Documentary: Early Non-Fiction Films and the 'View' Aesthetic." In *Uncharted Territory: Essays on Early Non-Fiction Film*, ed. Daan Hertogs and Nico de Klerk. Amsterdam: Nederlands Filmmuseum, 1997.

———. "Loïe Fuller and the Art of Motion." *La Decima Musa/The Tenth Muse*, 25–34. Udine: Forum, 2001.

———. "Modernity and Cinema: A Culture of Shocks and Flows." In *Cinema and Modernity*, ed. Murray Pomerance, 297–315. Newark, NJ: Rutgers University Press, 2006.

———. "New Thresholds of Vision: Instantaneous Photography and the Early Cinema of the Lumière." In *Impossible Presence: Surface and Screen in the Photogenic Era*, ed. Terry Smith, 71–99. Chicago: Chicago University Press, 2001.

———. "Phantasmagoria and the Manufacturing of Illusions and Wonder: Towards a Cultural Optics of the Cinematic Apparatus." In *The Cinema, a New Technology for the 20th Century*, ed. André Gaudreault, Catherine Russell, and Pierre Veronneau, 31–44. Lausanne: Editions Payot, 2004.

Ha, Marie-Paule. *Figuring the East: Segalen, Malraux, Duras, and Barthes*. Albany: SUNY Press, 2000.

Hammond, Paul, ed. *The Shadow and its Shadow: Surrealist Writings on the Cinema*. London: BFI, 1978.

Hamon, Philippe. *Imageries, littérature et image au XIXe siècle*. Paris: José Corti, 2001.

Hamot, Odile. "La Clef et la cithare: Gourmont et la réception saintpolienne." In *Actualité de Remy de Gourmont*. Paris: Le Clown lyrique, 2008.

Hamp, Pierre (Henri Bourillon). *La Peine des hommes, le rail*. Paris: NRF, 1912.

Hanna, Christophe. *Poésie action directe*. Romainville: Al Dante, 2003.

Hansen, Mark. *Embodying Technesis: Technology Beyond Writing*. Ann Arbor: University of Michigan Press, 2002.

Hansen, Miriam Brattu. "Benjamin and Cinema: Not a One-Way Street." In *Benjamin's Ghosts: Interventions in Contemporary Literary and Cultural Theory*, ed. Gerhard Richter, 41–73. Stanford: Stanford University Press, 2002.

Harper, Graeme, and Rob Stone, ed. *The Unsilvered Screen: On Surrealism and Film*. London and New York: Wallflower Press, 2007.

Hayles, N. Katherine. *How We Became Posthuman: Virtual Bodies in Cybernetics, Literature, and Informatics*. Chicago: Chicago University Press, 1999.

———. *Writing Machines*. Cambridge, MA: MIT Press, 2002.

Hayman, David. "An Interview with Maurice Roche." In *The Wake of the Wake*, ed. David Hayman and Elliott Anderson. Madison: University of Wisconsin Press, 1978.

Heidegger, Martin. *Being and Time*. Trans. John Macquarrie and Edward Robinson. San Francisco: Harper, 1962.

Hellens, Franz. "Avant-propos." *Le Disque vert* 4–5 (1924).

Heller-Roazen, Daniel. *The Inner Touch: Genealogy of a Sensation*. New York: MIT Press, 2007.

Henry, Maurice. *Philosophie et phénoménologie du corps*. Paris: PUF, 1965.

Heu, Pascal Manuel. *Le Temps du cinéma, Émile Vuillermoz père de la critique cinématographique, 1910–1930*. Paris: L'Harmattan, 2003.

Higgins, Lynn A. *New Novel, New Wave, New Politics: Fiction and the Representation of History in Postwar France*. Lincoln: University of Nebraska Press, 1996.

Hill, Leslie. *Blanchot: Extreme Contemporary*. London: Routledge, 1997.

Hillel-Erlanger, Irène. "Diaphragme." *Ms*. Bibliothèque du Film. Paris. GD4441.

———. "Par amour." *Littérature* 10 (1919).

———. "Tour du monde et coeur du monde." *Le Promenoir* 3 (1921) 12–14.

———. *Voyages en kaléidoscope*. Paris: Georges Crès, 1919; reprint, Paris: Éditions Allia, 1996.

Hirsch, Joshua. *Afterimage: Film, Trauma, and the Holocaust*. Philadelphia, PA: Temple University Press, 2004.

Histoire du surréalisme. Paris: Club des éditeurs, 1958.

Hochberg, Julian, and Virginia Brooks. "Movies in the Mind's Eye." In *Post-Theory: Reconstructing Film Studies*, ed. David Bordwell and Noël Carroll, 368–87. Madison: University of Wisconsin Press, 1996.

Hocquard, Emmanuel. *Une Journée dans le détroit, récit*. Paris: Hachette, 1980.

———. *Ma Haie*. Paris: POL, 2001.

———. *Théorie des tables*. Paris: POL, 1991.

Houppermans, Sjef. "Alain Robbe-Grillet et le photoroman." In *Le Roman-Photo: actes du colloques de Calaceite*, ed. Jan Baetens and Ana González, 112–30. Amsterdam: Rodopi, 1996.

Hubert, Étienne-Alain. *Circonstances de la poésie: Reverdy, Apollinaire, surréalisme*. Paris: Klincsieck, 2000.

Huet, Marie-Hélène. *Monstrous Imagination*. Cambridge, MA: Harvard University Press, 1993.

Hugnet, Georges. *La Hampe de l'imaginaire*. Paris: G.L.M., 1936.

Huret, Jules. "Concerts et spectacles." *Le Figaro* (February 11, 1896): 4.

———. "Le Courrier des théâtres." *Le Figaro* (April 23, 1896): 4.

Husserl, Edmund. *The Essential Husserl: Basic Writings in Transcendental Phenomenology*. Edited by Donn Welton. Bloomington: Indiana University Press, 1999.

Huysmans, Karl. *A Rebours*. Paris, Charpentier, 1884.

Huyssen, Andreas. *After the Great Divide: Modernism, Mass Culture, Postmodernism*. Bloomington: Indiana University Press, 1987.

Iampolski, Mikhaïl. "La danse, le cinéma et un peu de physique." *Cinémathèque* 9 (1996): 94–103.

———. *The Memory of Tiresias: Intertextuality and Film*. Berkeley: University of California Press, 1998.

Ibels, André. "Enquête sur le roman illustré par la photographie." *Mercure de France* 92 (January 1898): 97–115.

Icart, Roger. *Abel Gance*. Lausanne: L'Age d'homme, 1983.

Illouz, Jean-Nicolas. *Le Symbolisme*. Paris: LGF, 2004.

Irigaray, Luce. *Speculum, de l'autre femme*. Paris: Minuit, 1974.

Iser, Wolfgang. *The Fictive and the Imaginary: Charting Literary Anthropology*. Baltimore, MD: Johns Hopkins University Press, 1993.

Isou, Isidore. *L'Agrégation d'un nom et d'un messie*. Paris: Gallimard, 1947.

———. *Esthétique du cinéma*. Paris: Ur, 1953.

———. *Introduction à une nouvelle poésie et une nouvelle musique*. Paris: Gallimard, 1947.

———. *Œuvres de spectacle*. Paris: Gallimard, 1964.

———. *Traité d'économie nucléaire. Le Soulèvement de la jeunesse*. Lausanne: Escaliers de Lausanne, 1949.

Jacob, Max. *Cinématoma*. Paris: Éditions de la Sirène, 1920.

———. "Petite chronique cinématographique." *L'Élan* 10 (December 1, 1916): 5.

———. "Printemps et cinématographe mêlés." *Les Soirées de Paris* 75 (April 15, 1914): 219.

———. "Théâtre et cinéma." *Nord-Sud* 12 (February 1918): 9–12.

Jameson, Fredric. *Postmodernism, or The Cultural Logic of Late Capitalism*. Durham, NC: Duke University Press, 1991.

Janicot, Christian. *Anthologie du cinéma invisible: 100 scénarios pour cent ans de cinéma*. Paris: Jean-Michel Place/Arte éditions, 1995.

Jarry, Alfred. *Œuvres complètes*, vol. 1. Paris: Gallimard, 1972.

———. *Œuvres complètes*, vol. 2. Paris: Gallimard, 1987.

Jay, Martin. *Downcast Eyes: The Denigration of Vision in Twentieth-Century French Thought*. Berkeley: University of California Press, 1994.

Jeanne, Max. *Western. Ciné-poème guadeloupéen*. Paris: L'Harmattan, 1978.

Jenkins, Bruce. "Un Peu tard: Cita en el cine de Marcel Broodthaers." In *Marcel Broodthaers: Cinéma*, ed. Manuel J. Borja-Villel and Michael

Compton, Exhibition catalog 289–310. Barcelona: Fundació Antoni Tàpies, 1997.

Kahn, Gustave. "Essai sur le vers libre." *Premiers poèmes.* Paris: Mercure de France, 1897.

Kaplan, Nelly. *Le Collier de ptyx, ciné-roman.* Paris: Jean-Jacques Pauvert, 1971.

———. *Manifeste d'un art nouveau: la Polyvision.* Paris: Caractères, 1955.

Kearney, Richard. *The Wake of Imagination.* Oxon: Century Hutchinson, 1988.

Kirsten, Guido. "Genèse d'un concept et ses avatars: La naissance de la théorie du dispositif cinématographique." *Cahiers Louis Lumière 4: Les Dispositifs.* Noisy-Le-Grand: 2007, 8–16.

Kitayama, Kenji. "Raymond Roussel et le cinéma des origines." In *Raymond Roussel: Nouvelle impressions critiques* 1. Paris: Minard, 2001.

Kittler, Friedrich A. *Gramophone, Film, Typewriter.* Trans. Geoffrey Winthorp-Young and Michael Wutz. Stanford: Stanford University Press, 1999.

Klerk, Nico de. "Program Formats." In *Encyclopedia of Early Cinema*, ed. Richard Abel, 533–35. London: Routledge, 2005.

Kluitenberg, Eric. "Second Introduction to an Archaeology of Imaginary Media." *Book of Imaginary Media: Excavating the Dream of the Ultimate Communication Medium.* Rotterdam: NAi, 2006.

Kojève, Alexandre. *Introduction à la lecture de Hegel.* Paris: Gallimard, 1947.

Kotz, Liz. *Words to Be Looked At.* Cambridge, MA: MIT Press, 2008.

Krauss, Rosalind. *Bachelors.* Cambridge, MA: MIT Press, 2000.

———. *A Voyage on the North Sea: Art in the Age of the Post-Medium Condition.* New York: Thames and Hudson, 2000.

Krell, David Farrell. *Daimon Life: Heidegger and Life-Philosophy.* Bloomington: Indiana University Press, 1992.

Krueger, Cheryl. "Surgical Imprecision and the Baudelairean *poèm en prose*," French Forum 27:3 (Fall 2002): 55–72.

Kuenzli, Rudolf E., ed. *Dada and Surrealist Film.* New York: Willis Locker & Owens, 1987.

Kyrou, Ado. *Le Surréalisme au cinéma.* Paris: Le Terrain vague, 1952.

Lacan, Jacques. *Les quatre concepts fondamentaux de la psychanalyse.* Paris: Seuil, 1973.

———. *Le Séminaire* I. Paris: Seuil, 1975.

Lacassin, Francis. *A la recherche de l'empire caché. Mythologie du roman populaire.* Paris: Julliard, 1991.

Lacoue-Labarthe, Philippe. *La Fiction du politique.* Paris: Christian Bourgois, 1987.

Lacoue-Labarthe, Philippe, and Jean-Luc Nancy. *The Literary Absolute: The Theory of Literature in German Romanticism*. Trans. Philip Barnard and Cheryl Lester. Albany: SUNY Press, 1988.

Lakoff, George. *Women, Fire and Other Dangerous Things: What Categories Reveal About the Mind*. Chicago: University of Chicago Press, 1990.

Lamartine, Alphone de. *Œuvres complètes*, vol. 1. Paris: chez l'auteur, 1860.

Lange, André. *Histoire de la télévision*. http:/histv2.free.fr (accessed November 11, 2011).

Latour, Bruno. *We Have Never Been Modern*. Trans. Catherine Porter. Cambridge, MA: Harvard University Press, 1993.

Laugier, Emmanuel. *Son Corps flottant*. Brussels: Didier Devillez Éditeur, 2000.

Lawder, Standish. *The Cubist Cinema*. New York: New York University Press, 1975.

Lawlor, Leonard. *The Challenge of Bergsonism*. London: Continuum, 2003.

Le Forestier, Laurent. "Entre cinéisme et filmologie: Jean Epstein, la plaque tournante." In *La Filmologie, de nouveau,* ed. François Albera and Martin Lefebvre, *Cinémas* 19, nos. 2–3 (spring 2009): 113–40.

———. "*Le Roi de la pédale*: La projection muette comme état transitoire au coeur d'un événement." In *Le muet a la parole: Cinéma et performance à l'aube du XXe siècle*, ed. Giusy Pisano and Valérie Pozner, 259–77. Paris: AFRHC, 2005.

Lemaître, Maurice. *Carnets d'un fanatique II*. Paris: Jean Grassin Éditeur, 1960.

———. *Au-delà du déclic*. Paris: Centre de créativité, 1965.

———. *Le Film est déjà commencé?* Paris: André Bonne, 1952.

———. *Maurice Lemaître*. Paris: Du Centre Georges Pompidou, 1995.

Lermina, Jules. *La Deux Fois Morte*. Paris: Fayard, 2003 [1895].

Lernout, Geert, and Wim Van Mierlo. *The Reception of James Joyce in Europe*. London: Continuum, 2004.

Leroi-Gourhan, André. *Le geste et la parole: la mémoire et les rythmes*. Paris: Albin Michel, 1965.

Leroy, Claude, and Jean-Carlo Flückiger. *Cendrars, le bourlingueur des deux rives*. Paris: A. Colin, 1995.

Lespiau, David. *Ouija Board*. Trans. Cole Swensen and Cosima Weiter. Genève: Héros-Limite, 2008.

Levinas, Emmanuel. "La réalité et son ombre." *Les Temps Modernes* (November 1948): 769–89.

———. *Totalité et infini: essai sur l'extériorité*. Paris: Kluwer Academic, 1998.

Lévy, Pierre. *Becoming Virtual: Reality in the Digital Age*. Trans. Robert Bononno. New York: Basic Books, 1998.

Leys, Ruth. *Trauma: A Genealogy*. Chicago: University of Chicago Press, 2000.

L'Herbier, Marcel. "Le Cinématographe et l'espace." In *L'Art cinématographique* IV. Paris: Alcan, 1927.

Liebman, Stuart. "Un Chien Andalou: The Talking Cure." In *Dada and Surrealism Film*, ed. Rudolf E. Kuenzli, 143–58. New York: Willis Locker & Owens, 1987.

Lippit, Akira Mizuta. *Atomic Light (Shadow Optics)*. Minneapolis: University of Minnesota Press, 2005.

Lista, Giovanni. *Loïe Fuller, danseuse de la Belle-Époque*. Paris: Stock, 1994.

Llinás, Rodolfo. *I of the Vortex: From Neurons to Self*. Cambridge, MA: MIT, 2002.

Loreau, Max. *La peinture à l'oeuvre et l'énigme du corps*. Paris: Gallimard, 1980.

Lowry, Edward. *The Filmology Movement and Film Study in France*. Ann Arbor: University of Michigan Press, 1985.

Lukasiewicz, Jan. *Du Principe de contradiction chez Aristote*. Trans. Dorota Sikora. Paris: L'Éclat, 2000.

Lupton, Catherine. *Chris Marker: Memories of the Future*. London: Reaktion Books, 2005.

Lynn, Kenneth Schuyler. *Charlie Chaplin and His Times*. New York: Simon & Schuster, 1997.

Lyotard, Jean-François. *Discours, figure*. Paris: Klincksieck, 1971.

Mac Orlan, Pierre. *François Villon, un film*. Paris: Maréchal, 1945.

Magno, Luigi, and Jean-Marie Gleize, eds. *Denis Roche: l'un écrit, l'autre photographie*. Paris: ENS Éditions, 2007.

Malabou, Catherine, ed. *La Plasticité*. Paris: Léo Scheer, 2000.

———. *La Plasticité au soir de l'écriture: dialectique, destruction, déconstruction*. Paris: Léo Scheer, 2005.

Mallarmé, Stéphane. *Correspondance*. 12 vols. Edited by Henri Mondor, Jean-Pierre Richard, and Lloyd James Austin. Paris: Gallimard, 1959–85.

———. *Le "Livre" de Mallarmé*. Edited by Jacques Scherer. Paris: Gallimard, 1977.

———. *Œuvres complètes*, vol. 1. Edited by Bertrand Marchal. Paris: Gallimard, 1998.

———. *Œuvres complètes*, vol. 2. Edited by Bertrand Marchal. Paris: Gallimard, 2003.

Malraux, André. *Esquisse d'une psychologie du cinéma.* Paris: Gallimard, 1945.

Mannoni, Laurent. *The Great Art of Light and Shadow: Archaeology of the Cinema.* Trans. Richard Crangle. Exeter: University of Exeter Press, 2000.

———. "Une féerie de 1896: *La Biche au bois.*" *Cinémathèque* 10 (1996): 117–23.

Marcel Broodthaers: Cinéma. Exhibition catalogue. Barcelona: Fundació Antoni Tàpies, 1997.

Marchal, Bertrand. *Mallarmé: Mémoire de la critique.* Paris: Presses de l'Université de Paris-Sorbonne, 1998.

Marcus, Greil. *Lipstick Traces: A Secret History of the Twentieth Century.* Cambridge, MA: Harvard University Press, 1989.

Marcus, Laura. *The Tenth Muse: Writing About Cinema in the Modernist Period.* Oxford: Oxford University Press, 2007.

Marey, Étienne-Jules. *Le Mouvement.* Nîmes: Jacqueline Chambon, 2002 [1894].

Margulis, Ivone, ed. *Rites of Realism: Essays on Corporeal Cinema.* Durham: Duke University Press, 2003.

Mariën, Marcel. *L'Imitation du cinéma.* Bruxelles: Les Lèvres nues, 1992 [1961].

Marker, Chris. *Commentaires* I. Paris: Seuil, 1961.

———. *Coréennes*, Paris: Le Seuil, 1959.

Marks, Laura U. *The Skin of the Film: Intercultural Cinema, Embodiment, and the Senses.* Durham, NC: Duke University Press 2000.

Martin-Schmets, Victor. "Céline Arnauld, épouse Paul Dermée, poète dadaïste." In *Les Oubliés des avant-gardes*, ed. Barbara Meazzi and Jean-Pol Madou. Chambéry: Université de Savoie, 2006.

Massumi, Brian. *Parables for the Virtual: Movement, Affect, Sensation.* Durham, NC: Duke University Press, 2002.

Maurier, George du. "Edison's Telephonoscope." *Punch's Almanack* (December 8, 1879).

Maynard, Patrick. *The Engine of Visualization: Thinking Through Photography.* Ithaca, NY: Cornell University Press, 1997.

McCabe, Susan. *Cinematic Modernism: Modernist Poetry and Film.* Cambridge: Cambridge University Press, 2005.

McCarren, Felicia. *Dance Pathologies: Performance, Poetics, Medicine.* Stanford: Stanford University Press, 1998.

———. "Mallarmé at the Movies." *L'Esprit créateur* 40, no. 3 (2000): 25–38.

McDonough, Tom. *"The Beautiful Language of My Century": Reinventing the Language of Contestation in Postwar France, 1945–1968*. Cambridge, MA: MIT Press, 2007.

McGann, Jerome. *Black Riders: The Visible Language of Modernism*. Princeton, NJ: Princeton University Press, 1993.

McGinn, Colin. *Mindsight: Image, Dream, Meaning*. Cambridge, MA: Harvard University Press, 2004.

———. *The Power of Movies: How Screen and Mind Interact*. New York: Vintage Books, 2005.

Meersxt, Joëlle, and Benoît Peeters. *Fugues*. Photographs by Marie-Françoise Plissart. Paris: Éditions de minuit, 1983.

Merleau-Ponty, Maurice. "Le Cinéma et la nouvelle psychologie." *Les Temps modernes* 3, no. 26 (November 1947): 930–43.

———. *Husserl at the Limits of Phenomenology*. Edited by Leonard Lawlor. Evanston: Northwestern University Press, 2002.

———. *L'oeil et l'esprit*. Paris: Gallimard, 1964.

———. *La phénoménologie de la perception*. Paris: Gallimard, 1945.

———. *Le visible et l'invisible*. Paris: Gallimard, 1964.

———. *The Visible and the Invisible*. Trans. Alphonso Lingis. Evanston, IL: Northwestern University Press, 1969.

Meschonnic, Henri. *Le Langage Heidegger*. Paris: PUF, 1991.

———. "Mallarmé au-delà du silence." In *Écrits sur le livre*, ed. Michel Valensi. Paris: Éditions de l'éclat, 1985.

Meusy, Jean-Jacques. *Paris-Palaces, ou le temps des cinémas* (1894–1918). Paris: CNRS, 1995.

Michaux, Henri. *Face aux verrous*. Paris: Poésie/Gallimard, 1992.

———. *Misérable miracle*. Paris: Poésie/Gallimard, 1972.

———. *Œuvres complètes*, 1. Paris: Gallimard, 1998.

———. *Œuvres complètes*, 2. Paris: Gallimard, 2001.

———. *Œuvres complètes*, 3. Paris: Gallimard, 2004.

———. *Paix dans les brisements*. Paris: Flinker, 1959.

Michelson, Annette. "On the Eve of the Future: The Reasonable Facsimile and the Philosophical Toy." *October* 29 (1988): 3–20.

Milner, Max. *Fantasmagorie, essai sur l'optique fantastique*. Paris: PUF, 1982.

Missac, Pierre. *Walter Benjamin's Passages*. Trans. Shierry Weber Nicholsen. Cambridge, MA: MIT Press, 1995.

Møller, Aage R. *Sensory Systems: Anatomy and Physiology*. Amsterdam: Academic Press/Elsevier, 2003.

Mondor, Henri. *Autres précisions sur Mallarmé et inédits*. Paris: Gallimard, 1961.

———. *Vie de Mallarmé.* Paris: Gallimard, 1941.

Moore, Rachel O. *Savage Theory: Cinema as Modern Magic.* Durham, NC: Duke University Press, 2000.

Moran, Dermot. *Introduction to Phenomenology.* London: Routledge, 2000.

Morel, Jean-Paul. "Artaud et le cinéma." *Obliques* 11–12 (1976): 117–32.

Morin, Edgar. *Le cinéma ou l'homme imaginaire. Essai d'anthropologie.* Paris: Minuit, 1956.

———. *The Cinema, or The Imaginary Man.* Trans. Lorraine Mortimer. Minneapolis: University of Minnesota Press, 2005.

———. *The Stars.* Trans. Richard Howard. Minneapolis: University of Minnesota Press, 2005.

Morris, David. *The Sense of Space.* Albany: SUNY Press, 2004.

Mourier, Maurice. "Michaux cinémane et cinématicien." In *Méthodes et savoirs chez Henri Michaux*, ed. Gérard Dessons. *La Licorne* 25 (1993): 43–62.

Moussinac, Léon. *Panoramique du cinéma.* Paris: Au sans pareil, 1929.

———. "Le scénario." *Le Crapouillot* (March 16, 1922): 11–13.

Mouton, Joseph. *Delenda West.* Postface by Patrice Ménaglier. Paris: Les Petits Matins, 2007.

Nemer, François. "Cocteau s'amuse." *Cinéma 04* (fall 2002): 74–82.

Némirovsky, Irène. *Films parlés.* Paris: NRF, 1934.

Nesbitt, Molly. *Their Common Sense.* London: Black Dog Publishing, 2000.

Noë, Alva. *Action in Perception.* Cambridge, MA: MIT Press, 2004.

Noël, Bernard. *Journal du regard.* Paris: POL, 1988.

———. *Poèmes 1.* Paris: Flammarion, 1983.

Noguez, Dominique. "Gide et le cinéma." *Revue des Lettres modernes* 1033–38 (1992): 151–87.

Noland, Carrie. *Poetry at Stake: Lyric Aesthetic and the Chalenge of Technology.* Princeton, NJ: Princeton University Press, 1999.

Oberthür, Mariel. *Henri Rivière. Connu, méconnu.* Semur-en-Auxois: Spiralinthe, 2004.

Oliver, Kelly. *Witnessing: Beyond Recognition.* Minneapolis: University of Minnesota Press, 2001.

Olson, Charles. "Projective Verse." In *Collected Prose*, ed. Donald Allen and Benjamin Friedlander. Berkeley: University of California Press, 1997.

Ong, Walter. *Orality and Literacy: The Technologizing of the Word.* London: Routledge, 1982.

Ortel, Philippe. *La Littérature à l'ère de la photographie, enquête sur une révolution invisible.* Nîmes: Jacqueline Chambon, 2002.

Parsons, Melinda Boyd, and Gary Joseph Pascuzzo. "Bernard Shaw, 'Unmechanical' Photography and Unconventional Science." *History of Photography* 2, no. 3 (autumn 2002): 170–77.

Pasolini, Pier Paolo. "The Cinema of Poetry" [1965]. In *Post-War Cinema and Modernity*, ed. John Orr and Olga Taxidou. New York: New York University Press, 2001.

———. "The Screenplay as a 'Structure That Wants To Be Another Structure.'" In *Heretical Empiricism*, ed. Ben Lawton and Louise K. Barnett, 186–96. Bloomington: University of Indiana Press, 1988.

Peeters, Benoît, and Marie-Françoise Plissart. "A La Recherche du roman-photo." *Photo-littérature, Revue des sciences humaines* 210 (1988): 77–82.

Péret, Benjamin. *De Derrière les fagots*. Paris: G.L.M. 1934.

———. "The Dishonor of Poets." In *Literary Debate: Texts and Contexts, Postwar French Thought*, vol. 2, ed. Denis Hollier and Jeffrey Melhman. New York: The New Press, 2001.

———. "Pulchérie veut une auto." *Littérature* 10 (May 1923): 17–23.

Perloff, Marjorie. *Radical Artifice: Writing Poetry in the Age of Media*. Chicago: University of Chicago Press, 1991.

Perrot, Victor. "Le cinéma est-il une écriture?" *Le Crapouillot* (May 1, 1920) 17.

Pichette, Henri. "Préface à un film." *La Délirante* 7 (1967).

———. *Rond-Point*. Paris: Mercure de France, 1950.

Pittolo, Véronique. *Gary Cooper ne lisait pas de livre*. Romainville: Al Dante, 2004.

———. *Montage*. Paris: Fourbis, 1992.

Polizzotti, Mark. *A Revolution of the Mind: The Life of André Breton*. New York: Farrar, Straus & Giroux, 1995.

Pomerand, Gabriel. *Saint ghetto des prêts, grimoire*. Brooklyn: Ugly Duckling Press, 2006.

Ponge, Francis. *Œuvres complètes* 1. Paris: Gallimard, 1999.

———. "Le sérieux défait." *Le Disque vert* 4–5 (1924): 50.

Portugal, Anne, and Suzanne Doppelt. *Dans la reproduction en 2 parties égales des plantes et des animaux*. Paris: POL, 1999.

Poulaille, Henry. "Charlie Chaplin écrivain." In *Cahiers Henry Poulaille*, 2–3. Bassac: Plein Chant, 1990.

———. *Charlot*. Paris: B. Grasset, 1927.

Prédal, René. *50 ans de cinéma français*. Paris: Nathan, 1997.

Prieur, Jérôme, and Jean-Paul Morel. "La machine à l'œil buté." *Obliques* [on Artaud] 10–11 (1976): 107–35.

Proust, Marcel. *Sodome et Gomorrhe*, vol. 1. Paris: Gallimard, 1988.

Queneau, Raymond. *Œuvres complètes* 1. Paris: Gallimard, 1989.

Quillier, Patrick, ed. *Court-métrage, quatre arguments pour le cinématographe*. Paris: Chandeigne, 2007.

Quintane, Nathalie. *Grand ensemble*, Paris: POL, 2008.

———. *Mortinsteinck, le livre du film*. Paris: POL, 1999.

Quintyn, Olivier. "Clicks n'Cuts." In *Denis Roche: l'un écrit, l'autre photographie*, ed. Luigi Magno and Jean-Marie Gleize, 287–98. Paris: ENS Éditions, 2007.

———. *Dispositifs/dislocations*. Marseille: Al Dante, 2007.

Rabinach, Anson. *The Human Motor: Energy, Fatigue, and the Origins of Modernity*. Berkeley: University of California Press, 1992.

Rancière, Jacques. "The Distribution of the Sensible." In *The Politics of Aesthetics*, trans. and introduction Gabriel Rockhill. London: Continuum, 2004.

———. *L'Espace des mots. De Mallarmé à Broodthaers*. Nantes: Édition Musée des beaux-arts de Nantes, 2005.

———. *La Fable cinématographique*. Paris: Le Seuil, 2001.

———. *Film Fables*. Trans. Emiliano Battista. London: Berg, 2006.

———. *The Flesh of Words*. Trans. Charlotte Mandell. Stanford: Standford University Press, 2004.

———. *The Future of the Image*. Trans. Gregory Elliott. London: Verso, 2007.

———. *Mallarmé, la politique de la sirène*. Paris: Hachette, 1996.

Ramirez, Francis. "Poésie et cinéma." In *Le Cinéma au rendez-vous des arts, France années 20 et 30*, ed. Emmanuelle Toulet. Paris: Bibliothèque Nationale de France, 1995.

Ramirez, Francis, and Christian Rolot. "Apollinaire et le désir de cinéma." *Cinémathèque* 7 (1995): 50–60.

Ray, Robert B. *How a Film Theory Got Lost and Other Mysteries in Cultural Studies*. Bloomington: Indiana University Press, 2001.

Rebourg, Michel. "Entre graphe et scope: Roussel au cinéma." *Europe* 714 (1988): 131–37.

Reynolds, Dee. *Symbolist Esthetics and Early Abstract Art*. Cambridge: Cambridge University Press, 1995.

Reverdy, Pierre. *Cette émotion appelée poésie*. Paris: Flammarion, 1974.

———. *Flaques de verre*. Paris: Flammarion, 2009.

———. *La Lucarne ovale*. Paris: Théâtre typographique, 2001.

———. "Le cinématographe." *Nord-Sud* 16 (October 1918): 8.

———. *Plupart du temps*, vol. 1. Paris: Gallimard, 1969.

———. "Ponctuation." *Nord-Sud* 8 (October 1917): 2.

Richard, Jean-Pierre. *L'Univers imaginaire de Mallarmé*. Paris: Seuil, 1961.

Richardson, Michael. *Surrealism and Cinema*. Oxford: Berg, 2006.

Richir, Marc. *Phantasia, imagination, affectivité*. Grenoble: Millon, 2004.

Richter, Gerhard, ed. *Benjamin's Ghosts: Interventions in Contemporary Literary and Cultural Theory.*. Stanford: Stanford University Press, 2002.

Rittaud Huttinet, Jacques, and Chantal Rittaud Huttinet. *Dictionnaire des cinématographes en France (1896–1897)*. Paris: Champion, 1999.

Robbe-Grillet, Alain. *Glissements progressifs du plaisir, ciné-roman illustré de 56 photographies du film*. Paris: Éditions de minuit, 1973.

Robinson, David. *Chaplin: His Life & Art*. New York: Da Capo Press, 1985.

Roche, Denis. *Dépôts de savoir & technique*. Paris: Le Seuil, 1980.

———. *La Poésie est inadmissible, œuvres poétiques complètes*. Paris: Le Seuil, 1995.

Roche, Maurice. "Calques. Récit." In *Montage*, ed. M. Roche, J. Roubaud, and J.-P. Faye, 107–20. Paris: Seuil, 1968.

———. *Circus*. Paris: Le Seuil, 1972.

———. *Compact*. Paris: Seuil, 1966.

———. *Compact*. Annecy: Tristram, 1996.

Rockmore, Tom. *Heidegger and French Philosophy: Humanism, Anti-Humanism, and Being*. New York: Routledge, 1994.

Rodanski, Stanislas. *Ecrits, sous le signe du soleil noir*. Paris: Christian Bourgois, 1999.

———. "Poèmes, notes, etc." *La Polygraphe* 30–31 (January 2004).

Rolland, Romain. *La Révolte des machines ou la pensée déchaînée*. Genève: n.p., 1921.

Rolot, Christian. "Cocteau spectateur." In *Le cinéma de Jean Cocteau* suivi de *Hommage à Jean Marais*, ed. Christian Rolot. Montpellier: CELF du XXème siècle, 1994.

Romains, Jules. *Donogoo Tonka, conte cinématographique*. Paris: NRF, 1920.

———. "La Foule au cinématographe." In *Puissance de Paris*, 103–5. Paris: NRF, 1911.

———. *La Vie unanime*. Paris: Gallimard, 1982.

———. *La Vie unanime. Poème*. Paris: Mercure de France, 1913.

———. *La Vision extra-rétinienne et le sens paroptique*. Paris: Gallimard, 1964 [1920].

Ropars-Wuilleumier, Marie-Claire. *Écraniques*, Villeneuve d'Ascq: Septentrion, 1995.

———. *Le Texte divisé, essai sur l'écriture filmique*. Paris: PUF, 1981.

Ross, Kristin. *Fast Cars, Clean Bodies: Decolonization and the Reordering of French Culture*. Cambridge, MA: MIT Press, 1996.

Rostand, Edmond. "Le Bois sacré." *L'Illustration* 3432 (December 5, 1908): n.p.

Rothwell, Andrew. "The 'Querelle du poème en prose': Pierre Reverdy's Polemical Portraits of Max Jacob, 1915–1925." *Nottingham French Studies* 31, no. 1 (spring 1992): 51–66.

Rotman, Brian. *Becoming Besides Ourselves: The Alphabet, Ghosts, and the Distributed Human Being*. Durham, NC: Duke University Press, 2008.

Roussel, Raymond. *How I Wrote Certain of My Books*. Trans. Trevor Winkfield. New York: Exact Change, 2004.

———. *Impressions d'Afrique*. Paris: Jean-Jacques Pauvert, 1963.

———. *Locus Solus*. Paris: Jean-Jacques Pauvert, 1965.

———. *Œuvres*, vol. 4. Paris: Pauvert/Fayard, 1998.

Roustang, François. *Influence*. Paris: Minuit, 1990.

Royet-Journoud, Claude. *La Poésie entière est préposition*. Marseille: Étic Pesty Éditeur, 2007.

———. *Théorie des prépositions*. Paris: POL, 2007.

Russo, Adelaide. "Le Propre du temps: Le retour de Marcelin Pleynet à la question du langage." In *Contemporary French Poetics*, ed. Michael Bishop and Christopher Elson, 167–77. Amsterdam: Rodopi, 2002.

Rutsky, R. L. *High Techné: Art and Technology from the Machine Aesthetic to the Posthuman*. Minneapolis: Minnesota University Press, 1999.

Sadoul, Georges. *Lumière et Méliès*. Paris: Pierre Lherminier, 1985.

Saint-Pol-Roux. *De l'art magnifique*. Mortemart: Rougerie, 1978.

———. *Cinéma vivant*. Mortemart: Rougerie, 1972 [ca. 1925–30].

———. *La Répoétique*. Mortemart: Rougerie, 1971.

———. *Vitesse*. Mortemart: Rougerie, 1973 [ca. 1930].

Sallis, John. *Force of Imagination: The Sense of the Elemental*. Bloomington: Indiana University Press, 2000.

Sanouillet, Maurice. *Dada à Paris*. Paris: CPEDERF, 2001.

Sanyal, Debarati. "Auschwitz as Allegory in *Night and Fog*," in *Concentrationary Cinema: Aesthetics and Political Resistance In and Beyond Alain Resnais's* Night and Fog," eds. Griselda Pollock and Max Silverman. Oxford: Berghahn Books, 2012.

Sartre, Jean-Paul. "Apologie pour le cinéma." In *Écrits de jeunesse*, 385–404. Paris: Gallimard, 1990.

———. *L'Imaginaire, psychologie phénoménologique de l'imagination.* Paris: Gallimard, 1940.

———. "Présentation," *Les Temps modernes* 1, no. 1 (1945): 34–42.

———. *Qu'est-ce que la littérature?* Paris: Gallimard, 1973.

Schehr, Lawrence. *French Gay Modernism.* Urbana-Champaign: University of Illinois Press, 2004.

Schlatter, Christian. "Canailles, roman hypergraphique (1950)." *Maurice Lemaître,* 120.

Schwartz, Vanessa R. "Cinematic Spectatorship before the Apparatus: The Public Taste for Reality in *Fin-de-Siècle* Paris." In *Cinema and the Invention of Modern Life,* ed. Leo Charney and Vanessa R. Schwartz, 297–319. Berkeley: University of California Press, 1995.

———. *It's So French: Hollywood, Paris, and the Making of Cosmopolitan Film Culture.* Chicago: University of Chicago Press, 2007.

Schwenger, Peter. *Fantasm and Fiction: On Textual Envisioning.* Stanford: Stanford University Press, 1999.

Scott, David. *Pictorialist Poetics: Poetry and the Visual Arts in Nineteeth-Century France.* Cambridge: Cambridge University Press, 1988.

Sebbag, Georges. *Le point sublime: Breton, Rimbaud, Kaplan.* Paris: Jean-Michel Place, 1997.

Segalen, Victor. *Correspondance,* vol. 1, 1893–1912. Paris: Fayard, 2004.

———. *Correspondance,* vol. 2, 1912–1919. Paris: Fayard, 2005.

———. *Essai sur l'exotisme.* Montpellier: Fata Morgana, 1978.

———. *Imaginaires.* Mortemart: Rougerie, 1972.

———. *Odes,* suivi de *Thibet.* Paris: Poésie/Gallimard, 1979.

———. *Peintures.* Paris: Gallimard, 1983.

———. *Stèles.* Paris: Poésie/Gallimard, 1973.

———. *Stèles.* Translated and annotated by Timothy Billings and Christopher Bush, preface by Haun Saussy. Middletown, CT: Wesleyan University Press, 2007.

———. *Les Synesthésies et l'école symboliste.* Montpellier: Fata Morgana, 1981.

Shattuck, Roger. *The Banquet Years: The Origin of the Avant-Garde in France, 1885 to World War I.* New York: Vintage, 1968.

Shaw, Mary Lewis. *Performance in the Texts of Mallarmé: The Passage from Art to Ritual.* Pittsburg: Pennsylvania State University Press, 1993.

Short, Robert. *The Age of Gold: Surrealist Cinema.* N.p.: Creation Books, 2003.

Sicard, Monique. *L'Année 1895, l'image écartelée entre voir et savoir.* Le Plessis-Robinson: Synthélabo, 1994.

———. "Passage de Vénus: Le Revolver photographique de Jules Janssen." *Études photographiques* 4 (May 1998).

Sidoti, Antoine. "Genèse et dossier d'une polémique, La Prose du transsibérien." *Archives Blaise Cendrars* 4. Paris: Minard, 1987.

Singer, Ben. *Melodrama and Modernity: Early Sensational Cinema and Its Contexts.* New York: Columbia University Press, 2001.

Sitney, P. Adam. *Modernist Montage: The Obscurity of Vision in Cinema and Literature.* New York: Columbia University Press, 1992.

Smith, Stephen. "Fragments of Landscape, Scraps of Décor: Maurice Roche's *Compact.*" *Yale French Studies* 57 (1979): 48–57.

Sobchack, Vivian. *The Address of the Eye: A Phenomenology of Film Experience.* Princeton, NJ: Princeton University Press, 1992.

———. *Carnal Thoughts: Embodiment and Moving Image Culture.* Berkeley: University of California Press, 2004.

Solomon, Mathew. "'Twenty-Five Heads Under One Hat': Quick-Change in the 1890s." In *Meta-Morphing: Visual Transformation and the Culture of Quick-Change*, ed. Vivian Sobchack, 3–20. Minneapolis: University of Minnesota Press, 2000.

Soupault, Philippe. *Charlot.* Paris: Plon, 1931.

———. *Écrits de cinéma.* Paris: Plon, 1979.

———. "Indifférence, poème cinématographique" and "Note sur le cinéma." *SIC* 25 (January 1918): 1–2.

———. "Observation présentée par M. Philippe Soupault," *La Révolution surréaliste* 4 (1925), 8.

———. "Photographies animées." *SIC* 32 (October 1918): 2.

———. "Photographies animées." *SIC* 33 (November 1918): 1.

Stafford, Hélène. *Mallarmé and the Poetics of Everyday Life: A Study of the Concept of the Ordinary in his Verse and Prose.* New York: Rodopi, 2000.

Staller, Natasha. "Melies' 'Fantastic' Cinema and the Origins of Cubism." *Art History* 12, no. 2 (June 1989): 202–32.

Stam, Robert. *A Companion to Literature and Film.* New York: Wiley-Blackwell, 2004.

Stiegler, Bernard. *Le Temps du cinéma et la question du mal-être.* Paris: Galilée, 2001.

Stockwell, Peter. *An Introduction to Cognitive Poetics.* London: Routledge, 2002.

Stout, John C. "Writing (at) the Limits of Genre: Danielle Collobert's Poetics of Transgression." *Symposium* 53, no. 4 (winter 2000): 299–309.

Sudre, Alain-Alcide. "Pensées sur l'oeuvre cinématographique de Maurice

Lemaître, replacée dans le champ du cinéma expérimental de l'après-guerre." *Maurice Lemaître* 57.

Suleiman, Susan. "Surrealist Black Humour: Masculine/Feminine." *Papers on Surrealism* 1 (winter 2003): 9.

Supervielle, Jules. "Les lettres, la pensée moderne, et le cinéma (enquête)." *Les Cahiers du mois* 16–17 (1926): 183–84.

Süssekind, Flora. *Cinematograph of Words: Literature, Technique, and Modernization in Brazil.* Stanford: Stanford University Press, 1997.

Tajima, Renee. "Moving the Image: Asian American Independent Filmmaking 1970–1990." In *Moving the Image: Independent Asian Pacific American Media Arts*, ed. Russell Leong. Los Angeles: UCLA AACP, 1992.

Tamagne, Florence. *History of Homosexuality in Europe: Berlin, London, Paris, 1919–1939.* New York: Algora Publishing, 2004.

Tarde, Gabriel. "Fragment d'histoire future." *Revue française de sociologie* 4, nos. 8–9 (August–September 1896): 603–54.

———. *Les Lois de l'imitation.* 2d ed. Paris: Félix Alcan, 1895.

Taves, Brian. "The Novels and Rediscovered Films of Michel (Jules) Verne." *Journal of Film Preservation* 62 (April 2001): 25–39.

———. "With Williamson Beneath the Sea." *Journal of Film Preservation* 25, no. 52 (April 1996): 54–61.

Tissandier, Gaston. "Le Kinétoscope d'Edison." *La Nature* (June–December, 1894): 323–26.

Tortajada, Maria. "Alfred Jarry: Le cinématographe contre la photographie." *La Decima Musa/The Tenth Muse* 101–13. Udine: Forum 2001.

———. "Machines cinématiques et dispositifs visuels. Cinéma et "pré-cinéma" à l'oeuvre chez Alfred Jarry." *1895* 40 (July 2003): 5–23.

———. "L'Ombre projetée de la vitesse. Le cinématographe et la course des dix mille milles dans *Le Surmâle* d'Alfred Jarry." In *Etudes de lettres, On a touché à l'espace! 1900–1930. Actes du colloque interdisciplinaire, Lausanne, 3–4 juin 1999*, ed. D. Chaperon and P. Moret, 109–33. Lausanne: Payot, 2000.

Torwanicki, Frédéric de. *Les Aventures de Harry Dickson.* Nantes: Capricci, 2007.

Toulet, Emmanuelle. "Le cinéma à l'exposition universelle de 1900." *Revue d'Histoire moderne et contemporaine* 33 (1986): 179–206.

———, ed. *Le Cinéma au rendez-vous des arts, France années 20 et 30.* Paris: Bibliothèque Nationale de France, 1995.

Tournadre, Claude, and Alain Virmaux. *La Bréhatine, cinéma-drame. Archives des lettres modernes* 126. Paris: Minard, 1971.

Tovgornick, Mariana. *Gone Primitive: Savage Intellects, Modern Lives.* Chicago: University of Chicago Press, 1990.

Trotter, David. *Cinema and Modernism.* Oxford: Blackwell, 2007.

Trouillot, Michel-Rolph. *Silencing the Past:Power and the Production of History.* Boston: Beacon Press, 1995.

Tsivian, Yuri. "Some Historical Footnotes on the Kuleshov Experiment." In *Early Cinema: Space—Frame—Narrative*, ed. Thomas Elsaesser, 245–55. London: BFI, 1990.

Tsur, Reuven. *Towards a Theory of Cognitive Poetics.* Amsterdam: North Holland, 1992.

Tulvey, Malcolm. "Jean Epstein's Cinema of Immanence: The Rehabilitation of the Corporeal Eye." *October* 83 (1998): 25–50.

Usai, Poalo Cherchi. "Pornography." In *Encyclopedia of Early Cinema*, ed. Richard Abel, 525–26. London: Routledge, 2005.

Uzanne, Octave. *Vingt jours dans le Nouveau Monde.* Paris: May & Motteroz, 1893.

———. "Une visite chez Edison." *Le Figaro* (May 8, 1893): 1.

Vaché, Jacques. *Lettres de guerre.* Paris: Au sans pareil, 1919.

Valéry, Paul. *Cahiers*, vol. 24. Paris: CNRS, 1961.

———. "L'Enseignement de la poétique au Collège de France." *Œuvres complètes,* vol. 1: 1438–43. Paris: Gallimard, 1957.

———. *Œuvres complètes,* 1. Paris: Gallimard, 1957.

———. *Œuvres complètes,* 2. Paris: Gallimard, 1960.

———. "La Photopoétique," *Œuvres complètes*, vol. 1: 395. Paris: Gallimard, 1957.

Van Wert, William. *The Theory and Practice of the Ciné-Roman.* New York: Arno Press, 1978.

Vernier A. "Causerie scientifique." *Le Temps* 10982s (June 12, 1891): 1.

Verschueren, Jef. *Understanding Pragmatics.* London: Arnold, 1999.

Vidal, Agustin Sanchez. *Luis Buñuel, Obra literaria.* Zaragoza: Heraldo de Aragon, 1982.

Villiers de L'Isle-Adam. *Contes cruels.* Paris: Gallimard, 1983.

———. *L'Ève future.* Paris: Mercure de France, 1922; reprint, Paris: Garnier-Flammarion, 1992.

Vinen, Richard. *The Unfree French: Life Under the Occupation.* New Haven, CT: Yale University Press, 2007.

Virmaux, Alain, and Odette Virmaux. *Artaud-Dulac, La Coquille et le clergyman: essai d'élucidation d'une querelle mythique.* Paris: Paris expérimental, 1999.

———. *Un Genre nouveau: le ciné-roman*. Paris: Edilio, 1983.

———. *Les Surréalistes et le cinéma*. Paris: Seghers, 1976.

———. "La Tentation du cinéma chez les poètes au temps du surréalisme d'Artaud à Supervielle." *Cahiers de l'Association des études françaises* 20 (May 1968): 257–74.

Wall-Romana, Christophe. "Danielle Collobert's '*Aux environs d'un film*'." *Sites: Contemporary French and Francophone Studies* 9, no. 3 (September 2005): 257–63.

———. "Epstein's Photogénie as Corporeal Vision: Inner Sensation, Queer Embodiment, and Ethics." In *Jean Epstein: Critical Essays and New Translations*, ed. Sarah Keller and Jason Paul. Amsterdam: Amsterdam University Press, 2012.

———. *Jean Epstein*. Manchester: Manchester University Press, 2012.

———. "Mallarmé's Cinepoetics: The Poem Uncoiled by the Cinématographe, 1893–98." *PMLA* 120, no. 1 (2005): 128–47.

———. "Poire, plume Douve et bob: les fantoches filmiques de la poésie." *French Review* 81, no. 2 (2007): 289–300.

Warner, Marina. *Phantasmagoria: Spirit Visions, Metaphors, and Media*. Oxford: Oxford University Press, 2006.

Wateau, Patrick. *Bernard Noël ou l'expérience extérieure*. Paris: José Corti, 2001.

Webber, Andrew J. *The European Avant-Garde* 1900–1940. Cambridge: Polity Press, 2004.

Weber, Samuel. *Mass Mediauras: Form, Technics, Media*. Stanford: Stanford University Press, 1996.

Wegner, Daniel M. *The Illusion of Conscious Will*. Cambridge, MA: MIT Press, 2002.

Weisberg, Gabriel P., ed. *Montmartre and the Making of Mass Culture*. Rutgers, NJ: Rutgers University Press, 2001.

Weiss, Gail. *Body Images: Embodiment and Intercorporeality*. New York: Routledge, 1999.

Welton, Donn, ed. *The Essential Husserl: Basic Writings in Transcendental Phenomenology*. Bloomington: Indiana University Press, 1999.

Williams, Alan. *The Republic of Images: A History of French Filmmaking*. Cambridge, MA: Harvard University Press, 1992.

Williams, James. *Jean Cocteau*. London: Reaktion Books, 2008.

Wilson, Emma. "Material Remains: Night and Fog." *October* 112 (spring 2005): 89–110.

Woodehouse, John. *Gabriele D'Annunzio*. Oxford: Oxford University Press, 1998.

Wourm, Nathalie. "Poetry in Moving Image: The French Avant-Garde." In *Porous Boundaries: Texts and Images in Twentieth-Century French Culture*, ed. Jérôme Game, 101–19. Oxford: Peter Lang, 2007.

Wyschogrod, Edith. *An Ethics of Remembering: History, Heterology, and the Nameless Others*. Chicago: University of Chicago Press, 1998.

Zachmann, Gail. *Frameworks for Mallarmé: The Photo and the Graphic of an Interdisciplinary Aesthetic*. Stony Brook: SUNY, 2009.

Zahavi, Dan. *Husserl's Phenomenology*. Stanford: Stanford University Press, 2004.

Ziarek, Krzysztof. *The Historicity of Experience: Modernity, the Avant-Garde, and the Event*. Evanston, IL: Northwestern University Press, 2001.

Zielinski, Siegfried. *Deep Time of the Media: Toward and Archaeology of Hearing and Seeing by Technical Means*. Cambridge, MA: MIT Press, 2008.

Zischler, Hanns. *Kafka Goes to the Movies*. Trans. Susan H. Gillespie. Chicago: Chicago University Press, 2003.

INDEX

Plates in the photo section are indicated by a "*p.*"